Communications in Computer and Information Science　　1241

Commenced Publication in 2007
Founding and Former Series Editors:
Simone Diniz Junqueira Barbosa, Phoebe Chen, Alfredo Cuzzocrea,
Xiaoyong Du, Orhun Kara, Ting Liu, Krishna M. Sivalingam,
Dominik Ślęzak, Takashi Washio, Xiaokang Yang, and Junsong Yuan

More information about this series at http://www.springer.com/series/7899

Arup Bhattacharjee · Samir Kr. Borgohain ·
Badal Soni · Gyanendra Verma ·
Xiao-Zhi Gao (Eds.)

Machine Learning, Image Processing, Network Security and Data Sciences

Second International Conference, MIND 2020
Silchar, India, July 30–31, 2020
Proceedings, Part II

Springer

Editors
Arup Bhattacharjee 🆔
National Institute of Technology Silchar
Silchar, India

Badal Soni 🆔
National Institute of Technology Silchar
Silchar, India

Xiao-Zhi Gao 🆔
University of Eastern Finland
Kuopio, Finland

Samir Kr. Borgohain 🆔
National Institute of Technology Silchar
Silchar, India

Gyanendra Verma 🆔
National Institute of Technology
Kurukshetra
Kurukshetra, India

ISSN 1865-0929   ISSN 1865-0937 (electronic)
Communications in Computer and Information Science
ISBN 978-981-15-6317-1   ISBN 978-981-15-6318-8 (eBook)
https://doi.org/10.1007/978-981-15-6318-8

This Springer imprint is published by the registered company Springer Nature Singapore Pte Ltd.
The registered company address is: 152 Beach Road, #21-01/04 Gateway East, Singapore 189721, Singapore

Preface

It is our great honor and privilege to present the proceedings of the Second International Conference on Machine Learning, Image Processing, Network Security and Data Sciences (MIND 2020), organized by the National Institute of Technology Silchar, India, and held during July 30–31, 2020. This conference is the second in a series which focuses on Machine Learning, Image Processing, Network Security, and Data Sciences. The papers included in these proceedings present original ideas and up-to-date discussions and directions regarding topics of interest of the conference.

MIND 2020 provided a platform to the researchers, practitioners, and technologists to present and discuss state-of-the-art novelties, trends, issues, and challenges in the area of Machine Learning, Image Processing, Network Security, and Data Sciences. Organization of this conference was primarily motivated by the need to promote research through sharing of ideas, technology, and trends at all levels of the scientific and technical community. Another motivation was the need for a common platform for building a framework for development of solutions to unresolved issues and challenges in different areas of computer engineering and engineering. This edition, continuing the spirit of the previous conference in this series, depicts the most important requirements of the academia and industry: quality and value. This was substantiated by the 219 high-quality submissions which posed a great challenge in the review and selection process. Each submission was subjected to at least three reviews under a double-blind peer review process mechanism. Based on the review results and recommendations of the Program Committee, 83 papers were accepted for presentation at the main conference. This resulted in an acceptance rate lower than 38%. Due to the COVID-19 outbreak, the conference was organized in a virtual format instead of as an onsite event. Further, though initially the conference was planned to be organized during April 23–24, 2020, the outbreak compelled the organizers to postpone the conference till July 30–31, 2020.

Any event of this nature needs sufficient time, complete support, and wholehearted cooperation and support of all, for success. We thank all the authors for submitting and presenting their quality paper(s) to/at MIND 2020. We are extremely thankful to the reviewers, who have carried out the most important and critical part of any academic conference, the evaluation of each of the submitted papers assigned to them. We also express our gratitude to the TPC members for their immense support and motivation in making MIND 2020 a success. We sincerely thank all the chairs for their hard work without which the success of MIND 2020 would not have been possible. We are also grateful to our invited speakers for enlightening and motivating the participants of the conference. We also express our sincere gratitude towards our publication partner,

Springer, for trusting and guiding us. We are obliged to TEQIP-III and DST-SERB for officially sponsoring MIND 2020.

May 2020   Arup Bhattacharjee

Organization

Executive Committee

Patron
Sivaji Bandyopadhyay   National Institute of Technology Silchar, India

Honorary Chair
Rajkumar Buyya   The University of Melbourne, Australia

General Chairs
Arup Bhattacharjee   National Institute of Technology Silchar, India
Salah Bourennane   École centrale de Marseille, France

Organizing Chairs
Samir Kr. Borgohain   National Institute of Technology Silchar, India
Badal Soni   National Institute of Technology Silchar, India

Technical Program Chairs
Xiao-Zhi Gao   University of Eastern Finland, Finland
Ching-Hsien Hsu   Asia University, Taiwan
Suganya Devi K.   National Institute of Technology Silchar, India
Gyanendra Verma   National Institute of Technology Kurukshetra, India
Bidyut Kumar Patra   National Institute of Technology Rourkela, India

Finance and Hospitality Chairs
Ujwala Baruah   National Institute of Technology Silchar, India
Pantha K. Nath   National Institute of Technology Silchar, India
Umakanta Majhi   National Institute of Technology Silchar, India

Publication and Publicity Committee

Publication Chairs
Shyamosree Pal   National Institute of Technology Silchar, India
Naresh Babu M.   National Institute of Technology Silchar, India
Rajesh Doriya   National Institute of Technology Raipur, India

Publicity Chairs
Rajib Kumar Jha   IIT Patna, India
Chiranjoy Chattopadhyay   IIT Jodhpur, India

Manish Okade	National Institute of Technology Rourkela, India
Poonam Sharma	National Institute of Technology Nagpur, India
Divya Kumar	National Institute of Technology Allahabad, India
Nabajyoti Medhi	Tezpur University, India
Sraban Kumar Mohanty	IIITDM Jabalpur, India

Steering Committee

Rajkumar Buyya	The University of Melbourne and Manjrasoft, Australia
Awadhesh Kumar Singh	National Institute of Technology Kurukshetra, India
B. B. Gupta	National Institute of Technology Kurukshetra, India
Gyanendra Verma	National Institute of Technology Kurukshetra, India
Rajesh Doriya	National Institute of Technology Raipur, India

Technical Program Committee

A. Chandrasekhar	IIT Dhanbad, India
A. Rajesh	Vellore Institute of Technology, India
A. Muthumari	University College of Engineering, Ramanathapuram, India
Aakanksha Sharaff	National Institute of Technology Raipur, India
Abdel Badi Salem	Ain Shams University, Egypt
Abdel-Hamid Ali Soliman	Staffordshire University, UK
Abdul Jalil M. Khalaf	University of Kufa, Iraq
Aditya Trivedi	IIITDM Gwalior, India
Alexander Gelbukh	National Polytechnic Institute, Mexico
Ali Jaoua	Qatar University, Qatar
Amr Ahmed	Google AI, UK
Anil Sao	IIT Mandi, India
Ankit Kumar Jain	National Institute of Technology Kurukshetra, India
Annappa	National Institute of Technology Karnataka, India
Anoop Patel	National Institute of Technology Kurukshetra, India
Anshul Verma	Banaras Hindu University, India
Antonina Dattolo	University of Udine, Italy
Anupam Shukla	IIITDM Gwalior, India
Aparajita Ojha	IIITDM Jabalpur, India
Ashish Ghosh	Indian Statistical Institute, India
Ashish Khare	University of Allahabad, India
Ashraf Hossain	National Institute of Technology Silchar, India
Atul Gupta	IIITDM Jabalpur, India
Awadhesh Kumar Singh	National Institute of Technology Kurukshetra, India
B. L. Velammal	Anna University, India
Balwinder Singh Sodhi	IIT Ropar, India
Basant Kumar	NIT Allahabad, India
Biswajit Purkayastha	National Institute of Technology Silchar, India

Bondu Venkateswarlu	Dayananda Sagar University, India
Brijesh Kumar Chaurasia	Indian Institute of Information Technology Lucknow, India
C. Bose	Anna University, India
C. Rani	Government College of Engineering, Salem, India
C. S. Sastry	IIT Hyderabad, India
Carlos Becker Westphall	University of Kentucky, USA
Ching-Hsien Hsu	Asia University, Taiwan
Chun-I Fan	National Sun Yat-sen University, Taiwan
Dalton Meitei Thounaojam	National Institute of Technology Silchar, India
David Klaus	University of Kassel, Germany
Davide Adami	University of Pisa, Italy
Davide Adami	Unipi, Italy
Debajyoti Choudhuri	National Institute of Technology Rourkela, India
Deep Gupta	National Institute of Technology Nagpur, India
Desineni Subbaram Naidu	University of Minnesota Duluth, USA
Dimitrios A. Karras	National and Kapodistrian University of Athens, Greece
Dinesh Vishwakarma	Delhi Technological University Delhi, India
Dipti Kapoor Sarmah	Utrecht University, The Netherlands
Eugénia Moreira Bernardino	Instituto Politécnico de Leiria, Portugal
Fateh Krim	Ferhat Abbas University of Setif, Algeria
Félix J. García Clemente	University in Murcia, Spain
G. Lavanya Devi	Andhra University, India
G. C. Nandi	IIIT Allahabad, India
G. Jaya Suma	JNTUK, University College of Engineering, India
Gaurav Varshney	Indian Institute of Technology Jammu, India
Gaurav Verma	National Institute of Technology Kurukshetra, India
Gautam Barua	IIIT Guwahati, India
Gyan Singh Yadav	Indian Institute of Information Technology Kota, India
H. K. Sardana	Central Scientific Instruments Organization (CSIR), India
Haimonti Dutta	State University of New York at Buffalo, USA
Ioannis Pitas	Aristotle University of Thessaloniki, Greece
Jalel Ben-Othman	CerraCap Ventures, France
Jayendra Kumar	Vellore Institute of Technology, India
John Jose	Indian Institute of Technology Guwahati, India
José Mario de Martino	Campinas State University, Brazil
Joseph Gladwin	SSN College of Engineering, India
Jukka K. Nurminen	University of Helsinki, Finland
Jupitara Hazarika	National Institute of Technology Silchar, India
K. K. Shukla	Indian Institute of Technology Banaras, India
K. Vivekanandan	Pondicherry Engineering College Puducherry, India
Kamran Arshad	Ajman University, UAE
Karthikeyan Subramanian	Sohar College of Applied Sciences, Oman

Klaus Moessner	University of Surrey, UK
Kolin Paul	Indian Institute of Technology Delhi, India
Kouichi Sakurai	National University Corporation Kyushu University, Japan
Koushlendra Kumar Singh	National Institute of Technology Jamshedpur, India
Krishn K. Mishra	NIT Allahabad, India
Kulwinder Singh	University of South Florida, USA
Laiphrakpam Dolendro Singh	National Institute of Technology Silchar, India
Latha Parthiban	Pondicherry University, India
Thomas D. Little	Boston University, USA
M. Sampath Kumar	Andhra University College of Engineering, India
Madhusudan Singh	Woosong University, South Korea
Mahalakshmi A.	Anna University, India
Mahendra Kumar Murmu	National Institute of Technology Kurukshetra, India
Malaya Dutta Borah	National Institute of Technology Silchar, India
Manjula Perkinian	Anna University, India
Manoj Kumar Singh	Banaras Hindu University, India
Mantosh Biswas	National Institute of Technology Kurukshetra, India
Marcelo S. Alencar	UFCG, Brazil
Marcelo Sampaio Alencar	Federal University of Campina Grande, Brazil
Mayank Dave	National Institute of Technology Kurukshetra, India
Mitul Kumar Ahirwal	National Institute of Technology Bhopal, India
Mohammed A. Qadeer	Aligarh Muslim University, India
Mohammed Bouhorma	Abdelmalek Essaâdi University, Morocco
Mullavisala Ravibabu	IIT Ropar, India
N. Malmurugan	Mahendra College of Engineering, India
N. Nasimuddin	Agency of Science Technology and Research, Singapore
Nabanita Adhikary	National Institute of Technology Silchar, India
Narendra Kohli	Harcourt Butler Technical University Kanpur, India
Navjot Singh	NIT Allahabad, India
Neminath Hubbali	Indian Institute of Technology Indore, India
Nidhi Gupta	Chinese Academy of Sciences, China
Nidul Sinha	National Institute of Technology Silchar, India.
Niharika Singh	UPES, India
Nityananda Sarma	Tezpur University, India
Niyati Baliyan	Indira Gandhi Delhi Technical University for Women, India
O. P. Vyas	IIT Allahabad, India
Onkar Krishna	NTT Coporation, Japan
P. V. Lakshmi	Gitam University, India
P. Ganesh Kumar	Anna University, India
P. Yogesh	Anna University, India
P. Sudhakar	Annamalai University, India

Pankaj Pratap Singh	Central Institute of Technology (CIT) Kokrajhar, India
Pao-Ann Hsiung	National Chung Cheng University, Taiwan
Paolo Crippa	Università Politecnica delle Marche, Italy
Partha Pakray	National Institute of Technology Silchar, India
Pascal Lorenz	University of Haute Alsace, France
Poonam Dhaka	University of Namibia, Namibia
Poonam Saini	PEC Chandigarh, CSE Punjab Engineering College, India
Prabir Kumar Biswas	IIT Kharagpur, India
Pradeep Singh	National Institute of Technology Raipur, India
Pradip K. Das	Indian Institute of Technology Guwahati, India
Prashant Giridhar Shambharkar	Delhi Technological University, Delhi
Pratik Chattopadhyay	Indian Institute of Technology (BHU), India
Pritee Khanna	IIITDM Jabalpur, India
R. Vasanth Kumar Mehta	SCSVMV University, India
R. Balasubramanian	Indian Institute of Technology Roorkee, India
R. Murugan	National Institute of Technology Silchar, India
Rajdeep Niyogi	IIT Roorkee, India
Rajesh Pandey	IIT BHU, India
Rajesh Prasad	IIT Delhi, India
Rajlaxmi Chouhan	Indian Institute of Technology Jodhpur, India
Rakesh Kumar Lenka	IIIT Bhubaneswar, India
Ram Bilas Pachori	Indian Institute of Technology Indore, India
Ranjay Hazra	National Institute of Technology Silchar, India
Ranjeet Kumar	Madanpalle Institute of Technology and Science, India
Ravi Panwar	Indian Institute of Information Technology, Design and Manufacturing, India
Rekh Ram Janghel	National Institute of Technology Raipur, India
S. Sridevi	Thiagarajar College of Engineering, India
Saber Abd-Allah	Beni Suef University, Egypt
Salah Bourennane	École centrale de Marseille, France
Samudra Vijaya K.	CLST, Indian Institute of Technology Guwahati, India
Sanasam Ranbir Singh	IIT Guwahati, India
Sanjaya Kumar Panda	Veer Surendra Sai University of Technology (VSSUT) Odisha, India
Santosh Rathore	National Institute of Technology Jalandhar, India
Saroj Kumar Biswas	National Institute of Technology Silchar, India
Saurabh Ranjan	Orange County, USA
Saurabh Tiwari	DAIICT Gandhinagar, India
Seetharaman K.	Annamalai University, India
Senthilkumar	Anna University, India
Shankar. K.	National Institute of Technology Silchar, India
Sugam K. Sharma	Iowa State University, USA
Shashi Shekhar Jha	Indian Institute of Technology Ropar, India

Sherif Rashad	Morehead State University, USA
Shitala Prasad	Nanyang Technological University, Singapore
Shivashankar B. Nair	Indian Institute of Technology Guwahati, India
Shuai Zhao	University of Missouri, USA
Shyamapada Mukherjee	National Institute of Technology Silchar, India
Simon Pietro Romano	University of Naples Federico, Italy
Soumen Bag	Indian Institute of Technology, Indian School of Mines, Dhanbad, India
Srinivas Koppu	Vellore Institute of Technology, India
Srinivas Pinisetty	IIT Bhubaneswar, India
Sriparna Saha	IIT Patna, India
Subhash Bhalla	University of Aizu, Japan
Subhrakanta Panda	BITS-PILANI Hyderabad, India
Sudarsan Sahoo	National Institute of Technology Silchar, India
Sudhir Kumar	IIT Patna, India
Sudipta Mukhopadhyay	Indian Institute of Technology Kharagpur, India
Sukumar Nandi	Indian Institute of Technology Guwahati, India
Suneeta Agarwal	MNNIT Allahabad, India
Swati Vipsita	IIIT Bhubaneswar, India
Syed Taqi Ali	Visvesvaraya National Institute of Technology Nagpur, India
T. G. Vasista	Mizan Tepi University, Ethiopia
Thanikaiselvan V.	Vellore Institute of Technology, India
Thoudam Doren Singh	National Institute of Technology Silchar, India
Tomasz Rak	Rzeszow University of Technology, Poland
Tracy Liu	AT&LABS, USA
Tripti Goel	National Institute of Technology Silchar, India
Uma Shanker Tiwary	IIIT Allahabad, India
Umashankar Subramaniam	Prince Sultan University, Saudi Arabia
Utpal Sharma	Tezpur University, India
V. Balaji	KCG College of Technology, India
V. M. Senthilkumar	Malla Reddy College of Engineering and Technology, India
V. Ramalingam	Annamalai University, India
Veenu Mangat	Panjab University, India
Venkateswari Palanisami	Sengunthar Engineering College, India
Vijay Bhaskar Semwal	Maulana Azad National Institute of Technology Bhopal, India
Vikram Singh	National Institute of Technology Kurukshetra, India
Viranjay M. Srivastava	University of KwaZulu-Natal, South Africa
Vishal Ramesh Satpute	VNIT Nagpur, India
Vishal Saraswat	Robert Bosch Engineering and Business Solutions Pvt. Ltd., India
Vivek Dikshit	IIT Kharagpur, India
Vivek S. Verma	AKGEC Ghaziabad, India
Wael Elmedany	University of Bahrain, Bahrain

Wai Ho Mow	Hong Kong University of Science and Technology, China
Warusia Mohamed	Technical University of Malaysia, Malaysia
Wei-Chiang Hong	Oriental Institute of Technology, Taiwan
Xiao-Zhi Gao	University of Eastern Finland, Finland
Yang Zhang	American University, USA
Youakim Badr	INSA-Lyon, France
Youcef Baghdadi	Sulta Qaboos University, Oman
Zhao Yang	Northwest University, China
Zoran Bojkovic	University of Belgrade, Serbia

Sponsors

- Technical Education Quality Improvement Programme (TEQIP-III)
- Science and Engineering Research Board, Department of Science and Technology, Government of India

Contents – Part II

Contents – Part I

Mining Composite Fuzzy Association Rules Among Nutrients in Food Recipe

Rajkamal Sarma and Pankaj Kumar Deva Sarma$^{(\boxtimes)}$

Department of Computer Science, Assam University, Silchar, Assam, India
rajkamal_sarma@rediffmail.com, pankajgr@rediffmail.com

Abstract. Association Rule Mining is a data mining technique to discover associations among attributes of data in the form of if.. then rules in large databases of transactions. Fuzzy Association Rule Mining (FARM) emerged as a significant research area and is an extension of classical association rule mining which applies Fuzzy set theory to address the uncertainty in the case of categorical data. Different algorithms are proposed for Fuzzy Association Rule Mining and applied in different domains. Composite Fuzzy Association Rule Mining (CFARM) is one of the algorithms based on the concept of composite data items. In this paper Composite Fuzzy association rule mining technique is applied on different recipes containing their nutrient values. The recipes considered are prepared from green leafy vegetables, other vegetables and recipes of Fish and Meat. The recipes are combination of nutrient attributes like moisture, protein, fat carbohydrates etc. and micronutrient combination of some nutrient attribute like calcium, iron, vitamin and moisture etc. The Composite Fuzzy Association Rule Mining algorithm is applied to discover association among the nutrients values in the recipes. This paper contains an overview of CFARM algorithm and a composite dataset is prepared to generate rules. Experimental results are presented and analyzed with different measures of interestingness along with scope of future works.

Keywords: Fuzzy association rule mining · Composite attributes · Nutrient composition · Food recipes

1 Introduction

With the tremendous growth of data in every application, it becomes a challenging issue to convert data into proper information. Knowledge Discovery in Databases (KDD) is the process of transformation of data into knowledge. Data mining is a step in the KDD process to mine data using different functions. Among these functions, discovery of association rules is concerned with finding interesting association relationships among different attributes [1]. Association Rule Mining technique was commonly applied in Market – Basket analysis to find the customer purchasing behavior in terms of association between items from the transaction of sales. An association rule is represented in the form of X –> Y, which describes an item containing attribute X is likely to contain attribute Y. For example, Bike –> Helmet, indicates that a customer who buys a Bike has tendency to buy a Helmet as well. However, two important

© Springer Nature Singapore Pte Ltd. 2020
A. Bhattacharjee et al. (Eds.): MIND 2020, CCIS 1241, pp. 1–10, 2020.
https://doi.org/10.1007/978-981-15-6318-8_1

user-specified interestingness measures *support* and *confidence* are required to specify the frequency and the strength of the generated association rule and also to avoid discovery of unnecessary rules.

There are different types of association rules like Boolean, generalized, categorical, quantitative etc. These are classified on the basis of different data representations. But, there are some limitations of these types of association rules in discovering nontrivial knowledge. One major drawback of classical association rule mining is the problem of sharp boundary. At this point, Fuzzy association rule mining has a better data representation than that for classical association rule. By using fuzzy sets imprecise terms and relations employed by humans in communication and understanding can be optimally modeled [2]. Therefore, fuzzy technique is used as component of data mining system because of their affinity with human knowledge representation [3].

In this paper, primary attention is paid on the representation of composite items with fuzzy association rule mining algorithm. For this a dataset consisting of nutrient values of regional food recipes of Assam is prepared [4, 5]. Then the Composite Fuzzy Association Rule Mining Algorithm [6] is applied on this dataset to generate association rules from composite nutrient attribute from large transaction of data. The term composite item means combination of several items. Here, by means of association rules, the intake behavior of different nutrients from different recipes are observed and it is tried to find out the per day consumption of those nutrients from meals that are taken by a person in a day. For this a list of normal diet containing some typical Assamese recipe is taken.

2   Background and Related Works

In literature the term "composite item" is defined as combination of several items. This concept of composite items has been used in data mining, especially in association rule mining, just to show how, combining two attributes more appropriate rules can be generated which otherwise may not be found individually from a single attribute because of low support. For example, if itemset {A, B} and {A, C} are not larger than specified support count then {B} → {A} and {C} → {A} will not be generated. But, if B and C are combined to make a new composite item {B, C} then it may be large and rules such as {B, C} → A may be generated. Composite items are defined as an item with properties or attributes [3]. In association rule mining, quantitative attributes are divided into various partitions and each partition is regarded as a binary valued attribute. But there is a major drawback regarding sharp boundary problem. Fuzzy association rule mining [7, 8] method has been applied to resolve this problem by using membership function for converting numeric values into membership degree on the basis of support count regardless of whether an item value belongs to one or more fuzzy sets.

2.1   Interestingness Measure

Interestingness measures are required to discover meaningful association rules in large datasets. Association rules are conventionally discovered based on support-confidence framework. Fuzzy Support (FS) [9] can be calculated as follows:

$$FS(A) = \frac{\text{sum of votes satisfying A}}{\text{Number of records in T}}$$

Where, $A(a1, a2, a3,\ldots\ldots, a|A|\}$ is a set of property attribute-fuzzy set (label) pairs such that $A \subseteq P \times L$. A record t'_i satisfies A if $A \subseteq t'_i$. The individual vote per record is calculated by multiplying the membership degree with an attribute –fuzzy set pair $[i[1]] \in A$:

Votes for t_i satisfying $A = \prod_{\forall [i[l]] \in A} t'i[i[l]]$

Therefore,

$$FS(A) = \frac{\sum_{i=1}^{i=n} \prod_{\forall [i[l]] \in A} t'i.[i[l]]}{n}$$

Frequent attribute sets with fuzzy support as given above with the specified threshold are used to generate all possible rules. A fuzzy association rule derived from a fuzzy frequent attribute set C is of the form:

$$A \rightarrow B$$

Where, A and B are disjoint subsets of the set $P \times L$ such that $A \cup B = C$.

Fuzzy Confidence (FC) of an association rule $A \rightarrow B$ is calculated as in the case of classical association rule and is given by

$$FC(A \rightarrow B) = \frac{FS(A \cup B)}{FS(A)}$$

3   CFARM Algorithm

Like A priori algorithm, the Composite Fuzzy Association Rule Mining (CFARM) algorithm also applies the breadth first search technique. The algorithm consists of four major steps:

1. Conversion of transaction dataset (T) into a property dataset (T^P).
2. Conversion of property dataset (T^P) into fuzzy dataset (T).
3. Application of an A priori like fuzzy association rule mining algorithm to T' using fuzzy support, confidence and correlation measures to generate a set of frequent itemset F.
4. Process F and generate a set of fuzzy association rules R such that $\forall r \in R$.

3.1 Mining Composite Fuzzy Association Rules Among Nutrients in Food Recipe

The quantity of nutrients in food recipes depends on the ingredients and association among the nutrients can be analyzed by applying the composite fuzzy association rule mining technique. For this purpose, a data set of nutrient composition of different food recipes is prepared based on the information available in [4, 10]. Then the CFARM algorithm is applied on this data set to discover the rules. It is illustrated below.

Example: Consider a dataset shown in Table 1 containing nutrient composition of different food recipes [4, 10]. The food items are typical Assamese foods represented in some recipe codes. The data set is prepared as a transaction dataset (T) in which a transaction includes a meal generally prepared for the lunch time. The data for a period of one week is shown below in Table 1.

Table 1. Recipe and nutrient value

Sl No	Recipes	Recipe code	Protein (g)	Fats (g)	Fiber (g)	Carbohydrates (g)	Energy (KJ)	Calcium (mg)	Iron (mg)	Vitamin C (mg)
1	Rice (white)	R1	7.1	0.66	1.3	80	1528	28	0.8	0
2	Wheat	R2	12.6	1.54	12.2	71	1369	29	3.19	0
3	Kasu thur patat diya	R3	0.7	1.6	5.2	4.3	143.9	109.3	2.6	24.1
4	Masundari patat diya	R4	1.2	0.8	0.4	12.6	261.1	192.8	6.2	6.3
5	Mandhania chutney	R5	1.7	0.6	0.6	6.3	156.5	75.5	2.2	6.1
6	Kalmou sak bhaji	R6	1.2	11.8	5.4	13.8	695.4	182.5	3.4	16.2
7	Dhekia sak bhaji	R7	1.7	7.8	4.6	10.7	501.2	73.5	3.1	8.1
8	Morisa sak bhaji	R8	1.6	12.9	3.2	9.9	678.2	342	7.8	6.5
9	Lai sak bhaji	R9	1.6	5.5	2	9	384.5	358.7	7.4	20.2
10	Aloo pitika	R10	3.3	1.3	0.5	14	338.5	52	1.7	6.5
11.	Pura aloo pitika	R11	3	1.3	0.3	22.8	480.7	107.2	5.8	6.3
12.	Aloo bilahi pitika	R12	3.5	0.8	0.3	10.9	271.1	153.5	4.8	6.2
13	Pura bengena aru sijua kani pitika	R13	4.9	3.6	0.4	9.7	379.9	391.7	3.7	15.5
14	Kaldil bhaji	R14	2.2	8.7	3.1	11.1	550.2	102	2.5	3.7
15	Kathalar tarkari	R15	1.3	8.1	2.9	12.2	530.9	128.9	11.8	1.7
16	Tita kerela bhaji	R16	0.9	8.9	6.5	15.5	609.6	212.5	4.6	8.2
17	Bhat kerela bhaji	R17	0.9	9.8	12.6	8.1	519.7	231.8	4.8	9.1
18	Rou masar tenga	R18	2	2.7	0.2	11.5	327.6	122.8	1.9	41.5
19	Rou mas bhoja	R19	21.2	11.6	0.1	6.9	907.1	287.2	5.1	12.2
20	Rou masar cutlet	R20	8.3	22.5	5.5	12.6	1197	489.5	3.7	14.8
21	Rou masar charchari	R21	8.9	13.8	1.2	13.3	891.2	219.3	3.9	14.3
22	Boriola mas bhoja	R22	27	26.7	–	8.2	1594	286.9	7.9	15.4
23	Murgi mansar jol	R23	4.1	13.8	1.8	13	805.8	230.5	2	26.
24	Bhoja murgi	R24	26.9	16.3	0.6	10.2	1235	230.5	6.5	9.4
25	Murgi mansar biryani*	R25	8.8	6.9	1	22.1	776.9	188.3	5.1	18.6
26	Kharikat diya murgi*	R26	31.6	15.1	0.9	10.2	1268	678.5	7.9	13

The input data termed as Raw Dataset D consists of a set of transaction $T = \{t_1, t_2, ..., t_n\}$, composite items $I = \{i_1, i_2, ..., i_{|I|}\}$ and properties $P = \{p_1, p_2, ..., p_n\}$. Each transaction t_i is some subset of I and each item $t_i[ij]$ is subset of P. Here, $t_i[ij]$ means the jth item in the ith transaction. The nutrient values of different properties of recipes can be represented as $t_i[ij] = \{v|v_1, v_2, ..., v_m\}$. Thus "$k^{th}$" property value for j^{th} item in the ith transaction is $t_i[ij[vk]]$. In this example each composite item is represented using the notation <label, value> as shown in the Table 3 based on the transaction dataset in Table 2 and the recipe and nutrient values shown in Table 1.

Table 2. Example of transaction dataset

TID	Day	Recipe codes
1	Sunday	$R_1,R_3,R_5,R_6,R_{10},R_{15},R_{19},R_{23}$
2	Monday	$R_1,R_7,R_{11},R_{14},R_{15},R_{16},R_{21}$
3	Tuesday	$R_1,R_4,R_8,R_{13},R_{17},R_{19},R_{20}$
4	Wednesday	$R_2,R_3,R_9,R_{12},R_{14},R_{23}$
5	Thursday	$R_1,R_3,R_5,R_7,R_{11},R_{15},R_{16}$
6	Friday	$R_1,R_9,R_{10},R_{13},R_{17},R_{18}$

Table 3. Example of raw dataset

TID	Record
1	{<R1,{7.1,0.66,1.3,80,1528,28,0.8,0.0}> <R3,{0.7,1.6,5.2,4.3,144,109,3,2.6,24.1}> <R5,{1.7,0.6,0.6,6.3,156.5,75.5,2.2,6.1}> <R6,{1.2,11.8,5.4,13.8,695,182.5,3.4,16.2}> <R10,{3.3,1.3,0.5,14.0,339.0,52.0,1.7,6.5}> <R15,{1.3,8.1,2.9,12.2,531.0,128.9,11.8,1.7}> <R19,{21.2,11.6,0.1,6.9,907.0,287.2,5.1,12.2}> <R23,{4.1,13.8,1.8,13.0,806.0,230.5,2.0,26.8}>}

According to the first step of CFARM algorithm raw dataset D is initially transformed into property Dataset D^P as shown in the Table 4. It includes property transaction T^P and property attributes P where $\forall t_i^p \sqsubset P$. The value for each property attribute $t_i^p[pj]$ is calculated by aggregating the values for all Pj in t_1 as follows:

$$\text{Prop Value}(t_j^p[pj]) = \frac{\sum_{j=1}^{|ti|} ti[ij[vk]]}{|ti|}$$

Table 4. Example of property dataset D_p generated from the raw dataset given in the Table 3.

Tid	X_1 (protein) (g)	X_2 (fats) (g)	X_3 (fiber) (g)	X_4 (carbohydrates) (g)	X_5 (energy) (KJ)	X_6 (calcium) (mg)	X_7 (iron) (mg)	X_8 (vitamin C) (mg)
1	5.0	6.1	2.2	9.8	638.3	136.7	3.7	11.7
2	2.6	5.4	2.7	23.4	649.0	110.7	4.3	9.9
3	6.4	8.8	3.3	19.9	781.5	280.4	4.5	9.2
4	4.1	5.3	4.1	19.3	587.5	163.8	3.7	13.5
5	2.3	4.1	3.0	21.6	564.5	104.9	4.4	7.7
6	3.3	3.9	2.8	22.0	580.0	197.5	3.3	15.4
7	6.3	8.4	4.8	18.0	712.3	185.4	3.9	9.2

Here the numerical values are taken up to one decimal place.

According to the second step, once a property dataset is defined, it is transformed into the fuzzy dataset D'. A fuzzy dataset includes fuzzy transaction T' and fuzzy property attributes P'. Each of fuzzy property attributes $t_i^p[pj]$ then represented into different linguistic labels $L = \{l_1, l_2, \ldots, l_{|l|}\}$. Linguistic labels are then represented using fuzzy membership degree in between 0 to 1. The user defined fuzzy ranges is expressed in properties table as given in Table 5.

Table 5. Fuzzy ranges of properties table for raw dataset

Property Attributes	Linguistic labels		
	Low	Medium	High
X_1	$V_k \leq 3.5$	$2.5 < V_k \leq 5.5$	$4.5 < V_k$
X_2	$V_k \leq 4.5$	$3.5 < V_k \leq 6.5$	$5.5 < V_k$
X_3	$V_k \leq 3.0$	$2 < V_k \leq 5$	$4 < V_k$
X_4	$V_k \leq 12$	$10 < V_k \leq 20$	$18 < V_k$
X_5	$V_k \leq 600$	$550 < V_k \leq 700$	$650\ V_k$
X_6	$V_k \leq 140$	$120 < V_k \leq 200$	$180 < V_k$
X_7	$V_k \leq 4$	$3.8 < V_k \leq 4.4$	$4.2 < V_k$
X_8	$V_k \leq 9$	$8 < V_k \leq 11$	$10 < V_k$

Using membership function $\mu(t_i^p[pj], I_k)$, the numeric value of each property attribute $t_i^p[pj]$ are mapped into the membership degree. Thus complete Fuzzy property attributes P' is given by $P \times L$. In Table 6, a fuzzy data set constructed from the property dataset is given.

Table 6. Fuzzy dataset (T′)

TID	X1			X2			X3			X4			X5			X6			X7			X8		
	L	M	H	L	M	H	L	M	H	L	M	H	L	M	H	L	M	H	L	M	H	L	M	H
1	0	0.5	0.5	0	0.4	0.6	0.8	0.2	0	1	0	0	0	1	0	0.2	0.8	0	1	0	0	0	0	1
2	0.9	0.1	0	0	1	0	0.3	0.7	0	0	0	1	0	1	0	1	0	0	0	0.5	0.5	0	1	0
3	0	0	1	0	0	1	0	1	0	0	0.1	0.9	0	0	1	0	0	1.0	0	0	1	0	1	0
4	0	1	0	0	1	0	0	0.9	0.1	0	0.1	0.9	0.3	0.7	0	0	0.8	0.2	1	0	0	0	0	1
5	1	0	0	0.4	0.6	0	0	1	0	0	0	1	0.7	0.3	0	1	0	0	0	0	1	1	0	0
6	0.3	0.7	0	0.6	0.4	0	0.2	0.8	0	0	0	1	0.4	0.6	0	0	0.1	0.9	1	\0	0	0	0	1
7	0	0	1	0	0	1	0	0.2	0.8	0	1	0	0	0	1	0	0.8	0.2	0.5	0.5	0	0	1	0
8	2.2	2.3	2.5	1.0	3.4	2.6	1.3	4.8	0.9	1.0	1.2	4.8	1.4	3.6	2.0	2.2	2.4	2.3	3.5	1.0	2.5	1.0	3.0	3.0

Now, according to the third step of the algorithm an a priori like algorithm FTDA [11] is applied on this fuzzy dataset. On the basis of user specified threshold like min support count frequent items are selected as given in Table 7.

Table 7. Frequent items

Itemset	Support
$X_2.M$	3.4
$X_3.M$	4.8
$X_4.H$	4.8
$X_5.M$	3.6
$X_7.L$	3.5
$X_8.M$	3.0
$X_8.H$	3.0

In the next step, using the intersection operator between each of two possible Itemsets and on the basis of the minimum support count various combinations are selected as frequent. These are shown in Table 8.

Table 8. Frequent item set

Itemset	Support
$(X_3.M, X_4.H)$	4.3
$(X_3.M, X_8.M)$	3.5
$(X_7.L, X_8.H)$	3.0

In the fourth and final step of the CFARM algorithm association rules are discovered from the frequent itemsets. Some of the possible rules are shown below.

If X_3 = Middle then X_4 = High. (Support = 4.3)
If X_4 = High then X_3 = Middle. (Support = 4.3)
If X_3 = Middle, then X_8 = Middle. (Support = 3.5)
If X_8 = Middle, then X_3 = Middle. (Support = 3.5)
If X_7 = Low, then X_8 = High. (Support = 3.0)
If X_8 = High, then X_7 = Low. (Support = 3.0)

Now, these rules are converted into rules involving property attributes by substituting the corresponding property attributes. The following are the rules:

If Fiber = Middle then Carbohydrates = High. (Support = 4.3)
If Carbohydrates = High, then Fiber = Middle. (Support = 4.3)
If Fiber = Middle then Vitamin C = Middle. (Support = 3.5)
If Vitamin C = Middle, then Fiber = Middle. (Support = 3.5)
If Iron = Low, then Vitamin C = High. (Support = 3.0)
If Vitamin C = High, then Iron = Low. (Support = 3.0)

The pre specified minimum confidence is considered to be 0.5. The confidence for the above association rules are calculated with respect to this value of minimum confidence. The first rule is taken as an example. The confidence for the association rule "If X_3 = Middle then X_4 = High" can be calculated by the formula

$$\sum_1^7 (\text{If X3. Middle then X4. High}) / \sum_1^7 \text{X3. Middle} = 0.8$$

That is, "If Fiber = Middle then Carbohydrates = High" has support = 4.3 and confidence = 0.8.

Similarly, the confidences of the other association rules are calculated and are given below.

"If X_4 = High then X_3 = Middle" has confidence 0.8
"If X_3 = Middle, then X_8 = Middle" has confidence 0.7
"If X_8 = Middle, then X_3 = Middle" has confidence 1.1
"If X_7 = Low, then X_8 = High" has confidence 0.8
"If X_8 = High, then X_7 = Low" has confidence 1.0.

4 Experimental Results

In this experiment, it is assumed that the minimum support count is 3.0 and minimum confidence is 0.5. However, different rules may be generated if the interesting measures are changed. If the value of minimum support is less, more number of frequent itemsets will be found and more rules will be generated. On the other hand higher values of pre specified minimum support if provided as threshold may generate less number of rules. Therefore, it is critical to fix a proper user specified threshold on minimum support so that unnecessary rules are not generated or sometimes meaningful rules are not omitted. There is another issue regarding size of the dataset which also can affect the entire process.

The association rules discovered as a result of the experiments expresses the inter relationships among the intake of nutrients in the diets of the people taken over a period of time. For example, the association rule "If Fiber = Middle then Carbohydrates = High" discovered from the above data has support = 4.3 and confidence = 0.8. This means the content of fiber and carbohydrates together in the diets has an occurrence of 4.3 and out of all these people who consume fiber also consume carbohydrates on 80% of the time in their diets. Similarly all the other association rules can be interpreted. Thus, these association rules provide an analysis of the nutrient contents in the diets of the people over a period of time.

5 Discussion and Conclusion

In this paper, to analyze the nutrient contents in the diets of people containing various food recipes a data set is constructed. As different recipes contain different ingredients and hence has different nutrients and a particular diet is a combination of different recipes, therefore, the diets of various people over a period of time are collected and is designed as a transaction data set. Then the concept of composite association rule is applied by incorporating the fuzzy approach in the process of mining the association rules which depict the nutrient intake of the people involved. Then the Composite Fuzzy Association Rule Mining algorithm (CFARM) is applied in the database of different recipes having different nutrient values. The CFARM algorithm is a better option when the dataset consists of multiple attributes. This algorithm is very useful to mine Fuzzy association rules for composite items. A framework of support, confidence as interesting measures is used in generating those rules. More experiments shall be carried out in future to justify it in more convincingly.

There are some other Fuzzy Association Rule Mining Algorithms like F-PNWAR [12] and E-FWARM [13] which are also useful to mine fuzzy association rules from transaction datasets and the results may also vary. In [14], a fuzzy based technique is used to choose the perfect association rules in medical data related to liver disorder.

However, there is a possibility to use some other interestingness measures to generate more meaningful rules in this regard. As future work, the present approach of mining fuzzy association rules shall be expanded by taking into account of the food habits of much larger group people and based on their age groups. This will include construction of larger datasets and carrying out more experiments in different areas of applications.

References

1. Agrawal, R., Imielinski, T., Swami, A.: Mining association rules between sets of items in large databases. In: Proceedings of ACM SIGMOD International Conference on Management of Data (1993)
2. Delgado, M., Marfin, N., Sanchez, D., Vila, M.A.: Fuzzy association rules: general model and applications. IEEE Trans. Fuzzy Syst. **11**(2), 214–225 (2003)

3. Maeda, A., Ashida, H., Taniguchi, Y., Takahashi, Y.: Data mining system using fuzzy rule induction. In: Proceedings of IEEE International Conference on Fuzzy Systems (1995)
4. Das, P., Devi, L.P., Gogoi, M.: Nutrient composition of some regional recipes of Assam, India. Stud. Ethno-Med. 3(2), 111–117 (2009)
5. Barooah, M.S., Das, M., Chatterjee, L., Baruah, C., Khatoniar, S.: Nutrient composition of some traditional breakfast cereals of Assam. Int. J. Chem. Stud. 6(3), 2535–2537 (2018)
6. Muyeba, M., Khan, M.S., Coenen, F.: A framework for mining fuzzy association rules from composite items. In: Chawla, S., et al. (eds.) PAKDD 2008. LNCS (LNAI), vol. 5433, pp. 62–74. Springer, Heidelberg (2009). https://doi.org/10.1007/978-3-642-00399-8_6
7. Kouk, C., Fu, A., Wong, H.: Mining fuzzy association rules in databases. ACM SIGMOD Record. 27(1), 41–46 (1998)
8. Chen, G., Wei, Q.: Fuzzy association rules and the extended mining association algorithms. Inf. Sci. 147(1–4), 201–228 (2002)
9. Gyenesei, A.: A Fuzzy approach for mining quantitative association rules. Acta Cybern. 15(2), 305–320 (2001)
10. Nutrient data laboratory. United States department of Agriculture. Accessed 10 Aug 2016
11. Hong, T.P., Kuo, C.S., Chi, S.C.: Mining association rules from quantitative data. Intell. Data Anal. 3(5), 363–376 (1999)
12. Mangayarkkarasi, K., Chidambaram, M.: F-PNWAR: fuzzy-based positive and negative weighted association rule mining algorithm (2018)
13. Mangayarkkarasi, K., Chidambaram, M.: E-FWARM: enhanced fuzzy–based weighted association rule mining algorithm (2018)
14. Thakur, R.S.: Intelligent decision making in medical data using association rules mining and fuzzy analytic hiearchy process. Int. J. Recent Technol. Eng. (IJRTE) 7(6) (2019). ISSN: 22777-3878

Evaluation of Multiplier-Less DCT Transform Using In-Exact Computing

Uppugunduru Anil Kumar(✉)(iD), Nishant Jain, Sumit K. Chatterjee, and Syed Ershad Ahmed

BITS Pilani Hyderabad Campus, Hyderabad, India
anilkumaruppugundur@gmail.com

Abstract. Discrete Cosine Transform (DCT) is an ubiquitous operation that tends to consume more power when implemented on hardware. In-exact computing, an emerging paradigm, aids to reduce the energy consumption in these error resilient image and video processing application. In this paper, we propose a new in-exact adder architecture which when implemented in DCT reduces the computational complexity that too without comprimising the peak signal-to-noise ratio (PSNR). Exhaustive PSNR and synthesis analysis prove that the proposed design performs better than existing adder architectures. The proposed design is implemented in 180 nm CMOS process technology node and results show that die area and power consumed are reduced upto 10% and 8% respectively.

Keywords: Discrete cosine transform · In-exact computing · In-exact adder

1 Introduction

Approximate computing is an emerging paradigm that yields a significant reduction in computation resources in media processing applications. This method is gaining importance particularly in the ubiquitous image and video applications that have power and area constraints.

To process image and video information, different types of image and video compression techniques and algorithms are extensively used in digital signal processing (DSP) systems. The Joint Photographic Experts Group (JPEG) technique is a generally used technique in image processing while for video processing, Moving Picture Experts Group (MPEG) is a broadly used technique. The fundamental block in image and video processing standards such as JPEG and MPEG compression is a discrete cosine transform (DCT). Different types of DCT algorithms [1] are implemented for image and video processing applications. These algorithms implementation requires more hardware resources due to floating-point multiplications. To mitigate this, Bouguezel and Cintra et al.

© Springer Nature Singapore Pte Ltd. 2020
A. Bhattacharjee et al. (Eds.): MIND 2020, CCIS 1241, pp. 11–23, 2020.
https://doi.org/10.1007/978-981-15-6318-8_2

[2–5] proposed integer multiplications based DCT which are faster than the conventional algorithms [6]. However, they still remain the power-hungry blocks in JPEG and MPEG standards. To reduce the power consumption, imprecise computations are carried out in DCT since image and video processing error-resilient applications [7]. By introducing the imprecise computations in the DCT improvements in the area, delay and power can be achieved [8–13].

In this paper, we propose a new in-exact adder architecture for multiplier-less DCT architectures with intend to reduce the computational complexity. The proposed adder in DCT compression achieves acceptable peak signal to noise ratio (PSNR) while simplifying the addition operation in hardware compared to the existing designs. The same has been quantified by carrying out an exhaustive error and hardware analysis. The rest of the paper is organized as follows. Preliminary information about existing multiplier-less approximate DCT and adder architectures are represented in Sect. 2. Section 3 presents the proposed framework while the evaluation of the proposed framework is provided in Sect. 4. Finally, conclusions are drawn in Sect. 5.

2   Related Work

Various multiplier-less DCT algorithms [2–5] targetted for image and video processing applications are present in literature. Most of the existing works implement DCT using simple shift-and-add operations which consumes less hardware [7]. Since these DCT blocks will be deployed in error-resilient image processing applications further improvement in hardware can be obtained by pruning the adder modules.

The transformation matrix for n-point 1D DCT is given as:

$$H(u,v) = \begin{cases} \sqrt{\dfrac{1}{n}}, & u = 0, 0 \le v \le n-1 \\ \sqrt{\dfrac{2}{n}} cos[(2v+1)\pi u/2n], & 1 \le u \le n-1, 0 \le v \le n-1 \end{cases}$$

The n-point 2D Conventional DCT of X (n * n matrix) is given as:

$$F = HXH'$$ (1)

The inverse DCT for Eq. 1 is given as:

$$X = H'FH$$ (2)

The n-point 2D approximate DCT of X (n x n matrix) is given as:

$$F = CXC^1 = D(TXT')D$$ (3)

where

$$C = D * T$$ (4)

T is a low complexity matrix whose elements belong to the set $\{0, -1/2, 1/2, 1, -1\}$ and D is a diagonal matrix of size $n*n$ is of the format of $1/\sqrt{r}$, where 'r' is a positive integer.

The inverse DCT for Eq. 3 is given as:

$$X = C^1 FC = T'(DFD)T \tag{5}$$

Section 2.1 discusses the mathematical description of various approximate DCT transforms while existing in-exact adders are presented in Sect. 2.2.

2.1 Approximate DCT Transforms

A large number of approximate DCT transforms are available that decrease the computation complexity with minimal effect on the image quality. The complexity of the approximate DCT transform depends on the low complexity matrix(T). Here multiplier-less implementation can be achieved as the low complexity transformation matrix consists of elements that are only powers of two.

Bouguezel et al. [2] proposed an approximate DCT matrix technique named BAS 2008 that eliminates the multiplication operation. BAS 2008 approximation defined the following mathematical structure for low complexity transformation:

$$C = D * T = D * \begin{bmatrix} 1 & 1 & 1 & 1 & 1 & 1 & 1 & 1 \\ 1 & 1 & 0 & 0 & 0 & 0 & -1 & -1 \\ 1 & \frac{1}{2} & -\frac{1}{2} & -1 & -1 & -\frac{1}{2} & \frac{1}{2} & 1 \\ 0 & 0 & -1 & 0 & 0 & 1 & 0 & 0 \\ 1 & -1 & -1 & 1 & 1 & -1 & -1 & 1 \\ 1 & -1 & 0 & 0 & 0 & 0 & 1 & -1 \\ \frac{1}{2} & -1 & 1 & -\frac{1}{2} & -\frac{1}{2} & 1 & -1 & \frac{1}{2} \\ 0 & 0 & 0 & -1 & 1 & 0 & 0 & 0 \end{bmatrix} \tag{6}$$

Where D $= \text{diag}(1/(2\sqrt{2}), 1/2, 1/\sqrt{5}, 1/\sqrt{2}, 1/(2\sqrt{2}), 1/2, 1/\sqrt{5}, 1/\sqrt{2})$

Hence DCT computation requires only addition and shift operations because matrix T consists only of 1, -1, 0, 1/2, -1/2. This method reduces the quality of decompressed image mariginally, while on the other hand giving immense benefits in the complexity area.

Work by Bouguezel et al. [3] named BAS11 proposed a low complexity parametric transform for image compression. These transform matrix contains one parameter, whose value is adjusted to trade quality for complexity. The transformation matrix is given as follows:

$$T = \begin{bmatrix} 1 & 1 & 1 & 1 & 1 & 1 & 1 & 1 \\ 1 & 1 & 0 & 0 & 0 & 0 & -1 & -1 \\ 1 & a & -a & -1 & -1 & -a & a & 1 \\ 0 & 0 & 1 & 0 & 0 & -1 & 0 & 0 \\ 1 & -1 & -1 & 1 & 1 & -1 & -1 & 1 \\ 0 & 0 & 0 & 1 & -1 & 0 & 0 & 0 \\ 1 & -1 & 0 & 0 & 0 & 0 & 1 & -1 \\ a & -1 & 1 & -a & -a & 1 & -1 & a \end{bmatrix}$$

and $D = \text{diag}(1/(2\sqrt{2}),\ 1/2,\ 1/\sqrt{(4+4a^2)},\ 1/\sqrt{2},\ 1/(2\sqrt{2}),\ 1/\sqrt{2},\ 1/2,$ $1/\sqrt{(4+4a^2)})$

The complexity of the transformation matrix depends on the parameter 'a'. The value of 'a' is selected to be either '0' or '1' to simplify the transformation matrix [3].

In [4], the authors proposed a matrix, which is derived by rounding the elements of the DCT matrix to the nearest integer. This method referred as CB11 method uses the following matrices

$$
T = \begin{bmatrix}
1 & 1 & 1 & 1 & 1 & 1 & 1 & 1 \\
1 & 1 & 1 & 0 & 0 & -1 & -1 & -1 \\
1 & 0 & 0 & -1 & -1 & 0 & 0 & 1 \\
1 & 0 & -1 & -1 & 1 & 1 & 0 & -1 \\
1 & -1 & -1 & 1 & 1 & -1 & -1 & 1 \\
1 & -1 & 0 & 1 & -1 & 0 & 1 & -1 \\
0 & -1 & 1 & 0 & 0 & 1 & -1 & 0 \\
0 & -1 & 1 & -1 & 1 & -1 & 1 & 0
\end{bmatrix}
$$

and $D = \text{diag}(1/(2\sqrt{2}),\ 1/\sqrt{6},\ 1/2,\ 1/\sqrt{6},\ 1/(2\sqrt{2}),\ 1/\sqrt{6},\ 1/2,\ 1/\sqrt{6})$

This simple yet clever approach to finding approximate DCTs gives better results than BAS08 and removes shift operations too.

In [5] authors searched the 8×8 matrix space for the lowest complexity matrix whose structure would be similar to that of the conventional 8×8 DCT. They found eight matrices and chose the best based on its performance in JPEG-like compression. This method named PEA14 employs the following transformation matrix

$$
T = \begin{bmatrix}
1 & 1 & 1 & 1 & 1 & 1 & 1 & 1 \\
0 & 1 & 0 & 0 & 0 & 0 & -1 & 0 \\
1 & 0 & 0 & -1 & -1 & 0 & 0 & 1 \\
1 & 0 & 0 & 0 & 0 & 0 & 0 & -1 \\
1 & -1 & -1 & 1 & 1 & -1 & -1 & 1 \\
0 & 0 & 0 & 1 & -1 & 0 & 0 & 0 \\
0 & -1 & 1 & 0 & 0 & 1 & -1 & 0 \\
0 & 0 & 1 & 0 & 0 & -1 & 0 & 0
\end{bmatrix}
$$

and $D = \text{diag}(1/(2\sqrt{2}),\ 1/\sqrt{2},\ 1/2,\ 1/\sqrt{2},\ 1/(2\sqrt{2}),\ 1/\sqrt{2},\ 1/2,\ 1/\sqrt{2})$

Since this DCT was found by extensive computational search, it is by far the best performing approximate DCT. PEA14 uses less number of additions compared to all other existing DCT methods. So computation complexity very low compared to other existing DCTs.

2.2 In-Exact Adders

Arithmetic operations are well suited for in-exact computing. One of the fundamental operations in the multiplier-less DCT techniques is an addition. The inexact adders, when deployed in DCT architectures, leads to a significant reduction in power, area and delay [8–13]. Most of the inexact adder splits the adder into two parts: exact portion and in-exact portion. Figure 1 shows an N-bit inexact adder with an in-exact portion of m bit width.

In a typical truncated adder [14], k least significant bits (LSB) are truncated while the remaining (n-k) MSB bits are processed using accurate adder. Truncation adder occupies less area and consumes less power though with a trade-off in precision. Mahdiani et al. proposed Lower-part OR Adder (LoA) with an intent to improve the precision of the lower part of the adder using OR gates [15]. Carry in for the MSB section is calculated by using AND operation between the kth bits of LSB section of two inputs. Therefore, the critical path delay of LoA adder depends on AND gate delay and accurate adder delay. LoA adder is the best adder architecture compared to all the existing in-exact adder architectures with respect to hardware and error tradeoff [16].

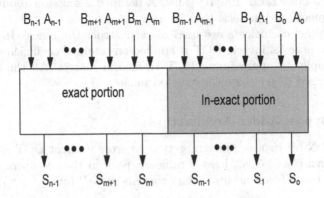

Fig. 1. A typical approximate adder architecture.

Work in [17] presents an adder design with high precision namely the Error tolerant adder (ETA1). The approximate lower part of ETA1 is implemented using half adders. In ETA1 LSB part sum is computed from the most significant bit k-1 to least significant bit position 0. If the carry out of k-1-bit position is "1" then sum bits of remaining least significant part is set to "1" otherwise sum result is the one computed by the half adder.

3 Proposed Work

Various DCT approximate methods are available in the literature to generate DCT coefficients. In this work, we focus on the existing multiplier-less techniques that involve addition and shifting operations. The existing DCT compression schemes [2–5] using exact addition operations tend to add to the computation complexity. Since DCT computation can tolerate errors up to a certain limit, replacing exact adders with in-exact adder will results in savings in area, power and delay.

The main contribution of this work involves designing an in-exact adder architecture targeted for error-tolerant DCT transform. The proposed adder improves the area, delay and power characteristics while achieving PSNR values to acceptable limit [18].

The typical image compression and reconstruction process using approximate DCT transform is shown in Fig. 2. In the image compression process, the input image is divided into 8 * 8 image sub-blocks. These sub-blocks are then approximated using low complexity approximate DCT transform matrix to obtain 64 coefficients. From these coefficients, ignore the DCT coefficients that generate high-frequency components, which are not sensitive to the human eye, while other DCT coefficients are retained. A different number of retained coefficients are considered when applied to image compression. By pruning the retained coefficients, the overall DCT circuit complexity can be reduced however it affects the peak signal-noise ratio (PSNR) value. A detailed discussion about the effect on PSNR as mentioned in Sect. 4.

These retained coefficients are used to reconstruct the image. In the image reconstruction process, inverse DCT is applied on retained coefficients using the same low complexity approximate DCT transform matrix. All the 8 * 8 sub-blocks are merged to get the reconstructed image.

3.1 New Bypass Adder Architecture

The proposed N-bit bypass adder targetted to error resilient DCT is composed of two portions: the in-exact least significant portion that comprises of P-bits while the most significant accurate part consists of N-P bits.

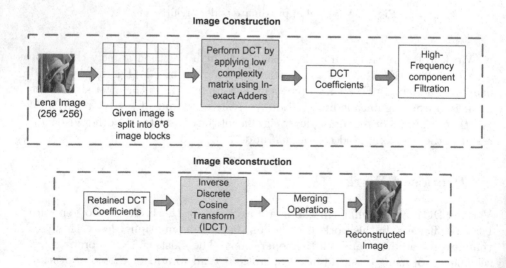

Fig. 2. Image construction and reconstruction process using DCT

The most significant adder is implemented using accurate adder such as ripple carry adder or any other fast adder while the in-exact adder will not include any computation blocks such as full adders or any other logic gates. It can be observed from Fig. 3 (highlighted in the circle section) that the outputs of the in-exact block are the same as one of it's respective inputs. The advantage of this technique is it does not require any hardware however has trade-off in accuracy. Work in [15] replaced the in-exact portion with OR gates in place of full adder block to reduce the hardware. Since the in-exact portion contributes least to the final result, we propose to bypass the complete in-exact portion. For example, the value of s_0 is equal to a_0 as depicted in Fig. 2. As shown in Table 1, the obtained sum (s_0) is four times correct out of the eight possible input combinations.

Table 1. Truth table 1-bit bypass adder architecture

a	b	Cin	Actual sum	Obtained sum
0	0	0	0	0 ✓
0	0	1	1	0 ✗
0	1	0	1	0 ✗
0	1	1	0	0 ✓
1	0	0	1	1 ✓
1	0	1	0	1 ✗
1	1	0	0	1 ✗
1	1	1	1	1 ✓

As shown in the Fig. 3, if the two inputs to the in-exact portion of bypass adder module are $a_{p-1} a_{p-2} ..a_1 a_0$ while other input is $b_{p-1} b_{p-2} ..b_1 b_0$, the sum ($s_{p-1}$ to s_0) out of this block is $a_{p-1} a_{p-2} ..a_1 a_0$. The most significant bit (b_{p-1}) from the in-exact adder forms the carry-in (c_{p-1}) to the precise adder as shown in Fig. 3. As a result, the critical delay of the proposed bypass adder depends on the precise portion of the adder. The proposed adder consumes less power and occupies less area since no full adder or logic gates are used in the in-exact portion of the adder. Based on the size of the in-exact portion of the adder (P), the saving in area, delay and power changes however with the trade-off in precision. The computation complexity of approximate DCT using the proposed bypass adder is less compared to existing in-exact adders because no operation is performed in the in-exact portion of the proposed adder.

4   Results

The various multiplier-less DCT approximate algorithms [2–5] are implemented in MATLAB and the exact adder architectures in these algorithms are replaced with existing in-exact adders [14,15,17] and the proposed adder. These algorithms are then evaluated using various images such as Lena image and Cameraman using proposed and existing in-exact adders to compute PSNR. The value of MSE is used to compute PSNR which is mentioned below:

$$MSE = \frac{1}{pq} \sum_{m=0}^{p-1} \sum_{n=0}^{q-1} [I(m,n) - K(m,n)]^2 \tag{7}$$

and PSNR can be found using MSE, as given below:

$$PSNR(dB) = 10log_{10}(\frac{MAX_I^2}{MSE}) \tag{8}$$

Where MAX_I is the maximum pixel value of the image. The Plots in Fig. 4 and 5 shows that PSNR values of compressed Cameraman images by executing using BAS08, BAS11 with a = 0 & a = 1, CB11, PEA14 using existing [14,15,17] and proposed bypass adder. As shown in the figures, the considered existing DCT methods are arranged in rows from top to bottom as BAS08, BAS11 with

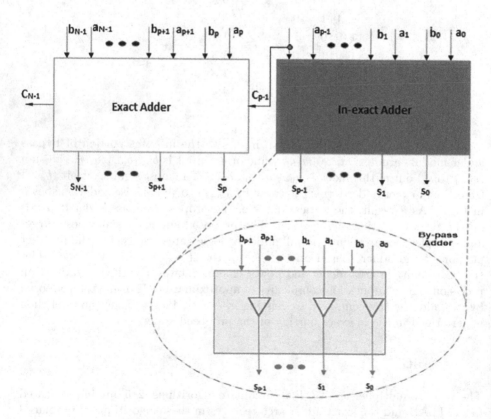

Fig. 3. Proposed bypass adder architecture.

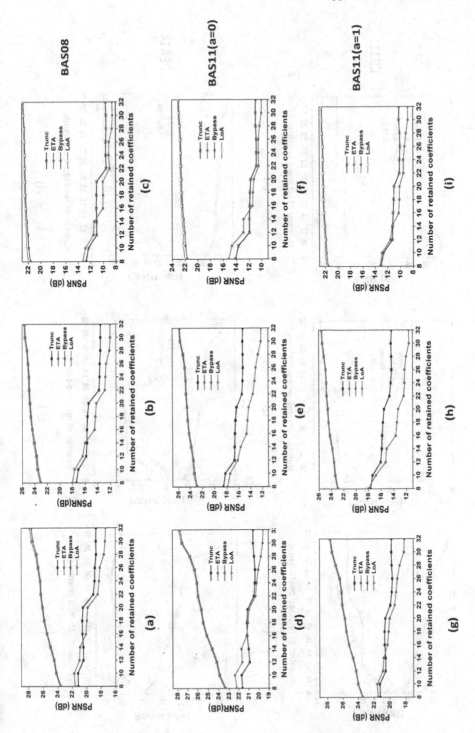

Fig. 4. In-exact DCT compression of Cameraman image using BAS08, BAS11 with a = 0 and a = 1 with different values of P.

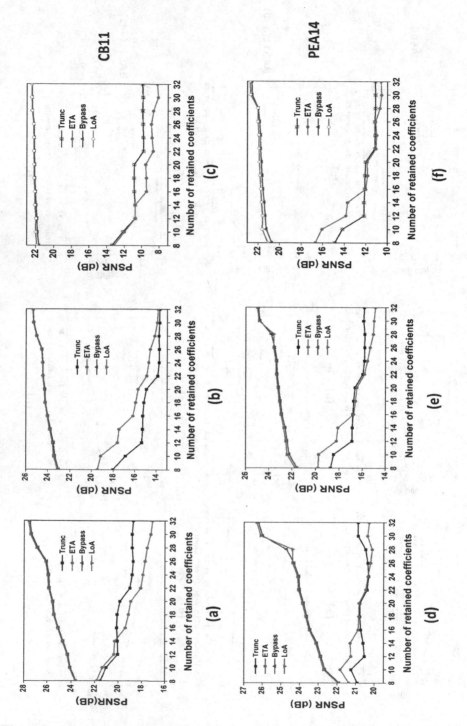

Fig. 5. In-exact DCT compression of Cameraman image using CB11 and PEA14 with different P values.

a=0 & a = 1, CB11 and PEA14 respectively. Each column represents the quality of a compressed image with different width of approximate bits (P) values. The leftmost column (Fig. 4 and 5) corresponds to P = 3, middle one represents to P = 4 while the rightmost column corresponds to P = 5.

The BAS08 [2] method implemented using the proposed and existing inexact adders corresponding to P = 3 is shown in Fig. 4 (a). The graph depicts the respective PSNR values obtained by varying the number of retained coefficients (C) for various adder architectures. It is evident from the graphs that the proposed and LoA [15] adder out-performs all the other adders. Further, related to the proposed design and LoA it can be observed that PSNR value increases with the value of C. However, in case of ETA and truncation adders the final result is rounded up and rounded down respectively, the resulting error is large and hence the PSNR values achieved is less. Similar results are obtained in other methods (BAS11 with a = 0 & a = 1,CB11 and PEA14) for different values of P. Though, LoA and the proposed adder achieves similar PSNR values, LoA adder tends to occupy more area and consume more power as discussed in Sect. 4.1.

It can be observed from Fig. 4 and 5 that PSNR values of approximate DCT using the proposed in-exact adder was more compared to existing in-exact adders except for LoA architecture. Compared to proposed one the PSNR values obtained with LoA are marginally better however it tends to occupy more area and power. In case of ETA since the result is rounded up in most of the cases then the final result is more than the correct result. In truncation, since the result is rounded down the result in all the cases is less than the correct result

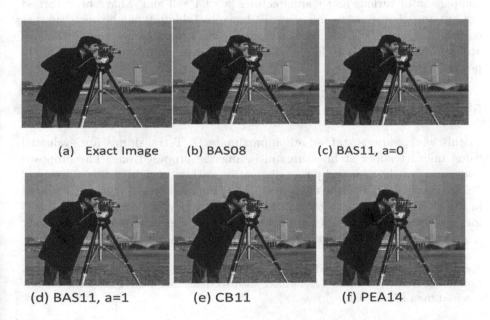

(a) Exact Image   (b) BAS08   (c) BAS11, a=0

(d) BAS11, a=1   (e) CB11   (f) PEA14

Fig. 6. (a) Exact adder output image (b-f) Processed images for P = 3 using DCTs.

Table 2. Synthesis results of various adder achitectures for P = 3 & 4.

Adder	P = 3			P = 4		
	Area(μm^2)	Power(nW)	Delay(ps)	Area(μm^2)	Power(nW)	Delay(ps)
Trunc [14]	215.914	8575.911	2106	198.274	7898.90	1928
ETA [17]	236.376	8976.70	2106	227.909	8504.81	1928
LoA [15]	237.082	9304.436	2288	222.970	8695.04	2109
Proposed Bypass	222.97	9141.76	2261	205.330	7995.395	2083

except for the case when both the operands are zero. From Fig. 4 and 5 it can be observed that if the number of approximate bits (P) increases then the PSNR value is decreased i.e. quality of the image is decreased. For P = 4, an acceptable level [18] of PSNR is obtained.

The same can be validated using exact and various approximate DCT compression techniques using the proposed in-exact adder for the Cameraman image and is shown in Fig. 6.

4.1   Synthesis Results

Various adder schemes are modeled in Gate level Verilog-HDL and simulated using Cadence incisive unified simulator (IUS). The synthesis has been carried out at 180 nm process technology nodes using the TSMC library. An exhaustive comparison of various adder architectures w.r.t P = 3 and 4 have been carried out in terms of area, delay and power is shown in Table 2. It can be observed that corresponding to P = 4, the proposed adder with bypass adder module achieves an improvement of 7 to 10% in area and achieves an improvement of 6 to 8% in power.

5   Conclusion

In this work, various state-of-art approximate DCT transforms are evaluated using in-exact adder architectures including the proposed one. The proposed adder reduces the area and power dissipation without a significant reduction of PSNR values. To prove the efficiency of the proposed adder, it is implemented in the DCT compression algorithm. Results prove that the proposed adder performs better than existing designs. The proposed design achieves area and power improvement 10% and 8% respectively without significant reduction in PSNR.

Acknowledgment. This work is supported by BITS Pilani under Research Initiation Grant (RIG) pro-gram. The authors wish to thank and acknowledge the support received from BITS Pilani.

References

1. Vladimir, B., Patrick, C.Y., Rao, K.R.: Discrete cosine and sine transforms: general properties, fast algorithms and integer approximations. Elsevier (2010)
2. Bouguezel, S., Ahmad, M.O., Swamy, M.N.S.: Low-complexity 8×8 transform for image compression. Electron. Lett. **44**(21), 1249–1250 (2008)
3. Bouguezel, S., Ahmad, M.O., Swamy, M.N.S.: A low-complexity parametric transform for image compression. In 2011 IEEE International Symposium of Circuits and Systems (ISCAS), pp. 2145–2148. IEEE (2011)
4. Cintra, R.J., Bayer, F.M.: A dct approximation for image compression. IEEE Signal Process. Lett. **18**(10), 579–582 (2011)
5. Potluri, U.S., Madanayake, A., Cintra, R.J., Bayer, F.M., Kulasekera, S., Edirisuriya, A.: Improved 8-point approximate dct for image and video compression requiring only 14 additions. IEEE Trans. Circ. Syst. I Regul. Papers **61**(6), 1727–1740 (2014)
6. Arai, Y., Agui, T., Nakajima, M.: A fast dct-sq scheme for images. IEICE Trans. (1976–1990) **71**(11), 1095–1097 (1988)
7. Liang, J., Tran, T.D.: Fast multiplierless approximations of the dct with the lifting scheme. IEEE Trans. Signal Process. **49**(12), 3032–3044 (2001)
8. Shin, D., Gupta, S.K.: Approximate logic synthesis for error tolerant applications. In: 2010 Design, Automation & Test in Europe Conference & Exhibition (DATE 2010), pp. 957–960. IEEE (2010)
9. Gupta, V., Mohapatra, D., Raghunathan, A., Roy, K.: Low-power digital signal processing using approximate adders. IEEE Trans. Comput.-Aid. Des. Integr. Circ. Syst. **32**(1), 124–137 (2012)
10. Liang, J., Han, J., Lombardi, F.: New metrics for the reliability of approximate and probabilistic adders. IEEE Trans. Comput. **62**(9), 1760–1771 (2012)
11. Jiang, H., Han, J., Lombardi, F.: A comparative review and evaluation of approximate adders. In: Proceedings of the 25th Edition on Great Lakes Symposium on VLSI, pp. 343–348 (2015)
12. Yang, Z., Jain, A., Liang, J., Han, J., Lombardi, F.: Approximate xor/xnor-based adders for inexact computing. In 2013 13th IEEE International Conference on Nanotechnology (IEEE-NANO 2013), pp. 690–693. IEEE (2013)
13. Almurib, H.A.F., Kumar, T.N., Lombardi, F.: Inexact designs for approximate low power addition by cell replacement. In 2016 Design, Automation & Test in Europe Conference & Exhibition (DATE), pp. 660–665. IEEE (2016)
14. Behrooz, P.: Computer Arithmetic, vol. 20. Oxford University Press, Cambridge (2010)
15. Mahdiani, H.R., Ahmadi, A., Fakhraie, S.M., Lucas, C.: Bio-inspired imprecise computational blocks for efficient vlsi implementation of soft-computing applications. IEEE Trans. Circ. Syst. I Regul. Papers **57**(4), 850–862 (2009)
16. Najafi, A., Weißbrich, W., Payá Vayá, G., Garcia-Ortiz, A.: A fair comparison of adders in stochastic regime. In: 2017 27th International Symposium on Power and Timing Modeling, Optimization and Simulation (PATMOS), pp. 1–6. IEEE (2017)
17. Zhu, N., Goh, W.L., Zhang, W., Yeo, K.S., Kong, Z.H.: Design of low-power high-speed truncation-error-tolerant adder and its application in digital signal processing. IEEE Trans. Very Large Scale Integr. (VLSI) Syst. **18**(8), 1225–1229 (2010)
18. Almurib, H.A.F., Kumar, T.N., Lombardi, F.: Approximate dct image compression using inexact computing. IEEE Trans. Comput. **67**(2), 149–159 (2017)

Legal Amount Recognition in Bank Cheques Using Capsule Networks

Nisarg Mistry[✉], Maneesh Darisi, Rahul Singh, Meet Shah,
and Aditya Malshikhare

Veermata Jijabai Technological Institute, Mumbai 400019, India
nisargbm@gmail.com, maneeshdarisi97@gmail.com,
singhrahul1497@gmail.com, meetshah145@gmail.com,
malshikhareaditya@gmail.com

Abstract. Legal amount detection is a decade old conundrum hindering the efficiency of automatic cheque detection systems. Ever since the advent of legal amount detection as a use-case in the computer vision ecosystem, it has been hampered by the deficiency of effective machine learning models to detect the language-specific legal amount on bank cheques. Currently, convolutional neural networks are the most widely used deep learning algorithms for image classification. Yet the majority of deep learning architectures fail to capture information like shape, orientation, pose of the images due to the use of max pooling. This paper proposes a novel way to extract, process and segment legal amounts into words from Indian bank cheques written in English and recognize them. The paper uses capsule networks to recognize legal amounts from the bank cheques, which enables the shape, pose and orientation detection of legal amounts by using dynamic routing and routing by agreement techniques for communication between capsules and thus improves the recognition accuracy.

Keywords: Legal amount detection · Capsule networks · Bank check recognition · Handwriting recognition · Image processing

1 Introduction

Automated cheque detection systems are an active field of research. This topic has high relevance in the finance industries, wherein an enormous number of cheques are processed on a daily basis. Legal amount extraction and recognition problem is a language-specific problem. People widely have divided the detection of legal amount from bank cheques into three major phases: 1. Location of legal amounts on the bank cheques and preprocessing them. 2. Segmentation of preprocessed bank cheques image into legal amount words. 3. Recognition of segmented legal amount words using diverse machine learning techniques.

Indian bank cheques have fixed layouts for various fields on the bank cheque and provide two baselines for writing the legal amount. The most basic step for legal amount detection is identifying the zones of interest. Identification of the baselines based on the layout of the bank cheque and extracting the legal amount based on the baselines is the primary task. Various techniques such as binarization [1], recursive

© Springer Nature Singapore Pte Ltd. 2020
A. Bhattacharjee et al. (Eds.): MIND 2020, CCIS 1241, pp. 24–37, 2020.
https://doi.org/10.1007/978-981-15-6318-8_3

thresholding [2], Arnold transforms [3], Least Square fitting, Hough transform [4], Gaussian filtering [5], noise elimination are used to detect legal amounts from the baselines. After the detection of the legal amount baselines, the next step is to segment the legal amount into subunits using either the holistic or analytical approach.

The next step is to recognize the segmented legal amounts. The field of handwriting recognition is a field under development with many innovative techniques coming up to tackle the problem. In recent times, CNNs or Convolutional neural networks [6] are used as the optimal and efficient deep learning neural network algorithms in most of the image classification tasks. One of the drawbacks of CNN is it uses max-pooling for down-sampling the data before it is passed to the next layers within the CNN architecture. They ignore the spatial details between objects and fail to capture spatial relationships between pixels of the image [7]. Capsule network architecture [8] was proposed to tackle the problem of invariance. It is a deep learning architecture that preserves spatial information. The paper proposes to use capsule networks for handwriting recognition of legal amounts.

2 Literature Survey

The development of every computer vision problem lies in the variety of data sets that it has been trained or tested on. Few of the common datasets that are used for legal amount detection are CENPARMI [9], ISIHWD. ISIHWD [10] consists of 62 legal words which are written by 105 writers. It consists of 31124 handwritten words, which are split into a training set of 24924 words and a test set of 6200 words to provide a writer agnostic word recognition and a common platform in writer independent word recognition. This paper also uses the IDRBT [11] dataset, which is a cheque image dataset consisting of 112 cheque leaves from four different banks in India with diverse texture and ink colors.

A method based on baselines (guidelines) is used in [12] and [13] to extract the handwritten date, courtesy and legal amounts of Canadian bank cheques. The guideline for the legal amount is found by analyzing the lengths of the lines extracted through edge detection. A searching region and a bounding region are decided for each field, and the grey-scale distributions of the handwritten strokes related to each item are extracted by tracing the connected components.

For segmentation, two of the most popular approaches are analytic approach [14] and holistic approach [15] The analytic approach involves segmenting of the entire zone of interest into multiple subparts and then recognizing the subparts. The overall accuracy of the zones of interest is found by aggregating the individual accuracy of the subparts. Thus, proper segmentation is an essential step of the analytic approach, which impacts the accuracy of the recognition of subparts. The holistic approach revolves around the detection of the legal amounts by extracting features from the legal amount without dividing them into subunits. However, both the above methods used for segmentation fall into the problem of over-segmentation and under-segmentation.

Various approaches have been put forward for legal amount recognition. [16] uses slant correction, noise detection, and smoothing for preprocessing and Hidden Markov Model(HMM) model trained using the Baum-Welch Algorithm and the Cross-Validation process for detection of legal amounts. Accuracies vary from 82%–93% depending on the classification of handwritten words but suffers from the fact that the legal amounts detected are not case-invariant.

[17] provides a holistic method of segmentation to avoid segmentation and stage and segmentation errors. It uses a graph numerical recognizer based input subgraphs to graphs of symbol prototypes. The approach finds similarities between the courtesy and legal amount recognition accuracies using cross-validation, which achieves a 20% improvement in recognition. [18] involves creating a legal amount vocabulary which could be used to handle mixed cursive and discrete legal amount. Pre-processing and feature extraction of mixed cursive and discrete features are used to improve the recognition accuracy. The accuracies using the approach given in this paper varied from 75%–81%. This approach is unable to handle the spatial orientation features of the handwritten legal amounts. Previous works also utilize multidimensional LSTMs to recognize handwriting [19] however, more recent works suggest that similar performances can be achieved with a 1D-LSTM [20]. Briefly, [20] utilized a CNN for image feature extraction and fed the features into a bidirectional LSTM and trained the network to optimize the Connectionist Temporal Classification (CTC) loss.

3   Implementation

3.1   Preprocessing

Preprocessing is used to remove unnecessary details from the cheques and locate and extract zones of interest. The pre-printed straight lines on the cheque, also called guidelines, are used to locate interest zones for detecting the legal amount on the cheques (Fig. 1).

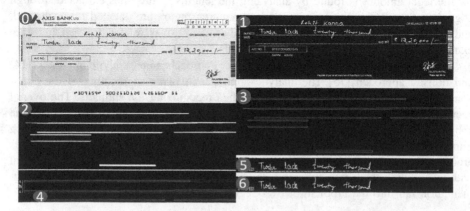

Fig. 1. Preprocessing phases

Implementation Details

0. Input image cheque in RGB color format.
1. Conversion of the colored bank cheque image to a grayscale image using thresholding followed by the binarization of the grayscale image. The threshold has been taken as the average of the minimum (0) and maximum (255) possible value of the intensity of image pixels in the range of grayscale values.
2. Then pass the binarized gray image to a gaussian blur filter to remove the noise and smoothen the sharp baselines. Then 3 iterations of a dilation using the Morph cross operator of size (5,2) are applied. Based on the layout analysis of the bank cheque, baselines whose length is less than (cheque image length)/5 using a horizontal kernel are eliminated. The output of these operations leaves us with payee and legal amount baselines on the cheque.
3. The edges of the payee and legal amount baselines were detected using the Canny detector. Hough Transform was used to isolate the baselines of a particular length from the image to obtain the coordinates of the baselines.
4. After the detection of baselines, the baselines are sorted according to the y-coordinates. The bottom and top sections of the cheque are truncated. The area between the extracted baseline contours is the zone of interest, which contains handwritten fields. Height h is the distance between two adjacent contours. But the height of the first line of handwritten field is taken as the distance between the top of the sliced image and first baseline contour. The final contours extracted are of height $h' = h + (2 *\Delta)$, where Δ is the margin of error field. The optimal value of delta should be in the range [0.1* h', 0.2* h']. The contours obtained in this step are stored in set C. Set C denotes a set of contours $[c_1, c_2 ... c_k]$
5. Create a 2d matrix of zeros whose size corresponds to the size of the sliced cheque image. The set C contains contours c_i of the previous step. Apply the algorithm as in Code Snippet 1.
6. For every contour, find all the lines whose length is less than cheque image length/2 using a horizontal kernel and subtract those from the original contour image.

Code Snippet. 1.

```
Consider two lists previous P and next N and set
C = [c₁, c₂ ... cₖ].
P → c₁
Foreach Contour cᵢ ∈ C i ←1 to i ←n-1 step do
    N = cᵢ
    If (overlap(P, N)) then
        i = i + 1
    Else
        P = N
```

```
Overlap function
   Input: Two contours C₁ and C₂
   Each Cᵢ is four-tuple(x,y,w,h) where x: top left contour
x coordinate of Contour i
   Y: top left contour y coordinate of Contour i
   w: width of the contour of Contour i
   h: h height of the x contour of Contour i

Matrix m is of size (W, H), where W is the width of
sliced cheque and height of sliced cheque.
m[0:W][0:H]=0
Foreach Contour cᵢ ∈ C i ← 1 to i ← 2 step do
   m[Cᵢ.x : Cᵢ.x + Cᵢ.w][Cᵢ.y : Cᵢ.y + Cᵢ.h] += 1
   number_of_2s = Σnumber of 2s in m
     where "number of 2s in m" represents the number of
pixel coordinates where contours overlap
   number_of_1s = Σnumber of 1s in m
     where "number of 1s in m" represents the number of
pixel coordinates where contours are present but do not
overlap
   If (number_of_2s/ number_of_1s > threshold)
     Return true
   Else
     Return false
   Where the threshold is taken as the ratio of overlap-
ping regions and non-overlapping regions
```

The payee and legal amount baselines found in the previous step can be discontinuous in nature. Therefore, these discontinuous lines are merged into a single smooth baseline based on the coordinates of the legal amount baseline. The mechanism to merge the discontinuous baselines is as follows. Consider a bank cheque image I

1. GB, a gaussian blur filter, is used on this grayscale image to remove the noise smoothen the sharp baselines. $I_2 \rightarrow GB(I)$
2. Apply 3 iterations of dilation with a (5,1) kernel to merge the discontinuous baselines.
3. Apply horizontal kernel on the image to find all long horizontal lines. Eliminate all the horizontal lines by converting all pixels of horizontal lines to black.

The below terminologies defined would be used ahead

Perfectly Segmented. A word is said to be perfectly segmented if the bounding box contains exactly one word Fig. 2.

Under-Segmented. A word is said to be under segmented if the bounding box contains one word along with auxiliary content (characters/lining/dots/ligatures) Fig. 2.

Over-Segmented. A word is said to be over segmented if the bounding box does not contain all the characters of the word on which segmentation was applied Fig. 2.

Threshold. Threshold is the maximum horizontal distance of pixels between two bounding boxes on an image matrix.

Fig. 2. 1. Perfectly segmented 2. Under-segmented 3. Over-segmented

3.2 Segmentation

This is the phase wherein the extracted zones of interest are broken down into subunits. These subunits are then provided as input for recognition (Table 1).

Implementation

In this phase, the legal amount is segmented into words. The main concern of this phase is the writer's handwriting, which varies in size, height, width, skewness and style of the content written. The main steps followed to produce the optimal results out of the workflow as per Fig. 3:

1. Contour detection technique is used for extracting out the handwritten fields within the legal amount image. Based on the handwriting of the writer, the detected content varies from a single stroke of an alphabet to multiple words of legal amount leading to under-segmented and over-segmented contours. Eg. Fig. 2

2. The approach used to handle these highly varying contours is to merge or split the contours based on the horizontal distance between the contours.

3. The next step is to eliminate all contours, which are detected due to noise within the image. Minute contours are not required and hence, are eliminated.

4. The contours are then sorted based on x coordinates.

5. The next step is to merge all the adjacent contours with overlapping x-coordinates so that they do not interfere in minimum distance calculation between words.

6. Minimum distance(Min_distance) is the product of threshold and the average distance between 2 adjacent contours(avg_distance). Take the width of the largest contour as the maximum possible width(Max_word_width) of any possible word.

7. The next step is to compare the distance between adjacent contours. If the distance is less than min_distance (threshold * avg_distance), then merge the adjacent contours.

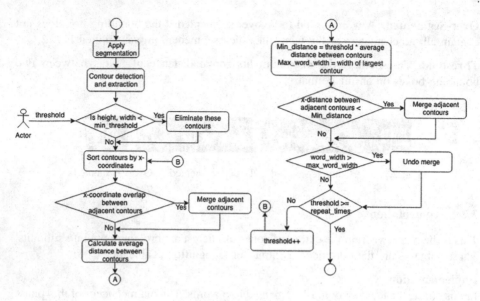

Fig. 3. Segmentation steps

8. However, if the width of the newly formed contour is greater than the maximum possible width of a word(Max_word_width), then undo the merge of contours.
9. Repeat steps 1 to 8 for n iterations where the user defines n.

Table 1. IDRBT[11] dataset legal amount segmentation results

Threshold	Perfectly segmented (Number ‖ %)	Under-segmented (Number ‖ %)	Over-segmented (Number ‖ %)	Total
2	382 ‖ 75.94	70 ‖ 13.92	51 ‖ 10.14	503
3	383 ‖ 76.14	79 ‖ 15.71	41 ‖ 8.15	503
4	382 ‖ 75.94	82 ‖16.3	39 ‖ 7.76	503

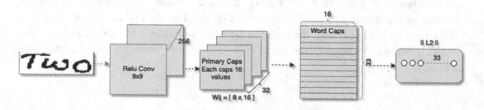

Fig. 4. CapsNet architecture

3.3 Capsule Networks

Convolutional Neural Network (CNN) [21] is considered state-of-the-art for any image classification task such as facial recognition, document analysis, geographic and meteorologic analysis, object detection for self-driving cars etc. However, the use of max-pooling in CNNs leads to loss of necessary info and makes CNNs invariant to rotations and translations, which has been tackled by Capsule Networks. The Capsule Networks architecture is composed of capsules [22], and each capsule is a group of neurons. Each capsule represents an activity vector that encodes entity properties like position, shape, rotation, stroke thickness, skew, width, etc. also called as instantiation parameters. This architecture uses Routing by Agreement algorithm [8] to train the capsules. For legal amount recognition, this paper uses Capsule networks to take advantage of the positional information of various handwritten legal amount words within the input image and provide a better recognition rate. The architecture used in this paper is as per Fig. 4.

Architecture

1. Dimensions of the input provided: 30*100*1.
2. The first convolution layer is a convolutional layer(Conv1), which has 256, 9 × 9 convolution kernels with a stride of 1 and ReLU activation. This layer converts pixel intensities to the activities of local feature detectors. These are provided as inputs to the primary capsules.
3. The second layer is a convolution capsule layer called the Primary capsule layer, having 32 channels of 8D capsules. Each capsule contains 8 convolutional units with 9 x 9 kernel and a stride of 2. The inputs are 256 × 81 Conv1 units from the previous layer whose receptive fields overlap with the location of the center of the capsule. The output of the primary capsule layer consists of [32 × 6 × 6] capsule outputs (each output is an 8D vector), and each capsule in the [6 × 6] grid is sharing their weights with each other.
4. The final layer (WordCaps) consists of a single 16D capsule per class. These capsules receive input from all the capsules in the previous layer.

The Capsule Network architecture uses a **squashing function** [23] as a non-linear activation function, which provides a probability of whether a particular feature is present within the image or not. This function shrinks the length of the output vector into a value between 0 and 1. Greater the length of the vector higher the probability of that particular capsule related to that object. The squashing function is given by:

$$V_j = \parallel s_j \parallel^2 * s_j / (1 + \parallel s_j \parallel^2) * \parallel s_j \parallel \tag{1}$$

Where s_j = Total input, v_j = Vector Output of capsule j.

Capsule networks use **routing by agreement algorithm** [24]. Unlike max-pooling, routing-by-agreement algorithm passes only useful information and throws away the data that would add noise to the results. The routing algorithm takes care of the selection and routing relevant results to further layers. The capsules which are at a higher level represent complex entities having more degrees of freedom.

$$s_j = \sum c_{ij} u_{j|i} \tag{2}$$

Where S_j = summation matrix, $u_{j|i}$ = prediction vector, and c_{ij} = coupling coefficients determined by iterative dynamic routing.

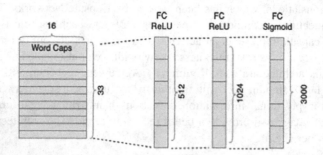

Fig. 5. Reconstruction architecture for regularization

Reconstruction as a Regularization Method. Reconstruction loss is used to encourage the word capsules to encode the instantiation parameters of the input. During the training phase, the output of the word capsule is classified as a specific word, and this activity vector is used to reconstruct the input image. The reconstruction architecture consists of 3 fully connected layers and uses minimization of the sum of the squared error loss function. Reconstruction loss is scaled down by 0.0005 so that it does not dominate the margin loss during training. The reconstructions are done using the 16D output vector from the CapsNet (Fig. 5).

Margin Loss. Longer the output vector greater the probability of the presence of capsule entity. The model uses margin loss for correctly classifying the capsule outputs. For different classes, separate margin loss is used, L_k for each class capsule k:

$$L_k = T_k \max(0, m^+ - \| v_k \|)^2 + \lambda(1 - T_k)\max(0, \| v_k \| - m^-)^2 \tag{3}$$

where $T_k = 1$ if a word of class k is present and $m^+ = 0.9$, $m^- = 0.1$ and $\lambda = 0.5$. λ is a regularization parameter that helps prevent the shrinking of the activity vectors during the learning phase. The total loss is the summation of the losses of all capsules.

For the training of the CapsNet[22] model, ISIHWD[10] dataset has been used. Capitalized words and lower case words have been taken into a single category. The dataset consists of 31124 handwritten words split into a training set of 24924 words and a test set of 6200 words to provide a common platform in writer independent word recognition.

This model has been trained for a total of 30 epochs and the Adam optimizer has been used with a learning rate of 0.001 and a learning rate decay factor of 0.9 after every epoch. Mean squared error (MSE) has been used as the reconstruction loss and the coefficient for the loss is loss_recon = 0.0005 x (Image dimensions) = 0.0005 x 30 x 100 = 1.5 which is equivalent to using SSE (sum squared error) and loss_recon = 0.0005.

Capsule Network Result

The trained Capsnet Model has achieved 98.05% test accuracy and 98.13% training accuracy after 29 epochs on the ISIHWD dataset. Figure 6 shows the epochs vs. accuracy graph for the training phase and test phase.

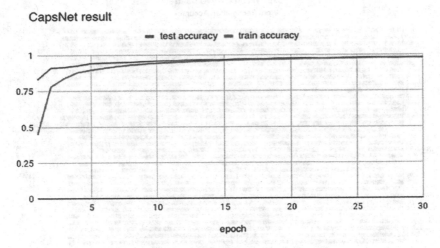

Fig. 6. CapsNet result on ISIHWD dataset

Table 2. ISIHWD dataset [14] performance comparison.

	Approach	Classes	Training size	Test size	Training epochs	Recognition accuracy (%)
Das Gupta et al. [14]	DCNN + SVM	33	24925	6200	40	95.35%
Proposed system	CapsNet [8]	33	24738	6386	29	98.06%

[10] uses a DCNN + SVM architecture, which is a deep convolutional neural network and classifier approach. This approach is able to achieve a recognition accuracy of 95.35% over 40 training epochs. The capsule network architecture is able to achieve a recognition accuracy of 98.06% over just 29 epochs. The Table 2 provides a comparison of word wise accuracy obtained on the ISIHWD dataset for CapsNet and the DCNN-SVM approach mentioned in [10].

Figure 7 provides the accuracy of the 33 legal amount words is predicted on the ISIHWD dataset. Words like hundred, thousand, lakh, five are predicted with the highest accuracy. Certain words like forty and crore are predicted with an accuracy of 93%. This is due to the ambiguity between specific pairs of words like (forty, fifty) and (one, crore) written in cursive handwriting.

Figure 8 compares the word wise accuracy of the CapsNet architecture vs DCNN-SVM approach on the ISIHWD dataset. Based on the results, certain words are predicted better by DCNN-SVM, and certain words are predicted better by CapsNet. The model performs better in cases that have common word suffixes like 'teen' in thirteen, fourteen, fifteen, and so on.

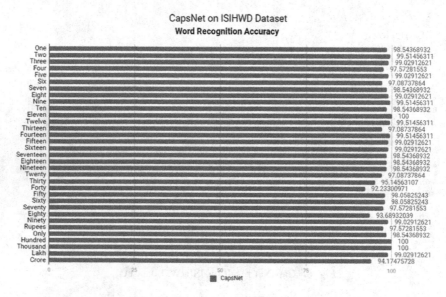

Fig. 7. CapsNet on ISIHWD dataset

The trained model has been used on the extracted words from the segmentation phase Table 3 shows the results of CapsNet on IDRBT bank for perfectly segmented and over-segmented category of words. On analysis, the experimentation proves that under segmented category words could not be recognized by CapsNet as it contained more than one legal amount word.

4 Improvements and Future Scope

This paper proposes a solution that is relevant for Indian bank cheques written in the English language and could be improved to provide support for language and layout agnostic legal amount bank cheque detection. The extraction process can be simplified by using the template matching techniques. A way to extract the desired handwritten fields is by using a blank cheque template and subtracting it from the original cheque image. With the absence of guidelines in the above approach, it will be challenging to identify the handwritten field.

This paper relies on the user for multiple threshold values for the legal amount extraction and segmentation phase. This user dependency provides fine-grained control over-extraction and segmentation phases presently. However, for complete automation of the algorithm, the solution could compute accuracies for an optimal range of values for these thresholds. Data Quality and variance plays a crucial role in deciding the accuracy of the computation. This solution's classification accuracy can be fine-tuned further by training on more extensive and diversified bank cheque databases, which consist of several bank cheque layouts.

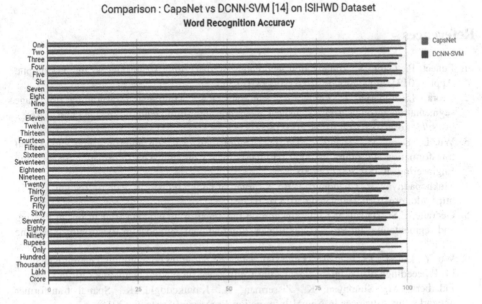

Fig. 8. CapsNet vs DCNN + SVM

Table 3. IDRBT bank cheque dataset [11] legal amount recognition results

Threshold	Perfectly segmented recognition accuracy (%)	Over segmented recognition accuracy (%)
Default	82	16.8
1	84.5	30
2	84.7	31
3	85	28
4	84.7	23.8

5 Conclusion

This paper provides an end to end legal amount extraction solution for Indian bank cheques written in English. This paper has emphasized its experimentation on the segmentation and preprocessing algorithms used for extracting the legal amounts. The root cause of the decrease in detection accuracy is identified as inaccuracies in the segmentation algorithms used in previous works. Thus, the paper has attempted to improve the segmentation algorithms and has obtained around 76% accuracy on the

IDRBT dataset. This paper uses a promising deep learning architecture known as CapsNet for detecting legal amounts and has achieved 98.05% on training datasets and around 85% accuracy on the testing datasets. The further goals of this paper would be to provide language-agnostic mechanisms to detect the legal amount and to use myriad deep learning architectures to improve the detection accuracy.

References

1. Puneet, P., Garg, N.: Binarization techniques used for grey scale images. Int. J. Comput. Appl. (2013). https://doi.org/10.5120/12320-8533
2. Arora, S., Acharya, J., Verma, A., Panigrahi, P.K.: Multilevel thresholding for image segmentation through a fast statistical recursive algorithm. Pattern Recogn. Lett. (2008). https://doi.org/10.1016/j.patrec.2007.09.005
3. Wu, L., Deng, W., Zhang, J., He, D.: Arnold transformation algorithm and anti-Arnold transformation algorithm. In: 2009 1st International Conference on Information Science and Engineering, ICISE 2009 (2009)
4. Mukhopadhyay, P., Chaudhuri, B.B.: A survey of hough transform. Pattern Recogn. (2015). https://doi.org/10.1016/j.patcog.2014.08.027
5. Gedraite, E.S., Hadad, M.: Investigation on the effect of a Gaussian Blur in image filtering and segmentation. In: Proceedings Elmar - International Symposium Electronics in Marine (2011)
6. Wu, Y., Liu, Y., Li, J., et al.: Traffic sign detection based on convolutional neural networks. In: Proceedings of the International Joint Conference on Neural Networks (2013)
7. Jaderberg, M., Simonyan, K., Zisserman, A., Kavukcuoglu, K.: Spatial transformer networks. In: Advances in Neural Information Processing Systems (2015)
8. Sabour, S., Frosst, N., Hinton, G.E.: Dynamic routing between capsules. In: Advances in Neural Information Processing Systems (2017)
9. Haghighi, P.J., Nobile, N., He, C.L., Suen, Ching Y.: A new large-scale multi-purpose handwritten farsi database. In: Kamel, M., Campilho, A. (eds.) ICIAR 2009. LNCS, vol. 5627, pp. 278–286. Springer, Heidelberg (2009). https://doi.org/10.1007/978-3-642-02611-9_28
10. Gupta J.D., Samanta, S.: ISIHWD: A database for off-line handwritten word recognition and writer identification. In: 2017 9th International Conference on Advances in Pattern Recognition, ICAPR 2017 (2018)
11. Dansena, P., Bag, S., Pal, R.: Differentiating pen inks in handwritten bank cheques using multi-layer perceptron. In: Shankar, B.U., Ghosh, K., Mandal, D.P., Ray, S.S., Zhang, D., Pal, S.K. (eds.) PReMI 2017. LNCS, vol. 10597, pp. 655–663. Springer, Cham (2017). https://doi.org/10.1007/978-3-319-69900-4_83
12. Liu, K.E., Suen, C.Y., Cheriet, M., et al.: Automatic extraction of baselines and data from check images. Int. J. Pattern Recogn. Artif. Intell. (1997). https://doi.org/10.1142/S0218001497000299
13. Liu, K., Suen, C.Y., Nadal, C.: Automatic extraction of items from cheque images for payment recognition. In: Proceedings - International Conference on Pattern Recognition (1996)
14. Dimauro, G., Impedovo, S., Pirlo, G., Salzo, A.: Automatic bankcheck processing: a new engineered system. Int. J. Pattern Recogn. Artif. Intell. (1997). https://doi.org/10.1142/S0218001497000214

15. Kim, K.K., Kim, J.H., Chung, Y.K., Suen, C.Y.: Legal amount recognition based on the segmentation hypotheses for bank check processing. In: Proceedings of the International Conference on Document Analysis and Recognition, ICDAR (2001)
16. De Almendra Freitas, C,O., El Yacoubi, A., Bortolozzi, F., Sabourin, R.: Brazilian bank check handwritten legal amount recognition. In: Brazilian Symposium of Computer Graphic and Image Processing (2000)
17. Dzuba, G., Filatov, A., Gershuny, D., et al.: Check amount recognition based on the cross validation of courtesy and legal amount fields. Int. J. Pattern Recogn. Artif. Intell. (1997). https://doi.org/10.1142/S0218001497000275
18. Han, K., Sethi, I.K.: An off-line cursive handwritten word recognition system and ITS application to legal amount interpretation. Int. J. Pattern Recogn. Artif. Intell. (1997). https://doi.org/10.1142/s0218001497000330
19. Graves, A., Schmidhuber, J.: Offline handwriting recognition with multidimensional recurrent neural networks. In: Advances in Neural Information Processing Systems 21 - Proceedings of the 2008 Conference (2009)
20. Puigcerver, J.: Are multidimensional recurrent layers really necessary for handwritten text recognition? In: Proceedings of the International Conference on Document Analysis and Recognition, ICDAR (2017)
21. Jmour, N., Zayen, S., Abdelkrim, A.: Convolutional neural networks for image classification. In: 2018 International Conference on Advanced Systems and Electric Technologies, IC_ASET 2018 (2018)
22. Xiang, C., Zhang, L., Tang, Y., et al.: MS-CapsNet: a novel multi-scale capsule network. IEEE Signal Process. Lett. (2018). https://doi.org/10.1109/LSP.2018.2873892
23. Hinton, G., Sabour, S., Frosst, N.: Matrix capsules with EM routing. In: 6th International Conference on Learning Representations, ICLR 2018 - Conference Track Proceedings (2018)
24. Peer, D., Stabinger, S., Rodriguez-Sanchez, A.: Training Deep Capsule Networks (2018). arXiv

Log Periodic Power Law Fitting on Indian Stock Market

Nagaraj Naik$^{(\boxtimes)}$ and Biju R. Mohan

IT Department, National Institute of Technology, Surathkal, India
nagaraj21.naik@gmail.com
http://www.nitk.ac.in

Abstract. Stock price prediction is one of the challenging tasks for researchers and academics due to frequent changes in stock prices. The stock prices are speculation, and it purely depends on the demand and supply of the market during the trading session. Most of the existing work approach is foresting stock prices using machine learning methods. There has been a limited number of studies on stock crisis identification. Log periodic power law (LPPL) is one of the approaches to identify bubbles in the stock market before crises happened. By looking at existing work, we found that LPPL has not applied in the Indian stock market. In this paper, we have considered LPPL to identify a bubble in the Indian stock market. Due to fluctuation in the market, stock price follows the nonlinearity behavior, hence LPPL is considered to fit the equations. The experiment is carried out R Studio platform.

Keywords: LPPL · Nonlinearity · Bubble · Stock market

1 Introduction

The stock crisis is a period where stock prices drop continuously. During the period of crisis, the stock follows a lower low at every trading session. It creates panic for investors, and they start selling the stock or equity from its portfolio. Financial crisis identification is a complex task because the crisis can occur in the following conditions. First is government policy. If the government policy is not stable, then the investor may be less confident in the market, and there is a possibility of more sellers in the market than buyers. Second is the failure of bank repayment from a corporate or industry. In such a situation bank is not able to raise the liquidity, then the market may face liquidity issues. These are possible probability where investors lose their confidence and pull out the money from the stock market. The bubble pattern has been found before the stock market crisis. A bubble is nothing but exponential growth or infinite growth of particular equity or stock [5,6,14]. This bubble burst at a particular period, which leads to a crisis in the market. Stock price fluctuations are motivated us to identify the bubble in the stock market before it crashes. LPPL is one of the popular methods to identify a bubble in the stock market. The goal of this paper is

© Springer Nature Singapore Pte Ltd. 2020
A. Bhattacharjee et al. (Eds.): MIND 2020, CCIS 1241, pp. 38–43, 2020.
https://doi.org/10.1007/978-981-15-6318-8_4

whether India stock indices follow the LPPL or not. If indices fit in LPPL, that indicates the stock crisis can be predicted [15]. Therefore, we studied LPPL to identify a bubble in the Indian stock market.

2 Background Work

2.1 Machine Learning Based Prediction

Zhong et al. [18] proposed a stock price prediction model. In this work, various parameters of stock data have considered in the experiment, which increases the dimension of data. To reduce the dimension in data, kernel principal component techniques have been considered. The stock forecasting can be carried out in two ways. First is classification methods to classify the stock price movements, i.e., up and down. Second is the regression analysis method to forecast future stock prices. Artificial neural network and support vector machine method has used to classify the stock prices [7]. The different Machine learning approaches considered to classify stock price movements, namely random forest, naive-bayes [13]. There have been several studies on the stock price movement classification based on deep neural networks [10,16]. The related work is described in Table 1.

Table 1. Related works

Author	Techniques	Outcome
Werner Kristjanpoller et al. [8]	ANN-GARCH	Currency Price Prediction
Mehmet Orhan et al. [12]	GARCH	Stock Index Prediction
Nikolay Y. Nikolaev et al. [11]	GARCH	Currency volatility Prediction
David Enke et al. [2]	Neural Network	Stock Price Prediction
Chenn Huanget et al. [4]	ANN, SVM	Stock Price Classification
Sotirios P. Chatzis et al. [1]	DNN	Stock Crises
Qun Zhang et al. [17]	Quantile Regressions of Log- Periodic Power Law	Financial Crises
Jan Wosnitzag et al. [15]	LPPL	Liquidity crisis
Chong Li [9]	LPPL	Chinese market bubble identification

2.2 LPPL for Bubble Diagnose

LPPL Singular method has been used to diagnose the bubble [17]. The work proposed the quantile regression method to diagnose bubbles instead of using standard least squares and maximum likelihood estimation. The experiment demo stared that standard least squares or maximum likelihood estimation are not able to fit for outliers.

In this work [3], discussed the transformation of a log-periodic power law, which reduces nonlinear parameters in the model. The advantage of reducing nonlinear parameters which significantly decreases the complexity of the model. Therfore, the work proposed two nonlinear parameters and rewrites in the log-periodic power law equation.

3   Data Specification

We have considered Indian stock exchange data for the experiments. These data are openly available on the National Stock Exchange website. Stock data contains five different values are open price, close price, high price, low price, and traded volume. In this experiment we considered stock prices range from 2007 to 2019.

4   Methodology

4.1   LPPL

LPPL model is used to identify the bubble in the stock or stock price index. In this context, the bubble is nothing but an exponential growth of stock prices. Hence there is a possibility of profit booking in the stock market and decreases the stock prices, which may lead to stock crises event. The log-periodic power law equation is defined below 1. It consists of seven parameters in that three parameters are linear, namely (A, B, C), and four parameters are nonlinear are (t_c, m, ω, ϕ) [3].

$$T[lnp(t)] = A + B(t_c - t)^m + C(t_c - t)^m cos(\omega ln(t_c - t) - \phi) \qquad (1)$$

where:
$[lnp(t)] \rightarrow$ log stock price termination of the bubbles
$t_c \rightarrow$ critical-time
$A \rightarrow$ log price at the peak
$B \rightarrow$ power-law accelerations
$C \rightarrow$ log-periodic oscillation
$m \rightarrow$ exponential growth
$\omega \rightarrow$ temporal hierarchy of oscillations
$\phi \rightarrow$ time scale of the oscillations

For fitting the LPPL models, we have three parameters that are linear, and four parameters are nonlinear, and the goal is the minimize the error between

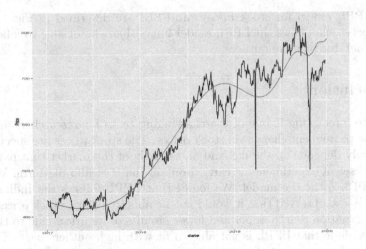

Fig. 1. Infosys stock follows LPPL model

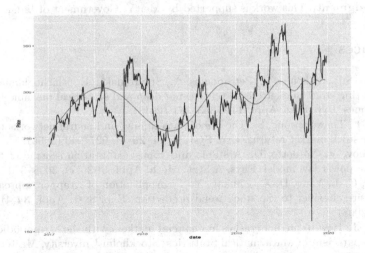

Fig. 2. SBI stock follows LPPL model

actual and predicted. Ordinary least squares method is used to minimize the sum of squared residuals and it is defined in Eq. 2. The experimental results of LPPL fitting on stock prices are described in Figs. 1 and 2.

$$T(t_c, m, \omega, \phi, A, B, C) = \sum_{t=1}^{n} [lnp(t) - A - B(t_c - t)^m - C(t_c - t)^m cos(\omega ln(t_c - t) - \phi)]^2$$

(2)

The LPPL model for stock Infosys and SBI are described in Fig. 1 and 2. The Infosys stock follows the LPPL model but SBI stock not able to follows the LPPL model due to more outliers.

5   Conclusion

Stock price forecasting is one of the challenging tasks for researchers and academics due to frequent changes in stock prices. The stock prices are speculation, and it purely depends on the demand and supply of the market that particular trade. The set of experiments is carried out in the R studio platform. We considered LPPL to fit the model. We found that LPPL follows the Indian stock market. We also observed that it would not be able to fit for a stock price, which is more fluctuation due to upper and lower circuits of its price. Due to this reason, we conclude that LPPL is not able to fit with high outliers data. Therefor more parameter optimization needs to be performed for future work.

Acknowledgment. This work is supported by MeitY, Government of India.

References

1. Chatzis, S.P., Siakoulis, V., Petropoulos, A., Stavroulakis, E., Vlachogiannakis, N.: Forecasting stock market crisis events using deep and statistical machine learning techniques. Exp. Syst. Appl. **112**, 353–371 (2018)
2. Enke, D., Thawornwong, S.: The use of data mining and neural networks for forecasting stock market returns. Exp. Syst. Appl. **29**(4), 927–940 (2005)
3. Filimonov, V., Sornette, D.: A stable and robust calibration scheme of the log-periodic power law model. Phys. A Stat. Mech. Appl. **392**(17), 3698–3707 (2013)
4. Huang, C.-J., Yang, D.-X., Chuang, Y.-T.: Application of wrapper approach and composite classifier to the stock trend prediction. Exp. Syst. Appl. **34**(4), 2870–2878 (2008)
5. Emilie, J.: How to predict crashes in financial markets with the log-periodic power law. Department of Mathematical Statistics, Stockholm University, Master dissertation (2009)
6. Johansen, A., Sornette, D.: Log-periodic power law bubbles in latin-american and asian markets and correlated anti-bubbles in western stock markets: an empirical study. arXiv preprint cond-mat/9907270 (1999)
7. Kara, Y., Boyacioglu, M.A., Baykan, O.K.: Predicting direction of stock price index movement using artificial neural networks and support vector machines: the sample of the Istanbul stock exchange. Exp. Syst. Appl. **38**(5), 5311–5319 (2011)
8. Kristjanpoller, W., Minutolo, M.C.: A hybrid volatility forecasting framework integrating garch, artificial neural network, technical analysis and principal components analysis. Exp. Syst. Appl. **109**, 1–11 (2018)
9. Li, C.: Log-periodic view on critical dates of the Chinese stock market bubbles. Phys. A Stat. Mech. Appl. **465**, 305–311 (2017)
10. Long, W., Zhichen, L., Cui, L.: Deep learning-based feature engineering for stock price movement prediction. Knowle.-Based Syst. **164**, 163–173 (2019)

11. Nikolaev, N.Y., Boshnakov, G.N., Zimmer, R.: Heavy-tailed mixture garch volatility modeling and value-at-risk estimation. Exp. Syst. Appl. **40**(6), 2233–2243 (2013)
12. Orhan, M., Köksal, B.: A comparison of garch models for var estimation. Exp. Syst. Appl. **39**(3), 3582–3592 (2012)
13. Patel, J., Shah, S., Thakkar, P., Kotecha, K.: Predicting stock and stock price index movement using trend deterministic data preparation and machine learning techniques. Exp. Syst. Appl. **42**(1), 259–268 (2015)
14. Sornette, D.: Dragon-kings, black swans and the prediction of crises. arXiv preprint arXiv:0907.4290 (2009)
15. Jan Henrik Wosnitza and Cornelia Denz: Liquidity crisis detection: an application of log-periodic power law structures to default prediction. Phys. A Stat. Mech. Appl. **392**(17), 3666–3681 (2013)
16. Yu, P., Yan, X.: Stock price prediction based on deep neural networks. Neural Comput. Appl., pp. 1–20 (2019)
17. Zhang, Q., Zhang, Q., Sornette, D.: Early warning signals of financial crises with multi-scale quantile regressions of log-periodic power law singularities. PloS one **11**(11), e0165819 (2016)
18. Zhong, X., Enke, D.: Forecasting daily stock market return using dimensionality reduction. Exp. Syst. Appl. **67**, 126–139 (2017)

An Automated Algorithm for Estimating Respiration Rate from PPG Signals

Kinjarapu Manojkumar$^{(\boxtimes)}$, Srinivas Boppu$^{(\boxtimes)}$,
and M. Sabarimalai Manikandan$^{(\boxtimes)}$

Biomedical System Lab, School of Electrical Sciences, Indian Institute of Technology
Bhubaneswar, Jatani, Khordha 752050, India
{km18,srinivas,msm}@iitbbs.ac.in

Abstract. Objective: This paper presents a simple automated method
to estimate respiration rate (RR) from the photoplethysmography (PPG)
signals. **Methods:** The method consists of preprocessing, extremely
low-frequency two-pole digital resonator, fast Fourier transform, spectral magnitude computation, prominent spectral peak identification and
respiration rate computation. **Validation Dataset:** The proposed RR
estimation method is evaluated using standard PPG databases including
MIMIC-II and CapnoBase. **Results:** The proposed method had estimation accuracy with absolute error value (median, 25th–75th percentiles)
of 0.522 (0, 1.403) and 0.2746 (0, 0.475) breaths/minute for the PPG
recordings from the MIMIC-II and CapnoBase databases, respectively
for the 30 s segment. Results showed that the proposed method outperforms the existing methods such as the empirical mode decomposition
and principal component analysis (EMD-PCA), ensemble EMD-PCA,
and improved complete EEMD with adaptive noise-PCA methods. **Conclusion:** Results demonstrate that the proposed method is more accurate
in estimating RR with less processing time of 0.0296 s as compared to
that of the existing methods. This study further demonstrate that the
two-pole digital resonator with extremely low-frequency can be simple
method to estimate the RR from the PPG signals.

Keywords: Photoplethysmography (PPG) signal · Respiratory
signal · Respiration rate (RR) · Digital resonator · Fast Fourier
transform

1 Introduction

Respiration rate (RR) is an essential parameter for understanding the breathing
patterns under normal and abnormal conditions [1–25]. The RR ranges between
5 and 24 breaths/min (i.e., 0.08–0.4 Hz) at resting condition for adult subjects,
and that of neonates at resting ranges from 10 to 80 breaths/min (0.17–1.33 Hz)

This research work is carried out with the support of IMPRINT-II and MHRD Grant,
Government of India.

[23]. During exercise, the RR can increase to approximately 45 breaths/min [24]. For children with age ranging between 1–5 years, the RR value above 40 breaths/min (age) is recommended as per the guidelines [12]. The PPG signal contains cardiac rhythm with synchronous respiratory component [21].

In the past studies, it was observed that the PPG waveform is modulated by the breathing in three ways such as the baseline wander (BW), amplitude modulation (AM), and frequency modulation (FM) [10, 14, 20]. The respiration induces variations in pulse rate (PR), amplitude and width of the pulsatile waveform. The PR is increased and decreased during inspiration and expiration, respectively which causes respiratory-induced frequency variation (RIFV) in the PPG signal [3]. The PRV is modulated by respiration, which is well known as respiratory sinus arrhythmia (RSA). The respiratory synchronous blood volume variations cause the respiratory-induced intensity variation (RIIV) [21], which indicates variations in absolute amplitude of peaks of the PPG waveform [8, 12]. A decrease in cardiac output with reduced ventricular filling causes change in peripheral pulse strength, which is termed as the respiratory-induced amplitude variation (RIAV) which indicates the height of pulsatile waveform [12]. The pulse amplitude is modulated due to variations in stroke volume and stiffness of the blood vessel that can also modulate the pulse width variability (PWV) [7].

1.1 Existing Respiration Rate Estimation Methods

In the past studies, different methods were presented for estimating respiration rate (RR) (or breathing rate (BR)) from the PPG signals recorded in different locations under different physical activity conditions. Most methods perform analysis of respiratory signals derived from the respiration-induced variations (intensity, frequency and amplitude) of the pulsatile waveform. Existing methods use signal processing technique(s), such as digital filters, Fourier transforms, wavelet transforms, empirical mode decomposition (EMD) and its variants, short-time Fourier transform (STFT), wavelet synchrosqueezing transform (WSST), Fourier SST (FSST), vertical second-order SST (VSST), variable-frequency complex demodulation (VFCDM), autoregressive (AR) models, feed-forward neural network (FFNN) and principal component analysis (PCA). In this section, we summarize some of the RR estimation methods.

In [2], Motin et al. (2019) investigated the effect of all variants of EMD ((EMD-, ensemble EMD (EEMD)-, complementary EEMD (CEEMD)-, complete EEMD with adaptive noise (CEEMDAN)-, and improved CEEMDAN (ICEEMDAN)-) PCA for extracting BR from the PPG signal. The PPG signal was first processed using the Savitzky-Golay based smoothing filter with third order polynomial. The PCA was applied to the selected embedded intrinsic mode functions (IMFs) of PPG signal. The fast Fourier transform (FFT) was used to estimate the breathing rate. The IMFs are selected based on the BR ranges between 8 and 45 breaths/min. The method had median absolute error between 0 and 5.03 and between 2.47 and 10.55 breaths/min for the MIMIC and CapnoBase datasets, respectively. It was noted that the EEMD-PCA and ICEEMDAN-PCA methods had better performance for both datasets as compared with all the EMD variants. In [3], Dehkordi et al. (2018)

presented a method based on the SST to extract the respiratory-induced intensity, amplitude and frequency variation signals to extract the instantaneous RR values. The SST algorithm had $O(nlog(n))$ computations per scale and peak-conditioned fusion algorithm had $O(n)$ computations, where n is the number of samples. In [4], M. Pirhonen et al. (2018) studied the use of amplitude variability to estimate the RR using time-frequency (TF) representation and particle filter. The spectral estimation methods are STFT, WSST, FSST, and VSST techniques. Results showed that the Synchrosqueezing methods performed more accurately than the STFT method when the particle filter was employed. In [6], M. A. Motin et al. (2017) presented an algorithm based on EEMD with PCA (EEMD-PCA) to estimate HR and RR simultaneously from PPG signal. The EEMD-PCA-based method had the median RMS error (1st and 3rd quartiles) of 0.89 (0, 1.78) breaths/min for RR estimation and of 0.57 (0.30, 0.71) beats/min for HR on the MIMIC dataset. The method had the median RMS error of 2.77 (0.50, 5.9) breaths/min and 0.69 (0.54, 1.10) beats/min for RR and HR, respectively on the CapnoBase dataset.

In [7], Hernando et al. (2017) investigated the PPG signals recorded from forehead and finger sites for estimating the RR using pulse amplitude variability (PAV). Results suggested that the forehead PAV is not useful as a signal to extract the RR parameter. In [8] Pimentel et al. (2017) studied the multiple autoregressive models of different orders to determine the respiratory frequency from the RIFV, RIAV, and RIIV waveforms, which were derived from the PPG signal. The algorithm used the existing peak and trough points detection approach. From the peaks and troughs, the three waveforms were computed and then resampled to 4 Hz by using the linear interpolation to estimate RR values using multiple AR models. For the CapnoBase and BIDMC datasets, the method had mean absolute errors (in terms of median, 25th–75th percentiles) of 1.5 (0.3–3.3) and 4.0 (1.8–5.5) breaths/min (for each dataset respectively) for 32 s segment. The method had the average processing time of 1.6 s on the 2.4 GHz single processor computer.

In [12], Karlen et al. (2013) presented a method to real-time estimation of RR from the PPG signal. The average processing time was 0.36 s on the 1.8 GHz single processor computer. In [15], Li et al. (2013) investigated correlations between six respiratory-induced variations (RIVs), including (i) the systole period, (ii) the diastole period, (iii) the pulse period, (iv) the amplitude of systole, (v) the amplitude of diastole, and (vi) the intensity variation. Results showed that the systole and diastole periods had poor correlation with respiration as compared with the pulse period. In [16], Karlen et al. (2011) investigated the estimation of RR by extracting respiratory sinus arrhythmia (RSA) from the pulse rate variability (PRV) measurement. In [17], Chon et al. (2009) presented the method based on the TF spectral estimation, VFCDM to identify frequency modulation of the PPG signal. The VFCDM method was tested for breathing frequencies ranging from 0.2 to 0.6 Hz. The average processing time of the VFCDM method was 0.3 s on 1-min data segment. In [18], Fleming et al. (2007) presented a comparison of different techniques to extract breathing rate from the PPG signal. The first method was based on the 3rd order Butterworth band-pass filter with a pass-band frequency ranging from 0.1 to 0.3 Hz (6 to 18 breaths/min). The second method was based on the three different low-pass filters with cut-off frequencies at 0.3, 0.4 and 0.55 Hz to obtain the breathing signal. The choice of cut-off frequency was adapted based on the estimated pulse rate. In [19], P. Leonard et al. (2004) studied WT based method for detecting breaths from the pulse oximeter waveform. In [20], Johansson et al. (2003) presented neural network based method based on the five features of the PPG components. The RIIV component was obtained using a 16th-order bandpass Bessel filter with pass-band of 0.13–0.48 Hz for each 2 min segment. The cardiac synchronous component was derived using a 5th-order bandpass Butterworth filter with pass-band of 0.50–2.0 Hz. From each cardiac cycle, five values are extracted, including the systolic peak value, diastolic valley value, peak-to-peak interval (PPI), pulse height PULSEi, and RIIV value. These features were fed to the fully connected feed-forward neural network (FFNN) for RR estimation. In [21], Nilsson et al. (2000) presented an automated breath detection algorithm based on the band-pass filter with cut-off frequency ranging between 0.13 to 0.48 Hz to suppress the cardiac-related variations and the frequency components below the respiratory frequency. The extreme peaks of each curve were used to identify the breaths.

1.2 Motivation and Key Contributions

In existing RR estimation methods, the first stage is the extraction of a respiratory-induced variation (RIV) signal from the PPG signal. Different methods were presented to extract RIV signal(s). Most methods were based on the detecting peaks and troughs of the PPG signal. Under different morphological variations, detection of peaks and troughs is still challenging tasks. Further, the RR estimation accuracy depends on accurate determination of peaks and troughs and also the effective interpolation techniques. Most methods did not provide complete peak and trough algorithms. Some of methods mentioned that publicly available peak and trough detection algorithms were used at the preprocessing stage. Some of the methods mentioned that the peak and trough locations were manually annotated to study the effectiveness of the RIV based RR estimation methods. Moreover, complex signal decomposition techniques were presented for removal of artefacts and noises and also to obtain respiratory related signal for RR estimation. Such RR estimation methods demand more energy and memory resources which are major constraints of wearable health monitoring devices.

In this paper, we attempt to explore a simple automated RR estimation algorithm based on the two-pole digital resonator and fast Fourier transform. In the first stage, the PPG signal is processed by using the two-pole resonator to extract a respiratory signal. In the second stage, Fourier magnitude spectrum of the extracted respiratory signal is computed. In the third stage, the respiratory frequency F_R is computed by finding the location of a maximum spectral peak within a predefined spectral window ranging between 0.1 to 0.8 Hz. Finally, the RR is computed as $F_R * 60$ breaths/ min. We study the performance of the proposed method with different block lengths such as 10, 20, and 30 s. For the

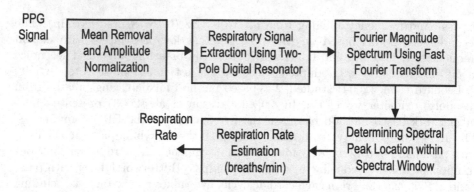

Fig. 1. Block diagram of the proposed method for estimating respiration rate from the PPG signal.

standard datasets, the performance of the proposed method is compared with the other methods in terms of absolute error (AE) represented as median (25th–75th percentiles) and computational time (ms).

The rest of this paper is organized as follows. Section 2 presents the proposed RR estimation method. Section 3 presents the evaluation results of the proposed method on four datasets and also presents the performance comparison with the current state-of-the-art methods. Finally, conclusions are drawn in Sect. 4.

2   Materials and Methods

In order to evaluate the performance of the proposed method, we used three publicly-available datasets such as Multiparameter intelligent monitoring in intensive care (MIMIC) [26], and CapnoBase [27], as described below:

- **The MIMIC Dataset**: The MIMIC dataset [26] includes 72 simultaneously recorded PPG, blood pressure, respiratory and electrocardiogram (ECG) signals. The signals were digitized with a sampling rate of 125 Hz. In this study, 266 epochs of 30 s duration are manually selected from simultaneously recorded PPG and respiratory signals. For each of the epochs, we have compared RR estimated from the PPG signal with reference RR derived from the respiratory signal. In addition, we tested the algorithm's performance with 406 epochs of 20 s duration and 826 epochs of 10 s duration.
- **The CapnoBase Dataset**: The capnoBase dataset [27] contains simultaneously recorded respiratory, ECG, and PPG signals. The signals were digitized with a sampling rate of 300 Hz. In this study, 336 epochs of 30 s duration are manually selected from simultaneously recorded PPG and respiratory signals. In addition, we tested the algorithm's performance with 504 epochs of 20 s duration and 1008 epochs of 10 s duration.

2.1 Proposed RR Estimation Method

Figure 1 depicts a block diagram of the proposed method, which consists of the following steps:

(1) Preprocessing for mean subtraction and amplitude normalization
(2) Respiratory signal extraction using two-pole digital resonator
(3) Finding Fourier magnitude spectrum using fast Fourier transform
(4) Determining maximum spectral peak location within specified spectral range
(5) Respiration rate determination

Each of the steps of the proposed method is described in the next subsections.

Preprocessing. The preprocessing is performed to subtract mean from the PPG signal $y[n]$ and to normalize the zero-mean signal amplitude between -1 to 1. In this study, we consider three block duration values such as 10, 20 and 30 s to estimate the respiration rate. The mean subtraction is implemented as

$$x[n] = y[n] - \mu_y, \tag{1}$$

where μ_y denotes the mean of the signal $y[n]$. Then, the zero-mean signal amplitude is normalized as

$$\widehat{x}[n] = \frac{x[n]}{max_{n=0}^{N-1}\{|x[n]|\}}, \tag{2}$$

where N is the number samples within a block, which is computed as $\lfloor D * F_s \rfloor$ where D is the block duration, F_s is the sampling rate (samples/second) and $\lfloor \bullet \rfloor$ denotes the floor.

Respiratory Signal Extraction. In past studies, many signal processing techniques such as digital filters, wavelet transforms, EMD, ensemble EMD, synchrosqueezing transform, complementary EEMD, complete EEMD with adaptive noise (CEEMDAN), and improved CEEMDAN (ICEEMDAN), empirical wavelet transform (EWT), Fourier-Bessel series expansion-based EWT (FBSE-EWT), AR models, and PCA were used for extracting respiratory signal from the PPG signal. Although the RR estimation methods based on the above signal processing technique(s) showed promising estimation results, real-time implementation of the methods was not addressed on the wearable devices which are constraint with limited resources such as processor speed, memory and battery power. Therefore, in this study, we attempt to explore a simple filtering technique to extract a respiratory component from the PPG signal.

Past studies showed that the pole-zero placement is effective method for designing narrow bandwidth band-pass and band-stop filters. The placement of poles emphasizes the magnitude response and of zeros provides zero gains. A two-pole band-pass filter with the pair of complex conjugate poles near the unit circle, i.e., poles at $p_{1,2} = re^{\pm j\omega_o}$, where ω_o denotes the resonant frequency and r denotes magnitude of the poles, which controls the bandwidth of the filter.

The transfer function of the two-pole digital resonator with zeros at the origin is given by

$$H(z) = \frac{b_0}{(1 - re^{j\omega_o}z^{-1})(1 - re^{-j\omega_o}z^{-1})} \tag{3}$$

where b_0 is the gain of the resonator. The magnitude response of the function has a large magnitude for the frequency of f_o. By choosing suitable band-pass parameters such as r and f_o, we can extract the respiratory signal having frequency range between 0.1 to 0.8 Hz (6–48 breaths/min). The $|H(e^{j\omega_o})|$ has its peak at or near $\omega = \omega_o$. The width of the resonance centered at ω_o can be controlled by using the parameter r. The Eq. (3) can be rewritten as

$$H(z) = \frac{b_0}{1 - (2r\cos\omega_o)z^{-1} + r^2 z^{-2}} \tag{4}$$

The above transfer function can be further simplified as

$$H(z) = \frac{b_0}{1 + a_1 z^{-1} + a_2 z^{-2}} \tag{5}$$

where, the desired normalization factor b_0 can be computed as

$$b_0 = (1 - r)\sqrt{1 + r^2 - 2r\cos 2\omega_o} \tag{6}$$

$$a_1 = -2r\cos\omega_o \quad and \quad a_2 = r^2. \tag{7}$$

In this study, the resonant frequency ω_o and the bandwidth controlling parameter r are fixed as 0.3 Hz and 0.997 empirically. Then the feed backward coefficients a_1 and a_2 and the gain factor b_0 are computed by using the Eqs. (6) and (7). The magnitude response and phase response of the two-pole resonator are shown in Fig. 2. From Eq. (5), the difference equation of the two-pole digital resonator can be expressed as

$$y[n] = -a_1 y[n] - a_2 y[n-2] + b_0 x[n]. \tag{8}$$

For the PPG signals taken from the MIMIC and CapnoBase datasets, the extracted respiratory signals are shown in Fig. 3. From the extracted respiratory signals, it is noted that the period of the respiratory signal is approximately similar to the period of the original respiratory signal. Further, the extracted signal contains the pulse waveform which is superimposed on the respiratory signal. Thus, it can be used for extracting both pulse rate (PR) and respiration rate (RR) from the extracted signals by using Fourier magnitude spectrum. However, this study restricts to perform RR estimation by limiting the peak analysis of the Fourier spectrum within the range between 0.1 to 0.8 Hz.

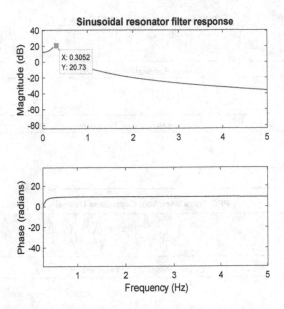

Fig. 2. Magnitude and phase response of the two-pole digital resonator with $w_o = 0.3\,\text{Hz}$ and $r = 0.997$.

Fourier Magnitude Spectrum: In this study, we use FFT for computing the magnitude spectrum of the extracted respiratory signal. Depending on the block duration and sampling rate to be analyzed, the number of points is fixed for FFT computation. For each of the datasets and their sampling rates, the Fourier magnitude spectra of the extracted respiratory signals are shown in Figs. 4 and 5. From the results, it is observed that the dominant spectral peak corresponds to the frequency of the respiratory signals. Results further show that the estimated respiratory frequency matches with the respiratory frequency estimated from the original respiratory signal.

Spectral Peak Finding Logic: In this study, we assume that the respiration rate varies from 6 to 48 breaths/min which equals to the frequency range between 0.1 to 0.8 Hz. Thus, we find a location of the dominant spectral peak within the Fourier spectrum ranging from 0.1–0.8 Hz. From this we find the respiratory frequency F_R to compute the respiration rate.

Respiration Rate Estimation: From the estimated frequency F_R, the respiration rate can be computed as

$$\text{RR} = F_R * 60 \quad (\text{breaths/min}). \tag{9}$$

In this paper, we study the performance of the proposed method using three standard datasets and PPG dataset created by using the BioRadio. The estimation

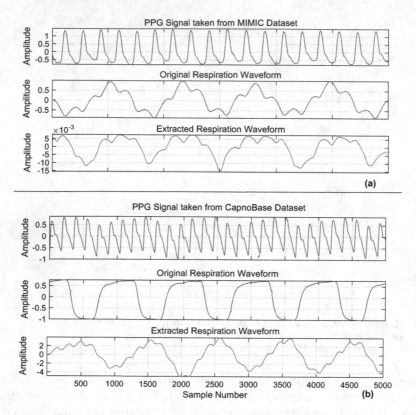

Fig. 3. Extracted respiratory signals from (a) the PPG signal taken from the MIMIC dataset and (b) the PPG signal taken from the CapnoBase dataset.

accuracy is measured in terms of absolute error (AE) and root mean square error (RMSE) (breaths/min).

2.2   Performance Metrics

In past studies, the root mean square error (RMSE) [12] and absolute error (AE) metrics [2] were used for performance evaluation. The RMSE is computed as

$$\text{RMSE}_i = \sqrt{\frac{1}{N} \sum_{i=1}^{N} \left(RR_{ref}(i) - RR_{est}(i) \right)^2}. \tag{10}$$

The RMSE is computed for each of the subjects. The AE was used to find the difference between the reference and derived BR. The AE is computed as:

$$\text{AE}_i = |RR_{ref}(i) - RR_{est}(i)|, \tag{11}$$

where $RR_{ref}(i)$ denotes the RR of the original respiratory signal and $RR_{est}(i)$ denotes the RR of the extracted respiratory signal for for i^{th} observation.

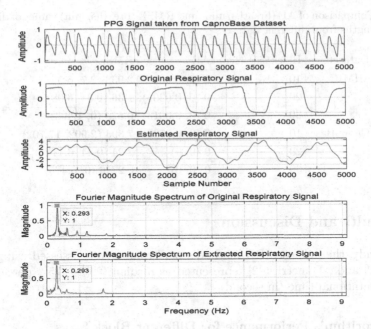

Fig. 4. Results of the two-pole digital resonator and Fourier magnitude spectrum of the extracted respiratory signal from the PPG signal taken from CapnoBase dataset.

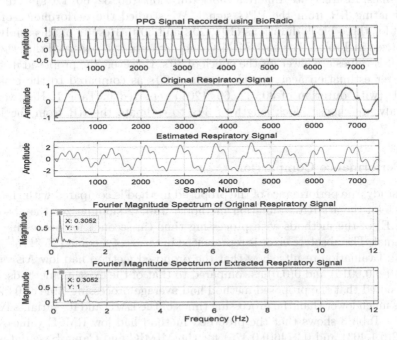

Fig. 5. Results of the two-pole digital resonator and Fourier magnitude spectrum of the extracted respiratory signal from the PPG signal recorded using the BioRadio system.

Table 1. Comparison of AE (breaths/min) and RMSE (breaths/min) values of different segment lengths from different datasets

Dataset	Block size (sec)	AE	RMSE
MIMIC	10	0 (0, 0.061)	2.938 (2.7, 6.55)
	20	0 (0, 0.0305)	1.36 (0.34, 6.98)
	30	0 (0, 0.0015)	0.522 (0, 1.403)
CapnoBase	10	0 (0, 0.0732)	7.393 (2.902, 17.702)
	20	0 (0, 0)	2.24 (0.44, 6.11)
	30	0 (0, 0)	0.2746 (0, 0.475)

3 Results and Discussion

In this study, the proposed RR method's performance was assessed using both RMSE [12] and AE metrics [2] represented as median ($25^{th} - 75^{th}$ percentiles) and computational time (in second).

3.1 Algorithm's Performance for Different Block Sizes

Most methods used the segment length greater than 30 s to estimate RR from PPG signals. In literature, different block durations (30, 32, 60, 120 s) were used for estimating RR from the PPG signal. We studied the performance of our method for three block durations (10 s, 20 s and 30 s). Results of this study are summarized in Table 1. For both MIMIC and datasets, it is observed that the AE and RMSE values are lower for the epoch of 30 s. However, the proposed method had better estimation accuracy for epoch of 20 s as compared to the existing methods (with duration of 30, 32, 60, 120 s) reported in Table 1. However, in this study, we choose block length of 30 s to estimate the RR from the PPG signal.

3.2 Performance Comparison

In this study, the performance of the proposed method is compared with the current state-of-the-art RR estimation methods. Table 2 summarizes the absolute error (AE) of the methods with processing time (in second) for processing 30 s PPG signal. The absolute error is represented in terms of median (25th, 75th percentiles). Evaluation results show that the proposed method had low AE values such as 0(0,0.0015) and 0(0,0) as compared to that of the existing methods. It is further noted that the proposed method had average processing time of 0.0296 s which is much lower than the processing times of the EMD and its variants based methods. Table 3 shows that the proposed method had low RMSE values such as 0.522(0,1.403) and 0.2746(0,0.475) for the MIMIC and CapnoBase datasets, respectively as compared to that of the existing methods. It is also noted that the proposed method had better accuracy in estimating the RR from the 30 s

Table 2. Comparison of AE (breaths/min) values represented as median (25th–75th percentiles) of different segment lengths from different datasets: PT: Processing time.

Methods	AE (MIMIC)	AE (CapnoBase)	PT* (sec) for 30 s block
Proposed method	**0 (0–0.0015)**	**0 (0–0)**	0.0296
Pimentel et al. [8]	4.0 (1.8–5.5)	1.5 (0.3–3.3)	NAN
Karlen et al. [12]	5.8 (1.9–9.7)	1.2 (0.5–3.4)	NAN
Shelley et al. [9]	3.5 (1.5–9.4)	4.5 (0.8–10.5)	NAN
Nilsson et al. [21]	5.4 (3.4–9.2)	10.5 (4.9–12.4)	NAN
EMD-PCA [2]	0.9 (0.2–5)	9.9 (3.4–19.8)	2.8
CEEMD-PCA [2]	5 (0.9–10.9)	105 (6.7–19)	3.2
CEEMDAN-PCA [2]	0 (0–0.9)	3.6 (1–8.9)	10.5
EEMD-PCA [2]	0 (0–0.5)	2.4 (0.7–8.6)	4.2
ICEEMDAN-PCA [2]	0 (0–0.5)	3.3 (0.8–8.9)	6.2

Table 3. Comparison of RMSE (breaths/min) values of different segment lengths from different datasets. Correntropy spectral density (CSD); Power spectral density (PSD)

Method and database	RMSE (breaths/min)	Data length (in sec)
Proposed method, MIMIC	**0.522 (0, 1.403)**	**30**
Proposed method, CapnoBase	**0.2746 (0, 0.475)**	**30**
EEMD-PCA [6], MIMIC	0.89 (0, 1.78)	30
EEMD-PCA [6], CapnoBase	2.77 (0.50, 5.9)	30
CSD [11], CapnoBase	0.95 (0.27, 6.20)	120
PSD [11], CapnoBase	3.18 (1.20, 11.3)	120
Smart fusion [12], CapnoBase	1.56 (0.60, 3.15)	32
EMD [13], CapnoBase	3.5 (1.1, 11)	60

PPG signal. Evaluation results demonstrate that the proposed method is much simpler than the other signal processing techniques used to estimate the RR from the PPG signal.

4   Conclusion

A simple method is presented for estimating the RR from a PPG signal. The proposed method is based on the two-pole digital resonator and fast Fourier transform (FFT) algorithms. The proposed method is evaluated using the benchmark metrics on the standard PPG datasets. The proposed method had low RMSE values such as 0.522(0,1.403) and 0.2746(0,0.475) for the MIMIC and CapnoBase datasets, respectively. The proposed method had low AE values such as 0(0, 0.0015) and 0(0,0). Results show that the proposed method outperforms the existing methods such as the EMD-PCA, ensemble EMD-PCA, and improved

CEEMDAN-PCA methods. Results further showed that the proposed method had average processing time of 0.0296 s, which is lower as compared to the existing methods for 30 s PPG signal.

References

1. L'Her, E., N'Guyen, Q.T., Pateau, V., Bodenes, L., Lellouche, F.: Photoplethysmographic determination of the respiratory rate in acutely ill patients: validation of a new algorithm and implementation into a biomedical device. Ann. Intensive Care **9**(1), 1–10 (2019). https://doi.org/10.1186/s13613-019-0485-z
2. Motin, M.A., Karmakar, C.K., Palaniswami, M.: Selection of empirical mode decomposition techniques for extracting breathing rate from PPG. IEEE Signal Process. Lett. **26**(04), 592–596 (2019)
3. Dehkordi, P., Garde, A., Molavi, B.: Extracting respiratory rate from multiple photoplethysmogram respiratory-induced variations. Front. Physiol. **9**, 1–10 (2018)
4. Pirhonen, M., Peltokangas, M., Vehkaoja, A.: Acquiring respiration rate from photoplethysmographic signal by recursive Bayesian tracking of intrinsic modes in time-frequency spectra. Sensors **18**(06), 1693 (2018)
5. Charlton, P.H., et al.: Breathing rate estimation from the electrocardiogram and photoplethysmogram: a review. IEEE Rev. Biomed. Eng. **11**, 2–20 (2018)
6. Motin, M.A., Karmakar, C.K., Palaniswami, M.: Ensemble empirical mode decomposition with principal component analysis: a novel approach for extracting respiratory rate and heart rate from photoplethysmographic signal. IEEE J. Biomed. Health Inf. **22**(3), 766–774 (2017)
7. Hernando, A., Peláez, M.D., Lozano, M.T., Aiger, M., Gil, G., Lázaro, J.: Finger and forehead PPG signal comparison for respiratory rate estimation based on pulse amplitude variability. In: 2017 25th IEEE European Signal Processing Conference (EUSIPCO), pp. 2076–2080 (2017)
8. Pimentel, M.A., et al.: Toward a robust estimation of respiratory rate from pulse oximeters. IEEE Trans. Biomed. Eng. **64**(08), 1914–1923 (2017)
9. Shelley, K.H., Awad, A.A., Stout, R.G., Silverman, D.G.: The use of joint time frequency analysis to quantify the effect of ventilation on the pulse oximeter waveform. J. Clin. Monit. Comput. **20**(02), 81–87 (2016)
10. Charlton, P.H., Bonnici, T., Tarassenko, L., Clifton, D.A., Beale, R., Watkinson, P.J.: An assessment of algorithms to estimate respiratory rate from the electrocardiogram and photoplethysmogram. Physiol. Meas. **37**(4), 610 (2016)
11. Garde, A., Karlen, W., Ansermino, J.M., Dumont, G.A.: Estimating respiratory and heart rates from the correntropy spectral density of the photoplethysmogram. PloS One **9**(1), 1–11 (2014)
12. Karlen, W., Raman, S., Ansermino, J.M., Dumont, G.A.: Multiparameter respiratory rate estimation from the photoplethysmogram. IEEE Trans. Biomed. Eng. **60**(7), 1946–1953 (2013)
13. Garde, A., Karlen, W., Dehkordi, P., Ansermino, J., Dumont, G., Empirical mode decomposition for respiratory and heart rate estimation from the photoplethysmogram. In: Computing in Cardiology, pp. 799–802 (2013)
14. Addison, P.S., Watson, J.N., Mestek, M.L., Mecca, R.S.: Developing an algorithm for pulse oximetry derived respiratory rate (RR(oxi)): a healthy volunteer study. J. Clin. Monit. Comput. **26**(1), 45–51 (2012)

15. Li, J., Jin, J., Chen, X., Sun, W., Guo, P.: Comparison of respiratory-induced variations in photoplethysmographic signals. Physiol. Meas. **31**(3), 415–425 (2010)

16. Karlen, W., Brouse, C.J., Cooke, E., Ansermino, J.M., Dumont, G.A.: Respiratory rate estimation using respiratory sinus arrhythmia from photoplethysmography. In: Proceedings of IEEE Annual International Conference in Medicine and Biology Society, Boston, MA, USA, pp. 1201–1204 (2011)

17. Chon, K.H., Dash, S., Ju, K.: Estimation of respiratory rate from photoplethysmogram data using time-frequency spectral estimation. IEEE Trans. Biomed. Eng. **56**(8), 2054–2063 (2009)

18. Fleming, S., Tarassenko, L.: A comparison of signal processing techniques for the extraction of breathing rate from the photoplethysmogram. Int. J. Biol. Med. Sci. **2**(4), 232–236 (2007)

19. Leonard, P., Grubb, N.R., Addison, P.S., Clifton, D., Watson, J.N.: An algorithm for the detection of individual breaths from the pulse oximeter waveform. J. Clin. Monit. Comput. **18**(5–6), 309–312 (2004)

20. Johansson, A.: Neural network for photoplethysmographic respiratory rate monitoring. Med. Biol. Eng. Comput. **41**(3), 242–248 (2003)

21. Nilsson, L., Johansson, A., Kalman, S.: Monitoring of respiratory rate in postoperative care using a new photoplethysmographic technique. J. Clin. Monit. Comput. **16**(04), 309–315 (2000)

22. Olsson, E., Ugnell, H., Oberg, P.A., Sedin, G.: Photoplethysmography for simultaneous recording of heart and respiratory rates in newborn infants. Acta Paediatr. (Oslo, Norway: 1992) **89**(7), 853–861 (2000)

23. Lindberg, L.G., Ugnell, H., Oberg, P.A.: Monitoring of respiratory and heart rates using a fibre-optic sensor. Med. Biol. Eng. Comput. **30**(5), 533–537 (1992)

24. Nakajima, K., Tamura, T., Miike, H.: Monitoring of heart and respiratory rates by photoplethysmography using a digital filtering technique. Med. Eng. Phys. **18**(5), 365–372 (1996)

25. Nakajima, K., Tamura, T., Ohta, T., Miike, H., Oberg, P.A.: Photoplethysmographic measurement of heart and respiratory rates using digital filters. In: Proceedings IEEE Annual International Conference in Medicine and Biology Society, pp. 1006–1007 (1993)

26. Moody, G.B., Mark, R.G.: A database to support development and evaluation of intelligent intensive care monitoring. In: Proceedings Computer in Cardiology, pp. 657–660 (1996). https://physionet.org/physiobank/database/mimicdb/

27. Karlen, W., Turner, M., Cooke, E., Dumont, G.A., Ansermino, J.M.: CapnoBase: signal database and tools to collect, share and annotate respiratory signals. In: Proceedings Annual Meeting Society for Technology Anesthesia, West Palm Beach, FL, USA, p. 25 (2010). http://www.capnobase.org/

28. Saeed, M., et al.: Multiparameter intelligent monitoring in intensive care II (MIMIC-II): a public-access intensive care unit database. Critical Care Med. **39**, 952–960 (2011). https://physionet.org/physiobank/database/bidmc/

29. BioRadio Wireless Data Acquisition System. https://glneurotech.com/bioradio/exercise-science/

Phonemes: An Explanatory Study Applied to Identify a Speaker

Saritha Kinkiri[1]([⊠]), Basel Barakat[2], and Simeon Keates[2]

[1] University of Greenwich, Chatham ME4 4TB, UK
s.kinkiri@gre.ac.uk
[2] Edinburgh Napier University, Edinburgh EH11 4DY, UK
B.N.Bakarat@gre.ac.uk, S.Keates@napier.ac.uk

Abstract. Speaker Identification (SI) is a process of identifying a speaker automatically via a machine using the speaker's voice. In SI, one speaker's voice is compared with n- number of speakers' templates within the reference database to find the best match among the potential speakers. Speakers are capable of changing their voice, though, such as their accent, which makes is more challenging to identify who is talking. In this paper, we extracted phonemes from a speaker's voice recording and investigated the associated frequencies and amplitudes to be assist in identifying the person who is speaking. This paper demonstrates the importance of phonemes in both speech and voice recognition systems. The results demonstrate that we can use phonemes to help the machine identify a particular speaker, however, phonemes get better accuracy in speech recognition than speaker identification.

Keywords: Accent · Human speech · Phonemes and speaker identification

1 Introduction

Speaker recognition is used to identify an individual person who is speaking, independent of what has been said. The production of speech involves the brain, vocal cords, lips, tongue, lungs, diaphragm, mouth and nasal/sinus cavities. The two steps in speaker recognition are perception and recognition. The brain receives a sound wave principally through the ears. The wave is transformed into electrical nerve impulses in the cochlea and those impulses are sent to the brain for processing and recognition.

Digital systems need to be given training on speech samples to identify a speaker. These speech samples are collected from each person speaking through a microphone and processed by a processor to recognise the voice/speech. Voice characteristics include both physical and behavioral components. The shape of the vocal tract is fundamental in the physiological component. The vocal tract is made up of the mouth, tongue, jaw, pharynx and larynx which articulate and control speech production by manipulating the airflow generated by the lungs and diaphragm. The behavioral component comprises emotion, accents, rate of speech and pronunciation. Some elements of speech, such as the ability to roll the letter 'r,' are controlled genetically.

Human speech conveys two levels of information [11]. At the primary level, speech signal conveys the words being spoken by a user, which helps us to recognise a user's

© Springer Nature Singapore Pte Ltd. 2020
A. Bhattacharjee et al. (Eds.): MIND 2020, CCIS 1241, pp. 58–68, 2020.
https://doi.org/10.1007/978-981-15-6318-8_6

pronunciation, accent, age and language. On secondary level, the signal conveys information that can identify a speaker on more fundamental characteristics rather than what has been said. Humans are generally good at identifying a speaker in very limited time by listening to their speech/voice [1] especially if the speaker is familiar to them. However, even when the speaker is not known to the listener, it is still possible to learn a lot about the person from how they speak. For example, if you are in a flight and some people are sitting behind you and they started talking with people who are sitting beside them; by listening to their speech, you would be able to identify the gender, predict their age, emotion and accent (if you are familiar with their accent), even though if you may have not seen them before).

Humans can even identify intent by listening to a sound that does not have any obvious semantic meaning [15]. For example, parents of young children can often under- stand what the child or infant wants, irrespective of the fact that the child is not using proper words, or merely making sounds to indicate what they need or how they feel. Speech conveys different types of information such as message, language infor- mation, emotional and physiological characteristics [3, 9].

Machines can process audio signals in real-time such as speech recognizers e.g.: Siri and Alexa. However, it is difficult for a machine to distinguish sounds from different resources such as music, human voice, animal sound etc. as humans do. Thus, to make an algorithm that can identify the speaker, it is important to understand the components of the human voice. Current speaker identification systems extract short-term acoustic features from a human speech [2], as shown in Fig. 1.

In this paper, we are investigating the differences in the frequencies of phonemes. Hence, we conducted an experiment, which includes collecting voice samples from ten participants and extracted phonemes. This paper is organized as follows, Sect. 2 presents a brief overview of the background of the speaker identification system, followed by results, discussion and given the conclusion of using phonemes to identify a speaker.

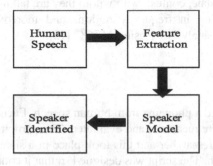

Fig. 1. Speaker identification system

2 Background

The sounds of human speech are complex and have been studied for centuries and are still being researched [e.g., 12, 13]. Research suggests that phonetics has always been an important part of sound production. Phonetics is derived from a Greek word, '*phōnētikós*'; phone means a sound or voice. The small units of sounds are called phonemes, with each language having their own phonetic set. Phonetics have played the main role in learning and understanding a language rather than identifying a speaker. There are 20 letters that are considered to be "voiced," which, in English, include consonants B, D, G, J, L, M, N, NG, R, SZ, TH, V, W, Y, Z and vowels A, E, I, O and U. There are 8 "unvoiced" sounds: CH, F, K, P, S, SH, T and TH [4, 5].

There are three types of phonetics: acoustic, auditory and articulatory phonetics [5]. Acoustic phonetics is the physical property of the sounds of a language; that is the volume of sound, frequency of the sound waves, frequency of vibrations, etc. Auditory phonetics is focused on how speakers perceive the sounds of a language, with the help of the ears and the brain. Articulatory phonetics conveys how the vocal tract produces the sounds of a language that is, with the help of moving parts of our mouth and throat, also known as the articulators [5, 7]. Phonetics helps when learning and distinguishing within a language, or between multiple languages. By uttering a sequence of discrete sounds (or phonemes) with the help of our articulators, words are composed [2, 10]. A combination of coherent words leads to a sentence. Phonemes are discrete or different sounds within a particular language but make up the building blocks of all speech. Thus, all words and sentences are ultimately collections of phonemes [8].

Feature extraction plays a crucial part in speech processing. Features should provide the necessary information to be able to identify a speaker. There are numerous feature extraction methods are available such as: Linear Predictive Codes (LPC), Perceptual Linear Prediction (PLP), Mel Frequency Cepstral Coefficients (MFCC), PLP-RASTA (PLP-Relative Spectra) etc. The most popular feature extraction method is MFCC, but extraction features would be difficult when speaker changes their voice such as: their emotional state, context, with whom they are talking etc. MFCC does not provide enough resolution in frequency regions and moreover, signal cannot be reverted from frequency analysis by using MFCC [13].

3 Experiment

In this paper, we extracted a phoneme from human speech. Each phoneme's amplitude and frequency values were measured and evaluated. The participant's task was to read a script provided by the researcher and this took place in a silent/quiet room allocated especially for the research. The script was designed so that it could be read easily by all participants and prevented the use of foul language as well.

3.1 Data Collection

The speech was recorded from ten participants reading a script. Participants were asked to read the script, which comprised of ten sentences, which are shown below. They aimed to cover the main phonemes used within the English language (there are 44 in total), these sentences are:

1. The boys enjoyed playing dodgeball every Wednesday.
2. Please give me a call in ten minutes.
3. I love toast and orange juice for breakfast.
4. There is heavy traffic on the highway.
5. If you listen closely, you will hear the birds.
6. My father is my inspiration for success.
7. I will be in the office in 10 min.
8. I will go India to meet my parents.
9. Turn the music down in your headphones.
10. It all happened suddenly.

3.2 Instructions to Use Recording Equipment

The researcher will offer participants the option to do some trial recordings before the actual recording to allow the participant to become comfortable with the process. The equipment used in this research includes an audio recorder which in itself was not harmful, nevertheless, the researcher gave clear instructions on how to use the recording equipment (e.g. distance to the microphone) before the start of the recording.

In the case that the participant becomes anxious, the researcher would remind the participant that they are not obliged to take part in the study. Since one of the recording locations was enclosed (anechoic chamber), there was a chance that a participant did not want to record their voice in this location. The lead researcher was available in the anechoic chamber to calm the participants down if they were to appear to become anxious since it was an enclosed space. If the participant was still uncomfortable to do the recordings in that environment, then an alternative space could have been used. The alternative space would be outside of the anechoic chamber or any of the classrooms on campus. It was explained to the participants how his/her data would be used and handled in the project before the task started.

The participants were given a choice to not take part if they decided to do so. The participants were given the option to leave the study at any point of the research. Assuming they gave their consent, their recorded voices were added anonymously to the database. Since the recorded voices could be used as a biometric identification means, there could be a consequent potential security risk [14]. However, as all data was anonymized before storage and usage this risk was minimised as there was no personal ID linked with the recordings. All data was stored safely and will be deleted once the project is completed. The following were used for the recording as shown in Table 1.

Table 1. The equipment used in this research

Number of participants	10
Recording place	Anechoic chamber, Nelson building
Recording equipment	Scarlett 2i2 studio, MacBook
Software	Audacity
Programming language	Python
Headphone/headset	Participant choice/option

3.3   Methodology

After recording the voices of all participants, the next step was to extract phonemes from a script. There is no software available to do extract phonemes from a speech, so it was extracted manually. To observe how the frequency and relative amplitude values changed for a specific phoneme a Fast Fourier Transform (FFT), was applied to the voice signal to observe the frequency spectrum. The FFT was applied to phonemes of all 10 participants.

Phonemes play an important role in human's speech as shown in Fig. 2. Phonemes help us to recognise the sound, as soon one's heard a sound [6]. For example, when one speaks/say, "Hello". What is the first sound that comes first in the human's brain? The sound which comes as "/h". Identification of a phoneme helps to identify a common sound in different words [15]. For example, when some say: boys, breakfast, birds and ball. The first sound one can hear is "/b".

In this experiment, the frequency of phonemes in words has been observed at various points such as the position of a phoneme in several words. In this experiment, participants were asked to read a list of sentences. Participant read a bunch of sentences from a script which consists of several words, and then words have the same phoneme in different positions. For example, phoneme 'B' was read in different words by the same participant. However, their frequency and amplitudes values were changed drastically for a few participants which were noted in Table 2. The hypothesis of this experiment was, phonemes would be individual to a speaker, then one can use phonemes to identify a speaker-independent of a language. But then, once experiment was conducted and results were observed, one can use phonemes to identify a speaker but with some boundaries, as explained in the conclusion.

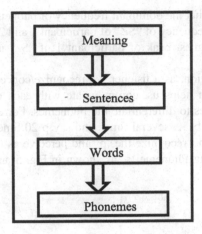

Fig. 2. Description of phonemes

4 Results

The voiced phonemes are extracted from participants and FFT is applied to observe how relative amplitude and frequency values of a phoneme vary for different words from the same participant. The highest peak of the frequency does not change. Each phoneme represents a different visual representation of the phonemes of a participant. Once the voiced phonemes of one participant are compared with another participant, it is observed that some phonemes are very similar to others and some of them are very distinctive. The frequency and relative amplitude values were derived and recorded, from each phoneme.

Next, voiceless phonemes of all participants are extracted to find out if there is any consistency, sufficient enough to identify a speaker. Surprisingly, voiceless phonemes of some participants are very distinctive to recognize a person. FFT graphs are prepared for both phonemes of all participants and voiced versus voiceless phonemes is compared to draw a conclusion. Moving forward, voiced and voiceless phonemes of all participants are compared. Participants voices are used as an initial data set and only their phonemes are extracted. Participant 1 and participant 3 have the same similarity, when they pronounce the letter "P" as shown in Fig. 3 and 4; on the other hand, participant 6 and participant 9 have 100% of similarity of producing phonemes "r". Participant 1 is similar to participant 4 when pronouncing the phoneme "th". Lastly, participant 5 is the only one with a distinctive pronunciation of the phoneme "SZ".

There are several factors, which make a phoneme sound different and represent different relative amplitude and frequency values. Another phenomenon that will be questioned is how easy it is for a participant to pronounce a phoneme?

Phonemes are extracted for ten participants. For each participant, a boundary is set up for dominant frequency, independent of phonemes, meaning he/she can say any phoneme but, the dominant frequency should lie between the range. For several phonemes, like Sz, Y, P, W and TH, the dominant frequency lies between 50 to 200 Hz. For the phoneme T and V, the dominant frequency lies between 200 to

285 Hz. It was observed that the dominant frequency of phoneme "V" of participant 1 and 2 are the same. The frequency of "SZ" of participant 1 and 2 are same but differs in amplitude values. The highest peak of participant 1 of "Sz" is same as "w" of participant 2.

In our daily conversation, as a listener we recognize/concentrate words to understand the meaning, which helps us, communicate with each other. Hence, it is not practical to use frequencies to differentiate the phonemes. For example, if someone is continuously saying b, b, b, … several times and say p 20 times in between and then continue saying b, we don't recognize the 'p' and perceive as if the participant said b only. Participants of saying Phoneme 's' as shown in Fig. 5 and 6.

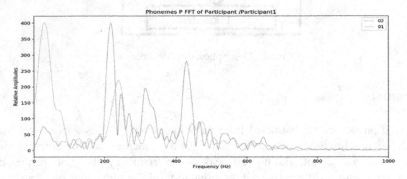

Fig. 3. Spectrograph of phoneme 'p' of a participant

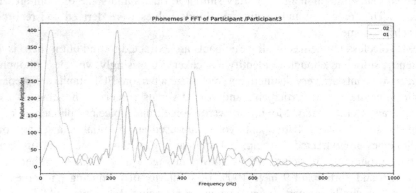

Fig. 4. Spectrograph of phoneme 'p' of a participant 3

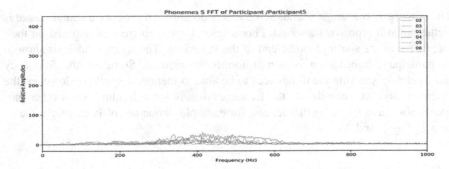

Fig. 5. Spectrograph of phoneme 'S' of a participant 5

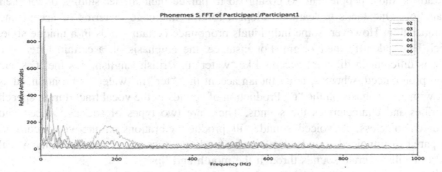

Fig. 6. Spectrograph of phoneme 'S' of a participant 1

5 Discussion

Several questions arise about the recording of the above data. These questions include: why phonemes are changing even though the same person is speaking? Why some phonemes are distinctive to a participant and a few of them are very similar between different participants?

There are several limitations of using phonemes as a fundamental factor that affects voice recognition: Phonemes produce different sounds because of the exaltation of air from our mouth. It is hard to keep track of how these different sounds are produced, as it is dependent on many factors such as how much air is exhaled whilst speaking, how big the vocal cord is open, the shape of lips, placement of tongue etc.

Some of the other factors included are the actual placement of the phoneme in a word; emotions can alter the phonetic emphasis on a word and context of the word (paint and pain/sell and cell). Phonemes are good enough to identify their origin, but not consistent to identify a person. Even in the linguistics, the aim of the listener is not to concentrate on individual phoneme, but to understand the meaning of the words/sentences. It is difficult to extract phonemes from a voice signal manually.

The same sound may be represented by different letters or combination of letters. One should be knowledge of phonemes completely or can use of IPA to find out the phonemes in a word. The same letter produces a different sound. Different combination of letters represents a single sound. Some letters do not even produce a sound. There is no letter but still represents a sound. Phonemes change their frequency based on their place, that is in the starting/middle/end of the sentences. The spectral analysis showed that, participant information is non-uniformly distributed. Some of the frequency domains clearly showing the differences to be able to identify a speaker. However, the problem is, how one can decide the frequency bands for individual when other participants also have the same differences, for example phoneme 'p' is exactly same as shown in Fig. 3 and 4.

6 Conclusion

Nowadays, most people tend to go abroad to pursue their higher studies or for their dream job. One tends to learn or adopt a foreign language in terms of accent and pronunciation. However, some individuals pronounce certain words in a unique style, which helps identify their origin. For instance, the emphasis on a certain letter of a word is different in different accents like 'water' in British English, has the 't' silent when pronounced, whereas, in an Indian accent that "ter" in 'water' is pronounced as turr, with an emphasis on the "r". Production of sounds in the vocal tract during speech describes and characterizes the sounds. There are two types of sounds, voiced and unvoiced/voiceless. A voiced sound will produce vibrations in the vocal cord as compared to unvoiced sounds. Unvoiced sounds produce no vibrations in the vocal cord but still generate sounds through the mouth and lips.

Participants can adjust the boundaries of a phonemes' frequency based on the context. For example, the participant will learn how to say words in different ways. There are numerous papers focused on how phonemes are used to identify a person, but it is only available for a few languages [4, 5, 10]. This is mainly because they have their own systems because of know which phonemes are used very often. Phonemes mainly arise from a language perceptive. As humans, we don't listen to phonemes on its own, however, we do listen to complete phonemes to understand the language, but not to identify a speaker. Language carries information from a human speech, by using words. Changes in the position of a phoneme create a lot of difference that would reflect a different pattern of a human speech. Then it would become more difficult to identify a speaker. Moreover, English is not a phonetical language. In the English language, one phoneme can be represented by using other letters. For example, \k\ in Cat, kite, KitKat. \k\ is represented by using 'c'.

Participants have used knowledge of phonemes from their original language that helps us identify which country they belong to. It is difficult to extract a phoneme, if you don't know observe/listen what has been said. For example, /p/in cap and /b/in cab. If system is trained based on phonemes only, without context/situation system cannot figure out which phoneme is pronounced. The dominant frequency of phoneme 'p' did not change for all ten participants as shown in Fig. 6.

Phoneme "B" of participant 1 and 2 were extracted from word: boys, ball, breakfast and birds. The frequency values were varied, even though same person is speaking the same phoneme were noted in the Table 2 and spectrum of a phoneme 'B, for all ten participants were shown in Fig. 7.

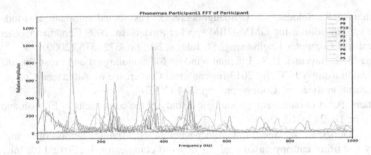

Fig. 7. Spectrograph of phoneme 'B' of 10 participants

Table 2. Frequency of phoneme "B".

Phoneme "B"	Boys	Ball	Breakfast	Birds	Mean	Median
Participant 1	248	528	482	242	375	365
Participant 2	100	32	108	32	68	66
Participant 3	409	343	366	551	417.25	387.5
Participant 4	335	345	381	472	383.25	363
Participant 5	336	342	480	285	360.75	339
Participant 6	449	370	348	336	375.75	359
Participant 7	222	236	280	240	246.5	242
Participant 8	280	450	320	440	372.5	380
Participant 9	270	150	320	440	247.5	260
Participant 10	320	387	420	450	394.25	403.5

When we consider the Chinese language, it is a tonal language. The way of expressing phonemes would be different to convey the message/information. After observing the data, it is concluded that phonemes will not help us identify a speaker, but instead help us find out their nativity. Phonemes can play an important role in the linguistic theory of speech. One of the main problems with phonemes is that participants had an influence from their native language on the other familiar language (English). Participants pronounced differently or mispronounced, phonemes in words. They tend to use their native language phonology skill on other languages that helped us recognise their nativity. If would be helpful to understand the language, so we can use it in speech recognition and language identification. we can presume which language a person is speaking and/or what is their origin (for example, Indians, British and so.).

References

1. Bazyar, M., Sudirman, R.: A new speaker change detection method in a speaker identification system for two-speakers segmentation. In: 2014 IEEE Symposium on Computer Applications and Industrial Electronics (ISCAIE), Penang, pp. 141–145 (2014)

2. Chowdhury, F.R., Selouani, S., O'Shaughnessy, D.: Distributed automatic text-independent speaker identification using GMM-UBM speaker models. In: 2009 Canadian Conference on Electrical and Computer Engineering, St. John's, NL, pp. 372–375 (2009)
3. Nagaraja, B.G., Jayanna, H.S.: Efficient window for monolingual and cross lingual speaker identification using MFCC. In: 2013 International Conference on Advanced Computing and Communication Systems, Coimbatore, pp. 1–4 (2013)
4. Al-Hattami, A.: A phonetic and phonological study of the consonants of English and Arabic. Lang. India **10**, 242–365 (2010)
5. Bacha, S., Ghozi, R., Jaidane, M., Gouider-Khoujia, N.: Arabic adaption of phonology and memory test using entropy-based analysis of word complexity. In: 2012 11th International Conference on Information Science, Signal Processing and their Applications, (ISSPA), Montreal, QC, pp. 672–677 (2012)
6. Ngo, G.H., Nguyen, M., Chen, N.F.: Phonology-augmented statistical framework for machine transliteration using limited linguistic resources. IEEE/ACM Trans. Audio Speech Lang. Process. **27**(1), 192–211 (2019)
7. Shih, S.S., Inkelas, S.: Auto segmental aims in surface-optimizing phonology. Linguist. J. **50**(1), 137–196 (2018)
8. Uma Maheswari, N., Kabilan, A.P., Venkatesh, R.: Speaker independent speech recognition system based on phoneme identification. In: 2008 International Conference on Computing, Communication and Networking, St. Thomas, VI, pp. 1–6 (2008)
9. Rashid, R.A., Mahalin, N.H., Sarijari, M.A., Abdul Aziz, A.A.: Security system using biometric technology: design and implementation of voice recognition system (VRS). In: 2008 International Conference on Computer and Communication Engineering, Kuala Lumpur, pp. 898–902 (2008)
10. Akhila, K.S., Kumaraswamy, R.: Comparative analysis of Kannada phoneme recognition using different classifies. In: 2015 International Conference on Trends in Automation, Communications and Computing Technology (I-TACT 2015), Bangalore, pp. 1–6 (2015)
11. Panda, S.P.: Automated speech recognition system in advancement of human-computer interaction. In: 2017 International Conference on Computing Methodologies and Communication (ICCMC), Erode, pp. 302–306 (2017)
12. Xue, M., Zhu, C.: A study and application on machine learning of artificial intelligence. In: 2009 International Joint Conference on Artificial Intelligence, pp. 272–274 (2009)
13. Zhao, C., Wang, H., Hyon, S., Wei, J., Dang, J.: Efficient feature extraction of speaker identification using phoneme mean F-ratio for Chinese. In: 2012 8th International Symposium on Chinese Spoken Language Processing, pp. 345–348 (2012)
14. Lavan, N., Burton, A.M., Scott, S.K., McGettigan, C.: Flexible voices: identity perception from variable vocal signals. Psychon. Bull. Rev. J. **26**(1), 90–102 (2019)
15. Kinkiri, S., Keates, S.: Identification of a speaker from familiar and unfamiliar voices. In: 2019 5th International Conference on Robotics and Artificial, pp. 94–97 (2019)

Nutritional Status Prediction in Neonate Using Machine Learning Techniques: A Comparative Study

Zakir Hussain[✉] and Malaya Dutta Borah

Department of Computer Science and Engineering,
National Institute of Technology Silchar, Cachar, Silchar 788010, Assam, India
zak08hussain@gmail.com, malayaduttaborah@gmail.com

Abstract. For proper physical and mental development, nutrition has vital role to play. Proper development of child both physically and mentally is essential for building a peaceful society. This study has focused on prediction of nutritional status in neonate using the features of mother. The machine learning techniques namely Logistic Regression, Decision Tree, K-Nearest Neighbor, Linear Discriminant Analysis, Gaussian Naïve Bayes and Support Vector Machine have been implemented using a self created dataset having 445 instances and eighteen features. The dataset has a label with two classes- under weight and normal weight. We have got an accuracy of 88% for Logistic Regression, 99% for Decision Tree, 85% for K-Nearest Neighbor, 93% for Linear Discriminant Analysis, 86% for Gaussian Naïve Bayes and 88% for Support Vector Machine. All the techniques have shown magnificent performance.

Keywords: Nutritional status · Nutritional status in neonate · Nutritional status in new born · Features of mother · Malnutrition · Under-weight

1 Introduction

In low-and-middle-income countries like India, both extremes of malnutrition are faced by the children due to rapid change in food system [8]. Most of the times the term malnutrition is used to mean under-nutrition, but actually it mean both under-nutrition and over-nutrition [3]. There are many reasons to develop malnutrition. Some of those are intake of diet or amount of calorie consumption, imbalanced calorie intake while suffering from disease, complications occurred due to illness such as less absorption and excessive loss of nutrient and sometimes all these causes can also be combined [14]. Also malnutrition influences in losing physical and mental potential and decreases the potential to handle stress [4]. Food is the main source of nourishing the body by supplying the necessary chemicals. Refusal to the food increases the probability to suffer from malnutrition. Early identification of the susceptibility toward suffering from malnutrition in

© Springer Nature Singapore Pte Ltd. 2020
A. Bhattacharjee et al. (Eds.): MIND 2020, CCIS 1241, pp. 69–83, 2020.
https://doi.org/10.1007/978-981-15-6318-8_7

latter ages is very necessary as almost 80% of brain development happens within two years from the birth. If this development is disturbed by any means, then the children is likely to be the victim of the consequences of less development of the brain. Other consequences like higher infection, higher complication, increased loss of muscle, reduced wound healing, increased morbidity and mortality are also associated. As a result the performance of the children in all aspect gets reduced. This will create a human resource with less efficiency and less compatibility in certain fields. This will hamper the economic development of the country.

As stated in the report of World Health Organization (WHO), India is one of the countries having large number of children and adults suffering from the consequences of malnutrition [15]. The degree of malnutrition is very high in India. A WHO and UNICEF review in 2018 suggested that the Sustainable Development Goals (SDG) of eliminating all types of malnutrition by 2030 was desirable but not achievable and, on the basis of trends so far, recommended targets for the malnutrition indicators up to 2030 [13]. To ensure a curative measure for this problem is- early detection of the possibility for a child to be affected by malnutrition and treat accordingly. For early detection, the study and experiment can be carried out on the mother carrying the child in her womb. Some unique features are visible on the mother who is going to deliver a child with certain probability of getting affected by malnutrition. Those features can be considered for machine learning techniques to classify the children in certain classes for similar kind of treatment.

1.1   Motivation

If we look back we find that a large number of unsocial, inhuman and menacing activities happen in the under developed and developing countries like India. The count of abduction, kidnapping, accident, addiction, theft, extremist activity and other crimes have got an enhancement from past few years. Many causes are there to foster these activities but nutritional state of the body can be thought of as one of the major causes. If the above cases are analysed it can be found that the assailant is a victim of some sort of physical or mental disorder. Among other reasons, nutritional state of the body is highly responsible for these disorders. It is always said that a healthy mind resides in a healthy body. For a healthy body there must have proper balance in the nutrients. A person with good health and good mental state posses the ability to analyse the situations and causes with positive note and can handle those with positive attitude. A healthy mind can help a person to get right direction to decide what to accept and what to reject. Malnutrition in either the form of under-nutrition or over-nutrition can disrupt the development of physical and mental health. It has been expected that if the malnutrition can be overcome in early ages, then the rate of these irksome activities can be reduced significantly and we can dream for a better society.

1.2 Problem Statement

As the above mentioned problem is a problem that must be addressed for better society, many theoretical researches have been carried out. Causes of the problem is also assumed and medical science is trying to identify and solve the problems with their traditional approaches. The traditional approach is very time consuming and costly, and people underlying in Below Poverty Line (BPL) can not afford. Use of the improved techniques in this area is very less. Application of machine learning techniques in addressing these problems can be expected to reduce the cost as well as time. Machine learning techniques have the potential to predict the nutritional status in neonate better and as a result doctors can take quality decision for right treatment. In this research, machine learning techniques namely Logistic Regression, Decision Tree, K-Nearest Neighbor, Linear Discriminant Analysis, Gaussian Naïve Bayes and Support Vector Machine have been used to get maximum possible prediction using some important features. Since this is considering the prediction for the neonate, so the study will mainly focus on the mother.

The main objective of this research is to alert the parent by predicting nutritional status of neonate. The aim of this research is to find the solution for the following research questions to achieve the above objectives:

- Is it possible to identify the nutritional status of neonate?
- Is it possible to predict nutritional status of neonate before birth by using features of mother?
- Can machine learning techniques correctly predict nutritional status of neonate?

The first and the second questions are totally dependent on medical science. To get the answers of these questions, two Medical and Health Officers have helped a lot. To answer the third question, data were collected from Geramari MPHC, Dhubri, Assam and Kazigaon SD, Kokrajhar, Assam and machine learning techniques were applied.

2 Literature Review

Literature review for this study has focused on the prediction of nutritional status of neonate. Some surveys have also been carried out for the babies under the age of five years and also for adults suffering from the consequences of malnutrition. This is to extract the analysis reports and different techniques used for prediction. The study has covered a vast area related to prediction and classification considering different aspects. In [5], the authors have studied about the prediction of infant's weight in maternal hypertensive and non-hypertensive condition with Naïve Bayes method. For performance measurement they have used WEKA [5]. In [12], the authors have worked on a model based on the logical decision tree algorithm and decision tree algorithm. They have claimed that logical decision tree algorithm had the highest predictive capabilities with respect to recall [12]. Also they have mentioned that the model based on the decision tree algorithm with low pruning had the highest precision [12]. The study in [1] aimed to asses maternal risk factors linked with low birth weight neonates. Also they have intended to compare Random Forest with Logistic Regression. They had carried out the experiment on 600 volunteer pregnant women [1]. They have identified four top rank variables: age of pregnancy, body mass index during the third three months of pregnancy, mother's age and body mass index during the first three months of pregnancy [1]. In their experiment they have claimed that Random Forest outperformed Linear Regression. The study in [7] aimed at prediction and classification of low birth weight data in Indonesia. They have used Binary Logistic Regression and Random Forest approach in IDHS (Demographic and Public Health Survey in Indonesia) data of 2012 [7]. They have considered the features like place of residence, time zone, wealth index, education level of mother, education level of father, age of the mother, job of the mother, number of children [7]. They have claimed that Linear Regression showed good performance in prediction, but poor performance in classification but Random Forest had good performance for both prediction and classification [7]. The study in [11] aims to compare logistic regression and data mining techniques. They also aimed to identify promising predictor variables as well as to come up with a decision support system to help the physicians for making better decision in case of low weight child birth [11]. They have used Logistic Regression, Support Vector Machine, Neural Network, Naïve Bayes, Decision Tree, Random Forest, and Data mining techniques [11]. They have carried out the experiment on data from Baystate Medical centre, Springfield, Massachusetts of 1986. They had used 189 instances with 11 attributes like ID-identification number, Mother's age in years (AGE), the weight before pregnancy (LWT), number of doctor visits during the first trimester of pregnancy (FTV), race (RACE), lifestyle information such as smoking (SMOKE), a history of previous preterm delivery (PTL), the existence of uterine irritability (UI), and hypertension (HT) [11]. They have identified highly influenced variables to predict LBW as- Mother's last weight before becoming pregnant, Mother's age, Number of doctor visits during the first trimester, parity [11]. The study in [17] has concentrated on extracting useful information from health indicators of pregnant woman for early detection of potential low birth weight cases using machine learning techniques. They have used Bayes minimum error rate and Indian healthcare data was used to construct decision rules [17]. They have used 18 attributes and got an accuracy of 96.77%. In study [2], they have mentioned about the development of Artificial Neural Network for predicting birth weight. They used Multi-layer concept topology on some birth cases in hospitals [2]. They have used the features like age, smoke, race, weight (lbs) before pregnancy, uterine irritability, number of doctor visits in 1st trimester, hypertension and claimed 100% accuracy. The study in [6] attempts to analyse malnutrition based on food intake, wealth index, age group, educational level, occupation. They have applied Decision tree, Artificial Neural Network in a dataset of family health survey having 254 instances and 9 attributes [6]. They have carried out the experiment for children under age of five and found 68.50% accuracy for ID3, 77.17% for Random Forest and 77.17% for Multilayer perceptron. In [14], the authors have studied about the prediction of the mortality rate in surgical patients suffering from malnutrition. they have used data mining models like J48, ADTree and KNN [14]. In [3], the author has used decision tree technique for rule generation to help the medical experts to reduce the malnutrition condition among children under the age of 5 in developing countries. In [16], the authors have talked about the use of rule based classification along with agent technology to detect malnutrition in children. In [6], the authors have used decision tree and artificial neural networks to classify dataset of family health survey. They have studied about the nutritional status of children aged under five [6]. In [9], the authors have carried out logistic regression to identify the probabilities of explaining malnutrition by the features extracted by machine learning techniques from Indian Demographic and Health Survey dataset. In [10], the authors have used Bayesian Gaussian regression model for analysing the effect of selected socio-economic, demographic, health and environmental covariates on malnutrition for child under five years of age.

3   Methodology

3.1   Proposed Architecture

The proposed architecture in Fig. 1 shows the work flow from the data collection to the performance evaluation of different machine learning techniques. The required dataset has been created from the collected data and then the same has been inspected, cleaned, transformed and modelled as per the need of the used methods or techniques.   After pre-procession the required features have

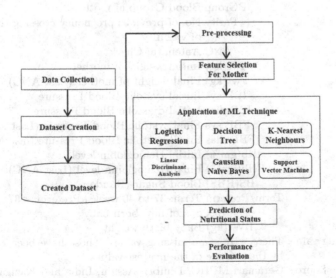

Fig. 1. Block diagram of proposed approach

been selected. Next the machine learning techniques have been applied on the dataset. The applied techniques have predicted and created the result. Based on the result, performance evaluation has been carried out for different methods using statistical tools.

3.2   Data Collection and Dataset Creation

The required data for this experiment has been collected from two government health centres. The authority of the health centres provided the hand written registers maintained for recording the information. The health centres keep track of a mother right from the start of pregnancy to the baby reaches 5 years of age. The work is for prediction and identification of nutritional status of neonate. So we have collected data of mothers. We have collected the data up to the birth of the baby as our objective is to predict the nutritional status of the neonate. The necessary data have been picked up and the dataset has been created on our own. The dataset is named as CBWDB.csv. The details of the dataset can be found in Table 1.

Table 1. Details of the created dataset

Name of the dataset: CBWDB.csv	
No. of instances: 445	
No. of class labels:	02 L and N: L-under weight, N-normal weight
No. of attributes: 18	
Details of attributes:	SEC Socio-Economic Condition
	Age(years) Age of mother at the time of pregnancy
	Height(cm) Height of mother at the time of pregnancy
	BGroup Blood Group of mother
	Parity No. of previous pregnancy crossing the period of viability
	ANC Antenatal Check
	Iwt(kg) Initial weight of mother
	Fwt(kg) Final weight of mother (Last ANC)
	IBP_sys Initial systolic Blood Pressure
	IBP_dias Initial diastolic Blood Pressure
	FBP_sys Final systolic Blood Pressure (Last ANC)
	FBP_dias Final diastolic Blood Pressure (last ANC)
	IHb(gm%) Initial Hemoglobin level
	FHb(gm%) Final Hemoglobin level (Last ANC)
	BS(RBS) Blood Sugar (Random)
	Term/Preterm Term: 37 to 40 weeks, Preterm: <37 weeks
	Sex Sex of new born baby
	BWt(kg) Baby birth weight
Missing value:	There were some missing values. Those have been replaced by the average of the nearest values.
Source:	Geramari MPHC, Dhubri, Assam, India and Kazigaon SD, Kokrajhar, Assam, India

3.3   Pre-processing and Feature Selection

While collecting the data from the health centres we noticed that there were so many columns recording different types of information about mother and child. All the information recorded in the register were not suitable for applying the machine learning techniques. Finally we have selected eighteen number of features and one label for classification. While creating the dataset, it was noticed that some data were not inserted in the register. As a result the data were missing in the created dataset. To get rid of the null value in the created dataset, the blank spaces were filled with the average of the values present in the nearby cells.

After thorough study and discussion with doctors, eighteen features were selected for the application of machine learning techniques. Those features are: SEC, Age(years), Height(cm), Bgroup, Parity, ANC, Iwt(kg), Fwt(kg), IBP_sys, IBP_dias, FBP_sys, FBP_dias, IHb(gm%), FHb(gm%), BS(RBS), Term/Preterm, Sex, BWt(kg). Along with these features one more column namely LNH has been considered for recording the nutritional status of the neonate. Table 1 can be referred for the details of these features.

3.4   Used Machine Learning Techniques

There are many machine learning algorithms available to implement classification and prediction problems. This study is about the prediction of the nutritional status of neonate. The following machine learning techniques have been implemented in a dataset created considering the features of mother. The dataset has a field denoting two different labels.

Logistic Regression. Logistic regression works when target is categorical. Here, output is strictly 1 or 0. For linear regression the hypothesis is $z = wx + b$, but for logistic regression it is the sigmoid of hypothesis of linear regression. That is, $h_\theta(x) = sigmoid(z)$. The hypothesis used here is the estimated probability. Mathematically this can be represented as-

$$h_\theta(x) = P(Y = 1|X; \theta) \tag{1}$$

This means, probability that $Y = 1$ given X which is parameterized by θ. From the above equation we can write-

$$P(Y = 1|X; \theta) + P(Y = 0|X; \theta) = 1$$
$$\text{or } P(Y = 0|X; \theta) = 1 - P(Y = 1|X; \theta)$$

In this case, linear regression model is fitted with the data, then the data is acted upon by a logistic function. This logistic function predicts the targeted categorical dependent variable. Logistic regression comes in different categories like Binary, Multinomial and Ordinal Logistic Regression. Decision boundary is used to predict the class of a data. This means, a threshold can be fixed and based on that threshold, obtained estimated probability can be classified into classes.

Decision Tree. Decision tree are grown through an iterative splitting of data into discrete groups [5]. Decision tree which are used to predict categorical variables are called classification tree because it plays instances in categories [5]. Decision tree which is used to predict continuous variables are called regression tree [5]. Some of the decision tree are ID3, C4.5, C5.0, Quest, CART, and CHAID [5]. The tree is formed by selecting some attributes using Attribute Selection Measures. The attribute with best score is considered as splitting attribute. Information gain, Gain ratio and Gini index are the popular selection measures.

Information gain can be expressed as follows:

Information gain = Entropy before split of the dataset − Average entropy after split of the dataset

Mathematically information gain can be represented as follows:

$$Info(K) = -\Sigma_{i=1}^{m} p_i log_2 p_i \tag{2}$$

where, p_i is the probability that a random tuple in K belongs to class C_i.

$$Info_B(K) = \Sigma_{j=1}^{V} \frac{|K_j|}{|K|} \times Info(K_j) \tag{3}$$

$$Gain(B) = Info(K) - Info_B(K) \tag{4}$$

where, $Info(K)$ is the "average amount of information" that is needed to identify the class label of a tuple in K.

$\frac{|K_j|}{|K|}$ is the weight of jth partition.

$Info_B(K)$ is the "expected information" that is required to classify a tuple in K based on partition by B.

The attribute B with the highest information gain i.e. $Gain(B)$ is chosen as the "splitting attribute" at node N.

This is generally used by ID3 (Iterative Dichotomiser) decision tree algorithm.

Gain Ratio normalizes the information gain to manage the issue of bias. The mathematical expression for this is as follows:

$$SplitInfo_B(K) = -\sum_{j=1}^{v} \frac{|K_j|}{|K|} \times \log_2 \left(\frac{|K_j|}{|K|} \right) \tag{5}$$

where, $\frac{|K_j|}{|K|}$ is the weight of the jth partition, and v denotes number of discrete values in attribute B

The gain ratio can be defied as

$$GainRatio(A) = \frac{Gain(A)}{SplitInfo_A(D)}$$

This index is used by C4.5 algorithm. C4.5 algorithm is familiar as J48, and it is available in WEKA data mining tool.

Gini Index is to consider a binary split for each attribute. The mathematical expression for this is as follows:

$$Gini(K) = 1 - \Sigma_{i=1}^{m} P_i^2 \tag{6}$$

This index is basically used by CART (Classification and Regression Tree). This study has been implemented using Scikit-Learn and Scikit-Learn uses an optimized version of CART.

K-Nearest Neighbours. K-Nearest Neighbours (KNN) algorithm is supervised in nature. This algorithm can be used for both classification and regression problems. This algorithm works with an assumption that similar objects exist in close proximity. KNN uses the idea of similarity. Sometimes similarity is also called as distance, proximity, or closeness. Depending on the problem, there may have many ways of calculating the distance. However, Euclidean distance or straight line distance is familiar. So, it can be concluded that the working principle of KNN is to find distances between a query and all other examples in the data and to select K number of examples nearest to the query.

Linear Discriminant Analysis. Linear Discriminant Analysis (LDA) works by reducing the number of dimensions (i.e. variables or feature) in a dataset keeping as much information as possible. Basic steps along with mathematical representation followed by LDA can be as follows:

- Calculation of the "within class scatter matrix" using

$$M_w = \sum_{i=1}^{c} M_i \tag{7}$$

where c is the total number of distinct classes and

$$M_i = \sum_{s \in K_i} (s - m_i)(s - m_i)^T$$

and

$$m_i = \frac{1}{n_i} \sum_{s \in K_i}^{n} s_k$$

where s is a sample (i.e. row) and n is the total number of samples for a given class.
"Between class scatter matrix" is calculated using

$$M_B = \sum_{i=1}^{c} N_i (m_i - m)(m_i - m)^T \tag{8}$$

where,

$$m_i = \frac{1}{n_i} \sum_{x \in K_i} s_k$$

$$m = \frac{1}{n} \sum_{i}^{n} s_i$$

- Solving the generalized eigenvalue problem for $M_W^{-1} M_B$ to obtain the linear discriminant.
- Sorting of the eigenvalues from highest to lowest and selection of k eigenvectors. These are sorted as the eigenvectors having highest eigenvalues convey the most information.
- Creation of a matrix M_{new} with first two eigenvectors. Then

$$Y = X \cdot M_{new}$$

where X is a $s \times d$ matrix with s samples and d dimensions, and Y is a $s \times t$ matrix with s samples and $t(t < s)$ dimensions. That means Y is composed of the LDA components. Y can now be called as the new feature space.

Gaussian Naïve Bayes. Naïve Bayes classifier is a probability based machine learning model. Its crux is based on the Bayes theorem. i.e.

$$P(c|F) = \frac{P(F|c)P(c)}{P(F)} \tag{9}$$

Here, c can be considered as class variable which is supposed to be predicted and F can be considered as parameters or features. In this case, it is assumed that the predictors or features or parameters are independent, i.e. the presence of one particular feature does not affect the other. Hence it is called naive. There can have many instances of F. Let us consider that F has n number of instances denoted by $f_1, f_2, \ldots, f_n$. So, substituting F by its instances, we can write the above equation as

$$c = argmax_c P(c) \Pi_{i=1}^n P(f_i|c) \tag{10}$$

For Gaussian Naïve Bayes classifier, the above equation changes to a equation containing Gaussian function and looks like the following:

$$P(f_i|c) = \frac{1}{\sqrt{2\pi\sigma_c^2}} exp\left(\frac{(f_i - \mu_c)^2}{2\sigma_c^2}\right) \tag{11}$$

Support Vector Machine. Though Support Vector Machine (SVM) can be used for both regression and classification tasks, but it is widely used in classification. It has the ability to produce significant accuracy with less computation power. SVM basically finds a hyper-plane in an K-dimensional space (K is the number of variables or features) that distinctly classify the data points. To distinguish two classes of data points, there may have many hyper-plane. But the objective is to choose a plane that has maximum margin from the data points of both the classes. Maximum distance helps to classify the future unseen data points with more confidence. The dimension of the hyper-plane is dependent on the number of features. Data points that are closer to the hyper-plane, influence the orientation and position of the hyper-plane are called the support vectors.

In case of logistic regression, the output of linear function is squashed to the range of [0,1] using sigmoid function. In case of SVM, the output of linear function is considered directly. One class is maintained for the values greater than 1 and another is for the value -1. So, the range of SVM is $[-1, 1]$.

3.5   Experimentation

We have carried experiments on our proposed method using python. The popular tool called Scikit-Learn that comes with python has been used to implement different machine learning algorithms. The details of the experimental setup is shown in Table 2. The dataset has some fields that are containing alphanumeric values. The implemented algorithms don't work with alphanumeric values. That is why some of the attributes like SEC, BGroup, Term/Preterm and Sex has not been considered during the implementation. So, out of eighteen attributes we have selected fourteen attributes for the experimentation.

Table 2. Details of system and software packages used

Operating System	: Ubuntu 16.04 LTS
Language	: Python 3.5
Core Library	: Pandas
Library for visualisation	: Matplotlib and Seaborn
Library for ML	: Scikit-Learn
IDE	: jupyter notebook

4   Results and Discussions

The background study shows that limited works have been carried out in predicting the nutritional status of the neonate. Most of the studies have been carried out to predict and analyse the nutritional status of the child under the age of five years. Here, a novel study has been carried out to predict the nutritional status of the neonate with two labels namely under weight and normal weight using the features of mother. One more label called over-weight was also been included but due to less number of samples in the dataset for this category, the prediction accuracy for this label was very less. This level has been omitted for the time being and that has been left for the future work. This study had expected that certain features or attributes of mother during the pregnancy (from conceive to birth) can give a platform to predict the nutritional status of the neonate. In this study, six numbers of machine learning algorithms have been implemented in our created dataset and as expected we have got impressive results. The Table 3 shows the performance of six algorithms trained and tested on this dataset. Figure 2 can be referred for the pictorial view of the performance measures.

Now let us see whether the answers for the research questions are obtained or not. The first question was about the identification of the nutritional status of neonate. This is a theoretical question based on medical science. After thorough study and discussion with the doctors, it has been found that it is possible to identify the nutritional status of neonate from the birth weight. Birth weight of neonate has lot to say about the health status.

Table 3. Performance of different ML algorithms

ML Algorithm	Accuracy(%)		Precision		Recall		F1 Score	
	Train	Test	Label1	Label2	Label1	Label2	Label1	Label2
Logistic Regression	86	88	1.00	0.87	0.36	1.00	0.53	0.93
Decision Tree	98	99	1.00	0.99	0.95	1.00	0.98	0.99
K- Nearest Neighbour	87	85	0.69	0.87	0.41	0.96	0.51	0.91
Linear Discriminant Analysis	94	93	0.89	0.94	0.73	0.98	0.80	0.96
Gaussian Naïve Bayes	86	86	0.64	0.91	0.64	0.91	0.64	0.91
Support Vector Machine	90	88	0.83	0.88	0.72	0.88	0.76	0.86

The second question was about the possibility of predicting nutritional status of neonate by using features of mother. As we know, before birth the baby is totally dependant on mother for nutrition. The physical and mental status of mother will have significant influence on the baby. The physical status of mother can be understood by investigating some features of the mother. It is clear that by analysing the features of mother, the birth weight can be predicted and so the nutritional status.

The third question was about the correctness of prediction by machine learning techniques. To get the answer, this experiment has been carried out and for six number of popular classification and prediction algorithms of machine learning has been trained and tested. It has been found that among Logistic Regression, Decision Tree, K-Nearest Neighbours, Linear Discriminant Analysis, Gaussian Naïve Bayes and Support Vector Machine; Decision Tree has shown the best performance in terms of Accuracy, Precision, Recall and F1-Score. From Table 3, it is clear that machine learning techniques can predict the nutritional status with very good accuracy.

4.1   Comparison with Other Studies

It has been found that limited studies have been carried out for nutritional status prediction for neonate. Most of the studies are for the nutritional status of child below five years of age. Different researchers have implemented different algorithms on different datasets and varied number of attributes. One of the researchers has obtained 95% accuracy for Random Forest [1], another researcher has used Minimum Error Rate classifier and got an accuracy of 96.77% [17], another researcher got 80.372% of accuracy using Naïve Bayes classifier [5]. A researcher has claimed 100% accuracy using Artificial Neural Network [2]. In our study we have implemented six algorithms. We have got the accuracy of 88% for Logistic Regression, 99% for Decision Tree, 85% for K-Nearest Neighbors, 93% for Linear Discriminant Analysis, 86% for Gaussian Naïve Bayes and 88% for Support Vector Machine. Figure 3 can be referred for the plot of the features for Support Vector Machine using Principal Component Analysis.

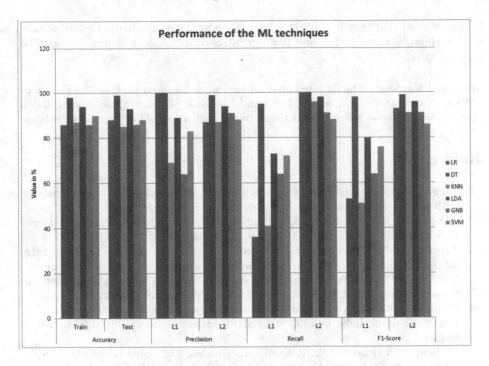

Fig. 2. Bar chart of performance measures

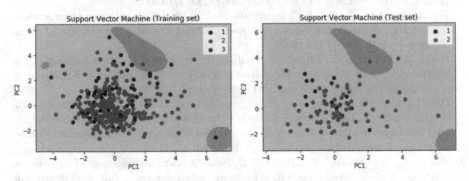

Fig. 3. Plot of the features for SVM using PCA

5   Conclusion and Future Work

Nutritional status plays vital role in signaling the development of physical and mental health. Proper development of child both physically and mentally is essential for building a peaceful society. Prediction regarding the nutritional status of neonate can alert the parent and doctors to take preventive and curative measures. In this study, six machine learning techniques have been implemented using a small dataset. All the techniques have shown impressive accuracy in prediction. As a future work, the dataset will be expanded and the third level of nutritional status will be taken into consideration. Also other state-of-the-art machine learning techniques like neural network, deep learning can also be implemented.

Acknowledgment. The data required for this work has been provided by Geramari MPHC, Gauripur, Dhubri, Assam, India and Kazigaon SD, Kokrajhar, Assam, India. Authors would like to offer heartfelt thank to the authorities of both the organizations.

References

1. Ahmadi, P., et al.: Prediction of low birth weight using random forest: a comparison with logistic regression. J. Paramedical Sci. (JPS) **8**, 36–43 (2017)
2. Al-Shawwa, M., Abu-Naser, S.S.: Predicting birth weight using artificial neural network. Int. J. Acad. Health Med. Res. (IJAHMR) **3**(1), 9–14 (2019)
3. Ariyadasa, S.N., Munasinghe, L.K., Senanayake, S.H.D., Fernando, M.: Knowledge extraction to mitigate child malnutrition in developing countries (Sri Lankan context). In: 2013 4th International Conference on Intelligent Systems, Modelling and Simulation, pp. 321–326, January 2013. https://doi.org/10.1109/ISMS.2013.23
4. Dalal, A.: DC Dutta's textbook of gynaecology and textbook of obstetrics. J. Obstet. Gynecol. India **66**, 303–304 (2016). https://doi.org/10.1007/s13224-016-0848-4
5. Desiani, A., Primartha, R., Arhami, M., Orsalan, O.: Naive Bayes classifier for infant weight prediction of hypertension mother. J. Phys. Conf. Ser. **1282**, 012005 (2019). https://doi.org/10.1088/1742-6596/1282/1/012005
6. Duraisamy, T.D., Sudha, P.: Identification of malnutrition with use of supervised datamining techniques-decision trees and artificial neural networks. Int. J. Eng. Comput. Sci. **3**, 2319–7242 (2014)
7. Faruk, A., Cahyono, E., Eliyati, N., Arifieni, I.: Prediction and classification of low birth weight data using machine learning techniques. Indonesian J. Sci. Technol. **3**, 18–28 (2018). https://doi.org/10.17509/ijost.v3i1.10799
8. Haughton, P., Drysdale, C.: Twin presence of obesity and under-nutrition reflects shifts in food systems (2019). https://www.who.int/news-room/detail/16-12-2019-more-than-one-in-three-low-and-middle-income-countries-face-both-extremes-of-malnutrition. Accessed 20 Jan 2020
9. Khare, S., Kavyashree, S., Gupta, D., Jyotishi, A.: Investigation of nutritional status of children based on machine learning techniques using Indian demographic and health survey data. Procedia Comput. Sci. **115**, 338–349 (2017). https://doi.org/10.1016/j.procs.2017.09.087
10. Mohammed, S., Asfaw, Z.: Bayesian Gaussian regression analysis of malnutrition for children under five years of age in Ethiopia, emdhs 2014. Arch. Public Health **76**, 21 (2018). https://doi.org/10.1186/s13690-018-0264-6
11. Senthilkumar, D., Paulraj, S.: Prediction of low birth weight infants and its risk factors using data mining techniques. In: Proceedings of the 2015 International Conference on Industrial Engineering and Operations Management Dubai, United Arab Emirates (UAE), March 2015
12. Sudha, P.: An efficient identification of malnutrition with unsupervised classification using logical decision tree algorithm. Int. J. Innov. Res. Comput. Commun. Eng. **4**, 1311–1315 (2016)

13. Swaminathan, S., et al.: The burden of child and maternal malnutrition and trends in its indicators in the states of India: the global burden of disease study 1990–2017. Lancet Child Adolesc. Health **3**, 855–870 (2019). https://doi.org/10.1016/S2352-4642(19)30273-1
14. Watcharapasorn, P., Kurubanjerdjit, N.: The surgical patient mortality rate prediction by machine learning algorithms. In: 2016 13th International Joint Conference on Computer Science and Software Engineering (JCSSE), pp. 1–5, July 2016. https://doi.org/10.1109/JCSSE.2016.7748844
15. WHO: 2018 global nutrition report: Shining a light to spur action on nutrition (2019). https://www.unicef.org/rosa/press-releases/2018-global-nutrition-report-reveals-malnutrition-unacceptably-high-and-affects. Accessed 26 Dec 2019
16. Xu, D., Ganegoda, U.: Rule based classification to detect malnutrition in children. Int. J. Comput. Sci. Eng. **3**, 423–429 (2011)
17. Yarlapati, A.R., Roy Dey, S., Saha, S.: Early prediction of LBW cases via minimum error rate classifier: a statistical machine learning approach. In: 2017 IEEE International Conference on Smart Computing (SMARTCOMP), pp. 1–6 (May 2017). https://doi.org/10.1109/SMARTCOMP.2017.7947002

Handwritten Bengali Character Recognition Using Deep Convolution Neural Network

Suprabhat Maity[1](✉), Anirban Dey[2](✉), Ankan Chowdhury[3](✉),
and Abhijit Banerjee[4](✉)

[1] B. P. Poddar Institute of Management and Technology, Kolkata, India
suprabhatmaity@gmail.com
[2] RCC Institute of Information Technology, Kolkata, India
adey60906@gmail.com
[3] L & T Infotech, Mumbai, India
ankan.chowdhury007@gmail.com
[4] Infosys Limited, Bhubaneshwar, India
abhijit17.1997@gmail.com
https://www.bppimt.ac.in, https://www.rcciit.org

Abstract. Recognition of Handwritten Character had been one of the promising area of research for its applications in diverse field, it appear to be a challenging research. In our paper, we focus specifically on offline handwritten character recognition of regional language (Bengali) by first detecting individual characters. The principal approaches for offline handwritten character recognition may be divided into two classes, segmentation and holistic based. In our method we applied segmentation based handwritten word recognition and to identify individual characters neural network have been used. We have used 15,000 instances of Bengali alphabets to create a recognition model, which when provided with images of physical pieces of handwritten texts, it is able to segment and extract characters from the said image of a physical handwritten text with 65% accuracy, and recognize the properly segmented alphabets with 99.5% accuracy.

Keywords: Convolution Neural Network (CNN) · Floodfill algorithm

1 Introduction

Handwritten character recognition is being considered to be a research domain for its different kind of applications in diverse field. The applications starts from zip code recognition to author identification, from identifiying numerals and alphabets in vehicle's number plate for traffic surveillance to automated processing of check in bank, etc. There is ample number of research works has been done on Handwitten English text (other languages), but research work taken by the researcher on Bengali handwritten character recognition is very nominal. Bengali literature comprises of a vast range of characters which are very

© Springer Nature Singapore Pte Ltd. 2020
A. Bhattacharjee et al. (Eds.): MIND 2020, CCIS 1241, pp. 84–92, 2020.
https://doi.org/10.1007/978-981-15-6318-8_8

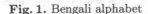

	vowels				
অ	আ	ই	ঈ	উ	ঊ
ঋ	এ	ঐ	ও	ঔ	

					consonants				
ক	খ	গ	ঘ	ঙ	চ	ছ	জ	ঝ	ঞ
ট	ঠ	ড	ঢ	ণ	ত	থ	দ	ধ	ন
প	ফ	ব	ভ	ম	য	র	ল	শ	ষ
স	হ	ড়	ঢ়	ৎ	ং	ঃ	ঁ		

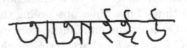

Fig. 1. Bengali alphabet   **Fig. 2.** Handwritten Bengali word

complex in their structure. There are few characters in this language which are comprises of two or more characters (known as compound character), which creates the challange for recognitionizing handwritten characters. In our paper, we first create a disjoint Bengali character sets (digits, vowels and compound letters, etc.) and deep convolutional neural network model is trained and used to identify the handwritten characters at a stretch. For each set we have build separate classifier, and then the model is executed on an aggregated dataset taken from web resources. The techniques for offline handwritten bengali character recognition can be separated in two classes those are holistic and segmentation based approach. The holistic approach is confined to limited size vocabulary where it is considered the global features extracted from the entire image of handwritten character. Now the vocabulary size increases, the recognition rate decreases rapidly and increases complexity. In segmentation-based approach it's employ bottom-up fassion, the character stroke has been considered starting level towards producing a significant word. The problem gets optimized after segmentation for identifying a separate characters, strokes and therefore any vocabulary can adopt our system for the recognition of handwritten text.

Bengali literature consists of a wealthy character set having 10 numerals, 11 vowels, 39 consonants, and few more than 30 compound letters. Their shapes and structures are given in Fig. 1 and Fig. 2. We choose 11 vowels and 39 consonants of the literature in our model. Convolutional neural networks (CNN) is considered for their impact in recognition of handwriten character from images. LeCun proposes back propagation network for their handwritten digit recognition [9]. This architecture is executed in MNIST digit classes and successful recognized the MNIST digit classes [10]. CNN works perfectly with image due to their scale and translational variance of the features of images. It is proven CNN successfully recognizing the character for other languages and they are rightly fit to be used in Bengali literature.

The challange in any visual recognition task is how to getthe optimal set of features from the image, Trier proposed character recognition by feature extraction [8,18]. Different kind of methods like support vector machines (SVMs) which is also applied in different literature, Lauer, Sarkhel and Drewnik uses SVM for their character recognition model [5,8,13]. But CNN is very much effective at lower layer, appropriate features are extracted for them, Niu develop CNN-SVM model for character recognition [11]. There are many clustering techniques being applied in the literature along with K-Nearest Neighbour algorithm, Zhang proposed K-Nearest Neighbour using cluster based trees [19]. Traditional neural networks fails to accomply with these techniques compared to CNN. They were considered more for their efficiency rather than accuracy. The declining execution time of machines obscureing their efficiency. Histogram of oriented gradient (HOG) is also an eminant feature extractor in literature, Khan and Banjare uses HOG features for character recognition [3, 7]. The recognition task fully depends on the accuracy of how local features variance is adapted. CNNs solves this adaptability in the lower layers by using replicative feature detectors.

CNNs also have been tried for Bengali character recognition, Sharif, Shopon and Adak uses CNN for their recognition task [1, 14–16]. Ghosh develop a model using HMM [6]. All these works, in hiatus, either confined to 10 numerals or to a subset (of size 50) of alphabets, have not yet proposed a system that can extract sentences, words and finally characters from images taken of physical handwritten pieces of text and literature, then recognized the said text and ultimately provided a digital translation by piecing together the segments. In this paper, we attempt to develop such a system, which will be able to provide digital translation of real world handwritten piece of text with the help of multilayered CNN based classification/recognition model and flood-fill based segmentation algorithm added to histogram based approach, alphabet width estimation and 'matra' detection and removal technique.

2 Preliminaries

2.1 Convolutional Neural Network (CNN)

Feature vectors are extracted from the image by using CNN. The two module of CNN consists of: feature extraction and output prediction. It consists of two layers in feature extraction: convolution layer and sub sampling (max pooling) layer. And one fully connected layer is used for classification or prediction of output. After obtaining the features from convolution layer it supplied to an activation function. The convolutional layer comprises of a set of matrix multiplications accompany with summation arithmetics. The complete process given in Fig. 3.

2.2 Floodfill Algorithm

Flood fill is an algorithm in Fig. 4 is used to identifying the bounded area connected to a given pixel in a multi-dimensional array. It is a close resemblance to the bucket tool in paint programs.

Stack-based recursive function is the most appropriate implementation of this algorithm.

– Take the starting point.
– Make decisions on wether it is going in 4 directions (N, S, W, E) or 8 directions (N, S, W, E, NW, NE, SW, SE).

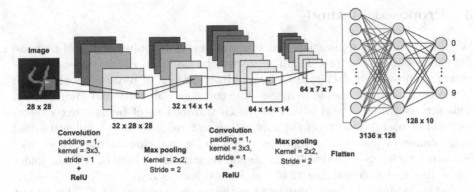

Fig. 3. Convolution Neural Network

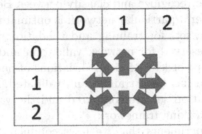

Fig. 4. Floodfill algorithm

- Choose the target color and replacement color.
- Move forward in those directions.
- If the pixel is a target then reaplce it with the replacement color.
- Continue 4 and 5 until it process everywhere within the boundaries.

2.3 Machine Learning and Deep Learning

With the help of computer engineers Machine Learning has been explored to the extent that whether computers can be teached and learn to play games, and a field of computation power of Statistics not that much taken care, to a broad discipline fundamental theories of learning processes in statistical-computation has been developed, has build learning algorithms are regularly applied in commercial systems for computer vision, speech recognition and a various other kind of tasks, and state of the art technology is used in industry for data mining to discover hidden pattern in the large volumes of online datasets.

Deep Learning is a subfield of machine learning confined with algorithms motivated by the process and structure of the human brain often says artificial neural networks (ANN) given in Fig. 5.

3   Proposed Method

We aim to build an application that is useful in making online copies of physical Bengali books and scripts. This feature will be useful in restoration or preservation purposes, will facilitate making online versions of physical books which will make it more accessible to masses due to easy availability and lowered cost. This project will also help in text-to-speech translations of Bengali texts therefore will be useful as a travel aid application to foreign tourists to identify road signs, names of places and buildings, etc. The Bengali character set consists of 50 basic characters - 11 vowels and 39 consonants. It consists of a Train folder and a Test folder, containing 12,000 and 3,000 images respectively.

In this module, the basic framework of the model is implemented. The dataset is used to train the neural networks which is implemented as a part of this module which will be used to recognize and classify between Bengali characters. The main to evaluate whether a particular network is optimal for any given problem is to have separate data sets for training and validation. Trained networks are fed with the data set reserved for network validation and the prediction accuracy measurements are recorded. After all variations of neural networks deemed suitable for the problem has been trained and validated, their prediction measurements on the validation set are compared and the variation with the best value is chosen as the working framework.

Now, as per the experiments that we have conducted on our main framework, the CNN structure given in Eq. 1, with layer quantity or variations of non-linearity and add-ons, it has shown positive growth in fitness with the introduction of maxpooling given in Eq. 2, ReLU given in Eq. 3 and fully-connected layers in the backend.

Due to hardware limitations, we are being unable to construct a really dynamic model that will not only incorporate all the features and facilities provided by our afore-described model, but also it will automate the model to an extent such that it will decide which kernel size and which filter to choose in what layer depending upon the given set of inputs while training. Such a dynamic

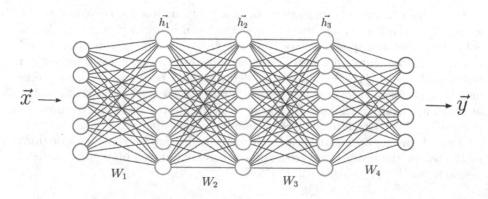

Fig. 5. Deep Learning

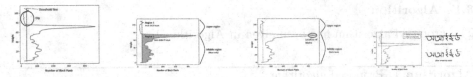

Fig. 6. Row wise sum of black pixels   **Fig. 7.** Region of character   **Fig. 8.** Location of "Matra"   **Fig. 9.** Removal of "Matar"

construct is known as Inception net [17] and it is certainly has much more volume and computational complexity than the model we have described earlier. Given the limitations we possess, the tradeoff between software complexity and runtime goes against the idea of using such high profile mechanism. But it will definitely make the model more stable and accurate.

For recognizing a character Floodfill algorithm have been used to identify each word and then we have used the "matra" feature to extarct each character from the handwritten bengali script. First identified the location of "matra" then extracted the lower protion which is the body of the character. Second we have removed the "matra" to extract each character and generated the feature vector. The above said process has been explained in Fig. 6, 7, 8 and 9.

The final neural network is a multi-CNN layer model with maxpooling layers and nonlinear ReLU layers in between each convolution layer, and a fully-connected layer at the very end appended with dropout, with softmax being applied at the very end for the classifier to predict class of any input alphabet Figs. 10, 11 and 12.

$$c_{i,j} = \sum_{p=1}^{m}\sum_{q=1}^{m} w_{p,q} x_{i+p-1,j+p-1} \tag{1}$$

$$c_{i,j} = \max\{x_{i+p-1,j+p-1} \ \forall 1 \le p \le m \text{ and } 1 \le q \le m\} \tag{2}$$

$$Relu\,(r) = \{0 \ if \ r < 0 \text{ and } r \ if \ r \ge 0\} \tag{3}$$

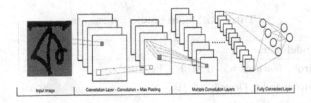

Fig. 10. CNN layer configuration

3.1   Algorithm

The proposed algorithm has been given in Algorithm 1.

Algorithm 1. Proposed algorithm

1: Preprocessing of Bengali Scripts
2: Extracting Individual Character
    – Morphological Operations performed in specific cases
    – 8-Way Floodfill algorithm for word extraction
    – "Matra" detection and removal using row-wise intensive histogram
    – Character segmentation using column-wise intensive histogram
3: Neural Network Model for Training and Recognition
    – Input
    – Layer1: 1 i/p, 32 o/p, 5 × 5 Kernel
    – Layer2: 32 i/p, 64 o/p, 2 × 2 Kernel
    – Layer3: 64 i/p, 128 o/p, 3 × 3 Kernel
    – Layer4: 128 i/p, 256 o/p, 2 × 2 Kernel
    – Fully Connected Layer
    – Output Layer with 50 nodes (Softmax)

Fig. 11. Identifying words

Fig. 12. Handwritten separate Bengali word

4   Results

We have compared our results with other methods applied. As CNN is applied by many other researcher we have proposed a different approach and compared the results given in Table 1.

Table 1. Model prediction results

Model name	Accuracy
Stroke features based MLP Classifier [4]	81.4%
Autoencoder Deep-CNN [15]	99.5%
Deep CNN [12]	98.6 %
Skeletal Convexity & Dynamic Programming [2]	60.6%
Proposed Model (Deep CNN)	99.5%

5   Conclutions

We built an application which can be useful in making online copies of physical Bengali books and scripts. This feature will be useful in restoration or preservation purposes will facilitate making online versions of physical books which will make it more accessible to masses due to easy availability and lowered cost. This project will also help in text-to-speech translations of Bengali texts therefore will be useful as a travel aid application to foreign tourists to identify road signs, names of places and buildings, etc. A deep CNN is very promising for handwritten character recognition. The shapes of Bengali character set likelihood is creating future challange. With the advent of state of the art infrastructure more distinctive features can be extracted by building networks having more capacity. Recent state of the art infrastructure (GPU) can be used to train the Deep CNN model with large datasets having all kind of shapes.

References

1. Adak, C., Chaudhuri, B.B., Blumenstein, M.: Offline cursive Bengali word recognition using CNNS with a recurrent model. In: 2016 15th International Conference on Frontiers in Handwriting Recognition (ICFHR), pp. 429–434. IEEE (2016)
2. Bag, S., Bhowmick, P., Harit, G.. Recognition of Bengali handwritten characters using skeletal convexity and dynamic programming. In: 2011 Second International Conference on Emerging Applications of Information Technology, pp. 265–268. IEEE (2011)
3. Banjare, K., Massey, S.: Numeric digit classification using hog feature space and multiclass support vectore machine classifier. Int. J. Sci. Res. Educ. **4**, 5339–5345 (2016)
4. Bhowmik, T.K., Bhattacharya, U., Parui, S.K.: Recognition of Bangla handwritten characters using an MLP classifier based on stroke features. In: Pal, N.R., Kasabov, N., Mudi, R.K., Pal, S., Parui, S.K. (eds.) ICONIP 2004. LNCS, vol. 3316, pp. 814–819. Springer, Heidelberg (2004). https://doi.org/10.1007/978-3-540-30499-9_125
5. Drewnik, M., Pasternak-Winiarski, Z.: SVM Kernel configuration and optimization for the handwritten digit recognition. In: Saeed, K., Homenda, W., Chaki, R. (eds.) CISIM 2017. LNCS, vol. 10244, pp. 87–98. Springer, Cham (2017). https://doi.org/10.1007/978-3-319-59105-6_8
6. Ghosh, R., Roy, P.P.: Comparison of zone-features for online Bengali and Devanagari word recognition using HMM. In 2016 15th International Conference on Frontiers in Handwriting Recognition (ICFHR), pp. 435–440. IEEE (2016)
7. Khan, H.A.: MCS HOG features and svm based handwritten digit recognition system. J. Intell. Learn. Syst. Appl. **9**(02), 21 (2017)
8. Lauer, F., Suen, C.Y., Bloch, G.: A trainable feature extractor for handwritten digit recognition. Pattern Recognit. **40**(6), 1816–1824 (2007)
9. LeCun, Y., et al.: Handwritten digit recognition with a back-propagation network. In: Advances in Neural Information Processing Systems, pp. 396–404 (1990)
10. LeCun, Y., Cortes, C., Burges, C.: MNIST handwritten digit database, vol. 2, p. 18. AT&T Labs (2010). http://yann.lecun.com/exdb/mnist
11. Niu, X.-X., Suen, C.Y.: A novel hybrid CNN-SVM classifier for recognizing handwritten digits. Pattern Recognit. **45**(4), 1318–1325 (2012)

12. Purkaystha, B., Datta, T., Islam, M.S.: Bengali handwritten character recognition using deep convolutional neural network. In: 2017 20th International Conference of Computer and Information Technology (ICCIT), pp. 1–5. IEEE (2017)
13. Sarkhel, R., Das, N., Saha, A.K., Nasipuri, M.: A multi-objective approach towards cost effective isolated handwritten Bangla character and digit recognition. Pattern Recognit. **58**, 172–189 (2016)
14. Sharif, S., Mohammed, N., Mansoor, N., Momen, S.: A hybrid deep model with hog features for Bangla handwritten numeral classification. In: 2016 9th International Conference on Electrical and Computer Engineering (ICECE), pp. 463–466. IEEE (2016)
15. Shopon, M., Mohammed, N., Abedin, M.A.: Bangla handwritten digit recognition using autoencoder and deep convolutional neural network. In: 2016 International Workshop on Computational Intelligence (IWCI), pp. 64–68. IEEE (2016)
16. Shopon, M., Mohammed, N., Abedin, M.A.: Image augmentation by blocky artifact in deep convolutional neural network for handwritten digit recognition. In: 2017 IEEE International Conference on Imaging, Vision & Pattern Recognition (icIVPR), pp. 1–6. IEEE (2017)
17. Szegedy, C., et al.: Going deeper with convolutions. In: Proceedings of the IEEE Conference on Computer Vision and Pattern Recognition, pp. 1–9 (2015)
18. Trier, Ø.D., Jain, A.K., Taxt, T.: Feature extraction methods for character recognition-a survey. Pattern Recognit. **29**(4), 641–662 (1996)
19. Zhang, B., Srihari, S.N.: Fast k-nearest neighbor classification using cluster-based trees. IEEE Trans. Pattern Anal. Mach. Intell **26**(4), 525–528 (2004)

Lexical Feature Based Feature Selection and Phishing URL Classification Using Machine Learning Techniques

Bireswar Banik[✉] and Abhijit Sarma

Department of Computer Science, Gauhati University, Guwahati, India
bireswarbanik02@gmail.com, abhijit_gu@yahoo.com

Abstract. Phishing is an illegitimate method to collect secret information of any person or organization. Information like debit card, credit card details, PIN no, OTP, passwords, etc. are stolen by the attackers through phishing sites. Researchers have used different techniques to detect those phishing sites. But it is difficult to stay on a particular technique as attackers come with new tactics. In this paper, phishing and legitimate URL classifications are performed based on the lexical features of URLs. Feature selection technique is used to select the relevant features only. Accuracy for all combination of features with different numbers of features each time was evaluated to find the best possible combination of features. Performances are analyzed for different datasets with various parameters using four different machine learning techniques.

Keywords: Network security · Phishing URLs · Legitimate URLs · Lexical features of URL · Feature selection · Machine learning classification methods

1 Introduction

Dependency on the web is increasing speedily. Along with this, the malicious attacks are also happening at a high rate and our security within the internet is in peril. Phishing is a kind of activity that tries to gather personal credentials through some fraudulent sites that seem like legitimate [1]. By assuming such sites as legitimate, the users are lured to enter their personal information through some forms available there. It is hard to identify such sites visually, so users can become victim of those sites.

The domains from which attacks are made are of limited lifetime. Attackers change the domains frequently to steal the information. As per the Anti Phishing Working Group (APWG) phishing trends reports [2] from 2017 to 2019, the number of phishing attacks increases gradually. The total number of phish detected in the second half of 2018 was 289,342 where as the total number of phish detected in the first half of 2019 was 363,223. Since fourth quarter of 2016, highest number of phishing sites detected in the third quarter of 2019 and it was approximately 46% more than total number of detected phishing sites in second quarter of 2019. Brazilian commercial sites faced huge loss during FIFA World Cup, 2018 held as cyber criminals used this opportunity for stealing and selling TVs illegally. In 2019, they utilized the advantage of holiday shopping to steal personal detail of the consumers.

© Springer Nature Singapore Pte Ltd. 2020
A. Bhattacharjee et al. (Eds.): MIND 2020, CCIS 1241, pp. 93–105, 2020.
https://doi.org/10.1007/978-981-15-6318-8_9

Many anti-phishing solutions are implemented to detect and prevent phishing attacks, but still people are becoming victim of these attacks in their daily life. It is difficult to differentiate between the phishing and legitimate sites visually. Different techniques have been implemented to detect phishing URLs by accessing content of the webpages. But for limited set of URLs also these procedures need to analyze a huge amount of data. So, this paper focuses on classifying phishing and legitimate URLs based on only the static properties of URLs taking considerably larger datasets.

In this paper, phishing URL detections are performed based on lexical features of URLs using different machine learning classification techniques. The performances are analyzed using three different datasets. Chi-square feature selection technique is used to rank the features based on their importance to detect phishing URLs. As per our knowledge, Chi-square feature selection algorithm is used for the first time to select the features for phishing URL detection.

The rest of the paper is structured as follows. Section 2 describes the related works based on URL detection. In Sect. 3, our working model is defined with the detail features, different datasets and machine learning techniques. Performances are analyzed in Sect. 4. In Sect. 5, conclusion of our works is stated.

2 Related Studies

Many solutions are proposed and implemented by different researches for detection of phishing URLs. Since the attackers change the domain and techniques for attacking at regular interval of time, so fix a perfect method for detecting phishing URLs is difficult. Some previous works to detect phishing sites using different methods are discussed here:

One of the simplest methods to detect phishing URLs is blacklisting. It contains the list of phishing URLs and IP addresses which are detected earlier. Google safe browsing API [3] is one of the blacklisting techniques which checks whether an URL is in the unsafe list or not. Google maintains the list of unsafe URLs which are updated continuously [4]. But if the URL is modified a bit, it would not be detected by this method. A technique called Phishnet is proposed by Prakash et al. [5] to detect phishing URL even it is changed slightly from the blacklisted URLs. It is based on five possible heuristics namely, replacement in Top Level Domain, changed in query string, similarity in IP addresses, directory structure and brand names.

Another alternative to blacklisting is whitelisting. It is a technique used by different researchers where a list of legitimate sites is maintained. Han et al. [6] proposed a technique known as Automated Individual White List (AIWL) which alerts a user if he or she tries to submit any information to a site whose URL is not present in the whitelist. It maintains the automated whitelist using Naïve Bayes classifier. Jain and Gupta [7] also proposed a whitelist technique to protect from phishing attacks. The list contains domain names and IP addresses. If an URL is not present in the list, it decides whether that the URL is phishing URL or not based on three different parameters related to hyperlinks present in the webpage. The experiment is performed using a dataset of 1525 URLs only.

Main problem with the listing approaches are that the lifetime of phishing domains are small. Attackers may attack with new domain or may target a domain present in a safe list. So, it is difficult to detect a zero day phishing attack using list based approaches. Heuristics based techniques have better performance against zero-day phishing attacks. Common web browsers like Internet Explorer, Mozilla Firefox uses heuristic based approaches [4].

Attackers may create phishing sites based on the same appearance with any popular legitimate sites to confuse users. Phishing URL detection based on the visual similarity is proposed by Jain and Gupta [8] which stated URLs can be classified based on Visual features, style, HTML code etc. The text and images like text content, background color, background image, image features are considered as visual features.

Sahoo et al. [9] proposed machine learning techniques to detect malicious URLs. They provide a detailed study of different features that can be useful like blacklisted technique, lexical features, host-based features, content based features, visual features and other related features.

Vanhoenshoven et al. [10] performed classification of malicious URLs using different machine learning classifiers on different datasets. Three different feature sets are used based on binary attributes, real value attributes and a combination of binary and real attributes. Random Forest and Multi Layer Perception achieved higher accuracy.

Mamun et al. [11] proposed to detect malicious URLs like spam, phishing, malware and defacement URLs using different lexical features. They obtained precision value of 92.6% for multiclass classification of phishing URLs for dataset of approximately 10000 phishing URLs and 35000 legitimate URLs only.

An automated self structured neural network is proposed by Mohammad et al. [1] for the phishing sites prediction. Along with URL based features they extract the features accessing WHOIS database, availability of DNS record, age of the URL, use of pop-up window etc. For this, the content of the webpages need to accessed. They evaluated the performance by using 1400 URLs only.

Many of the researches to detect phishing URLs are based on the features related to content of the webapges, domain registration and properties related to URLs. We concentrate on only the lexical properties of URLs with an aim to implement a fast and efficient phishing URL detection system.

3 Proposed Methodology

We present a system for classifying phishing and legitimate URLs using lexical features of URLs only. Experiments have been performed on different datasets using four machine learning techniques. As only the lexical features are selected so the space required to hold the URL data and processing time is reduced considerably. A filter based feature selection technique known as Chi-square feature selection is used to rank the features based on the scores obtained by each feature using statistical measures and select only the appropriate features which contribute most for classification. The block diagram of our proposed system is shown in Fig. 1.

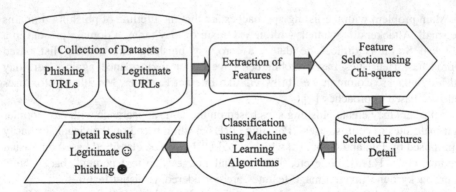

Fig. 1. Block diagram of the proposed system

3.1 Collection of Datasets

The performances of the proposed system are analyzed using three different datasets and with a dataset consist of URLs from all three datasets as in Table 1. Datasets contain two classes: Phishing and Legitimate. Each of these three datasets consists of different number of URLs collected from different sources. For Dataset1 Phishing URLs are collected from Phistank repository [12] at three different dates and legitimate URLs from DMOZ directory [13]. Dataset2 consists of the URLs considered by Banik and Sarma [14]. Dataset3 is a standard dataset for benchmarking proposed by Chiew et al. [15]. A fourth dataset namely Dataset4 is created by combining all three datasets used here.

Table 1. Detail of different datasets used

Dataset name	No. of phishing URLs	No. of legitimate URLs
Dataset1 [12, 13]	63997	149991
Dataset2 [14]	12799	19853
Dataset3 [15]	15000	15000
Dataset4	91796	184844

3.2 Feature Extraction

Lexical features based on statistical properties of URLs which are mostly used and have been found more relevant for classifying phishing URLs by different researchers [11, 14, 16] are only considered. 17 different lexical features are extracted from URLs. These features are considered with an aim to perform a detail study on the importance of different lexical features and implement a fast and efficient phishing URL classification system. Since we do not depend on any external software or websites to extract features, so time taken for feature extraction is also lesser. The detail of the features is given in Table 2.

3.3   Feature Selection

This process is performed to choose only the relevant features for classification. Less important features are removed through this process to reduce the size of the dataset. We want to assign score for each feature based on their contribution to predict the outcome class correctly. For this, filter based feature selection technique is suitable which treats each feature as independent and uses statistical measures to find the scores based on the relationship between a feature and the class labels. Chi-square, Mutual Information and F-test based techniques are commonly used in filter based method [17, 18]. In our work, Chi-square feature selection algorithm is considered since it is widely used for feature selection in categorical data. The performance of Chi-square technique is compared with other two techniques.

Chi-Square Feature Selection. Chi-square test is a statistical method for finding a score based on the dependency of the features. This feature selection method is used to remove the unimportant features which have less dependency towards the class labels. It assumes that any two features are independent by null hypothesis and tries to find most relevant features [19, 20]. Higher Chi-square value indicates that the importance of the feature is higher. It is calculated using Eq. (1):

$$\chi^2 = \sum_{i=1}^{m} \sum_{j=1}^{n} \frac{(O_i - E_i)^2}{E_i} \tag{1}$$

Where m stands for number of features, n stands for the number of classes, O_i is the observed frequency and E_i is the expected frequency. Here, Chi-square score is calculated for all the 17 features using three datasets separately. Overall rank of each feature is evaluated by finding the average of Chi-square score percentage obtained in each dataset as shown in Table 2.

3.4   Machine Learning Techniques

In this paper, Phishing URL detections are performed using four commonly used machine learning techniques for binary classification viz. Random Forest algorithm (RF), Decision Tree (DTREE), Naive Bayes classification method (NB) and Support Vector Machine (SVM) [9]. In following, we discuss the working of these algorithms:

Random Forest. Random Forest algorithm is selected since it is one of the mostly used techniques for classification. It follows the concept of bagging technique of ensemble learning methods where multiple decision trees are created based on the randomly chosen set of training records and randomly selected features. In our case, 100 number of decision trees are created. The class which obtained majority votes for a particular test record is predicted as of that class [10, 21].

Decision Tree. Decision Tree algorithm creates a tree like structure where the non-leaf nodes are the decision points and the leaf nodes contain the class labels. The whole path takes the decisions based on if-then-else rules on feature values for each record. A particular record is predicted as of the leaf node class. The training dataset is split into several subsets. Different algorithms are used to select the decision nodes and simplify the tree to fit suitably for the test data [9, 10].

Table 2. Feature sets, descriptions, ranks based on Chi-square score

Features name	Description	Chi-square score (%)				Overall rank
		Dataset			Avg. score	
		1	2	3		
Path length to URL length ratio	Finds the ratio of length of the URL path to the length of URL	31.8	13.0	17.8	20.9	1
Length of URL	Takes the length of the URL string	12.6	22.7	16.4	17.2	2
Special chars to URL length ratio	Finds the ratio of total number of special characters to the length of URL	9.3	17.6	8.8	11.9	3
No. of suspicious characters	Total number of suspicious chars [i.e. % # ^ $ * & ! ' , : etc.] and other symbols present	7.0	6.7	17.1	10.3	4
No. of slashes	Counts total number of slashes (/) present	8.1	1.4	17.8	9.1	5
No. of suspicious keywords	Counts number of words mostly used in phishing sites like 'submit', 'confirm', 'account', 'login', 'signin', 'logon', 'suspend', 'secure' etc. as in [14]	10.0	11.8	3.3	8.4	6
No. of dots	Finds number of dots (.) present	5.3	4.9	9.7	6.6	7
Presence of query	Checks whether any query is there in URL	4.5	8.2	3.9	5.5	8
No. of question marks	Calculates number of question marks (?) present	4.6	7.3	1.7	4.5	9
No. of dashes	Counts number of dash/hyphen (-) present	4.2	3.9	2.7	3.6	10
Presence of @	Checks whether @ is present or not	1.3	1.3	0.3	1.0	11
Presence of symbol in last char	Checks is there any symbol present at the last character of the URL (except '/')	0.4	0.9	0.0	0.4	12
Presence of http in middle	Checks whether the word 'http' is present in domain name or path of the URL	0.4	0.0	0.3	0.3	13
Presence of // (redirection)	Checks the occurrence of redirection in URL	0.3	0.1	0.1	0.2	14
Presence of IP address	Sees whether the URL contains any IP address or not	0.2	0.2	0.1	0.1	15
Presence of unicode	Checks the presence of UNICODE characters	0	0	0	0	16
Presence of port number	Checks ant port no. is present or not in the URL	0	0	0	0	17

Support Vector Machine. SVM is widely used for binary classification in supervised machine learning [9]. The concept is to put the training data points in n-dimensional space where n is the number of features and identify the support vectors. The support vectors are the extreme data points near the hyperplane. The hyperplane(s) may linear or non-linear is drawn in such a way that it maintains the maximum distance from the support vectors and reduces the incorrect appearance of data points in both classes [10, 14]. Here, RBF kernel is used to implement the SVM to classify phishing and legitimate URLs.

Naïve Bayes. Naïve Bayes classifier is based on the concept of Bayes theorem. Bayes theorem is used to find the probability of an event if the probability of an already occurred event is given. This classifier assumes each feature is independent and makes equal contribution to the result [9, 10]. It finds the probability of a record for each class based on probability of all the feature values. The record is predicted as of that class which results the highest probability.

3.5 Performance Metrics

Performances of the experiments are evaluated using different metrics namely True Positive Rate (TPR), True Negative Rate (TNR), Accuracy (ACC), Precision (PRE) and F-Score (FSC) using Eqs. (2) to (7) as given below [22, 23]:

$$TPR = \frac{TP}{TP + FN} * 100\% \tag{2}$$

$$TNR = \frac{TN}{TN + FP} * 100\% \tag{3}$$

$$ACC = \frac{TP + TN}{TP + FP + TN + FN} * 100\% \tag{4}$$

$$REC = TPR \tag{5}$$

$$PRE = \frac{TP}{TP + FP} * 100\% \tag{6}$$

$$FSC = 2 * \left(\frac{PRE * REC}{PRE + REC}\right) \tag{7}$$

Where True Positive (TP) is number of phishing URLs correctly detected as phishing, True Negative (TN) is number of legitimate URLs correctly detected as legitimate, False Positive (FP) is number of legitimate URLs wrongly detected as phishing and False Negative (FN) is number of phishing URLs wrongly detected as legitimate.

4   Results and Analysis

First, the features are selected using Chi-square feature selection technique for three different datasets. Percentage of score obtained by each feature in a dataset are considered and overall rank is assigned to each feature based on the average score obtained by the features for those three datasets as shown in Table 2. Path length to URL ratio and length of URL obtained top two ranks. It is found that phishing URLs usually contain feature values more than the legitimate URLs for the features like length of URL, number of slashes, number of suspicious characters etc.

The performance of Chi-square feature selection is compared with Mutual Information based and F-test based methods in Table 3. Here, Random Forest algorithm is used for classifying URLs using top five features selected by each feature selection method for different datasets. Experiment is performed using 10 fold cross validation. Chi-square performs slightly better than the other two.

Figures 2, 3 and 4 shows the changing accuracy for three datasets for different techniques as the number of features increases from Rank 1 to Rank 17 using 10 fold cross validation. Random Forest shows the highest accuracy. As seen, in most cases accuracy increases with the increasing number of features using Random Forest and Decision Tree algorithm however accuracy do not improve significantly for the lower rank features. So, features with low Chi-square values are removed to reduce the dimensionality, only the top 9 features are considered for further evaluation. But it could be possible that any combinations among these 9 features perform better results than the results have been found considering top ranked 9 features. So, detail study of features are performed to obtain the best combination of features and validate the rank of features evaluated based on Chi-square score.

For this, n number of features are considered each time (where n = 3, 4, ..., 9) and accuracy of all possible combination, a total of 466 combination of features among these 9 features are evaluated. Experiments are performed using Random Forest algorithm for 10 fold cross validation on Dataset4 which is created with combination of all three datasets. The detail of our experiment is shown in Table 4.

In 10 fold cross validation, the dataset is equally split into ten parts and execute ten times by taking each part once as testing data and remaining nine parts as training data. Final result is calculated by finding the average results of all executions.

Table 3. Accuracy using RF for top 5 features selected using different selection methods

Dataset name	Chi-square	Mutual information	F-test
Dataset1	98.87	98.79	96.06
Dataset2	94.96	94.72	94.21
Dataset3	99.99	99.99	99.99

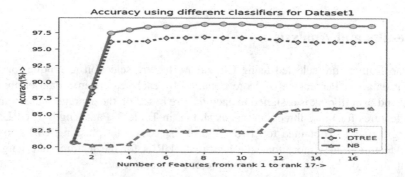

Fig. 2. Feature wise accuracy of classifiers for Dataset1

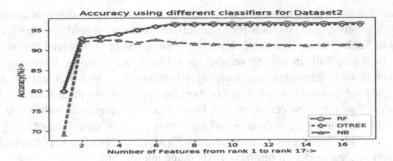

Fig. 3. Feature wise accuracy of classifiers for Dataset2

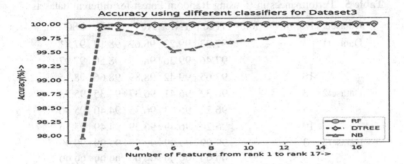

Fig. 4. Feature wise accuracy of classifiers for Dataset3

Table 4. Accuracy with combination of all features

No. of features (n)	Total possible combination of features	Group of features obtained highest accuracy	Rank on Chi-square of these features as in Table 2	ACC obtained
3	84	URL length, Path length to URL ratio, Special chars to URL ratio	1–3	97.83
4	126	Previous Group of Features (PGF) + No. of suspicious chars	1–4	97.92
5	126	PGF + No. of slashes	1–5	98.02
6	84	PGF + No. of keywords	1–6	98.16
7	36	PGF + No. of dots	1–7	98.49
8	9	PGF + Presence of query	1–8	98.48
9	1	PGF + No. of question marks	1–9	98.57

It has been observed that the combinations of the features which have shown highest accuracy for particular value of n (number of features) are the top n ranked features based on the Chi-square rank calculated in Table 2. These experiments justify the ranks assigned based on Chi-square score to the lexical features mostly used by different researchers for classifying phishing URLs.

Table 5 depicts the comparison of performances using three different cross validation folds namely 3, 5, 10 folds for three different datasets considering top 9 lexical features of Table 2 using Random Forest algorithm. It has been observed that accuracy slightly increases with increasing number of folds. Table 6 shows a comparison of performances of different machine learning algorithms for three different cross validation folds for Dataset4 which is a combination of all these three datasets. Naïve Bayes algorithm performs comparatively faster but its performance values are lesser compare to other three algorithms. Random Forest and Decision Tree obtain greater accuracy and take lesser time to execute than SVM. A comparison is performed with some other related works on phishing URL detection in Table 7.

Table 5. Performances in % using Random Forest for different datasets

Datasets	No. of CV folds	TPR	TNR	ACC	PRE	FSC
Dataset1	3	97.23	99.22	98.62	98.19	97.71
	5	97.46	99.36	98.78	98.50	97.97
	10	97.65	99.42	98.89	98.66	98.15
Dataset2	3	96.32	96.41	96.37	94.35	95.33
	5	96.22	96.43	96.35	94.40	95.30
	10	96.24	96.49	96.39	94.49	95.36
Dataset3	3	99.99	99.99	99.99	99.99	99.99
	5	99.99	99.99	99.99	99.99	99.99
	10	99.99	99.99	99.99	99.99	99.99

Table 6. Performances in % using different algorithms for different Dataset4

Algorithm	No. of CV folds	TPR	TNR	ACC	PRE	FSC
RF	3	97.81	97.37	98.38	97.37	97.59
	5	97.96	98.81	98.52	97.61	97.78
	10	98.06	98.82	98.57	97.63	97.84
DTREE	3	92.14	97.73	95.87	95.27	93.71
	5	92.29	97.90	96.04	95.61	93.92
	10	92.41	92.41	96.05	95.55	93.95
NB	3	82.23	81.56	82.46	61.74	70.28
	5	82.23	81.56	82.46	61.74	70.28
	10	82.23	81.57	82.46	61.74	70.28
SVM	3	84.06	96.85	92.61	92.98	88.29
	5	85.55	96.85	93.09	93.08	89.16
	10	86.11	96.74	93.21	92.91	89.38

Table 7. Comparison of our work with other related works

Paper	Approaches	No. of URLs	ACC (%)
Banik and Sarma [14]	Using SVM	32652	96.35
Hutchinson et al. [21]	Using Random Forest	11055	96.50
Sonowal and Kuppusamy [22]	PhiDMA model	1662	92.72
Mao et al. [23]	Using RF on page layout similarities	24051 samples	97.31
Our proposed method	Using Random Forest on Lexical features of URL	276640	98.57, Precision 97.63%

Our approach has proved to be an efficient detection system for phishing URLs. Accuracy of 98.57% is achieved for the dataset combining three different datasets for only 9 lexical features based on URL using Random Forest algorithm. Other papers as in Table 7 have less accuracy compare to our approach and the number of URLs considered by them in the experiment is also lesser.

5 Conclusion

This system works on classifying phishing and legitimate URLs using machine learning techniques based on lexical features of URLs only with an eye to develop a fast and efficient classification system. Experiments are performed using three different datasets. Chi-square feature selection is used to select only the features which have high dependency towards classification. Performances are measured using different parameters for four different machine learning algorithms. Random Forest algorithm produces better result for all the datasets. Our final result is evaluated by combining three datasets together. Random Forest algorithm has shown F-score value greater than 97.5% and low false positive rate of 1.18%. So, our approach can be considered as an efficient phishing URL classification system.

References

1. Mohammad, R.M., Thabtah, F., McCluskey, L.: Predicting phishing websites based on self-structuring neural network. Neural Comput. Appl. **25**(2), 443–458 (2013). https://doi.org/10.1007/s00521-013-1490-z
2. Phishing Activity Trends Reports. https://www.antiphishing.org/trendsreports/. Accessed 13 Nov 2019
3. Overview Safe Browsing APIs (v4) Google Developers. https://developers.google.com/safe-browsing/v4. Accessed 18 Dec 2019

4. Gupta, B.B., Arachchilage, N.A.G., Psannis, K.E.: Defending against phishing attacks: taxonomy of methods, current issues and future directions. Telecommunication Systems **67** (2), 247–267 (2017). https://doi.org/10.1007/s11235-017-0334-z

5. Prakash, P., Kumar, M., Kompella, R.R., Gupta, M.: PhishNet: predictive blacklisting to detect phishing attacks. In: 2010 Proceedings IEEE INFOCOM (2010). https://doi.org/10.1109/infcom.2010.5462216

6. Han, W., Cao, Y., Bertino, E., Yong, J.: Using automated individual white-list to protect web digital identities. Expert Syst. Appl. **39**, 11861–11869 (2012). https://doi.org/10.1016/j.eswa.2012.02.020

7. Jain, A.K., Gupta, B.B.: A novel approach to protect against phishing attacks at client side using auto-updated white-list. EURASIP J. Inf. Secur. **2016**(1), 1–11 (2016). https://doi.org/10.1186/s13635-016-0034-3

8. Jain, A.K., Gupta, B.B.: Phishing detection: analysis of visual similarity based approaches. Secur. Commun. Netw. **2017**, 1–20 (2017). https://doi.org/10.1155/2017/5421046

9. Sahoo, D., Liu, C., Hoi, S.C.H.: Malicious URL detection using Machine Learning: a survey. arXiv:1701.07179v2 (2017)

10. Vanhoenshoven, F., Napoles, G., Falcon, R., Vanhoof, K., Koppen, M.: Detecting malicious URLs using machine learning techniques. In: 2016 IEEE Symposium Series on Computational Intelligence (SSCI) (2016). https://doi.org/10.1109/ssci.2016.7850079

11. Mamun, M.S.I., Rathore, M.A., Lashkari, A.H., Stakhanova, N., Ghorbani, A.A.: Detecting malicious URLs using lexical analysis. In: Chen, J., Piuri, V., Su, C., Yung, M. (eds.) NSS 2016. LNCS, vol. 9955, pp. 467–482. Springer, Cham (2016). https://doi.org/10.1007/978-3-319-46298-1_30

12. Phishtank-Join the fight against phishing. https://www.phishtank.com/. Accessed 09 Nov 2019

13. DMOZ URL gr33ndata: gr33ndata/dmoz-urlclassifier. https://github.com/gr33ndata/dmoz-urlclassifier/. Accessed 27 Oct 2019

14. Banik, B., Sarma, A.: Phishing URL detection system based on URL features using SVM. Int. J. Electron. Appl. Res. **5**, 40–55 (2018). https://doi.org/10.33665/ijear.2018.v05i02.003

15. Chiew, K.L., Chang, E.H., Tan, C.L., Abdullah, J., Yong, K.S.C.: Building standard offline anti-phishing dataset for Benchmarking, International Journal of Engineering & Technology, vol. 7, no. 4.31, pp. 7–14, (2018). https://doi.org/10.14419/ijet.v7i4.31.23333

16. Althobaiti, K., Rummani, G., Vaniea, K.: A review of human- and computer-facing URL phishing features. In: 2019 IEEE European Symposium on Security and Privacy Workshops (EuroS&PW) (2019). https://doi.org/10.1109/eurospw.2019.00027

17. Brownlee, J.: How to Choose a Feature Selection Method For Machine Learning. https://machinelearningmastery.com/feature-selection-with-real-and-categorical-data/. Accessed 05 Jan 2020

18. Asaithambi, S.: Why, How and When to apply Feature Selection. https://towardsdatascience.com/why-how-and-when-to-apply-feature-selection-e9c69adfabf2. Accessed 05 Jan 2020

19. Liu, H., Setiono, R.: Chi2: feature selection and discretization of numeric attributes. In: Proceedings of 7th IEEE International Conference on Tools with Artificial Intelligence (1995). https://doi.org/10.1109/tai.1995.479783

20. Meesad, P., Boonrawd, P., Nuipian, V.: A Chi-Square-test for word importance differentiation in text classification. In: International Conference on Information and Electronics Engineering (2011)

21. Hutchinson, S., Zhang, Z., Liu, Q.: Detecting phishing websites with random forest. In: Meng, L., Zhang, Y. (eds.) MLICOM 2018. LNICSSITE, vol. 251, pp. 470–479. Springer, Cham (2018). https://doi.org/10.1007/978-3-030-00557-3_46

22. Sonowal, G., Kuppusamy, K.: PhiDMA – a phishing detection model with multi-filter approach. J. King Saud Univ. Comput. Inf. Sci. **32**, 99–112 (2017). https://doi.org/10.1016/j.jksuci.2017.07.005
23. Mao, J., et al.: Phishing page detection via learning classifiers from page layout feature. EURASIP J. Wirel. Commun. Network. **2019**(1), 1–14 (2019). https://doi.org/10.1186/s13638-019-1361-0

Feature Selection Using PSO: A Multi Objective Approach

Jyoti Vashishtha[(✉)], Vijay Hasan Puri[(✉)], and Mukesh[(✉)]

Guru Jambheshwar University of Science and Technology, Hisar, Haryana, India
jyoti.vst@gmail.com, vijay.hasanpuri@gmail.com,
mukeshnimbiwal@gmail.com

Abstract. Feature selection is a pre-processing technique in which a subset or a small number of features, which are relevant and non-redundant, are selected for better classification performance. Multi-objective optimization is applied in the fields where finest decisions need to be taken in presence of trade-offs between two or more differing objectives. Therefore, feature selection is considered as a multi-objective problem with conflicting measures like classification error rate and feature reduction rate. The existing algorithms, Non-dominated Sorting based particle swarm optimization for Feature Selection (NSPSOFS) and Crowding Mutation Dominance based particle swarm optimization for Feature Selection (CMDPSOFS) are the two multi-objective PSO algorithms for feature selection. This work presents the enhanced form of NSPSOFS and CMDPSOFS. A novel selection mechanism for gbest is incorporated and hybrid mutation is also added to the algorithms in order to generate a better pareto optimal front of non-dominated solutions. The experimental results show that the proposed algorithm generates non-dominated solutions and produce better result than existing algorithms.

Keywords: Feature selection · Multi-objective optimization · PSO

1 Introduction

Data mining has an important task known as classification which is concerned to construct a model from training set to distinguish and describe data classes or concepts to predict objects whose class label is unknown [1, 2]. The real world datasets comprise of irrelevant and redundant features also stated as noisy features. These noisy features are problematic for classification task and make it indeed a challenging task [3, 4]. In such cases, selection of relevant features is necessary [5, 6]. Therefore, elimination of noisy data and enhancement of performance of classifier by selecting relevant subset of features is main concept for feature selection. Filter approach, wrapper and embedded approach are three methods of feature selection [7–9].

Filter Approach
Filter Approach provides a general view of feature space and does not classify features by learning any algorithm. In this approach, features are analyzed and evaluated individually on the basis of evaluation function. Evaluation function measures the feature's selective ability in order to differentiate class labels. In addition,

© Springer Nature Singapore Pte Ltd. 2020
A. Bhattacharjee et al. (Eds.): MIND 2020, CCIS 1241, pp. 106–119, 2020.
https://doi.org/10.1007/978-981-15-6318-8_10

computational cost of filter approach is less as compared to wrapper approach. However, if the evaluation criterion unmatched or does not satisfy the conditions of the classifier well then the approaches may suffer from low performance.

Wrapper Approach

Wrapper approach uses classification/learning algorithm to select optimal feature subset. Evaluation function considers classification error rate or classification accuracy, induced by the learning algorithms [10, 11]. This characteristic of wrappers approach results in higher classification performance than filter approach. However, this approach is often much more time consuming since a classifier have to train for each subset evaluation.

Embedded Approach

It combines the advantages of both wrapper and filter approach. The term "embedded" indicates the involvement of two different evaluation methods. So, using both independent measure and data mining algorithm, feature set is evaluated. The independent measure is concerned to choose the best subset for a cardinality which is already given and the data mining algorithm chooses the best or finest subset among the best subsets.

Feature selection includes two main objectives i.e. minimization of number of features and maximization of classification accuracy. Therefore, number of methodologies has been introduced to handle the problems of multi-objective feature selection. To deal with the combinatory problems, evolutionary techniques are being used which are helpful for efficient and effective exploration of the solution space for the generation of solution which is optimal and effective with the supreme classification performance [12, 13]. Xue *et al.* [14] have designed an effective and optimal approach using PSO for multi-objective feature selection.

1.1 Particle Swarm Optimization (PSO)

PSO is a population-based optimization algorithm inspired by intelligent collective behavior of animals such as flocks of birds [15]. In 1995, Kennedy and Eberhard worked hard to develop PSO which is effectively based on swarm's intelligence and movement. It uses the concept of natural social behavior of swarm's to solve problems. Concept of PSO can be understood from the following example. When a group of birds starts moving in some area for the search of food, initially, they are not aware of food's location. After each iteration, birds get the knowledge about the distance of the food and every bird start rushing towards neighboring bird which is closest to the food the bird which is nearest to the food. Bird, as an individual, has limited potential but it is their cooperative work that makes their behavior intelligent.

Continuous PSO

A randomly generated population of particles is considered in PSO and position and velocity are associated to each particle. By iteratively changing the velocity and position based on the flying experience towards pbest and gbest location, PSO determines the optimal solution. Gbest value is most right fitness value in cluster while pbest value is best fitness value of each particle which is accomplish by that specific particle so far. Velocity and Position of particle is to be changed as per Eqs. (1) & (2) resp.

$$v_{id} = w \times v_{id} + c_1 \times rand() \times (p_{id} - x_{id}) + c_2 \times rand() \times (p_{gd} - x_{id}) \qquad (1)$$

$$x_{id} = x_{id} + v_{id} \qquad (2)$$

In dimension d, v_{id} assigned as the ith particle velocity and x_{id} assigned as is the ith particle position the position of particle at time t, p_{id} is location of pbest and p_{gd} is the location of gbest. Each particle updates their velocity on the basis of its previous distance and velocity of current location from gbest and pbest location. *Cognitive part,* c_1 describes particle's learning from its own flying experience while *Social part,* c_2 represents particle's learning from flying experience of group. The function rand() is the name of random function that create random values in the range [0, 1]. Suitable value of w, inertia weight ensures balance among global and local exploration and exploitation [16, 17].

Binary PSO

PSO was originally aimed to solve real value problem. It was further extended to discrete/binary space to solve discrete problem where velocity was squashed using logistic function. The state space has restrictions in the range from 0 to 1 in each dimension where the particle moves [18]. A particle changes its velocity according to equation number (1) except that v_{id} must be in interval [0, 1] and x_{id}, p_{id} and p_{gd} are integers in $\{0, 1\}$. Sigmoid function S(v) is used to do this and particle's position in changed on basis of following rule:

If $rand() < S(v_{id})$

$x_{id} = 1$

else

$x_{id} = 0$

Where, $S(v) = \dfrac{1}{(1 + e^{-v})}$

rand() is a number which is randomly selected form uniform distribution in [0, 1] and S(v) is a sigmoid limiting transformation.

1.2   Multi-objective Optimization

An optimization problem involve multiple objective function that need to be optimize or amend concurrently is termed as multi objective optimization. This problem needs to take some optimal decisions in existence of compensation between one or more than one dissident objectives. This optimization includes minimizing or maximizing of more than one conflicting objective functions. Formulation of multi-objective optimization problem in mathematical terms that can be done as minimization problem having more than one objective functions can be reported as [14]:

$$Minimize, F(x) = [f_1(x), f_2(x), \ldots, f_n(x)] \qquad (3)$$

subject to

$$g_i(x) \leq 0, i = 1, 2, \ldots k$$

$$h_i(x) = 0, i = 1, 2, \ldots l$$

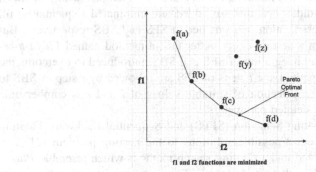

Fig. 1. Minimization problem with two objective functions

Figure 1 illustrating the pareto optimal front for two objective functions (f_1 and f_2). Where x represents the vector of decision variables, $g_i(x)$ and $h_i(x)$ are the constraint functions, $f_i(x)$ is taken as a function of x, and n represents the no. of objective functions which are to be minimized. It has effectively practices in various ground of science fields of science which includes engineering, economics and logistics where it has been applied in various fields of science, along with economics, engineering and logistics. A solution x dominates solution y if it fulfil the condition:

$$f_i(x) < = f_i(y) \ \&\& \ f_i(x) < f_i(y) \tag{4}$$

If x and y solution of n objective problem satisfy the Eq. (4), then these are called dominated solution. A solution is termed as non-dominated or pareto optimal, if a solution remains non-dominated by any other solution. Non dominated solutions form trade-offs surface in search space termed as Pareto front. Features selection problem can be defined two conflicting objectives, one is to minimize number of features and other is to minimize classification error or maximize classification accuracy. Multi-objective approach is the most studied field in the recent years [19, 20]. It is being applied in most of the data mining problems. Multi-objective approach is being used in the area of feature selection using PSO to obtain pareto optimal solutions [14].

Rest of the paper is structured as follows. Section 2 illustrates the necessary related work for feature selection and multi-objective optimization methods. Section 3 specifics of the proposed algorithm: MOFSPSO for feature selection. Section 4 gives experimental results and discussions. The last Sect. 5 concludes the paper.

2   Related Work

Traditional feature selection methods are classified in to three parts: wrapper, filter and embedded approach. Wrapper approach which are used commonly are Sequential Forward Selection (SFS) and Sequential Backward Selection (SBS) [11, 21] which perform feature subset selection sequentially. However, these two algorithms completely differ in their working. SFS initialize with a blank set of features while SBS with the set of all features. Candidate features are added and eliminated sequentially, till there is improvement in classification performance in SFS and SBS respectively. But these algorithms suffer from a nesting effect. After this, a method named *Plus-l-take-away-r*, which is basically an integration of SFS and SBS, introduced to overcome the nesting effect [22]. In this method, the l steps of SFS are followed by r step of SBS to select the features. However, selection of suitable values of l and r is cumbersome problem as l and r are user-defined parameters.

Sequential Forward Floating Selection (SFFS) and Sequential Backward Floating Selection (SBFS) are two other possible solutions to the nesting problem [21, 22]. These methods are categorized under floating search methods which resemble *Plus-l-take-away-r* method but has dynamic control. They are capable of selecting or removing the features at different stages of feature selection procedure until desired numbers of features are obtained. Relief is a filter method based algorithm that rank the features based on feature relevance property and a threshold is used to select feature subset [23, 24]. However, it considers only relevant features not redundant features. Another filter algorithm, FOCUS initialize with all features and uses exhaustive approach to get optimal subset [25]. It suffers from high computational cost due to exhaustive approach used.

Traditional feature selection methods rarely provide satisfactory results for large dataset. By using them we obtain either optimal or computationally effective feature subset but not the both. Many Nature inspired methods like Ant colony, PSO etc. have been used in past for Feature Selection due to their global search ability. Few of the works discussing feature selection using PSO have been reviewed in this subsection.

Two new algorithms (BPSO-P, BPSO-G) are developed by Liam *et al.* [26] which are based on information theory and BPSO algorithm. Both are introduced to find more optimal feature subset. To evaluate the relevance between features and class labels, mutual information is used as a measure in BPSO-P while entropy of group of features in BPSO-G. Experiment results show that both algorithms with suitable weight of relevance and redundancy perform better. However, these algorithms have not been compared with other algorithms. Several strategies have been adopted to change update strategy other than that of standard PSO. Chuang *et al.* [27] proposed an approach to reset value of the parameter gbest, if gbest remains unchanged after several iterations. KNN method with LOOCV has been used using gene expression data to estimate fitness value of particle. Experimental results illustrate that better classification accuracy has been achieved by modified approach.

Another parameter has been suggested by Yang *et al.* [28] to reset the gbest value. Boolean function is used to replace old gbest with new gbest fitness value, if it remains identical during three successive generations. In comparison to GA and original BPSO, proposed modifications lead to better results. In order to prevent BPSO from getting stuck in local optima, chaotic map embedded with BPSO (CBPSO) by Chuang et al. [29] that adjusts the inertia weight. Different equations are used by chaotic map including logistic and tent map, to update inertia weight which affects the search ability of CBPSO. CBPSO with tent map achieved higher value of classification accuracy as compare to CBPSO with logistic map.

To enhance the performance of BPSO, Catfish effect introduced by Chuang et al. [30]. Particles with worst fitness in a number of consecutive iterations are replaced by new particles. Catfish-BPSO simplifies process of Feature selection and outperforms BPSO and deterministic algorithms. There is also work being made regarding multi-objective feature selection (MOFS). Although MOFS have been investigated frequently using evolutionary algorithms, no work has been done on this using PSO. PSO first time has been used for MOFS problem by Xue et al. [14]. Continuous PSO is opted for feature selection rather than binary PSO because in BPSO, particle's position is changed according to only velocity. However, Standard PSO considers both velocity and current position when changes are made to particle's position. In this paper, two new methods NSPSOFS, CMDPSOFS are proposed for feature selection based on multi-objective PSO. NSPSOFS uses the concept of non-dominated sorting [29] while CMDPSOFS uses crowding, mutation and dominance [30] to find non-dominated solutions for optimal feature subset.

3 Proposed Algorithm

Proposed algorithm is an extension of CMDPSOFS. In the modified multi-objective approach, MOFSPSO, a new selection mechanism for gbest and hybrid mutation is incorporated to obtain a pareto front of non-dominated feature subsets. The algorithm has two main objectives, one is to minimize number of features and other is to minimize classification error. Since Basic PSO algorithm is not built for more than one objective problem so that those algorithms are unable to optimize multi-objective problems directly [31]. PSO for multi-objective optimization problem has been introduced by Sierra [32]. However, it is not used for multi-objective feature selection.

Xue et al. [14] uses PSO first time for multi-objective feature selection. In this algorithm, to update velocity of particles, gbest is chosen using binary tournament selection that randomly selects gbest from the leader set. Instead of this selection mechanism, roulette wheel selection is employed with which gbest is selected on the basis of probability corresponding to crowding factor from LeaderSet. Moreover, hybrid mutation has been effectively and successfully applied in cost based feature selection. However, it has not been used in feature selection without cost. This encourages using hybrid mutation for feature selection without cost. To enhance the search ability of algorithm, a Hybrid mutation operator [20] is adopted. Pseudo-code of MOFSPSO is shown by algorithm shown in Fig. 2. The main steps of CMDPSOFS except selection of gbest and hybrid mutation are followed by the new algorithm. The steps: Selections of gbest and hybrid mutation are described in details as follows.

Initialization of swarm includes generation of a population of particles. In PSO algorithm, each candidate solution of the problem is considered as a particle which is encoded by an array or a vector (n real numbers), where n is the number of features available.

Algorithm : MOFSPSO
Input: Training Dataset
         Test dataset
Output: Pareto optimal solution.

Begin
  Initialize swarm;
  Initialize LeaderSet and Archive
  Evaluate
      crowding distance (Leader Set);
  while i=1 to max_iter
     do
       for j=1 to pop_size
       do
           Select leader (gbest); // *using roulette wheel selection.*
         Update velocity, position(j);
         Apply hybrid mutation operator;
         Estimate two objective value of each particle;
         Update pbest; //*for every particle*
      End
      Identify non-dominated solutions
      Update LeaderSet;
      Copy leaders to archive.
      Evaluate crowding distance //*of every particle.*
    End
    Evaluate classification error rate //*of solutions in Archive on testset;*
 End

Fig. 2. Proposed algorithm (MOFSPSO)

A threshold value (θ), is needed to make the decision about the selection of feature i.e. selected or not. LeaderSet is employed to store all non-dominated solution of population as the potential leaders and crowding distance corresponding to each solution is calculated. Archive is retained to store non dominated solutions conveyed by algorithm. This process is carried out on training dataset. Classifier error rate of solution in archive is determined on test dataset.

4 Results and Discussion

The proposed Continuous PSO approach for multi-objective feature selection is implemented using MATLAB. The performance of the proposed algorithm is validated on five datasets with distinct number of features, classes and instances from UCI machine learning repository. Since missing values in a particular dataset degrades its classification performance, therefore these values are being removed using tool WEKA. Normalization of dataset is a necessary step particularly to standardize dataset. All datasets used for experiment have different sizes and functionality and are described in Table 1.

Table 1. Datasets used for experimental work

S. No.	Dataset	Instances	Features	Classes
1.	Ionosphere	351	34	2
2.	Australian	690	14	2
3.	Wine	178	13	3
4.	WBCD	569	30	2
5.	Lung cancer	32	56	3

Ionosphere dataset has 351 instances with 34 attributes and corresponding 2 classes named as good or bad. No missing value is contained in this dataset. Australian dataset has 690 instances, 14 features and two classes named as class 1, class 2. Out of 14 features, 6 are numerical and 8 are categorical attributes. Missing values present in this dataset are removed using WEKA. Wine dataset have 178 instances with 3 classes and 13 features. Class distribution of wine Dataset is as follow: Class 1 (59 instances), class 2 (71 instances) and class 3 (48 instances). There is no missing value in this dataset. WBCD dataset consists of 30 features with 569 instances having two classes benign and malignant. There are 357 instances of benign and 212 of malignant. This dataset do not have any missing values. Lung Cancer dataset consists of 32 instances, 56 features and 3 classes. Class distribution of lung cancer dataset as follows: 9 instances (class 1), 13 instances (class 2) and 10 instances (class 3).

In the experiment, every dataset is randomly divided into two parts by 70–30 ratio. Each particle in PSO corresponds to a feature subset and corresponding classification performance is determined by ANN classifier on training set.

To achieve the testing classification error rate, features selected are calculated on the test set after the training process. The proper working of algorithm requires values of each parameter to be set accordingly. The parameters along with their values are explained in Table 2. 'max_iter' refers to maximum hundred iterations. 'pop_size' refers to total number of particles i.e. population size, here pop_size is set to 30. 'arc_size' refers to the max. no. of non-dominated solution that can be placed in archive and used 15 non-dominated solutions.

Table 2. Parameters used for proposed algorithm

Sr. No.	Parameters	Description	Values
1	max_iter	Max. iterations	100
2	pop_size	Population size	30
3	arc_size	Max. No. of non-dominated solutions that can place in archive	15
4	θ	Threshold value that can be used to decide a feature to be selected or not	0.6
5	P_m	Probability by which velocity of one tenth of particles in population	0.1
6	J_m	Jumping mutation probability	$\frac{1}{nVar}$
7	w	Weight of inertia	[0.1, 0.5]
8	C_1	Cognitive and social part	1.5
9	C_2	Cognitive and social part	2.0

Particle is serve as or show by nVar bit string and contains number of available features. 'θ' is a threshold value that is adopted to decide in case feature is selected or not. If $p_k > \theta$, then corresponding k^{th} feature is selected where p_k is position value in the kth dimension in the interval [0, 1], p_k indicates the probability of the kth feature being selected. 'P_m' represents probability by which velocity of one tenth of particles in population is set to 0.001. 'J_m' represents jumping mutation probability whose value is set to $\frac{1}{nVar}$ due to which each particle may uniformly jump in any dimensional space. Inertia weight, w is chosen randomly between [0.1, 0.5]. C_1 is cognitive part with value 1.5 and C_2 is social part with value 2.0. Proposed algorithm achieve a pareto front of non-dominated results including set of fewer number of features and reduced classification error rate.

4.1   Comparison of MOFSPSO with NSPSOFS and CMDPSOFS

Pareto frontiers of MOFSPSO, NSPSOFS and CMDPSOFS are obtained using MATLAB and the spectacular results are obtained. Algorithms are performed on benchmark datasets which are mentioned in Table 1 and parameters are used according to Table 2. The pareto frontiers are shown in Fig. 3. As NSPSOFS and CMDPSOFS performs far better than the other existing approaches, so the results of these algorithms enclosed in this section as a standard to test the proposed algorithm. Figure 3 illustrates the experimental results of NSPSOFS, CMPSOFS and MOFSPSO.

As shown in Fig. 3, pareto front of MOFSPSO includes more than one nondominated solutions which selects fewer number of features and achieved lower classification error rate than NSPSOFS and CMDPSOFS. There are number of combination of same number of features with the distinct classification performance. So MOFSPSO

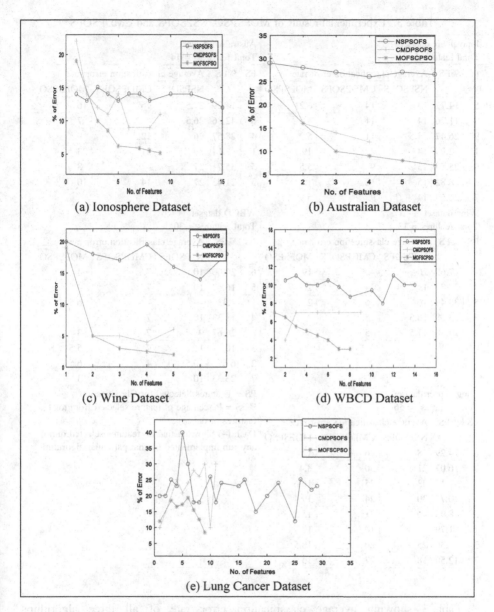

Fig. 3. Results obtained from MOFSPSO, NSPSOFS and CMDPSOFS.

can obtain same number of features with different error rate in different runs. So the average of classification error rate is included in the Fig. 3. In most of the datasets, MOFSPSO discloses a feature subset which is preferred less features but obtained lower error rate that other algorithms.

Table 3. Experimental results of MOFSPSO, NSPSOFS and CMDPSOFS

Ionosphere dataset Total features = 34					Australian dataset Total features = 14				
FS	%FS	Average classification error rate			FS	%FS	Average classification error rate		
		NSPSOFS	CMDPSOFS	MOFSPSO			NSPSOFS	CMDPSOFS	MOFSPSO
5	14.71	13	14	6.2	2	14.29	27.5	16	16
4	11.76	14	11	8.5	6	42.86	26.5	–	7
9	26.47	13.5	11	5.2	4	28.57	26	12.5	9
1	2.94	14	22	19	1	7.14	29	31	23
8	23.53	13	9	5.5	5	35.71	27	–	8
3	8.82	15	12.5	10	3	21.43	27	14	10
7	20.59	14	9	5.9					

Wine dataset Total features = 13					WBCD dataset Total features = 30				
FS	%FS	Average classification error rate			FS	%FS	Average classification error rate		
		NSPSOFS	CMDPSOFS	MOFSPSO			NSPSOFS	CMDPSOFS	MOFSPSO
1	7.69	20	–	19	6	20.00	10.5	7	4
4	30.77	19.5	4	2.5	5	16.67	10	7	4.5
5	38.46	16	6	2	1	3.33	–	–	6.5
3	23.08	16.5	5	3	4	13.33	10	7	5
2	15.38	17.5	5	5	8	26.67	9	7	3
					3	10	11	7	5.5
					2	6.67	10.5	4	6.5
					7	23.33	10	7	3

Lung cancer dataset Total features = 56				
FS	%FS	Average classification error rate		
		NSPSOFS	CMDPSOFS	MOFSPSO
8	14.29	18	26	12
9	16.07	21	30	8.4
4	7.14	23	25	16.6
6	10.71	30	24	19.4
5	8.93	40	21	15.5
1	1.79	20	10	12
3	5.36	25	20	18.5
7	12.50	18	27	15

FS = Features Selected for Classification
%FS = Percentage of feature selected from total features of dataset
Dash (–) Showing that no features selected during any run implemented by that particular algorithm
**

Table 3 showing average classification error rate of all three algorithms (NSPSOFS, CMDPSOFS and MOFSPSO), MOFSPSO selects only around 7.14% of features (1 from 14) in Australian dataset and 3.33% (1 from 30) in WBCD dataset but obtained lower classification error than NSPSOFS and CMDPSOFS. MOFSPSO performed better in almost all cases except 1 feature selection in Ionosphere, selecting subset of 2 features in WBCD dataset and subset with 1 feature in Lung Cancer dataset.

To evaluate proposed algorithm's performance, the proposed algorithm is compared with NSPSOFS and CMDPSOFS. These entire algorithms is performing better and selecting less no. of features and showing high classification performance. But in some cases, MOFSPSO is performed better than other algorithms by selecting less number of features and obtained more improved classification performance. Figure 3 shows that proposed algorithm conclude better Pareto front than other algorithms in terms of multi-objective features. MOFSPSO overcomes the limitations of other two algorithms.

5   Conclusions

In a dataset, all feature are not favorable for classification. Extraneous, irrelevant and redundant features may reduce the performance of classification. This paper conducted an enhanced research on multi-objective PSO for feature selection. In this work a new algorithm MOFSPSO is designed and its performance is evaluated on standard benchmark datasets. Result that are obtained from experiment shows that MOFSPSO showed better results in comparison with NSPSOFS and CMDPSOFS. Selection mechanism (Roulette Wheel Selection) for gbest in MOFSPSO used less computing and feature features and less computational time than the selection mechanism (Binary Tournament Selection) used in these two existing algorithms. MOFSPSO obtains a pareto front of nondominated results rather than obtaining a single result. This pareto optimal front can end-users to select better solutions to achieve their goal. Hybrid mutation operator incorporated to maintain control the diversification of swarm and to effectively deal with global and local search abilities. Roulette wheel selection mechanism and hybrid mutation operator in MOFSPSO achieve paramount performance over NSPSOFS and CMDPSOFS.

This work achieved good subset of feature and performance but it is not known whether it can achieve an enhanced pareto optimal front. In future, we will be investigating for further improvement. A new selection mechanism can be used to select gbest value and it would also be interesting to extend PSO based feature selection algorithms to cope with binary PSO.

References

1. Han, J., Kamber, M., Pei, J.: Data Mining: Concepts and Techniques, 3rd edn. Morgan Kaufmann, Burlington (2011)
2. Vashishtha, J., Kumar, D., Ratnoo, S.: An evolutionary approach to discover intra- and inter-class exceptions in databases. IJISTA **12**, 283 (2013)
3. Vashishtha, J., Kumar, D., Ratnoo, S.: Revisiting interestingness measures for knowledge discovery in databases. In: 2012 Second International Conference on Advanced Computing & Communication Technologies, Rohtak, Haryana, India, pp. 72–78. IEEE (2012)
4. Ratnoo, S., Pathak, A., Ahuja, J., Vashishtha, J.: Exception discovery using ant colony optimisation. Int. J. Comput. Syst. Eng. **4**, 46–57 (2018)
5. Lin, S.-W., Ying, K.-C., Chen, S.-C., Lee, Z.-J.: Particle swarm optimization for parameter determination and feature selection of support vector machines. Expert Syst. Appl. **35**, 1817–1824 (2008)
6. Neha, N., Vashishtha, J.: Particle swarm optimization based feature selection. IJCA **146**, 11–17 (2016)

7. Liu, H., Sun, J., Liu, L., Zhang, H.: Feature selection with dynamic mutual information. Pattern Recogn. **42**, 1330–1339 (2009)
8. Pathak, A., Vashistha, J.: Classification rule and exception mining using nature inspired algorithms. Int. J. Comput. Sci. Inf. Technol. **6**, 3023–3030 (2015)
9. Butler-Yeoman, T., Xue, B., Zhang, M.: Particle swarm optimisation for feature selection: a size-controlled approach. In: AusDM, pp. 151–159 (2015)
10. Visalakshi, S., Radha, V.: Wrapper based feature selection and classification for real time dataset. Int. J. Emerg. Technol. Comput. Appl. Sci. **3**, 306–311 (2015)
11. Lane, M.C., Xue, B., Liu, I., Zhang, M.: Particle swarm optimisation and statistical clustering for feature selection. In: Cranefield, S., Nayak, A. (eds.) AI 2013. LNCS (LNAI), vol. 8272, pp. 214–220. Springer, Cham (2013). https://doi.org/10.1007/978-3-319-03680-9_23
12. Kim, G., Kim, S., Tek, T., Kyungki, S.: Feature selection using genetic algorithms for handwritten character recognition. In: Schomaker, L.R.B., Vuurpijl, L.G. (eds.) Nijmegen: International Unipen Foundation, Amsterdam, Netherland, pp 103–112 (2000)
13. Cvetkovic, D., Parmee, I.C.: Preferences and their application in evolutionary multiobjective optimization. IEEE Trans. Evol. Comput. **6**, 42–57 (2002)
14. Xue, B., Zhang, M., Browne, W.N.: Particle swarm optimization for feature selection in classification: a multi-objective approach. IEEE Trans. Cybern. **43**, 1656–1671 (2012)
15. Kennedy, J., Eberhart, R.: Particle swarm optimization. In: Proceedings of ICNN 1995 - International Conference on Neural Networks, Perth, pp. 1942–1948. IEEE (1995)
16. Shi, Y.: Particle swarm optimization. In: Proceeding of International Conference on Neural Networks Society, vol. 4, pp. 8–13. IEEE (2004)
17. Shi, Y., Eberhart, R.: A modified particle swarm optimizer. In: 1998 IEEE International Conference on Evolutionary Computation Proceedings. IEEE World Congress on Computational Intelligence (Cat. No. 98TH8360), pp. 69–73. IEEE (1998)
18. Unler, A., Murat, A.: A discrete particle swarm optimization method for feature selection in binary classification problems. Eur. J. Oper. Res. **206**, 528–539 (2010)
19. Zitzler, E., Thiele, L., Laumanns, M.: Performance assessment of multiobjective optimizers: an analysis and review. IEEE Trans. Evol. Comput. **7**, 117–132 (2003). https://doi.org/10.1109/TEVC.2003.810758
20. Zhang, Y., Gong, D., Cheng, J.: Multi-objective particle swarm optimization approach for cost-based feature selection in classification. IEEE/ACM Trans. Comput. Biol. Bioinform. **14**, 64–75 (2017). https://doi.org/10.1109/TCBB.2015.2476796
21. Lane, M.C., Xue, B., Liu, I., Zhang, M.: Gaussian based particle swarm optimisation and statistical clustering for feature selection. In: Blum, C., Ochoa, G. (eds.) EvoCOP 2014. LNCS, vol. 8600, pp. 133–144. Springer, Heidelberg (2014). https://doi.org/10.1007/978-3-662-44320-0_12
22. Xue, B., Zhang, M., Browne, W.N.: Particle swarm optimization for feature selection in classification: novel initialization and updating mechanisms. Appl. Soft Comput. **18**, 261–276 (2014)
23. Dash, M., Liu, H.: Feature selection for classification. Intell. Data Anal. **1**, 131–156 (1997)
24. Chandrashekar, G., Sahin, F.: A survey on feature selection methods. Comput. Electr. Eng. **40**, 16–28 (2014)
25. Wang, X., Yang, J., Teng, X.: Feature selection based on rough sets and particle swarm optimization. Pattern Recogn. Lett. **28**, 459–471 (2007)
26. Cervante, L., Xue, B., Zhang, M., Shang, L.: Binary particle swarm optimisation for feature selection: a filter based approach. In: 2012 IEEE Congress on Evolutionary Computation, Brisbane, QLD, pp. 1–8. IEEE (2012)
27. Chuang, L.-Y., Chang, H.-W., Tu, C.-J., Yang, C.-H.: Improved binary PSO for feature selection using gene expression data. Comput. Biol. Chem. **32**, 29–38 (2008)

28. Yang, C.-S., Chuang, L.-Y., Ke, C.-H., Yang, C.-H.: Boolean binary particle swarm optimization for feature selection. In: 2008 IEEE Congress on Evolutionary Computation. IEEE World Congress on Computational Intelligence, Hong Kong, pp. 2093–2098. IEEE (2008)

29. Yang, C.-S., Chuang, L.-Y., Li, J.-C., Yang, C.-H.: Chaotic maps in binary particle swarm optimization for feature selection. In: 2008 IEEE Conference on Soft Computing in Industrial Applications, Muroran, pp. 107–112. IEEE (2008)

30. Chuang, L.-Y., Tsai, S.-W., Yang, C.-H.: Improved binary particle swarm optimization using catfish effect for feature selection. Expert Syst. Appl. **38**, 12699–12707 (2011)

31. Deb, K., Pratap, A., Agarwal, S., Meyarivan, T.: A fast and elitist multiobjective genetic algorithm: NSGA-II. IEEE Trans. Evol. Comput. **6**, 182–197 (2002)

32. Sierra, M.R., Coello Coello, C.A.: Improving PSO-based multi-objective optimization using crowding, mutation and ∈-dominance. In: Coello Coello, C.A., Hernández Aguirre, A., Zitzler, E. (eds.) EMO 2005. LNCS, vol. 3410, pp. 505–519. Springer, Heidelberg (2005). https://doi.org/10.1007/978-3-540-31880-4_35

An Empirical Study to Predict Myocardial Infarction Using K-Means and Hierarchical Clustering

Md. Minhazul Islam, Shah Ashisul Abed Nipun, Majharul Islam,
Md. Abdur Rakib Rahat, Jonayet Miah, Salsavil Kayyum$^{(\boxtimes)}$,
Anwar Shadaab, and Faiz Al Faisal

Department of Electrical and Computer Engineering (ECE),
North South University, Dhaka, Bangladesh
{minhazul.islam01, shah.aa.nipun, majharul.islam02,
abdur.rahat, jonayet.miah, salsavil.kayyum,
anwar.shadaab, faiz.faisal}@northsouth.edu

Abstract. The target of this research is to predict Myocardial Infarction using unsupervised Machine Learning algorithms. Myocardial Infarction Prediction related to heart disease is a challenging factor faced by doctors & hospitals. In this prediction, accuracy of the heart disease plays a vital role. From this concern, the authors have analyzed on a myocardial dataset to predict myocardial infarction using some popular Machine Learning algorithms K-Means and Hierarchical Clustering. This research includes a collection of data and the classification of data using Machine Learning Algorithms. The authors collected 345 instances along with 26 attributes from different hospitals in Bangladesh. This data have been collected from patients suffering from myocardial infarction along with other symptoms. This model would be able to find and mine hidden facts from historical Myocardial Infarction cases. The aim of this study is to analyze the accuracy level to predict Myocardial Infarction by using Machine Learning techniques.

Keywords: Machine learning · K-means · Hierarchical clustering · Myocardial infarction · Heart disease

1 Introduction

Myocardial Infarction (MI) which known as a heart attack is a very common disease in the world. A significant number of people are suffering from multiple kinds of heart diseases. An extensive amount of patient deaths due to heart diseases (Myocardial Infarction-MI) is increasing day by day. This is a perplexing mission to scan Myocardial Infarction (heart attack) with the help of reports from the patients. The physician reaches to a conclusion based on their past experiences and knowledge to circle the causes of heart attack. In 2019 SB Cho, SC Kim and MG Chung [7] used

© Springer Nature Singapore Pte Ltd. 2020
A. Bhattacharjee et al. (Eds.): MIND 2020, CCIS 1241, pp. 120–130, 2020.
https://doi.org/10.1007/978-981-15-6318-8_11

Risk-based Clustering on a dataset of 10,023 instances and 5 attributes. So it is the high time to think about this problem and try to find out possible best solutions. Machine Learning (ML) is a division of algorithms that enables applications to be more accurate in predicting results without being explicitly programmed [9].

Machine Learning holds great potential to explore the hidden patterns in huge information that can be used for clinical diagnosis. Machine Learning permits model of human healthiness to use facts and figures systematically and do the analysis for identifying inefficiencies, finest practices that progress carefulness and lower the cost rates. Chaitali S. Danger [3] has suggested a heart disease estimation model depending on Neural Networks (NN). The H.D.P.S scheme assume the chances of having a Heart diseases. W. Chen, et al. [8] introduced an estimation model for Type 2 diabetes with the help of k-means and J48. Therefore the authors conducted a search based on machine learning algorithms to find out the chances of occurrence of Myocardial Infarction disease before it occurs. The purpose of our study is to do an analysis on heart disease dataset to identify Myocardial Infarction accurately using Machine Learning techniques namely K-Means Clustering and Hierarchical Clustering.

2 Related Works

In 2018, in the United States of America, **Williams et al.** [2] utilized J48 and Naive Bayes to predict breast cancer symptoms. They used WEKA as primary tool for their work. They stated as a result that J48 has given the best results for the estimation which is a 94.2% accuracy, whereas Naive Bayes performed a bit low and provided an accuracy of 82.6%. **Chaitrali S. Dangare** [3] prepared a NN model for heart disease prediction. In order to conduct the prediction, attributes like gender, blood pressure, cholesterol, sugar level, age and more 13 have used by the method. A fresh algorithm has been presented by **M. Akhil Jabbar et al.** [4] which contains differences of the instances using K-Nearest Neighbor method with genetic algorithms. A worldwide exploration on composite large and multimodal set of data have been done to obtain a highly accurate result. From the outcomes the authors made assumption that cross-breeding GA with KNN achieves expected accuracy in heart disease estimation. **Rajkumar et al.** [5] used Tanagra tool to complete their study for prediction of heart attack. This was used to compare the accuracies of different data processing techniques to predict heart disease. According to their research, Naive Bayes is gave faster compact time for processing the set of data and performed the best with highest accuracy among the other algorithms. A 52.33% was obtained as the overall accuracy level for the model. **Milan Kumari et al.** [6] suggested a system for prediction of circulatory illness dataset with the assistance of diverse Data Mining Techniques. The precision proportions for different data mining techniques are Support Vector Machine-81.08%, Artificial Neural Networks-80.06%, Decision Tree-79.05% and RIPPER classifier-84.12%.

3   Methodology

The analysis can be divided into four vital phases which are given as follows:

- Data Collection
- Data Preprocessing
- Data Training
- Machine Learning Algorithms

A flow-chart of overall analysis has been demonstrated in the below Fig. 1 -

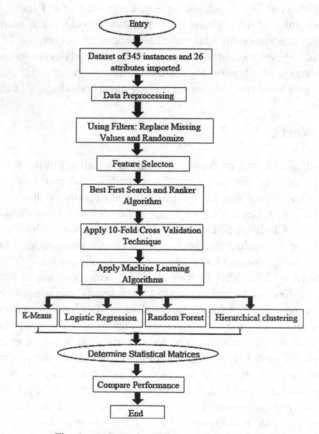

Fig. 1. A flow chart of the complete study

3.1   Data Collection

The data have been taken from different hospitals in Dhaka. Heart attack patients got the most priority to collect the data from them. Table 1 shows the factors which are responsible for the Distinctive and Non-Distinctive class. Table 2 shows the hospitals which helped the team in collecting the data. A total of 345 instances and 26 attributes which is shown in Table 4 have been collected in which there is information for an individual patient. The dataset contains the class attribute which is categorized by three types, Distinctive, Non-Distinctive and Both.

3.2 Data Preprocessing

After collecting the data, the authors completed the preprocessing. In the preprocessing phase, the authors used two unsupervised filters in the broadly used machine learning platform Waikato Environment for Knowledge Analysis (WEKA 3.8.3). At first, the authors filtered the Missing Values and then replaced on the dataset. This filtering process replaced the values which was missing in professed and numerical attributes using the mean, medians and modes. Secondly, the authors have used the Randomize filter which replaces the missing information without giving up much of the performance. Another one is median () to find out the most middle value of the dataset [10].

3.3 Data Training

WEKA: The training of the data have been done using the K-Fold Cross Validation technique of WEKA. It is a resampling technique to evaluate the prediction model by dividing the main dataset into a training dataset and a testing data set. The parameter K determines the number of groups the dataset will be divided into by shuffling the dataset randomly.

Rapid Miner: Rapid Miner is used for research, education and training. The authors applied this application for the data mining techniques- data processing, visualizations results, model validity and optimization. It is one of the most analytical tools used predictive Gartner's rapid recognition of the knife in the leadership of the advanced magic quadrant analytical platforms.

3.4 Machine Learning Algorithms

After the training phase, classification has been using various machine learning algorithms among which K-MEANS Algorithm and Hierarchical Clustering outperformed. Therefore, the authors determined those two algorithms to be their model. The performances of the two algorithms on the dataset are as follows-

K-Means Algorithm Method: K-Means known as the humblest learning algorithms to explain the clustering complications'-Means clustering is a division depended clustering practice. In K-Means clustering method is the specified set of data which divided into a stationary quantity of clusters. K-means algorithm practices the iteration technique that lessens the summation of distances from each entity to its cluster centroid. This algorithm involves two segments –

1. Determine the value of K and select K centers in an arbitrary fashion.
2. Allot the given set of data entity to the nearby midpoint.

Pseudo code:

1. A Numeral of preferred clusters K and a data set is provided as input.
2. Distance, D = {A1, A2... An} comprising n data items.
3. A set of K clusters will be given as output.

The multiple stages that should be done are given as follows:

1. State the midpoint of the clusters.
2. State the distance between each data entity to the centroids.
3. Fix the location of individual cluster to mean of all data points belonging to that cluster.
4. Repetition of stage 2 and 3 until merging.

Hierarchical Clustering: Here, the objective is to harvest a hierarchical sequences of nested clusters. Hierarchical clustering constructs prototypes grounded on distance connections. Connections based clustering, likewise recognized as hierarchical clustering, and is based on the essential notion of entities being more related to nearest entities than to entities at a distance. As such these events connect entities to form clusters grounded on their expanse. A cluster can be labelled fundamentally by the extreme distance desirable to connect portions of the cluster. At unlike distances, many unlike clusters will be created, which can be characterized using a dendrogram which clarifies where the common name "hierarchical clustering" is derived [11].
   Pseudo code:

1. Shift each input entry for single items in a cluster.
2. Calculate the distance between every pair of clusters (c1, c2)
3. Take the smallest distance between the clusters or combine the pair of similar clusters.
4. Continue the step-2 till the finale standard shows up to the mark.
5. The finale standard most generally known as a finale of the distance value. Before any clustering is done, it is compulsory to decide the immediacy matrix comprising the parting between each point by means of a separation function. Then, the matrix is revitalized to display the parting between each cluster. Three methods are given below for verifying the separation in every cluster

Single Linkage: In all clusters, the path between two clusters is categorized as smallest path between two closest points [11].

$$L(s, t) = \min (D(xsi, xtj))$$

The length of the path from cluster to cluster s and t which in the left is equivalent to the span of arrow in their two closest points.

Complete Linkage: In all clusters, the path from clusters to clusters is categorized as largest path between two farthest points [11].

$$L(s, t) = \max\left(D(xsi, xtj)\right)$$

The length of the path from cluster to cluster s and t which in the left is equivalent to the span of the arrow in their two farthest points.

Average Linkage: In the clusters, the path from cluster to cluster is categorized as average path from one point in one cluster to any points in another cluster.

This continues until all the clusters are joint together. Comparisons between the two clustering techniques [12] are illustrated in Table 3.

Table 1. Illustrates the criteria for the symptoms

Distinctive	Non-distinctive
Weakness	Headache for blood pressure
Weight loss	Weakness

Table 2. The Hospitals which helped to collect data

1. Holy Family Red Crescent Hospital	4. US Bangla Hospital
2. BSMMU- Bangabandhu Sheikh Mujib Medical University	5. Impulse Hospital
3. Uttara Adhunik Hospital	6. Asian Medical College Hospital

Table 3. Comparison between K-means clustering and hierarchical clustering

Properties	K-means cluster	Hierarchical clustering
Complexity	(n)	(n^2)
Quality	Low	High
Efficiency	Less	More
Number of clusters	Predefined	Not predefined
Repeatability	May not repeatable	Repeatable
Performance	High	Low
Handling big dataset	Yes	No
Dataset types	Numeric	Numeric
Noisy data handling	No	No
High dimension handling	No	No

4 Experimental Outcomes

The graph below Fig. 2 shows classification accuracy of different algorithms for collected data. Here X axis shows different classifier algorithms and Y axis show the classification accuracy in percentage (%). The highest peak of classification accuracy is 97% and the lowest peak of classification accuracy is 75%. The graph below Fig. 3 shows classification accuracy of different algorithms for reference data. Here X axis shows different classifier algorithms and Y axis show the classification accuracy in percentage (%). The highest peak of classification accuracy is 60% and the lowest peak of classification accuracy is 55%.

Table 4. Features list

Features	Subcategory	Data Distribution
Sex	Male	56.81%
	Female	43.19%
Age	Lowest: 14	*Mean ± SD*
	Highest: 86	45.28 ± 14.80
Profession	Lowest: Rickshaw-Puller, Garments Worker, Magistrate, Receptionist, Political Leader, Assistant Accountant, Major General, Model, Unemployed, Servant, Farmer, Miscellaneous, Banker, Military	4.06%
	Highest: Housewife	20.87%
	Rest	75.07%
Marital Status	Married	82.61%
	Unmarried	17.39%
Height	Lowest: 142 cm	165.81 ± 8.47
	Highest: 193 cm	
Weight	Lowest: 41 kg	67.23 ± 11.64
	Highest: 99 kg	
Breathing Problem	Yes	23.19%
	No	76.81%
Stress	Yes	62.32%
	No	37.68%
Work Load	Low	33.04%
	Normal	25.80%
	Medium	30.14%
	High	11.01%
Food Habit	Non –Vegetarian	77.68%
	Vegetarian	10.43%
	Mixed	11.88%
Heart-Rate (bpm)	Lowest: 50 bpm	176.12 ± 12.42
	Highest: 124 bpm	
Systolic (mmHg)	Lowest: 90 mmHg	126.60 ± 15.85
	Highest: 200 mmHg	
Diastolic (mmHg)	Lowest: 10 mmHg	81.22 ± 12.29
	Highest: 110 mmHg	
Blood Sugar Rate Before Meal	Lowest: 3.1 mmol/L	8.61 ± 4.56
	Highest: 23.8 mmol/L	
Blood Sugar Rate After Meal	Lowest: 3.7 mmol/L	12.55 ± 6.00
	Highest: 28.8 mmol/L	

*SD – Standard Deviation

Features	Subcategory	Data Distribution
Urine-Color-Before- Meal	Normal	24.64%
	Straw	3.48%
	Yellow	11.01%
	Pale Yellow	14.20%
	Deep Amber	6.38%
	Green	30.72%
	Orange	3.19%
	Blue	5.80%
	Light Green	0.58%
Urine-Color-After- Meal	No Significant Change	31.59%
	Normal	14.78%
	Red	1.16%
	Orange	4.64%
	Blue	1.74%
	Green Yellow	0.58%
	Light Green	1.74%
	Pale Yellow	3.19%
	Yellow	8.12%
	Green	32.17%
Drug History	Yes	94.78%
	No	5.22%
Physical-Activity	Normal	44.93%
	Hard	18.84%
	Medium	36.23%
Smoking (per day)	Lowest: 0	2.83 ± 3.42
	Highest: 12	
Headache-for-High-Blood-Pressure	Yes	62.32%
	No	37.68%
Weakness	Yes	87.83%
	No	12.17%
Diabetes Mellitus	Yes	8.41%
	No	31.59%
Chest Pain	Yes	3.62%
	No	26.38%
Weight Loss	Yes	69.86%
	No	30.14%
Class	Distinctive	51.01%
	Non-Distinctive	26.09%
	Both	22.90%

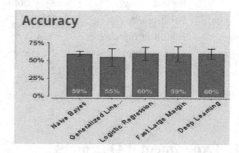

Fig. 2. Accuracy graph using collected data

Fig. 3. Accuracy graph using reference data [1]

The graph below Fig. 4 shows the classification error of different algorithm for collected data. Here X axis shows different classifier algorithm and Y axis show the classification error in percentage (%). The highest peak of classification error is 25% and the lowest peak of classification error is 3%. The graph below Fig. 5 shows classification error of different algorithms for reference data. Here X axis shows different classifier algorithms and Y axis show the classification error in percentage (%). The highest peak of classification error is 45% and the lowest peak of classification error is 40%.

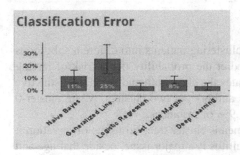

Fig. 4. Classification error for the algorithms using collected data

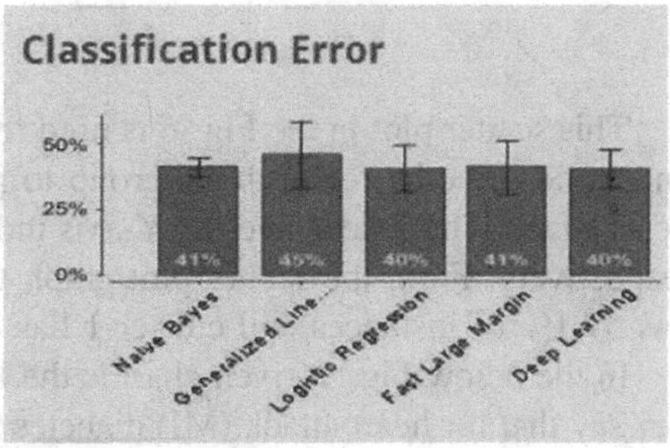

Fig. 5. Classification error for the algorithms using reference data [1]

Here Table 5 and Table 6 shows the accuracy for collected and reference data respectively. In the tables, it shows the model names and accuracy level with standard deviation. Also the training and scoring time and total timings are shown in the below tables

Table 5. Accuracy chart of data analysis

Models	Accuracy level	Standard deviation	Total timing	Training time	Scoring time
Naïve Bayes	88.8%	±5.4%	443 ms	10 ms	43 ms
Generalized linear model	74.9%	±11.6%	1 s	3 s	152 ms
Logistic regression	97.0%	±2.7%	2 s	348 ms	464 ms
Fast large margin	91.8%	±2.9%	2 s	92 ms	87 ms
Deep learning	96.9%	±2.8%	2 s	2 s	51 ms

128   Md. M. Islam et al.

Table 6. Accuracy chart of data analysis using reference data [1]

Models	Accuracy level	Standard deviation	Total timing	Training time	Scoring time
Naïve Bayes	59.2%	±3.7%	576 ms	113 ms	1 s
Generalized linear model	54.5%	±12.4%	798 ms	2 s	∼0 ms
Logistic regression	59.9%	±8.9%	999 ms	1 s	926 ms
Fast large margin	59.3%	±10.3%	2 s	196 ms	96 ms
Deep learning	59.9%	±7.3%	996 ms	2 s	29 ms

This scatter plot in the Fig. 6 is used for clustering patients into different subgroups and build a model for each subgroup to predict the probability of the risk of having heart attack. The X-axis and the Y-axis indicates the class-both and the class distinctive respectively. From the scatter plot graph the authors got two clusters, where cluster-0 has 57.1% of instances and cluster-1 has 42.9% of instances.

In the below Fig. 7 given chart is the k-means cluster tree. From the observation it can say that for heart attack (MI) diabetes mellitus is a major issue, beside that age and sex also play the imperative rule for heart attack (MI). Therefore the root attribute shows diabetes mellitus when positive. Which eventually indicates that this attribute is the most vital among the other attributes for predicting heart attack (MI).

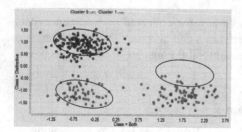

Fig. 6. Scatter plot graph generated by K-means algorithm

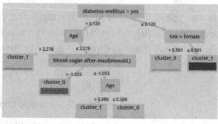

Fig. 7. K-means cluster tree

The analysis in Fig. 8 and Fig. 9 has been done using Hierarchical clustering (HC) and the clustering model is built on the full training set. Cluster 0 represents the both class and Cluster 1 represents the Distinctive class. In the Fig. 8 the percentage of correctly clustered instances is 51.3053%. Beside that in the Fig. 9 the values which is estimated using reference data [1], the percentage of correctly clustered instances obtained from the Hierarchical Clustering is 59.1176%. For collected data, if the authors ignore 'both' case data and use only cluster for 'distinctive' and 'non-distinctive' case the percentage of correctly clustered instances increased to 76.36%.

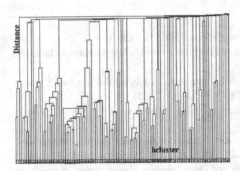

Fig. 8. Dendrogram of HC (for collected data)

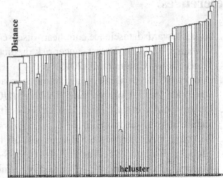

Fig. 9. Dendrogram of HC (for reference data [1])

5   Conclusion

In contrast to accuracy, the collected data shows the highest accuracy which is 97% for Logistic Regression and deep learning algorithm. On the other hand, the highest accuracy for reference data is 60% using the Logistic Regression and Deep Learning algorithm. The maximum classification error for collected data is 25% and for the reference data, the highest classification error is 45% using the Generalized Linear Model. By using the distinctive and non-distinctive case, the hierarchical clustering can correctly classify up to 76.36%, on the other hand in the K-Means section the percentage of correctly classify is only 53%. From experimental result it can be said that Hierarchical clustering is more useful for prediction and more correctly clustered than the K-Means clustering.

The general motive of the study is to predict the occurrences of heart disease (MI) more efficiently applying machine learning techniques. In this paper, the authors have offered a fresh approach grounded on k-means and hierarchical clustering. After using the algorithms and techniques the experimental results indicate that Hierarchical Clustering techniques are more efficient to predict heart attack than K-Means. Hierarchical Clustering has expanded the effectiveness of the output. This technique is one of the most efficient process to predict Myocardial Infarction or Heart Diseases. During the study the authors facing the limitation of collecting information about patients and the number of instances, a limited number of clusters. In spite of having these limitations for future implementation, the authors want to use some more algorithms in this dataset such as ANN, more specifically Neuron Fuzzy Interface System, CNN (Convolution Neural Network). To predict Myocardial Infarction disease more efficiently & effectively, developing an expert system using Machine Learning techniques would be a good idea for future purposes.

References

1. https://towardsdatascience.com/heart-disease-prediction-73468d630cfc
2. Williams, K., et al.: Breast cancer risk prediction using data mining classification techniques. Trans. Netw. Commun. **3** (2015)
3. Dangare, C.S., et al.: A data mining approach for prediction of heart disease using neural networks. Int. J. Comput. Eng. Technol. (IJCET) **3**, 30–40 (2012)
4. Jabbar, M.A., et al.: Heart diseases classification using nearest neighbor classifier with feature subset selection (2013)
5. Rajkumar, A., Reena, S.: Diagnosis of heart disease using data mining algorithms. Global J. Comput. Sci. Technol. **10**(10), 38–43 (2010)
6. Kumari, M., Godara, S.: Comparative study of data mining classification methods in cardiovascular disease prediction. Int. J. Comput. Eng. Technol. **2** (2011)
7. Cho, S.B., Kim, S.C., Chung, M.G.: Identification of novel population clusters with different susceptibilities to type 2 diabetes and their impact on the prediction of diabetes. Sci. Rep. **9** (2019)
8. Chen, W., Zhang, S., Wu, T.: A hybrid prediction model for type 2 diabetes using K-means and decision tree. In: "ICSESS" International Conference in Beijing, China (2017)
9. Rouse, M.: The essential guide to managing HR technology trends. (2018). www.searchenterpriseai.techtarget.com. Accessed 15 July 2019
10. "Median", RDocumentation (2019). www.rdocumentation.org/median. Accessed 01 July 2019
11. Sayad, D.: Hierarchical Clustering, clustering hierarchical. www.saedsayad.com. Accessed 17 July 2019
12. Shakeel, P.M., Baskar, S., Dhulipala, V.R.S., Jaber, M.M.: Cloud based framework for diagnosis of diabetes mellitus using K-means clustering. Health Inf. Sci. Syst. **6**(1), 1–7 (2018). https://doi.org/10.1007/s13755-018-0054-0

A Robust Technique for End Point Detection Under Practical Environment

Nirupam Shome[1](✉), Rabul Hussain Laskar[2](✉),
Richik Kashyap[1](✉), and Sivaji Bandyopadhyay[2]

[1] Assam University, Silchar 788011, Assam, India
nirupam_shome@yahoo.com, rknits2010@gmail.com
[2] National Institute of Technology, Silchar 788010, Assam, India
rhlaskar@ece.nits.ac.in,
sbandyopadhyay@cse.jdvu.ac.in

Abstract. Speech end point detection is the process of identifying speech boundary by digital processing technique. The performance of many of the speech processing applications largely depends on accurate end point detection. In this paper, we try to address this important issue and proposed an algorithm to identify the speech boundary. The algorithm based on frame-wise pitch and energy estimation to detect the onset and the terminus of an utterance. The performance of proposed algorithm has been evaluated for three databases and results were compared with the three state of art technique of end point detection. Experimental results reveal the validity of the proposed method and prove the significant improvement in end point detection over other techniques under observation. An accuracy of 71 to 87.6% in start point detection and 59 to 76.6% in end (termination) point detection is achieved by proposed Pitch and Energy based Detection (PED) for ±60 ms resolution window. In terms of error in detection, an average improvement of 26.9 ms in start point and 200.5 ms in end point is attained in compare to other methods for different speech corpus. This investigation clearly indicates that the PED technique offers superior results in terms of accuracy and error in detection for different data conditions.

Keywords: Voice activity detection · Glottal activity detection · Vowel on set point detection · Pitch and energy based detection · Accuracy in end point detection · Error in end point detection

1 Introduction

The performance of a system mainly depends on input signal condition. The input signal may contain redundant parts along with valuable information. The redundant information primarily present before and after the region of interest and it drastically degrade the performance of many speech processing applications [1–3]. It is essential to remove these unwanted portions in order to improve the system performance of a speech based application. The removal of these unwanted parts by identifying the speech boundary is called end point detection. Precise end point detection reduces the computational complexity by optimizing the dimensionality of speech signal [4], which is very much essential in application like speech and speaker recognitions. Moreover, end point

© Springer Nature Singapore Pte Ltd. 2020
A. Bhattacharjee et al. (Eds.): MIND 2020, CCIS 1241, pp. 131–144, 2020.
https://doi.org/10.1007/978-981-15-6318-8_12

detection finds application in fundamental frequency estimation, stop consonant identification, and formant extraction. The overall system performance of text-dependent speaker verification is largely dependent on proper end point detection [5–8].

End point detection can be broadly classified into two categories, threshold based approaches and pattern matching approaches. In the threshold based approach, acoustic features are extracted and compared with predefined threshold to identify speech frames. And for pattern matching, speech and noise models are created. Based on these models speech and non-speech classification are done. Several features have been reported in literature that are useful for end point detection, are STE [9], ZCR [10], Entropy [11], MFCC [12], HMM [13], and wavelet transform [14]. To identify the end points of speech signal several end point detection techniques have been reported in literature. Among all techniques, energy based voice activity detection (VAD) [4, 15] are most popular for end point detection. Energy base methods perform well for clean data conditions but with degraded data performance became poor [16]. In [17], periodicity based VAD was used and it shows better results than conventional energy based VAD. Another technique proposed in [6], used vowel onset point (VOP) to detect end points of speech signal. This method gives better result than energy based methods but have some problems in detecting begin and end points from first and last VOPs. An improvement in VOP can be achieved by glottal activity detection (GAD) as it includes sonorant consonants. This is helpful in accurate end point detection. As we know, the entropy of noise and speech are different and it is used to identify the end points of speech sample in [11]. An improvement on this algorithm has been achieved by changing the spectral probability density function [18]. A linear pattern classifier based one-dimensional Mahalanobis distance function [19, 20] has been used to find the end point of speech in [4]. This method relies on the statistical properties of background noise and physiological aspect of speech production. In most of the algorithms energy is one of the major criterions for speech activity detection and high frequency regions are considered as speech regions. But as we know most of the noises are in high frequency range, so it significantly affects the overall performance of any system.

In this article, we propose a new algorithm based on frame-wise energy and pitch estimation. As we know that the voiced segments contains high energy compare to unvoiced and silent part, here we calculate segmented energy and compare it with mean energy of whole signal. Under the influence of noise and other background signal, segmented energy can be large in unvoiced part. To compensate this error, segmented pitch information has been incorporated with segmented energy. Pitch detection has been done by normalized cross correlation function (NCCF) as it is appropriate than normal auto correlation function [21] and it is frequently used in various pitch detection algorithm [22]. The speech frames that satisfying both energy and pitch criterion are considered as voiced frame. The first and last voiced frames are taken as starting and ending point of the utterance respectively. The performance of the proposed algorithm has been evaluated for different dataset having practical noise.

The rest of the article is organized as follows. In Sect. 2 we explain the baseline system for end point detection. Section 3 presents the detailed discussion of proposed PED method alon with algorithm. Section 4 illustrates several experimentation and comparative analysis along with description of speech databases used for our analysis. The conclusion is given in Sect. 5.

2 Baseline Methods for End Point Detection

For detecting the end point of speech signal, there are numerous algorithms developed till now. Here we have chosen three state of art techniques to assess the performance. The results of the state of art techniques are compared with the proposed method in subsequent sections.

2.1 Methods Used to Evaluate the Performance of End Point Detection

The techniques used for performance evaluation are as follows:

Energy Based Voice Activity Detection (VAD) [23]. In this technique, energy based VAD has been used for end point detection. Here input speech signal are segmented in short frames of 20 ms with 50% frame shift. Then the energy of each frame has been calculated and compared with a predefined threshold. If frame energy is more than that of threshold value, it is considered to be a speech frame otherwise non-speech frame.

Glottal Activity Detection (GAD) [24]. GAD method discussed here can be divided into mainly two parts. In the first part, ZFFS is obtained from the zero frequency filter and applying adaptive threshold on ZFFS, glottal regions are identified. And in the second part, for GAD low threshold is set and it is increasing in finite steps until the number of samples identified is less than that of VAD. Finally, glottal and non-glottal regions are decided by applying an optimum threshold for the energy frame of ZFFS.

Vowel on Set Point Detection (VOP) [6]. This vowel onset point detection method combined the evidences from spectral peaks, excitation source and modulation spectrum energies. This VOP detection technique is used in our study of end point detection. Complementary information about the VOPs can be obtained from each of these three features. So, combining these individual evidences VOPs are detected. Out of the detected VOPs, the first and the last VOPs are taken as the anchor point. Since the speech utterances are starts before the first on set point and ends after the last on set point, the start and end point are selected 500 ms before and after the first and last VOP respectively.

3 Proposed End Point Detection Method

To improve the performance, a new end point detection technique is proposed and explained here.

3.1 Pitch and Energy Based Detection (PED)

Speech coding is an essential part of digital communication system. With the increase in telecommunication services, speech coding development progressed simultaneously. A good quality, low bit-rate speech codecs become essential and substantial amount of research [25] has been done to meet this requirement. For speech synthesis applications features extraction from speech signals is very crucial and become challenging. The fundamental frequency is one of the significant features and commonly known as pitch. The rate of vibration of human vocal cords corresponds to the fundamental frequency

(F0). In various speech processing systems accurate pitch detection is very much essential. For speech coding, pitch provides essential information about the nature of the excitation source and from pitch contour, speaker recognition, emotion state determination, speech activity detection, and many others task can be performed [22]. In literature many pitch detection methods have been reported: autocorrelation method [25], HPS [22], RAPT [26], SIFT [21]. The error rate considering voicing decision is quite high for most of the methods, but in case of voiced pitch estimation accuracy is high. Pitch detection algorithms can be categorized into three fundamental categories as time-domain based tracking, frequency domain based tracking and joint time-frequency domain based tracking.

Pitch and Energy Based Algorithm to Detect End Points. In the proposed methodology, the end points of speech signal are detected by the pitch information along with the energy associated with the speech signal. Short term analysis of speech signal is used for our study. Short term analysis is used because the speech signal exhibits quasi-periodic behavior. Since speech signals are non-stationary over a long period, short term analysis is used. In short frame, some similarities can be observed in speech signal.

In this proposed method, the signal is first divided into frames of length 20 ms with 50% overlap and then averaged energy of i-th frame is calculated as,

$$([S_E]_F)_i = \frac{1}{M} \sum_{n=0}^{M-1} s^2(n) \tag{1}$$

Where, $s(n)$ is n-th speech sample and M denotes number of samples/length of i-th frame.

The energy of the complete signal can be measured by averaging the frame-wise energies of all frames

$$[S_E]_T = \frac{1}{N} \sum_{i=o}^{N-1} ([S_E]_F)_i \tag{2}$$

Where, N represents total number of frames in speech signal

The segmented energy has been compared with the predefined threshold. The threshold is determined by multiplying energy of whole signal with a scaling factor of suitable value.

$$E_{th} = \alpha * [S_E]_T \tag{3}$$

Where, E_{th} represents energy threshold and α is the scaling factor.

The scaling factor (α) is decided experimentally, the best performing value has taken for our analysis.

At the same time, frame wise pitch is calculated using normalized cross correlation function method (NCCF) [15] as,

$$([S_P]_F)_i = \frac{\sum_{n=0}^{M-m-1} s(n).s(n+m)}{\sqrt{\sum_{n=0}^{M-m-1} s^2(n). \sum_{n=0}^{M-m-1} s^2(n+m)}}, 0 \le m \le Q \tag{4}$$

Where, $s(n)$ is the speech frame with length M, m is a lag and Q is the number of auto correlation points to be computed.

The averaged pitch of whole signal can be found out by,

$$[S_P]_T = \frac{1}{N} \sum_{i=o}^{N-1} ([S_P]_F)_i \tag{5}$$

This averaged pitch value is scaled with a suitable scaling factor to get the pitch threshold and can be represented as,

$$P_{th} = \beta * [S_P]_T \tag{6}$$

Where, β is the scaling factor and its value can be obtained by experimental analysis.

The energy and the pitch of each window have been calculated simultaneously and compared with the respective thresholds. If both frame energy and frame pitch satisfies the threshold value, the frame is considered as the speech frame otherwise non-speech frame.

$$\text{Speech frames,} \, S_F = [S_E]_F \geq E_{th} \wedge [S_P]_F \geq P_{th} \tag{7}$$

This process is continued for the entire signal and identifies the speech and non-speech frames. To decide the start point and end point, minimum of four consecutive speech frames has been explored. The first sample of the first quad of speech frame taken as the start point and the last sample of the last quad of speech frames considered as the end point. The end points of the speech signals have been decided by the method described above and results of our proposed method based on this technique. The steps involved in the proposed algorithm are discussed below.

Sequence of steps	Pitch and Energy based detection (PED)
1	The speech signal analyzed at 8 kHz sampling frequency and window size of 20 ms with frame shift of 10 ms
2	The total energy and frame wise energy of the signal has been calculated
3	The average of the total energy with suitable scaling factor has been used to set the energy threshold
4	Frame wise pitch has been calculated using NCCF and average of pitch values of the whole signal has been measured
5	Average pitch value with suitable scaling factor has been chosen for the threshold evaluation
6	Frame wise energy and pitch value has been compared with the energy and pitch threshold, if it exceeds both the threshold then the frame is considered as speech frame otherwise non-speech frame
7	Check for four consecutive such frames, the first sample point of the first quad is taken as start point and the last sample point of the last quad is taken as end point

Figure 1 illustrates the comparison of different end point detection techniques. Long vertical dotted lines represents ground truth manual marking. Performance analysis of all the methods has been done by taking this dotted line as anchor points. Figure 1(a) shows speech signal with detected end point by energy based VAD. Figure 1(b) shows speech signal and it's begin and end point identified by GAD method. Speech sample with first and last VOPs as end point are shown in Fig. 1(c). And Fig. 1(d) illustrates end points marked by the proposed PED technique along with the speech sample.

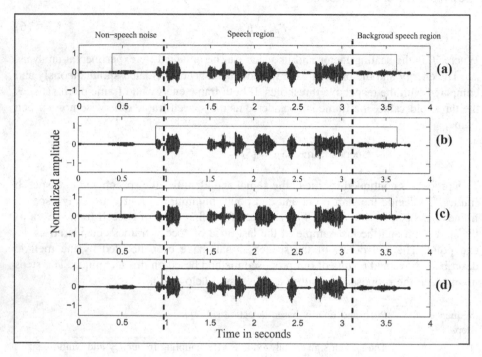

Fig. 1. Illustration of begin and end point detection by four methods. **a** End points detected by Energy based VAD. **b** End points detected by GAD. **c** End points detected by VOP. **d** End points detected by Proposed PED. Long vertical dotted lines represents ground truth manual marking of end points.

4   Experimental Results and Discussion

In this section, experimental results are discussed and comparative analyses of proposed method with existing methods are provided. To perform experiments, here we chose CSLU database [27], IITG-MV SR database [28] and database collected at NIT Silchar [29]. The CSLU corpus consists of telephonic speech from about 500 contributors.

This corpus has been recorded in twelve sessions within two year period. In this database different types of utterances are there viz. Limited vocabulary utterances, Numbers, Words, Phrases, Spontaneous Speech. Our experimental results are on phrases as we are interested to evaluate end points of speech samples. IITG-MV SR database has been recorded by the telephone network, for remote person authentication using speech mode. The data was collected for one academic semester from 325 speakers (286 males and 39 females) of 25–35 years age groups. Data recording was done in different degraded environmental conditions, which includes background speech, background noise, and other environmental conditions. To cover the practical dimensions data has been recorded through the personal mobile handsets. To facilitate the development of online speaker verification system through the telephone network, data collection has been done at NIT Silchar,. An interactive voice response system (IVRS) was developed to guide the user during data collection. Data collection was performed in three different modes namely text dependent, text independent and voice password. Here number of speakers are 298, out of which 247 Male speakers and 51 female speakers. The speakers include students and research scholars of NIT Silchar in the age group of 22–28. Speakers are indorsed to talk in their normal mode of speaking. The database collected in uncontrolled environments: laboratory, corridor, class room and hostel room etc. To study the effect of practical noise, this noisy speech corpus expected to be suitable.

In this study, three state of art techniques: energy based voice activity detection (VAD), glottal activity detection (GAD), and vowel on set point detection (VOP) has been chosen to identify the start and end point of a speech signal. The results of these methods are compared with the proposed PED method of end point detection. Manually detected end points have taken as the anchor points for each experiment. For each data sample, end points are evaluated manually to perceive the performance of different end point detection approaches. The performances of all techniques are expressed in terms of accuracy in detection and error in detection. To calculate the accuracy resolution windows of different size has been chosen and put across the manually detected end points. The end points detected by the algorithms within the resolution window considered as true end point, otherwise not. For our study resolution windows of ±10 ms, ±20 ms, ±30 ms, ±40 ms, ±50 ms, and ±60 ms has been taken to evaluate performance of all the methods. Accuracy is measured for each speech sample and averaged value is taken as final result. Another parameter to represent the performance is error in detection. Same as the earlier case, here also manually detected end points have taken as the reference point to calculate the error in detection. From the reference point, the deviation of detected end point has been calculated in millisecond. Large detection error means more deviation from anchor point and vise-versa.

With the help of formula given below error in end point detection has been estimated.

$$\text{Error in start point detection, } E_s = |s_M - s_A| \tag{8}$$

$$\text{Error in end point detection, } E_e = |e_M - e_A| \tag{9}$$

Where s_M is manually identified start point, e_M is manually identified end point, s_A is algorithmically detected start point, e_A is algorithmically detected end point. For our analysis three databases has been chosen. The performance of the different end point detection methods under three different dataset explained in subsequent sections.

4.1   Result Analysis for CSLU Database

Phonetically rich phrases have been selected for our analysis. This study is mainly concentrated on short speech analysis to identify the speech boundary effectively.

The performance of the various end point detection techniques on CSLU database is presented in Table 1. It can be seen that, for ±10 ms and ±20 ms resolution window, the start point detection using VAD is comparatively much better than the other methods. When the resolution window increased gradually from ±30 ms to ±60 ms, the performance of the proposed technique improves compare to other techniques under observation in case of start point detection. For lower resolution window GAD performs better than VOP and the proposed method in case of start point detection. The VOP based end point detection technique shows very poor results in case of both start and end point detection. However for resolution window greater than ±40 ms, the start point detection performance improved quite a bit, but not close enough to other methods. In case of ending point detection, VOP based approach utterly fails in every cases. Even for ±60 ms window resolution the accuracy is under 2%, which is very much undesirable. End (Termination) point detection based on GAD is also not very convincing, as it can achieve only 27.6% accuracy even for ±60 ms resolution window. The performance of VAD in ending point detection is much better than that of VOP and GAD based techniques. In case of the proposed method, the accuracy in ending point detection indications best result irrespective of resolution window. For ±10 ms window accuracy is 61.9% and it is increases gradually with the increase in observation window. Hence, the accuracy of the proposed method outperforms both in start and end point detection for observation window is greater than ±20 ms.

Table 1. Performance comparison of end point detection methods for CSLU database in terms of accuracy (SP = Start Point; EP = End Point)

End point detection method	Accuracy (in %) in specified resolution window (in millisecond)											
	±10		±20		±30		±40		±50		±60	
	SP	EP	SP	EP	SP	EP	SP	EP	SP	EP	SP	EP
VAD [23]	66.6	36.19	79.0	58.0	80	63.8	81.9	65.7	83.8	70.47	84.7	73.3
GAD [24]	33.3	2.85	54.2	9.5	61.9	15.2	72.3	20.9	74.2	25.7	82.8	27.6
VOP [6]	8.5	0	18.0	0	31.4	0	49.5	0	62.8	1.9	69.5	1.9
PED [Proposed]	19.0	61.9	48.5	62.8	78.0	62.8	84.76	71.4	86.6	74.2	87.6	75.2

Another way to characterize the result is error in end point detection and it gives an overall idea the performance of each method. Comparisons of error in detection for various techniques are given in Fig. 2. From the figure, it is observed that the error in case of starting point is minimum for VAD, whereas maximum for VOP. And for GAD and proposed methods results almost equal, little bit higher than VAD. The error value in case of end (termination) point is minimum for proposed method as compare to other methods. The proposed PED method is suitable for end point detection as its start point detection performance is much closer to the best result and end (termination) point detection gives finest result as compare to other methods.

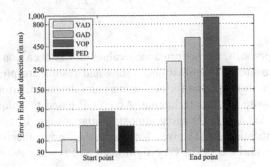

Fig. 2. Performance analysis of end point detection methods for CSLU database in term of error in end point detection (in millisecond)

4.2   Result Analysis for IITG-MV SR Database

In this set of experiments, IIG-MV SR database has been used check the performance of different methods under practical environment. The results of these experiments are presented in Table 2 and observations are discussed here.

In the first approach, accuracy in end point detection has been explicated for different resolution window. In case of VAD based end point detection, accuracy for smaller window (±10 ms, ±20 ms, ±30 ms) is better than any other methods. With the increase in the window size proposed PED methods gives better result than VAD. For GAD, it has been witnessed that the performance is poor than VAD and PED but better than VOP for higher resolution windows (±40 ms, ±50 ms, ±60 ms). For lower window GAD performs better than VOP and PED. Even in higher resolution window performance of VOP is very bad. When PED is used to identify the speech boundary, it has been observed that though it shows poor result in small window but for large window PED outperforms all the techniques. Here an improvement of 6–17% in case of start point and 4–15% in case of end point can be observed compare to VAD and GAD.

Table 2. Performance comparison of end point detection methods for IITG-MV SR database in terms of accuracy (SP = Start Point; EP = End Point)

End point detection Method	Accuracy (in %) in specified resolution window (in millisecond)											
	±10		±20		±30		±40		±50		±60	
	SP	EP	SP	EP	SP	EP	SP	EP	SP	EP	SP	EP
VAD [23]	34	24	42	38	48	44	50	48	53	50	58	55
GAD [24]	8	18	22	30	35	34	48	38	51	41	54	48
VOP [6]	2	4	9	5	13	8	18	9	23	10	31	12
PED [Proposed]	7	5	13	15	37	22	56	40	66	56	71	59

In the second approach, the performance evaluation has been done in term of error in detection from manually identified end points and results are presented in Fig. 3. From the figure, it is observed that for beginning point detection, error in PED method is minimum in compare to other technique. And VOP based technique error is maximum among all. VAD and GAD show almost similar results. In case of end (termination) point identification, GAD gives less error than any other methods. But the difference of error with PED is not very significant and is only about 20 ms.

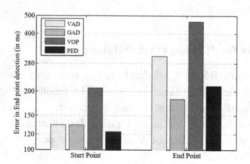

Fig. 3. Performance analysis of end point detection methods for IITG-MV SR database in term of error in end point detection (in millisecond)

4.3 Result Analysis for Database Collected at NIT Silchar

In this subsection performance analysis has been done using data collected at NIT Silchar premises. The phonetically rich sentences are chosen to develop this database with fully uncontrolled environment. The result analysis is shown in Table 3.

In case of accuracy evaluation, the performance of VAD based system gives similar results as it is for IITG MV SR dataset. For smaller resolution window (±10 ms, ±20 ms) this method provide better results. But with the increase in the resolution window other methods shows improved results. When window size of ±30 ms, ±40 ms, ±50 ms, ±60 ms are chosen, GAD shows superior results in compare to VAD and VOP but inferior to PED in case of start point detection. For end (termination) point detection, VOP based technique not shown convincing result for every resolution window. For lower window size VAD gives improved results. With the increment in window size above ±30 ms, beginning point detection with PED improved significantly compare to other methods. It reaches up to 85.1% for ±60 ms window, which is more than 22–25% than others. For termination point detection also an improvement of 8–14% can be achieved with PED over VAD and GAD.

Table 3. Performance comparison of end point detection methods for NIT Silchar database in terms of accuracy (SP = Start Point; EP = End Point)

End point detection method	Accuracy (in %) in specified resolution window (in millisecond)											
	±10		±20		±30		±40		±50		±60	
	SP	EP	SP	EP	SP	EP	SP	EP	SP	EP	SP	EP
VAD [23]	43.5	35.6	50.4	51.4	51.4	58.4	56.4	62.3	58.4	65.3	62.3	68.6
GAD [24]	13.8	19.8	37.6	31.6	52.4	39.6	60.4	52.4	62.3	58.4	63.3	62.3
VOP [6]	12.8	0	19.8	2.98	26.7	2.9	31.6	7.9	38.6	7.9	57.4	12.8
PED [Proposed]	20.2	13.8	34.0	21.2	52.2	32.9	74.4	50.8	85.1	64.9	85.1	76.6

It can be seen from Fig. 4 that the error in detection for VAD and PED are quite similar. For starting point detection with PED, reduction in error (10–28 ms) can be achieved over other methods. Whereas for ending point detection, an improvement of 12–70 ms compare to GAD and VOP can be achieved and in case of VAD results are similar. Overall speech boundary marking is better with PED in terms of accuracy and error in detection.

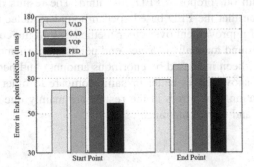

Fig. 4. Performance analysis of end point detection methods for NIT Silchar database in term of error in end point detection (in millisecond)

4.4 Comparative Investigation of the Four Methods

In the last three subsections, we have presented and analyzed the performance of three state of art methods along with our suggested method. It is observed that for lower resolution windows (±10, ±20, ±30 ms) energy based VAD shows much better results compare to other methods for all dataset but for higher resolution windows (±40, ±50, ±60 ms) PED and GAD performs better. It is concluded that for noise free signal VAD shows better result but in case of non-uniform (in time) noise results are not satisfactory. GAD and PED gives similar results in terms of accuracy and error in detection as both the methods uses source information to locate speech activities. When we compare VOP with other methods, results are unsatisfactory for all databases. VOP cannot be the criterion for end point detection of a sentence as every vowel must be surrounded by consonants. And duration of the consonants is not same and should be considered carefully in case of speech end point detection.

From these analyses, it can be observed that PED provides enhanced results for all dataset in both performance evaluation parameters. We have used practical corpus and it contains various unwanted signals. When a speech sample got affected by noise, amplitude increases significantly but these regions have no periodicity /repetition pattern. So pitch information is absent for these regions. PED combines both the energy and pitch information to identify the end points, so it gives improved results. Failure of PED algorithm is due the speech samples having background speech or speech like noise.

5 Conclusion

In this paper we have discussed some well-known techniques that can be used to identify begin and end point of speech sample. With help of these state of art techniques, we have traced the speech boundary and evaluate the performance for different datasets. As the performances of these methods have some limitations, we have developed an algorithm which is based on pitch and energy detection (PED) from speech sample to detect speech boundaries. We have performed a comparative analysis of these methods with our proposed PED algorithm. The results of our experiments give a clear indication that the PED based speech boundary detection method shows significant amount of improvement over other methods. With the compromise in large resolution window around manually detected end points, performance of our system in terms of accuracy has been increased by enormous amount. And performance in terms of error in detection shows either better or same compare to other methods for each experimental observation. The errors in the results are mainly due the noise and low energy during begin and end of utterances.

References

1. Campbell, J.: Speaker recognition: a tutorial. Proc. IEEE **85**, 1437–1462 (1997)
2. Karray, L., Martin, A.: Towards improving speech detection robustness for speech recognition in adverse conditions. Speech Commun. **40**, 261–276 (2003)
3. Sangwan, A., Chiranth, M., Jamadagni, H., Sah, R., Venkatesha Prasad, R., Gaurav, V.: VAD techniques for real-time speech transmission on the internet. In: 5th IEEE International Conference on High Speed Networks and Multimedia Communication, pp. 46–50 (2002)

4. Saha, G., Chakroborty, S., Senapati, S.: A new silence removal and endpoint detection algorithm for speech and speaker recognition applications. In: Proceedings of the 11th National Conference on Communications (NCC), pp. 291–295 (2005)
5. Furui, S.: Cepstral analysis technique for automatic speaker verification. IEEE Trans. Acoust. Speech Signal Process. **29**, 254–272 (1981)
6. Prasanna, S.R.M., Zachariah, J., Yegnanarayana, B.: Begin-end detection using vowel onset points. In: Proceedings of Workshop on Spoken Language Processing, TIFR, Mumbai (2003)
7. Rabiner, L., Juang, B.: Fundamentals of Speech Recognition. Pearson Education, Delhi (2005)
8. Yegnanarayana, B., Prasanna, S., Zachariah, J., Gupta, C.: Combining evidence from source, suprasegmental and spectral features for a fixed-text speaker verification system. IEEE Trans. Speech Audio Process. **13**, 575–582 (2005)
9. Lamel, L., Rabiner, L., Rosenberg, A., Wilpon, J.: An improved endpoint detector for isolated word recognition. IEEE Trans. Acoust. Speech Signal Process. **29**, 777–785 (1981)
10. Rabiner, L., Sambur, M.: An algorithm for determining the endpoints of isolated utterances. Bell Syst. Tech. J. **54**, 297–315 (1975)
11. Shen, J., Hung, J., Lee, L.: Robust entropy-based endpoint detection for speech recognition in noisy environments. In: 5th International Conference on Spoken Language Processing (ICSLP 1998). ISCA Archive, Sydney (1998)
12. Wu, G., Lin, C.: Word boundary detection with mel-scale frequency bank in noisy environment. IEEE Trans. Speech Audio Process. **8**, 541–554 (2000)
13. Sohn, J., Kim, N., Sung, W.: A statistical model-based voice activity detection. IEEE Signal Process. Lett. **6**, 1–3 (1999)
14. Aghajani, K., Manzuri, M., Karami, M., Tayebi, H.: A robust voice activity detection based on wavelet transform. In: Second International Conference on Electrical Engineering, pp. 1–5 (2008)
15. Savoji, M.: A robust algorithm for accurate endpointing of speech signals. Speech Commun. **8**, 45–60 (1989)
16. Pradhan, G.: Speaker verification under degraded conditions using vowel-like and nonvowel-like regions (2013)
17. Hautam, V., Tuononen, M., Niemi-Laitinen, T., Fränti, P.: Improving speaker verification by periodicity based voice activity detection. In: Proceedings of 12th International Conference on Speech and Computer (SPECOM 2007), pp. 645–650 (2007)
18. Jia, C., Xu, B.: An improved entropy-based endpoint detection algorithm. In: International Symposium on Chinese Spoken Language Processing (ISCSLP), Beijing (2002)
19. Duda, R., Hart, P., Stork, D.: Pattern Classification. Wiley, New York (2001)
20. Sarma, V., Venugopal, D.: Studies on pattern recognition approach to voiced-unvoiced-silence classification. In: IEEE International Conference on Acoustics, Speech, and Signal Processing, ICASSP 1978, vol. 3, pp. 1–4 (1978)
21. Rabiner, L., Cheng, M., Rosenberg, A., McGonegal, C.: A comparative performance study of several pitch detection algorithms. IEEE Trans. Acoust. Speech Signal Process. **24**, 399–418 (1976)
22. Benesty, J., Sondhi, M.M., Huang, Y.A. (eds.): Springer Handbook of Speech Processing. SH. Springer, Heidelberg (2008). https://doi.org/10.1007/978-3-540-49127-9
23. Freeman, D., Boyd, I.: Voice Activity Detection, US Patent, Patent No. US 276765 A (1994)
24. Rama Murty, K., Yegnanarayana, B., Anand Joseph, M.: Characterization of glottal activity from speech signals. IEEE Signal Process. Lett. **16**, 469–472 (2009)
25. Kondoz, A.: Digital Speech: Coding for Low Bit Rate Communication Systems. Wiley, New York (2005)

26. Talkin, D.: A robust algorithm for pitch tracking (RAPT). In: Kleijn, W., Paliwal, K. (eds.) Speech Coiling and Synthesis, pp. 495–518. Elsevier Science (1995)
27. Cole, R., Noel, M., Noel, V.: The CSLU speaker recognition corpus. In: Fifth International Conference on Spoken Language Processing, pp. 3167–3170 (1998)
28. Haris, B.C., Pradhan, G., Misra, A., Prasanna, S.R.M., Das, R.K., Sinha, R.: Multivariability speaker recognition database in Indian scenario. Int. J. Speech Technol. **15**, 441–453 (2012). https://doi.org/10.1007/s10772-012-9140-x
29. Das, R., Jelil, S., Prasanna, S.: Multi-style speaker recognition database in practical conditions. Int. J. Speech Technol. **21**, 409–419 (2017)

An Explainable Machine Learning Approach for Definition Extraction

Priyanshu Kumar⬩, Aadarsh Singh⬩, Pramod Kumar(✉)⬩,
and Chiranjeev Kumar⬩

Department of Computer Science and Engineering,
Indian Institute of Technology (Indian School of Mines), Dhanbad, Jharkhand, India
kpriyanshu256@gmail.com, aadarshsingh191198@gmail.com,
k.pramod.iitdhn@gmail.com, chiranjeev@iitism.ac.in

Abstract. With the outburst of available data, Definition Extraction has emerged as an important technique as it is a precursor to many other tasks like ontology generation, glossary creation, and question answering. Definition Extraction is most commonly treated as a binary classification problem of definitional and non-definitional sentences. Traditional techniques for definition extraction involve rule-based approaches, which did not yield good results because of the overwhelming complexity of natural language. Incorporating linguistic information via syntactic dependencies turned out to be useful in identifying sentences containing a definition. In this paper, we explore the performance of Transformer based architectures, like Bidirectional Encoder Representations from Transformers (BERT), which produce state-of-the-art results on many Natural Language Processing (NLP) tasks. Experiments on an annotated dataset of definitional sentences prove that BERT obtains results comparable to the state-of-the-art benchmark. In further experiments, we look under the hood of BERT, trying to figure out the reason for its success. Analyzing the outputs of the attention heads reveals that BERT captures not only syntactic dependencies but many other relevant dependencies within the words of the sentence, which proves beneficial in Definition Extraction.

Keywords: BERT · Self attention · Definition Extraction · NLP · Syntactic dependencies

1 Introduction

Over time, the informational sources and informational contents have increased exponentially. In this vast sea of information, dictionaries and glossaries play an essential role in human life. However, constructing and compiling these dictionaries and glossaries is a tedious task, given the time constraints. Definition Extraction (DE), the process of identifying definitions from free-text, helps us

The authors Priyanshu Kumar and Aadarsh Singh have equal contribution in the work.

© Springer Nature Singapore Pte Ltd. 2020
A. Bhattacharjee et al. (Eds.): MIND 2020, CCIS 1241, pp. 145–155, 2020.
https://doi.org/10.1007/978-981-15-6318-8_13

in constructing dictionaries efficiently. In the paper's context, the task of Definition Extraction is solved as classifying text sentences into whether they contain a definition or not. In general, a definition has the following components.

- The DEFINIENDUM field (DF) i.e., the word being defined.
- The DEFINITOR field (VF) i.e., the verb phrase used to introduce the definition.
- The DEFINIENS field (GF) i.e., genus phrase or the hypernym.
- The REST field (RF) i.e., additional clauses that help to distinguish the definiendum from its genus.

Figure 1 shows an example definition with the fields present in it.

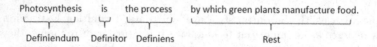

Fig. 1. Fields in a sample definition

Many researchers have used DE for developing question answering systems [13], ontology generation [21], supporting terminology applications [10,14,15] and for developing e-learning applications [1,18].

In recent years, most of the methods proposed for DE require explicit creation of a feature vector from the text data. Despite the advent of the deep learning era, proposed methods work better when provided with external features like syntactic dependencies. A syntactic dependency is a relation between two words in a sentence with one word being the governor and the other being the dependent of the relation We believe that since NLP's ImageNet moment has arrived, we can get away with external feature creation for definition extraction and focus more on text preprocessing, which seems more necessary in today's scenario.

Since the performance of Transformer [17] based architectures has not been explored for Definition Extraction, we propose to explore BERT [4]. BERT produces state of the art results in many NLP tasks with limited fine-tuning on task-specific training data. BERT consists of the Transformer architecture, which relies on Attention rather than conventional Long Short Term Memory (LSTM) or Convolutional Neural Network (CNN) units. It has deep bidirectional representations that have been learned from an unlabeled corpus by a Masked Language Model (MLM) inspired by the Cloze task [16]. An MLM randomly masks a token in the input sentence and tries to predict it using both the left and right contexts. Moreover, BERT also utilizes a "next sentence prediction" task (to be discussed later in the Proposed Methodology section of the paper) that jointly pre-trains text-pair representations for a better understanding of the corpus.

With a bit of data preprocessing, BERT helps us to achieve results comparable to the state of the art results on a benchmark dataset for Definition Extraction. Thus, BERT avoids the requirement for external features for training.

Next, we try to understand our model as per Machine Learning Explainability i.e. to extract human-understandable insights from any machine learning model such as, what features in the data did the model think are most important, etc. For this, we analyze the attention weights of the model when predicting a query sentence. We observe that the attention mechanism is strong enough to capture dependencies between the tokens of a sentence implicitly.

The rest of the paper is organized as follows: Related work with its limitations has been discussed in Sect. 2. The proposed methodology has been elaborated in Sect. 3. Section 4 comes up with the experimental result on the dataset along with its validation. Section 5 concludes the paper.

2   Related Work

Kobyliński & Przepiókowski [8] used a "Random Forest-based classifier" to classify definitions, with their main focus being the imbalance in the definition data.

Navigli & Velardi [11], did a major work in the field of definition extraction using a generalization of word lattices to model textual definitions in the form of Definiendum, Definitor, Definiens and Rest. However, this approach fails for generalization of definitions, especially the ones that do not follow the conventional semantics i.e common definition formats.

Jin et al. [7] in their work, built DefMiner, a supervised sequence labelling system that used shallow parsing and dependency features. The use of dependency features gave a considerable improvement in the scores on the WCL dataset [12].

Borg et al. [3] explored the performance of genetic algorithms (GA) on the task of definition extraction with definition sentences containing *"is a"*. They created a feature vector for sentences using patterns and tags found in the sentences. Later, GA was applied to find out the corresponding weights of these features. However, the model was not generic enough for unseen definitions.

Anke & Saggion [1] tried to achieve superior performance using CRF (Conditional Random Fields) on definition extraction. They trained CRF with lexical, terminological, and structural features extracted from data and obtained promising results and observations from the results.

Anke & Schockaert [5] took advantage of the subtrees in the dependency parsing of a sentence. Using the subtrees, they formed the feature vector of a sentence. These vectors were then used for training various classification algorithms available in Weka.

Anke et al. [6] extended the idea of machine learning techniques of having classifiers trained with data incorporated with linguistic patterns. In addition to linguistic patterns, they also used semantic information into the training classifiers. The use of SensEmbed helped to reveal the semantic compactness of definition containing sentences.

Li et al. [9] attempted the problem of definition extraction using deep learning. By applying some data preprocessing (replacing some selected words with POS tags), they carried out Sentence Feature Generation using LSTM (Long

Short Term Memory) cells and obtained brilliant results. The LSTM cells are capable of extracting definitional structures from sentences.

Authors in [2] incorporated syntactic information (syntactic dependencies and dependency labels) along with the text sentences as input. Pre-trained word embeddings were used, followed by convolutional filters in series with a layer of Bi-LSTM (Bidirectional Long Short Term Memory). They used convolutional filters to extract important features at a local level and then Bi-LSTM to extract the long term dependencies among these features in both directions of time sequence.

Most of the methods mentioned above rely on manually created features or features created using linguistic knowledge. Engineering such features requires extra effort. The features engineered by the use of dependency parsing utilize only a part of the information provided by the dependency trees. The methods fail to exploit the entire structure of the dependency trees. Moreover, these features are created with the help of dependency parsers which may lead to error propagation i.e, any error in extracting the dependencies will automatically propagate to the final task of DE.

Our method helps us to focus more on the data preprocessing part of the NLP pipeline and leaves the implicit feature engineering part to the neural network.

3   Proposed Methodology

3.1   Data Preprocessing

Some preprocessing has been applied to the data before training a model. Sentences with length less than five words are considered as outliers and are hence, removed from the dataset. Since the dataset has been mined from Wikipedia, some of the sentences contain the translated text of the Definiendum or some other information within parentheses. Since we are not working in a multilingual context (English only), we remove the translated text from the sentences. For example, the instance "The Achaeans (in Greek Ἀχαιοί, Akhaioi) is one of the collective names used for the Greeks in Homer's Iliad (used 598 times) and Odyssey." is converted to "The Achaeans is one of the collective names used for the Greeks in Homer's Iliad and Odyssey.". The experiments are done with both lower cased and upper cased data. However, pretrained models trained on a specific case of data are fine-tuned with data of the corresponding case.

3.2   Methodology

Li et al. [9] experimented with the use of LSTM trained using POS tags for the task. However, with the discovery of Attention, we anticipate that instead of using the POS tags, the Attention layer can prove more beneficial. We try out a model consisting of LSTM armed with Self-Attention. The results were not as we expected. Li et al. achieved a 10-fold cross validation F1 score of 0.912 whereas our model was able to achieve a score of 0.907 only. However, the inspection of the self-attention weights revealed that the model had a good understanding of the relation between the words in the sentence. Moreover, the self-attention layer also helps in capturing the information related to the definition, as shown in Fig. 2. The greater the intensity of the color highlighting the word, the greater is the attention weight of the word. Thus, the self attention layer seems to put great stress on the Definiendum and the Rest fields, which is a positive sign as per the Definition Extraction point of view.

the aardwolf proteles cristatus is a small insectivorous hyenalike mammal native to eastern and southern africa

classics or classical studies is the branch of the humanities dealing with the languages literature history art and other aspects of the ancient mediterranean world especially ancient greece and ancient rome during the time known as classical antiquity roughly spanning from the ancient greek bronze age in 1000 bc to the dark ages circa ad 500

in christianity docetism from the greek $\delta o \kappa \omega$ to seem is the belief that jesus ' physical body was an illusion as was his crucifixion that is jesus only seemed to have a physical body and to physically die but in reality he was incorporeal a pure spirit and hence could not physically die

Fig. 2. Weights of the words in a sentence based on the self attention layer

The above observation paved the way for our further experiments with more powerful Attention models, such as BERT. The classification experiments are carried out using BERT. The model consists of multi-head attention that apply a sequence-to-sequence transformation, just like LSTM cells, except for the fact that they are not recurrent. The key features of BERT have already been discussed in the Introduction Section and details about Masked Language Model and Next Sentence Prediction are discussed in the following paragraphs.

For training the MLM of BERT, either of the following operations is performed on the sentences:

- Randomly replace some tokens with the MASK token (happens in majority of the input sentences).
- Leave the sentence intact (happens in some sentences).
- Replace some of the tokens with some random token (happens in very few sentences).

The MLM's task is to learn to predict the masked tokens in an input sequence. The addition of noise in the input by randomly replacing some tokens with some other tokens, is done in a controlled manner to make the model robust.

BERT's training process also incorporates the ability of Next Sentence Prediction. Given two sentences separated by a SEP token, BERT can predict whether they occur together or not. BERT receives two sentences as input and learns to predict whether the second sentence is in continuation of the first sentence. For example, BERT learns that "The car is not working." followed by "It is unable to start." makes sense, whereas "The car is not working." followed by "Food is delicious." does not make much sense. This ability of BERT to learn the context of the corpus helps in boosting the performance of the model.

BERT learns many embeddings, namely Token Embedding (for the tokens of a sequence), Segment Embedding (for different parts of the input sequence), and Positional Embedding. The Positional Embedding helps BERT to keep track of the order of tokens in a sequence. In order to reduce the vocabulary size, BERT uses Wordpiece [20], which breaks up the words into sub-words. For example, "Photosynthesis" is tokenized as "Photo","##sy","##nt" and "##hesis".

We experiment with bert-base-uncased and bert-base-cased, as provided in Huggingface's Transformers[1] implementation [19]. Both the models have 12 hidden layers in the encoder of the Transformer, with 768 as the dimensionality of the encoder output. With 12 attention heads, there are around 110 million parameters in both the models. The only difference between bert-base-uncased and bert-base-cased is that the former is pre-trained on lower cased English text while the latter is pre-trained on cased English text. The Transformers library provides an efficient implementation of Transformer based architectures along with their pre-trained weights.

For the analysis experiments, we use an open-source project bertviz[2] to visualize the attention weights of BERT. The library provides Attention-Head view, Model view, and Neuron view. We use the Attention Head view to analyze the weights layer-by-layer and head-by-head.

4   Experiments, Results, and Validation

The WCL (World-Class Lattices) dataset is used for validation. The dataset contains a total of 4,718 manually annotated Wikipedia sentences out of which 1,871 are definitions while the remaining 2,847 are non-definitional sentences. Since many authors have performed a 10-fold cross-validation experiment on the classification task, we do the same to compare our results against the existing baselines.

In Table 1, we compare the performance of BERT against the considered baselines using the average F1 score of the 10-fold cross-validation as metric.

The following baselines have been considered:

1. **WCL** [11]: An algorithm using the concept of Word-Class lattices for modeling higher-level features over shallow parsing and part of speech.

---

[1] https://huggingface.co/transformers/.
[2] https://github.com/jessevig/bertviz.

2. **DefMiner** [7]: A CRF model trained with lexical, terminological and structural (e.g., document position) features.
3. **E&S** [5]: A system incorporating complex features from subtrees of the dependency tree, obtained from dependency parsing.
4. **LSTM-POS** [9]: LSTM network which represents each sentence as a mixture of infrequent words and frequent words' associated part-of-speech.
5. **E&SS** [2]: CNN-BiLSTM model using syntactic dependencies incorporated in the training data.

Table 1. Performance on WCL dataset

Model	Precision	Recall	F1 score
WCL	0.988	0.607	0.752
DefMiner	0.920	0.790	0.850
E&S	0.859	0.853	0.854
LSTM-POS	0.904	0.820	0.912
E&SS	0.942	0.942	0.942
BERT-uncased	0.968	0.973	0.970
BERT-cased	0.967	0.979	0.974

From Table 1, it is evident that BERT, with its attention layers, is superior than the proposed techniques.

For BERT-base-uncased and BERT-base-cased, we get an average F1 score of 0.97 and 0.974 for the positive class, respectively. The difference in the results of the two BERT versions can be attributed to the fact that lowering the text data leads to loss of information. For example, BERT-cased tokenizes "Photosynthesis" as "Photo","##sy","##nt" and "##hesis" (WordPiece). Since the data is cased, it helps the model to understand that "Photo" in this context (referring to photon or light) is not the same as "photo" (referring to images). The BERT cased model captures this lost information, which helps it to produce better results.

Although both BERT and E&SS are based on deep learning, the latter is also dependent upon engineered features in the form of syntactic dependencies. The reason for BERT outperforming the E&SS baseline (in spite of the additional input) can be attributed to the fact that BiLSTMs (present in E&SS architecture) encode an input sequence from "left-to-right" and "right-to-left" but are unable to do them both at once. BERT, on the other hand, takes the help of both the previous and the subsequent tokens at the same time.

Next, we carry out further experiments analyzing the attention weights of our best model on the WCL dataset. For this, we analyze the attention weights of each head for each layer for the input "Photosynthesis is the process by which

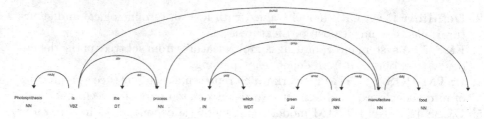

Fig. 3. Syntactic dependencies extracted using SpaCy.

green plants manufacture food." Moreover, correspondingly we also extract the syntactic dependencies present in the input sentence using SpaCy[3] as shown in Fig. 3.

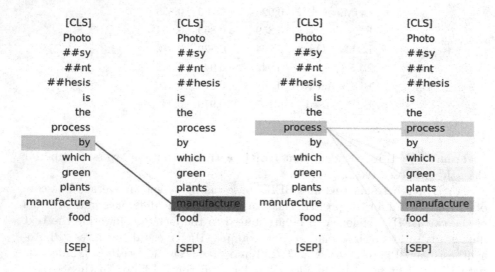

Fig. 4. BERT capturing long-range dependencies.

We observe that the attention weights of BERT capture the syntactic dependencies automatically. Figure 4 shows that "by" and "manufacture" are correlated with each other. Similarly, "process" and "manufacture" is another long-range syntactic dependency that has been captured by BERT. The boldness of the lines depicts the magnitude of the weight.

Figures 4 and 5 also provide strong evidence that the Transformer architecture is carrying out the task of CNNs (capturing local dependencies) and LSTMs (capturing long-range dependencies) in a much better manner. Thus, despite the absence of CNNs and LSTMs in the architecture, Transformers are capable of extracting the important information from the data.

---

[3] https://spacy.io/.

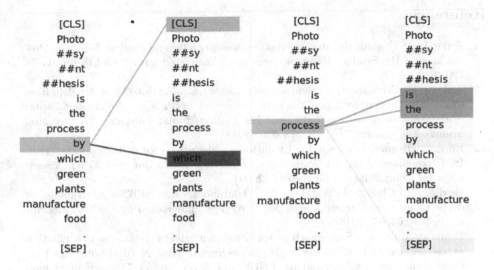

Fig. 5. BERT capturing local dependencies

The same syntactic dependencies are captured in the heads of many layers, thus increasing the robustness of the model. Multiple occurrences of syntactic dependencies highlight the fact that they are indeed important for definition extraction, as proved by previous works in this domain.

The weights capture many other dependencies (as shown in Figs. 4 and 5) that seem meaningful but are not a part of the syntactic dependencies, thus improving the performance of the model. The self-attention mechanism is a soft dependency measure between two tokens present in a sentence. Thus, implicitly BERT is capturing many dependencies of variable strength and using them for better definition extraction. This is the essential reason for BERT's good performance on the task.

5   Conclusion

In this paper, we try to explain the intricacies of definition extraction using the power of self-attention. We start off by showing what self-attention is able to capture and then move on to test out BERT on the task of definition extraction. We observe that despite not using features engineered from syntactic information, BERT outperforms the existing proposed methods. More importantly, we discover that the multi-head attention mechanism of BERT is powerful enough to incorporate the information of syntactic dependencies implicitly, thus relieving us from the process of feature engineering. However, deployment of BERT can be difficult in systems with limited resources since BERT has millions of parameters. The complexity of the model leads to low inference-time which makes it unsuitable for real-time applications. So, as future work, one can adopt the concept of distillation, i.e. training a student model that mimics the behaviour of the teacher model, to speed up the process of definition extraction.

References

1. Anke, L.E.: Towards definition extraction using conditional random fields. In: Proceedings of the Student Research Workshop Associated with RANLP, pp. 63–70 (2013)
2. Anke, L.E., Schockaert, S.: Syntactically aware neural architectures for definition extraction. In: Proceedings of the 2018 Conference of the North American Chapter of the Association for Computational Linguistics: Human Language Technologies, Volume 2 (Short Papers), pp. 378–385 (2018)
3. Borg, C., Rosner, M., Pace, G.: Evolutionary algorithms for definition extraction. In: Proceedings of the 1st Workshop on Definition Extraction, pp. 26–32. Association for Computational Linguistics (2009)
4. Devlin, J., Chang, M.W., Lee, K., Toutanova, K.: BERT: pre-training of deep bidirectional transformers for language understanding. arXiv preprint arXiv:1810.04805 (2018)
5. Espinosa-Anke, L., Saggion, H.: Applying dependency relations to definition extraction. In: Métais, E., Roche, M., Teisseire, M. (eds.) Natural Language Processing and Information Systems. LNCS, vol. 8455, pp. 63–74. Springer, Cham (2014). https://doi.org/10.1007/978-3-319-07983-7_10
6. Espinosa-Anke, L., Saggion, H., Delli Bovi, C.: Definition extraction using sense-based embeddings. In: Gupta, P., Banchs, R.E., Rosso, P. (eds.) International Workshop on Embeddings and Semantics (IWES 2015), Alicante, Spain, 15 September 2015. CEUR (2015). 6 p
7. Jin, Y., Kan, M.Y., Ng, J.P., He, X.: Mining scientific terms and their definitions: a study of the ACL anthology. In: Proceedings of the 2013 Conference on Empirical Methods in Natural Language Processing, pp. 780–790 (2013)
8. Kobyliński, Ł., Przepiórkowski, A.: Definition extraction with balanced random forests. In: Nordström, B., Ranta, A. (eds.) GoTAL 2008. LNCS (LNAI), vol. 5221, pp. 237–247. Springer, Heidelberg (2008). https://doi.org/10.1007/978-3-540-85287-2_23
9. Li, S.L., Xu, B., Chung, T.L.: Definition extraction with LSTM recurrent neural networks. In: Sun, M., Huang, X., Lin, H., Liu, Z., Liu, Y. (eds.) CCL/NLP-NABD -2016. LNCS (LNAI), vol. 10035, pp. 177–189. Springer, Cham (2016). https://doi.org/10.1007/978-3-319-47674-2_16
10. Meyer, I.: Extracting knowledge-rich contexts for terminography. In: Recent Advances in Computational Terminology, vol. 2, p. 279 (2001)
11. Navigli, R., Velardi, P.: Learning word-class lattices for definition and hypernym extraction. In: Proceedings of the 48th Annual Meeting of the Association for Computational Linguistics, pp. 1318–1327. Association for Computational Linguistics (2010)
12. Navigli, R., Velardi, P., Ruiz-Martínez, J.M., et al.: An annotated dataset for extracting definitions and hypernyms from the web. In: LREC (2010)
13. Saggion, H., Gaizauskas, R.J.: Mining on-line sources for definition knowledge. In: FLAIRS Conference, pp. 61–66 (2004)
14. Seppälä, S.: A proposal for a framework to evaluate feature relevance for terminographic definitions. In: Proceedings of the 1st Workshop on Definition Extraction, pp. 47–53. Association for Computational Linguistics (2009)
15. Sierra, G., Alarcón, R., Aguilar, C., Barrón, A.: Towards the building of a corpus of definitional contexts. In: Proceeding of the 12th EURALEX International Congress, Torino, Italy, pp. 229–240 (2006)

16. Taylor, W.L.: "Cloze procedure": a new tool for measuring readability. Journal. Bull. **30**(4), 415–433 (1953)
17. Vaswani, A., et al.: Attention is all you need. In: Advances in Neural Information Processing Systems, pp. 5998–6008 (2017)
18. Westerhout, E., Monachesi, P.: Extraction of Dutch definitory contexts for elearning purposes. LOT Occas. Ser. **7**, 219–234 (2007)
19. Wolf, T., et al.: Transformers: state-of-the-art natural language processing. arXiv preprint arXiv:1910.03771 (2019)
20. Wu, Y., et al.: Google's neural machine translation system: bridging the gap between human and machine translation. arXiv preprint arXiv:1609.08144 (2016)
21. Zhang, C., Jiang, P.: Automatic extraction of definitions. In: 2009 2nd IEEE International Conference on Computer Science and Information Technology, pp. 364–368. IEEE (2009)

Steps of Pre-processing for English to Mizo SMT System

Chanambam Sveta Devi[(⊠)] and Bipul Syam Purkayastha

Department of Computer Science, Assam University, Silchar 788011, India
ch.sveta666@yahoo.com, bipul_sh@hotmail.com

Abstract. The idea behind this present paper is to construct the pre-processing techniques on Bilingual Parallel Corpus. The parallel corpus is a common essential resource for the application of NLP. The parallel corpus is a huge number of parallel sentences or text of two different languages. We propose a new framework for the pre-processing steps of the Bilingual Corpus of SMT System. The purpose of this study the virtue of the pre-processing methods which are mainly used for training the translation. The pre-processing technique contributes to a main part of the Statistical Machine Translation. In this paper, we survey the various steps of pre-processing methods used for the translation system and also how the complication of the translation method has succeeded in society so far. Experimental results of the pre-processing steps on Bible Domain (https://www.bible.com/kjv). 'English-Mizo' parallel corpus (on bible domain) are discussed and all the results of pre-processing steps are mentioned.

Keywords: English language · Mizo language · Statistical Machine Translation · Parallel corpus · Domain

1 Introduction

Machine translation is a subfield of computer Sciences and NLP, also it is the most important application of Natural Language Processing. MT investigates the uses of computer software that translates the speech or words from one source to another target language. In MT, the basic idea is the simple performances of a word's substitution in one natural language to another. Many times, translation System software allows for the personalization by a domain or profession and provides better results by limiting the field of acceptable swapping. This particular method is effectively used in a set of domains or language formulaic. The translation system follows the authority and valid documents process more feasible output from that discussion or from less normalized text [5]. There are two classifications of Machine translation (MT) i.e. Bilingual MT and Multilingual MT. Bilingual MT entails one source and one target language whereas Multilingual MT entails two or more languages of source to two or more target languages [20]. This paper proposes in the framework of developing Pre-processing steps of Bilingual parallel corpus for English and Mizo language. And also there are several approaches to MT viz. Direct, Rule-Based, Statistical, Example-Based etc. However, Statistical Machine Translation system has generated more interest over the past few years. This system is entirely automatic and requires less human work than traditional

A. Bhattacharjee et al. (Eds.): MIND 2020, CCIS 1241, pp. 156–167, 2020.
https://doi.org/10.1007/978-981-15-6318-8_14

Rule-Based approach. SMT is based on the parallel corpus which has been trained. Parallel corpus consists of 2 texts, one is translation of the other. Other NLP problems such as Word Sense Disambiguation, Information Retrieval, Named Entity Recognition etc., are used in this parallel corpus. The process of training of the TM component of SMT system is dependent on large size of parallel corpus, where the training data of pre-processing can make better quality of Statistical Machine Translation modules such as Language model, Translation model and Decoder. Its importance for pre-processing methods for SMT like Sentences splitting, Tokenization, Truecasing and Cleaning techniques has been discussed. There are other various pre-processing methods such as Speech segmentation, Morphological Analysis, POS Tagging, Parsing, Text-to-Speech, WSD, NER, Automatic Summarization etc. but basic SMT pre-processing methods are also discussed in this technique.

The English Bible parallel corpus has been used for testing in our proposed system.

2 Related Works

There are few works that we have discussed to collect the possible idea for our pre-processing methods of the Machine translation system.

The literature on Translation of English to Mizo was referred, recalling the paper [23] presented a Multi-word Expression (MWE) for Mizo language, [22] paper shows the Identifying rules for recognition of Name Entity Classes in Mizo language, A report is given [24] reported Resource building and POS tagging for Mizo language and recently on English-Mizo Machine Translation using Neural and Statistical approaches [25].

In paper [15], presented English to Malayalam translation model using a Hybrid-based approach combined with Statistical Machine Translation. In this work, Tokenization, Truecasing and Cleaning pre-processing techniques are used. For the translation model, the training phrase is built from the corpus which is provided by a collection of aligned sentences in two file format, they are in English and Malayalam language. The Statistical Model consists of the Language Model, Translation Model and Decoding Model that are implemented by using the Data set of corpus and the process tools such as GIZA++, IRSTLM, Moses Decoder, while Moses allows automatically the train Translation system.

In paper [13], Alignment-Based Recording for SMT, mainly presented the word alignment for phrase-based SMT and initial word alignment discussed source recorder words according to another target word order. And then, a 100 k set of small sentences and a 700 k set of large sentences are used for comparing the effect of recording on two data sets. Also evaluated manually different translations of that recorded system, as well as word order differences, as are known from the recorded and baseline systems. This paper states that the problem of translation can be minimized between the steps of pre-processing corpus that achieve the grouping and word splitting.

In paper [2], Pre-processing Techniques for SMT used Data Pre-processing that included (a) **Normalization** that convert all the characters of source and target sentences to uppercase or lowercase characters in a sentence. (b) **Tokenization** for both the parallel corpus data that split a sentence into word or character, and the split sentences return in a list, by inserting spaces between words and punctuation. (c) **Truecasing** that provides the probability in the parallel corpus and builds a model for all the set of words data and this model is used for this truecasing for giving the file of each language Truecasing. Truecasing is applied to both target language and source also. (d) **Cleaning**, it is the action of deleting long or empty sentences or misaligned sentences from the document, which can affect the quality of translation. Other components like the Language Model, Translation Model, and Tuning. This paper used various tools as IRSTLM, KenLM, GIZA++, and Moses toolkits to generate the final model.

In paper [9], the process of corpus filters for normalization is used. Normalization used the MOSES toolkit to provide *truecase.Perl* model. And for normalization of Hindi corpus we used NLP Indic Library. Both the corpus data used, to store in the extension with .en for the English language and the corresponding Hindi language with .hi for parallel corpus. Also, this paper performed data splitting and used MOSES for translation.

Paper [18] constructs the parallel text corpus and implements English to Bodo SMT system. This paper designs the architecture of E-BPTC construction and translates in different ways like manual translation (generating the first steps of English-Bodo parallel corpus), Manual validation (translator checks the correction of spelling, fluency, and adequacy) and Parallel corpus generator (translate English sentences to Bodo sentences). This paper also implements English-Bodo SMT and the operation performed using Corpus Preparation (i.e. Tokenization, Truecasing, and Cleaning), Language Model, Translation and Decoder.

In this paper [8], the author presents the Pre-processing steps of the data for training.

The steps of Pre-processing are stated below:

1. The corpus of Assamese and English are Tokenized.
2. The English corpus converts to lowercase.
3. Cleaning the data removes the extra space, empty lines that the lines have been too short or too long.

In paper [17], the author presents the pre-processing steps of SMT using the techniques of Tokenization, Truecasing, and Cleaning and gives both the accuracy percentage of Language Model using Pre-processing to be having 100% and without using Pre-processing to be having 73%. Finally, he has given the translation model using pre-processing having 94% correct translation and without using pre-processing having 66% of correct translation.

3 Mizo

The name of the language is Mizo is the lingua-franca of Mizoram, widely spoken by local people of Mizoram and state of Chin hill in Burma and there are 1,200,000 in India, 200,000 in Myanmar and 1,500 in Bangladesh. The Mizo language is formerly known as the Lusei dialect and is allied to the group of Kuki-chin language. The sentence construction of Mizo language is in the form of a object-subject-verb.

4 Corpus

A parallel text is the form of a collection of text and its translation. The parallel corpus is used in various parts of the research linguistic and computational area. The state corpus has been contentious in linguistics. The parallel corpus is a huge parallel text in two languages and usually are stored and worked electronically. It can be used for analysis, teaching, and research in translation, bilingual lexicography and linguistics. Mainly, the corpus has three types such as Monolingual, Bilingual and Multilingual. These types of corpora work in different ways of machine translation. Parallel corpus plays the main role in building a Statistical Approach System.

5 Statistical Machine Translation

Common approach is Statistical Machine Translation of MT system and the basic translation is done in Statistical models. The state-of-the-art SMT which comes under the corpus-Based (or Empirical) MT system used a huge number of the bilingual parallel corpus from the source language to get good target translation language. The paper shows the background of the Statistical Machine translation i.e., we consider a given source sentence as English language *'e'* which indicates to translate into a target Mizo sentence as Mizo language *'m'*. According to the Bayes Rule.

$$\arg \max P(m/e) = P(m) * P(e/m)/P(e)$$
$$= P(m) * P(e/m)$$

Here, $P(m)$ indicates the Language Model Probability and $P(e/m)$ also indicates the Probability of Translation Model.

Considered all the likely Mizo sentences *'m'* and chose the maximizes product $P(m)$ $P(e/m)$. the $P(e)$ factor can be ignored since for every 'e' it is same.

The SMT approach proposal is an excellent solution to the ambiguity problem. This approach consists of various models that are stated below:

1) **Language Model (LM):** The Language Model assigns a probability of the Target language and practically SMT uses n-gram language and uses simple frequency counts over a huge monolingual text corpus with back-off and smoothing.
2) **Translation Modes (TM):** The Translation model easily enumerates the probabilities of source sentences and Target sentence of this two languages.
3) **Decoder:** In the decoder process is the maximum probability of LM and TM.

6 Pre-processing

Nowadays, the pre-processing steps is an important part of the application of NLP. Preprocessing is the word to word convert processing, prior to actual processing by something else. In the NLP work, a pre-processor is also a machine program where input gives the output data which is used as input data to another program. The steps of pre-processing for Translation system are as follows:

6.1   Tokenization

Tokenization is the process of splitting a sentence into words or numbers or punctuation marks called tokens. In any task, tokenization is considered as the first step.

6.2   Stemming

It is also a necessary process of Text Mining application, Spelling checker and Machine Translation. The stemming is another process of finding the word root of a word and removal of variant affix viz, prefix and suffix [16].

6.3   Morphological Analysis

Morphological analysis is the study of a variety of structural analysis of morphemes and at the same time determines if in a sentence a word has all the grammatical characteristics. In the Machine Translation for any pair of languages between them, the different language and the amount of the parallel data and most of the morphological richness and different word order can affect the Machine Translation [14].

6.4   Part of Speech Tagging

It is the action of giving the lexical categories of each word based on its context. POS tagger plays an important role in training parts for building the Machine Translation for low resource language [11].

6.5   Parsing

It is the task of changing the sentences of Natural language to parse tree or syntax tree. And this is the important phrase used to understand the syntax and semantics of any sources that are limited to the grammar. And most useful technique is parsing for machine translation to recognize the structure of source language for pre-ordering likewise structure of target language for post-ordering [3].

6.6   Named Entity Recognition

Recently Named Entity of correct identity is a serious problem for Machine translation and often causes translation failure [4]. In the Machine Translation, Named Entity Recognition (NER) works an important role in translation from one source language to another and often the NER is transliterated rather than translated.

6.7   Word Sense Disambiguation

In the field of NLP, it is an activity of determining the word sense from a specific condition. The performance of the MT can improve by the correct word sense is used in a sentence [21].

7   Proposed System on Steps Pre-processing for English to Mizo Corpus

The main purpose of these frameworks is the pre-processing steps to implement the Machine Translation using Statistical Corpus-based approach. Finding of the pre-processing methods like word sense and the structure of word arrangement are done by the basic elements of the SMT system like LM, TM and Decider. The English to Mizo pre-processing output will be helpful for the implementing of the English to Mizo SMT system. This section shows the pre-processing techniques in figure follows:

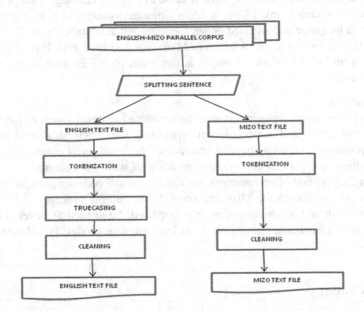

Fig. 1. Flow-chart of pre-processing steps of parallel corpus.

The above Fig. 1 shows the overview of the purposed automated pre-processing system that will be helpful for developing the English to Mizo SMT system. Here, the step wise description of the pre-processing steps is shown.

Step 1: Splitting Sentences
The parallel corpora have been collected from the bible domain (https://www.bible.com/kjv) and the corpora file store in the **.xl** file format. The total number of sentences in this file is 25482 (12741 English sentences and 12741 Mizo sentences). The

sentences split using a python program that takes the file as an input and output and two distinct document files is also produces, one document contains English sentences and another one contains Mizo sentences.

Step 2: Tokenization

Most common pre-processing step is Tokenization, the process of breaking up the big quantity of raw text into words which means there will be spaces inserted between the words and punctuation. However, tokenizer of the English language is available easily in the network but it is not in the Mizo language. So, we need to write a code using Perl scripts for Tokenization from Moses inbuilt Toolkits.

Step 3: Truecasing

Truecasing is the distinction of words that occurs in the raw text of lowercase or uppercase form. And it is correlated with Tokenization. We take an item capital, Capital and CAPITAL which can exist from the large collection of texts, it consist in the middle, at the beginning or headline of a sentence. It is useful in the same word to the case normalize, that is their most likely cases are converted by lowercase or truecasing. In this respect Mizo language is same as English language, except the 'i' in 'I am' which is written in small letter in Mizo language as opposed to how it is written in the English language and we used uppercase letter when we talk about 'God' i.e., all individual 'I' are written in small letters in Mizo, not just in 'I am'. But all the 'i's in both English and Mizo Tokenizer output is the input file of English Truecasing and Mizo Truecasing.

Step 4: Cleaning

Cleaning is the action of replacing or deleting unwanted sentences such as long, empty sentences, and misaligned sentences from truecasing file. These unwanted sentences can create problems in training parallel sentences. The small script *clean-corpus-n.perl* is used to clean up a parallel corpus, so it works well with the training script. For the Cleaning of English and Mizo sentences, we used the small code script *clean-corpus-n. perl,* so it works well with the Mizo and English file training process.

These English and Mizo Pre-processing Steps will be needed to develop the Statistical Machine Translation primary elements i.e. Language model, Translation Model, and Decoder.

8 Experiment

These parts show the observation result. The file format of the parallel corpus is only six pairs of sentences shown below:

I have sewed sackcloth upon my skin, and defiled my horn in the dust.
Ka vun chungah saiip puanka bel a Ka Id chu vaivutah ka tal a.
But his flesh upon him shall have pain, and his soul within him shall mourn.
A taksa na chu a hre ch auh va A thlarauvin amah a sûn a.
And he shall flay the burnt offering, and cut it into his pieces.
A vun chu a lip ang a, a sachu a chan sawm ang a.
And the water ran round about the altar; and he filled the trench also with water.

Tin, tui chu maichâm vêlah chuan a luang ta dûldûl a; tin, laih khuar chu tuiin a tikhat ha-vdc a.
Thou shall not have in thy bag divers weights, a great and a small.
In ipah chuan khîn chi dang dang, a ritleh a zâng in neitur a ni lo.
And Jokmeam with her suburbs, and Beth-horon with her suburbs,
Gezer a daivêlte nên; Jokmeam a daivelte nen Beth-horon a Daivêlte nên,

Result 1: Sentences Splitting
English Corpus File

I have sewed sackcloth upon my skin, and defiled my horn in the dust.
But his flesh upon him shall have pain, and his soul within him shall mourn.
And he shall flay the burnt offering, and cut it into his pieces.
And the water ran round about the altar; and he filled the trench also with water.
Thou shall not have in thy bag divers weights, a great and a small.
And Jokmeam with her suburbs, and Beth-horon with her suburbs,

Mizo Corpus File

Ka vun chungah saiip puanka hel a Ka ki chu vaivutah ka tal a.
A taksa na chu a hrechauhva A thlarauvin amah a sûn a.
A vun chu a lip anga, a sachu a chan sawm ang a.
Tin, tui chu maicham velah chuan a luang ta dûldûl a; tin, laih khuar chu tuiin a tikhat battk a.
In ipah chuan khin chi dang dang, a ritleh a zâng in neitûr a ni lo.
Gezer a daivêlte nên; Jokmeam a daivelte nen Beth-horon a daivêlte nên,

Result 2: Tokenization
English Corpus File

I have sewed sackcloth upon my skin, and defiled my horn in the dust.
But his flesh upon him shall have pain, and his soul within him shall mourn.
And he shall flay the burnt offering, and cut it into his pieces.
And the water ran round about the altar; and he filled the trench also with water.
Thou shall not have in thy bag divers weights, a great and a small.
And Jokmeam with her suburbs, and Beth-horon with her suburbs,

Mizo Corpus File

Ka vun chungah saiip puanka bel a Ka ki chu vaivutah ka tal a.
Ataksa na chu a hrechauhva A thlarauvin amah a sun a.
A vun chu a lip anga, a sachu a chan sawm ang a.
Tin, tui chu maichâm vêlah chuan a luang ta dûldûl a; tin, laih khuar chu tuiin a tikhat ba-vdc a.
In ipah chuan khîn chi dang dang, a ritleh a zâng in neitûr a ni lo.
Gezer a daivêlte nên; Jokmeam a daivelte nen Beth-horon a daivêlte nên,

Table 1. Result of Tokenization

Corpora	Total size of tokens
Normal English Corpus	349619
Tokenized English Corpus	403911
Normal Mizo Corpus	345098
Tokenized Mizo	404061

Result 3: Truecasing for English Corpus

i have sewed sackcloth upon my skin, and defiled my hom in the dust.
but his flesh upon him shall have pain, and his soul within him shall moum.
and he shall flay the burnt offering, and cut it into his pieces.
and the water ran round about the altar; and he filled the trench also with vrater.
thou shalt not have in thy bag divers vteights, a great and a small.
and jokmeam with her submbs, and beth-horon with her suburbs,

Result 4: Cleaning
English Corpus File

i have sewed sackcloth upon my skin, and defiled my hom in the dust.
but his flesh upon him shall have pain, and his soul within him shall momn.
and he shall flay the burnt offering, and cut it into his pieces.
and the vrater ran round about the altar; and he filled the trench also with water.
thou shalt not have in thy bag divers weights, a great and a small.
and jokmeam with her suburbs, and beth-horon with her suburbs,

Mizo Corpus File

ka vun chungah saiip puanka bei a ka ki chu vaivutah ka tal a.
a taksa na chu a hre chauh va a thlarauvin amah a sûn a.
a vun chu a lip ang a, a sachu a chan sawm ang a.
tin, tui chu maicham velah chuan a luang ta dûldûl a; tin, laih khuar chu tuiin a tikhat bawk a.
in ipah chuan khîn chi dang dang, a ritleh a zâng in neitûr a ni lo.
gezer a daivêlte nên; jokmeam a daivelte nen beth-horon a daivêlte nên;

Result. The process of Cleaning works in the sentence only to reduce and truncate the space unwanted between sentences as well as between the words.

9   Language Mode (LM)

The Language Model presents the computed probability of a sentence using n-gram. It can be compared as the computational probability of selected words to all the given words preceding it in a sentence [1]. And LM can also be used to make a better quality of the target sentences of the proposed model for testing in these two models we used 6 input sentences.

Table 2. Result of Language Model

	Accuracy
Without using pre-processing	65%
Using pre-processing	100%

10   Translation Model (TM)

The translation Model determines Conditional Probability. A Translation model trained using the parallel corpus for target-sources pair and it builds the phrase table, which contains a phrase or English words translated into Mizo. Both the translation models are prepared, using English to Mizo test files containing 88 and 101 tokens while normal English to Mizo files consist of 70 and 80 tokens from those 6 input sentences respectively. The models checked the result manually as given below:

Table 3. Result of Translation Model

	Accuracy
Without using pre-processing	60%
Using pre-processing	95%

11   Conclusion

The concept of Machine translation is the oldest application of NLP and there are many available translating texts from similar languages (i.e., Indian to Indian language) and Indian language to English, English to Indian language for MT system in India. Here, we described the collection of the Bible corpus and its application in building statistical Machine Translation. The experimental result in Table 1 shows the Tokenization of parallel Corpus and the Tables 2 and 3 show the result of LM (Language model) and TM (Translation Model).

In the future work of this study, more parallel corpus can be provided and work on a different type of implementation can be done to achieve better results and better performing works of pre-processing on the parallel corpus model and for development of the basic components of SMT. All the work in these areas will be considered in future research work.

References

1. Abiola, O.B., Adetunmbi, A.O., Oguntimilehin, A.: Using hybrid approach for English to Yoruba text machine system (proposed). Int. J. Comput. Sci. Mob. Comput. (IJCSMC) **4**, 308–313 (2015). www.ijcsmc.com
2. ElSayed, A.G.M., Salama, A.S., El-Ghazali, A.E.-D.M.: A hybrid model for enhancing lexical statistical machine translation (SMT). Int. J. Comput. Sci. IJCS **12** (2015)
3. Bisazza, A., Federico, M.: A survey of word reordering in statistical machine translation: computational models and language phenomena. Comput. Linguist. **42**, 163–205 (2016)
4. Babych, B., Hartle, A.: Improving machine translation quality with automatic named entity recognition. In: Proceeding of the 7th International EAMT Workshop on MT and Other Language Technology Tools, Improving MT Through Other Language Technology Tools: Resources and Tools for Building MT, EAMT, Stroudsburg, pp. 1–8 (2003)

5. Bhattacharyya, P.: Machine Translation. CRC Press, Boca Raton (2015)
6. Brown, P.E., Pietra, S.A.D., Pietra, V.J.D., Mercer, R.L.: The mathematics of statistical machine translation: parameter estimation. Comput. Linguist. **19**(2), 263–311 (1993)
7. Chhangte, L.: A preliminary grammar of the Mizo language. Master's thesis, University of Texas Arlington (1986)
8. Das, P., Baruah, K.K.: Assamese to English statistical machine translation integrated with a transliteration module. Int. J. Comput. Appl. **100**(5), 20–24 (2014)
9. Dungarwal, P., Chatterjee, R., Mishra, A., Kunchukutta, A., Shah, R., Bhattacharyya, P.: The IIT Bombay Hindi, English translation system at WMT. In: Workshop on Machine Translation (2014)
10. Fanai, L.: Some aspects of the lexical phonology of Mizo and English: an auto segmental approach. Ph.D. Dissertation, CIEFL, Hyderabad, India (1992)
11. Sánchez-Martínez, F., Amentano-Oller, C., Pérez-Ortiz, J.A., Forcada, M.L.: Training part-of-speech taggers to build machine translation systems for less-resourced language pairs. Procesamiento del Lenguaje natural **39**, 257–264 (2007). (XXIII congreso de la Sociedad Espanola de Procesamiento del Lenguaje Natural)
12. Fournier, B.: Preprocessing on bilingual data for statistical machine translation, The Netherlands (2008)
13. Holmqvist, M., Stymne, S., Ahrenberg, L., Merkel, M.: Alignment-based reordering for SMT. In: Chair, N.C.C., et al. (eds.) Proceedings of the 8th International Conference on Language Resources and Evaluation (LREC), Istanbul, Turkey, May 2012. European Language Resources Association ELRA (2012)
14. Koehn, P., Birch, A., Steinberger, R.: 462 Machine translation system for Europe. In: MT Summit XII (2009)
15. Nithya, B., Shibily, J.: A hybrid approach to English to Malayalam machine translation. Int. J. Comput. Appl. **81**, 11–15 (2013)
16. Paul, A., Dey, A., Purkayastha, B.S.: An affix removal stemmer for natural language text in Nepali. Int. J. Comput. Appl. **91**(6), 1–4 (2014)
17. Paul, A., Purkayastha, B.S.: Pre-processing steps on bilingual corpus for SMT. Int. J. Adv. Res. Comput. Sci. (2010)
18. Islam, S., Paul, A., Purkayastha, B.S.: Construction of English-Bodo parallel text corpus for statistical machine translation. Int. J. Nat. Lang. Comput. (IJNLC) **7** (2018)
19. Sarmah, P., Wiltshire, C.R.: A preliminary acoustic study of Mizo vowels and tones. Acoust. Soc. Ind. **37**, 121–129 (2010)
20. Jindal, S., Goyal, V., Bhullar, J.S.: English to Punjabi statistical machine translation using moses (corpus-based). J. Stat. Manag. Syst. **21**(4), 553–560 (2018). https://doi.org/10.1080/09720520510.2018.1471265
21. Vickey, D.: Word-sense disambiguation for machine translation. In: Proceedings of the Conferences on Human Language Technology and Empirical Methods in Natural Language Processing. Association Computational Linguistics (2005)
22. Bentham, J., Pakray, P., Majumder, G., Lalbiaknia, S., Gelbukh, A.: Identification of rules for recognition of name entity classes in Mizo language. In: 15th Mexican International Conference on Artificial Intelligence (MICAI). Springer, Cancun (2016)
23. Majumder, G., Pakray, P., Khiangte, Z., Gelbukh, A.: Multiword expressions (MWE) for Mizo language: literature survey. In: International Conference on Intelligent Text Processing and Computational Linguistics, pp. 623–635. Springer, Konya (2016)

24. Pakray, P., Pal, A., Majumder, G., Gelbulk, A.: Resource building and POS tagging for Mizo language. In: 14th Mexican International Conference on Artificial Intelligent (MICAI), Cuernavaca, Mexico, pp. 3–7 (2015)
25. Pathak, A., Pakray, P., Bentham, J.: English–Mizo machine translation using neural and statistical approaches. Neural Comput. Appl. **31**(11), 7615–7631 (2018). https://doi.org/10.1007/s00521-018-3601-3

Efficient Human Feature Recognition Process Using Sclera

Raghav Kachhawaha[1], Pragya Gupta[1], Tushar Kansal[1],
Amitava Chaudhary[1(✉)], and Tanmay Bhowmik[2]

[1] School of Computer Science, University of Petroleum and Energy Studies,
Dehradun, India
a.choudhury2013@gmail.com
[2] Computer Science and Engineering, Bennett University, Greater Noida, India

Abstract. This paper proposes a biometric system that works on a new promising idea of sclera recognition. Sclera is the white part which is evenly present in the human eye with a unique blood vessel pattern. Therefore, it can be used as a new biometric feature or human ID. In this paper different methods are proposed which will help in making a sclera-based biometric system. Firstly, the captured image is undergone image segmentation for further analysis. Secondly, these images are converted into grayscale for complexity reduction and then Gaussian blur and median blur will be applied to reduce the high-frequency components of the image. Thirdly, Otsu's method and adaptive thresholding are applied to the grayscale images for thresholding. The images obtained after applying thresholding methods are superimposed for better image. After this, CNN is used for classification of the dataset into sclera or not. The proposed model achieved 86.84% training accuracy as well as 85.27% testing accuracy.

Keywords: Sclera · Biometric · Blood vessels · Segmentation

1 Introduction

A biometric system, as the name suggests, is a system that takes biological information and measurements of a person to recognize that person [1]. The advent of biometric systems too appears in the scene, to secure the organizations. Not only security, managerial issues in different organizations have also been addressed through biometric systems. It makes the task of identification of people way easier as compared to traditional manual methods. This saves a lot of human effort and time. There are different biometric systems like face recognition, fingerprint, hand geometry, iris detection, etc [2]. Face recognition system is used for identification of a person. However, extraction of facial feature becomes a big challenge as human faces possess complex and multidimensional features [3]. Different angles of the face are required to be stored for accurate results, which is practically very difficult to accomplish. The image of a person captured in different environments produce results that differ in levels of accuracy [4, 5]. Nowadays, one of most important biometric features is fingerprint. But in today's world, fabricating of any person's finger print is a big security issue. Although fingerprint of a person does not change throughout the

© Springer Nature Singapore Pte Ltd. 2020
A. Bhattacharjee et al. (Eds.): MIND 2020, CCIS 1241, pp. 168–181, 2020.
https://doi.org/10.1007/978-981-15-6318-8_15

lifetime, but if there is an accident or a bruise, the fingerprint recognition system might fail [6–8]. Hand geometry is also used as a biometric feature and it works by identifying the geometry or shape of the person's hand. The limitation of this system is that it can be used for verification and not for identification. The efficiency of the system will be low for differently abled persons [9]. Iris-based biometric systems are trusted to be one of the better biometric systems. However, the accuracy decreases dramatically if the image is taken in visible light [10, 11]. To observe dark pigmented iris, it is required to have NIR (near-infrared) wavelength [12].

The proposed biometric feature, sclera can reduce the problems faced in other systems [13]. Sclera is an opaque, fibrous and protective outer layer of the human eye. The sclera that is uniformly present in the human eye contains the multilayered blood vessel patterns with complex, nonlinear deformations. The four layers of sclera are episclera, stroma, lamina fusca and endothelium. Since it is difficult to copy the sclera portion of an individual, therefore, sclera recognition is promising new biometrics for positive human ID [14].

Identification of a person by the vessel pattern of the sclera is possible because, these patterns possess a high degree of randomness, which is never the same for any two individuals, even for identical twins. This makes it an ideal choice for personal identification [15]. Recognition will be done through the unique connective tissues and blood vessels of each individual. The pattern of these tissues and vessels remain fixed throughout a person's lifetime. Although the color of the sclera might change due to diseases, but the pattern formed by the tissues and vessels remains unchanged. The sclera has these patterns, which differ for left eye and right eye of a person, and these patterns are there because the connective tissues and blood vessels are in different orientation and layers.

The biometric system will have the images captured from a high definition camera in its database. Those images will be associated with each individual for unique and accurate identification. The original image is converted into a grayscale image to reduce the color-complexity of the image. After the image is converted into grayscale, Gaussian blur and median blur is applied for noise reduction of image. Noise reduction improves the extracted pattern of the connective tissues and blood vessels in the sclera.

Otsu's method is an exhaustive algorithm for searching the global optimal threshold [16]. Otsu's thresholding consumes less time compared to any other thresholding method [20]. This method is applied on grayscale images to perform cluster-based image thresholding. This thresholding method converts the grayscale images to binary images to find the region of interest in the image on which further processing is to be done. Adaptive method is used to change the threshold of the image dynamically.

Convolution neural network (CNN) is used for binary classification of sclera. The classification task has been performed based on two output class as "sclera" and "not sclera". Binary classification is done to improve the efficiency of the system [23]. The efficiency here signifies the ability to classify the objects into their respective classes, and the binary classifier works effectively in classifying the objects. CNN is a part of neural networks and it is majorly used in image recognition or image classification [24]. The superimposing process [22] has been applied to find more clear structure of the blood vessels thus detection can be easier.

2 Proposed Methodology

The steps involves to recognizing sclera from human eyes are shown in below working flow diagram.

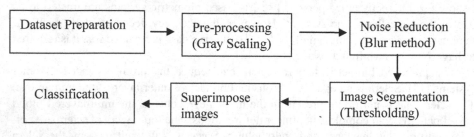

2.1 Dataset Preparation

The dataset consists of the images of human eye. The image is not of single human eye. It is collection of different human eyes since sclera of each pair of human eyes is different. Figure 1 shows the images of human eye on which further work is done.

Fig. 1. The original images of human eye

2.2 Pre-processing

As part of image processing, the images are converted from RBG format to grayscale format so that the system can manipulate it. The images have multiple shades of gray and each dot of pixels can have a different shade of the color (gray). These images are also known as binary images as the grayscale images are kind of black and white images where black has weakest intensity and white has the highest intensity. The intensity of an image is very important for image processing [17] and hence gray scaling is used to reduce the intensity so that the result is obtained without much complexity. Figure 2 is the grayscale-converted image of Fig. 1.

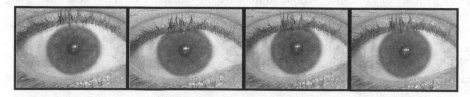

Fig. 2. The gray scale images

2.3   Noise Reduction

In image processing, noise in images is the major problem because it distorts the image and the fine details are also damaged. Two methods have been used for the noise-reduction: Gaussian blur and median blur. Gaussian blur is used with Otsu's method to detect the area of sclera whereas median blur is used with the adaptive thresholding method to detect the vein structure.

Gaussian Blur

The Gaussian function is used which was named after the mathematician and scientist C.F Gauss. It is used to reduce the noise and details from the images. It is known to be linear and low-pass filter. When noise reduction is done in an image, the edges are not preserved in this method. The Gaussian function used in Gaussian blur is shown in Eq. (1).

$$G(x) = \frac{1}{\sqrt{2\pi\sigma^2}} e^{-\frac{x^2}{2\sigma^2}} \tag{1}$$

The Eq. (1) is Gaussian function in one dimensional. The Gaussian function in two-dimensional form is shown in Eq. (2)

$$G(x,y) = \frac{1}{\sqrt{2\pi\sigma^2}} e^{-\frac{x^2+y^2}{2\sigma^2}} \tag{2}$$

Here, variance of Gaussian filter is σ^2, and x is the distance from the origin in horizontal axis, y is the distance from origin in vertical axis. The two dimensional formula results in concentric circles with a Gaussian distribution from the centre point. The Fig. 3 illustrates images after applying Gaussian blur method.

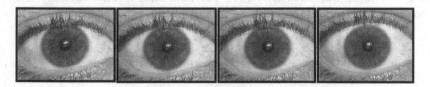

Fig. 3. Images after applying Gaussian blur

Median Blur

Median blur is also used for noise reduction from an image without blurring the fine details of the image [18]. It is a non-linear digital filtering technique. Median blur preserves the edges when reducing noise from an image that is the reason it is widely used in image processing. The noise is removed by changing the intensity value of central pixel value of the window by median intensity value, which is calculated within the window [19]. The median value is calculated by the formula given in Eq. (3).

$$S(i,j) = median(k,l) \in w_{m,n}\{D(i+k,j+l)\} \tag{3}$$

Here, w is used for the window and *mxn* is the window size and central pixel coordinates are (i, j). The coordinates of median intensity value of pixel are (k, l). The Fig. 4 shows the result after applying median blur method.

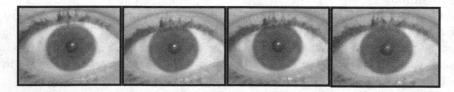

Fig. 4. Images after applying median blur

2.4   Thresholding

The image thresholding is done using two methods: Otsu's method and Adaptive thresholding method. Thresholding of any image is done for its segmentation. To implement image processing, the complexity of the image is reduced and to obtain a better result the image is segmented into smaller parts.

Otsu's Method
In 1979, the maximum classes' variance method was proposed by N. Otsu. It has great stability and is used as a threshold selection method that consumes less time than any other thresholding methods [20]. Figure 5 shows the result after Otsu's method is applied on the original images. The limitation of Otsu's method is that if the image is a small-sized or image's background is uneven then incorrect thresholding is determined which results in segmentation error [21]. For bimodal images, threshold value (t), weighted within-class variance can be as defined by below mentioned equation:

$$\sigma_w^2(t) = q_1(t)\sigma_1^2(t) + q_2(t)\sigma_2^2(t) \tag{4}$$

Where q_1 and q_2 are the probabilities of two classes differentiated by threshold t, and σ_1^2 *and* σ_2^2 are the variances of these two classes.
Where, Class probability $q_{1,2}(t)$ is computed as

$$q_1(t) = \sum_{i=1}^{t} P(i) \, and \, q_2(t) = \sum_{i=t+1}^{I} P(i) \tag{5}$$

And Class mean is computed as

$$\mu_1(t) = \sum_{i=1}^{t} \frac{P(i)}{q_1(t)} \, and \, \mu_{12}(t) = \sum_{i=t+1}^{I} \frac{P(i)}{q_2(t)} \tag{6}$$

Finally, the individual class variances are

$$\sigma_1^2(t) = \sum\nolimits_{i=1}^{t} [i - \mu_1(t)]^2 \frac{P(i)}{q_1(t)} \, and \, \sigma_2^2(t) = \sum\nolimits_{i=t+1}^{I} [i - \mu_1(t)]^2 \frac{P(i)}{q_2(t)} \qquad (7)$$

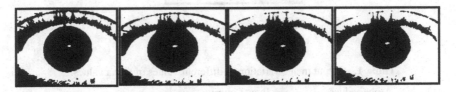

Fig. 5. Images after applying Otsu's method

Adaptive Thresholding Method

Adaptive thresholding is also used for image segmentation. Otsu's method is an exhaustive algorithm it gives global optimal threshold, but the adaptive method changes the threshold of the image dynamically. The images are segmented based on the intensity of each pixel in the image. The pixel value is set to foreground value if its intensity is above the threshold or else it is set to the background value. Figure 6 illustrates images after applying adaptive thresholding.

Fig. 6. Images after applying adaptive method

2.5 Superimposing Result Images

The images obtained after applying Otsu's and adaptive thresholding respectively, are superimposed and a new image is obtained as a result shown in Fig. 7. The technique of superimposing an image is suitable for images having similar as well as various nature [22]. The formula used for superimposing the images is called linear blend operator.

$$g(x) = (1 - \alpha)f_0(x) + \alpha f_1(x) \qquad (8)$$

The image generated is g(x), $f_0(x)$ and $f_1(x)$ are the source images taken after applying Otsu's and adaptive thresholding. The value of α can vary from 0 to 1 and to perform temporal cross dissolve between the two images obtained after Otsu's and adaptive thresholding the value of α taken is between the given range. The value of α is taken as 0.85 and the resultant image is shown below in Fig. 7. The input image also tested with various value of alpha as shown in Table 1.

Fig. 7. Superimposed image

Table 1. Output image variation in different values of alpha values.

Alpha values	Image output
0.2	
0.4	
0.6	
0.8	
0.85	
0.9	

2.6   Binary Classification

Binary classification is used when there are two sets of groups in which the data is to be divided. The data will fall in which group is decided on the basis of some classification rules. Binary classification is done to improve the efficiency of the system [23].

2.6.1 Dataset Preparation

The dataset that contains the images of the human eye through which the sclera is being detected is divided into two parts. Some of the images in the dataset are such from which the detection of sclera becomes difficult so those images are segregated from the images from which sclera is detected. The dataset is divided into a training dataset and testing dataset.

2.6.2 Convolutional Neural Network (CNN)

Today the capability of machines to view and detect object in images, image analysis and classification have become an easy process as compared with the earlier cumbersome methods when the computer processing speed was slow. But as the computer processing speed increased the process of processing the image in the computer becomes much easier and it paved the path for Convolutional Neural Network. All the advancements in computer vision in today's era is possible due to Convolutional Neural Network.

The inspiration behind CNN is from our visual cortex system and is analogous to it, the CNN takes input of an image, assign learnable weights and is able to differentiate one image from another. The CNN has huge advantage over simple feed forward neural network as the CNN takes the image matrix as input which results in better capturing of features of the image as compared to the feed forward neural network which will fail to capture complex images. The CNN performs better for image classification and identification purposes because taking matrix as input reduce the number of parameters and increase the reusability of weights.

2.6.3 Layers

These layers are a part of CNN (convolutional neural network). CNN is a part of neural networks and it is majorly used in image recognition or image classification [24]. An image is given as an input in CNN image classification and it is classified under some categories whereas in the neural network input is a vector. The input in CNN is three dimensional, that is, it has height, length, and breadth. The different layers of CNN are mentioned below.

Convolutional Layer

It is the first layer of CNN which is basically used to extract the features from the images that are used as input. The convolution is carried out by the formula:

$$g(x,y) = h(x,y) * f(x,y) \tag{9}$$

$$g(x,y) = \text{2-D output}$$

$$h(x,y) = \text{Kernel}$$

$$f(x,y) = \text{2-D input}$$

This is called kernel convolved with the image.

For example – Convoluting a $5 \times 5 \times 1$ image with $3 \times 3 \times 1$ image to get a $3 \times 3 \times 1$ convolved feature.

For example – Convoluting a $5 * 5 * 1$ image with $3 * 3 * 1$ image to get a $3 * 3 * 1$ convolved feature.

The kernel K is traversed all around the image and then performs the matrix multiplication operation. In the above examples the kernel K is traversed with stride 1 where it shifts to one side left after performing the multiplication operation and carries on shifting until the entire image is traversed.

The primary objective of convolutional layer is to identify the high-level features of the image like edges. The first layers of convolutional neural network is responsible for capturing lower level features of the image like color gradient, orientation etc. but as we increase the layers in the network, the architecture adapts in capturing the high level features of the image similar to how we would perceive the image.

However, there are some tweaks applied to the network when the network is large as if the network gets larger the dimensions of the image also shrunk. Therefore, there is necessity of a tweak called padding to keep the image dimension sufficient for last layers to capture the features from the image else it would be a futile process to increase the network size. There are two types of padding: Same and Valid padding.

Same Padding – When the image of dimension $5 \times 5 \times 1$ is augmented to $6 \times 6 \times 1$ and then the kernel of dimension $3 \times 3 \times 1$ is traversed over it, the resulting convolved matrix comes out to be of dimension $5 \times 5 \times 1$. Hence, the name is same padding.

Valid Padding - When the image of dimension $5 \times 5 \times 1$ is convolved with kernel of dimension $3 \times 3 \times 1$ the result of convolved matrix comes out to be of $3 \times 3 \times 1$ itself. Hence, the name is valid padding.

Pooling Layer

When the image is too large then the pooling factor reduces the numbers of parameters. It is used for down-sampling to reduce the complexity of layers [25]. Moreover, it is useful for extracting dominant features like rotational and positional features of the image, and maintaining the process effectively and efficiently training the model. There are different types of pooling: Mean pooling, Max pooling, and Sum pooling. Max pooling returns the maximum value from the portion of the image over which the kernel is traversed whereas mean pooling returns the average of all the values in the portion of the kernel. Max pooling is used because along with dimensionality reduction it also works as a noise suppressant, discarding the noisy activations and performing de-noising in the feature map of the image.

Fully Connected Layer

This layer is used as it is the cheap way of learning the non-linear combinations from the output of convolutional layer. After the image has been converted suited for passing onto the feed forward network, the image feature is flattened for feeding it into the feed forward neural network and then applied back propagation in every epochs of training.

Over the number of epochs the network is able to identify the low and high level features of the sclera image and is successfully able to classify the sclera and not sclera part using soft max classification technique. The number of parameters is very large in this layer and hence it takes lots of training time [25].

```
Layer (type)                  Output Shape              Param #
=================================================================
conv2d_1 (Conv2D)             (None, 62, 62, 32)        896

max_pooling2d_1 (MaxPooling2  (None, 31, 31, 32)        0

conv2d_2 (Conv2D)             (None, 29, 29, 32)        9248

max_pooling2d_2 (MaxPooling2  (None, 14, 14, 32)        0

flatten_1 (Flatten)           (None, 6272)              0

dense_1 (Dense)               (None, 128)               802944

dense_2 (Dense)               (None, 2)                 258
=================================================================
Total params: 813,346
Trainable params: 813,346
Non-trainable params: 0
```

Fig. 8. Output after applying CNN

3   Result and Discussion

3.1   Accuracy Graph

The graphs shown below in Fig. 9 respectively describe the accuracy in each epoch, that is, iteration. When the number of iterations increases the accuracy of system to recognize the sclera also increases. Figure 9 show that each time the number of iteration is increased the accuracy has also increased. The dataset was divided into training and testing datasets and the accuracy for both datasets in iterations has been shown in the two below mentioned graphs.

The training of the network was done for the 30 epochs and these graphs shows the transition of accuracy during the training process. The training loss graph indicates that as the training progressed the loss value decreased whereas the accuracy over the training dataset increased. Similar behavior is noticed in the graphs of validation loss and validation accuracy which is calculated over the validation set.

Figure 9 explains the how the accuracy has increased when the number of iteration has increased for the testing dataset. In the graph for all iteration, the accuracy of sclera recognition has gone up. This tells the efficiency of the system and also that the number of iterations is directly proportional.

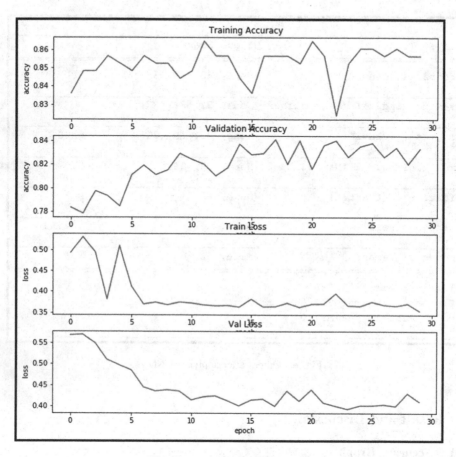

Fig. 9 Accuracy vs epoch graph

The initial dataset was trained on which Gaussian blur along with Otsu's method and median blur with adaptive method was applied. This resulted in the extraction of sclera portion as well as vein structure of the sclera. Since there were lots of images in which detection of sclera portion was not clearly possible so, later that dataset is divided into two sub-datasets, that is, the training and testing dataset so that the images can be segmented. The images are segmented into two categories, which are "sclera" and "not sclera". This is done by using convolutional neural networks (CNN). This resulted into segregation of the data into two categories and that improved the efficiency of the system.

The images captured form high definition camera, are converted into grayscale images first. Further these grayscale images are used for image recognition process. The noise reduction of these images is done by using Gaussian and median blur techniques. The two methods give different results that are shown in Fig. 3 and Fig. 4 respectively. After the noise is removed the images are used for thresholding. The images are segmented into smaller parts to reduce the complexity of the image. Again the two methods of thresholding used are, Otsu's method and adaptive thresholding. Otsu's thresholding resulted in extraction of sclera portion whereas adaptive method resulted into extraction of vein structure. Since there were lots of distorted images in the database as well, therefore CNN is applied to segregate the data into two classes, that is, "sclera" and "not sclera". After that, the resultant images of Otsu's and adaptive methods are superimposed which resulted in a new image. The superimposed images show better vein structure or pattern which makes it easy to detect them.

Proposed work is compared with literature [14] proposed by the Zhou *et.al*. It observed that proposed work based a machine learning approach, Convolutional Neural Network (CNN) has been used for classification of the dataset into different classes. After which segmentation has been done using two methods and later the resultant images are superimposed to get a conspicuous vein pattern.

4 Conclusion and Future Work

In this paper, we have discussed a new biometric feature, sclera. Image processing has been applied on human eye image dataset to identify the region of interest, that is, the sclera region. The dataset contains numerous human eye images that are preprocessed. Two methods have been used for noise reduction of the images namely; Gaussian blur and median blur method, where both the methods produce different resulting images. The region of the image that contains sclera is extracted and the vein structure is obtained by applying the two different thresholding methods – Otsu's thresholding and Adaptive thresholding method. After applying thresholding methods, the resultant images are superimposed to obtain a clear vein pattern. The linear blending operator is used for superimposing the images where the value of α taken is 0.85. The accuracy achieved after applying classification is 86% and hence the new biometric feature sclera can be used in various organizations effectively.

In future, to capture the veins, a microscopic camera is required, through which the images being captured. The microscopic images will help in achieving accuracy of more than 86%. Hence, it can be used for security purpose in many organizations.

References

1. More, S.B., Ubale, A.B., Jondhale, K.C.: Biometric security. In: 2008 First International Conference on Emerging Trends in Engineering and Technology, pp. 701–704 (2008)
2. Femila, M.D., Irudhayaraj, A.A.: Biometric system. In: 2011 3rd International Conference on Electronics Computer Technology, pp. 152–156 (2011)

3. Masupha, L., Zuva, T., Ngwira, S., Esan, O.: Face recognition techniques, their advantages, disadvantages and performance evaluation. In: 2015 International Conference on Computing, Communication and Security (ICCCS), pp. 1–5 (2015)
4. Siswanto, R.S., Nugroho, A.S., Galinium, M.: Implementation of face recognition algorithm for biometrics based time attendance system. In: 2014 International Conference on ICT for Smart Society (ICISS), pp. 149–154 (2014)
5. Zhen, C., Su, Y.: Research about human face recognition technology. In: 2009 International Conference on Test and Measurement, pp. 420–422 (2009)
6. Ivanov, V.I., Baras, J.S.: Authentication of fingerprint scanners. In: 2011 IEEE International Conference on Acoustics, Speech and Signal Processing (ICASSP), pp. 1912–1915 (2011)
7. Qiu, L.: Fingerprint sensor technology. In: 2014 9th IEEE Conference on Industrial Electronics and Applications, Hangzhou, pp. 1433–1436 (2014)
8. Aguilar, G., Sanchez, G., Toscano, K., Salinas, M., Nakano, M., Perez, H.: Fingerprint recognition. In: Second International Conference on Internet Monitoring and Protection (ICIMP 2007), p. 32 (2007)
9. Singh, K., Agrawal, A.K., Pal, C.B.: Hand geometry verification system: a review. In: 2009 International Conference on Ultra Modern Telecommunications & Workshops, pp. 1–7 (2009)
10. Polash, P.P., Monwar, M.M.: Human iris recognition for biometric identification. In: 2007 10th International Conference on Computer and Information Technology, pp. 1–5 (2007)
11. Daugman, J.: How iris recognition works. IEEE Trans. Circuits Syst. Video Technol. 14(1), 21–30 (2004)
12. Daugman, J.: How iris recognition works. In: Proceedings. International Conference on Image Processing, Rochester, p. I (2002)
13. Alkassar, S., Woo, W.L., Dlay, S.S., Chambers, J.A.: A novel method for sclera recognition with images captured on-the-move and at-a-distance. In: 2016 4th International Conference on Biometrics and Forensics (IWBF), pp. 1–6 (2016)
14. Zhou, Z., Du, E.Y., Thomas, N.L., Delp, E.J.: A new human identification method: sclera recognition. IEEE Trans. Syst. Man Cybern. - Part A Syst. Hum. 42(3), 571–583 (2012)
15. Das, A., Pal, U., Blumenstein, M., Ballester, M.A.F.: Sclera recognition - a survey. In: Proceedings - 2nd IAPR Asian Conference on Pattern Recognition, ACPR 2013, pp. 917–921 (2013). https://doi.org/10.1109/acpr.2013.168
16. Liu, D., Yu, J.: Otsu method and K-means. In: 2009 Ninth International Conference on Hybrid Intelligent Systems, pp. 344–349 (2009)
17. Papamarkou, I., Papamarkos, N.: Conversion of color documents to grayscale. In: 21st Mediterranean Conference on Control and Automation, pp. 1609–1614 (2013)
18. Wichman, R., Neuvo, Y.: Multilevel median filters for image processing. In: IEEE International Symposium on Circuits and Systems, vol. 1, pp. 412–415 (1991)
19. Vishaga, S., Das, S.L.: A survey on switching median filters for impulse noise removal. In: 2015 International Conference on Circuits, Power and Computing Technologies [ICCPCT 2015], pp. 1–6 (2015)
20. Qu, Z., Zhang, L.: Research on image segmentation based on the improved Otsu algorithm. In: 2010 Second International Conference on Intelligent Human-Machine Systems and Cybernetics, pp. 228–231 (2010)
21. Chan, F.H.Y., Lam, F.K., Zhu, H.: Adaptive thresholding by variational method. IEEE Trans. Image Process. 7(3), 468–473 (1998)
22. Efimov, I., Novikov, A.I., Sablina, V.A.: Image superimposition technique in computer vision systems using contour analysis methods. In: 2016 5th Mediterranean Conference on Embedded Computing (MECO), pp. 132–136 (2016)

23. Tung, H., Cheng, C., Chen, Y., Chen, Y., Huang, S., Chen, A.: Binary classification and data analysis for modeling calendar anomalies in financial markets. In: 2016 7th International Conference on Cloud Computing and Big Data (CCBD), pp. 116–121 (2016)
24. Dahia, G., Santos, M., Segundo, M.P.: A study of CNN outside of training conditions. In: 2017 IEEE International Conference on Image Processing (ICIP), pp. 3820–3824 (2017)
25. Albawi, S., Mohammed, T.A., Al-Zawi, S.: Understanding of a convolutional neural network. In: 2017 International Conference on Engineering and Technology (ICET), pp. 1–6 (2017)

Optimization of Local Ordering Technique for Nearest Neighbour Circuits

Lalengmawia Chhangte$^{(\boxtimes)}$ ⓘ and Alok Chakrabarty ⓘ

Department of Computer Science and Engineering,
National Institute of Technology Meghalaya, Shillong, India
{moya,alok.chakrabarty}@nitm.ac.in

Abstract. Most quantum architectures restrict qubit interactions. They allow a qubit to interact with another qubit only if they are directly connected, and this constraint is the nearest neighbour (NN) constraint. If the interacting qubits are not adjacent, we need to insert swap gates appropriately to make them adjacent. Since the insertion of swap gates increases the circuit cost, a minimal number of swaps has to be performed. This paper illustrates the possibility of swap gate reduction for 2D NN circuits by better re-ordering of qubits using a multi-window look-ahead approach. Using this technique, near optimal solutions for NN circuit conversion are obtained. Experimental evaluation shows the effectiveness of our proposed local re-ordering algorithm for the reduction of swap requirements. We have compared our results with the most recent results, and a significant improvement is observed, with a maximum of 37.5% swap gate reduction.

Keywords: Quantum computing · Nearest neighbour · 2D architecture · Quantum circuit · Optimization · Local ordering algorithm

1 Introduction

Quantum computing is a promising technology for solving today's computationally hard problems. It will be most welcomed in the field of security, artificial intelligence, simulation of molecules and financial modelling. Different technologies have been proposed for the implementation of quantum computers. The typical limitations of quantum computing technologies like ion traps [15], quantum dots [8], and superconducting technology [16] are the limited connectivity between qubits and the constraint that computations can be performed between adjacent qubits only. We need to ensure that a gate's qubits are nearest neighbour (NN) compliant before a gate operation is performed. For qubits that are not adjacent, we move them towards each other until they become adjacent; a swap gate is used for this purpose. Recently, real quantum computers have been deployed in the cloud by IBM [7]. The initial versions imposed more restrictions on qubit connectivity where a CNOT gate can be applied only in one direction. The latest version, however, allows bi-directional connectivity of CNOT gates.

© Springer Nature Singapore Pte Ltd. 2020
A. Bhattacharjee et al. (Eds.): MIND 2020, CCIS 1241, pp. 182–192, 2020.
https://doi.org/10.1007/978-981-15-6318-8_16

Table 1. NCV quantum gates

NOT gate	V gate	$V^\dagger$ gate
$\begin{pmatrix} 0 & 1 \\ 1 & 0 \end{pmatrix}$ $a \longrightarrow \oplus \longrightarrow x$	$\begin{pmatrix} \frac{1+i}{2} & \frac{1-i}{2} \\ \frac{1-i}{2} & \frac{1+i}{2} \end{pmatrix}$ $a \longrightarrow \boxed{v} \longrightarrow x$	$\begin{pmatrix} \frac{1-i}{2} & \frac{1+i}{2} \\ \frac{1+i}{2} & \frac{1-i}{2} \end{pmatrix}$ $a \longrightarrow \boxed{v^\dagger} \longrightarrow x$

In this work, we focus on reducing the number of swaps required. The effectiveness of the algorithm is decided based on the number of swap gates inserted, which we try to minimize. On studying the reported results from the existing works, we can see that no one technique can optimize all classes of circuits. We found that the existing algorithms can give an optimal solution for some benchmark circuits, while they give bad results for others. In this paper, we propose a qubit re-ordering technique, motivated by a window-based look-ahead scheme, to reduce swap requirements. The window defines the gates to be considered from circuit tail for cost evaluation. A circuit tail is the netlist of gates in a quantum circuit that is not yet processed. For swap cost estimation, we use multiple window sizes where the sizes increase linearly until the optimal swap is obtained; an alternative to existing methods which used a fixed window size [22]. Determining the best window size for a given circuit is a question that cannot be answered unless we analyze all possible window sizes.

The rest of the paper is organized as follows: Sect. 2 explains the fundamentals of quantum computing. Section 3 discusses the literature review on circuit mapping problem and describes the proposed algorithm. Section 4 discusses the experimental results; and, finally, Sect. 5 provides the conclusion and future works.

2   Background

Classical computers operate on a bit that can store the states 0 or 1, one at a time. Likewise, a quantum computer operates on a qubit, that can have the basis states $|0\rangle$ and $|1\rangle$ or a state which can be a superposition of these basis states. A superposition state can be represented as $|\psi\rangle = \alpha|0\rangle + \beta|1\rangle$ such that $|\alpha^2| + |\beta^2| = 1$, where α and β are complex numbers. The states of a qubit can be formally represented in a 2D complex Hilbert space, where $|0\rangle = \begin{pmatrix} 1 \\ 0 \end{pmatrix}$ and $|1\rangle = \begin{pmatrix} 0 \\ 1 \end{pmatrix}$.

Any computation on a quantum computer is represented in the form of quantum circuits (algorithms). A quantum circuit is a basic design for performing a task in a quantum system. In a diagram of a quantum circuit, a solid line represents a qubit. The gates [2] are applied on the qubits to perform an operation. Table 1 shows some NCV quantum gates. A controlled gate can be formed with these single-qubit gates, as shown in Table 2, column 1. The symbol U for Controlled gate represents any unitary operation gate like NOT gate, V gate and $V^\dagger$ gate; thus, two-qubit gates such as Controlled NOT (CNOT) gate, Controlled $V^\dagger$ gate and Controlled V can be formed. The control qubit q_c is represented as a

Table 2. Multi-qubit gates

Controlled gate		Swap gate	
$\begin{pmatrix} 1 & 0 & 0 & 0 \\ 0 & 1 & 0 & 0 \\ 0 & 0 & & \\ 0 & 0 & U & \end{pmatrix}$	$q_c \longrightarrow\!\bullet\!\longrightarrow x$ $q_t \longrightarrow\boxed{U}\longrightarrow y$	$\begin{pmatrix} 1 & 0 & 0 & 0 \\ 0 & 0 & 1 & 0 \\ 0 & 1 & 0 & 0 \\ 1 & 0 & 0 & 0 \end{pmatrix}$	$a \longrightarrow\!\times\!\longrightarrow b$ $b \longrightarrow\!\times\!\longrightarrow a$

dot on the qubit line. If q_c is set, the operation U is performed on q_t. Otherwise, there is no change in output. A swap gate is also shown in Table 2, column 2. As the name suggests, it simply interchanges two qubits.

The physical arrangement of qubits can be represented as a grid or a graph. The nodes represent physical qubits, and the edges between two nodes represent the connectivity (nearest neighbour connectivity) between two qubits. A real quantum architecture [7] in current technology has more constraints which make a graph more suitable for representing qubit coupling.

The NN satisfaction of a gate is checked using the metric called Nearest Neighbour Cost (NNC) [23]. In general, the NNC of a gate $g(q_c, q_t)$ is the shortest distance between q_c and q_t, minus one.

$$NNC(g) = mindist(q_c, q_t) - 1 \tag{1}$$

If the arrangement of qubits is interpreted as a grid, the minimum distance would be the Manhattan distance between q_c and q_t. The NNC of a circuit or sub-circuit C is calculated as the sum of NNC values of all gates,

$$NNC(C) = \sum_{g \in C} NNC(g) \tag{2}$$

2.1 Mapping Quantum Circuits to 2D Nearest Neighbour Architectures

The execution of a quantum algorithm requires satisfaction of every constraint imposed by the quantum architecture. The mapping problem starts with the determination of an initial qubit placement or permutation and then the re-ordering of qubits is done wherever required. The NN-constraint satisfiability problem may get highly alleviated by the determination of a suitable initial qubit placement, thus requiring minimal additional swap gates. However, to know the suitable permutation, we need to run a local qubit re-ordering algorithm separately for several permutations.

Example 1: Consider the input circuit shown in Fig. 1(a) and the initial arrangement of qubits in Fig. 2(a). The circuit gates are executed from left to right. The first three gates' qubits $(q3, q2)$, $(q1, q2)$ and $(q4, q6)$ are located adjacent to each other in the grid. On reading the fourth gate $g(q2, q4)$, the qubits $q4$ and $q2$ are found to be not adjacent. Before executing the gate, we need to make

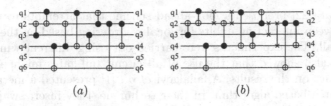

(a)   (b)

Fig. 1. Example of 2D NN conversion. (a) Input quantum circuit. (b) Output circuit

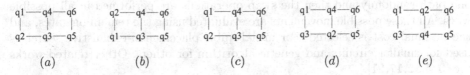

(a)   (b)   (c)   (d)   (e)

Fig. 2. (a) Initial placement of qubits. (b) After swapping q1 and q2 (c) After swapping q1 and q2 (d) After swapping q3 and q2 (e) After swapping q2 and q4

them adjacent by inserting swap gates. Here, we swap $q1$ and $q2$, and the fourth gate becomes NN-compliant (see Fig. 2(b)). On reading the next gate $g(q1, q4)$, we find that $q1$ and $q4$ are not adjacent; again, we need to insert swap gates to make them adjacent. A swap is performed between $q1$ and $q2$, see Fig. 2(c). The same process continues until the last gate is reached. Figure 1(b) shows the corresponding NN-compliant circuit.

3 Re-ordering of Qubits

In this section, we summarise the existing works on qubit re-ordering (or, local ordering) and later explain how a swap reduction can be further improved. In the past, several approaches have been discussed to reduce the swap requirements for NN satisfaction. The primary problem is to select the best swap option from several permutations. Most of the existing approaches are heuristic-based, which do not guarantee optimal solutions. Heuristic-based algorithms are adopted to reduce the execution time because finding the best solution requires a significant amount of time. An exhaustive search analyses all possible options for swap gate insertions while a greedy search finds an acceptable solution from smaller search space.

Works on mapping problem for Linear Nearest Neighbour (1D NN) architectures were earlier presented in [6,13,14,18,24]. Several works on LNN were summarized in [23]. Later, 2D architectures were considered by Shafaei et al. [19], Lin et al. [10] and Lye et al. [11]. In these works, scalability and longer runtime were identified as the most common drawbacks. For two-dimensional Nearest Neighbour (2D NN) architectures, [11] reported optimal swap counts for small NCV circuits. Shrivastwa et al. [20] proposed a fast local re-ordering technique that performs routing by moving qubits vertically and then horizontally until the interacting qubits become adjacent.

Wille *et al.* [22] proposed a look-ahead scheme that attempts to reduce the distance between interacting qubits for local re-ordering based on the effects on the circuit tail. The experiments were carried out using different window sizes. The authors also showed that the use of all circuit tail gates might not have a positive impact on the results. Alfailakawi *et al.* [1] presented a meta-heuristic harmony search-based algorithm. In their technique, they insert swap gates by exploring all possible paths, and the best swap option is selected. Kole *et al.* [9] proposed a heuristic where the re-ordering of qubits is performed by selecting one path randomly and then the swap operations are performed in all possible ways. All these possible movements are evaluated using the remaining gates, and the minimal cost is selected. For initial qubit placements, exhaustive search is used for smaller circuits and genetic algorithm for others. Other related works are [3–5,12,17,21].

3.1   Proposed Algorithm for Local Re-ordering

The proposed algorithm is a window-based look-ahead approach; wherein multiple windows are applied for cost estimation. The circuit is processed from left to right, and the gates are checked for the NN-constraint satisfiability. Swap gates are inserted before the gate if it does not satisfy the NN-constraint. Consider $g_i(q_c, q_t)$ is the current gate that does not satisfy the NN-constraint, that is, $NNC(g_i) > 0$. We obtain all possible movements of q_c and q_t such that the distance between them is reduced by exactly one. The best movement of qubits is selected. To decide the best swap, a linearly increasing window size is used. Among several swap options, the one with the minimum cost wins over the others. The cost is the sum of all the NNC values of the gates within the window. Initially, the window size (w) is set to 1; that is, the first gate g_{i+1} from the circuit tail is considered. To calculate the cost, we first apply the swap on the current grid separately for each swap option j, and we calculate the cost as follows:

$$C_{g_i, w=1}^j = NNC(g_{i+1}) \tag{3}$$

After calculating the cost for all the swap options, we check the minimum cost. If there is one minimum cost, then we select the swap pair with minimum cost. Otherwise, we calculate the cost again with increased window size, $w = 2$, and check for minimum cost. If there is one swap pair with minimum cost, it is applied. Else, the window size is increased by one, and the process continues until one minimum cost is found, or until the circuit tail is exhausted. If there is no distinct minimum cost even after reaching the end of the circuit tail, we select one option randomly. The cost calculation for window size, n, is

$$C_{g_i, w=n}^j = NNC(g_{i+1}) + NNC(g_{i+2}) + \ldots + NNC(g_{i+n}) \tag{4}$$

The proposed technique avoids all possible permutations by considering only the neighbouring qubits for swap evaluation, one at a time. It gradually reduces the distance by one until the interacting qubits become adjacent. By incorporating multiple windows for swap selection, a locally optimal solution is

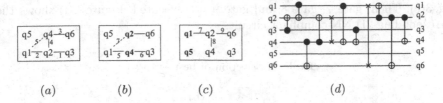

(a) (b) (c)   (d)

Fig. 3. Local ordering of qubits. (a)–(c) Steps for swap gate insertion (d) Output circuit

---

Algorithm 1: Selection of swap

 Input: S, all swap options; $Grid$, current grid;
1 $W \leftarrow 1$; //Initialize window size to 1
2 $C \leftarrow [\,]$;
3 **while** *true* **do**
4   **foreach** s *in* S **do**
5    $|$ $C(s) \leftarrow CalculateCost(s, W, Grid)$;
6   **end**
7   $MINCOST \leftarrow GetMinimumCost(C)$;
8   $min\_cnt \leftarrow Count\ MINCOST\ in\ C$;
9   **if** $min\_cnt = 1$ **then**
10    $|$ *break*;
11   **end**
12   $W \leftarrow W + 1$
13 **end**
14 Return S_i where $C(S_i) = MINCOST$

---

obtained. The use of a fixed window size does not guarantee local best solution. Algorithm 1 shows the procedure for selecting the best swap.

Example 2: Consider the same circuit in Fig. 1(a). The swap process is shown in Fig. 3. The first four gates satisfy the NN-constraint, but gate 5 $g(q1, q4)$ does not; $q1$ and $q4$ are not neighbours, indicated by a dotted line in Fig. 3(a). The neighbours of $q1$ and $q4$ are $q2$ and $q5$. The possible swaps are $(q1, q2)$, $(q1, q5)$, $(q4, q2)$, $(q4, q5)$. Among these four options, we select the best one based on the analysis shown in Table 3(a). The selection process starts with window size, $w = 1$. For $w = 1$, the minimum cost is 1, shared by three options (*namely, j = 1, 2, 4*). Since minimum cost is shared by more than one options, we increase the window size by 1. On applying window size, $w = 2$, the minimum cost is 1, and it is shared by two options (*namely, j = 2, 4*). Next, for window size $w = 3$, we have one minimum cost, $min(C_{w=3}^j) = 1$ for $j = 4$. We apply the swap option $(q4, q2)$ in the current grid. Figure 3(b) shows the new grid arrangement.

  Now, gate 5 $(q1, q4)$ and gate 6 $(q3, q4)$ are NN-compliant, but gate 7 $g(q1, q2)$ does not satisfy the NN-constraint; the same process is applied. Neighbours of both $q1$ and $q2$ are $q4$ and $q5$; the swap options are $(q1, q4)$, $(q1, q5)$, $(q2, q4)$, $(q2, q5)$. Cost calculation is shown in Table 3(b). The best option is $C_{w=2}^1 = 0$; thus, we perform a swap between $q1$ and $q4$; the resultant ordering is shown in

Fig. 3(c). Then, gate 7, gate 8 and gate 9 are executed. Figure 3(d) shows the corresponding 2D NN-compliant circuit.

Table 3. Selection of best swap

(a)				(b)		
Swap option j	Cost			Swap option j	Cost	
	$C^j_{w=1}$	$C^j_{w=2}$	$C^j_{w=3}$		$C^j_{w=1}$	$C^j_{w=2}$
1: (q1, q5)	**1**	2	3	1: (q1, q5)	**0**	**0**
2: (q1, q2)	**1**	**1**	3	2: (q1, q4)	**0**	1
3: (q4, q5)	2	2	3	3: (q2, q5)	1	2
4: (q4, q2)	**1**	**1**	**1**	4: (q2, q4)	1	1

Table 4. Comparison of swap counts for small benchmarks having up to six qubits

Benchmark			Swap count			Proposed		% Impr		
Name	n	#2QG	[1]	[22]	[9]	Grid	Swap	[1]	[22]	[9]
3_17_13	3	13	4	5	4	2×2	5	−25	0	−25
4_49_17	4	30	–	–	9	2×2	12	–	–	−33.3
4gt10-v1_81	5	36	11	15	13	2×3	11	0	+26.67	+15.38
4gt11_84	5	7	1	–	2	2×3	1	0	–	+50
4gt12-v1_89	6	52	16	–	22	2×3	16	0	–	+27.27
4gt13-v1_93	5	16	–	–	3	2×3	3	–	–	0
4gt4-v0_80	6	43	13	–	18	2×3	11	+15.38	–	+38.89
4gt5_75	5	22	6	–	–	2×3	5	+16.67	–	+28.57
4mod5-v1_23	5	24	8	–	10	2×3	7	12.50	–	+30
4mod7-v0_95	5	40	9	–	14	2×3	9	0	–	+35.71
aj-e11_165	5	59	15	–	24	2×3	16	−6.67	0	+33.33
alu-v4_36	5	31	8	–	9	2×3	7	+12.50	–	+22.22
decod24-v3_46	4	9	2	–	2	2×2	2	0	–	0
hwb4_52	4	23	7	–	7	2×2	6	+14.29	–	+14.29
hwb5_55	5	109	38	37	44	2×3	39	−5.41	−2.63	+11.36
hwb6_58	6	146	63	59	62	2×3	54	+14.29	+8.47	+12.9
mod5adder_128	6	81	28	33	35	2×3	25	+10.71	+24.24	+28.57
mod8-10_177	6	108	39	–	41	2×3	36	+7.69	–	+12.2
QFT5	5	10	3	–	3	2×3	3	0	–	0
QFT6	6	15	5	–	8	2×3	5	0	–	+37.5
rd32-v0_67	4	8	–	–	2	2×2	2	–	–	0

4   Experimental Results

We perform the experiments in two stages. In the first experiment, we consider benchmark circuits that are composed of qubits up to six in count. For the initial placement, all permutations are used. The effectiveness of our proposed algorithm is evaluated by comparing our results with the most recent results reported in [1,9] and [22]. These are known to be the best performing algorithms, to the best of our knowledge. We implemented our proposed algorithm in Python and executed that on a system with Intel Core i5 microprocessor and Windows 10 operating system. Each row in Table 4 shows benchmark name, number of qubits, number of 2-qubit gates, swap count of existing works, grid size and swap count of the proposed result and the percentages of improvements. The average improvements over [1,22] and [9] are 9%, 3.87%, 16.18%, respectively. For all the circuits shown in Table 4, the average execution time is less than 0.1 s.

Table 5. Comparison of swap counts for benchmarks having more than six qubits

Benchmark			Swap count			Proposed			% Impr		
Name	n	#2QG	[1]	[22]	[9]	Grid	Swap	Time(s)	[1]	[22]	[9]
cnt3-5_180	16	125	–	–	67	4 × 4	54	0.033	–	–	+19.41
cycle10_2_110	12	1212	467	483	598	4 × 4	456	0.136	+2.36	+5.59	+23.75
ham15_108	15	458	199	223	249	4 × 6	194	0.08	+2.51	+13	+22.09
ham7_104	7	87	26	37	34	2 × 4	30	0.0121	−15.38	+18.93	+11.76
hwb7_62	8	2659	1162	1050	1292	3 × 3	958	0.18	+17.56	+8.76	+25.85
hwb8_118	9	16608	6787	6316	8091	3 × 4	6386	1.429	+5.91	−1.11	+21.07
hwb9_123	10	20405	9230	8522	10749	4 × 3	8467	1.913	+8.27	+0.65	+21.23
plus127mod8192_162	14	65455	30435	27549	37626	4 × 4	27951	8.984	+8.16	−1.46	+25.71
plus63mod4096_163	13	29019	13031	11764	16072	4×4	11799	3.604	+9.45	-0.30	+26.59
plus63mod8192_164	14	37101	17346	15484	21206	4 × 4	15479	4.998	+10.76	+0.03	+27.01
QFT10	10	45	31	37	43	3 × 4	32	0.008	−3.23	+13.51	+25.58
QFT7	7	21	10	13	13	3 × 3	11	0.002	−10	+15.38	+15.38
QFT8	8	28	16	17	16	3 × 3	15	0.003	+6.25	+11.76	+6.25
QFT9	9	36	19	22	25	3 × 3	19	0.005	0	+13.64	+24
rd53_135	7	78	28	30	40	2 × 4	30	0.011	−7.14	0	+25
rd73_140	10	76	21	–	31	4 × 3	20	0.008	+4.76	–	+35.48
rd84_142	15	112	42	–	64	4 × 4	40	0.024	+4.76	–	+37.5
Shor3	10	2076	1042	1010	1210	4 × 3	993	0.279	+4.70	+1.68	+17.93
Shor4	12	5002	2925	2757	3255	3 × 5	2590	0.67	+11.45	+6.06	+20.43
Shor5	14	10265	6246	6344	7608	5 × 3	6569	1.794	+4.43	+5.91	+21.54
Shor6	16	18885	12888	12468	14801	4 × 4	12048	4.109	+6.52	+3.37	+18.6
sym9_148	10	4452	–	1446	2065	4 × 3	1445	0.31	–	+0.07	+30.02
sys6-v0_144	10	62	–	–	32	4 × 4	24	0.011	–	–	+25
urf1_149	9	57770	30279	29252	29084	3 × 3	27080	8.313	+10.57	+7.43	+6.89
urf2_152	8	25150	12982	12872	12532	4 × 3	11406	2.937	+12.14	+11.39	+8.98
urf3_155	10	132340	56055	69693	70985	4 × 3	64551	20.662	−15.16	+7.38	+9.06
urf5_158	9	51380	26778	25887	25645	4 × 3	23850	7.142	+10.93	+7.87	+7.0
urf6_160	15	53700	32681	31540	33152	4 × 6	29430	15.19	+9.95	+6.69	+11.23

The results for the second set of experiments are reported in Table 5. The labelling of columns is the same as for Table 4; the average execution times (in seconds) are also presented. The table consists of benchmark circuits with more than six qubits. For initial placement, we used pseudo-randomly generated initial permutations. The qubits of the beginning gates of the circuits are placed towards the middle positions of grids and the remaining qubits at random positions. The average improvements over [1,22] and [9] are 6.51%, 4.02% and 20.37%, respectively. On analysing the results presented in Table 4 and Table 5, it is not possible to point out the best performing algorithm. All the algorithms give good and bad solutions for different benchmark circuits. It is also observed that the proposed algorithm performs better for larger circuits. We also compared the optimal results reported by [9]. As reported, their algorithm requires a long runtime, and therefore only a few circuits were executed. On comparing their results with ours, we achieved better results for some circuits; and, the swap differences for most circuits are comparable.

The proposed algorithm applies multiple windows for determining the best swap, which is very effective when compared to using one window. The costs estimated by one window also results in multiple choices in the selection of the best option, in many cases. Alternatively, in the proposed work, larger window sizes are applied iteratively until the best or near-optimal solution is found. The elimination of supplying window size as user input is another advantage of the proposed algorithm.

5   Conclusion and Future Works

In this paper, we discussed work on nearest neighbour optimization for quantum circuits for 2D nearest neighbour architectures. We reviewed the existing approaches and proposed a local re-ordering method for optimized mapping of the quantum circuits. The re-ordering scheme of qubits has a significant impact on the overall circuit cost. To insert a swap gate for nearest neighbour satisfaction, we apply a window several times wherein the window size increases linearly, and then halts when one minimal cost is obtained. The use of multiple windows ensures locally optimal swap gate insertion. The experimental results proved the effectiveness of the proposed algorithm for swap reduction. The future work is to propose an excellent initial placement technique for the presented local ordering algorithm; at present, random permutations are used for larger circuits.

References

1. Alfailakawi, M.G., Ahmad, I., Hamdan, S.: Harmony-search algorithm for 2D nearest neighbor quantum circuits realization. Expert Syst. Appl. **61**(C), 16–27 (2016). https://doi.org/10.1016/j.eswa.2016.04.038
2. Barenco, A., et al.: Elementary gates for quantum computation. Phys. Rev. A **52**, 3457–3467 (1995). https://doi.org/10.1103/PhysRevA.52.3457

3. Bhattacharjee, A., Bandyopadhyay, C., Wille, R., Drechsler, R., Rahaman, H.: A novel approach for nearest neighbor realization of 2D quantum circuits. In: 2018 IEEE Computer Society Annual Symposium on VLSI (ISVLSI), pp. 305–310 (2018). https://doi.org/10.1109/ISVLSI.2018.00063

4. Bhattacharjee, A., Bandyopadhyay, C., Mondal, B., Wille, R., Drechsler, R., Rahaman, H.: An efficient nearest neighbor design for 2D quantum circuits. In: Singh, A.K., Fujita, M., Mohan, A. (eds.) Design and Testing of Reversible Logic. LNEE, vol. 577, pp. 215–231. Springer, Singapore (2020). https://doi.org/10.1007/978-981-13-8821-7_12

5. Bhattacharjee, D., Chattopadhyay, A.: Depth-optimal quantum circuit placement for arbitrary topologies. CoRR abs/1703.08540 (2017)

6. Hirata, Y., Nakanishi, M., Yamashita, S., Nakashima, Y.: An efficient method to convert arbitrary quantum circuits to ones on a linear nearest neighbor architecture. In: 2009 Third International Conference on Quantum, Nano and Micro Technologies, pp. 26–33 (2009). https://doi.org/10.1109/ICQNM.2009.25

7. IBM QX device. https://quantumexperience.ng.bluemix.net/qx/devices

8. Jones, N.C., et al.: Layered architecture for quantum computing. Phys. Rev. X **2**, 031007 (2012). https://doi.org/10.1103/PhysRevX.2.031007

9. Kole, A., Datta, K., Sengupta, I.: A new heuristic for N-dimensional nearest neighbor realization of a quantum circuit. IEEE Trans. Comput. Aided Des. Integr. Circuits Syst. **37**(1), 182–192 (2018). https://doi.org/10.1109/TCAD.2017.2693284

10. Lin, C., Sur-Kolay, S., Jha, N.K.: PAQCS: physical design-aware fault-tolerant quantum circuit synthesis. IEEE Trans. Very Large Scale Integr. (VLSI) Syst. **23**(7), 1221–1234 (2015). https://doi.org/10.1109/TVLSI.2014.2337302

11. Lye, A., Wille, R., Drechsler, R.: Determining the minimal number of swap gates for multi-dimensional nearest neighbor quantum circuits. In: The 20th Asia and South Pacific Design Automation Conference, pp. 178–183 (2015). https://doi.org/10.1109/ASPDAC.2015.7059001

12. Marbaniang, L., Kole, A., Datta, K., Sengupta, I.: Design of efficient quantum circuits using nearest neighbor constraint in 2D architecture. In: Phillips, I., Rahaman, H. (eds.) RC 2017. LNCS, vol. 10301, pp. 248–253. Springer, Cham (2017). https://doi.org/10.1007/978-3-319-59936-6_19

13. Maslov, D., Falconer, S.M., Mosca, M.: Quantum circuit placement. IEEE Trans. Comput. Aided Des. Integr. Circuits Syst. **27**(4), 752–763 (2008). https://doi.org/10.1109/TCAD.2008.917562

14. AlFailakawi, M., AlTerkawi, L., Ahmad, I., Hamdan, S.: Line ordering of reversible circuits for linear nearest neighbor realization. Quantum Inf. Process. **12**(10), 3319–3339 (2013). https://doi.org/10.1007/s11128-013-0601-1

15. Nickerson, N.H., Li, Y., Benjamin, S.C.: Topological quantum computing with a very noisy network and local error rates approaching one percent. Nat. Commun. **4** (2013). https://www.nature.com/articles/ncomms2773. Article no. 1756

16. Ohliger, M., Eisert, J.: Efficient measurement-based quantum computing with continuous-variable systems. Phys. Rev. A **85**(6) (2012). https://doi.org/10.1103/physreva.85.062318

17. Rahman, M.M., Dueck, G.W., Chattopadhyay, A., Wille, R.: Integrated synthesis of linear nearest neighbor ancilla-free MCT circuits. In: 2016 IEEE 46th International Symposium on Multiple-Valued Logic (ISMVL), pp. 144–149 (2016). https://doi.org/10.1109/ISMVL.2016.54

18. Shafaei, A., Saeedi, M., Pedram, M.: Optimization of quantum circuits for interaction distance in linear nearest neighbor architectures. In: 2013 50th ACM/EDAC/IEEE Design Automation Conference (DAC), pp. 1–6 (2013). https://doi.org/10.1145/2463209.2488785
19. Shafaei, A., Saeedi, M., Pedram, M.: Qubit placement to minimize communication overhead in 2D quantum architectures. In: 2014 19th Asia and South Pacific Design Automation Conference (ASP-DAC), pp. 495–500 (2014). https://doi.org/10.1109/ASPDAC.2014.6742940
20. Shrivastwa, R.R., Datta, K., Sengupta, I.: Fast qubit placement in 2D architecture using nearest neighbor realization. In: 2015 IEEE International Symposium on Nanoelectronic and Information Systems, pp. 95–100 (2015). https://doi.org/10.1109/iNIS.2015.59
21. Taha, S.M.R.: Fundamentals of reversible logic. Reversible Logic Synthesis Methodologies with Application to Quantum Computing. SSDC, vol. 37, pp. 7–16. Springer, Cham (2016). https://doi.org/10.1007/978-3-319-23479-3_2
22. Wille, R., Keszocze, O., Walter, M., Rohrs, P., Chattopadhyay, A., Drechsler, R.: Look-ahead schemes for nearest neighbor optimization of 1D and 2D quantum circuits. In: 2016 21st Asia and South Pacific Design Automation Conference (ASP-DAC), pp. 292–297 (2016). https://doi.org/10.1109/ASPDAC.2016.7428026
23. Wille, R., Lye, A., Drechsler, R.: Exact reordering of circuit lines for nearest neighbor quantum architectures. IEEE Trans. Comput. Aided Des. Integr. Circuits Syst. 33(12), 1818–1831 (2014). https://doi.org/10.1109/TCAD.2014.2356463
24. Wille, R., Saeedi, M., Drechsler, R.: Synthesis of reversible functions beyond gate count and quantum cost. In: International Workshop on Logic Synthesis (2009)

Attention-Based English to Mizo Neural Machine Translation

Candy Lalrempuii[✉][iD] and Badal Soni[iD]

National Institute of Technology Silchar, Silchar, Assam, India
candy@rs.cse.student.nits.ac.in, badal@nits.ac.in
http://www.nits.ac.in/

Abstract. Machine Translation alleviates the need of human translators for source to target languages translation by enabling instant translation in multiple languages. Neural Machine Translation (NMT) has exhibited remarkable results in case of high-resource languages. However, for resource scare languages, NMT does not perform equivalently well. In this paper, various NMT models based on different configurations such as unidirectional and bidirectional Long Short Term Memory (LSTM), deep and shallow networks and optimization methods like Stochastic Gradient Descent (SGD) and Adam has been trained and tested for resource scare English to Mizo language pair. The quality of output translations have been evaluated using automatic evaluation metrics and analyzed the predicted translations based on best and worst performances of test data.

Keywords: Machine translation · Neural machine translation · Mizo language

1 Introduction

Research in Machine Translation (MT) approaches over the years have evolved from simple word-to-word translations using bilingual dictionaries to rule-based transfer and interlingua methods and on to more sophisticated corpus-based approaches.

While rule-based instances such as interlingua-based approach performs translation using an additional interlingual representation without the need of a transfer component, interlingua definition becomes more challenging for a wider domain. Corpus-based approaches set out to eliminate a number of these shortcomings by doing away with complex linguistic rules and wholly relying on the availability of a parallel dataset.

Neural Machine Translation (NMT) is a corpus-based technique which depends entirely on the parallel corpus. NMT systems comprise of an end-to-end framework that integrates all the processes involved in the translation process into a single model [2,3,16], as opposed to Statistical Machine Translation (SMT), a corpus-based approach where the sub-components are separately

A. Bhattacharjee et al. (Eds.): MIND 2020, CCIS 1241, pp. 193–203, 2020.
https://doi.org/10.1007/978-981-15-6318-8_17

trained. A primary sequence-to-sequence NMT model relies on an Recurrent Neural Network (RNN) pair used as encoder and decoder, to perform translation of a source-side sentence into its corresponding target sentence. LSTM networks, a special kind of RNN capable of handling long term dependencies for sequence to sequence tasks has been employed. The encoder reads input sequence and transforms it into a fixed vector representation. The decoder utilizes this vector representation to predict the target sequence. Incorporating attention mechanism with NMT systems have been found to outperform earlier MT approaches such as SMT on several grounds [8]. This has been mainly attributed to the ability of NMT systems to analyze the context of the input sequence and therefore, produce fluent translations [11,12].

Mizo language is the native language of the state of Mizoram, India, with approximately 830,000 speakers of the language[1]. Mizo language is a tonal language and is a part of the Sino Tibetan language family. The advantages of NMT over other NMT approaches has motivated us to train and test various configurations of NMT system for English to Mizo language pair. Different NMT models including LSTM and Bidirectional LSTM (BiLSTM), shallow and deep networks as well as SGD and Adam optimizers have been trained. The results of translation have been evaluated using automatic translation metrics such as Bilingual Evaluation Understudy (BLEU) [10], Translation Error Rate (TER) [15], METEOR [5] and F-measure. The performance of best performing NMT model has been analyzed based on best and worst translations for short, medium and long sentences.

The rest of the paper is structured as follows. Section 2 gives the related works in MT. Section 3 describes the NMT system alongwith the dataset used for training the system. Section 4 details the results of various automatic evaluation metrics and analysis of predicted translations. Section 6 gives the conclusion and future work.

2   Related Works

Research in MT of Indian languages specifically in English-Mizo language pair has been very limitedly explored. The effectiveness of predicted translations has been analyzed using Phrase-based SMT (PBSMT) and NMT for English-Mizo language pair and performed a detailed comparative analysis [12]. PBSMT has been found to lay more emphasis on adequacy whereas NMT tends to produce fluent translations. Neural-based translation of Indian languages such as Hindi, Punjabi and Tamil has been performed and analyzed based on the variations of size of training data and length of sentences [11]. The performance of NMT system has been found to increase with the increase in training data as well as increase in length of test sentences.

Two encoder-decoder NMT architectures namely, convolutional sequence to sequence model (ConvS2S) and recurrent sequence to sequence model (RNNS2S) has been compared for English-Hindi language pair in both directions [14]. The

---

[1] http://en.wikipedia.org/wiki/Mizo_language/.

BLEU scores of Hindi-English direction has been found to be greater for ConvS2S than RNNS2S whereas RNNS2S outperforms ConvS2S in the English-Hindi direction. An NMT system employing the attention mechanism for Bengali-Hindi language pair has been found outperform the existing SMT model of MOSES and post-processing steps have been implemented to improve errors in translation of named entities and rare words [4]. NMT system has been trained using LSTM and Bi-LSTM and tested using automatic and manual metrics for four language pairs, English–Malayalam, English–Hindi, English–Tamil, and English–Punjabi [1].

A model based on bidirectional recurrent neural network encoder employing a gated recurrent unit (GRU) has been used to generate parallel sentences [13]. The model applied on low resource language pairs, English- Tamil and English-Hindi has been used to improve BLEU scores using the parallel sentence pairs extracted from comparable corpora. A code-mixed to monolingual translation has been proposed by exploiting a strategy in order to translate code-mixed source data in English and Bengali into their equivalent Bengali target data achieving a BLEU score of 16.47 [9].

Incorporating a context-aware recurrent encoder (CAEncoder) has been shown to have better context analyzing ability using two hierarchy levels [18]. The bottom level, which summarizes the information that has been read, and the upper level which utilizes the summarized information and future context for the source sequences has been found to improve on Chinese–English and English–German pairs. Task interference issues in Multi-Task Learning (MTL) has been addressed using multiple blocks and a trainable routing network for low-resource languges English-Farsi and English-Vietnamese [17]. Increasing the parallel data using filtering of pseudo-parallel corpus has been proposed to address the problem of low resource languages [6]. By utilizing quality estimation based on sentence-level round-trip translation, BLEU scores have been found to increase for data, particularly with low resources.

3   System Description

NMT directly models the conditional probability using an encoder-decoder architecture to process source sequences and transform them into target sequences. Let A and B represent the source and target sequences and $A_1, A_2, A_3, ..., A_N$ denotes the fixed vector representations. Using conditional probability,

$$P(B|A) = P(B|A_1, A_2, A_3, ..., A_N) \tag{1}$$

Using chain rule, Eq. 1 can be re-written as below, in which the fixed vector from the encoder is used by the decoder to predict the next word in the target sequence.

$$P(B|A) = P(b_i|b_0, b_1, b_2, b_3, ..., b_{i-1}; A_1, A_2, A_3, ..., A_N) \tag{2}$$

A softmax is applied on all the words in the vocabulary represented by each distribution.

The primary steps in building the NMT system are data preprocessing, system training and translation which has been elaborated in the subsequent subsections. The python port of OpenNMT [7] toolkit has been employed for system training and testing. OpenNMT is an open-source framework for NMT which is based on sequence to sequence MT.

3.1 Data Preprocessing

The corpus has been classified into source and target train data and source and target validation data respectively. The source and target data comprises of parallel pairs of sentences. To preprocess the data, source and target sentences have been subjected to tokenization and lowercasing. The data preprocessing stage has also been used to generate serialized train, validation and vocabulary data. A vocabulary size of 19843 and 27060 for source and target respectively, has been generated for the purpose of indexing. Validation data has been used to check the convergence of the training data.

Dataset. The data used for NMT system comprises of English and Mizo parallel sentences as source and target languages. The corpus has been manually prepared from various government websites, online blogs, the Bible and English to Mizo dictionary. The data collected has been properly aligned and various preprocessing tasks have been performed to ensure good quality of the corpus. Table 1 indicates the detailed corpus description. Validation and train data has been set aside from the training data.

Table 1. Dataset description

Data	No. of parallel sentences
Training data	62247
Validation data	4000
Test data	1000

3.2 System Training

The NMT system has been trained using OpenNMT's sequence to sequence RNN. A global attention mechanism has been incorporated in order to handle long sequences. The key components of the NMT system includes the encoder and decoder. The baseline encoder is composed of a two layer LSTM with 500 hidden units using SGD as optimizer. Each variable-length input sequence has been converted into a vector representation which is representative of the input sentence using the encoder. The decoder which is also composed of a two layer LSTM having 500 hidden units in each layer, takes the vector representation and predicts the target sequence using the vector information. A softmax is then applied to produce target words.

NMT architecture with input feeding for a two layer LSTM is shown in Fig. 1. The English sentence *"Come here !"* has been fed token-wise into the LSTM encoder, marked in blue. The decoder LSTM then predicts the target sentence *"Lo kal rawh !"* after it encounters the end of sentence ($< eos >$) symbol.

We have also experimented with a deep network with four layers LSTM, each layer composed of 500 hidden units. Adam optimizer has also been used in place of SGD with learning rate set to 0.001, beta1 to 0.9 and beta2 to 0.999. Adam is used as an optimization method since it effectively combines the benefits of other SGD extensions. It calculates the squared gradient as well as exponential moving average of the gradient. The decay rates of the moving averages are adjusted using parameters beta1 and beta2.

LSTM has also been replaced with two layer bidirectional LSTM as well as a deep network bidirectional LSTM with four layers. A bridge, which is an additional layer between the last encoder state and the first decoder state is also added in order to analyze and compare the performance with other NMT models.

The number of train steps has been set to 10000 for each setup and the train model for which the learning curve reaches highest point has been chosen. The NMT system has been trained on a single NVIDIA Quadro P2000 GPU.

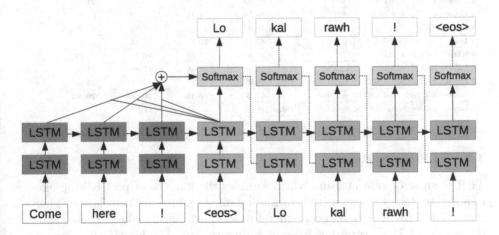

Fig. 1. NMT architecture

3.3 Translation

The trained models obtained from the system training stage has been used to translate the test data in order to assess the performance of each model. The translation takes place using a beam search, which generates a set of most probable candidate translations. The beam width has been set to 5 in our experiments.

4   Experimentation Results

This section compares the various models based on different configurations for English-Mizo language pair using automatic evaluation metrics.

4.1   BLEU Score Results

For our experiments, BLEU score has been considered upto 3-gram. An average of BLEU scores for $n = 1, 2, 3$ has been computed since the minimum length of test sentences is 3. Table 2 indicates the BLEU score results as well as the average BLEU scores. We have experimented with different configurations namely, LSTM and Bi-LSTM, shallow and deep networks and SGD and Adam optimizers. Surprisingly, a deep Bi-LSTM network with SGD optimizer has obtained the lowest average BLEU score of 16.84. A four layer BiLSTM with Adam optimizer has obtained a highest average BLEU score of 29.84.

Table 2. BLEU score results for various configurations

Configuration	BLEU (1-g)	BLEU (2-g)	BLEU (3-g)	Average BLEU
2 Layers LSTM + SGD	31.33	19.67	13.3	21.4
2 Layers LSTM + Adam	36.20	24.09	16.77	26.69
2 Layers Bidirectional LSTM + SGD	39.8	25.64	17.32	27.59
2 Layers Bidirectional LSTM + Adam	40.18	27.37	19.55	29.03
4 Layers LSTM + SGD	30.84	17.25	10.76	19.62
4 Layers LSTM + Adam	34.30	22.35	15.46	24.04
4 Layers Bidirectional LSTM + SGD	26.21	15.04	9.37	16.84
4 Layers Bidirectional LSTM + Adam	**41.3**	**28.19**	**20.03**	**29.84**
4 Layers Bidirectional LSTM + Adam + Bridge	38.9	25.03	17.08	27

4.2   TER Score Results

TER is an error rate measure which signifies the amount of post-editing effort required to change the predicted translation into the reference translation. Therefore, a low TER score would correspond to less post-editing effort. Table 3 shows the results of TER scores for different configurations. The high TER scores can be mainly attributed to the fact that only one reference translation has been used since TER finds the number of edits to the closest reference. A four layer BiLSTM with Adam optimizer obtains a minimum TER score of 71.88 among various configurations used.

Table 3. TER score results for various configurations

Configuration	TER Score
2 Layers LSTM + SGD	80.15
2 Layers LSTM + Adam	75.95
2 Layers Bidirectional LSTM + SGD	77.3
2 Layers Bidirectional LSTM + Adam	72.86
4 Layers LSTM + SGD	88.56
4 Layers LSTM + Adam	76.42
4 Layers Bidirectional LSTM + SGD	83.04
4 Layers Bidirectional LSTM + Adam	**71.88**
4 Layers Bidirectional LSTM + Adam + Bridge	77.47

4.3 METEOR and F-Measure Score Results

METEOR scores predicted translations against reference translations based on the exact, stemmed, synonyms and paraphrases between sequences. F-measure computes the harmonic mean between recall and precision. In our experiment, since our target language is not supported by METEOR we compare only exact matches between the predicted and reference translations. Table 4 presents the METEOR scores for the different configurations. METEOR score has been found to be consistent with BLEU scores and maximum METEOR score of 0.17 and F-measure score of 0.4 has been achieved by four layer BiLSTM with Adam configuration. Figure 2 shows a Meteor alignment for Segment 562 where the reference

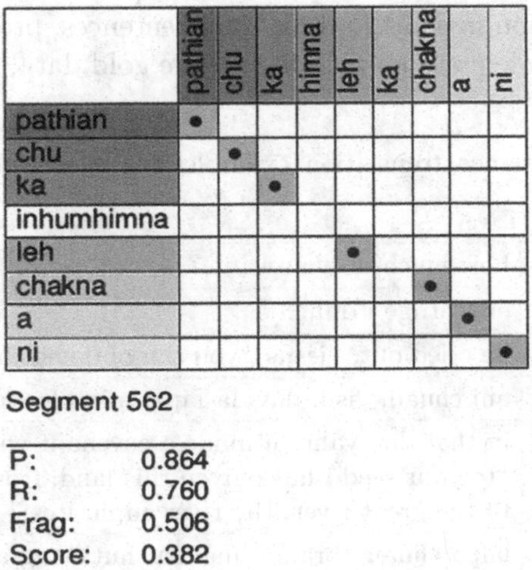

Segment 562

P: 0.864
R: 0.760
Frag: 0.506
Score: 0.382

Fig. 2. Meteor alignment for segment 562 with precision, recall, fragmentation and METEOR scores.

Table 4. METEOR score and F-measure results for various configurations

Configuration	METEOR score	F-measure
2 Layers LSTM + SGD	0.13	0.32
2 Layers LSTM + Adam	0.15	0.37
2 Layers Bidirectional LSTM + SGD	0.16	0.37
2 Layers Bidirectional LSTM + Adam	0.12	0.32
4 Layers LSTM + SGD	0.1	0.24
4 Layers LSTM + Adam	0.14	0.35
4 Layers Bidirectional LSTM + SGD	0.1	0.26
4 Layers Bidirectional LSTM + Adam	**0.17**	**0.4**
4 Layers Bidirectional LSTM + Adam + Bridge	0.15	0.36

translation is placed on the top row and predicted translation on the left column. The solid dots with green colour indicate exact matching of words between reference and predicted translations. In the given example, the words *"inhumhimna"* and *"himna"* are synonymous. However, since synonyms for target language has not been provided, the two words has been shown as a mismatch.

5   Analysis and Discussion

To analyze predicted translations by the best performing model, we have considered the best and worst translation examples from our test set. Table 5 and 6 shows the best and worst performance translation examples for short, medium and long sentences from test set compared to the predicted translation. For best performance translation in short and medium sentences, predicted translation is perfectly fluent and adequate and similar to the gold data.

Table 5. Best performance translation examples for short, medium and long test sentences

Source test	how much do you want ?
Predicted translation	engzatnge i duh ?
Source test	he cried out, "jesus , you son of david, have mercy on me !"
Predicted translation	ani chuan, "isu, davida fapa, min khawngaih rawh," a ti a.
Source test	in that day yahweh made a covenant with abram, saying, "to your seed i have given this land, from the river of egypt to the great river, the river euphrates:"
Predicted translation	lalpa chuan abrama hnênah thuthlung a siam a, "i thlahte hi eufretis lui chhak lama lui thlengin he ram hi ka pe a ni."

Table 6. Worst performance translation examples for short, medium and long test sentences

Source test	i can't sit, i have to move on
Predicted translation	ka ko thei lo va, ka kal thei lo
Source test	i will not go outside since the weather is too hot today
Predicted translation	vawiin chu thim takah a awm lo vang a, vawiinah hian
Source test	at evening, behold, terror ! before the morning, they are no more. This is the portion of those who plunder us, and the lot of those who rob us
Predicted translation	tlaiah hian en teh u, tûk zîngah chuan awm teh se, tûk zîngah chuan awm rawh se; zîngah chuan kan zînga mi tam tak a awm a, kan zînga mi tam tak a ni

However, for the long sentence, predicted translation is perfectly fluent. The named entity has also been mistranslated. In general, it has been observed that long sentences are often mistranslated as compared to short and medium length sentences. In case of worst performance translation, the predicted example for short sentence is partially fluent but inadequate. The predicted translation for medium sentence example is incomplete and completely inadequate. Furthermore, the long sentence predicted example results in over-translation of the same words and is inadequate. This can be attributed to the incompetency of LSTM in handling long sequences, even with the use of attention. However, NMT systems has been found to perform poorly in case of low-resource languages as NMT is a data hungry approach.

6 Conclusion

NMT provides an end-to-end neural based model for source to target language translation. NMT systems tend to produce fluent translations and outperform SMT in a number of settings which motivated us to employ NMT systems for English to Mizo translation. We have trained and tested NMT models using various configurations and bidirectional LSTM with Adam optimizer has been found to outperform other NMT models for the given language pair. The performance of NMT models have been evaluated using automatic evaluation metrics and our analysis shows that performance of the NMT system decreases with long sentences. In future, NMT system can be improved for low-resource scenarios by experimenting with transfer-learning approach, use of monolingual data and incorporating target language specific linguistic features.

References

1. Premjith, B., Kumar, M.A., Soman, K.P..: Neural machine translation system for English to Indian language translation using MTIL parallel corpus: special issue on natural language processing. J. Intell. Syst. **28** (2019). https://doi.org/10.1515/jisys-2019-2510

2. Bahdanau, D., Cho, K., Bengio, Y.: Neural machine translation by jointly learning to align and translate. In: 3rd International Conference on Learning Representations, ICLR 2015, San Diego, CA, USA, May 7–9, 2015, Conference Track Proceedings (2015)

3. Cho, K., et al.: Learning phrase representations using RNN encoder-decoder for statistical machine translation. In: Proceedings of the 2014 Conference on Empirical Methods in Natural Language Processing (EMNLP), pp. 1724–1734. Association for Computational Linguistics, Doha (2014). https://doi.org/10.3115/v1/D14-1179

4. Das, A., Yerra, P., Kumar, K., Sarkar, S.: A study of attention-based neural machine translation model on Indian languages. In: Proceedings of the 6th Workshop on South and Southeast Asian Natural Language Processing (WSSANLP2016), pp. 163–172. The COLING 2016 Organizing Committee, Osaka (2016)

5. Denkowski, M., Lavie, A.: Meteor universal: language specific translation evaluation for any target language. In: Proceedings of the Ninth Workshop on Statistical Machine Translation, pp. 376–380. Association for Computational Linguistics, Baltimore (2014). https://doi.org/10.3115/v1/W14-3348, https://www.aclweb.org/anthology/W14-3348

6. Imankulova, A., Sato, T., Komachi, M.: Filtered pseudo-parallel corpus improves low-resource neural machine translation. ACM Trans. Asian Low Resour. Lang. Inf. Process. **19**(2), 1–16 (2019). https://doi.org/10.1145/3341726

7. Klein, G., Kim, Y., Deng, Y., Senellart, J., Rush, A.: OpenNMT: open-source toolkit for neural machine translation. In: Proceedings of ACL 2017 System Demonstrations, pp. 67–72. Association for Computational Linguistics, Vancouver (2017)

8. Luong, T., Pham, H., Manning, C.D.: Effective approaches to attention-based neural machine translation. In: Proceedings of the 2015 Conference on Empirical Methods in Natural Language Processing, pp. 1412–1421. Association for Computational Linguistics, Lisbon (2015). https://doi.org/10.18653/v1/D15-1166

9. Mahata, S.K., Mandal, S., Das, D., Bandyopadhyay, S.: Code-mixed to monolingual translation framework. In: Proceedings of the 11th Forum for Information Retrieval Evaluation, FIRE 2019, pp. 30–35. Association for Computing Machinery, New York (2019). https://doi.org/10.1145/3368567.3368579

10. Papineni, K., Roukos, S., Ward, T., Zhu, W.J.: Bleu: a method for automatic evaluation of machine translation. In: Proceedings of the 40th Annual Meeting on Association for Computational Linguistics, ACL 2002, pp. 311–318. Association for Computational Linguistics, Stroudsburg (2002). https://doi.org/10.3115/1073083.1073135

11. Pathak, A., Pakray, P.: Neural machine translation for indian languages. J. Intell. Syst. **28**(3), 465–477 (2019). https://doi.org/10.1515/jisys-2018-0065

12. Pathak, A., Pakray, P., Bentham, J.: English–Mizo Machine Translation using neural and statistical approaches. Neural Comput. Appl. **31**(11), 7615–7631 (2018). https://doi.org/10.1007/s00521-018-3601-3

13. Ramesh, S.H., Sankaranarayanan, K.P.: Neural machine translation for low resource languages using bilingual lexicon induced from comparable corpora. In: Proceedings of the 2018 Conference of the North American Chapter of the Association for Computational Linguistics: Student Research Workshop, pp. 112–119. Association for Computational Linguistics, New Orleans (2018). https://doi.org/10.18653/v1/N18-4016

14. Singh, S., Panjwani, R., Kunchukuttan, A., Bhattacharyya, P.: Comparing recurrent and convolutional architectures for English-Hindi neural machine translation. In: Proceedings of the 4th Workshop on Asian Translation (WAT 2017), pp. 167–170. Asian Federation of Natural Language Processing, Taipei (2017)

15. Snover, M., Dorr, B., Schwartz, R., Micciulla, L., Makhoul, J.: A study of translation edit rate with targeted human annotation. In: Proceedings of Association for Machine Translation in the Americas, pp. 223–231 (2006)

16. Sutskever, I., Vinyals, O., Le, Q.V.: Sequence to sequence learning with neural networks. In: Proceedings of the 27th International Conference on Neural Information Processing Systems, NIPS 14, vol. 2, pp. 3104–3112. MIT Press, Cambridge (2014)

17. Zaremoodi, P., Buntine, W., Haffari, G.: Adaptive knowledge sharing in multi-task learning: Improving low-resource neural machine translation. In: Proceedings of the 56th Annual Meeting of the Association for Computational Linguistics, vol. 2: Short Papers, pp. 656–661. Association for Computational Linguistics, Melbourne (2018). https://doi.org/10.18653/v1/P18-2104

18. Zhang, B., Xiong, D., Su, J., Duan, H.: A context-aware recurrent encoder for neural machine translation. IEEE/ACM Trans. Audio Speech Lang. Process. **25**(12), 2424–2432 (2017). https://doi.org/10.1109/TASLP.2017.2751420

In Depth Analysis of Lung Disease Prediction Using Machine Learning Algorithms

Ishan Sen, Md. Ikbal Hossain$^{(\boxtimes)}$, Md. Faisal Hossan Shakib$^{(\boxtimes)}$,
Md. Asaduzzaman Imran$^{(\boxtimes)}$, and Faiz Al Faisal$^{(\boxtimes)}$

Department of Electrical and Computer Engineering (ECE),
North South University, Dhaka 1229, Bangladesh
{ishan.sen,ikbal.hossain,faisal.shakib,
asaduzzaman.imran,faiz.faisal}@northsouth.edu

Abstract. The objective of this examination is to investigate and foresee the Lung Diseases with assistance from Machine Learning Algorithms. The most common lung diseases are Asthma, Allergies, Chronic obstructive pulmonary disease (COPD), bronchitis, emphysema, lung cancer and so on. It is important to foresee the odds of lung sicknesses before it happens and by doing that individuals can be causes and make fundamental strides before it occurs. In this paper, we have worked with a collection of data and classified it with various machine learning algorithms. We have collected 323 instances along with 19 attributes. These data have been collected from patients suffering from numerous lung diseases along with other symptoms. The Lung diseases attribute contains two types of category which are 'Positive' and 'Negative'. 'Positive' means that the person has a lung disease and so forth. The training of the dataset has been done with K-Fold Cross Validation Technique and specifically, five Machine Learning algorithms have been used which are Bagging, Logistic Regression, Random Forest, Logistic model tree and Bayesian Networks. The accuracy for the above mentioned machine learning algorithms are 88.00%, 88.92%, 90.15%, 89.23%, and 83.69% respectively.

Keywords: Machine learning algorithm · Lung diseases bagging · Logistic Regression · Random Forest · Logistic model tree · Bayesian Networks

1 Introduction

Respiratory diseases are among the critical reasons for death around the world. Lung contaminations (for the most part pneumonia and tuberculosis), carcinoma and chronic obstructive pulmonary disease (COPD) together represented 9.5 million passing overall during 2008, one-6th of the overall aggregate, the planet Health Organization evaluates that a proportional four maladies represented one-tenth of disability-adjusted life-years (DALYs) lost worldwide in 2008. Likewise among the 25 most fundamental causes were COPD (positioned sixth in 1990 and ninth in 2010), tuberculosis (positioned eighth in 1990 and thirteenth in 2010) and carcinoma (positioned 24th in 1990 and 22nd in 2010) [1]. Forecast of Lung related malady is a difficult factor looked by specialists and clinics. Right now, the exactness of lung sickness assumes an indispensable job.

© Springer Nature Singapore Pte Ltd. 2020
A. Bhattacharjee et al. (Eds.): MIND 2020, CCIS 1241, pp. 204–213, 2020.
https://doi.org/10.1007/978-981-15-6318-8_18

Machine Learning methods are widely utilized in medical sectors. Data mining holds great potential to explore the hidden patterns in huge information which will be used for clinical diagnosis. Data mining allow health systems to use data systematically and do the analysis for identifying inefficiencies, best practices that improve care and reduce costs. Detection of lung disease is one among the vital issues and lots of researchers are developing intelligent medical decision support systems to urge better the power of the physicians. Therefore we conducted an enquiry supported machine learning algorithms to seek out the probabilities of occurrence of lung disease before it actually occurs, the only purpose of this analysis is that the identify the accuracy levels of Bagging, Logistic Regression and Random Forest algorithms and to integrate this leads to such a system which is user friendly in order that people can use it whenever they feel convenient.

2 Related Works

In 2002, in the United Kingdom, Martin J Wildman et al. [2] and his team worked on to assess whether the results found in terms of survival were the prognoses among physicians of patients with intense poignancy with obstructive lung malady focused on serious consideration. They have been worked on over 832 patients who were matured 45 years and more with a breathing problem, respiratory flunk, and variation of mental health because of suffering from COPD and asthma, or a conjunction of both. Their yielding is calculated by the physicians and they need around 180 days to predict this outcome. D J Hole et al. [3] and his group worked on determining the connection between the one-second forced expiratory volume (FEV1) and subsequent death. They directed this research on 7058 men and 8353 women who were aged between 45–64 years. They wanted to find fatality rate from all causes, ischemic heart illness, lung cancer, and other cancers, sudden stroke, disease of respiratory organ, and different reasons for death following 15 years of development. They found that 2545 men and 1894 women have died in this period with critical patterns of expanding hazard with lessening FEV1 for both genders, the reasons for death studied afterwards age change, smoking, blood pressure, weight record and social groups are clear. Timor Kadir, Fergus Gleeson [4] had given a review about fundamental lung disease expectation ways to deal with date and feature a portion from their comparative qualities and shortcomings in this paper. AI based lung malignant development expectation models have been offered to help medical practitioners in overseeing unknown or recognized uncertain aspiratory knobs. They have used CNN using trained data, which is a class of deep neural network. While evaluating there were needed to be informed about some limitations whether the patients were smoker or with history of lung nodule. Before testing their system, their works concluded with some related questions for future works that if it were to implement, which output or who should use this system. Anuradha et al. [5] proposed a model, which uses machine learning that is to recognize and analyze the lung disease as ahead of schedule as conceivable which will assist the specialist with saving the patient's life. They used binary classification with different parameter like age, gender, X-ray images and view position. And the expected output is to find whether the patient has lung disease or not. For their particular dataset, they have used mainly CNN and capsule network algorithm for extraction since their chosen dataset of chest x-ray may have many unnecessary data. This paper portrays how lung maladies were anticipated and controlled, utilizing Machine Learning. With pre-trained model they would improve their accuracy level. Jason et al. [6] and his team in their work they gathered information from aspiratory nodule(s) patients and they were about 1500 and their nodules were till 15 mm identified and distinguished on routinely performed CT chest filters matured 18 years of age or else more established from three scholastic focus in the United Kingdom were utilized for creating risk lamination models. For developing their model, they have used Artificial Intelligence (AI) based dataset. Aiyesha et al. [7] have examined the current clinical system and they have suggested how AI based strategies might be utilized for analysis differentially on Phthisis and Pneumonia. Here they presented a classification model using three machine learning algorithm which are Naïve Bayes, Decision Tree and Random forest. In this paper we also used these algorithms to show different results.

3 Methodology

The examination can be partitioned into four crucial stages which are given as follows:

- Data Collection
- Data Processing
- Data Training
- Application of ML algorithms

3.1 Data Collection

The data for this analysis has been collected from some hospitals in Dhaka. National Institute of Diseases of the Chest and Hospital, National Institute of Cancer Research & Hospital (NICRH) helped us by providing us with the majority of the data. A total of 323 instances and 19 attributes have been collected in which there is information for an individual patient. The dataset contains the lung diseases attribute which is categorized by two types; Positive (have lung diseases) and Negative (Doesn't have any lung diseases) (Table 1).

Table 1. The hospitals which helped us to collect data are mentioned below

1. National Institute of Diseases of the Chest and Hospital
2. National Institute of Cancer Research & Hospital (NICRH)

3.2 Data Preprocessing

In the wake of gathering the information, we did the preprocessing inside the preprocessing stage, we utilized the two unsupervised filters inside the extensively utilized AI stage WEKA 3.8.3 (Waikato Environment for Knowledge Analysis). From the start, we applied the Replace MissingValues filter on our dataset. This replaces all the missing qualities for ostensible and numerical traits utilizing the modes and means. Besides, we've utilized the Randomize filter which replaces the missing data without surrendering a great part of the exhibition.

3.3 Data Training

The preparation of the data has been finished utilizing the K-Fold Cross Validation method of WEKA. It is a resampling procedure to evaluate the forecast model by parting the first dataset into two sections preparing the set and a test set. The parameter K decides the number of groups the dataset will be separated into by rearranging the dataset haphaz-ardly.

3.4 Application of Machine Learning Algorithms

After the training phase, classification has been done using various machine learning algorithms among them Bagging, Logistic

Table 2. Features list

Features	Subcategory	Data distribution
Sex	Male	46.62%
	Female	53.08%
Age	Lowest: 7	Mean ± SD
	Highest: 85	43.412 ± 17.475
Hemoglobin (Hb)	Lowest: 5 gm/dl	11.526 ± 1.491
	Highest: 16.9 gm/dl	
Erythrocyte sedimentation rate (ESR)	Lowest: 2 mm	59.105 ± 33.893
	Highest: 165 mm	
White Blood Cell (WBC)	Distinct: 102	Unique: 22(07%)
Platelet Count (PC)	Distinct: 131	Unique: 43(13%)
Hematocrit (HCT)	Lowest: 9.3%	33.979 ± 4.718
	Highest: 54.6%	
Neutrophils	Lowest: 6%	68.006 ± 14.591
	Highest: 96%	
Lymphocytes	Lowest: 2%	24.035 ± 13.588
	Highest: 90%	
Monocytes	Lowest: 1%	5.168 ± 2.82
	Highest: 17%	
Eosinophil	Lowest: 0%	4.342 ± 2.662
	Highest: 16%	
Basophils	Lowest: 0%	0
	Highest: 0%	
Blood-Glucose-After-Meal	Lowest: 40 mg/dl	106.099 ± 48.443
	Highest: 312.25 mg/dl	
Serum-creatinine	Lowest: 0.3 mg/dl	0.868 ± 0.236
	Highest: 2 mg/dl	
Serum-bilirubin	Lowest: 0.2 mg/dl	1.085 ± 2.249
	Highest: 12 mg/dl	
Serum glutamic pyruvic transaminase (SGPT)	Lowest: 6 u/l	33.049 ± 25.767
	Highest: 178 u/l	
Height	Lowest: 130 cm	160.157 ± 9.608
	Highest: 176 cm	
Weight	Lowest: 20 kg, Highest: 75 kg	50.231 ± 8.989
Cancer-Test-Result {Negative, Positive}	Negative: 307	94.17%
	Positive: 18	5.83%
Lung-Disease-Result	Positive: 285	87.423%
	Negative: 40	12.577%

Regression and Random Forest Logistic model tree and Bayesian Networks outperformed. Therefore, we determined those five algorithms to be our model.

4   Workflow

Figure 1 represents the overall workflow of the entire analysis illustrated in brief. We collected a dataset comprising of 323 instances from hospitals mentioned in Table 2 along with 19 attributes. After that, we preprocessed the data and used the feature selection option in WEKA. The next thing we did was to train the dataset using K-fold Cross-Validation Technique. Afterward, we applied various machine learning algorithms among which three of the above mentioned algorithms stood out. In the end, we concluded our analysis by comparing the performances of the five algorithms.

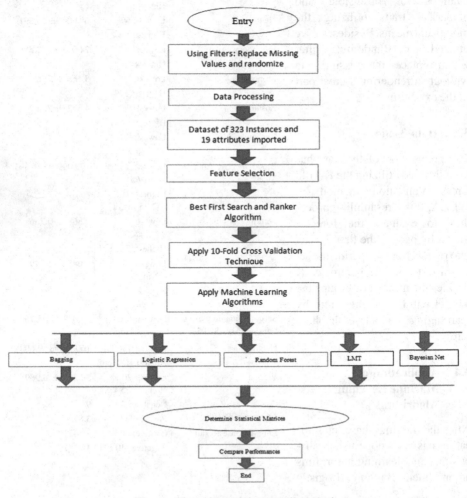

Fig. 1. Flow chart of the overall analysis

Performance Parameters

The outcomes of this analysis are based on the following performance parameters:

A. Seed:

It indicates changing numbers haphazardly and getting an alternate outcome.

B. Correctly Classified Instances (CCI):

The precision of the model relies upon the test information.

$$Accuracy = \frac{Tp + Tn}{Tp + Tn + Fp + Fn}$$

Here, Tp = True Positive, Fp = False Positive, Fn = False Negative, Tn = True Negative.

C. Kappa Statistics (KS):

The Kappa Statistics is used to quantify the proclamation among predicted and observed provisions of a dataset.

$$K = \frac{R0 - Re}{1 - Re}$$

Here, R_0 = Relative watched understanding among raters, Re = Theoretical likelihood of chance assertion.

D. Mean Absolute Error (MAE):

Without assessing the sign it normalizes the size of individual mistakes.

$$MAE = \frac{|p1 - b1| + \cdots + |pn - bn|}{n}$$

Here, p = Predicted Value, b = Actual Value.

E. Relative Absolute Error (RAE):

It is the absolute error with the similar manner of normalization.

$$RAE = \frac{|p1 - b1| + \cdots + |pn - bn|}{|b1 - b| + \cdots + |bn - b|}$$

F. Specificity:

It is the proportion of patients without the disease who test negative.

$$Specificity = \frac{Tn}{Fp + Tn}$$

G. Precision (PRE):

It is denoted as PRE $\left(PRE = \frac{Tp}{Tp + FP}\right)$.

H. Recall (REC):

It is denoted as REC and the cohesion between PRE and REC is MCC.

$$REC = \frac{Tp}{Tp + Fn}$$

I. F-Measure:

It is denoted by FM.

$$FM = 2 \times \frac{PRE \times REC}{PRE + REC} = \frac{2 \times Tp}{2 \times Tp + Fp + Fn}$$

5 Results Analysis

The examination was finished in 3 seeds utilizing every calculation for 2 classes titled as Positive and Negative. In Figs. 2 and 3, where the x-axis shows to the False positive rate (Fp) and the y-axis connotes the True positive rate (Tp). Tp is likewise perceived as Recall and it is utilized to quantify the real level of accurately ordered cases. Fp is the proportion between the number of negative cases that are inaccurately delegated positive and the quantity of really negative examples. (0, 1) a point on the diagram is where the classifier gives the ideal outcome for example it orders the genuinely positive and negative cases effectively.

In Fig. 3a, 3b given below illustrates the percentage of correctly classified instances and incorrectly classified instances respectively from 5 different algorithms. From Fig. 3a, it has clearly seen that the Random Forest (RF) gives the highest accuracy results whereas Bayes Net gives the lowest accuracy; the figure is approximately 90.1538% and 83.6929% successively. On the other hand, Logistic Regression (LR) gives us nearly 88.9231% which is higher than Bagging which gives us almost 88% accuracy. However, the logical model tree (LMT) is slightly higher than LR and the figure is around 88.2308%. From Fig. 3b it can be said that Bayes Net has given us the highest incorrect instances and the percentage is around 16.30 whereas the RF and LMT give us almost lowest incorrect instances and the figure are almost 10%. Table 3 represents the comparison of five different algorithms on various evaluation matrix. It can be observed that the KS value for Bagging, LR, RF, LMT, Bayes Net are 0.2821, 0.3803, 0.501, 0.4052, 0.2974 respectively.

The MAE for Bagging, LR, RF, LMT, Bayes Net are 0.1785, 0.1592, 0.1551, 0.197 successively whereas the Root Mean Squared Error are 0.3102, 0.3038, 0.2888, 0.3015 and 0.3258 respectively for these algorithms. In terms of RAE, it can be said that the Bayes Net gives the highest percentage of error, which is 90.4575% whereas

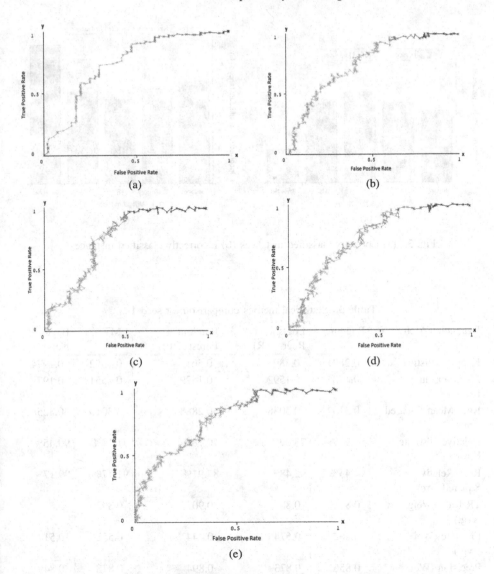

Fig. 2. (a) BAG curve for positive class (b) LR curve for positive class (c) RF curves for positive class (d) LMT curve for positive class (e) Bayes net curve for positive class

the lowest proportion of these errors is 70.1852% percentage, which is for RF. On the other hand, this proportion is slightly lower which is for LMT and the figure is 71.1941%. If it comes to Bagging the error is 81.9378% which is the second-lowest error after Bayes Net. Now if we talk about the Root Relative Squared Error then the Bayes Net gives 99.1762% whereas RF gives 87.9163%. On the other hand, Bagging, LR, KMT give 94.4328%, 92.4839%. 91.7746% respectively.

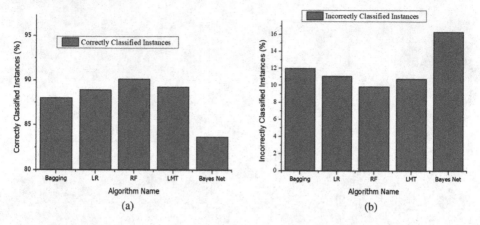

Fig. 3. (a) Correctly classified instances (b) Incorrectly classified instances

Table 3. Statistical metrics comparison for seed 1

Evaluation Metrix	Bagging	Logistic Regr. (LR)	Random Forest (RF)	LMT	Bayes Net
Kappa Statistic	0.2821	0.3803	0.501	0.4052	0.2974
Mean absolute Error	0.1785	0.1592	0.1529	0.1551	0.197
Root Mean Squared Error	0.3102	0.3038	0.2888	0.3015	0.3258
Relative absolute Error	81.93%	73.09%	70.18%	71.19%	90.45%
Root Relative Squared error	94.43%	92.48%	87.91%	91.77%	99.17%
TR Rate (Weighted Avg.)	0.880	0.889	0.902	0.892	0.837
FR Rate (Wei. Avg.)	0.662	0.574	0.444	0.552	0.517
Precision (Wei. Avg.)	0.856	0.873	0.894	0.878	0.849
Recall (Wei. Avg.)	0.880	0.889	0.902	0.892	0.837
F-Measure (Wei. Avg.)	0.861	0.877	0.897	0.881	0.842

6   Conclusion

In conclusion, our study shows that lung diseases can be correctly classified using the machine learning techniques. However, obtaining the real time data was one of the primary concerns that we had faced at the initial stages. In addition to that, we could not able to get similar data from existing works to compare our results. However it is worth to mention that our dataset has many attributes, which is rare to find from online sources. Among the five algorithms, Random Forest gives the best performance than LR, Bagging, LMT and Bayes Net. The accuracy level are 88.00%, 88.9231%, 90.1538%, 89.2308% and 83.6929% respectively. In addition to work, future researches like, study with deep learning methods like - Neuron Advanced Ensemble Learning, Fuzzy Inference System, and Convolution Neural Network would be useful and beneficial.

References

1. The burden of lung disease. https://www.erswhitebook.org/chapters/the-burden-of-lung-disease/
2. Wildman, M.J., et al.: Implications of prognostic pessimism in patients with chronic obstructive pulmonary disease (COPD) or asthma admitted to intensive care in the UK within the COPD and asthma outcome study (CAOS): multicenter observational cohort study (2007). https://doi.org/10.1136/bmj.39371.524271.55
3. Hole, D.J., et al.: Impaired lung function and mortality risk in men and women: findings from the Renfrew and Paisley prospective population study (1996). https://doi.org/10.1136/bmj.313.7059.711
4. Kadir, T., Gleeson, F.: Lung cancer prediction using machine learning and advanced imaging techniques (2018). https://doi.org/10.21037/tlcr.2018.05.15
5. Gunasinghe, A.D., Aponso, A.C., Thirimanna, H.: Early prediction of lung diseases. Conference Paper, March 2019
6. Oke, J.L., et al.: Development and validation of clinical prediction models to risk stratify patients presenting with small pulmonary nodules: a research protocol. Diagn. Progn. Res. **2**, 22 (2018)
7. Sadiya, A., et al.: Differential diagnosis of tuberculosis and pneumonia using machine learning. Int. J. Innov. Technol. Explor. Eng. (IJITEE) **8**(6S4), 245–250 (2019). ISSN 2278-3075

Improve the Accuracy of Heart Disease Predictions Using Machine Learning and Feature Selection Techniques

Abdelmegeid Amin Ali, Hassan Shaban Hassan,
and Eman M. Anwar$^{(\boxtimes)}$

Faculty of Computer and Information, Department of Computer Science,
Minia University, Minya, Egypt
{abdelmageed.ali,hassanshaban}@mu.edu.eg,
emyanwar616@gmail.com

Abstract. In the age of today, cardiac disease is becoming a significant problem, with a large population in the world suffering from this problem. Despite the death rate and huge numbers of people with heart disease, it has been shown How significant is the early diagnosis of cardiac diseases. Machine learning classification techniques can make a significant contribution to the medical field by Making disease diagnoses accurate and quick. The goal of a paper is to enhance the predictive performance of cardiac disease by using machine learning algorithms (decision tree (DT), support vector machine (SVM), naive Bayes (NB), Random Forest (RF) and K nearest neighbor (KNN)), two feature selection algorithms, the cross-validation methods that classify patients whether or not they have heart disease. The results indicated considerable improvement in predictive accuracy that achieve the highest accuracy at 98.4%. The efficacy of the classifier being proposed is investigated through a comparison of performance with different techniques of research.

Keywords: Heart disease · Machine learning · Classification first section

1 Introduction

1.1 Heart Disease

Cardiac disease is a significant cause of death worldwide on average. In accordance with the World Health Organization, 17,7 million deaths from heart diseases estimated for around 31% Around the world in 2016. In the light of this estimate, of these, 82% are in low and medium-revenue areas, under the age of 70, there are 17 million people are vulnerable to infectious diseases, 6.7 million people are affected by stroke and 7.4 million are causing coronary cardiac disease (WHO, 2016) [1]. Examining the heart disease mischance, the specific lifestyle factors which must to be addressed. Patients will consider this, therefore, undergo Significant tests including cholesterol, chest pain, average heart rate, electrocardiograms, blood pressure and high sugar levels, which can easily disclose and predict effective therapy circumstances.

© Springer Nature Singapore Pte Ltd. 2020
A. Bhattacharjee et al. (Eds.): MIND 2020, CCIS 1241, pp. 214–228, 2020.
https://doi.org/10.1007/978-981-15-6318-8_19

1.2 Traditional Ways

The principal reason for this huge death number is that the issue has not been identified at an early stage [2]. When heart disease is predicted at an early stage, several patients may be saved from dying. Early prediction of cardiac disease also gets to a prominent role in the detection of cardiovascular disease. Effective and more accuracy treatment may be offered to the patient by early prediction. There is, therefore, a need to develop such an early prediction and medical diagnosis system day by day and the methods which are invasive for heart disease diagnosis are building on a medical history examination of the patient, Study on physical exam, and medical expert analyzes of the Physical symptoms concerned. All of these methods cause often imprecise diagnoses and the results of diagnostic are often delayed owing to human mistake. It is also more costly and computationally intensive which takes time for evaluations to be carried out [3].

1.3 The Classification Techniques

Since we have a large number of medical databases, machine learning will help us uncover trends and useful knowledge from them. Although it has many uses, Machine-learning is used mostly for disease prediction on the medical field. Many researchers have become interested in using machine learning to diagnose diseases because it helps to reduce diagnostic time and improves accuracy and efficiency. Many diseases can be diagnosed using machine learning methods, but the focus of this paper will be regarding diagnosing cardiac disease. Because cardiovascular disease is the primary which causes death in around The Earth today, and a good treatment of cardiac disease is extremely useful in saving lives [4].

There will be many advantages of machine learning in Healthcare, e.g. the benefits of grouping patients with similar types of diseases or health problems can be provided with effective treatments, tested or made available for medical solutions. Safe health-care treatment for patients at a lower cost, reduction of time for medical treatment, detecting disease causes, determining the Healthcare treatment methods and efficient use of other resources, etc. It also helps health care organizations and experts to develop effective health policies. Developing computer technology allowed the auto-mated recording and analysis of cardiac diseases. Many used the popular UCI heart disease dataset to train and test their classifier, while others used data from other hospitals that were available to them.

Heart diseases are a major challenge in medical science, and Machine Learning can be a good choice for predicting any heart disease in humans [5]. Heart disease can be predicted by the use of Neural Network, Decision Tree, KNN, etc. Earlier in this article, we'll see how machine learning Is utilized to assessing the accuracy of cardiac disease. It also reveals how ML can help with heart disease in our future.

The research suggested aims to explored these techniques with regards to the operation of the prediction. It is accordingly, suggested that Predicting cardiac disease method be built and implemented. The proposed method for predicting cardiac disease Uses supervised learning to predict class labels of the heart dataset input sequence.

In this study, predictive models were learned using various algorithms, for instance, SVM, K-NN, NB, RF, and DT, to identify cardiac patients and people who are healthy. Moreover, two algorithms for feature selection, Linear Discriminant Analysis (LDA) and principal component analysis (PCA). Cross-validation approach was also utilized, such as k-fold. In addition, preprocessing methods for data was used on the dataset for cardiac disease. The system proposed had been trained and tested on the 2016 Cleveland dataset of cardiac disease. The remainder of the paper is set out as; contains literature review of the study actually proposed in this field in Sect. 2; the proposed system architecture and methodology will be described in Sect. 3, Experimental results and the comparison between techniques for classification will be exhibited in Sect. 4. Finally, the study is finished under Sect. 5.

2 Literature Review

Literature includes many works that diagnose cardiac disease utilizing machine learning and data mining. Analytical research on the techniques for data mining predicting cardiac disease has the efficacy of NN, DT, NB proved and composable classification in cardiovascular prediction. Classification of associative gives high accuracy and versatility compared with traditional classification, even when dealing with unstructured data [6, 7]. A comparative study of the classification strategies found that the classification of decision tree is easy and reliable [8]. The best algorithm was described by NB next to by NN and DT [6]. In addition, ANN are used to predict disease. For diagnosis, Supervised learning was utilized for training by the Back-Propagation Algorithm can be used to practice. demonstrated satisfactory precision of the experimental results [9].

A cardiac disease diagnostic method that is on the basis of a support vector machine and a minimal sequential optimization algorithm, are featured. This method also uses the network manufacturing of the Radial Basis Function and is equipped with the Orthogonal Least Square algorithm and implemented to an Indian patient data set. The results in SVM being equally good detecting cardiac disease compared with radial bias with an accuracy reach at 86.42% [10]. Anbarasi et al. are also using genetic algorithms in a different approach. Where the amount of checks to be carried out by the person is decreased by the determination of the attributes involved in cardiac prediction. Three classifiers were used in this process, and Such classifiers have been provided with fewer attributes, but the system takes longer to build the model [11].

A classification system of multilayer perception with the algorithm of back-propagation learning in the UCI dataset with 8 attributes and achieved the accuracy 80.99% [12]. The two approaches to diagnosis cardiac disease are Adaptive neuro fuzzy inference (ANFSI), ANN and the ANN achieved the maximum accuracy of 87.04% [13]. Chen et al. [14] Proposed the idea of predicting cardiac disease. They used Vector Quantization, one of the artificial intelligence methods used for classification and prediction purposes. Initially, 13 clinical features are identified for prediction. Second, ANN is utilized for classification purposes. Finally, performant of the neural network training using backpropagation for evaluating cardiac disease prediction system. Approximately 80% accuracy is achieved with the cardiac disease prediction test set by the system. Sonawane and Patil [15] Proposed a further approach to ANN-based cardiac disease prediction. It is in this situation that the ANN is trained using the Vector Quantization Algorithm using incremental training in random order. A total of 13 neurons are used to represent the clinical characteristics of the cardiac disease data set in the input layer. To achieve fewer errors and best accuracy, just one single neuron is used as the output layer showing that there is a cardiac disease or not. The system Efficiency is enhanced with NN training through a high number of epochs. This predictive model achieves 85.55% accuracy.

[16] introduced a classifier-based logistical regression system of decision support for classifying cardiac disease and accuracy reach at 77%. Using of The Cleveland data with global evolutionary methods and obtained predictions of high performance in precision [17]. [17] used SVM and multilayer perceptron (MLP) algorithms for the classification of cardiac disorder. The accuracy of the suggested classification reaches 80.41%. [18] developed a classification system for cardiac disease that utilized a hybrid strategy that blends a NN with fuzzy neural network and ANN. And the classification proposed was reached at 87.4%. [4] developed an expert system for cardiac disease diagnosis and implemented methods of machine learning as, for example, NB, ANN, and DT in the proposed system.

3 Proposed Technique

The proposed system for the classification of person with cardiac disorder and healthy people was developed. The performance of various predictive methods of machine learning for cardiac disorder prediction was tested at all of the features and subset of selected features. Selecting important features using algorithms of feature selection such as PCA and LDA, and on these selected features the classification efficiency was tested. The system utilized the popular machine learning classifier SVM, NB, K-NN, and DT. The measurements for the validation and efficiency evaluation for the model were determined. The proposed technique is divided into steps including (1) the pre-processing, (2) the selecting features, (3) the method of K-fold cross-validation, (4) the machine learning classification, and (5) The methods for assessing performance of classifiers. Its portrayed is shown in Fig. 1.

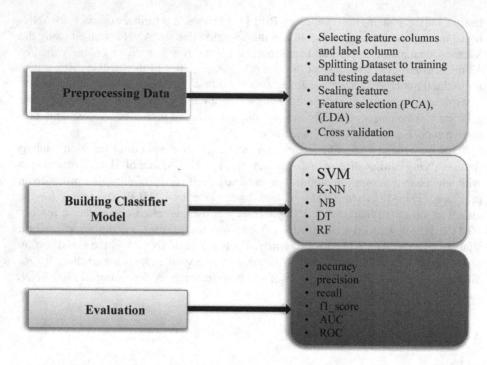

Fig. 1. The proposed techniques methodology

Now we will describe in details the stages of the Proposed Techniques Methodology as follows:

3.1 Pre-processing Data

Data set is prepared for building the suitable model. firstly, Data is split into independent value that is considered feature and dependent value is a target then categorical encoder that is dummy value converted string value to int value. The feature scaling of data set functions is a technique which standardizes the different scales and dynamic varieties of different examples and improvement in classification efficiency has been demonstrated. We shifted and scaled the data to 0 and 1 for all records. The attribute row of missing values is simply removed from the data set.

3.2 Feature Selection Algorithms

To the process of machine learning, the selection of features is important because features of irrelevant also affect machine learning classification effectiveness. The selection of features increases the accuracy of classification and decreases model execute times. We used two algorithms for the selection of features in our system and these algorithms select important features such as LDA and PCA algorithms.

3.3 Building Classifier Model

In this section, some classifier algorithms are introduced for comparison with the proposed techniques:

Support Vector Machine (SVM) is a supervised learning algorithm which utilizes a mathematical function collection that is kernel defined. The kernel function is to collect the data as input and transform it into the form needed. it can be utilized for both regression or classification challenges [19].

K-Nearest Neighbors (K-NN) is a supervised learning algorithm which may be used to solve regression problems and classification issues. Where KNN is used for classifying, the performance of output can be measured as the highest frequency class of instances like the K-most. Each case is held as the prediction in core votes for their class and the class with the most votes [20].

Decision Tree (DT) is a supervised learning algorithm which split its training collection of data into smaller parts, for extracting patterns utilize for the classification process. The knowledge is then showed in a tree form that can be facilely understood [21].

Random Forest (RF) is a classification composed of a set of tree-structured of classification. After a big number of trees is created, at input x they vote for the most public class. An error in the generalization of a tree classifier forest relied on the strength and relation between the individual forest trees [22].

Naive Bayes (NB) is a supervised learning. This model is utilized to compute backward probability of a class. The objective of the model is to predict future objects when a collection of objects is given to each class [23].

4 Experimental Results and Discussions

This partition introduces and describes the parameter settings, data set description, and results analysis and discussion.

Dataset Description: Dataset Description (processed. Cleveland. Data) was selected from the Kaggle heart disease datasets "https://www.kaggle.com/johnsmith88/heart-diseasedataset". It contains 1025 records of the patients with 14 attributes and two class variables. The class attribute indicates cardiac diseases (positive class) and non- cardiac diseases (negative class) patient records. Among 1025 patient records, 499 records belong to the negative class and 526 records belong to positive class. All the classifiers were trained using python on a workstation with a 4.0 GHz Core i3 4 CPU and 4 GB memory (Table 1).

Table 1. Parameter setting of the tested algorithms

Attribute	Description
Age	Years age
Sex	Sex, 0 for female, 1 for male
CP	Type of chest pain (1 = typical angina: 2 = atypical angina: 3 = non-angina pain: 4 = asymptomatic)
Trestbps	Blood pressure resting
Chol	Serum cholesterol in mg/dl
Fps	Fasting blood sugar larger 120 mg/dl (1 true)
Restecg	Electrocardiographic results Resting (1 = abnormality, 0 = normal)
Thalach	Maximum cardiac rate achieved
Exang	Exercise-induce angina (1 yes)
Oldpeak	ST depression induce: Exercise relative to rest
Slope	Peak exercise ST slope
CA	Major vessels number
Thal	No explanation provided, but probably thalassemia
Num	Cardiac disease diagnosis (angiographic disease status) 0 (<50% diameter narrowing) 1 (>50% diameter narrowing)

In this dataset patients ages, 29 to 79 were selected. Sex value 1 is denoted for male patients, and sex value 0 is denoted for female patients. Four types of cardiac disease can be viewed as examples of chest pain. Because of narrowed coronary arteries, Angina type 1 is induces a decreased blood flow to the cardiac muscles. Angina type 1 is a pain in the chest that happens during mental or emotional stress. Due to various reasons, Non-angina chest pain may occur and may not always occur as a result of actual cardiac failure.

The asymptomatic type fourth may not be a sign of cardiac disease. The next feature of the threetbps is blood pressure measurement at rest. Chol is the cholesterol-rate. FBS is the fasting blood sugar rate; The value is classified as 1 if the sugar in the fasting blood is less than 120 mg/dl and as above. Restecg is the result of electrocardiographic rest, thalach is the maximum cardiac rate, angina caused by stress is registered as 1 when pain occurs and 0 when pain is not present, Oldpeak is ST depression caused by stress, the slope is the ST peak stress part, ca is the big number fluoroscopic colored vessels, Thal is the stress duration check in minutes and number is the class features. The class function has a rating of 0 for patients diagnosed with usual and 1 for those diagnosed with cardiac disease.

Validation Method: For cross-validation of k-fold, the data set is split into k equal size of parts, where k − 1 group is utilized for training the classifying and the remaining portion was utilized to test the outperformance in each stage. Repeated k- times are the process of validation. Classifier performance is calculated according to the results of k. For CV multiple values of k are chosen. We have utilized in our study k = 10 Because good execution is achieved. 90% of the data was used for training in the process of 10-fold CV and 10% of the dataset was utilized for testing purposes.

4.1 Evaluation Criteria

Evaluation criteria is important step that are used for evaluation performance of trained model by utilizing testing data set. Different matrices are evaluated the model through accuracy, recall, precision, F-measure, ROC, and AUC.

Accuracy (Acc) It is one of the classification performances measures most frequently used and is described as the percentage of the samples accurately classified to the total sample number as indicated in Eq. (1)

$$Accuracy = \frac{TN + TP}{FP + FN + TP + TN} \tag{1}$$

Where, the number of true positive, false positive, true negative, and false negative samples is indicated by TP, TN, FP, and FN respectively.

A recall is defined as the percentage of the accurately classifier positive samples to the total number of positive samples as shown in Eq. (2).

$$Recall = \frac{TP}{TP + FN} \tag{2}$$

Precision is described as the percentage of positive samples classifier correctly to the total number of positive samples predicted as shown in Eq. (3).

$$Precision = \frac{TP}{TP + FP} \tag{3}$$

F-measure is also referred to as F1-score and is the harmonic mean of precision and recall as in Eq. (4). The F-measure value is reached from zero to one, and the good F-measure values imply a high classification efficiency.

$$F\text{-measure} = \frac{2 * Precision*Recall}{Precision + Recall} \tag{4}$$

The receiver operating characteristics (ROC) curve is a two-dimensional diagram where the y-axis is determined by the recall, and the x-axis is the False positive probability (FPR). The ROC curve was used to evaluate numerous systems, including diagnosis and treatment systems for medical decision-making, and machine learning [23].

The metric ROC Curve Area (AUC) is utilized for measuring the area below the ROC curve. The AUC value is always restricted by zero to one, and an AUC lower than 0.5 has no realistic classifier.

4.2 Result Analysis and Discussion

To assess the classification algorithms' performance, accuracy, recall, precision, f-measure, ROC, and AUC metrics are used for making a comparison among them. The results that are obtained from the comparison are recorded and summarized according to using dataset as the following samples.

This scenario compares between k-NN, SVM, DT, RF, NB and k-NN algorithms using data set which contains 13 features with Appling feature selection and finding the accuracy, recall, precision, F1 score and AUC percentages for predicting the cardiac diseases.

Performance Classifiers K-Fold Cross-validation Results on Full Features (n = 13)
In this test, the total features of the data set on machine learning algorithms were checked using 10-fold cross-validation technique. 90% was utilized in the 10-fold CV to the classifiers were trained and only 10% tested. Finally, it measured the 10-fold approaches average metrics. Furthermore, different parameter values were transferred via the classifications. Table 2 discusses the results of Cross-validation 10-fold to Full Function.

Table 2. Classification performance on full features

Method	Accuracy	Recall	Precession	F1 score	AUC
KNN (K = 3)	0.90	0.91	0.894	0.90	0.96
SVM	0.89	0.95	0.86	0.90	0.89
DT	0.86	0.87	0.87	0.87	0.868
RF	0.88	0.92	0.85	0.85	0.88
NB	0.89	0.95	0.86	0.90	0.89

In Table 2 we experimented with various values of k = 1, 2, 3, 5, and 9 to K-NN classifier. However, at k = 1, the efficiency of K-NN was excellent with a classification accuracy of 0.98%, 97% recall, 99% precession, 97% F1-score, and 98% AUC. The SVM has 86% Recall, 95% Precision, and 89% accuracy. The SVM and NB were the second-best classification that has Recall 95%, Precision 86%, and 89% for accuracy. The DT has 87% Recall, 87% Precision, and 86% accuracy. The RF has accuracy 88%, Recall 85%, and Precision 92% is shown. Figure 3 shows K-NN classification performance, with various value of K.

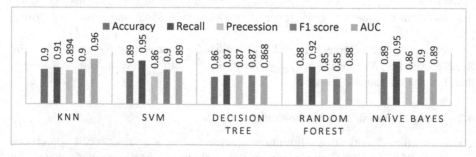

Fig. 2. Performance of various classification by 10-fold CV on full features

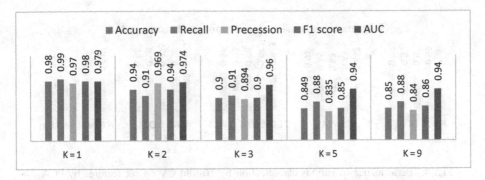

Fig. 3. K-NN performance on various K value.

AUC was 96% for K-NN, which shows that K-NN covered an area 96% larger than other classifications. The better AUC value indicates the greater efficiency of the classifier. The classifiers AUC is displayed in Fig. 2.

Results of Performance Classification by K-Fold Cross-validation (F = 10) on Feature Selection (n = 6) by PCA

Table 3. Performance of classification on feature selection (n = 6) by PCA

Method	Accuracy	Recall	Precession	F1 score	AUC
KNN (K = 1)	0.98	0.99	0.97	0.98	0.979
SVM	0.847	0.88	0.83	0.85	0.91
Decision tree	0.983	0.987	0.98	0.98	0.98
Random Forest	0.979	0.98	0.975	0.98	0.98
Naïve Bayes	0.837	0.88	0.819	0.85	0.92

According to Table 3, the DT Showed an extremely good accuracy, accuracy 98.3%, 98.7% Recall, and 98% Precision. The AUC value of DT is 98%. For K-NN, we experimented with various values of k = 1, 2, 3, 5, and 9. However, at k = 1, the efficiency of K-NN was excellent with a classification accuracy of 98%, However, the performance of K-NN was not good at k = 9. SVM efficiency was not good when compared with other algorithm values and as displayed in Table 3. SVM Achieved accuracy 84.7%, Recall 88%, Precision 83%, and AUC 91%. The NB obtained a classification accuracy of 83.7%, Recall 88%, and Precision 81.9%. For random forest was applied accuracy 97.9%, Recall 98%, and Precision 97.5%. The AUC value was 98%. Table 3 displayed performance classification by K-Fold Cross-Validation (F = 10) on feature selection by PCA algorithm.

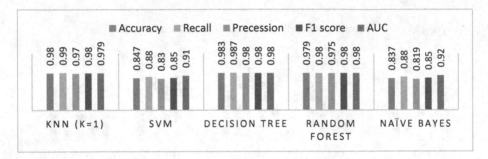

Fig. 4. Performance of various classification by 10-fold CV on six features by PCA

Figures 4 also display the classifiers values of ROC AUC at 6 selected features. The DT and RF AUC values are 98% large by comparison with other classifications. SVM, NB respectively have low value in AUC reach at 91% and 92%.

Results of Performance Classification by K-Fold Cross-validation (F = 10) on Feature Selection (n = 6) by LDA

Table 4. Performance classification on feature selection (n = 6) by LDA

Method	Accuracy	Recall	Precession	F1 score	AUC
KNN (K = 1)	0.984	0.985	0.98	0.98	0.98
SVM	0.87	0.93	0.84	0.88	0.93
Decision tree	0.984	0.985	0.98	0.98	0.98
Random Forest	0.984	0.985	0.98	0.98	0.986
Naïve Bayes	0.869	0.93	0.838	0.88	0.93

According to Table 4, the DT, KNN, and RF Showed an extremely good accuracy, accuracy reach at, 98.4%. The AUC value of RF, DT, and KNN are 98.6%, 98%, and 98%. For K-NN, we experimented with various values of k = 1, 2, 3, 5, and 9. However, at k = 1, the efficiency of K-NN was excellent with a classification accuracy of 98.4% accuracy, However, the performance of K-NN was not good at k = 9. NB efficiency was not good when compared with other algorithm values and as displayed in Table 4. SVM achieved 87% accuracy, Recall 93%, Precision 84%, and AUC 93%. The NB achieved 86.9%, accuracy Recall 93%, and Precision 83%. For random forest was applied accuracy 98.4%, Recall 98%, and Precision 98%. The AUC value was 98.6%. Table 4 displayed performance classification by K-Fold Cross-Validation (F = 10) on feature selection by the LDA algorithm.

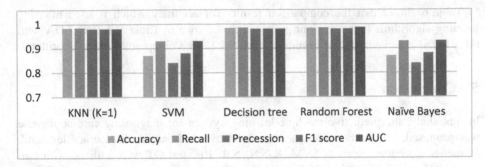

Fig. 5. Performance of various classification by 10-fold CV on six features by LDA

Figures 5 also display the classifiers values of ROC AUC at 6 selected features. The DT, KNN and RF AUC values are 98%, 98%, and 98.6%, respectively, which were large by comparison with other classifications. SVM and NB have low value in AUC reach at 93%.

Table 5. Measures for best performance evaluation

FS	The best accuracy	The best recall	The best precession	The best F1-score	The best AUC
PCA	98.3% DT	99% KNN	98% DT	98% KNN, RF, DT	98% RF, DT
LDA	98.4% KNN, RF, DT	98.5% KNN, RF, DT	98% KNN, RF, DT	98% KNN, RF, DT	98.6% RF
All features	90% KNN	95% SVM, NB	89% KNN	90% KNN, NB, SVM	96% KNN

Table 5 shows that on reduced features, the classification accuracy of RF increased from 88% to 98.4%. Similarly, DT accuracy increased with reduced features from 86% to 98%. Therefore, choose important features by the function selection algorithms that enhanced performance of classifiers. Designing the prediction of cardiac disease diagnostic system utilizing the selecting feature LDA with classifiers will effectively improve performance.

Table 6. Compared with different researches

Compared algorithms	RFRS [24]	NB [25]	J48 [26]	NB, DT, MLP, KNN, SCRL, RBF, SVM, bagging, boosting and stacking Boosting with SVM [27]	RF, LDA	DT, PCA
Best accuracy	92.6%	86.4%	56.76%	84.81%	98.4	98.3

Table 6 shows that the comparison results for accuracy which is used machine learning algorithms found that our proposed that shown in Table 5, 6 (RF, LDA) and (DT, PCA) are given highest accuracy reach 98.4, 98.3 compare to other algorithms.

5 Conclusion

In this study, the predictive machine-learning system for diagnosing cardiac disease was proposed. The study was trained on the data set of cardiac disease at Cleveland. Classifier algorithms such as SVM, K-NN, NB, RF, and DT were utilized with two selection function algorithms PCA, and LDA. The method of cross-validation has been utilized for validation in the study. Also, different evaluation metrics were adopted to inspect classifier performance. The feature selection algorithms choose significant features which improve the effectiveness of the classifier with respect to classification accuracy recall, and precision, AUC and F1-score. When selected by the LDA algorithm, the classifiers Random forest with cross-validation 10-fold displayed the better accuracy of 98.4%.

This research work is the development of a heart disease diagnostic system. The study used two feature selection algorithms, five classification algorithm, cross-validation method, and cardiac diseases diagnostic evaluation performance. The study was tested for classifying cardiac disease and healthy subjects on the Cleveland dataset of heart disease. Implementing a decision making for using the machine-learning approach will be better suited for cardiac diagnosis. In addition, other unrelated features reduced the diagnostic performance and efficiency. Thus, the use of selecting feature algorithms to select the best attributes was another groundbreaking aspect of this study Which would improve classification accuracy. We will be performing more experiments in the future to improve the efficiency of these classification predictive for cardiac diagnosis by utilizing additional feature selection methods and optimization algorithms.

References

1. World Health Organization: World Health Organization (2019). http://www.who.int/cardiovasculardiseases/en
2. Blair, S., et al.: Commentary on Wang Y et al. "an overview of non-exercise estimated cardiorespiratory fitness: estimation equations, cross-validation and application". J. Sci. Sport Exerc. 1(1), 94–95 (2019). https://doi.org/10.1007/s42978-019-0001-z
3. Vanisree, K., Singaraju, J.: Decision support system for congenital heart disease diagnosis based on signs and symptoms using neural networks. Int. J. Comput. Appl. 19(6), 6–12 (2011)
4. Al-Janabi, M.I., Qutqut, M.H., Hijjawi, M.: Machine learning classification techniques for heart disease prediction: a review. Int. J. Eng. Technol. 7(4), 5373–5379 (2018)
5. Gandhi, M.: Prediction in heart disease using techniques of data mining. In: International Conference on Futuristic Trend in Computational Analysis and Knowledge Management (ABLAZE-2015) (2015)

6. Mastoli, M.M.M., Pol, U.R., Patil, R.D.: Machine learning classification algorithms for predictive analysis in healthcare. Mach. Learn. **6**(12), 1225–1229 (2019)
7. Sudhakar, K.: Study of heart disease prediction using data mining. Int. J. Adv. Res. Comput. Sci. Softw. Eng. **4**(1), 1157–1160 (2014)
8. Thenmozhi, K., Deepika, P.: Heart disease prediction using classification with different decision tree techniques. Int. J. Eng. Res. Gen. Sci. **2**(6), 6–11 (2014)
9. Soni, S.N., Bhatt, N.: Forecasting of heart disease using hybrid algorithm. Int. J. Sci. Res. Eng. Trends **5**, 1234–1238 (2019)
10. Ghumbre, S., Patil, C., Ghatol, A.: Heart disease diagnosis using support vector machine. In: Proceedings of International Conference on Computer Science and Information Technology (ICCSIT), pp. 84–88, December 2011
11. Anbarasi, M., Anupriya, E., Iyengar, N.: Enhanced prediction of heart disease with feature subset selection using genetic algorithm. Int. J. Eng. Sci. Technol. **2**, 5370–5376 (2010)
12. Hasan, T.T., Jasim, M.H., Hashim, I.A.: Heart disease diagnosis system based on multi-layer perceptron neural network and support vector machine. Int. J. Curr. Eng. Technol. **77**(55), 2277–4106 (2017)
13. Abushariah, M.A.M., Alqudah, A.A.M., Adwan, O.Y., Yousef, R.M.M.: Automatic heart disease diagnosis system based on artificial neural network (ANN) and adaptive neuro-fuzzy inference systems (ANFIS) approaches. J. Softw. Eng. Appl. **7**(12), 1055–1064 (2014)
14. Chen, A.H., Huang, S.-Y., Hong, P.-S., Cheng, C.-H., Lin, E.-J.: HDPS: heart disease prediction system. Comput. Cardiol. **2011**, 557–560 (2011)
15. Sonawane, J.S., Patil, D.: Prediction of heart disease using learning vector quantization algorithm. In: 2014 Conference on IT in Business, Industry and Government (CSIBIG), pp. 1–5 (2014)
16. Detrano, R., Janosi, A., Steinbrunn, W.: International application of a new probability algorithm for the diagnosis of coronary artery disease. Am. J. Cardiol. **64**(5), 304–310 (1989)
17. Haq, A.U., et al.: A hybrid intelligent system framework for the prediction of heart disease using machine learning algorithms. Mob. Inf. Syst. **2018**, 1–21 (2018)
18. Kahramanli, H., Allahverdi, N.: Design of a hybrid system for the diabetes and heart diseases. Expert Syst. Appl. **35**(1–2), 82–89 (2008)
19. Fan, Q., Wang, Z., Li, D., Gao, D., Zha, H.: Entropy-based fuzzy support vector machine for imbalanced datasets. Knowl.-Based Syst. **115**, 87–99 (2017)
20. Brownlee, J.: K-nearest neighbors for machine learning. Understand machine learning algorithms, April 2016
21. Zhang, X., Treitz, P.M., Chen, D., Quan, C., Shi, L., Li, X.: Mapping mangrove forests using multi-tidal remotely-sensed data and a decision-tree-based procedure. Int. J. Appl. Earth Obs. Geoinf. **62**, 201–214 (2017)
22. Islam, M.M., Kim, J., Khan, S.A., Kim, J.M.: Reliable bearing fault diagnosis using Bayesian inference-based multi-class support vector machines. J. Acoust. Soc. Am. **141**(2), EL89–EL95 (2017)
23. Narayanan, U., et al.: A survey on various supervised classification algorithms. In: International Conference on Energy, Communication, Data Analytics and Soft Computing (ICECDS), pp. 2118–2124 (2017)
24. Liu, X., et al.: A hybrid classification system for heart disease diagnosis. Comput. Math. Methods Med. **2017**, 1–11 (2017)
25. Vembandasamy, K., Sasipriya, R., Deepa, E.: Heart diseases detection using Naive Bayes algorithm. Int. J. Innov. Sci. Eng. Technol. **2**(9), 441–444 (2015)

26. Patel, J., et al.: Heart disease prediction using machine learning and data mining technique. Heart Disease 7(1), 129–137 (2015)
27. Pouriyeh, S., et al.: A comprehensive investigation and comparison of machine learning techniques in the domain of heart disease. In: Proceedings of IEEE Symposium on Computers and Communications (ISCC), pp. 204–207. IEEE, Heraklion, July 2017

Convolutional Neural Network Based Sound Recognition Methods for Detecting Presence of Amateur Drones in Unauthorized Zones

Ungati Ganapathi[✉] and M. Sabarimalai Manikandan[✉]

Real-Time Embedded Signal Processing Lab, School of Electrical Sciences,
Indian Institute of Technology Bhubaneswar, Jatani, Khordha 752050, India
{ug12,msm}@iitbbs.ac.in

Abstract. Unmanned aerial vehicles (UAVs), or drones, have become an integral part of diverse civil and commercial applications. But illegal operations of UAVs pose serious risks to public safety, privacy and national security. Thus, the detection of these vehicles has become vital to identify and track amateur drones in unauthorized zones or restricted areas. This paper presents three sound event recognition (SER) methods developed based on the Mel-frequency cepstrum coefficients (MFCCs) and spectrogram features combined with three machine learning classifiers such as multi-class SVM, one-dimensional convolutional neural networks (1DCNN) and two-dimensional CNN (2DCNN) for recognizing drone sounds. The SER methods are evaluated using a wide variety of sounds such as music, speech, wind, rain, and vehicle. Results showed that the MFCC-SVM based and MFCC-1DCNN based SER methods had average recall rate (RR) = 92.53%, precision rate (PR) = 93.21% and F1-score = 92.84% and RR = 94.28%, PR = 96.57% and F1-score = 95.02% for a segment length of 1 s, respectively. The spectrogram-2DCNN based method had average RR = 73.27%, PR = 74.55% and F1-score = 73.37% for audio segment length of 500 ms. Preliminary results demonstrate that the MFCC-1DCNN based SER method achieves better recognition rates as compared to that of the MFCC-SVM based and spectrogram-2DCNN based methods in recognizing drone sounds.

Keywords: UAV detection · Acoustic based UAV detection · Convolutional neural networks · Audio event recognition

1 Introduction

Due to the rapid development of unmanned aerial vehicles ("UAV" - also known as "Drone" and "Quadcopter"), use of UAVs continues to grow in various com-

This research work is carried out with support of IMPRINT-II and MHRD grant, Government of India.

mercial and defence applications, such as border security, surveying and mapping, precision agriculture, construction and mining management, mineral explorations, wide area grid monitoring, mobile hot spots for broadband wireless access, traffic monitoring, aerial remote sensing for disaster management, media and entertainment, and product delivery [1–4]. Despite attracting a great wide attention in both military and civil applications, unmanned aerial vehicles pose a number of threats, such as airspace safety, air traffic, physical and cyber private/public property attacks, malicious entries to border and private land and other potential risks associated with a possible intrusion. Therefore, detection of UAVs has become most important to classify and track malicious UAVs that can be most essential for avoiding physical and cyber attacks, and preventing spying on private/public property [1–20]. Further, detection, classification and tracking UAVs have become most important for maintaining safe and collusion-free operation. Use of consumer mini and micro UAVs are exponentially growing in diverse applications, which lead to a new physical security threats in near future. In the past studies, various techniques including radar, radio frequency (RF) signals radiated from UAVs, acoustic sensors based signals, and imaging cameras (ultraviolet, visible, near-infrared and thermal) based computer vision methods were explored for detection and classification of UAVs [1–11]. However, different types of materials, sizes, speeds, ranges, RF interference, and application environment pose very challenging problems in accurate and reliable detection of mini and micro UAVs [1]. In [1], B. Taha and A. Shoufan presented a review of machine learning based methods for drone detection and classification with different modalities. In [2], M. Ezuma et al. investigated detection and classification of UAVs in the presence of wireless interference signals. In [2], M. Ezuma et al. presented micro-UAV detection and classification from RF fingerprints using machine learning techniques. In [4], a machine learning-based method was presented based on the features extracted from packet size and inter-arrival time of encrypted WiFi traffic.

1.1 Related Sound Recognition Methods

In [12], Lim et al. presented a method for classifying UAVs sound using convolutional neural networks (CNN) with spectrogram data collected with microphones by exploring Doppler shift of the sound components. The method had an accuracy of 91.972% for a single fully connected neural network and of 99.92%. In [14], Sara et al. presented drone detection and identification methods using acoustic fingerprints with deep learning techniques such as CNN, recurrent neural network (RNN) and convolutional recurrent neural network (CRNN). The signal was acquired with a sampling frequency of 16 kHz. Results showed that the CNN have outperformed RNN with a relative improvement of 21.38%, 20.32%, 20.32% and 27.59% in accuracy, F1 score, precision and recall, respectively. The CNN had shown an improvement of 1.66%, 1.98%, 1.21% and 1.98% in accuracy, F1 score, precision and recall, respectively as compared with that of CRNN. The precision and recall values are 75.0% and 75.92% (RNN based method), 96.38% and 96.24% (CNN based method) and 94.72% and 95.02% (CRNN based method).

In [15], Matson et al. proposed a UAV detector using multiple acoustic sensor nodes with the Mel-frequency cepstral coefficients (MFCC) and short-time Fourier transform (STFT) and support vector machines (SVM) and CNN classifiers. Microphones are placed at distance of 20 m. The CNN architecture includes two convolutional layers and two dense layers. Compared to MFCC-SVM, STFT-SVM model provides better results with clearer paths. In [16], Jeon et al. investigated effectiveness of sound classification methods based on the Gaussian Mixture Model (GMM), CNN, and RNN with the spectrogram for drone detection in real-time environments. The RNN models had F-Score of 80.09% with 240 ms duration input audio that provides better detection performance as compared to the CNN and GMM based methods (CNN > GMM: 0.6415 > 0.5232). For unseen types of data, the RNN based method had the best performance in terms of F-Score (0.6984) with the precision and recall (0.5477, 0.9635). In [17], Mezei et al. presented drone sound detection using correlation. The signal was digitized with sampling frequency of 44.1 kHz and 16-bit resolution. The digital audio segment was transformed using fast Fourier transform. Then transformed signal was filtered with characteristics of the band pass filter. Five correlation methods, such as the cross-correlation, normalized maximum correlation, Pearson correlation, Spearman rank-correlation and Kendall rank-correlation were studied for drone sound detection. In [18], Kim et al. presented a real-time drone detection and monitoring system to detect drones based on the Fourier transformed sound data and two different methods such as the plotted image machine learning (PIL) and K nearest neighbors (KNN). Results showed the accuracy rate of 83% and 61% were achieved by PIL and KNN methods, respectively. In [19], Bernardini et al. presented a drone detection method based on the short term parametrization in time and frequency domain of environmental audio and support 48 kHz and 16-bit resolution. The duration of audio segment is 5 s. The audio segment was normalized to −1 to 1. Each segment was segmented into sub-segments of 20 ms using a moving Hamming window with overlap of 10 ms. The temporal and spectral features such as the short-time energy (STE), the zero crossing rate (ZCR), the temporal centroid, the spectral centroid (SC), the spectral roll-off, and the Mel-frequency cepstrum coefficients (MFCCs) and mid term features were extracted for drone sound identification problem. The method had precision of 98.3%. In [20], Ellen E. Case et al. presented an acoustic array using commercial off-the-shelf (COTS) hardware to locate and track small UAVs. A band-pass filter was designed with frequency range between 450 Hz to 3 kHz to remove ambient clutter noise and suppress interference.

1.2 Major Contributions of This Paper

In the past studies, some of the drone detection methods have been presented using the single or multiple acoustic sensor nodes. Most drone detection methods were designed for classification of drone vs. no-drone by analysing their audio fingerprints, formulated as a binary sound event classification problem. Researchers have developed machine learning based methods to decide if the recorded sound is a drone's sound or not. Most methods fail to investigate the performance of the methods under diverse environmental sound sources such as music, speech, wind, rain, and vehicle which are unavoidable in practical scenarios.

In this paper, we present three sound event recognition (SER) methods for detecting the presence of drones. These SER methods are developed based on the MFCCs and STFT spectrogram features combined with three machine learning classifiers such as multi-class SVM, one-dimensional CNN (1DCNN) and two-dimensional CNN (2DCNN). The performance of the AER methods were validated using a large variety of drone's sounds and other environmental sounds. In this study, the performance of the SER methods are evaluated for different lengths of audio segment. The rest of this paper is organized as follows. Section 2 presents sound event recognition methods. Section 3 summarize the results of the three SER methods. Finally, Sect. 4 presents conclusions.

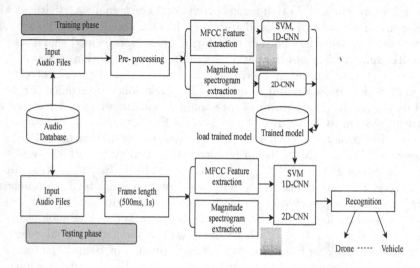

Fig. 1. A simplified block diagram of sound event recognition methods.

2   Materials and Methods

Block diagram of sound event recognition (SER) method is shown in Fig. 1. This paper presents three SER methods by using the MFCC and STFT spectrogram features and classifiers such as the multi-class SVM, 1DCNN and 2DCNN. The SER method classify audio segments into five classes such as *drone, nature (wind and rain), music, speech, vehicle* by choosing the suitable audio segment size. In this study, we consider two audio segment lengths (1 s, 500 ms) to investigate the performance of the AER methods.

2.1   MFCC Feature Extraction

The mel-frequency cepstrum coefficients (MFCCs) are most widely used for recognition of audio events. The MFCC feature extraction process is described as follows [21, 22].

– Apply pre-emphasis filter to amplify high frequency components which are having smaller amplitudes as compared to the lower frequency components. It is implemented as

$$y[n] = x[n] - \alpha x[n-1], \tag{1}$$

where α is fixed as 0.97.
– Multiply the filtered signal $y[n]$ with a hamming window $w[n]$, which is computed as

$$w(n) = 0.54 - 0.46 \ \cos\left(\frac{\pi n}{N}\right), \tag{2}$$

where N denotes the length of segment.
– Find the magnitude spectrum for the windowed segment $z[n]$ using the fast Fourier transform (FFT).
– Compute mel-frequency spectrum with a set of 26 triangular band-pass filters related to the linear frequency f by

$$M(f) = 1125 \ \ln\left(1 + \frac{f}{700}\right). \tag{3}$$

– Compute the decorrelated filter bank coefficients that are computed as

$$C_n = \sum_{k=1}^{k}(\log \ S_k)\left[n\left(k - \frac{1}{2}\right)\frac{\pi}{K}\right], \tag{4}$$

where K denotes number of triangular band-pass filters and $n = 1, 2......, K$, and S_k denotes the energy of the Kth triangular band-pass filter.

In this study, 13 MFFCs are used for each of the segments in both training and testing phases.

2.2   Fourier Magnitude Spectrogram

In this study, we present the 2DCNN classifier with the STFT based spectrogram of an audio segment. The magnitude spectrogram captures frequency components of each of the sounds. Therefore, many STFT features were extracted for recognizing different kinds of sounds. Recently, the magnitude spectrogram used as feature image for creating representation models to distinguish sounds.

The signal is divided into segments with duration of 500 ms and 1 s. Then, the spectrogram is computed with a hamming window. The magnitude spectrum are

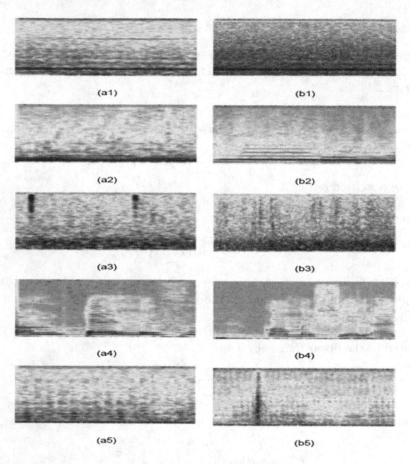

Fig. 2. Magnitude spectrogram images of five classes 500 ms (left side) and 1 s (right side): (a1)–(b1) Drone Sounds; (a2)–(b2) Music; (a3)–(b3) Nature (wind and rain); (a4)–(b4) Speech; and (a5)–(b5) Vehicle Sounds.

combined with 2DCNN classifier to obtain five sound models. The spectrogram of an audio segment is computed as [23]

$$s_i(k, m) = \sum_{n=0}^{N-1} x_i(n)w(m-n)e^{-j\frac{2\pi}{N}kn}, \tag{5}$$

where $w(.)$ is the window function, $s_i(k, m)$ is the spectrogram of x_i. Figure 2 illustrates the magnitude spectra of the sounds such as drone, music, speech, Nature (wind and rain), and vehicle. It can be seen that the magnitude spectrogram representations capture spectral components of sounds.

Table 1. Specifications of the MFCC-SVM based SER method

Parameters	Segment length	
	500 ms	1 s
Sound format	.wav	.wav
Number of channels	Mono	Mono
Resolution	16 bit PCM	16 bit PCM
Number of classes	5	5
Duration of training data	6 h	6 h
Duration of testing data	4 h	4 h
Sampling frequency	16 kHz	16 kHz
Sound feature	MFCC	MFCC
Segment length	8000 samples	16000 samples
SVM kernel	RBF	RBF
SVM penalty parameter, C	1	1
Gamma parameter	0.0769	0.0769
Degree parameter	3	3
Tolerance	0.001	0.001
Training time	84.83 min	89.96 min
Model size	8.28 MB	8.28 MB
Testing time	1.78 ms	1.85 ms

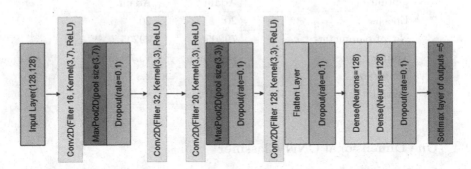

Fig. 3. Block diagram of the spectrogram-2DCNN based sound event recognition method.

2.3   Multi-class SVM Classifier

The SVM is implemented with the Gaussian radial basis function. Table 1 summarizes the specifications of the MC-SVM based SER method with the MFCC feature vector.

Table 2. Specifications of the MFCC-IDCNN based SER method

Parameters	Segment length	
	500 ms	1 s
Sound format	.wav	.wav
Number of channels	Mono	Mono
Resolution	16 bit PCM	16 bit PCM
Number of classes	5	5
Duration of training data	6 h	6 h
Duration of testing data	4 h	4 h
Sampling frequency	16 kHz	16 kHz
Sound Feature	MFCC	MFCC
Number of samples	8000	16000
Number of convolution layers	4	4
Number of drop-out layers	2	2
Number of Max-pooling layers	1	1
Fold	5	5
Activation functions	Softmax, Relu	Softmax, Relu
Number of neurons	1600	1600
Batch size	128	128
Learning rate	0.001	0.001
Optimizer	Adam	Adam
Epochs	20	20
No. of parameters	79205	79205
Training time	10.63 min	10.78 min
Model size	2.34 MB	2.35 MB
Testing time	85.03 usec	82.98 usec

2.4   One Dimensional CNN Classifier

In this study, the 1D-CNN includes the four convolutions, one max-pooling, two drop-out, one flatten and two fully-connected layers to obtain the models for each of the audio event classes. The number of layers and tuning parameters are tuned to achieve optimum performance. The max-pooling is used for reducing the feature map dimension and also for retaining the significant features of sound events. A drop-out layer is used to avoid the model over-fitting. The fully-connected layer is used in the last stage. The design parameters of the 1DCNN based SER method are summarized in Table 2.

2.5   Two Dimensional CNN Classifier

Figure 3 illustrates a block diagram of the spectrogram-2DCNN based SER method which includes 03 convolutional layers and 02 fully connected layers. The design parameters of the 2DCNN based SER method are summarized in Table 3.

Table 3. Specifications of spectrogram-2DCNN based SER method

Parameters	Segment length	
	500 ms	1 s
Sound format	.wav	.wav
Number of channel	Mono	Mono
Resolution	16 bit PCM	16 bit PCM
Number of classes	5	5
Training data	5 h	5 h
Testing data	5 h	5 h
Image width	128	128
Image height	128	128
Sampling frequency	16 kHz	16 kHz
Sound Feature	Spectrogram	Spectrogram
Number of convolution layers	4	4
Number of drop-out layers	4	4
Number of max-pooling layers	2	2
Activation function	Softmax, Relu	Softmax, Relu
Batch length	20	20
Learning rate	0.01	0.01
Optimizer	Adam	Adam
Epochs	30	30
Number of CNN parameters	379577	379577
Training time	4.56 h	5.21 h
Size of the model	11.7 MB	11.7 MB
Testing time	220.37 ms (avg)	227.19 ms (avg)

3   Results and Discussion

In this study, we evaluate the performance of the three sound event recognition methods by using a large scale of sound recordings.

3.1 Audio Database and Performance Metrics

In this study, we created 15 h audio database, including rain, wind, speech, music, vehicle, and drone sounds. The sounds are acquired by using different kinds of recording devices such as the H1n Handy recorder, EVISTR digital voice recorder and mobile handset (Samsung, Redmi) In addition, we also collected sounds from publicly accessible multimedia websites for performance study. We also included the drone sounds taken from publicly available sound database [24]. The sound signals are digitized at a sampling frequency of 44.1 kHz and 16 bit resolution. The sound signals are resampled to sampling frequency of 16 kHz for training and testing purposes.

To compute performance metrics, recognized sound classes are compared with ground-truth annotation files. An sound event is said to be correctly recognized true positive (TP) if the recognized sound event matches with its ground-truth annotation. If the sound event class is wrongly recognized then the sound event is considered to be a false positive (FP). If the correct sound event class is missed then the sound event is considered to be the false negative (FN). If the sound event class is correctly recognized then the event is considered as the true positive. Based on the TPs, FPs and FNs, three benchmark metrics such as precision rate (PR), recall rate (RR), and F1-score are computed as

$$PR = \frac{TP}{TP + FP} \times 100, \tag{6}$$

$$RR = \frac{TP}{TP + FN} \times 100, \tag{7}$$

$$\text{F1-score} = \frac{2(RR \times RR)}{PR + RR} \times 100. \tag{8}$$

3.2 Performance of SER Methods

In the past studies, some of the acoustic based drone detection methods were presented by recognizing drone sounds using the STFT and MFCC features combined with machine learning techniques. However, these drone sound detection methods were not evaluated under different outdoor sounds. It is difficult reproduce the detection results of the existing drone sound detection methods because the optimal parameters of existing methods are not available. Further, it is not pair to have direct comparison of existing methods since performance evaluations were performed with different sound databases with different sampling rates and segment lengths. Therefore, in this study, we investigate the performance three sound event recognition methods such as the MFCC-SVM based SER method, the MFCC-IDCNN based SER method and the spectrogram-2DCNN based SER method for recognizing the drone sounds and non-drone sounds such as speech, music, vehicle, wind and rain which are unavoidable in practical application of acoustic sensor based drone detection system.

Table 4. Confusion matrix for MFCC-SVM based SER method

	MFCC-SVM					
	TS	D	M	N	S	V
Audio segment length of 500 ms						
Drone (D)	12779	**10653**	1142	177	310	497
Music (M)	30034	430	**26939**	245	1002	1424
Nature (N)	34053	42	23	**33951**	14	23
Speech (S)	30408	489	1956	297	**26699**	967
Vehicle (V)	28079	376	1545	307	531	**25320**
Audio segment length of 1 s						
Drone (D)	12629	**10933**	840	136	244	476
Music (M)	30066	341	**27694**	185	679	1167
Nature (N)	34195	11	7	**34149**	17	11
Speech (S)	30267	245	1200	215	**28004**	603
Vehicle (V)	28172	373	1335	208	441	**25815**

Performance of MFCC-SVM Based SER Method: We study performance of the MFCC-SVM based SER method for the specifications summarized in Table 1. Evaluation results are summarized in Table 4 for segment lengths of 500 ms and 1 s. Results show that the MFCC-SVM based method with a segment length of 1 s provides better recognition rates as compared to that of a segment length of 500 ms. In the testing phase, the MFCC-SVM based method was tested with real-time sound signals that may includes some pause portions which may be added with some other background sounds. Further, 500 ms or 1 s duration sound segment may mimic like other sounds which are considered in this study. Such short duration sounds of one class may be misclassified into other classes. However, it is difficult to recognize such sounds through auditory perception. From the confusion matrix as shown in Table 4, the MFCC-SVM based AER method had false positives of 1337, false negatives of 1696 and true positives of 10653 for 500 ms segment duration with a total of 12779 drone sound segments. The false positive rate is 1.09% for a total of 122574 non-drone sound segments whereas the missed rate is 16.64% for a total of 12779 drone sound segments. For 1 s segment, the MFCC-SVM based SER method had false positives of 1334, false negatives of 2126 and true positives of 10653 for 500 ms segment duration with a total of 12779 drone sound segments. The false positive rate is 0.79% for a total of 122700 non-drone sound segments whereas the missed rate is 13.43% for a total of 12629 drone sound segments.

Performance of MFCC-IDCNN Based SER Method: We study performance of the MFCC-IDCNN based SER method for the specifications summarized in Table 2. Evaluation results are summarized in Table 5 for segment lengths

Table 5. Confusion matrix for MFCC-IDCNN based SER method

	MFCC-1DCNN based SER method					
	TS	D	M	N	S	V
Audio segment length of 500 ms						
Drone (D)	12930	**11565**	652	51	367	295
Music (M)	30532	222	**28315**	76	1153	766
Nature (N)	34482	4	16	**34447**	11	4
Speech (S)	30483	213	1596	52	**28059**	563
Vehicle (V)	28297	125	1131	70	466	**26507**
Audio segment length of 1 s						
Drone (D)	12929	**12209**	416	9	163	132
Music (M)	30384	12	**29424**	26	453	465
Nature (N)	34413	5	2	**34394**	10	2
Speech (S)	30497	127	1223	29	**28741**	377
Vehicle (V)	28347	129	752	23	156	**27287**

of 500 ms and 1 s. Results show that the MFCC-IDCNN based method with a segment length of 1 s provides better recognition rates as compared to that of a segment length of 500 ms. From the confusion matrix as shown in Table 5, the MFCC-IDCNN based AER method had false positives of 564, false negatives of 1365 and true positives of 11565 for 500 ms segment duration with a total of 12930 drone sound segments. The false positive rate is 0.46% for a total of 123794 non-drone sound segments whereas the missed rate is 10.55% for a total of 12930 drone sound segments. For 1 s segment, the MFCC-IDCNN based AER method had false positives of 273, false negatives of 720 and true positives of 12209 for 1 s segment duration with a total of 12929 drone sound segments. The false positive rate is 0.22% for a total of 123641 non-drone sound segments whereas the missed rate is 5.56% for a total of 12929 drone sound segments.

Performance of Spectrogram-2DCNN Based SER Method: We study performance of the spectrogram-2DCNN based SER method for the specifications summarized in Table 3. Evaluation results are summarized in Table 6 for segment lengths of 500 ms and 1 s. Results show that the spectrogram-2DCNN based method with a segment length of 500 ms provides better recognition rates as compared to that of a segment length of 1 s. From the confusion matrix as shown in Table 6, the spectrogram-2DCNN based SER method had false positives of 5951, false negatives of 3478 and true positives of 8522 for 500 ms segment duration with a total of 12000 drone sound segments. The false positive rate is 12.39% for a total of 48000 non-drone sound segments whereas the missed rate is 28.98% for a total of 12000 drone sound segments. For 1 s segment, the spectrogram-2DCNN based SER method had false positives of 6247, false neg-

Table 6. Confusion matrix for spectrogram-2DCNN based method

	Spectrogram-2DCNN based SER method					
	TS	D	M	N	S	V
Audio segment length of 500 ms						
Drone (D)	12000	**8522**	1706	199	214	1359
Music (M)	12000	1053	**9377**	64	732	774
Nature (N)	12000	2232	348	**8589**	12	819
Speech (S)	12000	490	562	19	**10737**	192
Vehicle (V)	12000	2176	1913	594	572	**6742**
Audio segment length of 1 s						
Drone (D)	12000	**9227**	1286	231	221	1035
Music (M)	12000	1291	**9567**	77	590	475
Nature (N)	12000	2875	1517	**6448**	14	1146
Speech (S)	12000	415	433	16	**11045**	91
Vehicle (V)	12000	1666	925	484	752	**7200**

Table 7. Performance comparison of the SER methods; SL: Segment Length

SL	Class	MFCC-SVM			MFCC-1DCNN			Spectrogram-2DCNN		
		RR	PR	F1	RR	PR	F1	RR	PR	F1
500 ms	Drone	83.36	88.84	86.01	89.44	95.34	92.29	71.01	58.88	64.39
	Music	89.67	85.23	87.39	92.73	89.29	90.97	78.14	67.43	72.39
	Nature	99.70	97.06	98.36	99.89	99.28	99.58	71.57	90.74	80.02
	Speech	87.80	93.49	90.55	92.05	93.37	92.70	89.47	87.52	88.48
	Vehicle	90.17	89.68	89.92	93.66	94.21	93.93	56.18	68.19	61.60
	Avg.	**90.14**	**90.86**	**90.44**	**93.55**	**94.29**	**93.89**	**73.27**	**74.55**	**73.37**
1 s	Drone	86.57	91.86	89.13	94.43	96.65	95.52	76.89	59.62	67.16
	Music	92.11	89.11	90.58	86.55	92.47	89.43	79.72	69.68	74.36
	Nature	99.86	97.86	98.84	99.94	99.94	99.74	53.73	88.86	66.96
	Speech	92.52	95.30	93.88	94.24	97.25	95.72	92.04	87.50	89.71
	Vehicle	91.63	91.95	91.78	96.26	96.54	94.72	60.00	72.38	65.61
	Avg.	**92.53**	**93.21**	**92.84**	**94.28**	**96.57**	**95.02**	**72.47**	**75.6**	**72.76**

atives of 2773 and true positives of 9227 for 1 s segment duration with a total of 12000 drone sound segments. The false positive rate is 13.01% for a total of 48000 non-drone sound segments whereas the missed rate is 23.11% for a total of 12000 drone sound segments.

3.3 Performance Comparison

Table 7 presents comparison of three SER methods for different segment lengths and same audio databases. Results showed that the MFCC-1DCNN based method achieves better results in terms of recall rate (RR), precision rate (PR) and F1-score. The MFCC-SVM based method had average RR = 92.53%, PR = 93.21% and F1-score = 92.84% for audio segment length of 1 s. The MFCC-1DCNN based method had average RR = 94.28%, PR = 96.57% and F1-score = 95.02% for audio segment length of 1 s. The spectrogram-2DCNN based method had average RR = 73.27%, PR = 74.55% and F1-score = 73.37% for audio segment length of 500 ms. This study shows that the MFCC-1DCNN based method outperforms the MFCC-SVM based and spectrogram-2DCNN based methods.

4　Conclusion

This paper presented three sound event recognition (SER) methods for detecting drone sounds in the presence of non-drone sounds, including speech, music, vehicle, rain and wind. The AER schemes are based on the MFCC and spectrogram features and the SVM, 1DCNN and 2DCNN classifiers. We investigated the performance of the MFCC-SVM based, MFCC-1DCNN based and spectrogram-2DCNN based methods using a wide variety of sound databases and different segment lengths. Our preliminary study demonstrated that the MFCC-1DCNN based method results in better recognition rates as compared to that of the MFCC-SVM based and spectrogram-2DCNN based methods. In the future directions, we further evaluate the performance these sound recognition methods on the mixture of background sounds with different levels.

References

1. Taha, B., Shoufan, A.: Machine learning-based drone detection and classification: state-of-the-art in research. IEEE Access **7**, 138669–138682 (2019)
2. Ezuma, M., Erden, F., Anjinappa, C.K., Ozdemir, O., Guvenc, I.: Detection and classification of UAVs using RF fingerprints in the presence of Wi-Fi and bluetooth interference. IEEE Open J. Commun. Soc. **1**, 60–76 (2020)
3. Ezuma, M., Erden, F., Anjinappa, C.K., Ozdemir, O., Guvenc, I.: Micro-UAV detection and classification from RF fingerprints using machine learning techniques. In: Proceedings of the IEEE Aerospace Conference, pp. 1–13, March 2019
4. Alipour-Fanid, A., Dabaghchian, M., Wang, N., Wang, P., Zhao, L., Zeng, K.: Machine learning-based delay-aware UAV detection and operation mode identification over encrypted Wi-Fi traffic. IEEE Trans. Inf. Forensics Secur. **15**, 2346–2360 (2019)
5. Zhang, W., Li, G.: Detection of multiple micro-drones via cadence velocity diagram analysis. Electron. Lett. **54**(7), 441–443 (2018)

6. Patel, J.S., Fioranelli, F., Anderson, D.: Review of radar classification and RCS characterisation techniques for small UAVs or drones. IET Radar Sonar Navig. **12**(9), 911–919 (2018)
7. Rozantsev, A., Lepetit, V., Fua, P.: Detecting flying objects using a single moving camera. IEEE Trans. Pattern Anal. Mach. Intell. **39**(5), 879–892 (2017)
8. Zhang, P., Yang, L., Chen, G., Li, G.: Classification of drones based on micro-Doppler signatures with dual-band radar sensors. In: Progress in Electromagnetics Research Symposium-Fall (PIERS-FALL), pp. 638–643, November 2017
9. Nguyen, P., Truong, H., Ravindranathan, M., Nguyen, A., Han, R., Vu, T.: Matthan: drone presence detection by identifying physical signatures in the drone's RF communication. In: Proceedings of the 15th Annual International Conference on Mobile Systems, Applications, and Services, pp. 211–224, June 2017
10. Nguyen, P., Ravindranatha, M., Nguyen, A., Han, R., Vu, T.: Investigating cost-effective RF-based detection of drones. In: Proceedings of the 2nd Workshop on Micro Aerial Vehicle Networks, Systems, and Applications for Civilian Use, pp. 17–22, June 2016
11. Taha, B., Shoufan, A.: Machine learning-based drone detection and classification: state-of-the-art in research. IEEE Access, 1–5 (2016)
12. Lim, D., et al.: Practically classifying unmanned aerial vehicles sound Using convolutional neural networks. In: Proceedings of IEEE International Conference on Robotic Computing (IRC), pp. 242–245, January 2017
13. Lim, D., et al.: A study on detecting drones using deep convolutional neural networks. In Proceedings of IEEE International Conference on Advanced Video and Signal Based Surveillance (AVSS), pp. 1–5, August 2018
14. Al-Emadi, S., Al-Ali, A., Mohammad, A., Al-Ali, A.: Audio based drone detection and identification using deep learning. In: Proceedings of IEEE International Wireless Communications and Mobile Computing Conference (IWCMC), pp. 459–464, June 2019
15. Matson, E., Yang, B., Smith, A., Dietz, E., Gallagher, J.: UAV detection system with multiple acoustic nodes using machine learning models. In: Proceedings of IEEE International Conference on Robotic Computing (IRC), pp. 493–498, February 2019
16. Jeon, S., Shin, J.W., Lee, Y.J., Kim, W.H., Kwon, Y., Yang, H.Y.: Empirical study of drone sound detection in real-life environment with deep neural networks. In: Proceedings of European Signal Processing Conference (EUSIPCO), pp. 1858–1862, February 2017
17. Mezei, J., Molnár, A.: Drone sound detection by correlation. In: Proceedings of IEEE International Symposium on Applied Computational Intelligence and Informatics (SACI), pp. 509–518, May 2016
18. Kim, J., Park, C., Ahn, J., Ko, Y., Park, J., Gallagher, J.C.: Real-time UAV sound detection and analysis system. In: IEEE Sensors Applications Symposium (SAS), pp. 1–5, March 2017
19. Bernardini, A., Mangiatordi, F., Pallotti, E., Capodiferro, L.: Drone detection by acoustic signature identification. Electron. Imaging **2017**, 60–64 (2017)
20. Case, E.E., Zelnio, A.M., Rigling, B.D.: Low-cost acoustic array for small UAV detection and tracking. In: Proceedings of IEEE National Aerospace and Electronics Conference, pp. 110–113, July 2019
21. Soni, S., Dey, S., Manikandan, M.S.: Automatic audio event recognition schemes for context-aware audio computing devices. In: Proceedings of IEEE International Conference on Digital Information Processing and Communications (ICDIPC), vol. 64, pp. 23–28 (2019)

22. Beritelli, F., Grasso, R.: A pattern recognition system for environmental sound classification based on MFCCs and neural networks. In: Proceedings of IEEE International Conference on Signal Processing and Communication Systems, pp. 1–4, December 2019
23. Soni, S., Dey, S., Manikandan, M.S.: SSQA: speech signal quality assessment method using spectrogram and 2-D convolutional neural networks for improving efficiency of ASR devices. In Proceedings of IEEE International Conference on Digital Information Processing and Communications (ICDIPC), pp. 29–34, May 2019
24. Drone database. http://dregon.inria.fr/datasets/dregon/

Comparison of Different Decision Tree Algorithms for Predicting the Heart Disease

Deepak Saraswat$^{(\boxtimes)}$ and Preetvanti Singh

Department of Physics and Computer Science, Dayalbagh Educational Institute,
Agra, India
deepakcsdei@gmail.com, preetvantisingh@gmail.com

Abstract. Data mining procedures are utilized to extract meaningful information for effective knowledge discovery. Decision tree, a classification method, is
an efficient method for prediction. Seeing its importance, this paper compares
decision tree algorithms to predict heart disease. The heart disease data sets are
taken from Cleveland database, Hungarian database and Switzerland database to
evaluate the performance measures. 60 data records for training and 50 data
records for testing were taken as input for comparison. In order to evaluate the
performance, fourteen attributes are considered to generate confusion matrices.
The results exhibited that the algorithm that highest accuracy rates for predicting
heart disease is Random forest, and thus can be considered as the best procedure
for prediction.

Keywords: Heart disease · Classification technique · Decision tree · Decision
tree algorithms · Performance measures

1 Introduction

The knowledge discovery process, now-a-days, has become more complex because of
increasing size and complexity of the data sets. Data mining procedures are utilized to
extract meaningful information for effective knowledge discovery. These procedures
can be classified as descriptive procedures and predictive procedures. Descriptive
procedures of data mining provide latest information on past or recent events, and for
validating results, necessitate post-processing methods. Predictive procedures, on the
other hand, predict the patterns and properties of vague information. Commonly used
data mining procedures are Clustering, Classification, Association, Outlier Detection,
Prediction, and Regression.

Classification is utilized for discovering knowledge based on different classes. It
determines a model to describe and distinguish data classes based on trained data set,
and identifies to which of the categories a new observation belongs to. Decision tree
fosters a classification model in a tree-like structure. This type of mining, where the
data set is distributed into smaller subsets and the associated Decision Tree (DT) is
incrementally built, belongs to supervised class learning. The benefits of decision trees
are:

© Springer Nature Singapore Pte Ltd. 2020
A. Bhattacharjee et al. (Eds.): MIND 2020, CCIS 1241, pp. 245–255, 2020.
https://doi.org/10.1007/978-981-15-6318-8_21

- Easy integration due to intuitively representing the data,
- Investigative discovery of knowledge
- High accuracy
- Easily interpretable, and
- Excludes unimportant features

Because of above mentioned benefits, decision tree classifier is utilized for knowledge extraction in areas like education [33, 40], tourism [18, 34], healthcare [30, 31] and others. The healthcare industry creates colossal information from which it becomes extremely difficult to extract useful information. Decision tree is an efficient method for extracting effective knowledge from this titanic of information and providing reliable healthcare decision. It has been utilized in making effective decisions in various medical science areas like cancer detection, heart disease diagnosis and others [9, 11, 32, 45]. Presenting a brief overview of the algorithms for developing decision trees, and then comparing these algorithms for predicting heart disease based on performance measures is the foremost goal of this paper.

Heart diseases are a major source of death worldwide. As of 2016 there have been more than 17.6 million deaths per year. The death toll is expected to exceed 23.6 million by 2030 [3]. India too is witnessing shocking rise in the occurrence of heart disease (HD) [12]. Researchers have developed various decision tree algorithms to effectively diagnosis and treat heart diseases. Decision trees and rough set approach was utilized by Son, Kim, Kim, Park and Kim [41] to develop a model for heart failure. Chaurasia and Pal [8], Sa [35], and Amin, Chiam, and Varathan [4] developed a prediction system for HD by utilizing decision tree in combination with other data mining algorithms. Mathan, Kumar, Panchatcharam, Manogaran, and Varadharajan [22] presented forecast frameworks for heart diseases using decision tree classifiers. Wu, Badshah and Bhagwat [45] developed prediction model for HD survivability. Saxena, Johri, Deep and Sharma [37] developed a HD prediction system using KNN and Decision tree algorithm. Shekar, Chandra and Rao [38] developed a classifier to provide optimized feature for envisaging the type of HD using decision tree and genetic algorithm. Vallée, Petruescu, Kretz, Safar and Blacher [43] evaluated the role of APWV index in predicting HD. Pathak and Valan [29] proposed a forecasting model for HD diagnosis by integrating rule-based approach with decision tree. Sturts and Slotman [42] predicted risks for the patients who are re-admitted within 30 days after hospital discharge for CHF by using decision trees analysis. Seeing the importance of decision tree in healthcare, this paper presents a brief overview and comparison of seven DT algorithms based on various evaluation measures to diagnosis the heart disease.

2   Material and Method

2.1   Overview of Decision Tree Algorithms

Decision tree algorithm is a supervised learning method which is implemented on the basis of the data volume, available memory space and scalability, in serial or parallel style. The DT algorithms considered in this study are: J48, Decision stump, LMT,

Hoeffding tree, Random forest, Random tree and REPTree. These are the most used algorithms for predicting various diseases (Table 1).

a. The J48 algorithm develops decision tree by classifying the class attribute based on the input elements.
b. The Hoeffding tree algorithm learns from huge data streams.
c. A Random tree algorithm draws a random tree from a set of possible trees and the distribution of trees is considered uniform.
d. A Random forest algorithm draws multiple decision trees using a bagging approach.
e. Logistic model tree (LMT) interprets combination of tree induction and linear logistic regression.
f. Decision stump builds simple binary decision stumps for both nominal and numeric classification task.
g. REPTree algorithm generates a regression or decision tree using information gain or variance.

Table 1. Different algorithms are applied in many areas.

S. No.	Authors name	Year	Algorithms	Areas
1	Vijiyarani and Sudha [44]	2013	Decision stump, Random forest, and LMT	Heart disease
2	Pandey, Pandey, Jaiswal and Sen [27]	2013	J48	
3	Chaurasia and Pal [7]	2014	J48	
4	Masethe and Masethe [20]	2014	J48 and REPTree	
5	Karabulut and Ibrikci [15]	2014	LMT	
6	Lohita, Sree, Poojitha, Devi and Umamakeswari [19]	2015	Random forest, J48, and REPTree	
7	Pachauri and Sharma [26]	2015	J48, Decision stump, and Random forest	
8	Bahrami and Shirvani [6]	2015	J48	
9	Kasar and Joshi [17]	2016	J48 and CART	
10	Alickovic and Subasi [2]	2016	Random forest	
11	Masetic and Subasi [21]	2016	Random forest	
12	Shrivas and Yadu [39]	2017	Decision stump	

(*continued*)

Table 1. (*continued*)

S. No.	Authors name	Year	Algorithms	Areas
13	Karthikeyan and Thangaraju [16]	2013	J48 and Random forest	Liver disorder
14	Novakovic and Veljovic [24]	2014	J48 and Decision stump	
15	Nahar and Ara [23]	2018	Decision stump, J48, REPTree, LMT, Random tree, Hoeffding tree, and Random forest	
16	Parimala and Porkodi [28]	2018	J48, LMT, Random tree, and REPTree	
17	Hasan, Bakar, Siraj, Sainin and Hasan [11]	2015	LMT, Random forest, and Random tree	Cancer
18	Azar, Elshazlyb, Hassanien and Elkorany [5]	2014	Random forest	Lymph diseases
19	Iyer, Jeyalatha and Sumbaly [13]	2015	J48	Diabetes
20	Perveen, Shahbaza, Guergachi and Keshavjeec [31]	2016	J48	
21	Alehegn, Joshi and Mulay [1]	2018	Decision stump	
22	Olayinka and Chiemeke [25]	2019	LMT, REPTree, Hoeffding tree, and J48	Malaria
23	Jena and Kamila [14]	2015	J48	Kidney disease
24	Gomathi and Narayani [10]	2018	Random forest, J48, and Hoeffding tree	Systemic Lupus Erythematous
25	Salih and Abraham [36]	2015	J48, LMT, Random forest, and Random tree	HD, Asthma, and Diabetes
26	Fatima and Pasha [9]	2017	J48	HD, Diabetes, Liver disease, and Dengue
27	Yang, Guo and Jin [46]	2018	J48, Decision stump, and Random tree	Cancer and Heart disease

2.2 Data Set

In order to attain the second goal of the present paper, three data sets from Cleveland database, Hungarian database and Switzerland database are considered for evaluating the performance measures of the DT algorithms. 60 data records for training and 50 data records for testing were taken as input for comparison. As shown in Table 2, fourteen attributes are considered for evaluating the performance measures.

Table 2. Description of the input attributes.

S. No.	Attributes	Description	Values
1.	Age	Years	Continuous
2.	Sex	M/F	1 if Male, 0 if Female
3.	CPT	Type of Chest pain	1 if Typical, 2 if Atypical angina, 3 if Non-angina pain, 4 if Asymptomatic
4.	RBP	Resting BP	Cont. (mm Hg)
5.	C	Cholesterol	Cont. (mm/dL)
6.	REG	Resting electrographic	0 = Normal, 1 = Abnormal, 2 = Probable
7.	BS	Blood sugar	True, when greater than or equal to 120 mg/dL and False, otherwise
8.	MHR	Maximum heart rate	Continuous
9.	EIA	Exercise induced angina	0 if no, 1 if yes
10.	OdPeak	Depression by exercise relative to rest	Cont.
11.	Slp	Slope	1 if unsloping, 2 if flat, 3 if downsloping
12.	Ca	Number of major vessels	Value (0–3)
13.	Tha	Type of Defect	3 if normal, 6 if fixed, 7 if reversible
14.	HDNum	The predicted attribute	0 = Heart Disease No, $1 \leq$ value ≤ 4 = Heart Disease Yes

3   Decision Tree Analysis

The performance measures are generated by using the information mining instrument Weka 3.9.3. Data pre-processing is done by means of the Replace Missing Values channel to filter all records and replace missing qualities. Next confusion matrices are developed by applying considered DT algorithms with 2 classes as Class 1 = YES (heart disease is present), and Class 2 = NO (heart disease not present), and True Positive = correct positive predicted; False Positive = incorrect positive predicted; True Negative = correct negative predicted; False Negative = incorrect negative predicted; P are Positive samples; and N are Negative samples.

These matrices are then utilized to compute the accuracy measures using the equations:

$$TPrate = \frac{TP}{TP + FP} \tag{1}$$

$$FPrate = \frac{FP}{FP + TN} \tag{2}$$

$$Accuracy = \frac{TP + TN}{P + N} \tag{3}$$

$$Errorrate = \frac{FP + FN}{P + N} \tag{4}$$

4 Results: Comparison

In Table 3 discussed the comparison of considered algorithms.

Table 3. Working comparison of decision tree algorithms.

Algorithms	Measure	Procedure	Pruning	Data type
J48	Information gain and Entropy	Top-down construction	Pre-pruning Single Pass Pruning Process	Discrete, Continuous, and can handle incomplete data
Hoeffding tree	Information gain and Hoeffding bound	Top-down construction	Pre-pruning	Data streams
Random tree	Hold-out set (back fitting)	Stochastic procedure	No Pruning	Discrete, Continuous, takes the input feature vector
Random forest	Receiver operating characteristic area under the curve	Class for constructing a forest of random trees	No pruning	Discrete, Continuous, takes the input feature vector
Logistic model tree	Logistic regression functions	Top-down	CART-based pruning	Numeric, Nominal, can contain missing values
Decision stump	Mean square error and Entropy	One-level decision tree	Post pruning	Discrete, Continuous, Binary
REPTree	Information gain	Top-down	Reduce error pruning with back-fitting	Binary, Numeric, Unary

Table 4 shows the computed performance measures using Eq. (3) and Eq. (4) for the data.

Table 4. Values of correctly classifier instances (CCI) and incorrectly classifier instances (ICI).

	Cleveland		Switzerland		Hungarian	
	CCI	ICI	CCI	ICI	CCI	ICI
Decision stump	81.167	18.833	76.167	23.833	81.833	28.167
J48	79.500	20.500	76.167	23.833	81.833	28.167
Hoeffding tree	86.167	13.833	83.333	16.667	86.167	13.833
LMT	96.667	3.333	76.167	23.833	75.500	22.000
Random forest	100.000	0.000	87.000	13.000	86.333	13.667
Random tree	100.000	0.000	82.000	18.000	79.333	19.000
REPTree	68.667	31.333	65.667	34.333	67.667	29.000

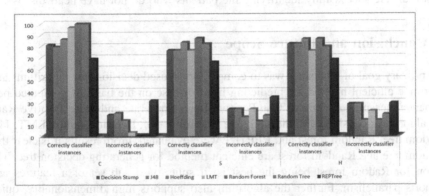

Fig. 1. Graph showing accuracy and error rate.

From the Fig. 1, it can be observed that for the considered data sets, Random Forest is showing max accuracy and least error rate.

Table 5. Class accuracy.

Algorithms	Class	Cleveland		Switzerland		Hungarian	
		TP rate	FP rate	TP rate	FP rate	TP rate	FP rate
J48	Yes	0.643	0.182	0.625	0.346	0.6	0.36
	No	0.818	0.357	0.654	0.375	0.64	0.4
Decision stump	Yes	0.786	0.182	0.625	0.396	0.6	0.36
	No	0.818	0.214	0.654	0.375	0.64	0.4
LMT	Yes	0.821	0.227	0.625	0.346	0.6	0.28
	No	0.773	0.179	0.654	0.375	0.72	0.4

(continued)

Table 5. (*continued*)

Algorithms	Class	Cleveland		Switzerland		Hungarian	
		TP rate	FP rate	TP rate	FP rate	TP rate	FP rate
Hoeffding tree	Yes	0.821	0.091	0.75	0.346	0.6	0.32
	No	0.909	0.179	0.654	0.25	0.68	0.4
REPTree	Yes	0	0	1	1	0.64	0.4
	No	1	1	0	0	0.6	0.36
Random tree	Yes	0.679	0.364	0.542	0.269	0.52	0.28
	No	0.636	0.321	0.731	0.458	0.72	0.48
Random forest	Yes	0.679	0.136	0.708	0.231	0.6	0.08
	No	0.864	0.321	0.769	0.292	0.92	0.4

From Table 5 it is clear that the TP Rate for the class = No is higher for Decision stump, Hoeffding tree, J48, Random forest, LMT and Random tree, which means the algorithms are successfully identifying the patients who do not have heart disease.

5   Conclusion and Future Scope

The primary goal of this paper was to compare most used decision tree algorithms and determine efficient method for predicting heart disease on the basis of computed performance measures Accuracy, True Positive Rate, Error rate and False Positive Rate. The algorithms considered in the study are Hoeffding tree, Decision stump, LMT, J48, Random tree, Random forest and REPTree were evaluated. From results it is clear that Random tree and Random forest are efficient method for generating decision tree. The reason for Radom forest being the best is, it splits on a sub set of a features and supports parallelism. Further the algorithm also supports high dimensionality, quick prediction, and outliners and non-linear data. However, the algorithm is less interpretable and can tend to over fit. In future, performance evaluation can be based on considering more attributes responsible for heart diseases. Other than healthcare, the framework can be utilized for evaluating performances in other domains also.

References

1. Alehegn, M., Joshi, R., Mulay, P.: Analysis and prediction of diabetes mellitus using machine learning algorithm. Int. J. Pure Appl. Math. **118**(9), 871–878 (2018)
2. Alickovic, E., Subasi, A.: Medical decision support system for diagnosis of heart arrhythmia using DWT and random forests classifier. J. Med. Syst. **40**(4), 108 (2016). https://doi.org/10.1007/s10916-016-0467-8
3. American Heart Association. Heart disease and stroke statistics 2018 (2017). http://www.heart.org/idc/groups/ahamahpublic/@wcm/@sop/@smd/documents/downloadable/ucm_491265.Pdf

4. Amin, M.S., Chiam, Y.K., Varathan, K.D.: Identification of significant features and data mining techniques in predicting heart disease. Telematics Inform. **36**, 82–93 (2019). https://doi.org/10.1016/j.tele.2018.11.007

5. Azar, A.T., Elshazly, H.I., Hassanien, A.E., Elkorany, A.M.: A random forest classifier for lymph diseases. Comput. Methods Programs Biomed. **113**(2), 465–473 (2014). https://doi.org/10.1016/j.cmpb.2013.11.004

6. Bahrami, B., Shirvani, M.H.: Prediction and diagnosis of heart disease by data mining techniques. J. Multidisc. Eng. Sci. Technol. (JMEST). **2**(2), 164–168 (2015)

7. Chaurasia, V., Pal, S.: Data mining approach to detect heart diseases. Int. J. Adv. Comput. Sci. Inf. Technol. (IJACSIT). **2**, 56–66 (2014)

8. Chaurasia, V., Pal, S.: Early prediction of heart diseases using data mining techniques. Carib. J. Sci. Technol. **1**, 208–217 (2013)

9. Fatima, M., Pasha, M.: Survey of machine learning algorithms for disease diagnostic. J. Intell. Learn. Syst. Appl. **9**(1), 1 (2017). https://doi.org/10.4236/jilsa.2017.91001

10. Gomathi, S., Narayani, V.: Early prediction of systemic lupus erythematosus using hybrid K-Means J48 decision tree algorithm. Int. J. Eng. Technol. **7**(1), 28–32 (2018)

11. Hasan, M.R., Abu Bakar, N.A., Siraj, F., Sainin, M.S., Hasan, S.: Single decision tree classifiers' accuracy on medical data (2015)

12. https://timesofindia.indiatimes.com/india/heart-disease-deaths-rise-in-india-by-34-in-15-years/articleshow/64924601.cms

13. Iyer, A., Jeyalatha, S., Sumbaly, R.: Diagnosis of diabetes using classification mining techniques (2015). arXiv preprint arXiv:1502.03774, https://doi.org/10.5121/ijdkp.2015.5101

14. Jena, L., Kamila, N.K.: Distributed data mining classification algorithms for prediction of chronic-kidney-disease. Int. J. Emerg. Res. Manag. Technol. **4**(11), 110–118 (2015)

15. Karabulut, E.M., Ibrikci, T.: Effective automated prediction of vertebral column pathologies based on logistic model tree with SMOTE preprocessing. J. Med. Syst. **38**(5), 50 (2014). https://doi.org/10.1007/s10916-014-0050-0

16. Karthikeyan, T., Thangaraju, P.: Analysis of classification algorithms applied to hepatitis patients. Int. J. Comput. Appl. **62**(15), 25–30 (2013)

17. Kasar, S.L., Joshi, M.S.: Analysis of multi-lead ECG signals using decision tree algorithms. Int. J. Comput. Appl. **134**(16) (2016). https://doi.org/10.5120/ijca2016908206

18. Kuzey, C., Karaman, A.S., Akman, E.: Elucidating the impact of visa regimes: a decision tree analysis. Tourism Manag. Perspect. **29**, 148–156 (2019). https://doi.org/10.1016/j.tmp.2018.11.008

19. Lohita, K., Sree, A.A., Poojitha, D., Devi, T.R., Umamakeswari, A.: Performance analysis of various data mining techniques in the prediction of heart disease. Indian J. Sci. Technol. **8**(35), 1–7 (2015)

20. Masethe, H.D., Masethe, M.A.: Prediction of heart disease using classification algorithms. In: Proceedings of the World Congress on Engineering and Computer Science, vol. 2, pp. 22–24 (2014)

21. Masetic, Z., Subasi, A.: Congestive heart failure detection using random forest classifier. Comput. Methods Programs Biomed. **130**, 54–64 (2016). https://doi.org/10.1016/j.cmpb.2016.03.020

22. Mathan, K., Kumar, P.M., Panchatcharam, P., Manogaran, G., Varadharajan, R.: A novel Gini index decision tree data mining method with neural network classifiers for prediction of heart disease. Des. Autom. Embedded Syst. **22**(3), 225–242 (2018). https://doi.org/10.1007/s10617-018-9205-4

23. Nahar, N., Ara, F.: Liver disease prediction by using different decision tree techniques. Int. J. Data Min. Knowl. Manag. Process (IJDKP) **8**, 1–9 (2018). https://doi.org/10.5121/ijdkp. 2018.8201
24. Novakovic, J.D., Veljovic, A.: Adaboost as classifier ensemble in classification problems. In: Proceedings Infoteh-Jahorina, pp. 616–620 (2014)
25. Olayinka, T.C., Chiemeke, S.C.: Predicting paediatric malaria occurrence using classification algorithm in data mining. J. Adv. Math. Comput. Sci. **31**(4), 1–10 (2019). https://doi. org/10.9734/jamcs/2019/v31i430118
26. Pachauri, G., Sharma, S.: Anomaly detection in medical wireless sensor networks using machine learning algorithms. Procedia Comput. Sci. **70**, 325–333 (2015). https://doi.org/10. 1016/j.procs.2015.10.026
27. Pandey, A.K., Pandey, P., Jaiswal, K.L., Sen, A.K.: A heart disease prediction model using decision tree. IOSR J. Comput. Eng. (IOSR-JCE) **12**(6), 83–86 (2013)
28. Parimala, C., Porkodi, R.: Classification algorithms in data mining: a survey. Proc. Int. J. Sci. Res. Comput. Sci. **3**, 349–355 (2018)
29. Pathak, A.K., Arul Valan, J.: A predictive model for heart disease diagnosis using fuzzy logic and decision tree. In: Elçi, A., Sa, P.K., Modi, C.N., Olague, G., Sahoo, M.N., Bakshi, S. (eds.) Smart Computing Paradigms: New Progresses and Challenges. AISC, vol. 767, pp. 131–140. Springer, Singapore (2020). https://doi.org/10.1007/978-981-13-9680-9_10
30. Paxton, R.J., et al.: An exploratory decision tree analysis to predict physical activity compliance rates in breast cancer survivors. Ethn. Health. **24**(7), 754–766 (2019). https://doi. org/10.1080/13557858.2017.1378805
31. Pei, D., Zhang, C., Quan, Y., Guo, Q.: Identification of potential type II diabetes in a Chinese population with a sensitive decision tree approach. J. Diabetes Res. (2019). https:// doi.org/10.1155/2019/4248218
32. Perveen, S., Shahbaz, M., Guergachi, A., Keshavjee, K.: Performance analysis of data mining classification techniques to predict diabetes. Procedia Comput. Sci. **82**, 115–121 (2016). https://doi.org/10.1016/j.procs.2016.04.016
33. Rizvi, S., Rienties, B., Khoja, S.A.: The role of demographics in online learning; a decision tree based approach. Comput. Educ. **137**, 32–47 (2019). https://doi.org/10.1016/j.compedu. 2019.04.001
34. Rondović, B., Djuričković, T., Kašćelan, L.: Drivers of E-business diffusion in tourism: a decision tree approach. J. Theor. Appl. Electron. Commer. Res. **14**(1), 30–50 (2019). https:// doi.org/10.4067/S0718-18762019000100104
35. Sa, S.: Intelligent heart disease prediction system using data mining techniques. Int. J. Healthcare Biomed. Res. **1**, 94–101 (2013)
36. Salih, A.S.M., Abraham, A.: Intelligent decision support for real time health care monitoring system. In: Abraham, A., Krömer, P., Snasel, V. (eds.) Afro-European Conference for Industrial Advancement. AISC, vol. 334, pp. 183–192. Springer, Cham (2015). https://doi. org/10.1007/978-3-319-13572-4_15
37. Saxena, R., Johri, A., Deep, V., Sharma, P.: Heart diseases prediction system using CHC-TSS evolutionary, KNN, and decision tree classification algorithm. In: Abraham, A., Dutta, P., Mandal, J., Bhattacharya, A., Dutta, S. (eds.) Emerging Technologies in Data Mining and Information Security, vol. 813, pp. 809–819. Springer, Singapore (2019). https://doi.org/10. 1007/978-981-13-1498-8_71
38. Chandra Shekar, K., Chandra, P., Venugopala Rao, K.: An ensemble classifier characterized by genetic algorithm with decision tree for the prophecy of heart disease. In: Saini, H.S., Sayal, R., Govardhan, A., Buyya, R. (eds.) Innovations in Computer Science and Engineering. LNNS, vol. 74, pp. 9–15. Springer, Singapore (2019). https://doi.org/10. 1007/978-981-13-7082-3_2

39. Shrivas, A.K., Yadu, R.K.: An effective prediction factors for coronary heart disease using data mining based classification technique. Int. J. Recent Innov. Trends Comput. Commun. **5**(5), 813–816 (2017)
40. Skrbinjek, V., Dermol, V.: Predicting students' satisfaction using a decision tree. Tert. Educ. Manag. **25**(2), 101–113 (2019). https://doi.org/10.1007/s11233-018-09018-5
41. Son, C.S., Kim, Y.N., Kim, H.S., Park, H.S., Kim, M.S.: Decision-making model for early diagnosis of congestive heart failure using rough set and decision tree approaches. J. Biomed. Inform. **45**(5), 999–1008 (2012)
42. Sturts, A., Slotman, G.: Predischarge decision tree analysis predicts 30-day congestive heart failure readmission. Crit. Care Med. **48**(1), 116 (2020). https://doi.org/10.1097/01.ccm. 0000619424.34362.bc
43. Vallée, A., Petruescu, L., Kretz, S., Safar, M.E., Blacher, J.: Added value of aortic pulse wave velocity index in a predictive diagnosis decision tree of coronary heart disease. Am. J. Hypertens. **32**(4), 375–383 (2019). https://doi.org/10.1093/ajh/hpz004
44. Vijiyarani, S., Sudha, S.: An efficient classification tree technique for heart disease prediction. In: International Conference on Research Trends in Computer Technologies (ICRTCT-2013) Proceedings published in International Journal of Computer Applications (IJCA), vol. 201, pp. 0975–8887 (2013)
45. Wu, C.S.M., Badshah, M., Bhagwat, V.: Heart disease prediction using data mining techniques. In: Proceedings of the 2019 2nd International Conference on Data Science and Information Technology, pp. 7–11 (2019). https://doi.org/10.1145/3352411.3352413
46. Yang, S., Guo, J.Z., Jin, J.W.: An improved Id3 algorithm for medical data classification. Comput. Electr. Eng. **65**, 474–487 (2018). https://doi.org/10.1016/j.compeleceng.2017.08. 005

Dynamic Speech Trajectory Based Parameters for Low Resource Languages

Parabattina Bhagath(✉)(iD), Megha Jain(iD), and Pradip K. Das(iD)

Department of CSE, Indian Institute of Technology Guwahati,
Guwahati 781039, Assam, India
{bhagath.2014,megha18,pkdas}@iitg.ac.in

Abstract. The speech recognition problem deals with recognizing spoken words or utterances to interpret the voice message. This domain has been investigated by many researchers for more than five decades. There are numerous techniques and frameworks made available to address this problem. Hidden Markov Modeling (HMM) being a popular modeling technique has been used in different tools to build speech-based systems. In spite of its vast usage and popularity, shortcomings have introduced some new challenges in designing the feature modeling techniques. One of the solutions is using trajectory models. They are efficient in capturing the intra-segmental temporal dynamics which helps to understand the continuous nature of the speech signal. Even though trajectories have been found to be an effective solution, the complexity of trajectory modeling is yet to be improved. In this paper, two trajectory parameter extraction methods are proposed. The methods are shown to be effective for speech classification. The detailed procedures with results are discussed in this paper.

Keywords: Fréchet distance · Peak attributes · Trajectory

1 Introduction

Speech recognition is an important domain that serves in human-machine interaction. It has various applications in fields like marketing, customer support, mobile phones, etc. There are many frameworks like Hidden Markov Modeling (HMM) [20], Gaussian Mixture Modeling (GMM) [15], Support Vector Machines (SVMs), Deep Neural Networks (DNNs) [21] that have been developed and have became popular in this area. The efficiency of the systems depends on the features modeling techniques. There are features like Linear Predictive Cepstral Coefficients (LPCCs) [10], Mel Frequency Cepstral Coefficients (MFCCs) [18] that have been proven to be successful in designing systems. Even though these methods are popular, they rely heavily on large datasets and an intensive training process. Therefore, it is required to develop new methods to address the problem of low resource languages. Researchers found that features that can capture the dynamic nature of the signals are useful for understanding the temporal

© Springer Nature Singapore Pte Ltd. 2020
A. Bhattacharjee et al. (Eds.): MIND 2020, CCIS 1241, pp. 256–270, 2020.
https://doi.org/10.1007/978-981-15-6318-8_22

structures of signals [16]. They are efficient in understanding the coarticulation properties over different phonetic units across an entire signal. These properties are significant in recognizing continuous sentences or words. Structural processing methods that model the data by understanding the shape of the signals are useful in designing systems for these languages [4]. There have been several attempts made by researchers on structural properties for speech signals that are useful in understanding the phonetic nature of speech. One such approach used in speech modeling is trajectory. Trajectory modeling helps in understanding the temporal dynamic nature of phonetic units. Syllable classification can also be done by using linguistic features such as syllable duration, lexical stress and difference between mono and poly-syllabic words [23]. The trajectory approaches that have been used are computationally expensive. To address these issues, the present work focuses on developing structural properties that can be used to model speech trajectories. The main contribution of the work is proposing two different types of features that can be used for speech modeling. The features are listed as follows:

1. Peak attributes
2. Fréchet distance based parameters for waveform trajectories

The first benefit of the parameters is reduction in the complexity of feature computation. Second is the comparatively less space requirement for the features than the popular methods like LPCCs and MFCCs. As a result, the training time required would be less. Parameter extraction methods are discussed in detail with implementation technicalities. To prove the effectiveness of these features, HMM was used for modeling. It is found in the study that the proposed parameters are effective for the speech classification problem.

The paper is organized as follows: Sect. 2 explains the proposed features. Section 3 describes the environment used for experiments. In Sect. 4, the results are discussed and the conclusions are given in Sect. 5. A brief overview of the trajectory and its application in similarity analysis is presented in the subsequent subsections respectively.

1.1 Trajectory Features for Speech Signal Analysis

A trajectory is a sequence that contains a number of entities where each entity can be a point or a segment. A speech signal can be represented using parametric trajectory models given by Eq. 1:

$$C(n) = \mu(n) + e(n), \forall n \in \{1, ..., N\} \tag{1}$$

where $C(n)$ is the set of cepstral properties in a speech segment of length N, $\mu(n)$ is the mean feature vector and $e(n)$ is the residual error term. H. Gish proposed a trajectory model for vowel classification that uses Gaussian Mixture Models and time-varying covariances [9]. Another variant of trajectory models is Polynomial trajectory Segmental Models (PSMs) that can be used for modeling co-articulation effects through context-dependent models. The PSM systems assume that the observations are generated by a Gaussian process and the covariance is assumed to be constant over a segment. The basic parameter that is used here is a time-varying vector mean trajectory and is expressed in Eq. 2:

$$\mu(t) = b_1 + b_2 t + ... + b_r t^{r-1}, \forall t \in [0,1] \tag{2}$$

where t is the normalized time [12]. Even though HMMs are successful, they use less knowledge of the underlying signal. HMM associates each state with a single frame of the speech signal which doesn't capture the intra-segmental temporal variations [20]. Therefore, an alternative process called Segmental HMMs has been used to model speech signals using parametric trajectories. In this process, a trajectory is obtained by using a design matrix based on transitional information of contiguous frames. The model of this system can be expressed by Eq. 3:

$$P(C_t|S_i, \lambda) = P(ZB_t|S_i, \lambda)P(C_t|ZB_t, S_i, \lambda) \tag{3}$$

where C_t is the observation vector, ZB_t is the unique trajectory at time t, λ is the observation probability of C_t that occur at state S_i [24]. M. Firouzmand proposed a discrete cosine model for amplitude trajectories of the form given by Eq. 4. Models are estimated using the amplitudes of trajectory using Minimum Mean Square error (MMSE) [8].

$$A_i(n) = \sqrt{\frac{2}{N}} \sum_{p=0}^{p_i} A_{ip} W(p) cos\left((n + \frac{1}{2})\frac{p\pi}{N}\right) \tag{4}$$

Modeling continuous signal is beneficial to capture dynamic nature over the entire signal. In the present approach, features are extracted over the entire signal where intra-segmental properties are captured effectively. In the next subsection, different works related to trajectories in finding similarities are described.

1.2   Trajectories in Similarity Analysis

A trajectory can represent spatiality and order of data in a time domain. Analyzing trajectories can help to classify similar entities based on the relationships found. They are useful in various applications that include GPS data, user profiling, location prediction, time series analysis, pattern mining, etc. Methods that are useful in finding the patterns are listed as follows:

- Merge Distance (MD)
- Multi Dimensional Scaling (MDS)
- Density based spatial clustering of applications with noise (DBSCAN)

Zelei et al. proposed a similarity finding method for predicting location based on a person's mobility features. This method is intended to find relationships between social relations of a person and variances in trajectory so that the moving location can be predicted aprior [17]. There have been applications in which spatial and temporal features alone cannot give sufficient information about system behavior. This requirement has lead to the use of multiple features based trajectories. In these approaches, a trajectory is represented through a combination of three or more features. These methods are called data fusion techniques. They merge the dynamic nature of different similarity properties to generate a model [22]. The model used in this approach is given in Eq. 5:

$$MMTD(t_1, t_2) = 1 - (w_1, w_2)\begin{pmatrix} dist_1(t_1, t_2) \\ dist_2(t_1, t_2) \end{pmatrix} \tag{5}$$

where $dist_1$ and $dist_2$ are different similarity measurements and each measure is treated with unequal weightages. MMTD is a maximum-minimum trajectory distance.

Zedong et al. proposed a method for predicting location based on user similarity that uses GPS trajectories. This approach combines spatio-temporal features and GPS coordinates data to extract the similarities among different users. The ordering of the points can be achieved by incorporating timestamps into the system. To understand the similarity, a Semantic Trajectory Distance (STD) was used. This distance is given by Eq. 6.

$$STD = 1 - \frac{|lcs(T_1, T_2)|}{|T_1| + |T_2| - |lcs(T_1, T_2)|} \tag{6}$$

where $|T_1|$ and $|T_2|$ represent the length of trajectories and $lcs(T_1, T_2)$ is a measurement used to define the longest common subsequence. This method was proven to be effective in finding the similarity between user mobility [14].

Trajectory data analysis has been used to improve navigation systems and traffic management also. Here, the navigation path was represented with features like traffic flow information, location and motion. To build rich navigation systems, clustering algorithms that are formed by the number of techniques have been used. One crucial similarity measurement used in such clustering algorithms is Merge Distance (MD) [13]. For a trajectory T that consists of a sequence of points where each point is represented by a time point and distance between these points is given by $l(p) = \sum d(p_i, p_j)$. Merge distance is the length of the shortest trajectory that can represent two different trajectories and is given by Eq. 7:

$$MD(t_i, t_j) = \frac{2l(t_i, t_j)}{l(t_i) + l(t_j)} \tag{7}$$

The present work focuses on proposing spatio-temporal features for speech trajectory analysis. A shape-based signal properties is proposed for characterizing speech signals. In the next section, the features and methodology are discussed in detail.

2   Dynamic Trajectory Features (Proposed Features)

As discussed earlier in the previous section, trajectory parameters have been used effectively for speech modeling. Even though trajectory HMMs model the dynamic features that reflect the changes in the signal, providing the features that capture the intra-segmental features are useful to improve the modeling. The proposed features give an insight into the dynamic nature of a signal which captures structural changes over the segments. Therefore, the variations of the entire signal can be reflected in the features. Each speech signal consists of various acoustic events and they can be characterized by the vibrations of the vocal tract. Usually, features are dependent on the motion of trajectory that varies at different instances of time. The major steps in the model generation for the signals are described in Algorithm 1. The features used in the process are the following:

1. Peak attributes
2. Similarity distance measures

In the following subsections, the procedure for feature extraction is explained.

Algorithm 1. Model Generation procedure

Input:
$S_n[N]$: Input speech signals
Output:
μ_n: Model parameters for given speech signals

1 **begin**
2   **for** $i \leftarrow 0$ **to** $N_{signals}$ **do**
3          $\chi_i \leftarrow Extract\_Features(S_n[i])$
4      $\pi \leftarrow start\_probability$
5      $A \leftarrow initial\_transition_p robability$
6      $\theta \leftarrow Emission\_probability$
7   Initialize the means and covariance matrices
8   Predict the model parameters using HMM process

2.1 Peak Attributes

These features concentrate on analyzing the dynamic nature of a signal in terms of its spatio-temporal structure. The shape of the signal is characterized by different primitives. They are listed as follows:

- Peak
- Valley
- Peak width

In a segment of speech let s_{i-1}, s_i and s_{i+1} be consecutive samples, the terms mentioned above are defined respectively as follows:

- s_i is said to be a peak if $s_{i-1} < s_i > s_{i+1}, \forall i \in \mathbb{Z}$

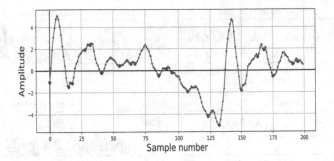

Fig. 1. Peaks and valleys in a speech segment of Vowel /a/

- s_i is said to be a valley if $s_{i-1} > s_i < s_{i+1}$, $\forall i \in \mathbb{Z}$
- The sample p_k being a peak point between any two valleys v_q and v_r, the difference $|r - q|$ is defined as width for the peak p_k $\forall k, q, r \in \mathbb{Z}$ and $q < k < r$.

A sample speech segment is shown in Fig. 1. A peak is a local maxima in the signal whereas local minima is a valley. The peaks and valleys are colored in red and green respectively.

The central idea of the present approach is that a speech signal is treated as a trajectory that records different acoustic events at various instances of time. The properties of these events are analyzed to find similarities among them. They are further modeled to form a generic representation for these trajectories. Peaks are considered as acoustic events and their attributes are used to understand temporal variations in a signal. When a moving object is observed in terms of the path that it forms in a trajectory, peak width is the duration that an object spends in a particular event. With the changes in its duration, a new peak forms in the path of a trajectory. The duration varies for each event by which a pattern can be observed for an object that can distinguish among different phonetic structures. Since each phonetic unit has a unique structure, the path that the spoken units can form is also distinct in its structure [19]. In the present study, this dynamic nature of the spoken units is taken and the similarity between them is used for classifying them. The classification is achieved by using Hidden Markov Modeling (HMM). The steps involved in parameter extraction are given in Algorithm 1. The peak widths of vowels /a/, /e/, /i/, /o/ and /u/ are shown in Fig. 2. The second proposed feature extraction method is explained in the next subsection.

2.2 Similarity Distance Measure Based on Fréchet Distance

Fréchet distance [6] is a measure of similarity between curves which preserves the order of data along with a time series. Let τ_1 and τ_2 be two trajectories that represent paths of any two objects with independent motions f and g respectively. The problem is to find the smallest distance between these two objects

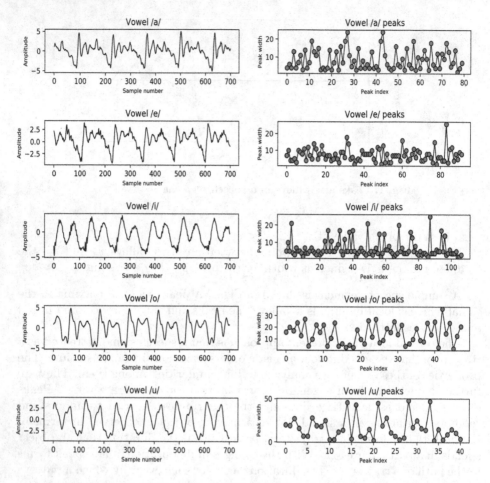

Fig. 2. Peak widths of vowels /a/, /e/, /i/, /o/ and /u/ respectively

while they move forward monotonically while preserving its orientation. This distance can be defined as Eq. 8:

$$\delta(\tau_1, \tau_2) = Max_{f,g}|\tau_1, \tau_2| \qquad (8)$$

This similarity measure was defined for a walking dog problem [1]. In the problem, a man walks with a dog where both follow different paths in the same direction but with different velocities. The constraint for movements is limited for two cases only. They can move forward or stop at any point of time as moving backward is not allowed. Therefore, the Fréchet distance between these two objects is the shortest possible length of the leash that is required to finish the walk. There are many algorithms available to solve this problem. In the present work, we used the approach proposed by Thomas and Heikki [7]. The algorithm considers three possible conditions at which man or dog can be. They are as follows:

Algorithm 2. Trajectory parameter extraction

Input:
S_n: Input speech signal
Output:
T_n: Trajectory vector that contains peak attributes

1 **begin**
2   **for** $i \leftarrow 0$ **to** $length(S_n)$ **do**
3   **if** $s_{i-1} > s_i < s_{i+1}$ **then**
4        $V_i \bigcup i$ ▷ *Find valley positions for the given signal*

5   **for** $j \leftarrow 0$ **to** $length(V_n)$ **do**
6      $T_i \bigcup |V_{j+1} - V_j|$ ▷ *Find the peak widths*

7   return T_n

- $Location_{man} = Location_{dog}$
- $Location_{man} < Location_{dog}$
- $Location_{man} > Location_{dog}$

In a trajectory space τ, let T_1, T_2 be two different trajectories and assume two points p_i and q_i on T_1 and T_2 respectively. Then the distance between these two points is given by Eq. 9:

$$\delta(p_i, q_i) = max(c[p_i, q_i], min(p_{i-1}, q_{i-1})) \tag{9}$$

where $c[p_i, q_i]$ is the cost between objects at the present location and $min(p_{i-1}, q_{i-1})$ is the minimum cost required in the previous move. This cost covers the effort needed to travel between the points in 3 possible ways. The next point to be understood is the representation of Fréchet metric for a speech signal. For a speech trajectory τ_s with a sequence of acoustic events $t_i, \forall i \in \mathbb{Z}$, i.e. $\tau_s = \{T_1, T_2, ..., T_n\}$. The pattern for τ_s is defined as a sequence of similarity distance between a pair of trajectories T_i and T_{i+1}. It is given in Eq. 10:

$$\tau_p = \delta(T_1, T_2), \delta(T_2, T_3), ..., \delta(T_{n-1}, T_n) \tag{10}$$

where as $\delta : \tau_s \longrightarrow \tau_p$ is a mapping function between τ_s and τ_p. In each step, δ gives the similarity between the consecutive pair of trajectories. The overall pattern of a trajectory is represented as a sequence of distances ($\delta_i s$). These values record the changes between acoustic events and thus the structural changes can be found.

The procedure for the feature extraction in this approach is described in Algorithm 2. The extracted similarity distance features using Algorithm 2 are used for classifying the signals. An example of Fréchet distance is shown in Fig. 3. From Fig. 3(b), it can be understood that the shape of the feature vector represents the shape of source signal as shown in Fig. 3(a). In the next section, the details of the dataset and environment used for the experiments are described.

Algorithm 3. Fréchet distance based feature extraction

Input:
S_n: Input speech signal
F_N: Length of frame in samples
Output:
FD_n: Vector of Fréchet distances between adjacent frames

1 **begin**
2   Normalize the input signal S_n
3   Divide S_n into number of frames with equal frame size
4     $n_{frames} = \frac{length(S_n)}{F_N}$
5   **for** $i \leftarrow 0$ **to** n_{frames} **do**
6        $FD_i \bigcup$ Fréchet distance(F_i, F_{i+1}) ▷ *Find the Fréchet distance between each adjacent frames in the signal*
7   return FD

---

3 Experimental Setup

The experiments were conducted on different datasets: vowels and digits. Each dataset contained 50 speaker's data. Each vowel and digit were recorded 15 times for all speakers. We have chosen speakers belonging to different regions in India. They included male and female speakers. The data was recorded using the CoolEdit software with 16 KHz sampling rate, 16 bits resolution and mono channel. The data used in experiments were normalized and DC component was removed. This dataset can be accessed using the link provided in [2] and [3]. The programs needed for experiments were implemented in Python 3.4. The libraries used are Numpy, Similarity measures [11]. The next section discusses the results observed in the study.

4 Results and Analysis

The study was conducted using two different features for the two different datasets as mentioned in the previous section. Each analysis is presented in subsequent subsections.

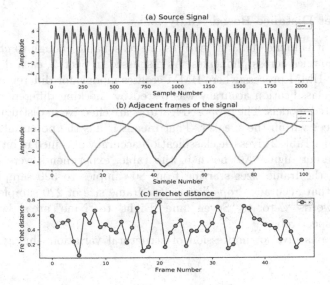

Fig. 3. Fréchet distance calculation for vowel /u/

4.1 Peak Width Analysis

The aim of the analysis is to find pattern by using peak widths. An interesting characteristic observed is that vowels /a/, /e/ and /i/ have peak widths up to 20 whereas vowels /o/ and /u/ has wider peak widths. This implies the number of peak components available in vowels /a/, /e/ and /i/ are comparatively more than vowels /o/ and /u/. It also means that the temporal variations are rapid in the vowels /a/, /e/ and /i/ and it is less in /o/ and /u/. The variations observed in the feature vectors reflect the changes in the source signals. So, it is inferred that the features are significant in identifying the patterns of speech trajectories.

The summary of peak attributes is shown in Table 1. Peak widths are effective in steady state segments like vowels. Vowels have similar behavior over time and therefore the patterns of vowels were captured by peak width properties efficiently. Table 1 presents the results for intra speaker variability and inter speaker variability. It shows that the features are useful in distinguishing vowels and digits in the intra-speaker data clearly. It gives a good classification for vowels also in the intra-speaker case.

Table 1. Accuracy with peak widths

Data base	Intra speaker	Inter speaker
Vowels	96%	75%
Digits	89%	58%

4.2   Fréchet Distance-Based Analysis

In the study, it is found that the features are reasonable enough to characterize temporal dynamics across phonemes. As discussed in Sect. 2, each digit data is trained using HMM process where HMM creates models for different digits separately. The classification accuracy was tested by checking different utterances with the created models. The proposed features are effective in distinguishing the digit utterances within the speaker. That means it has the potential to classify different words. Table 2 gives the classification accuracy obtained in intra-speaker data for different digits. As shown in the table, experiments were conducted with varying the frame sizes starting from 80 samples to 320 samples. It can be observed that accuracy drops down after frame size of 220 samples. Frèchet distance for words "Zero" to "Seven" and "Eight" to "Nine" are shown in Fig. 4 and Fig. 5 respectively.

These graphs give an impression of structural variation among the digits clearly.

Table 2. Accuracy with Frechet distance

S. No.	Frame size (in samples)	Accuracy
1	80	75%
2	120	85%
3	160	80%
4	**200**	**90%**
5	**220**	**90%**
6	240	85%
7	280	80%
8	320	55%

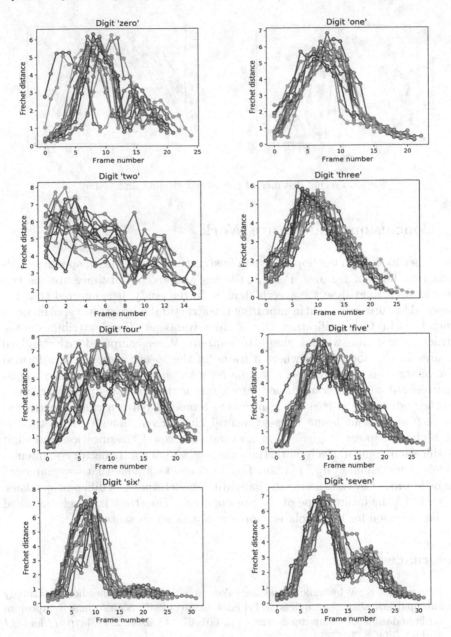

Fig. 4. Fréchet distance of the words "Zero" and "Seven"

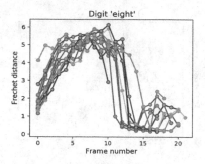
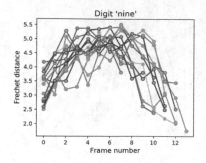

Fig. 5. Fréchet distance of the words "Eight" and "Nine"

5   Conclusions and Future Work

The paper focuses on developing dynamic structural properties of speech signals using two different features. Peak attributes and Fréchet distance are the two features used to analyse the speech signals. In the study, it is inferred that the proposed features are useful in capturing the structural properties of spoken units which is useful for classification. One of the advantages of peak attributes is the extraction procedure which is simple to compute. When compared with standard features LPCC and MFCC where a frame of the speech signal is transformed to a vector, this method gives a simple representation. Here, the entire signal is considered and it is transformed into a vector that contains peak attributes. Another advantage is that the continuous temporal pattern can be extracted in one pass without losing intra-segmental clues. Even though the method is not highly accurate, it gives good accuracy for vowel classification and digit classification comparatively with the existing parametric trajectory segmental models (approximately 75%) [5, 25]. The modeling technique that was employed can be improved by considering the individual model studies of different speakers. This will be the future scope of the present work. The study is being continued in that direction for both isolated words and continuous sentences.

References

1. Bringmann, K.: Why walking the dog takes time: Fréchet distance has no strongly subquadratic algorithms unless SETH fails. In: 2014 IEEE 55th Annual Symposium on Foundations of Computer Science, pp. 661–670, October 2014. https://doi.org/10.1109/FOCS.2014.76
2. CSEIITGUWAHATI: IITG digit database - Google drive, March 2020. https://drive.google.com/drive/folders/1px1p2p5QRNNvFvLJT9hgkA93N7_Utwzs. Accessed 05 Mar 2020
3. CSEIITGUWAHATI: IITG vowel data - Google drive, March 2020. https://drive.google.com/drive/folders/16BcS5cyOdE5oJChj6J8oQp1PmXvU7etV. Accessed 05 Mar 2020

4. Deng, L., Strik, H.: Structure-based and template-based automatic speech recognition - comparing parametric and non-parametric approaches. In: INTERSPEECH 2007, 8th Annual Conference of the International Speech Communication Association, Antwerp, Belgium, 27–31 August 2007, pp. 898–901 (2007). http://www.isca-speech.org/archive/interspeech_2007/i07_0898.html
5. Deng, L., Yu, D., Acero, A.: Structured speech modeling. IEEE Trans. Audio Speech Lang. Process. 14(5), 1492–1504 (2006)
6. Driemel, A., Har-Peled, S., Wenk, C.: Approximating the Fréchet distance for realistic curves in near linear time. Discrete Comput. Geom. 48(1), 94–127 (2012). https://doi.org/10.1007/s00454-012-9402-z
7. Eiter, T., Mannila, H.: Computing discrete Fréchet distance. Technical report, Citeseer (1994)
8. Firouzmand, M.Z., Girin, L.: Perceptually weighted long term modeling of sinusoidal speech amplitude trajectories. In: 2005 Proceedings of the IEEE International Conference on Acoustics, Speech, and Signal Processing (ICASSP 2005), vol. 1, pp. I/369–I/372, March 2005. https://doi.org/10.1109/ICASSP.2005.1415127
9. Gish, H., Ng, K.: A segmental speech model with applications to word spotting. In: 1993 IEEE International Conference on Acoustics, Speech, and Signal Processing, vol. 2, pp. 447–450, April 1993. https://doi.org/10.1109/ICASSP.1993.319337
10. Hubing, N., Yoo, K.: Exploiting recursive parameter trajectories in speech analysis. In: Proceedings ICASSP 1992: 1992 IEEE International Conference on Acoustics, Speech, and Signal Processing, vol. 1, pp. 125–128, March 1992. https://doi.org/10.1109/ICASSP.1992.225956
11. Jekel, C.F., Venter, G., Venter, M.P., Stander, N., Haftka, R.T.: Similarity measures for identifying material parameters from hysteresis loops using inverse analysis. Int. J. Mater. Form. (2018). https://doi.org/10.1007/s12289-018-1421-8
12. Kannan, A., Ostendorf, M.: A comparison of constrained trajectory segment models for large vocabulary speech recognition. IEEE Trans. Speech Audio Process. 6(3), 303–306 (1998). https://doi.org/10.1109/89.668825
13. Li, H., Liu, J., Wu, K., Yang, Z., Liu, R.W., Xiong, N.: Spatio-temporal vessel trajectory clustering based on data mapping and density. IEEE Access 6, 58939–58954 (2018). https://doi.org/10.1109/ACCESS.2018.2866364
14. Lin, Z., Zeng, Q., Duan, H., Liu, C., Lu, F.: A semantic user distance metric using GPS trajectory data. IEEE Access 7, 30185–30196 (2019). https://doi.org/10.1109/ACCESS.2019.2896577
15. Liu, S., Sim, K.C.: Implicit trajectory modelling using temporally varying weight regression for automatic speech recognition. In: 2012 IEEE International Conference on Acoustics, Speech and Signal Processing (ICASSP), pp. 4761–4764, March 2012. https://doi.org/10.1109/ICASSP.2012.6288983
16. Liu, S., Sim, K.C.: Temporally varying weight regression: a semi-parametric trajectory model for automatic speech recognition. IEEE/ACM Trans. Audio Speech Lang. Process. 22(1), 151–160 (2014). https://doi.org/10.1109/TASLP.2013.2285487
17. Liu, Z., Hu, L., Wu, C., Ding, Y., Zhao, J.: A novel trajectory similarity-based approach for location prediction. Int. J. Distrib. Sensor Netw. 12(11), 1550147716678426 (2016). https://doi.org/10.1177/1550147716678426
18. Manjunath, K.E., Kumar, S.B.S., Pati, D., Satapathy, B., Rao, K.S.: Development of consonant-vowel recognition systems for Indian languages: Bengali and Odia. In: 2013 Annual IEEE India Conference (INDICON), pp. 1–6, December 2013. https://doi.org/10.1109/INDCON.2013.6726109

19. Minematsu, N.: Mathematical evidence of the acoustic universal structure in speech. In: 2005 Proceedings of the IEEE International Conference on Acoustics, Speech, and Signal Processing, ICASSP 2005, vol. 1, pp. I/889–I/892, March 2005. https://doi.org/10.1109/ICASSP.2005.1415257

20. Russell, M.J., Holmes, W.J.: Linear trajectory segmental HMMs. IEEE Signal Process. Lett. 4(3), 72–74 (1997). https://doi.org/10.1109/97.558642

21. Wu, Z., King, S.: Improving trajectory modelling for DNN-based speech synthesis by using stacked bottleneck features and minimum generation error training. IEEE/ACM Trans. Audio Speech Lang. Process. 24(7), 1255–1265 (2016). https://doi.org/10.1109/TASLP.2016.2551865

22. Xiao, P., Ang, M., Jiawei, Z., Lei, W.: Approximate similarity measurements on multi-attributes trajectories data. IEEE Access 7, 10905–10915 (2019). https://doi.org/10.1109/ACCESS.2018.2889475

23. Han, Y., de Veth, J., Boves, L.: Trajectory clustering for automatic speech recognition. In: 2005 13th European Signal Processing Conference, pp. 1–4, September 2005

24. Yun, Y.-S., Oh, Y.-H.: A segmental-feature HMM using parametric trajectory model. In: 2000 Proceedings of the IEEE International Conference on Acoustics, Speech, and Signal Processing, (Cat. No. 00CH37100), vol. 3, pp. 1249–1252, June 2000. https://doi.org/10.1109/ICASSP.2000.861802

25. Zhao, B., Schultz, T.: Toward robust parametric trajectory segmental model for vowel recognition. In: 2002 IEEE International Conference on Acoustics, Speech, and Signal Processing, vol. 4, pp. IV-4165–IV-4165, May 2002. https://doi.org/10.1109/ICASSP.2002.5745596

Identification and Prediction of Alzheimer Based on Biomarkers Using 'Machine Learning'

Manash Sarma[1]([⊠]) and Subarna Chatterjee[2]

[1] Ramaiah University of Applied Sciences, Bangalore, India
smanash@hotmail.com
[2] Department of CSE, Ramaiah University of Applied Sciences,
Bangalore, India
subarna.cs.et@msruas.ac.in

Abstract. Alzheimer's disease is one form of dementia. It is characterized by progressive problems in thinking, learning and behavior. Since there is no cure till date, early detection and prediction of progressive stages of the disease may help preclude the severity. In this work, we have used Machine Learning techniques to identify the current stage and predict the progressive stages of this disease. Work in this paper has been carried out in two phases: first, identification of the disease based on 2092 samples, and second, prediction of the progressive stages based on 819 samples. The proposed feature selection technique selects 8 effective biomarkers out of 113 generic biomarkers for identification of disease stage. Our proposed data imputation approach is effective to handle missing records in periodic data used in stage prediction. We have achieved F1 score of 89% for CN, 84% for MCI, 80% for AD stage identification and F1 score of 96% for prediction of each stage of the disease.

Keywords: Alzheimer's disease · Stage prediction · Machine learning · Long short term memory model

1 Introduction

Named after Dr. Alois Alzheimer, an Alzheimer's Disease (AD) patient develops abnormal clumps called amyloid plaque, tangled bundles of fibers called neurofibrillary, or tau, tangles in brain. Loss of connection between neurons is another feature of AD. In the beginning, the problem seems to take place in the hippocampus, the part essential in forming memories. But as neurons die, other parts of the brain are affected. This causes progressive problems with short-term memory loss in the earlier stages, followed by a decline in other 'cognitive and behavioral functions' as the disease advances to next stages [1]. Generally, 50–75% of people above the age of 65 years are prone to AD. With increase in the life expectancy of middle-income category of people, number of AD patients is increasing worldwide.

Unfortunately, no cure is found for AD till date [2]. Only a rudimentary progress is made in identifying a cure. In spite of considerable effort, a failure rate of 99.6% is recorded in clinical trials of AD drugs [3]. In 2018, two groups were forced to end AD

A. Bhattacharjee et al. (Eds.): MIND 2020, CCIS 1241, pp. 271–284, 2020.
https://doi.org/10.1007/978-981-15-6318-8_23

clinical trials as their drugs failed in preventing progression of AD [4]. So, the viable alternative now is early detection of the current stage and prediction of the next stage so that the disease can be contained, and its progressive deterioration can be minimized. Prevention of further deterioration through early detection and prediction is the motivation for this work where ML (Machine Learning) can contribute enormously.

ML (Machine learning) helps in the identification of the present stage and prediction of the next stage of the disease based on biomarker (medical measurements that can indicate a disease) datasets. With the availability of AD datasets, ML is gaining popularity in recent times for the disease diagnosis. An AD dataset has a collection of biomarkers for each AD patient's record. AD biomarkers can be categorized as main cognitive tests, MRI ROIs (measures of brain structural integrity), FDG PET ROI averages (measure cell metabolism), AV45 PET ROI averages for amyloid-beta load measurement in brain, biomarkers for measuring tau load in the brain, DTI ROI measures used in measurement of microstructural parameters related to axons, CSF biomarkers for measuring tau levels and amyloid in cerebrospinal fluid, Others (APOE status, Demographic information, Diagnosis). Here APOE status is about APOE4, an allele of APOE gene, which is found to be one of major causes of late onset Alzheimer's disease [5]. The patients can be diagnosed in one of the stages namely Cognitive Normal (CN), Mild Cognitive Impairment (MCI), Cognitive Normal (CN), Alzheimer's Disease (AD) or dementia state.

However, a physician or clinical expert's diagnosis based on the values of this list of biomarkers can be subjective and is dependent on his/her experiences where he/she focusses on particular set of markers. The approach is manual, can take considerable amount of time and is prone to error at times (generally human error). So, health industry is additionally taking other approaches like Machine Learning, data-driven disease progression model. In this paper we are using Machine Learning and deep learning techniques for classifying the current state of Alzheimer's disease and predicting the evolutionary stage of the disease. Instead of exploring the few biomarkers solely based on experience, we are using the feature selection technique that helps automatically select only the essential biomarkers for classification and stage prediction of the disease.

There are various challenges in using the biomarker data. The dataset would have lots of missing and unformatted data. Different models trained with the same training data may respond differently with the same test data. Selecting the effective biomarkers from large number of available biomarkers is another challenge. It is noticed that research scholars select the few biomarkers based on their individual experience which is not generalized. Applying ML techniques to predict the disease stage is another challenge where biomarker data need to be collected over certain fixed time intervals. Dataset often misses out data of some interval. In this work, we have addressed every challenge individually and built the disease stage identification and prediction models with high accuracy and F1 score. Key contributions of this research work are as follows:

- Determine the essential 8 biomarkers from 113 biomarkers for AD detection and prediction using ML that reduces clinical diagnosis cost and increases reliability.
- Identify the current state of Alzheimer's disease with high 'F1 score' and accuracy by applying ML and DL techniques.

- Predict the progressive stages of the disease six-month prior with very high accuracy.

2   Related Work

This section briefly mentions some of the key research already done in Alzheimer's disease detection using machine learning techniques.

R. Chaves et al., introduced a classifier to diagnose AD with *association rule mining* [6–9]. They used SPECT dataset. The dataset had 97 samples where 43 were cognitive controls and 54 were dementia patients. Their work had accuracy of 95.87% with 100% sensitivity and specificity of 92.86%. However, dataset was pathologically unproven and total instance were actually low though performance was good. Liu, Zhang et al., (2012) proposed one Sparse representation-based classifier (SRC) [11]. The author's intention was to create *local patch based sub-classifiers*. These sub-classifiers are fused for better accuracy. Muehlboeck et al. worked on **baseline MRI** and **CSF data** combination for enhancing classification accuracy of AD [10]. The dataset had 96 samples of AD patients and 273 cognitive controls, labelled by experienced physicians. Their proposed classification method had a result of 91.8% accuracies for CSF and MRI combined. Veeramuthu et al. constructed a CAD tool. They used *Fisher Discriminants ratio* to do feature extraction to obtain ROI [12]. The samples were classified as normal when the extracted number of rules verified crossed final threshold. Otherwise the image was classified as AD. Their claim of 91.33% accuracy, 100% specificity, 82.67% sensitivity was in comparison of PCA+SVM, VAF and NFM+SVM. However, there was no discussion on handling missing data, class imbalance and validation method.

Regarding forecast of progression of the disease state, using ADNI dataset, Moore et al. achieved mAUC score of 0.82 with RF classifier [13]. Nguyen et al. achieved average mAUC score of 0.86 using RNN with forward-filling data imputation [14]. Recently, Jack Albright in his work on 'Forecasting the progression of Alzheimer's disease using neural networks and a novel preprocessing algorithm', took ADNI data from 1737 patients and processed using the **All-Pairs** technique [15]. ML models were trained with these processed data. Using Neural Network technique MLP, he claims mAUC score (0.866). However, he has not mentioned if the biomarkers he chose were based on some robust techniques used. Eufemia Lella et al., (2019) developed one ML framework for the feature importance analysis and classification of AD based on brain level communicability. They applied RF, ANN and SVM on connectivity networks using balanced samples of ADNI data records of AD and CN natives and achieved accuracy of 75% and AUC 83% [16].

Most of the researchers were focused on classifying the current state of the disease and not on the progressive stages till 2014. Because of lack of availability of pathologically proven, authentic dataset for public earlier or some other reasons, lots of research done earlier had to depend on unproven pathologically data. The datasets used were relatively small and lacked important disease state like MCI. Consequently, there was lack of sufficient validation process for the obtained results. It is easy to get good accuracy result with small datasets. But small dataset cannot represent actual population which often leads to overfitting. While some of the results of earlier research are impressive, they were based on small input, unproven dataset which could lead to uncertainty of the model.

3 Process Model Method

We have utilized the concept of **process model** mentioned in the article *The lightweight IBM Cloud Garage Method for data science* [17]. The **process model** comprises of tasks ETL (Extract, Transform and Load), exploration, cleaning and feature engineering, model definition, model evaluation and model deployment. The ETL (Extract, Transform and Load) step is not applicable here as the dataset used is in the form of csv file (details are mentioned in Sect. 3.1). Our methods and approaches are elaborated in subsequent sections of the documents and are broadly guided by **process model**.

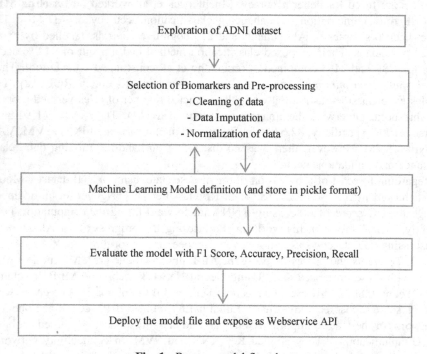

Fig. 1. Process model flowchart

3.1 Dataset Selection and Exploration

Dataset selection and exploration is the initial step of **process model** workflow shown in Fig. 1. In this research we have worked with two datasets. We have obtained **ADNI** (Alzheimer's Disease Neuroimaging Initiative) based **ADNIMERGE** dataset from LONI (Laboratory of Neuro Imaging) website https://ida.loni.usc.edu for identification of the stage of the disease. It is not directly downloadable. After registration and approval, the dataset is available for download. The **ADNIMERGE** dataset is comprised of several study phases, including ADNI-1, ADNI-GO, and ADNI-2 of year 2004, 2009, and 2011 respectively. TADPOLE (The Alzheimer's Disease Prediction of Longitudinal Evolution) grand challenge dataset is used for stage prediction. The **TADPOLE** dataset is based on ADNIMERGE dataset from **LONI**. ADNIMERGE dataset keep data collected from 2092 natives while TADPOLE dataset has data from 1737 natives. Both are almost same and did an exploratory data analysis (EDA) on ADNI dataset.

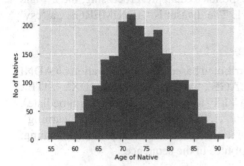

Fig. 2. Number of Natives with Age

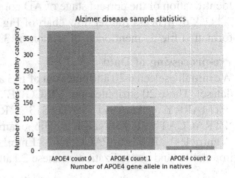

Fig. 3. Number of CN natives with APOE4 gene count

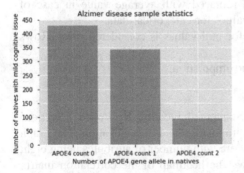

Fig. 4. Number of MCI natives with APOE4 gene count

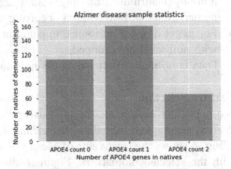

Fig. 5. Number of AD natives with APOE4 gene count

The dataset is explored with bar-chart visualization for an analysis on distribution of biomarkers **age** and **APOE4** gene. It is found that majority of the visitors belong to age group of 70–80 years as shown in the bar chart of Fig. 2. APOE4 allele impact on Alzheimer's disease is analyzed through next three figures. APOE4 is widely acknowledged as one of the major factors of causing Alzheimer's disease. The maximum number of APOE4 genes in a human genome can be 2. From Fig. 3, it is evident that a native labelled as CN (Cognitive Normal) is very less likely to have 2 numbers of APOE4 gene. Majority of the natives have no APOE4 gene as per Fig. 4. From Fig. 5, it appears that natives diagnosed with AD or dementia stage is likely to have 1 or 2 numbers of APOE4 gene allele. But there are some natives of dementia category without an APOE4 allele. So, APOE4 gene is not the only deciding factor for causing Alzheimer. Some other biomarkers are also responsible.

3.2 Method for Disease Stage Identification

Identification of the current stage of AD corresponds to data pre-processing, the 2nd and 3rd task of **process model** flow chart of Fig. 1. The dataset is 'ADNIMERGE', a 'csv' formatted file as mentioned in section of 3.1.

Pre-processing of Data

We initially selected 20 attributes out of 113 attributed based on our exploration on ADNI dataset. These 20 attributes are 'VISCODE', 'AGE', 'APOE4', 'MMSE','DX', 'SITE', 'PTMARRY', 'ADAS11', 'ADAS13', 'RAVLT_forgetting', 'RAVLT_immediate', 'PTRACCAT', 'PTGENDER', 'Hippocampus', 'PTETHCAT', 'RAVLT_learning', 'Ventricles', 'ICV', 'mPACCdigit', 'Entorhinal', 'Fusiform'. We apply data cleaning, imputation and normalization on these 20 attributes in the sequence:

- Data are present in diverse types, like int, float, string/object, date Values of type string/object are mapped to numeric type.
- Simple dropping of rows for missing values enormously reduces the dataset. For non-target attributes, missing values are replaced with average value in case of numeric data and 'maximum occurring value' for categorical data.
- For target or label attributes, imputation for null values is considered risky. Rows with null label are dropped.
- Data is normalized after data cleaning and imputation.

Feature Selection

We apply correlation matrix analysis and 'Sequential Floating Backward Selection' (SFBS) technique on the data after cleaning, imputation and normalization. The graph at Fig. 6 shows the least value of Mean CV score with number of attributes being eight with the selected biomarkers. Figure 7 shows the heatmap of the correlation matrix result. Red color indicates a negative correlation while green a positive correlation. Backward floating-point selection technique resulted the eight attributes. Both correlation matrix approach and attribute selection technique suggest the most effective biomarkers are namely AGE, APOE4, MMSE, SITE, ADAS11, ADAS13, PTRAC-CAT and mPACCdigit.

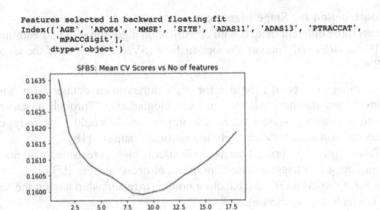

Fig. 6. Selected features and feature selection graph for CV scores at number of features

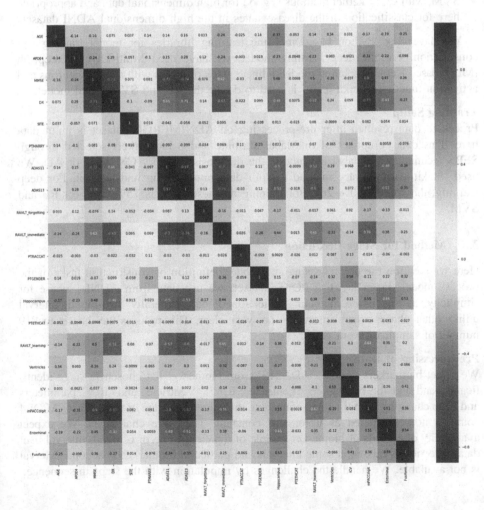

Fig. 7. Heatmap of correlation matrix of 20 biomarkers chosen from 113 (Color figure online)

Model Construction for Stage Identification

We construct three different models with classification algorithms Deep Learning (DL), Random Forest (RF) and Support Vector Machine (SVM). Strength of the algorithms are as follows:

- Deep learning is a good classifier for high dimensional dataset with nonlinear relationship among the predictors and the biomarkers. "Through a stacked and hierarchical learning system, deep learning methods could efficiently capture complex relationships between high-dimensional features" [18].
- Deep Learning is appropriate here as the dataset is high dimensional and nonlinear. Random Forest is a bagging-based ensemble of decision tress (DT).
- RF has the benefits of DT, like handling nonlinear relationship among the features, being insensitive to outliers etc.
- Some disadvantages of DT like overfitting, variance is taken care as RF is an ensemble of DTs. RF is also intrinsically suitable for multiclass problem.
- SVM, with set of kernel methods is good for high dimensional data and appropriate here for classification of the disease states in the high dimensional ADNI dataset.

We have used Python based machine learning libraries for model training and construction. For the deep learning model, we have used Multi-Layer Perceptron (MLP) based Keras sequential model, a linear stack of layers with a set of neurons and activation function. 'Scikit-learn' is used to define the RF and SVM based model.

Training Setup

Processed data resulted after pre-processing on ADNIMERGE dataset is input data here. This data comprises of one label attribute and 8 biomarkers selected through SFBS technique. The label attribute is the diagnosis category CN, MCI or AD. We used 'Scikit-learn' library method to split data into training and test set. For deep learning, the split is 80%–20% for training and testing. It is 75%–25% for RF and SVM.

3.3 Method for Stage Prediction

Here we mention the preprocessing and model definition or construction tasks of the process model. From the TADPOLE dataset, we use data from ADNI-1 phase for simplicity, as this phase maintains collection of data generally at 6-month interval unlike other phases where interval is not very clear. This reduces the dataset to 819 number of samples for our work.

Preprocessing of Data

We select biomarkers 'AGE', 'ADAS13' from biomarker list chosen in stage identification and add the biomarkers 'Ventricle', ICV'. 'Ventricle' and 'ICV' parameters and keep changing with time and contribute to progressive state of the disease. APOE4 count is not considered as it remains constant. There are challenges. We expect availability of records of biomarker sample of a patient to be of 6-month interval. But data collection is missed at some intervals and particular biomarker(s) at some interval is not available. We handle the challenges by imputation with the steps in sequence:

- Sort the records with patient roster ID and VISCODE.
- If a field in particular row(s) of the same patient is null, fill with the non-null field of next immediate or previous row with same roster ID.
- If a field in all the rows of the same roster id is null, remove the roster ID rows.
- If particular row(s) related to interval visit(s) of same roster ID is missing, impute a new row by copying immediate next or previous row of the roster ID.

At the end of preprocessing, each record of a patient reflects biomarker sample collection at approximately 6-month intervals.

Model for Stage Prediction

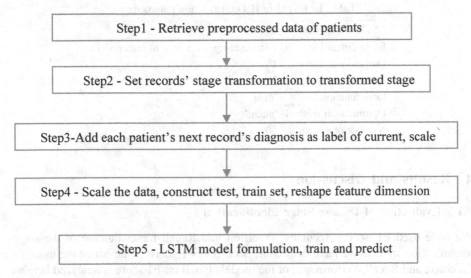

Fig. 8. LSTM model construction and evaluation flowchart

We have chosen RNN based LSTM to work on the periodic biomarker data. We explored other timeseries methods like ARMA (Auto Regressive Moving Average). LSTM works better when we have to deal with large data while ARIMA is good for small datasets. LSTM does well with enough nonlinear data. We build the LSTM model based on the periodic biomarker samples from preprocessing step. As samples collection is of 6-month interval, it is equivalent to 1 timestamp as considered in the LSTM model. Figure 8 mentions the steps of stage prediction model definition. From preprocessed data, the **stage transition** of **diagnosis** field is changed to stage transformed. So, the **diagnosis** values like **MCI to AD** is modified to **AD** in a patient's record as an example. In step 3, **diagnosis** value from next record (interval) is appended to the current biomarker record of the patient. So, existing biomarkers would have timestamp t unit and the appended **diagnosis** from next record has the timestamp $t + 1$. The biomarkers in a patient record can be represented as $var1(t)$, $var2(t)$, $var3(t)$, $var4(t)$, $var5(t)$ and $var1(t + 1)$. Here $var1(t)$ represents **diagnosis** information at time instant t and $var1(t + 1)$ represents **diagnosis** information at time instant $t + 1$. Then data is scaled within a value range between *0* to *1*.

Training Setup and Model Construction

At step 4, records are divided with 70% for training and 30% for testing. $var1(t + 1)$, the **diagnosis** information at time instant $t + 1$ is considered as label or target. At the end of step 4, data is reshaped because input data needs to be provided in an array structure in the form of: [samples, time steps, features] to the LSTM network. With $var1(t + 1)$ as target or label, our approach is sequence classification with LSTM (Table 1).

Table 1. LSTM model construction parameter

LSTM parameters	Values
Input dimension	1 (timestamp) × 5 (no. of features)
Output dimension	1
Number of layers	2
Loss function	'mae'
Optimization method	'adam'
Number of epochs	50

4 Results and Discussion

4.1 Evaluation of Disease Stage Identification

We have used F1 Score, Accuracy, Precision and Recall for evaluation of the stage identification models we have defined in Sect. 3.2. F1 score is the harmonic mean of Precision and Recall. Performance of the models based on F1 score is analyzed here as it is good for uneven class distribution and takes into account both Precision and Recall. We have used **classification_report** method of Scikit-learn.

Test Setup and Result Analysis

Please refer to training set-up of Sect. 3.2 where we split the data into training and test sets with a ratio of 75%–25% for RF and SVM and 80%–20% for the deep learning model.

Table 2 shows that deep learning classifier performs the best considering the accuracy score of 85%. F1-score, Precision and Recall considers success rate of classification for each category of patients diagnosed CN, AD, MCI. Again, DL model performs the best with F1-Score 89% for CN, 84% for MCI and 80% for AD. RF model has F1-Score 86% for CN, 81% for MCI and 77% for AD while SVM has 87% for CN, 81% for MCI and 79%. SVM and RF got same 'F1-Score' 81% for classification of MCI patients.

Table 2. Performance scores in percentage of different classifiers

Evaluation method	Deep learning	Random Forest	SVM
Accuracy	85	83	83
Precision (CN, MCI, AD)	91, 85, 75	88, 81, 77	84, 83, 81
Recall (CN, MCI, AD)	88, 83, 85	85, 82, 78	90, 80, 76
F1-Score (CN, MCI, AD)	89, 84, 80	86, 81, 77	87, 81, 79

4.2 Evaluation of Disease Stage Prediction

For evaluation we have used F1 Score, Accuracy, Precision and Recall. We have used 'classification_report' method of Scikit-learn (Figs. 9, 10, 11, 12, 13).

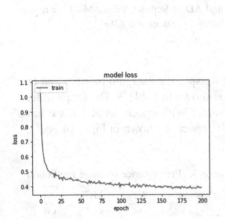

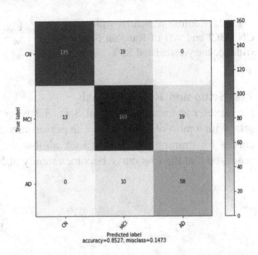

Fig. 9. Deep learning loss method values in each epoch

Fig. 10. Confusion matrix with categories CN, MCI and AD for Deep learning model with accuracy calculated 85%

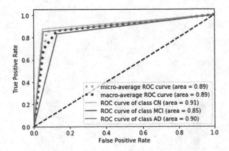

Fig. 11. ROC of each of CN, MCI and AD with deep learning model

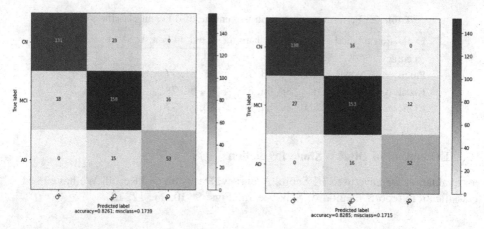

Fig. 12. Confusion matrix with categories CN, MCI and AD of Random Forest model with accuracy calculated 83%

Fig. 13. Confusion matrix with categories CN, MCI and AD of Support Vector Machine model with accuracy calculated 83%

Test Setup and Result Analysis

Please refer to training set-up of Sect. 3.3 where we split the data into training and test sets, with a ratio of 70%–30%. The performance is shown in Table 3. The shape of loss curves for training and testing look almost the same. With epoch set at 50, we have observed that the loss curve becomes steady at 50th epoch as shown in Figs. 14 and 15.

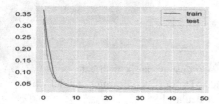

Fig. 14. Loss values in each epoch of LSTM model training

Table 3. Performance of stage prediction

Evaluation	CN	MCI	AD
Precision %	96	88	99
Recall %	96	97	86
F1 Score %	96	93	92
Accuracy %	93		

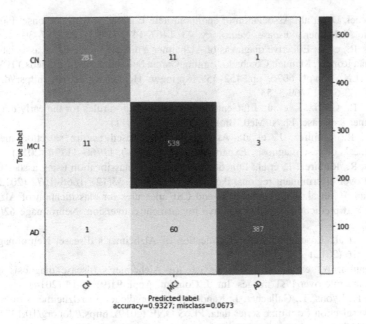

Fig. 15. Confusion matrix of LSTM model

5   Conclusion

In this work, we constructed three ML models for classification of current stage of AD and an RNN based LSTM model for prediction of the next stage of the disease. We handled multiple challenges as mentioned in the beginning and achieved F1 score and accuracy in stage prediction of the disease which is the best result so far. We also achieved competitive score in identifying the current stage of the disease. We could drastically minimize the number of biomarkers from 113 by applying appropriate feature selection technique and achieved the best results. It is envisaged that medical community will be benefitted from this research in future work on this disease. Our ML based techniques and the minimal set of effective biomarkers we found can be considered in clinical laboratories to diagnose this disease as a support to physicians.

References

1. Alzheimer's, Association: 2019 Alzheimer's disease facts and figures. Alzheimer's Dement. **15**(3), 321–387 (2019)
2. The need for early detection and treatment in Alzheimer's disease. EBioMedicine **9**, 1 (2016). https://www.ncbi.nlm.nih.gov/pmc/articles/PMC4972571/
3. Cummings, J.L., Morstorf, T., Zhong, K.: Alzheimer's disease drug development pipeline: few candidates, frequent failures. Alzheimer's Res Ther. **6**(4), 37 (2014)
4. Cortez, M.: Merck will end Alzheimer's trial as alternative approach fails (2018). https://www.bloomberg.com/news/articles/2018-02-13/merck-will-end-alzheimer-s-trial-as-alternative-approach-fails

5. Schmechel, D., et al.: Association of apolipoprotein E allele ε4 with late-onset familial and sporadic Alzheimer's disease. Neurology. **43**, 1467–1472 (1993). **63**, 287–303

6. Chaves, R., et al.: Effective diagnosis of Alzheimer's disease by means of association rules. In: Graña Romay, Manuel, Corchado, Emilio, Garcia Sebastian, M.Teresa (eds.) HAIS 2010. LNCS (LNAI), vol. 6076, pp. 452–459. Springer, Heidelberg (2010). https://doi.org/10.1007/978-3-642-13769-3_55

7. Chaves, R., Górriz, J., et al.: Efficient mining of association rules for the early diagnosis of Alzheimer's disease. Phys. Med. Biol. **56**(18), 6047 (2011)

8. Chaves, R., Ramírez, J., et al.: Association rule- based feature selection method for Alzheimer's disease diagnosis. Expert Syst. Appl. **39**(14), 11766–11774 (2012)

9. Chaves, R., Ramírez, J., et al.: Functional brain image classification using association rules defined over discriminant regions. Pattern Recogn. Lett. **33**(12), 1666–1672 (2012)

10. Westman, E., et al.: Combining MRI and CSF measures for classification of Alzheimer's disease and prediction of mild cognitive impairment conversion. Neuroimage **62**(1), 229–238 (2012)

11. Liu, Z., et al.: Ensemble sparse classification of Alzheimer's disease. Neuroimage **60**(2), 1106–1116 (2012)

12. Veeramuthu, A., et al.: A new approach for Alzheimer's disease diagnosis by using association rule over PET images. Int. J. Comput. Appl. **91**(9), 9–14 (2014)

13. Moore, P., Lyons, T., Gallacher, J.: Random forest prediction of Alzheimer's disease using pairwise selection from time series data. PLoS ONE (2019). https://doi.org/10.1371/journal.pone.0211558

14. Nguyen, M., Sun, N., Alexander, D.C., Feng, J., Yeo, B.T.: Modeling Alzheimer's disease progression using deep recurrent neural networks. In: 2018 International Workshop on Pattern Recognition in Neuroimaging (PRNI), pp. 1–4. IEEE (2018). https://doi.org/10.1109/PRNI.2018.8423955

15. Albright, J.: Forecasting the progression of Alzheimer's disease using neural networks and a novel preprocessing algorithm. Alzheimer's Dement. Transl. Res. Clin. Interventions **5**, 483–491 (2019)

16. Lella, E., Lombardi, A., et al.: Machine Learning and DWI Brain Communicability Networks for Alzheimer's Disease Detection (2019)

17. Kienzler, R.: The lightweight IBM cloud garage method for data science. https://developer.ibm.com/technologies/artificial-intelligence/articles/the-lightweight-ibm-cloud-garage-method-for-data-science/

18. Wu, Q., et al.: Deep learning methods for predicting disease status using genomic data. J. Biom. Biostat. **9**(5), 517 (2018)

Solving Quadratic Assignment Problem Using Crow Search Algorithm in Accelerated Systems

Manoj Kumar[⊠] and Pinaki Mitra

Department of Computer Science and Engineering, IIT Guwahati, Guwahati, India
{manoj.kumar,pinaki}@iitg.ac.in

Abstract. The Quadratic Assignment problem (QAP) is one of the most studied optimization problem. Although many direct and heuristic methods are used to give the solution of QAP for small size instances in reasonable time but it takes huge time for large size instances. So, solving QAP in massively parallel architecture like Graphics processing unit (GPU) by applying a noble metaheuristics Crow Search Algorithm (CSA) can further optimize the solution and their execution time. So, in this paper we analyse the QAP in accelerated systems by using CSA metaheuristics and CSA performs approximately 10 times faster on GPU as compared to CPU.

Keywords: Metaheuristics · QAP · GPU · CSA

1 Introduction

The Quadratic Assignment problem (QAP) is one of well known real life optimization problem. Due to its complexity and application in real life problems, many researchers started to find optimal solution of QAP. This problem comes under NP-Hard class [1]. There are many real life problems which have direct application of QAP. Some of these are- facility layout problem, the bin packing problem, keyboard layout problem, traveling salesman problem, scheduling problem, the max clique problem, graph partitioning, backboard wiring problem, memory layout in digital signal processors and many more became it more popular.

There are many exact and heuristics methods are available to solve QAP problem [2]. Although heuristics methods are able to solve and give near optimal solution but it takes huge amount of time for instances of size greater than 20. Also heuristics methods are problem specific but metaheuristics are suitable for all types of problems. So metaheuristics became the one of the alternate choice to solve QAP. There are many nature-inspired metaheuristics are available for solving the QAP in accelerated systems [3]. In this work, we have chosen a noble metaheuristics- crow search algorithm to find the best optimal solution of QAP and execution time by efficient parallelization of CSA metaheuristics

© Springer Nature Singapore Pte Ltd. 2020
A. Bhattacharjee et al. (Eds.): MIND 2020, CCIS 1241, pp. 285–295, 2020.
https://doi.org/10.1007/978-981-15-6318-8_24

in accelerated system. We have taken three architecture system- serial machine (CPU) multicore architecture, Posix thread (pthread) and graphics processing unit (GPU) many core architecture. We have mainly considered the instances from QAPLIB [4] as benchmark for QAP.

Rest of the paper is organized as follows: Sect. 2 presents the related work. Section 3 define the QAP. Section 4 explains the crow search algorithm. Section 5 presents the accelerated system used in this study. Section 6 explains the problem mapping to architecture. The next section presents the experimental results, followed by conclusion and future work.

2   Related Work

Evolutionary algorithm which is a population based metaheuristics is the first parallel algorithm developed on GPU. *Wong et al.* [5] proposed a first work of genetic algorithm on GPU. In their works, they implemented fast evolutionary programming based on mutation operator. They divide the work in three parts-first generate initial population in CPU and evaluate in GPU, second compare on either CPU or GPU and the final results is transferred from GPU to CPU. By using replacement and selection operators the next generation population that is neighbor solution is generated on CPU, so massive transfer of data from CPU to GPU limits the performance of algorithm. This drawback is removed by *Q. Yu et al.* [6] which was the first paper of full parallelization of genetic algorithm on GPU.

In paper [7], authors implemented a parallel evolution strategy algorithm based on pattern search on GPU. In this paper he used multiple kernels on GPU like selection and crossover operators run one kernel while mutation and evaluation run on other kernels of GPU and remaining processes are done on CPU.

Tsutsui et al. [8] used the memory management concept on GPU for solving a QAP by GA. Authors used the shared memory concept on GPU.

Luong et al. [9] proposed a hybrid evolutionary algorithm by mixing EA with local search on GPU. Authors divides their work on three layer-high level (memory allocation and data transfer), intermediate level (thread management) and low level layer (memory management). After this, authors tested proposed algorithm on QAP by taking standard *taillard* instances of size greater than 30, and noted the CPU time and GPU time and also on texture memory, analyses the performance and showed that GPU is much more efficient than CPU.

3   Quadratic Assignment Problem

The main objective of QAP is to minimize the assignment cost that is cost to assign n facilities among n locations. Where assignment cost is calculated as the sum of all pairs cost that is product of flows between facilities and distance between nodes which are assigned corresponding to that facilities.

Let $M_1 = (e_{ij})$ and $M_2 = (f_{ij})$ be two $n \times n$ matrices of positive integers. Then the solution of QAP is any permutation $\pi = (1, 2, \ldots, n)$ which minimize the objective function

$$z(\pi) = \sum_{i=1}^{n} \sum_{j=1}^{n} e_{ij} f_{\pi(i)\pi(j)} \tag{1}$$

Any permutation of number from 1 to size of the matrices that is $(1, 2, \ldots, n)$ represents the one of QAP solution. QAP solution is also called permutation representation from 1 to size of the matrix. Here on both matrices that is M_1 distance and M_2 flow matrices, the value of objective function Z depends and that dependency causes the QAP problem to became more harder and complex to solve. The solution after generating from each permutation represents a neighbor solution. In this paper we generated neighbor solution from initial solution by using adjacent pair-wise exchange method.

3.1 Solution Evaluation

For evaluating the solution, evaluation function is taking huge amount of time. Here in evaluation function we are passing one full solution at a time. The assignment cost is sum of the cost of all pairs of locations, so for calculating cost for one location it is searching all facilities and it takes $O(n)$ time. For calculating whole locations it takes $O(n^2)$ times. In incremental solution evaluation instead of passing one full solution at a time and calculating cost for every locations, here we are passing the only changed locations of neighbor solution and remaining locations are as it is. Hence instead of calculating cost for all locations only we calculated changed cost for that solution. So it takes only $O(n)$ times.

4 Crow Search Algorithm (CSA)

It is one of nature inspired metaheuristics which is based on intelligence of crows and their behaviour. This algorithm is developed by Askarzadeh [10] in 2016. Crows is very good in observing the other birds and when any other birds hide the excess food on some places they observe until they left and once left, crows steal their food. Once the crows committed theft they take more precautions by moving another position and to avoid for future victim. In a crows of flock size N, the crow i position at time (iteration) t in a d-dimensional environment is represented by a vector $x^{i,t}$ $(i = 1, 2, \ldots, N; t = 1, 2, \ldots, t_{max})$ where $x^{i,t} = [x_1^{i,t}, x_2^{i,t}, \ldots, x_d^{i,t}]$ and t_{max} denotes the maximum number of iteration. Each crow has a memory and $m^{i,t}$ denotes the memory (position of hiding place) of crow i at iteration t, and this is the best position obtained by crow i so far. Let us assume at any iteration t, crow j wants to visit its hiding place $m^{j,t}$ and crow i decides to follow crow j then at that situation two cases may happen:

Case 1: Crow j is unknown about the crow i is following it. As a result, crow i will approach to crow j hiding place. So crow i new position is represented as:

$$x^{i,t+1} = x^{i,t} + r_i \times f_l^{i,t} \times (m^{j,t} - x^{i,t}) \tag{2}$$

Where r_i denotes a random number between 0 and 1 with uniform distribution and $f_l^{i,t}$ represents the crow i flight length at iteration t.

Case 2: Crow j knows that crow i is following. Then in this situation crow j will fool crow i by moving to another position in the search space so that his hiding place remain protected. Now by combining the both cases 1 and 2 we can write the crow i position for next iteration:

$$x^{i,t+1} = \begin{cases} x^{i,t} + r_i \times f_l^{i,t} \times (m^{j,t} - x^{i,t}) & r_j \geq AP^{j,t} \\ \text{a random position} & \text{otherwise} \end{cases} \tag{3}$$

Where r_j represents any one random number between 0 and 1 with uniform distribution and $AP^{j,t}$ represents the crow j awareness probability at iteration t. Crow i next position will depends on flight length that is if $f_l < 1$ then the crow next position is between $x^{i,t}$ and $m^{j,t}$ and if $f_l > 1$ then next position of the crow can be any where on the line, that is it may exceed the position $m^{j,t}$. Hence small values of f_l move towards the local search where as a large value of f_l move towards the global search in search space.

5   Accelerated System

5.1   Multi cores System

In multi-core architecture generally ten or hundred number of cores are there. In multi-core processor two or more number of processors (also called *cores*) are built on a single computing platform and all cores run in parallel so that it enhanced the over all speed of the program. Each core is treated as a separate processor by operating system (OS) and maps to threads/processes by OS scheduler. Each processor is physically connected to the same memory. The first general-purpose multi-core processor POWER4 released by IBM in 2001 [11]. Multi-core processors executes multiple instructions and multiple data on different cores at time. In this study we have taken Intel(R) Core(TM) i7-7700HQ CPU which have 2.8 GHZ clock frequency, 64 bit and 8 CPU cores.

5.2   GPU Based System

Graphics Processing Unit (GPU) is not a stand alone single device but it is connected to CPU through a PCI-Express bus. NVIDIA's CUDA GPU architecture is a combination of several streaming multiprocessor (SM). Each SM consists of several scalar processors or cuda cores which runs in parallel. Each SM has a load/store unit, special functional unit (SFU), shared memory and caches (constant and texture caches) and shares a global memory of GPU. When any kernel is launched by GPU, the threads of that kernel is distributed among SM for execution.

In CUDA programming any program runs on CPU and GPU both. The task are divided among CPU host and GPU device. A program runs on CPU that is host code calls the program run on GPU that is device code that is called the kernel. As GPU threads are light weight so switching thread is a low cost operations. A cuda core runs a single instruction on multiple threads. In one *warps* group of 32 threads are there. Inside a warp all threads runs same instruction consecutively. In this study we used *Nvidia GeForce GTX* 1050 GPU with 640 cuda cores and 2 GB DDR5 memory, Streaming Processor (32*bits*) which is designed with Pascal architecture. We have install cuda tool-kit 10.1 on this device.

6   Mapping Crow Search Algorithm for QAP to Multicore, Pthread and GPU

6.1   CSA on Serial Machine

Many researchers solve the QAP problem by exact method for less than instance size 20, but as size of the instance increases solving QAP become more and more time consuming.

The most common approach for solving QAP using metaheuristics is, first we take the input data, as distance and flow matrices elements. After that we generated initial solution randomly, and from each initial solution, we generated all possible neighbor solution. Then we evaluate the cost of each neighbor solution using our objective function then we compared the cost of neighbor solution with the present solution. If that cost satisfies the objective function and improves their value then we considered that neighbor solution as present solution for next iteration of the metaheuristics. Metaheuristics algorithm will stop when it reaches termination criteria.

All the instances we have taken from standard online library QAPLIB [4]. This library is also available in website of QAPLIB. We mainly considered the *taillard* symmetric instances (type a) of size from 30 to 100 and *Nugent* instances of size from 14 to 30 for solving QAP using CSA metaheuristics.

For solving QAP using CSA some initial parameters are fixed like flight length and awareness probability (AP). Using AP search space is changing. By increasing and decreasing the value of AP will cause the search space exploration oriented that is explore the search space and exploitation oriented that is search in local region. For solving QAP in serial machine we have taken random initial solution which is generated on CPU. In each iteration we generated the neighbor solution by considering each initial solution serially. For neighbor solution generation we used adjacent pair wise exchange method that is if the size of solution is n then we will get $\binom{n}{2}$ neighbor solution. Then evaluate the neighbor solution using evaluation function. Among all these neighbor solution cost we find the best optimal cost of neighbor solution and that solution is considered as an initial memory for each crow corresponding to each initial solution. Each crow updating their memory as the number of iteration increases, and when the termination condition reached then, among all crows memory we find the best crow memory which is best optimal cost of the QAP. We have taken flight length 2, awareness probability 0.15, fixed number of iteration as 5000 for each solution.

6.2   CSA Using p-thread

Here for implementing on p-thread first we divide the number of initial solutions in available processors so that each processor will get the equal number of solutions and run the maximum number of fixed iteration and finally update the each crow memory. All processors starts running parallelly and inside each processor crow search algorithm running serially. When all processors completed their execution we get the best updated crow memory among all crows which gives the best optimal solution.

6.3   CSA on GPU Accelerated Machine

Metaheuristics implementation on massively parallel architecture requires huge effort at design and implementation level. For effective implementation on GPU three main issues must be considered- 1) communication among CPU and GPU is efficient so that transfer of data is minimized, 2) control of parallelization, such that efficient number of thread generated and mapped with data input, and 3) memory management of GPU is efficiently where required operation can be done on best suitable memory.

By parallelizing the metaheuristics for solving any combinatorial optimization problem like QAP, gives the huge performance effect on accelerated machine. Three major parallel design of meta-heuristics are classified by E. G. Talbi [12] which is: solution level, iteration level and algorithmic level. For running a program in GPU there are mainly three steps required: *first* copy the input data from CPU to GPU that is from host to device, *second* evaluate the results on GPU and last *third* send the computed result back from device to host that is copy results from GPU to CPU.

In GPU implementation of CSA, we firstly fixed the required initial parameters. Then we evaluated the assignment cost of each initial solution on CPU, and from each initial solution using adjacent pair wise exchange method, we generated neighbor solution, and the assignment cost of each neighbor solution is evaluated on GPU. Now for every initial solution, we find the best possible neighbor solution optimal cost, which will set to the memory for each crow, corresponding to each initial solution. Now the crow search algorithm starts running on CPU for find the next position of the crow, and evaluate the newly positioned solution cost, and compared with existing solution which is stored in their memory, if it gives best optimal solution then update memory of corresponding crow. CSA will continue to run until it reaches the terminating condition. Finally we find the best optimal solution cost among all crows memory and reported in Table 1 for taillard symmetric instances and in Table 2 for *Nugent* instances. The modified algorithm for CSA is described in algorithm 1.

Algorithm 1. Crow search algorithm (CSA) On GPU

Input: Distance matrix and Flow matrix
Output: Best optimal solution found.

1: Initialize the position of all crows randomly of flock size N in a search space
2: Evaluate the crows position
3: Initialize the each crow memory
4: Set initial parameters for CSA
5: Generate and evaluate neighbor solution on GPU
6: Update the memory for each crow with best neighbor solution cost
7: **while** $t < t_{max}$ **do**
8:     **for** $i = 1 : N$ **do**
9:         Among flock of size N randomly choose one of the crows to follow crows (for example j)
10:        Define an awareness probability
11:        **if** $r_j > AP^{j,t}$ **then**
12:            $x^{i,t+1} = x^{i,t} + r_i \times f_l^{i,t} \times (m^{j,t} - x^{i,t})$
13:        **else**
14:            $x^{i,t+1} =$ a random position in search space
15:        Check the new positions feasibility
16:        Evaluate the crows new position
17:        Update the crows memory

---

7 Experimental Results

7.1 Comparison on Serial, p-thread, and on GPU

In this paper we have taken *taillard* symmetric instances of size between 30 and 100 and *Nugent* instances of size between 14 and 30. For each *taillard* and *Nugent* instances we find the optimal assignment cost of QAP by using CSA metaheuristics in serial, p-thread and in GPU machine. We observed the percentage deviation of optimal cost from standard QAPLIB library for each taillard and Nugent instances and also execution time on CPU, p-thread and on GPU. Percentage deviation is calculated using $\frac{(ObtainedCost-QAPLIBCost)}{QAPLIBCost} * 100$. The percentage deviation from QAPLIB and execution time for taillard instances are observed in Table 1 and for Nugent instances in Table 2. In Table 1, we can see that execution time for *tai100a* instances on CPU is 4.868 s, on p-thread 4.345 s and on GPU is 0.5 s. Here we can see that GPU performs approximately 10 times faster than CPU. Also as the size of instances increases, speedup on GPU is also increases. In Table 2 for Nugent instances, execution time on p-thread is taking more time from CPU because of large overhead for creating and initializing the posix thread of small size instances. Here we can also see that for

Table 1. Percentage deviation and exec. time of QAP using CSA by taking taillard instances

Instance	CPU		Pthread		GPU	
	Deviation (%)	Exec. time	Deviation (%)	Exec. time	Deviation (%)	Exec. time
tai30a	0.71	0.152	13.58	0.694	14.79	0.144
tai35a	2.95	0.531	13.98	0.849	16.73	0.178
tai40a	15.72	1.027	14.55	0.838	15.80	0.193
tai50a	8.84	0.336	14.70	1.021	16.25	0.256
tai60a	15.45	2.200	14.25	1.955	15.49	0.290
tai80a	13.56	3.300	12.56	3.496	13.19	0.394
tai100a	12.81	4.868	11.75	4.345	12.53	0.500

Table 2. Percentage deviation and exec. time of QAP using CSA by taking Nugent instances

Instance	CPU		Pthread		GPU	
	Deviation (%)	Exec. time	Deviation (%)	Exec. time	Deviation (%)	Exec. time
Nug14	17.58	0.122	10.16	0.234	15.63	0.071
Nug15	21.91	0.112	14.26	0.268	13.57	0.130
Nug16a	14.97	0.228	11.93	0.288	17.39	0.166
Nug16b	22.42	0.185	11.45	0.300	21.77	0.207
Nug17	15.47	0.202	14.78	0.288	17.44	0.085
Nug18	25.85	0.174	15.65	0.313	20.62	0.091
Nug20	25.76	0.100	13.70	0.328	16.26	0.174
Nug21	29.29	0.299	20.26	0.427	23.95	0.260
Nug22	5.00	0.290	18.79	0.488	24.42	0.263
Nug24	29.39	0.241	18.75	0.472	23.51	0.254
Nug25	20.46	0.130	16.03	0.569	19.71	0.195
Nug27	22.68	0.402	19.03	0.565	22.54	0.216
Nug28	18.35	0.506	18.08	0.500	21.52	0.172
Nug30	7.81	0.396	19.40	0.646	22.70	0.162

some of the Nugent instances of size less than 20, *Nug20,Nug16b,and Nug15* on GPU is taking more time than CPU because of overhead for GPU set-up and initialization of parameters. In Fig. 1 we can see that for large size instances like-*tai100a* speedup increases because of less overhead in GPU. From Fig. 2 we can see that because instance size is less so overhead for initializing the p-thread and GPU device is taking more time.

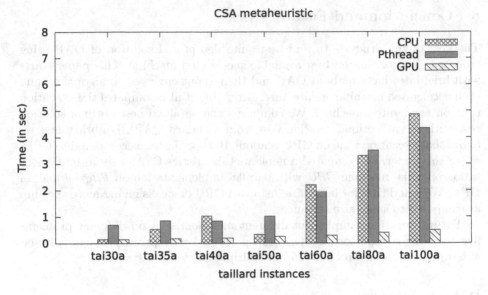

Fig. 1. Speed up for CSA Metaheuristics for taillard instances

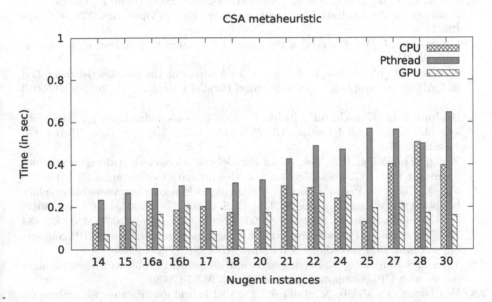

Fig. 2. Speed up for CSA Metaheuristics for Nugent instances

8   Conclusion and Future Work

The goal of this study is to find best suitable optimal solution of QAP using crow search algorithm on best available accelerated machine. This paper starts with brief introduction about QAP and then about crow search algorithm, and then accelerated machine architecture. After that it also compares the execution time on accelerated machine. We compared the obtained best optimal solution cost with recent optimal solution cost from standard QAPLIB library and we found that execution time on GPU is about 10 times faster as compared to CPU.

In this paper, we compared a noble metaheuristics CSA of serial implementation on serial machine *CPU* with parallel implementation on *Pthread* and on *GPU*. We found that for large size instances GPU device is giving more speedup as compared to small size instances.

Future work is to implement different metaheuristics on different problems like traveling salesperson problem [13], permuted perceptron problem [14] and weistrass continuous problem [15] on multiple accelerated systems.

References

1. Loiola, E.M., de Abreu, N.M.M., Boaventura-Netto, P.O., Hahn, P., Querido, T.: A survey for the quadratic assignment problem. Eur. J. Oper. Res. **176**, 657–690 (2007)
2. Commander, C.W.: A survey of the quadratic assignment problem, with applications (2005)
3. Abdelkafi, O., Idoumghar, L., Lepagnot, J.: A survey on the metaheuristics applied to QAP for the graphics processing units. Parallel Process. Lett. **26**(03), 1650013 (2016)
4. Burkard, R.E., Karisch, S.E., Rendl, F.: QAPLIB- a quadratic assignment problem library. J. Global Optim. **13**, 391–403 (1997). https://doi.org/10.1023/A:1008293323270
5. Wong, M.L., Wong, T.T., Fok, K.-L.: Parallel evolutionary algorithms on graphics processing unit. In: 2005 IEEE Congress Evolutionary Computation (2015)
6. Yu, Q., Chen, C., Pan, Z.: Parallel genetic algorithms on programmable graphics hardware. In: Wang, L., Chen, K., Ong, Y.S. (eds.) ICNC 2005. LNCS, vol. 3612, pp. 1051–1059. Springer, Heidelberg (2005). https://doi.org/10.1007/11539902_134
7. Zhu, W.: A study of parallel evolution strategy: pattern search on a GPU computing platform. In: Proceedings of the First ACM/SIGEVO (2009)
8. Tsutsui, S., Fujimoto, N.: Solving quadratic assignment problems by genetic algorithms with GPU computation: a case study. ACM (2009)
9. Van Luong, T., Melab, N., Talbi, E.: Parallel hybrid evolutionary algorithms on GPU. In: 2010 IEEE Congress Evolutionary Computation (CEC)
10. Askarzadeh, A.: A novel metaheuristic method for solving constrained engineering optimization problems: crow search algorithm. J. Comput. Struct. **169**, 112 (2016)
11. Vajda, A.: Multi-core and many-core processor architectures. In: Programming Many-Core Chips. Springer, Boston (2011). https://doi.org/10.1007/978-1-4419-9739-5_2
12. Talbi, E.G.: Metaheuristics: From Design to Implementation. Wiley (2009)

13. Dorigo, M., Gambardella, L.M.: Ant colony system: a cooperative learning approach to the traveling salesman problem. IEEE Trans. Evol. Comput. **1**, 53–66 (1997)
14. Pointcheval, D.: A new identification scheme based on the perceptrons problem. In: Guillou, L.C., Quisquater, J.-J. (eds.) EUROCRYPT 1995. LNCS, vol. 921, pp. 319–328. Springer, Heidelberg (1995). https://doi.org/10.1007/3-540-49264-X_26
15. Lutton, E., Vehel, J.L.: Holder functions and deception of genetic algorithms. IEEE Trans. Evol. Comput. **2**(2), 56–71 (1998)

Speech Signal Analysis for Language Identification Using Tensors

Shubham Jain⬦, Bhagath Parabattina(✉)⬦, and Pradip Kumar Das⬦

IIT Guwahati, North Amingaon, Guwahati 781039, Assam, India
{jain18,bhagath.2014,pkdas}@iitg.ac.in

Abstract. Language detection is the first step in speech recognition systems. It helps these systems to use grammar and semantics of a language in a better way. Due to these reasons, active research is being carried out in language identification. Every language has specific sound patterns, rhythm, tone, nasal features, etc. We have proposed an approach based on Tensor that uses MFCCs for determining the characteristic features of a language that can be used to identify a spoken language. Tensor based algorithms perform quite well for higher dimensions and scale quite well as compared to classic maximum likelihood estimation (MLE) used in latent variable modeling. Also, this approaches does not suffer from slow convergence and require fewer data points for learning. We have conducted language identification experiments on native Indian English and Hindi for some chosen speakers, and an accuracy of around 70% is observed.

Keywords: Language identification · Tensor analysis · MFCC

1 Introduction

Automatic Language Identification system aim is to identify a language from a speech signal of limited time duration. The language is to be identified from a finite set of languages.

Every language is a combination of some dialects. These dialects are specific to particular language and they share close grammatical and phonological systems with very similar vocabulary. At present, more than 7000 languages are identified comprising of nearabout 10000 dialects in world [1]. There are various linguistic factors like sentence length, stress, intonation that vary in different languages. They influence the speaking style that adds complexity to the language identification problem.

Language identification can also help to understand and know the background of a speaker without any prior information. This helps in systems like speaker verification and identification as the search space can be limited to a particular language.

In a multilingual country like India, people from different region speaks different languages. Here, automatic language identification system act as a medium

A. Bhattacharjee et al. (Eds.): MIND 2020, CCIS 1241, pp. 296–309, 2020.
https://doi.org/10.1007/978-981-15-6318-8_25

to simplify several existing processes. India is a growing nation where many service providers in different fields depend on automated services. In this context, identifying the language of the user helps to improve the services by providing service in their native language. In this way, the mean time to complete a call can be reduced significantly.

Quick Language identification can be useful in case of an emergency as it is always the case that in case of distress, a person prefers to speak in his/her native language. In current scenario, humans are trained to interpret the language and redirect calls, but tremendous responsibility is placed on them. If automatic language identification could be made fast and accurate, it could aid human operators.

Now-a-days, voice-based instruments like Google's Echo [10], Amazon's Alexa [9] have become household members. For the best customer experience, these devices can be tuned to detect the spoken language and subsequently grammar and semantic rules can be used for subsequent recognition of phonemes.

Each language has different prosodic features like intonation, stress, rhythm, etc. Language has its phonological units that are combined to form words. Languages differ in the way these phonological units are arranged and the frequency in which they occur. Understanding and exploitation of these differences is a key to language identification.

There are several methods proposed to identify the language of spoken speech. The machine learning algorithms include Deep Neural Networks (DNNs) [2], Hidden Markov Models (HMMs) [14], Support Vector Machines (SVMs) [6] and Gaussian Mixture Models (GMMs) [12]. Language characterization can be achieved using GMMs as it provides a relaxed approach to model a given language. The parameter estimation of GMM is usually done with Expectation Maximization (EM) [3]. EM method is based on the maximum likelihood ratio and is thus NP-hard. Also, this might get stuck in a local maximum and consume time to converge.

We explore the use of tensors for the language identification problem. Tensor [4] is simply a combination of arrays in which the elements can be numbers (features), functions that can transform according to certain rules specified. Thus tensor allows to represent data in a specific multidimensional form and gives the capability to reorder them accordingly. The multidimensional nature of tensors helps to analyze the latent features of the data.

This method has been used in domains like computer vision effectively. Tensor-based estimation algorithms for latent variable models like GMM are fast, consistent and can be executed in parallel. A method based on tensors is proposed to solve the problem of language identification.

2 Related Work

In recent decades, immense progress in language recognition has been made. This advancement is due to technological improvement in fields such as pattern recognition, signal processing and neural networks. At present state-of-the-art language recognition systems mainly comes into two categories: token-sequence-based and spectral approaches [15].

The main idea in Token sequence based approach is to identify the tokens which subsequently can be used to model different languages. A token can be a single feature vector, phoneme or a lexical word and may vary in size. It is also defined to describe a distinct acoustic phonetic activity.

Spectral-based methods for determination of language works by extracting measurements of the short-term speech spectrum over fixed frames (in contrast to token based) analysis and then modeling characteristics of these measurements, or features, for each language to be recognized.

Current state-of-the-art language identification systems use classifier based on Gaussian Mixture models (GMMs) or Support vector machines (SVM).

Among the various methods used for phone-tokenization, GMM tokenization technique operates at the frame level. It converts a sequence of speech frames into a sequence of Gaussian labels, each of which gives rise to the highest likelihood of the speech frame. GMM tokenizers [18] with 6 languages give an error rate of 17%.

SVMs [6] rely on separating data in high dimensions using margin and planes concept. SVM kernels provide a method for comparing sequences of feature vectors. SVM kernel is responsible for providing discrimination between two different languages. Given feature vectors from two samples, kernel produces a comparison that provides discrimination between the languages of the utterances.

Deep Neural Networks has gained much popularity in the past few years. [5] have proposed ALI system that solves problem of language identification in the image domain. A Hybrid Convolutional Recurrent Neural Network (CRNN) that operates on spectrogram images of the input audio samples is used for training and testing. The system gave 90% accuracy for 4 different languages.

[11] obtained accuracy of 68% for seven Indian languages using phonotactic as well as prosodic information. They used feature vectors that are obtained by concatenating the features of three consecutive syllables. A feed-forward neural network classifier is used at the back-end for obtaining the language identity of the given speech utterance.

3 Theoretical Background

The preliminary concepts of tensor analysis are described in this section.

3.1 Tensor Order

Tensor order is the number of dimensions. Scalars numbers are zeroth-order tensors, single dimension array are first-order tensors, and two dimension array (matrices) are second-order tensors as shown in Fig. 1. A pth order tensor is an object that is interpreted as a p-dimensional array. We can have tensor of any order, but we are focusing on third order tensor structure in our experiments.

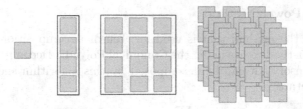

Fig. 1. Zeroth order tensor ($a \in \mathbb{R}$), 1st order tensor ($a \in \mathbb{R}^4$), 2nd order tensor ($A \in \mathbb{R}^{4 \times 3}$), 3rd order tensor ($\mathcal{A} \in \mathbb{R}^{4 \times 3 \times 5}$)

3.2 Outer and Inner Product

It is the element-wise product of two vectors which in turn generates a second-order tensor [13]. This operation is denoted by the ⊙ symbol Outer product of two n-sized vector is given by Eq. 1:

$$A = a \odot b = ab^T \tag{1}$$

The inner product of two vectors will lead to a scalar:

$$a = a^T b = \sum_{i=1}^{n} a_i b_i \tag{2}$$

3.3 Tensor Rank

Minimum number of rank-1 N order tensors that are needed which sum up to N order Tensor is defined as rank of N-order Tensor. If we can disintegrate an N order Tensor into an outer product of N vectors, then we say that the rank of that Tensor is 1 [13].

3.4 Tensor Decomposition

Breaking down objects into more straightforward and easy to handle pieces is a core base for decomposition. For tensor decomposition, two broad techniques are used - the Canonical Polyadic Decomposition (CPD) and the Tucker Decomposition. CPD [13] is mainly used for latent(hidden) parameter estimation and Tucker decomposition aims at dimensionality reduction. We have focused on CPD for our work.

3.5 Tensor Uniqueness and Rigidness

We can say that tensor decomposition using any of the above mentioned method is unique whenever there exists only one single combination of rank-1 tensors that sum to X(Tensor that is being decomposed) up to a common scaling factor. In other words there is one and only one decomposition into rank-1 tensor possible. The uniqueness of tensor decomposition is under much milder conditions than matrix decomposition [13].

3.6   Tensor Power Method

This is one of the method that is used for Tensor decomposition into simpler form and the method comes under the Canonical Polyadic Decomposition (CPD) family. The tensor that can be decomposed by this algorithm should have the following structure:

$$\mathcal{A} = \sum_{i=1}^{R} \lambda a_i \odot a_i \odot a_i \tag{3}$$

Here a_i and λ denotes eigenvector and eigenvalue respectively. In this special case, the factor matrices have to be identical and all a_i's needs to be orthogonal. It is very much similar to matrix power method. While the latter finds out singular vectors in the matrix, the former deals with top singular vector in tensors [13].

4   Proposed Method

An uttered sound of speech is a collection of feature vectors. Some of these vectors contains information that represent language characteristic while other forms the content of the speech. If we collect feature vectors of sentences in English and form a feature vector space from those, we shall get a vector space dominated by the factors of the English language. That is also true for Hindi. Now for a test utterance if there is a similar feature vector in either of two languages, we can infer the language of the utterance. The following section discuss about feature vector space generation of each language and the computation of language model vectors.

4.1   Pre-processing

The dataset we have gathered contains samples that have been recorded in different environments and contains background, unwanted and hardware noise. We have applied Normalization and DC shift for each sample of the training and testing recordings. DC shift is done to eradicate hardware system recording shift. Normalization is done to make sure that the maximum amplitude in each utterance is at same level so that each utterance is similar to other with respect to the environment.

4.2   Features Extraction

The performance and accuracy of a system depends heavily on the parameter extracted from the speech signal. We have used MFCC [7] (Mel-frequency cepstral coefficients) as they are most effective. MFCCs are based on the principle of the human's auditory system. These features concisely describe the overall shape of a spectral envelope. In MFCC, the frequency bands are equally spaced over the Mel scale (not linear) in contrast to linearly scaled band. Due to this non linearity these features more closely approximates the human auditory system's response.

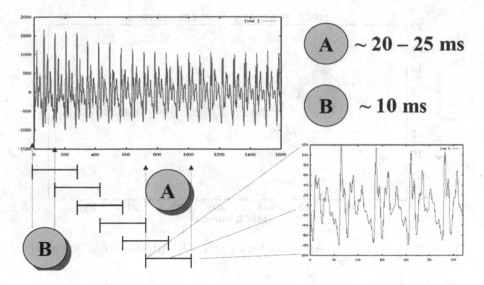

Fig. 2. Windowing

We have extracted these features from the speech samples considering a window size of 25 ms and overlapping of 10 ms for every training and testing sample segment (see Fig. 2). We have used total of 39 MFCC features (12 cepstral + 1(energy of frame) + 13 delta to capture changes in features from the previous frame to the next frame(velocity coefficient) + 13 that captures the dynamic changes of velocity coefficient from the last frame to the next frame). Delta coefficient are calculated using:

$$d_t = \frac{\sum_{i=1}^{N} i(c_{t+i} - c_{t-i})}{2\sum_{i=1}^{N} i^2} \tag{4}$$

Here d_t denotes delta (velocity) coefficient, from frame t. This is computed in terms of the static coefficients c_{t+N} to c_{t-N}. We have used N as 2. Delta-Delta (Acceleration) coefficients are calculated in similar manner, but they are calculated from the deltas coefficients, not the static coefficients (Fig. 3).

4.3 Refined Feature

Standard features extraction technique like Linear Predictive Cepstral Coefficient (LPCCs) [17], MFCC [7] gives a very good estimate of a spoken utterance, but these are not enough to capture the characteristics of a spoken language. Thus we need to convert the standard features into a useful feature set that we can feed to our model. We have focused on using Shifted Delta Coefficients (SDC) [16]. Shifted Delta operation allows us to extract pseudo prosodic features of a speech without having actually to model the structure and envelope of the speech signal. SDC captures long-term temporal features. They reflect the

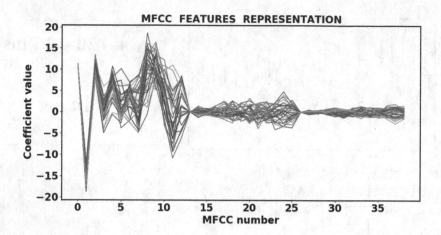

Fig. 3. 39 MFCC features representation for a "Hindi" utterance (first 30 frames).

dynamic characteristics of the spectral features. This shifting process is applied to MFCCs. The SD coefficients are useful due to the incorporation of multiple frames within a single feature vector. The process of applying the shifted Delta cepstral coefficient is as follows:

- First, all MFCCs are calculated by the usual method [7].
- Select N - Number of features for a single frame.
- Select D - represents delay and time advance for the delta computation.
- Select P - Distance between blocks (the gap between successive delta computation).
- Select K - It is the number of consecutive blocks stacked together to form a SDC vector.

The SDC vector at frame time t and block multiple n is given by:

$$\Delta C(t, n) = C(t + nP + D) - C(t + nP - D) \tag{5}$$

Feature vectors that are present D sample frames apart are differenced. After that we shift by P block. Again the feature vectors those are present D sample frames apart are differenced. This process is continued till we reach the end of the feature vector. Now group of K vectors that are obtained are stacked together to form new shifted Delta Feature Vector as shown:

$$SDC(t) = \begin{pmatrix} \Delta C(t, 0) \\ \Delta C(t, 1) \\ \Delta C(t, 2) \\ \cdot \\ \cdot \\ \Delta C(t, K-1) \end{pmatrix} \tag{6}$$

4.4   3D Feature Representation

The feature vectors obtained needs to be converted into 3rd order tensor; this is done by method of moments. The first moment is the mean, which is given by:

$$M_1 = \mu = E[x] = \frac{1}{N} \sum_{i=1}^{N} x_i \tag{7}$$

where N represent number of feature vectors in each language set.

Second ordinal moment is given by:

$$M_2 = E[x \odot x] - \sigma^2 I \tag{8}$$

where σ^2 smallest eigenvalue of the covariance matrix ($\Sigma = E[x \otimes x] - M_1 \odot M_1$) and I is the Identity matrix ($I \in \mathbb{R}^{d \times d}$). Similarly the third ordinal moment can be computed as:

$$M_3 = E[x \odot x \odot x] - \sigma^2 \sum_{i=1}^{d} (M_1 \odot e_i \odot e_i \\ + e_i \odot M_1 \odot e_i + e_i \odot e_i \odot M_1) \tag{9}$$

where e_i is the basis vector in i^{th} dimension.

[8] represent these moments using reduction in the following forms:

$$M_2 = \sum_{i=1}^{p} w_i a_i \odot a_i \tag{10}$$

$$M_3 = \sum_{i=1}^{p} w_i a_i \odot a_i \odot a_i \tag{11}$$

Thus M_3 is the scaled sum of p eigenvectors (a_i). We need to find the k dominant eigenvectors which are responsible for language property of the speaker.

4.5   Model Creation

Once we have the 3rd order tensor, tensor power method (described in Sect. 3) is applied to obtain dominant vector for each language and these vectors act as our saved model. Flow diagram of the proposed method is illustrated in Fig. 4.

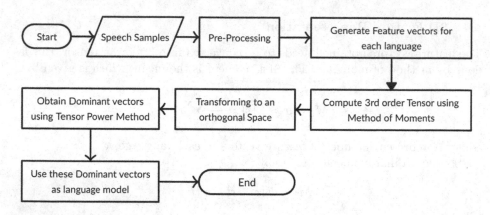

Fig. 4. Flow diagram of model creation

4.6   Model Testing

Vectors obtained from the above steps are used as reference model for English and Hindi language represented by L_E and L_H respectively.

For testing an unknown voice sample, distance between the dominant vector and feature vector of unknown sample is calculated. The language vector that gives minimum distance is reported as identified language.

$$D_i = \min_k \left(\sum_{j=1}^{d} (a_{kj} - x_{ij})^2 \right) \qquad (12)$$

Total distance from L_E and L_H can be computed using Eq. 13 and 14.

$$\mathcal{D}_E = \sum_{i=1}^{N} D_i \qquad (13)$$

$$\mathcal{D}_H = \sum_{i=1}^{N} D_i \qquad (14)$$

where N is total number of feature vectors (number of frames) for a voice.

Features vectors collected from English voice will be having more vectors which are affected by English dominant vectors, whereas it will be less affected by the other language (Hindi) dominant vectors. Thus $\mathcal{D}_E$ will be less than $\mathcal{D}_H$ for the English sample.

4.7   Algorithm Overview

Now that we are familiar with all the steps, we will give an overview of parameter estimation in our model.

- **Moment Calculation:** Once we have feature vectors for our language, we used method of moment to find model formulation in which the latent parameter are responsible for these moments.
- **Whiten the Data:** Obtaining second and third moment of our data is not sufficient to extract the latent information from these moments. This is because the vector producing these moments might not be orthogonal, which is the necessary condition to apply tensor power method. Thus orthogonalization (whiten) of third moment is done.
- **Decompose whiten tensor:** By using tensor power method, we can extract the latent factors v_is present in the whitened moment tensor.
- **Un-whiten the v_i's:** The resulting (latent) factors are obtained in whitened space. We tranform them back to original space by applying the inversion of the whitening transformation.

5   Dataset and Libraries

To realize our task of language identification we have collected speech samples of two languages from 30 people whose age lies between 20–25. Each person has spoken in English and Hindi. The dataset contains around 6000 recordings of English and Hindi with equal distribution of both gender speakers. Each recordings is of at least 5 seconds with inclusion of foreign words to make sure our system does not use some specific words for identification. 16-bit precision, 16 KHz sampling rate with mono channel output is used for storing the audio samples. Dataset can be accessed here[1].

We have implemented our proposed method in Python 3.6.7 with Ubuntu 18.10 environment, major libraries used are Numpy, Pandas, Seaborn, Matplotlib, Python_speech_features, Math, Scipy and Sklearn.

6   Experimental Setup and Results Analysis

We have carried out experiment with single speaker and with multiple speaker considering only two languages English and Hindi. All experiments are conducted using data-set collected. For single speaker experiments, we chose 5 speakers randomly, the training and testing for each speaker is done independently taking one speaker at a time. 90% utterances of single speaker are used for training and rest 10% for testing. We have used the configuration 7-1-3-7 for N-D-P-K while extracting SDC features. For every frame, MFCC coefficients along with 49 SDC coefficients are appended. We used these features for model creation. The accuracy was around 58%. Tabular representation is in Table 1 and the graphical representation is in Fig. 5.

In another experiment we used two speaker data for training in pair (speaker1 - English) (speaker2 - Hindi) with different speaker speaking different language, one speaks English and other Hindi, the accuracy was slightly more implying our model is capturing speaker characteristic along with the language. Thus we experimented with sufficient mixed data to rule out the above implication.

---

[1] http://bit.ly/lowResourceSpeechDataset.

Table 1. Accuracy for 5 randomly chosen speakers

Spk No.	Accuracy %		
	English	Hindi	Average
1	71	81	76
2	56	56	56
3	50	50	50
4	70	52	61
5	53	45	49
Average			58.4%

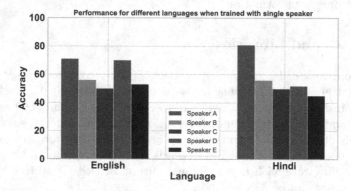

Fig. 5. Performance for different languages when trained with single speaker

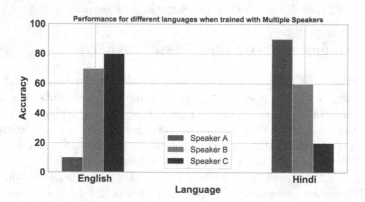

Fig. 6. Performance for different languages when trained with multiple speakers

When mixed data is provided as input to our model (30 speakers, 2 languages mixed), the training is done on 85% of data and rest 15% is used for testing. The overall accuracy of system was around 56%. On analysis of speech utterances, we figured out that accuracy was varying according to the speaker. For some of the speaker the system is able to recognize language 70% of the time but for other, distinction is not good in Fig. 6, the accuracy of 3 speakers is represented), thus bringing the overall accuracy down.

We then selected the speakers that were giving fairly good accuracy and then trained our model on this dataset. The accuracy obtained in this experiment came out to be 70.41%. These results are tabulated in Table 2.

These result imply that language characteristics are captured properly in our model and feeding speech utterance data of relatively good speakers to our model leads to good results. Overall experimentation is summarized in Table 3.

Table 2. Performance of system for 6 chosen speakers

Spk No.	Accuracy %		
	English	Hindi	Average
1	68.75	75	71.875
2	72.5	71.25	71.875
3	73.75	73.75	73.75
4	68.75	71.25	70
5	70	67.5	68.75
6	65	67.5	66.25
Average			70.41%

Table 3. Overall recognition summary

Speakers	Accuracy %		
	English	Hindi	Average
Single speaker	60	56.8	58.4
Multiple speakers	53	56	54.5
Chosen speaker	69.79	71.04	70.41

7 Conclusions and Future Work

We have proposed a tensor-based method to identify the language of spoken utterance. In order to carry out our experiment on native language we have gathered audio data for more than 40 speakers. A model for language identification system based on third order tensor and its decomposition which uses 39 MFCC and default SDC features is trained and tested. The similarity in voice origin, accent and overlapping phoneme sets imposes significant challenge in developing LID system. We have observed through experiments that; when multiple speakers are used the obtained accuracy is not satisfactory. For some speakers, language is being appropriately classified, but it is failing for other speakers. Also when tested with good chosen speakers, we were able to get satisfactory results, implying our dataset needs to be improved.

We are currently focusing on using modified coefficients to include information like intonation, stress and rhythm in speech and envisage to improve the accuracy by considering more language-specific features into the speech modeling process.

References

1. How many languages are there in the world in 2020? (surprising results). https://www.theintrepidguide.com/how-many-languages-are-there-in-the-world/#.Xlj1vHUzZuQ. Accessed 28 Feb 2020
2. Albawi, S., Mohammed, T.A., Al-Zawi, S.: Understanding of a convolutional neural network. In: 2017 International Conference on Engineering and Technology (ICET), pp. 1–6, August 2017. https://doi.org/10.1109/ICEngTechnol.2017.8308186
3. Biemond, J., Lagendijk, R.L.: The expectation-maximization (EM) algorithm applied to image identification and restoration. In: Proceedings of the ICCON IEEE International Conference on Control and Applications, pp. 231–235, April 1989. https://doi.org/10.1109/ICCON.1989.770513
4. Boyajian, A.: The tensor - a new engineering tool. Electr. Eng. **55**(8), 856–862 (1936). https://doi.org/10.1109/EE.1936.6539021
5. Bartz, C., Herold, T., Yang, H., Meinel, C.: Language identification using deep convolutional recurrent neural networks. arXiv preprint arXiv:1708.04811 (2017)
6. Hearst, M.A., Dumais, S.T., Osuna, E., Platt, J., Scholkopf, B.: Support vector machines. IEEE Intell. Syst. Appl. **13**(4), 18–28 (1998). https://doi.org/10.1109/5254.708428
7. Hossan, M.A., Memon, S., Gregory, M.A.: A novel approach for MFCC feature extraction. In: 2010 4th International Conference on Signal Processing and Communication Systems, pp. 1–5, December 2010. https://doi.org/10.1109/ICSPCS.2010.5709752
8. Hsu, D., Kakade, S.M.: Learning mixtures of spherical Gaussians: moment methods and spectral decompositions. In: Proceedings of the 4th Conference on Innovations in Theoretical Computer Science, ITCS 2013, pp. 11–20. ACM, New York (2013). https://doi.org/10.1145/2422436.2422439. http://doi.acm.org/10.1145/2422436.2422439
9. Lei, X., Tu, G.H., Liu, A.X., Li, C.Y., Xie, T.: The insecurity of home digital voice assistants-Amazon Alexa as a case study. arXiv preprint arXiv:1712.03327 (2017)
10. López, G., Quesada, L., Guerrero, L.A.: Alexa vs. Siri vs. Cortana vs. Google assistant: a comparison of speech-based natural user interfaces. In: Nunes, I. (ed.) AHFE 2017. AISC, vol. 592, pp. 241–250. Springer, Cham (2017). https://doi.org/10.1007/978-3-319-60366-7_23
11. Madhu, C., George, A., Mary, L.: Automatic language identification for seven Indian languages using higher level features. In: 2017 IEEE International Conference on Signal Processing, Informatics, Communication and Energy Systems (SPICES), pp. 1–6, August 2017. https://doi.org/10.1109/SPICES.2017.8091332

12. Mohamed, O.M.M., Jaïdane-Saïdane, M.: Generalized Gaussian mixture model. In: 2009 17th European Signal Processing Conference, pp. 2273–2277, August 2009
13. Rabanser, S., Shchur, O., Günnemann, S.: Introduction to tensor decompositions and their applications in machine learning. arXiv preprint arXiv:1711.10781 (2017)
14. Rabiner, L., Juang, B.: An introduction to hidden Markov models. IEEE ASSP Mag. **3**(1), 4–16 (1986). https://doi.org/10.1109/MASSP.1986.1165342
15. Reynolds, D.A., Campbell, W.M., Shen, W., Singer, E.: Automatic language recognition via spectral and token based approaches. In: Benesty, J., Sondhi, M.M., Huang, Y.A. (eds.) Springer Handbook of Speech Processing. SH, pp. 811–824. Springer, Heidelberg (2008). https://doi.org/10.1007/978-3-540-49127-9_41
16. Sinha, S., Jain, A., Agrawal, S.S.: Fusion of multi-stream speech features for dialect classification. CSI Trans. ICT **2**(4), 243–252 (2015). https://doi.org/10.1007/s40012-015-0063-y
17. Tierney, J.: A study of LPC analysis of speech in additive noise. IEEE Trans. Acoust. Speech Signal Process. **28**(4), 389–397 (1980). https://doi.org/10.1109/TASSP.1980.1163423
18. Torres-Carrasquillo, P.A., Reynolds, D.A., Deller, J.R.: Language identification using gaussian mixture model tokenization. In: 2002 IEEE International Conference on Acoustics, Speech, and Signal Processing, vol. 1, pp. I-757–I-760, May 2002. https://doi.org/10.1109/ICASSP.2002.5743828

Effective Removal of Baseline Wander from ECG Signals: A Comparative Study

Deepankar Nankani[✉][iD] and Rashmi Dutta Baruah[iD]

Computer Science and Engineering Department, Indian Institute of Technology
Guwahati, Guwahati 781039, Assam, India
{d.nankani,r.duttabaruah}@iitg.ac.in

Abstract. Electrocardiogram (ECG) signal classification is an essential task to diagnose arrhythmia clinically. For effective ECG analyses, it has to be decluttered from embedded low and high frequency noise. Low frequency noise include baseline wander and high frequency noise include power line interference. We provide a comparative study for the task of baseline wander removal from ECG signals using different variants of Empirical Mode Decomposition, Median Filtering and Mean Median Filtering with a major emphasis on variational mode decomposition as it is a relatively new technique and much more robust towards noise. The comparison between the aforementioned techniques depicted that variational mode decomposition estimates better baseline as compared to other techniques in terms of pearson correlation, percentage root mean square difference and maximum absolute error. However, the time required to decompose the signal is relatively higher than the filtering techniques.

Keywords: Electrocardiogram · Baseline wander · Empirical Mode Decomposition · Variational Mode Decomposition

1 Introduction

Electrocardiogram (ECG) represents the electrical activity of the heart. It is useful in detecting irregularities in the heart rhythm that occur sporadically in the patient's daily life [24]. An ideal ECG wave constitutes a P-wave, a QRS-complex, and a T-wave that represents atrial depolarization, ventricular depolarization, and ventricular repolarization, respectively. Low-frequency noise caused due to Baseline Wander corrupt ECG recordings. Baseline Wander (BW) ranges between 0.5 ± 0.5 Hz frequency and is caused due to respiration or motion of the subject, dirty leads and improper skin contact of electrode. BW hinders the doctors in analyzing the ST segment as both of them have a similar frequency spectrum [1,8] and introduces a gradual increase in the amplitude of ECG signal, thereby degrading the PQRST morphology.

© Springer Nature Singapore Pte Ltd. 2020
A. Bhattacharjee et al. (Eds.): MIND 2020, CCIS 1241, pp. 310–324, 2020.
https://doi.org/10.1007/978-981-15-6318-8_26

1.1 Related Work

Baseline wander removal from ECG signal is not a new problem and has been studied in the past. Papaloukas et al. employed cubic spline curve fitting method for BW removal [21]. Filtering techniques [5,12,16,19,22,25] including Non linear filter banks [16], Median Filtering [5], Mean Median Filtering [12], adaptive filters [25] and combination of wavelet and adaptive filters known as Wavelet Adaptive Filtering (WAF) [22] have been also used to reduce distortion in ST segment which is highly affected by BW. Lifting-based discrete wavelet transform [7], statistical techniques like independent component analysis [10] have also been used to remove artefacts from ECG. Filtered residue [13], independent component analysis [2,10] have also been used for BW removal from ECG singals. BW removal from ECG signal has also been performed using empirical mode decomposition (EMD) and its variants [3,4,14,15,29,30]. EMD itself is unable to remove BW as it distorts the QRS complex and attenuates R-peak. So, different techniques were employed in addition to EMD including mathematical morphology [14], adaptive filter [30], and wavelet transform [15]. Ensemble EMD was also used to remove noise [4]. Complete ensemble EMD with adaptive noise and wavelet threshold [29] was also used to remove BW. In most of the aforementioned techniques, filtering, wavelet transform and EMD based methods are prevalent for BW removal. The techniques based on EMD and its variants provide comparatively better results but require a high execution time. EMD performs signal decomposition into high and low frequency components that are commonly known as Intrinsic Mode Function (IMF). High frequency component denotes the QRS complex and high frequency noise such as the interference from power sources. Low frequency components are P, T waves, ST segments and BW. Direct removal of higher order IMF ruptures the ST segment morphology. Hence, EMD is used in tandem with different techniques. The problem with wavelet transform is the requirement of the P, T wave morphology that is difficult to obtain and also the methods fail in the presence of other noises. Recently, variational mode decomposition (VMD) was also used for baseline wander estimation and removal by Prabhakararao et al. [23]. They reported that VMD is better for BW estimation as compared to EMD and DWT.

1.2 Our Contributions

We present a detailed analysis for an efficient estimation of BW using Variational Mode Decomposition. In addition to [23], we varied different parameters of VMD, namely, the bandwidth constraint and number of modes for better decomposition of the input signal into a clean signal and BW. A comparison between different variants of Empirical Mode Decomposition, filtering techniques, namely, median, mean median filtering, and Variational Mode Decomposition, is also performed for an effective estimation of BW. The comparison between the techniques depicted that VMD estimates better BW in terms of pearson correlation, percentage root mean square difference, and maximum absolute error with slightly higher execution time required to decompose the signal.

1.3   Paper Organization

The rest of the paper is organized as follows. Section 2 provides a brief description of EMD along with its different variants, VMD, and mean median filtering. Section 3 describes the experimental setup that includes system configuration, data description and evaluation metrics. Section 4 explains the results and discussion followed by Sect. 5 that concludes the paper with the future scope.

2   Brief Description of Techniques

A brief description of the techniques including Empirical Mode Decomposition, Ensemble Empirical Mode Decomposition, Complete Ensemble EMD with Adaptive Noise, Variational Mode Decomposition, and Mean-Median Filtering is provided in subsequent subsections.

2.1   Empirical Mode Decomposition

Empirical Mode Decomposition(EMD) [11] is a data-driven technique that decomposes a non stationary signal (generated from non linear systems) in narrowband monocomponent signals also called as IMFs. IMFs are zero mean amplitude modulated frequency modulated (AMFM) components. However, it is not guaranteed that an IMF consists of a single oscillatory mode, and neither a narrow band signal nor its meaningfulness due to its limitations. The algorithm to calculate EMD of signal $y(t)$ is described as follows:

1. Determine all local maxima $y_{max}(t)$ and local minima $y_{min}(t)$ for $y(t)$.
2. Interpolate $y_{max}(t)$ and $y_{min}(t)$ using cubic spline.
3. Calculate mean $m(t)$: $m(t) = (y_{max}(t) + y_{min}(t))/2$.
4. Calculate $d(t)$: $d(t) = y(t) - m(t)$.
5. Check if $d(t)$ is an IMF using the stopping criteria, if it satisfies the criteria then goto step 6 or else goto step 1.
6. The above procedure is called sifting. After obtaining the first IMF, subtract it from $y(t)$ and obtain the remaining signal. Perform sifting on the obtained signal until the residue persists any meaningful frequency information.
7. The final decomposed signal can be obtained as a sum of IMF's $d_n(t)$ and a residue $r_n(t)$ as provided in Eq. 1.

$$y(t) = \sum_{n=0}^{N} d_n(t) + r_n(t) \qquad (1)$$

2.2   Ensemble Empirical Mode Decomposition

The IMFs obtained using EMD suffers from oscillation with multiple frequencies in a single mode or single frequency in multiple modes. This problem is commonly known as "mode mixing". Adding multiple realizations of a specific amount of noise removes mode mixing by utlizing the dyadic filter bank behaviour of EMD [9]. This phenomenon was given by Wu et al. [27] and was termed as ensemble EMD (EEMD). EEMD decomposes the original signal for multiple ensembles of noise and produces the modes by averaging. EEMD of signal $y(t)$ is described as follows:

1. Generate a new input by adding multiple noise realizations of $N(\mu = 0, \sigma = 1)$.
2. Decompose each new input using EMD and obtain the IMF d_k^n.
3. Assign d_k as the kth IMF obtained from $y(t)$ by averaging the corresponding IMFs as given in Eq. 2

$$D_k = \frac{1}{I} \sum_{i=1}^{I} d_k{}^i \qquad (2)$$

Each pair of signal + noise is individually decomposed and their residue $r_k{}^i = r_k{}^{i-1} - d_k{}^i$ is obtained thereby eliminating the estimation of local means.

2.3 Complete Ensemble EMD Using Adaptive Noise

EEMD alleviates mode mixing problem but introduces the problem of residual noise that corresponds to the difference between reconstructed and original signal. Another problem is that the averaging of IMFs is difficult due to the fact that varying number of IMFs are generated by EEMD. This led to the development of CEEMDAN [26] that achieved not only negligible reconstruction error but also solved the problem of varying number of modes for different noise realizations. The basic intuition of CEEMDAN comes from the fact that it utilises all final modes generated by multiple noise realization of signal for the calculation of the next mode.

This estimates the local means of modes in an efficient and sequential manner for each noise realization. Suppose $E_k(.)$ generates k^{th} IMF via EMD, where $w^{(j)}$ has $N(\mu = 0, \sigma = 1)$. Then CEEMDAN on signal $y(t)$ is calculated as follows:

1. For every $j = \{1 \ldots J\}$, decompose each $y^{(j)} = y + \beta_0 w^{(j)}$ using EMD until the first CEEMDAN mode is obtained. Then compute $\overline{d_1} = \frac{1}{J} \sum_{j=1}^{J} d_1^{(j)}$.
2. Calculate first residue using $r_1 = y - \overline{d_1}$.
3. Generate first mode of $r_1 + \beta_1 E_1(w^{(j)})$ by EMD, where $j = \{1 \ldots J\}$ and calculate second CEEMDAN mode as $\overline{d_2} = \frac{1}{J} \sum_{j=1}^{J} E_1(r_1 + \beta_1 E_1(w^{(j)}))$.
4. For $k = \{1 \ldots K\}$ calculate the kth residue as $r_k = r_{(k-1)} - \overline{d_k}$.
5. Calculate first mode of $r_k + \beta_k E_k(w^{(j)})$ by EMD, where $j = \{1 \ldots J\}$ and calculate the $(k+1)^{th}$ CEEMDAN mode as $\overline{d_{(k+1)}} = \frac{1}{J} \sum_{j=1}^{J} E_1(r_k + \beta_k E_k(w^{(j)}))$.
6. Goto step 4 for the calculation of next mode k.

Iterate steps 4 to 6 until the residue satisfies IMF conditions or it has less than 3 local extremum points. The last residue satisfies: $r_K = y - \sum\limits_{k=1}^{K} \overline{d_k}$, where K is the number of IMFs. Therefore, the overall signal can be represented by Eq. 3.

$$x = \sum_{k=1}^{K} \overline{d_k} + r_K \tag{3}$$

Modes extracted using CEEMDAN provide exact reconstruction of the original signal. Final number of IMFs is solely determined by the data and the stopping criterion. However, CEEMDAN also suffers from residual noise as the signal information appears in higher order IMF as compared to EEMD and some "spurious" lower order modes [26]. Theoretical and mathematical literature still lacks in finding out the number of ensembles and the amplitude of noise to be added in order to boost performance.

2.4   Variational Mode Decomposition

Variational Mode Decomposition (VMD) [6] is also a data adaptive technique that generates the variational modes from multicomponent signal $y(t)$ in an entirely non recursive and concurrent fashion. The variational modes (u_k) are quasi orthogonal and bandlimited around center frequency (ω_k) that are capable to reproduce the input signal. VMD comprises of a strong mathematical framework. It uses the concepts of Wiener filtering, Fourier transform, Hilbert transform, analytic signal and the frequency shifting through harmonic mixing. The algorithm to decompose a signal via VMD is described as follows:

1. For each mode, the analytical signal is computed using the hilbert transform to acquire a unilateral frequency spectrum.
2. The spectrum of the obtained mode is mixed with an exponential that shifts it to an estimated center frequency.
3. The bandwidth of the mode is estimated through the squared norm of the demodulated signal.

The above procedure is performed until convergence. Mathematically, VMD can be calculated using Eq. 4.

$$\min_{\{y_k\},\{\omega_k\}} \left\{ \sum_k \left\| \partial_t \left[\left(\delta(t) + \frac{j}{\pi t} \right) * y_k(t) \right] e^{-j\omega_k t} \right\|_2^2 \right\} \ s.t. \sum_{k=1}^{K} y_k(t) = y(t) \tag{4}$$

where, $y(t)$ is the signal to be decomposed, u_k are the modes obtained after decomposition, ω_k is the center frequency of each mode, δ is the dirac distribution, t is the time, K is the number of modes and $*$ is the convolution operator.

2.5   Mean-Median Filtering

Mean-Median Filtering (MMF) [20] utilizes the convex combination of the sample median and sample mean of signal $y(t)$ as provided in Eq. 5.

$$MMF = (1 - \alpha) * mean(y(t)) + \alpha * median(y(t)) \tag{5}$$

where, $\alpha \in [0, 1]$ is the 'contamination factor'.

3   Experimental Setup

This section describes the system configuration, database used for experimental purposes, proposed workflow, and the evaluation metrics used for comparison of techniques.

3.1   System Configuration

The experiments are performed on a workstation with Intel i5-6500 CPU with a clock frequency of 3.2 GHz and 16 GB of RAM. The code was developed in Python language.

3.2   Dataset Description

MIT-BIH database [17, 18] is used for experimental purposes. It consists of 23 normal ECG and 25 arrhythmic recordings with sampling frequency of 360 Hz for two channels, namely, modified limb lead II (MLII), and V1. We have used MLII lead signal for experimental purposes.

Figure 1a represents a normal sinus rhythm from record 103 that is contaminated with BW and Fig. 1b represents the clean normal sinus rhythm (NSR). Similarly, Fig. 2a represents a segment of ventricular tachycardia (VT) from record 205 that is contaminated with BW and Fig. 2b represents the clean segment of VT.

3.3   Proposed Workflow

The workflow followed in this paper is illustrated in Fig. 3. For testing the robustness of the models, artificially generated noise of frequency around 0.4 ± 0.4 Hz was added to the original signal. These frequencies were selected in particular because they correspond to the frequency of BW. The noisy signal was then provided to different baseline wander estimation techniques. The techniques include median filter [16], MMF [20], Blanco EMD [3], combination of MMF with EMD [28], EEMD with fixed cut off frequency [27], and VMD [6]. The estimated baseline is further subtracted from noisy signal producing the clean signal. The clean signal is compared to the noisy signal using the evaluation metrics provided in Sect. 3.4.

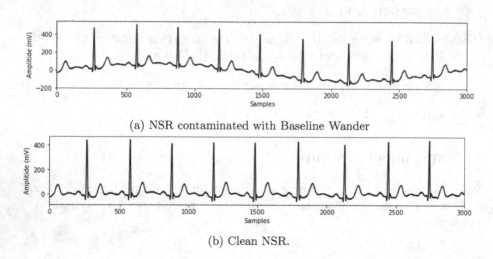

(a) NSR contaminated with Baseline Wander

(b) Clean NSR.

Fig. 1. Normal sinus rhythm from record 103 of MIT-BIH dataset.

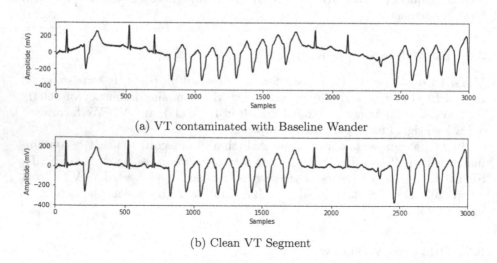

(a) VT contaminated with Baseline Wander

(b) Clean VT Segment

Fig. 2. Ventricular tachycardia segment from record 205 of MIT-BIH dataset.

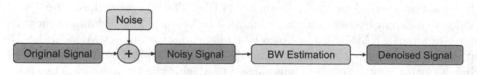

Fig. 3. Workflow followed

3.4   Evaluation Metrics

For comparing the clean and noisy signal, three evaluation metrics have been employed. In addition to the metrics, time taken by each technique for BW removal was also taken into account. The evaluation metrics employed are Percentage root mean square difference (PRMSD), Pearson Correlation (PC), and Maximum Absolute Error (MAE) as provided in Eq. 6, 7, and 8, respectively.

$$\text{PRMSD} = \sqrt{\frac{\sum\limits_{n=1}^{N} [x(n) - \tilde{x}(n)]^2}{\sum\limits_{n=1}^{N} [x(n)]^2}} \times 100\% \tag{6}$$

$$\text{PC} = \frac{N \sum\limits_{n=1}^{N} x(n)\tilde{x}(n) - \left(\sum\limits_{n=1}^{N} x(n) \sum\limits_{n=1}^{N} \tilde{x}(n) \right)}{\sqrt{\left[N \sum\limits_{n=1}^{N} x(n)^2 - \left(\sum\limits_{n=1}^{N} x(n) \right)^2 \right] \left[N \sum\limits_{n=1}^{N} \tilde{x}(n)^2 - \left(\sum\limits_{n=1}^{N} \tilde{x}(n) \right)^2 \right]}} \tag{7}$$

$$\text{MAE} = \max_{n=1}^{N}\{|x(n) - \tilde{x}(n)|\} \tag{8}$$

where, $x[n]$ represents the signal contaminated with baseline wander, $\tilde{x}[n]$ represents the clean signal and N represents number of samples in the signal. $x[n]$ and $\tilde{x}[n]$ are similar length signal.

4   Results and Discussion

The baseline wander estimation is performed for two signals from MIT-BIH dataset, namely 103 that represents normal sinus rhythm and 205 that represents ventricular tachycardia segment in this paper. Extensive experimentation is performed for BW removal from normal sinus rhythm using VMD in Sect. 4.1. A comparative analysis is then provided between different techniques: namely, median filter, mean median filter, EMD along with its other variants, and VMD for the task of baseline wander removal from both normal sinus rhythm and ventricular tachycardia segment in Sect. 4.2.

4.1   Analysis of VMD for BW Removal

A detailed analysis is performed for the use of VMD on the task of BW removal from normal sinus rhythm signal. The idea of choosing VMD as compared to other techniques, in particular, is because it is a relatively new technique and is not much explored for this particular task. Moreover, the variational modes extracted by VMD for the corresponding signal precisely captures their center frequencies The trend and mid frequency bands of the obtained modes consists of less spurious oscillations when compared to EMD. In addition to the above characteristics, no additional spectral and temporal feature estimates are required for discriminating the BW components from the ECG.

In [23], authors have used VMD for BW estimation, but the effect of the number of modes (K) and center frequency (ω) on the decomposition was not demonstrated. The authors specified that at $K = 8$ and $\omega = 1000000$ modes with least reconstruction error (in least square sense) are obtained. We analyze this effect for normal sinus rhythm having 3500 samples. We decomposed the signal into its variational modes/components using VMD and then reconstructed the original signal back from these variational modes. The difference between the original and reconstructed signal is illustrated with the help of Fig. 4. The number of modes/components varied from 2 to 15 and center frequencies varied from 1000 to 60000.

Few observations can be made from Fig. 4. The PRMSD and MAE are maximum when number of modes is less, and bandwidth constraint is very high. As variational modes increases, the bandwidth constraint should also be increased in order to obtain less error while reconstructing the original signal. As a precise value for number of variational modes and bandwidth constraint was difficult to determine, we choose $\omega = 8000$ and $K = 8$. At these two values least reconstruction error was error was obtained. As specified by [6], both over-binning and under-binning have advantages and disadvantages. During under-binning (less number of variational modes), mode sharing occurs between the neighbouring frequency for small center pulsation and high-frequency variational modes are discarded, as these modes are considered as noise for large pulsation. During over-binning (higher number of variational modes), larger values of pulsation allows a low-frequency band in the decomposed modes providing very compact band in frequency spectrum but with increased execution time for mode extraction. After the signal decomposition using VMD, the baseline wander was mostly present in the 1st component. A similar pattern can be observed for correlation where the PC increases as K and ω increase together. In the case of low K and high ω, the correlation becomes insignificant. The memory consumption also increases by 50 mega bytes for each additional variational mode. The time for mode extraction via VMD increases exponentially with each new mode as depicted in Fig. 4. Hence, for higher number of modes, the execution time of VMD algorithm limits the use in real world.

Therefore, we can infer that there exists a relation between the variational modes and bandwidth constraint such that if either of them increases then the other has to increase in order to produce consistent modes with least reconstruction error in least square sense. It is also clear that larger values of variational modes and bandwidth constraint produce modes with compact frequency spectrum when compared to smaller values, but the execution time and RAM requirement also increases.

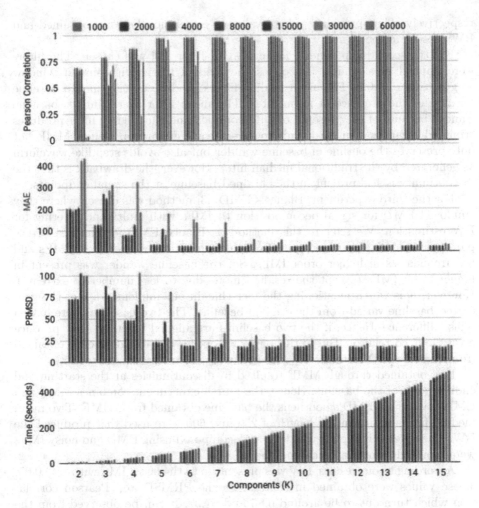

Fig. 4. Application of Variational Mode Decomposition on Normal Sinus Rhythm where the variational modes vary from 2 to 15 and center frequencies vary from 1000 to 60000.

4.2 Comparison of VMD with Other Techniques

After selecting parameters $K = 8$ and $\omega = 8000$ for VMD, we compare it with other BW removal techniques. For comparison, median filter, mean median filter and EMD along with its other variants are employed for BW removal in normal sinus rhythm and ventricular tachycardia.

For the first experiment, we employed two median filters [16] in a cascading fashion where the output of first filter was provided as input to second filter and a step like waveform is obtained as the resultant baseline wander. The window length for the filters was kept at 251 and 601 for first and second filter, respectively. Thus providing a high value of correlation between obtained and BW present in the signal.

For the second experiment, mean median filter [20] was chosen. The filters were applied in a similar fashion as the median filters with similar window length with $\omega = 0.6$. The mean median filters produce a very smooth baseline because of the presence of mean filter. The mean filter overestimates baseline wander because of the presence of QRS complex and the median filter produces trimmed mean that in turn leads to severe wave distortion. Hence, MMF not only preserves the outline of baseline wander but also avoids step like waveform as generated by the traditional median filter. However, the drawback is that the discontinuity is still present in the obtained baseline at the signal endpoints.

For the third experiment, Blanco's EMD. [3] method was chosen where they employed EMD for signal decomposition to IMFs with multiband filtering for BW estimation. We refer to this method as Blanco EMD for the rest of the paper. The EMD algorithm produces high frequencies in lower order IMFs and low frequencies in higher order IMFs. So, the baseline wander was present in higher order IMFs (except the residual mode due to less number of extrema). However, it is worth mentioning the fact that in our implementation, the generated baseline varied from the original baseline. The two baselines were have a phase difference. Hence, if the two baselines are aligned together, they produce a very high correlation. But in this paper we opt for the actual baseline obtained from Blanco EMD method.

BW obtained through MMF resulted in discontinuities at the starting and ending point of the baseline. Hence, the fourth experiment combines MMF and EMD [28], where EMD smoothens the baseline obtained from MMF. Two mean median filters with window length of 250 and 600 were used that produced the BW. The obtained baseline wander was decomposed using EMD and noisy IMFs were removed using statistical methods.

According to our results, BW was present up to the last 6 IMF with $L = 0.05$. These values were obtained in contrast to the PRMSD and Pearson correlation which turn out to be around 0.85 and 61.37. It can be observed from the Fig. 5 that due to the shifted baseline, the performance metrics deteriorated. We performed two more variations to the [3] approach by employing EEMD and CEEMDAN in place of EMD that helped in better estimation of baseline wander. However, the time required by CEEMDAN was very high making it unreasonable for real-time applications. Hence, we have not included the results of CEEMDAN in this study.

The performance for all the techniques for normal sinus rhythm for all evaluation metrics are provided in Fig. 5. The best PC was obtained for VMD at 0.98 followed by median filter, and EEMD with fix cut off frequency. Median Filter correlation constantly reduced from 0.97 to 0.83 as the artificially induced noise was increased. Except for Blanco EMD method, other techniques did not produce much change in MAE when the noise was increased. Here too, VMD produced least MAE among all at 27%. Median filter, EEMD_Fixcut, and Blanco EMD produced MAE in an increasing fashion as the noise was increased. For

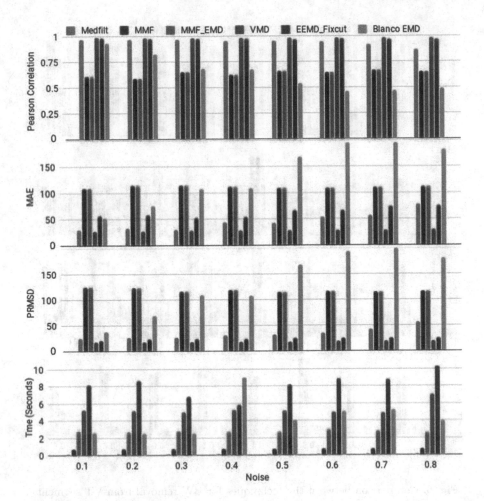

Fig. 5. Comparison between the techniques for BW removal from NSR.

PRMSD, median filter and Blanco EMD produced an increase in error as the noise increased. VMD again provided the least error irrespective of the noise. The time taken by decomposition techniques namely EMD, EEMD and VMD were higher than other techniques. Median filter, MMF and MMF-EMD took the least time at around 0.1, 0.6, and 3s, respectively. VMD took around 5s. The higher the complexity of the present baseline, the more execution time the algorithm took to decompose the signal. Hence, as the noise increased the time tom decompose also increased. Results for CEEMDAN are not included as its execution time exceeds by a huge margin as compared to other approaches.

Results on VT for all techniques for all evaluation metrics are provided in Fig. 6. The best PC was obtained for VMD at 0.97 followed by EEMD_Fixcut, and median filter. The PC values for MMF and MMF with EMD were better

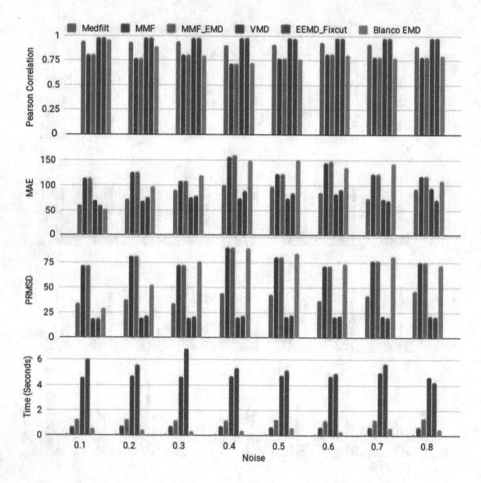

Fig. 6. Comparison between the techniques for BW removal from VT segment.

than the ones obtained for NSR. Blanco EMD method performed similar to MMF for high noise frequencies. MAE values kept varying for all the techniques at different noise frequencies. However, VMD provided less error at most of the noise frequencies and MMF, MMF-EMD and Blanco EMD method provided highest error at every noise frequency. VMD, EEMD fix cut constantly low PRMSD ranging between 20% to 25%. PRMSD for all other methods kept increasing with MMF, MMF-EMD, and Blanco EMD producing the highest PRMSD values. Median filter, MMF and MMF-EMD took the least time, whereas decomposition took relatively higher execution time.

5   Conclusions and Future Work

In this paper, we analysed variational mode decomposition for the task of baseline wander removal from normal and VT segment. An analysis between the relation of K and ω is also provided that affects the variational modes obtained from VMD. A comparative study for comparison between different decomposition methods, namely EMD along with its variants, VMD, median filter and MMF was also conducted. We found that VMD performs better in almost all aspects for both the signals at all noise frequencies. However, the time required by VMD was slightly higher than the filtering techniques.

For future research directions, we plan to use the baseline free ECG signal to produce features that characterize an ECG signal in an efficient way such that it can be used to predict different classes of arrhythmia in handheld mobile devices.

References

1. Agrawal, S., Gupta, A.: Fractal and EMD based removal of baseline wander and powerline interference from ECG signals. Comput. Biol. Med. **43**(11), 1889–1899 (2013)
2. Barros, A.K., Mansour, A., Ohnishi, N.: Removing artifacts from electrocardiographic signals using independent components analysis. Neurocomputing **22**(1–3), 173–186 (1998)
3. Blanco-Velasco, M., Weng, B., Barner, K.E.: ECG signal denoising and baseline wander correction based on the empirical mode decomposition. Comput. Biol. Med. **38**(1), 1–13 (2008)
4. Chang, K.M.: Arrhythmia ECG noise reduction by ensemble empirical mode decomposition. Sensors **10**(6), 6063–6080 (2010)
5. Chouhan, V., Mehta, S.S.: Total removal of baseline drift from ECG signal. In: 2007 International Conference on Computing: Theory and Applications, ICCTA 2007, pp. 512–515. IEEE (2007)
6. Dragomiretskiy, K., Zosso, D.: Variational mode decomposition. IEEE Trans. Signal Process. **62**(3), 531–544 (2014)
7. Ercelebi, E.: Electrocardiogram signals de-noising using lifting-based discrete wavelet transform. Comput. Biol. Med. **34**(6), 479–493 (2004)
8. Fasano, A., Villani, V.: ECG baseline wander removal and impact on beat morphology: a comparative analysis. In: 2013 Computing in Cardiology Conference (CinC), pp. 1167–1170. IEEE (2013)
9. Flandrin, P., Rilling, G., Goncalves, P.: Empirical mode decomposition as a filter bank. IEEE Signal Process. Lett. **11**(2), 112–114 (2004)
10. He, T., Clifford, G., Tarassenko, L.: Application of independent component analysis in removing artefacts from the electrocardiogram. Neural Comput. Appl. **15**(2), 105–116 (2006)
11. Huang, N.E., et al.: The empirical mode decomposition and the Hilbert spectrum for nonlinear and non-stationary time series analysis. Proc. R. Soc. Lond. A: Math. Phys. Eng. Sci. **454**, 903–995 (1998)
12. Huber, P.J.: John W. Tukey's contributions to robust statistics. Ann. Stat. **30**, 1640–1648 (2002)
13. Iravanian, S., Tung, L.: A novel algorithm for cardiac biosignal filtering based on filtered residue method. IEEE Trans. Biomed. Eng. **49**(11), 1310–1317 (2002)
14. Ji, T., Lu, Z., Wu, Q., Ji, Z.: Baseline normalisation of ECG signals using empirical mode decomposition and mathematical morphology. Electron. Lett. **44**(2), 1 (2008)

15. Kabir, M.A., Shahnaz, C.: Denoising of ECG signals based on noise reduction algorithms in EMD and wavelet domains. Biomed. Signal Process. Control **7**(5), 481–489 (2012)
16. Leski, J.M., Henzel, N.: ECG baseline wander and powerline interference reduction using nonlinear filter bank. Signal Process. **85**(4), 781–793 (2005)
17. Mark, R., Schluter, P., Moody, G., Devlin, P., Chernoff, D.: An annotated ECG database for evaluating arrhythmia detectors. IEEE Trans. Biomed. Eng. **29**, 600–600 (1982)
18. Moody, G.B., Mark, R.G.: The impact of the MIT-BIH arrhythmia database. IEEE Eng. Med. Biol. Mag. **20**(3), 45–50 (2001)
19. Nankani, D., Baruah, R.D.: An end-to-end framework for automatic detection of atrial fibrillation using deep residual learning. In: TENCON 2019–2019 IEEE Region 10 Conference (TENCON), pp. 690–695. IEEE (2019)
20. Nie, X., Unbehauen, R.: Edge preserving filtering by combining nonlinear mean and median filters. IEEE Trans. Signal Process. **39**(11), 2552–2554 (1991)
21. Papaloukas, C., Fotiadis, D., Liavas, A., Likas, A., Michalis, L.: A knowledge-based technique for automated detection of ischaemic episodes in long duration electrocardiograms. Med. Biolog. Eng. Comput. **39**(1), 105–112 (2001)
22. Park, K., Lee, K., Yoon, H.: Application of a wavelet adaptive filter to minimise distortion of the st-segment. Med. Biolog. Eng. Comput. **36**(5), 581–586 (1998)
23. Prabhakararao, E., Manikandan, M.S.: On the use of variational mode decomposition for removal of baseline wander in ECG signals. In: 2016 Twenty Second National Conference on Communication (NCC), pp. 1–6. IEEE (2016)
24. Spach, M.S., Kootsey, J.M.: The nature of electrical propagation in cardiac muscle. Am. J. Physiol.-Heart Circ. Physiol. **244**(1), H3–H22 (1983)
25. Thakor, N.V., Zhu, Y.S.: Applications of adaptive filtering to ECG analysis: noise cancellation and arrhythmia detection. IEEE Trans. Biomed. Eng. **38**(8), 785–794 (1991)
26. Torres, M.E., Colominas, M.A., Schlotthauer, G., Flandrin, P.: A complete ensemble empirical mode decomposition with adaptive noise. In: 2011 IEEE International Conference on Acoustics, Speech and Signal Processing (ICASSP), pp. 4144–4147. IEEE (2011)
27. Wu, Z., Huang, N.E.: Ensemble empirical mode decomposition: a noise-assisted data analysis method. Adv. Adapt. Data Anal. **1**(01), 1–41 (2009)
28. Xin, Y., Chen, Y., Hao, W.T.: ECG baseline wander correction based on mean-median filter and empirical mode decomposition. Bio-Med. Mater. Eng. **24**(1), 365–371 (2014)
29. Xu, Y., Luo, M., Li, T., Song, G.: ECG signal de-noising and baseline wander correction based on ceemdan and wavelet threshold. Sensors **17**(12), 2754 (2017)
30. Zhao, Z., Liu, J.: Baseline wander removal of ECG signals using empirical mode decomposition and adaptive filter. In: 2010 4th International Conference on Bioinformatics and Biomedical Engineering (iCBBE), pp. 1–3. IEEE (2010)

Face Recognition Based on Human Sketches Using Fuzzy Minimal Structure Oscillation in the SIFT Domain

Bibek Majumder[(✉)] and Sharmistha Bhattacharya (Halder)[(✉)]

Tripura University, Agartala, India
bibekmajumder6@gmail.com, halder_731@rediffmail.com

Abstract. Through this paper we present a new algorithm with the help of Scale Invariant Feature Transformation (SIFT) along with fuzzy m_X^* oscillation. We propose a fuzzy based similarity measurement technique i.e. fuzzy m_x^* oscillation for providing a better precision in face recognition area. First, apply SIFT for finding key points from sketch and digital images and then select the key points for feature extraction. After feature extraction fuzzy m_X^* oscillation based classification are used for these values. For experiment we have considered two scenarios which are described in the beginning of Sect. 4. So using this proposed algorithm we will easily able to identify the correct image as an output of face sketch to photo matching. Accuracy of our algorithm describes this work piece concerned on fuzzy m_x^* oscillation has achieved its aim of recognizing the face sketches in the SIFT domain.

Keywords: Scale Invariant Feature Transformation · Fuzzy minimal structure oscillation · Key points · Face recognition

1 Introduction

In [4] authors proposed an extensive inquiry of face recognition based on multiple stylistic sketches and they consider three kind of sketches and from their experimental results it is clear that hand draw sketches give more accurate result compare to other two scenarios. In [1–3] face sketch synthesis technique is beautifully described by the authors. Since our paper presents only the recognition techniques, so we consider only the hand draw sketches for our experiments. This sketch databases have been collected from freely available databases like IIIT Databases, CUHK Databases etc. (details given in Sect. 2). Through this paper we try to show use of fuzzy set in the field of face recognition and we received very good experimental results.

The work that we have done is highlighting the jotted aspects: (1) SIFT is used for finding keypoint region from sketches and digital images. (2) Then select these key points as a feature coordinates. (3) After feature extraction, call fuzzy m_X^* oscillation based classification for recognition part. (4) And lastly, for each pixel consider four different cases (In Sect. 2 these four cases described) for similarity measurement.

The method we have presented here as follows: the brief information about the notion and properties of fuzzy minimal structure is presented in Sect. 2, SIFT etc. and also in this section we discussed about the digital images and sketch images, which

A. Bhattacharjee et al. (Eds.): MIND 2020, CCIS 1241, pp. 325–335, 2020.
https://doi.org/10.1007/978-981-15-6318-8_27

have been used during our experiment. Section 3 contains the algorithm and detailed explanation about our algorithm. Next in Sect. 4 discussed the outcomes of proposed face recognition technique based SIFT and fuzzy m_X^* oscillation. Lastly, the conclusion is given in Sect. 5.

2 Preliminaries

Through this section we explain those notations which are the main background of our proposed algorithm. The notation and definition of fuzzy minimal structure, fuzzy oscillation, fuzzy m_X^* open and closed oscillatory operator etc. are to be described below-

Definition 2.1 [5]. In a universal set X, a family M of fuzzy sets is said to be a fuzzy minimal structure on X if $\alpha 1_X \in M$, where $\alpha \in [0, 1]$.

Definition 2.2 [6]. For defining Fuzzy m_X^* we need to define following operators from $I^X \rightarrow I^X$

(i) $\Lambda_{a_k}(X) = inf\{\mu_{a_k}(X_i) : \mu_{a_k}(X_i) \geq \mu_{a_k}(X), X_i \in G \quad G$ is an open
    set, $j = 1, 2, \ldots, n\}$
    $= \hat{1}$, otherwise;

(ii) $Int_{a_k}(X) = sup\{\mu_{a_k}(X_i) : \mu_{a_k}(X_i) \leq \mu_{a_k}(X), X_i \in G, \quad G$ is an open
    set, $j = 1, 2, \ldots, n\}$
    $= \phi$, otherwise;

(iii) $Cl_{a_k}(X) = inf\{\mu_{a_k}(X_i) : \mu_{a_k}(X_i) \geq \mu_{a_k}(X), X_i \in G, \quad G$ is an closed
    set, $j = 1, 2, \ldots, n\}$
    $= \hat{1}$, otherwise;

(iv) $V_{a_k}(X) = sup\{\mu_{a_k}(X_i) : \mu_{a_k}(X_i) \leq \mu_{a_k}(X), X_i \in G, \quad G$ is an closed
    set, $j = 1, 2, \ldots, n\}$
    $= \phi$, otherwise;

Where, $\mu_{a_k}(X_i)$ is the membership value for any characteristic X_i and for any attribute a_k.

Definition 2.3 [6]. A fuzzy m_X^* open oscillatory operator from $I^X \rightarrow I^X$ is denoted by O^o and defined by $O_{a_k}^o(X) = \Lambda_{a_k}(X) - Int_{a_k}(X)$. Similarly, a fuzzy m_X^* closed oscillatory operator from $I^X \rightarrow I^X$ is denoted by O^c and defined by $O_{a_k}^o(x) = Cl_{a_k}(X) - V_{a_k}(X)$.

Theorem 2.1 [6]. Suppose z is any object in fuzzy m_X^* structure then $O_{a_k}^o(z) = \alpha \Leftrightarrow O_{a_k}^o(z^c) = -\alpha$, where $\alpha \in I^X$.

Definition 2.4. On intuitionistic fuzzy m_X^* Oscillation (IF m_X^* Oscillation) a subfamily of IF sets in X is said to be IF m_X^{0*} structure if $1_\sim$ or $0_\sim$ belongs to m_X^* with $\alpha \in m_X^*$ where α is an IF set.

Definition 2.5. For defining Intuitionistic Fuzzy m_X^* we need to define following operators from $I^X \to I^X$

(i) $\Lambda_{a_k}(X) = Sup_\gamma \; inf_\mu \{ <\mu_{a_k}(X_i), \gamma_{a_k}(X_i) > \; : \mu_{a_k}(X_i) \geq \mu_{a_k}(X),$
$\gamma_{a_k}(X_i) \leq \gamma_{a_k}(X), \; X_i \in G$ is an open set, $j = 1, 2, \ldots, n\}$
$= \hat{I}$, otherwise;

(ii) $Int_{a_k}(X) = inf_\gamma \; Sup_\mu \{ <\mu_{a_k}(X_i), \gamma_{a_k}(X_i) > \; : \mu_{a_k}(X_i) \leq \mu_{a_k}(X),$
$\gamma_{a_k}(X_i) \geq \gamma_{a_k}(X), X_i \in G$ is an open set, $j = 1, 2, \ldots, n\}$
$= \phi$, otherwise;

Where, $\mu_{a_k}(X_i)$ and $\gamma_{a_k}(X_i)$ are the membership and nonmembership value of X_i.

Definition 2.6. m_X^* oscillatory operator O^o from $I^X \to I^X$ is defined as $O_{a_k}^o(X) = \Lambda_{a_k}(X) - Int_{a_k}(X)$. On Intuitionistic Fuzzy m_X^* the operator O^o is defined as $\langle \Lambda_{\mu_{a_j}}(x_i) - Int_{\gamma_{a_j}}(x_i), \; \Lambda_{\gamma_{a_j}}(x_i) - Int_{\mu_{a_j}}(x_i)\rangle$.

2.1 Fuzzy m_X^* Oscillation Based Face Recognition

The Detailed explanation of fuzzy m_X^* oscillation was introduced in [7–9]. In their work they introduced some pathway of decision about similar and difference.

At first, suppose we have an image set of consisting $I = I_1, I_2, \ldots, I_M$ images. The following cases might appear for comparing an unfamiliar image and the familiar image with the help of fuzzy m_X^* oscillation.

For $O_{I_K}^o(y_{ij}) = \Lambda_{I_K}(y_{ij}) - Int_{I_K}(y_{ij})$, the following cases may appear –

(1) $O_{I_K}^o(y_{ij}) = 0 \; or \; 1$
(2) $0 < O_{I_K}^o(y_{ij}) < 1$
(3) $O_{I_K}^o(y_{ij}) = \Lambda_{I_K}(y_{ij}) - \phi$
(4) $O_{I_K}^o(y_{ij}) = \hat{I} - \Lambda_{I_K}(y_{ij})$

Case (1): (i) Let, if possible $O_{I_K}^o(y_{ij}) = \Lambda_{I_K}(y_{ij}) - Int_{I_K}(y_{ij}) = 0$.

$\Leftrightarrow \Lambda_{I_K}(y_{ij}) = Int_{I_K}(y_{ij})$.
$\Leftrightarrow$ For training image the intensity of the pixel (i, j) = Intensity of the pixel (i, j) of the unfamiliar image.
$\Leftrightarrow$ Training image and the unfamiliar (rotated) image are same at the pixel (i, j).

(ii) Let if possible $O_{I_K}^o(y_{ij}) = \Lambda_{I_K}(y_{ij}) - Int_{I_K}(y_{ij}) = 1$.

$\Leftrightarrow \Lambda_{I_K}(y_{ij}) = 1$ and $Int_{I_K}(y_{ij}) = 0$.
$\Leftrightarrow$ i.e. at pixel (i, j) the intensity of the unknown image is not within a known position.

Therefore, these pixel is not comparable with the pixel (i,j) of known image. So we consider this pixel is undefined pixel.

Case (2): Let, if possible $0 < O^o_{I_K}(y_{ij}) < 1$.

(i)   If $O^o_{I_K}(y_{ij}) \leq 0.1$, There may be a similarity between the images of the pixel (i,j).

(ii) If $O^o_{I_K}(y_{ij}) \geq 0.1$, at pixel (i,j) and $\Lambda_{I_K}(y_{ij})$ Or $\text{Int}_{I_K}(y_{ij})$ we have to check the distinction among the intensity of the unknown image. If this difference is ≤ 0.1 then we take this pixel.

Case (3): Let, if possible $O^o_{I_K}(y_{ij}) = \Lambda_{I_K}(y_{ij}) - \phi$.

At pixel (i,j) and $\Lambda_{I_K}(y_{ij})$ Or $\text{Int}_{I_K}(y_{ij})$ we need to verify the distinction among the intensity of the unknown image. Suppose this oscillation is ≤ 0.1, then we take this pixel, otherwise different.

Case (4): Let, if possible $O^o_{I_K}(y_{ij}) = \hat{I} - \Lambda_{I_K}(y_{ij})$.

At pixel (i,j) and $\Lambda_{I_K}(y_{ij})$ Or $\text{Int}_{I_K}(y_{ij})$ we need to verify the distinction among the intensity of the unknown image. Suppose this oscillation is ≤ 0.1, then may be considered the image as similar at the pixel (i,j), otherwise different.

2.2   Scale Invariant Feature Transform (SIFT)

In [10], David G. Lowe beautifully described the algorithm for finding the key points using SIFT. Over the past 13 years Scale Invariant Feature Transformation (SIFT) used extensively in the face recognition branch. It is mainly detect and represents the Scale, the translation and the rotation invariant local features in any images. On face recognition it is used as a keypoints descriptor. Since, after enlarge the image, it would provide almost the same number of key points (in this paper key points considered as a feature coordinates), it is called scale invariant. Even for rotated images it would provide almost same number of key points (it is the another benefit of this algorithm). The essential steps of this algorithm are- Scale-Space Extrema Detection, remove the unreliable key points, orientation assignment and lastly key points descriptor calculation (Fig. 1).

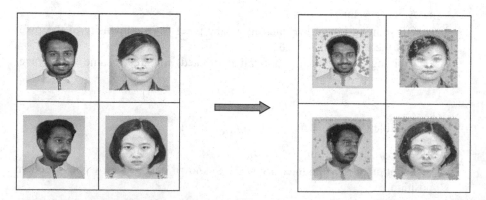

Fig. 1. Left images the gallery images and right images are the image after applying SIFT algorithm which indicates the key points.

Fig. 2. Keypoint region after applying SIFT

2.3   Facial Sketch-Image Databases

We have collected freely available sketch datasets namely CUHK [11] sketch database, it contains three separate databases that are CUHK database, AR database, and XM2VTS database, the database of CUHK student contains 188 pairs sketch photos, the database of AR [11] contains 123 sketch image pairs followed by XM2VTS database which contains 295 sketch images pairs. So, from here we managed to collect a total of 606 image database. We have used a total of 311 sketch database because here XM2VTS database is not a free one. Very well controlled illumination and fixed background are located in the CUHK sketch databases. We noticed that, we can't fully conclude that face recognition using these well-known databases are possible. Thus to overcome the complexity of sketch to face recognition, we collected various sketch and digital images from various sources, this set contains 231 sketch and digital images and these sketches are pictured by the artists. These databases include, FG-NET aging database [12] contain 67 sketch and digital image pairs, we have collected 92 sketch and its corresponding original image pairs from Labeled Faces in Wild database (LFW) [13], and lastly we have collected 568 sketch-digital image pairs from IIIT-Delhi databases [14]. IIIT-Delhi databases has contains their students and faculty members sketch and digital image pairs, moreover IIIT-Delhi databases contains more attractive and challenging databases compared to the CUHK databases [11]. Further, also we have collected some images with different facial expression, gesture and illumination (Fig. 3).

Fig. 3. Some sketch images (collected from different sources like IIIT-Delhi databases, CUHK databases etc.).

3   Face Recognition Based Sift, Fuzzy and IF m_X^* Oscillation

In our proposed method used fuzzy based similarity measurement technique. First we introduce Scale Invariant Feature Transformation and fuzzy m_X^* Oscillation and then introduced the procedure and algorithm for sketch to photo matching. For recognize the faces using Fuzzy m_X^* Oscillation initially we have collected probe sketch and digital images from gallery. Then Scale Invariant Feature Transform (SIFT) is applied for both the sketch and photos for finding key points (Fig. 4). At last, we need to correlate these pixel values of key points from known image matrix and unknown image matrix. The cl operator i.e. the operator Λ for negative images and the Int operator i.e. the V operator for negative images are measured (Fig. 5). The distinction among the Λ and Int operator i.e. Open Oscillatory Operator are calculated.

Fig. 4. Indicates the special coordinates.

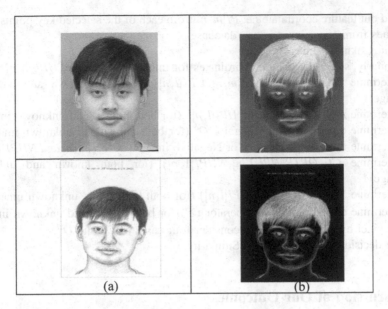

(a)   (b)

Fig. 5. Column (a) represents gallery image and its sketch and column (b) represents the negative images of input gallery and sketch images.

3.1   Face Recognition Procedure Based SIFT and Fuzzy m_X^* Oscillation

Step 1 : Let, we have a dataset which contains of N image. Then Scale Invariant Feature Transformation is applied for each image of the database. Then to find pixel values from the key points from each of the training images. Simultaneously feature coordinates were also collected from the unknown image after applying Scale Invariant Feature Transformation.

Step 2 : Now Λ operator and *Int* operator (INT_OPTR) with supremum value will be calculated.

Step 3 : CL_OPTR that is infimum value and V_OPTR that is Supremum value required to be determined for the negative(complementary) image. Then from the original image O^o that is open oscillatory value and O^{cl} that is closed oscillatory value from the negative images are determined.

Step 4 : The four cases of similarity measure are considered after calculated the open and closed oscillatory operators as stated in [6].

3.2   Algorithm

The algorithm used in this paper for face recognition using SIFT and Fuzzy m_X^* Oscillation is given below:-

1. Load any image database
2. Apply Scale Invariant Feature Transform for every input database

3. Find out feature coordinate i.e. $PI[m, n]$ from each of the selected key points (pixel values from every input image database)
4. Input Unknown Image
5. Similarly, select the feature coordinates for unknown image i.e. $UPI[m, n]$
6. Determine $LAMDA\_OPTR(PI[m, n], UPI[l, n])$ (for both known and unknown image)
7. Determine $INT\_OPTR(PI[l, n], UPI[l, n])$ (for both known and unknown image)
8. Determine open oscillatory operator O^o (for both known and unknown image)
9. Determine the Complementary or Negative image set $NPI[m, n]$ and $NUPI[I, n]$
10. Determine $CL\_OPTR(NPI[1, n], NUPI[1, n])$ (for both known and unknown image)
11. Determine $V\_OPTR(PI[l, n], UPI[l, n])$ (for both known and unknown image)
12. Determine closed oscillatory operator O^{cl} (for both known and unknown image)
13. For pixel by pixel comparison consider four cases of O^o and O^{cl}.
14. The decision for Difference or Similarity.

4 Discussion of Our Outcomes

We provide here the details representation of experimental results of our proposed algorithm (Tables 1 and 2). Here, we consider the two scenarios to check the accuracy of this proposed algorithm, these are (a) the different sketch face i.e. the sketch image which is different from the original suspect face and then compare it with the gallery photos (this gallery is not contain the face image of this sketch), (b) suspect original sketch face and similarly compare it with the gallery images (In gallery images we have the suspect face).

We have collected some images called Training image or Query sketch image for face recognition using fuzzy m_X^* oscillation and SIFT. The database contains various pose of an individual. Here we consider membership and non-membership values together to form the closed and open set oscillatory operator matrix. Therefore no need to calculate supremum and infimum operator separately for normal image and complementary image. In this paper we simultaneously form a non-membership images for each image. From which the closed set is formed with those feature point that are selected as the number of operation and calculation reduces the performance is better in case of intuitionistic fuzzy oscillation. Scale Invariant Feature transformation gives the key points as shown in Fig. 2.

Table 1. The accuracy calculation for distinct sketch face (correlate with an image of distinct individual)

Query set (training set)	Feature coordinate	Identical pixel	Different pixel	Accuracy
25	20	3(2)	16	0.762
30	20	4(1)	17	0.772
35	30	4	22	0.846
40	30	2(1)	32	0.914
45	35	2	39	0.951

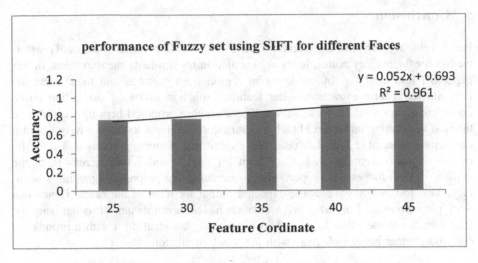

Fig. 6. Performance of fuzzy m_X^* oscillation with SIFT (for different faces)

Table 2. The accuracy calculation for identical sketch face (correlate with different image of similar images)

Query set (training set)	Feature coordinate	Identical pixel	Different pixel	Accuracy
25	20	13	2(2)	0.765
30	20	18	3(1)	0.818
35	30	23	3	0.885
40	30	30	2(1)	0.91
45	35	38	2	0.95

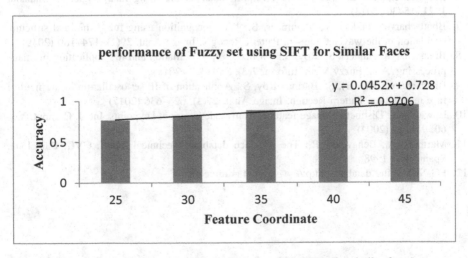

Fig. 7. Performance of fuzzy m_X^* oscillation with SIFT (for similar faces)

5 Conclusion

For developing our new algorithm we have used Scale Invariant Feature Transformation for finding key points, fuzzy m_X^* oscillation for similarity measurement. In this paper SIFT is used for finding keypoint region from sketches and then select the keypoits for feature extraction. After feature extraction fuzzy m_x^* oscillation based classification are used for these values. The algorithm proposed here by us has gone through verification under the Matlab program and additional to that we have tested it on various obtainable face database. The experiment of our algorithm was done by considering two scenarios. It is clear from the Figs. 6 and 7 that increasing of the number of coordinates has proportionately increased the proposed algorithm's accuracy. This fortunately gave us the expected output for most of the cases. Hence this work piece concerned on fuzzy m_X^* oscillation has achieved its aim of recognizing the face sketches in the SIFT domain. As we conclude, we shall do it with a promise to carry out further better endeavors with fuzzy m_X^* oscillation.

References

1. Wang, X., Tang, X.: Face photo-sketch synthesis and recognition. IEEE Trans. Pattern Anal. Mach. Intell. **31**(11), 1955–1967 (2009)
2. Wang, N., Gao, X., Li, J.: Random sampling for fast face sketch synthesis. Pattern Recogn. **76**, 215–227 (2018)
3. Jiao, L., Zhang, S., Li, L., Liu, F., Ma, W.: A modified convolutional neural network for face sketch synthesis. Pattern Recogn. **76**, 125–136 (2018)
4. Peng, C., Gao, X., Wang, N.: Face recognition from multiple stylistic sketches: scenarios, datasets, and evaluation. Pattern Recogn. **64**, 262–272 (2018)
5. Alimohammady, M.R.: Transfer closed and transfer open multimaps in minimal space. Chaos, Solitons Fractals **40**(3), 1162–1168 (2009)
6. Miry, A.H.: Face detection based on multi facial feature using fuzzy logic. AI-Mansour J. **21**, 15–30 (2014)
7. Bhattacharya (Halder), S., Majumder, B.: Face recognition using fuzzy minimal structure oscillation in the wavelet domain. Pattern RecogN. Image Anal. **29**(1), 174–180 (2019)
8. Bhattacharya (Halder), S., Roy, S.: On fuzzy m_X^* - oscillation and it's application in image processing. Ann. Fuzzy Math. Inform. **7**(2), 319–329 (2014)
9. Bhattacharya (Halder), S., Barman Roy, S.: Application of IF set oscillation in the field of face recognition. Pattern Recogn. Image Anal. **27**(3), 625–636 (2017)
10. Lowe, D.G.: Distinctive image features from scale-invariant keypoints. Int. J. Comput. Vis. **60**, 91–110 (2004)
11. Martinez, A., Benavente, R.: The AR face database. Technical report, CVC, Barcelona, Spain, June 1998
12. FG-NET aging database. http://www.fgnet.rsunit.com/

13. Huang, G., Ramesh, M., Berg, L.-M.T.: Labeled faces in the wild. A database for studying face recognition in unconstrained environment (2007)
14. Bhatt, H., Bharadwaj, S., Singh, R., Vatsa, M.: Memetically optimized MCWLD for matching sketches with digital face images. IEEE Trans. Inf. Forensics Secur. 7(5), 1522–1535 (2012)

An Ensemble Model for Predicting Passenger Demand Using Taxi Data Set

Santosh Rajak and Ujwala Baruah[(⊠)]

Department of Computer Science and Engineering,
National Institute of Technology, Silchar, Silchar, India
b.ujwala@gmail.com

Abstract. Prediction of the probable future pick-ups is one of the most beneficial and challenging tasks for taxi drivers. Efficient prediction of the same requires proper study of the past history. In this paper we have considered the past history of the New York Yellow Taxi Data Set to predict the number of pick-ups. Prediction of the passenger demand for cab driver is made based on the criteria- area of region, travel time, distance between each region and trip fare etc. By taking all these criteria into consideration the passengers demand is predicted which is expected to help build strong advanced traffic management system (ATMS) and intelligent traffic system (ITS) and also solve other challenges related to traffic. In all six modeling techniques have been taken into consideration. The modeling techniques used being Simple Moving Average, Weighted Moving Average, Exponential Moving Average, Linear Regression, Random Forest and XGBoost Regressor. Appropriate weights are assigned to the predictions from these models, depending on the accuracy of their prediction. A combined decision of the prediction is thereafter given.

Keywords: Taxi data set · Machine learning · Long short term memory · Exponential average

1 Introduction

A taxi driver would never want to drive his taxi without passengers. Predicting the number of passengers for a taxi driver is a challenging task. There are three main constraints for designing prediction model latency, interpretability and relative percentage error between predicted and actual value. Predicting the number of passengers for taxi drivers for a specific area is helpful to build a smart city and we can also establish Intelligent Transportation System for that region. In order to build a smart city we need to reduce carbon emissions and unnecessary traffic. Nowadays, most of the people look for private vehicle for their convenient travelling. Since the government transportation system have fixed pick-up and fixed drop-off locations, private vehicles are getting more preference. To predict the number of passengers for taxi drivers we must consider certain constraints such as road condition, earning and as well as reliability. In recent times, most of

© Springer Nature Singapore Pte Ltd. 2020
A. Bhattacharjee et al. (Eds.): MIND 2020, CCIS 1241, pp. 336–346, 2020.
https://doi.org/10.1007/978-981-15-6318-8_28

the cities which have some importance with regards to industry, popular market and other important places like movie theater, historical places, etc., suffer from heavy traffic congestion. Due to advancement in technology the taxi/cab are enabled with positioning system [8] and [9]. Since taxis are enabled with global positioning systems, it becomes possible for the taxi drivers to become aware of the location of the probable passengers. With the information received from the taxis, it is possible to predict the number of passengers in the surrounding area pertaining to a particular taxi-driver.

2 State of the Art

The recent past has seen a surge in the taxi demand prediction as one of the key interest areas for researchers for prediction for taxi drivers.

In [2] the authors have considered the road quality and the expected earning from the trip, to inform the driver as to where to find the next passenger with high probability. Deep neural network and t-SNE have been used to label the features. In this approach a geographical area has been divided into a grid of size $400 \times 400\,m$ based on average travel distance which is $1.57\,kilometers$ per trip. This method though works quite well in densely populated areas, fails to give satisfactory results in sparse area as well as in areas that does not preserve the average travelling distance of $1.57\,km$.

In [1] the authors have made use of the stack Auto Encoder which is based on Deep neural network for traffic flow forecasting. With dimensionality and sparsity constraints, auto encoders can learn traffic flow features. Here the flow of traffic is considered to be dependent on the historical data and traffic data collected from different sources like mobile Global Positioning system, crowd system and social media etc.

In [4] the methodology used by the authors to remove outliers is by counting the passengers in taxi and Global positioning system value only. With the help of the unified neural network the authors have tried to estimate the distance and time separately. For estimating the travel time they have made use of the segment based approach in which time travel is forecast on links straight subsection of a travel direction with no intersection.

In [3] the author have proposed a two layer deep learning architecture that influence word embeddings, convolution layer and other mechanisms for combining text information with time series data. In order to process data simple conventional text pre-processing techniques have been employed involving HTML tag removal, lowercase transformation, Tokenization and Lemmatization using Long Short Term Memory (LSTM), which is an upgraded version of Recurrent Neural Network (RNN).

In [7], the author have used time varying Poisson model and ARIMA technique. The main focus was on which taxi stand the cab driver has to go to after a passenger drop off. They try to find the best taxi stand where the passengers have to be found by cab driver. An intelligent approach to this issue would increase the efficiency of the network for both business and customer, decreasing the average by clever distribution of the vehicle throughout the stands.

In [5] the authors have proposed a method for predicting taxi pick-up and drop-off demand in different city regions, based on multi-task learning (MTL) and 3D convolutionary neural networks (3D CNN). The major thrust was on selecting the historical data of high significance at each time interval. Instead they viewed taxi pick-up demand prediction as related tasks and taxi drop-off demand prediction. We took advantage of MTL and 3D CNN's ability to derive spatiotemporal characteristics without separating the relationship between temporal correlation and spatial correlation.

In [6] they first collected and stored large amounts of geospatial data, including massive traces of the Global Positioning System (GPS), smart card data, cell phone records, user locations and social media trajectories, such as Facebook and others. Then they preprocessed them using image fusion and image selection techniques. In image fusion they merged two are more images in single image from different sources. In image selection, to predict the passenger demand they selected image such as image of the past few hours and image of the same time interval of the last weekend. After preprocessing images, they applied technique which was a combination of Convolution Neural Network (CNN/covnets) and Residual Network.

3   Problem Definition

For a given location, our goal is to forecast the number of passengers in a given location at a specific time interval. It has been observed that at a given point of time, certain locations need more taxis than other locations because of the presence of schools, hospitals and offices etc. The result of the prediction can be forwarded to the cab driver via smartphone application, and the taxi driver can thereafter move to the location where high pickups are predicted. Our main objective is to find the numbers of probable pickups as accurately as possible for a specific time period for each area. For forecasting a number of passengers for cab driver the following points have been considered:-

1. What is the minimum and maximum distance between any two regions?
2. The number and size of the clusters to be considered for a particular region.
3. The average speed of taxis in the city.

From the point of view of the cab driver the following issues are to be taken into consideration:

1. Latency: The time interval between the instant in which taxi driver sends his current location and the instant in which he receives the predicted pickups in his region and neighboring region should be in seconds.
2. Interpretability: Interpretability of the result bears no importance to taxi-drivers.
3. Relative Error: Relative error of the prediction is of prime importance to the taxi drivers.

3.1 Dataset Used

The dataset used in this work includes trip records from all trips completed in yellow taxis in New York city. Records include fields capturing pick-up and drop-off dates/times, pick-up and drop-off locations, trip distances, fares, rate types, payment types, and driver-reported passenger counts. The data used in the dataset has been collected and provided to the New York City Taxi and Limousine Commission (TLC) by technology providers authorized under the Taxicab Passenger Enhancement Program (TPEP) (Table 1).

Table 1. Data attribute.

Sr. no	Feature	Description
1	Vendor id	A code indicating the TPEP provider that provided the record
2	Pickup date time	The date and time when the meter was engaged
3	Pickup date time	The date and time when the meter was engaged
4	Passenger count	Number of the passenger in taxi
5	Trip distance	The elapsed distance in miles reported by the taxi meter
6	Pickup latitude	Latitude where the meter was engaged
7	Pickup longitude	Longitude where the meter was engaged
8	Store and fed flag	This flag indicates whether the trip record was held in vehicle memory before sending to the vendor because the vehicle did not have a connection to the server Y = store and forward N = not a store and forward trip
9	Dropoff longitude	Longitude where the meter was disengaged
10	Dropoff latitude	Latitude where the meter was disengaged
11	Trip fare	The time and distance fare calculated by the meter

3.2 Libraries Used

1. Dask: It does easy optimization to allow us work with a RAM size smaller than the database size. Instead of loading all the data in the RAM at once, Dask only loads those blocks of the file which are needed currently.
2. Folium: It is a powerful data visualization library in Python that is built primarily to help people visualize geospatial data. With Folium, one can create a map of any location in the world if its latitude and longitude values are known.
3. Xgboost: XGBoost (eXtreme Gradient Boosting) is a highly efficient, flexible and portable distributed gradient boosting library. Under the Gradient Boosting Framework it implements machine learning algorithms.
4. gpxpy: It is used to calculate a straight line between two pairs in miles (latitude, longitude).

3.3 Data Cleaning

A uni-variate analysis of the data is done and all outliers/ erroneous points are removed in the following way:

- Latitude and longitude Data: Every pickup has longitude and latitude, we'll use that to define the city's boundary. New York is bounded by the location coordinates (40.5774−, 74.15) and (40.9176, −73.7004) hence any coordinates including both pickup and drop-off not within these coordinates are not considered by us.
- Trip Duration: The maximum permitted trip length in a 24-h period is 12 h, according to the New York Taxi and Limousine Commission Regulations. Hence we eliminated all the records where the length of the trip exceeds 12 h.

$$Tripduration = Dropofftime - pickuptime \tag{1}$$

- Speed: We calculated speed as travel distance divided by total time taken to complete the journey. Records which had the average speed value as negative are considered to be outliers and removed.
- Trip distance: Trip distance values which are either very high or negative in value are considered to be outliers.
- Fare: We have eliminated all points where the fare for the trip is either extremely high or negative.

4   Proposed Method

See Fig. 1.

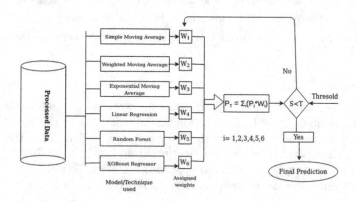

Fig. 1. Proposed model for predicting passenger demand.

4.1 Data Preparation

Clustering and Segmentation: Clustering is one of the most common exploratory data analysis techniques used to get an intuition about the structure of the data. During clustering the minimum inter-cluster distance considered is 0.5 mile and maximum distance considered is 2.0 mile as the taxi driver can travel 2 miles in 10 min time interval with an average speed of 12 mph (mile per hour). The K-means clustering algorithm has been used, based on the pickup size.

The number of clusters considered in an area is 40. In doing so it is observed that 9 out of 40 clusters maintain the inter-cluster distance of 2 miles. While the rest 31 clusters have an inter-cluster distance which is more than 2 miles. The minimum inter-cluster distance considered in this work is 0.506 as it has been experimentally observed that any inter-cluster distance below this value leads to the problem that the clusters will be very close to each other. We have experimented with bigger cluster sizes as well, but it is observed that the inter-cluster distance drops sharply which is not desirable.

Time Binning: Time is taken in the regular format and converted to the Unix timestamp and then divided by 600 to make bins of 10 min.

Smoothing Time-Series Data: As the data have been split into 10 min windows, while plotting the number of pickups versus time bins there may be a possibility that there will be zero pickups in any window which in turn will lead to zero issue divide. In order to get avoid this problem, some pickups from the neighboring bins are transferred to the bin containing zero pickups to make all the neighboring bin pickups equivalent. Smoothing is none other than zero avoidance. Ex: $(90, 0, 30)$ pickups can be converted as $(50, 50, 50)$.

4.2 Modeling

The modeling techniques taken into consideration in this work are:

Simple Moving Averages. Simple moving average is a technique for getting a general idea of the patterns in a data set. The moving average is of great help in predicting long-term patterns. The moving average model can be easily used in a controlled manner for prediction.

1. For ratio Feature: The first model used is the moving average model which uses the previous n values in order to predict the next value using the following formula:
$$R_t = (R_{t-1} + R_{t-2} + R_{t-3} + R_{t-n})/n \qquad (2)$$
   where, $R_{t-1} = p^{2016t} - 1/p^{2015t-1}$, n is the hyper parameter. The hyper parameter is the window size (n). It has been experimentally found that window size n = 3 is the optimal value for getting the best result using simple moving average. So the final formula used is:
$$R_t = (R_{t-1} + R_{t-2} + R_{t-3})/3 \qquad (3)$$

2. For previously known value the Moving averages of the 2016 values are used to predict the future values using the following formula:

$$P_t = (P_{t-1} + P_{t-2} + P_{t-3} \ldots P_{t-n})/n \tag{4}$$

In this method, the average value of n previously known values is used to predict the next known value. Here n is the hyper parameter. The hyper parameter is the manually tuned window-size (n) and it is found that the window-size of 1 is optimal to get the best results using Moving Averages using previous 2016 values, so the final formula used is:
$P_t = p_{t-1}$.

Weighted Moving Averages. In the Moving Average model used, equal importance is given to all the values within a window, but it is observed that the future is more likely to be similar to the latest values and less similar to the older ones. Weighted Averages supports this concept with the help of a statistical equation assigning the highest weight to the latest preceding value when measuring the averages and declining weights to the older ones that follow. Weighted Moving Averages using Ratio Values is given by the following formula:

$$R_t = (N*R_{t-1} + (N-1)*R_{t-2} + (N-2)*R_{t-3} \ldots 1*R_{t-n}/(N*(N+1)/2) \tag{5}$$

where R_t is the ratio, N is the weight distribution.

For ratio feature: The window size (n) is manually calibrated and it is found that the window size of 5 is ideal for achieving the best results using Weighted Moving Averages with previous Ratio values, therefore, we use the following formula:

$$R_t = (5*R_{t-1} + 4*R(t-2) + 3*R_{t-3} + 2*R_{t-1} + R_{t-5}/15 \tag{6}$$

For previously known value Weighted Moving Averages using Previous 2016 Value

$$P_t = (N*P_{t-1} + (N-1)*P_{t-2} + (N-2)*P_{t-3} \ldots 1*P_{t-n}/(N*(N+1)/2) \tag{7}$$

P_t is the predicted value. The hyper parameter is the manually adjusted window size (n) and it is found that a window size of 2 is ideal for achieving the best results using Weighted Moving Averages using previous values for 2016, so the final formula used is:

$$P_t = (2*P_{t-1} + P_{t-2})/3 \tag{8}$$

Exponential Weighted Moving Averages. In exponential moving average more weight is assigned to recent data points. By weighted average the analogy/equality of giving the latest value higher weighted is achieved. The subsequent weights are decreased for older points. But it is still unknown as to which scheme for assigning the weights will work best, as there are infinitely many possibilities for assigning weights in an increasing order and changing the window size of the hyper parameter. To simplify this process, the Exponential Moving Average has been next explored. This method is found to be a more logical way to assign weights while using an optimal window size at the same time. In the exponential moving average a single hyper parameter α is used whose value lies between 0 and 1. The weights and window sizes are configured based on the value of the hyper parameter alpha. The formula (9) is used to find the ratio and (10) is used to find the previous time bins.

Ratios:

$$R'_t = (\alpha * R_{t-1} + (1 - \alpha) * R'_{t-1}) \tag{9}$$

Previous Time Bins:

$$p'_t = (\alpha * p_{t-1} + (1 - \alpha) * p'_{t-1}) \tag{10}$$

4.3   Prediction Accuracy

For calculation of prediction accuracy Mean squared error and Mean absolute percentage error have been used.

Mean Squared Error: Mean Squared Error (MSE) or Mean Squared Deviation (MSD) calculates the cumulative squared difference between the predicted and actual values. It is a risk function, which corresponds to the expected value of the loss of squared error. It is always non-negative and near-zero values are better. The MSE is the second error moment (over the origin). MSE incorporates both the variance of the estimator and its bias using the following formula:

$$MSE = (1/N) \sum_{i=1}^{N} [Y_i - \hat{Y}_i]^2 \tag{11}$$

where, Y_i is the actual value $\hat{Y}_i$ is the predicted value.

Mean Absolute Percentage Error (MAPE): MAPE is also referred to as the Mean Absolute Percentage Error (MAPD). It is a method to measure predictive system accuracy in statistics, such as trend estimation. Due to its very straightforward definition of relative error, MAPE is commonly used as a loss function for regression problems and model evaluation. The formula for calculation of MAPE is as follows:

$$MSE = (100\%/n) \sum_{i=1}^{n} |A_t - F_t|/A_t \tag{12}$$

Where, A_t is the actual value and F_t is the predicted value.

5   Results

5.1   Error Metric Matrix (Forecasting Methods) - MAPE & MSE

Moving Averages (Ratios)
MAPE: 0.182115517339 MSE: 400.0625504032258
Moving Averages (2016 Values)
MAPE: 0.14292849687 MSE: 174.84901993727598 ——————

Weighted Moving Averages (Ratios) -
MAPE: 0.178486925438 MSE: 384.01578741039424
Weighted Moving Averages (2016 Values) -
MAPE: 0.135510884362 MSE: 162.46707549283155 ——————

Exponential Moving Averages (Ratios) -
MAPE: 0.177835501949 MSE: 378.34610215053766
Exponential Moving Averages (2016 Values) -
MAPE: 0.135091526367 MSE: 159.73614471326164

See Fig. 2.

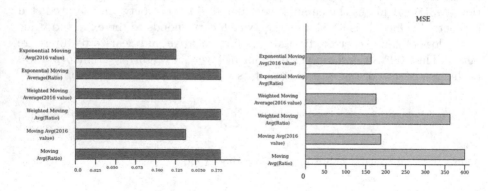

Fig. 2. Left side figure represents error metric matrix (MAPE) and right side figure represents error metric matrix (MSE).

5.2   Feature Engineering

Feature engineering is the method of extracting features from raw data using data mining techniques and domain knowledge. Such features may be used to improve machine learning algorithms performance. Feature engineering can be regarded as learning applied to the system itself. Based on the baseline model, it has been observed that the previous known value is efficient in forecasting pickups in the same area in the next time bin. So the last five time bins are added for next time bin in the same area to predict the pickups. The previous five features are used in data cleaning and modeling so the next sixth and seven features are the latitude and longitude of the origin of the region. The eight feature is the number of pickups in a day of the week. The ninth feature is the best model that gives the minimum error value. Frequency and amplitude for different time intervals are also considered using Fourier Transform.

Models Used: To test and train the data pertaining to 3 months of 2016 pickups are taken into consideration and split so that for each region 70% data is used for training and 30% data for testing.

1. Regression Model: To predict the number of pickups linear regression is employed on test and train data and then MAPE is calculated.
2. Random Forest Regressor: The Random Forest Regressor is used on the test and train data to predict the number of pickups and then to determine the MAPE.
3. XGboost Regressor: To predict the number the pickups the XGboost regressor is employed on the test and train data and then to determine the MAPE.

Error Metric Matrix (Tree Based Regression Methods) - MAPE

Baseline Model - Train: 0.14005275878 Test: 0.13653125704

Exponential Averages - Train: 0.1328996843 Test: 0.12936180420

Linear Regression - Train: 0.1333157201 Test: 0.12912029940

Random Forest Regression - Train: 0.091761954419 Test: 0.12724464713

XgBoost Regression - Train: 0.12938735567 Test: 0.126861699

6   Conclusion

In the forecasting methods used in this work it is observed that Exponential Weighted Moving Average gives the best prediction. This is because of the fact that the most recent data points are given the highest weight and the weights are subsequently decreased for the older data points. In the Feature Engineering methods XgBoost performs the best as with the additional features being included it works quite well for the prediction of the next pick-up locations.

7   Future Scope

An effort has been made to minimize the mean absolute percentage error. In future Long Short Term Memory which is extended version of Recurrent Neural Network may be explored. Long Short Term Memory is a type of Deep Neural Network and is a powerful technique to reduce the error. It has also been reported that LSTM works very well with time-series data based problems.

References

1. Lv, Y., Duan, Y., Kang, W., Li, Z., Wang, F.: Traffic flow prediction with big data: a deep learning approach. IEEE Trans. Intell. Transp. Syst. **16**(2), 865–873 (2015)
2. Huang, Z., et al.: PRACE: a taxi recommender for finding passengers with deep learning approaches. In: Huang, D.-S., Hussain, A., Han, K., Gromiha, M.M. (eds.) ICIC 2017. LNCS (LNAI), vol. 10363, pp. 759–770. Springer, Cham (2017). https://doi.org/10.1007/978-3-319-63315-2_66
3. Rodrigues, F., Ioulia, M., Pereira, F.: Combining time-series and textual data for taxi demand prediction in event areas: a deep learning approach. Inform. Fusion **49** (2018). https://doi.org/10.1016/j.inffus.2018.07.007
4. Jindal, I., Qin, T., Chen, X., Nokleby, M., Ye, J.: A Unified Neural Network Approach for Estimating Travel Time and Distance for a Taxi Trip (2017)
5. Kuang, L., Yan, X., Tan, X., Li, S., Yang, X.: Predicting taxi demand based on 3D convolutional neural network and multi-task learning. Remote Sens. **11**, 1265 (2019). https://doi.org/10.3390/rs11111265
6. Jiang, W., Zhang, L.: Geospatial data to images: a deep-learning framework for traffic forecasting. Tsinghua Sci. Technol. **24**(1), 52–64 (2019)
7. Moreira-Matias, L., Gama, J., Ferreira, M., Mendes-Moreira, J., Damas, L.: Predicting taxi-passenger demand using streaming data. IEEE Trans. Intell. Transp. Syst. **14**(3), 1393–1402 (2013)
8. Li, B., et al.: Hunting or waiting? Discovering passenger-finding strategies from a large-scale real-world taxi dataset. In: 2011 IEEE International Conference on Pervasive Computing and Communications Workshops (PERCOM Workshops), Seattle, WA, pp. 63–68 (2011)
9. Zheng, Y., Liu, Y., Yuan, J., Xie, X.: Urban computing with taxicabs. In: UbiComp 2011 – Proceedings of the 2011 ACM Conference on Ubiquitous Computing, pp. 89–98 (2011). https://doi.org/10.1145/2030112.2030126

A Novel Approach to Synthesize Hinglish Text to English Text

Ujwala Baruah[(✉)], N. Harini, Supraja Venkatesh, Khushbu Maloo,
and Rahul Debnath

National Institute of Technology, Silchar, Silchar, India
b.ujwala@gmail.com, harininarayanan1012@gmail.com, vsupraja98@gmail.com,
khushbumaloo96@gmail.com, rdebnath93@gmail.com

Abstract. The world is moving towards a communication based society and no natural language is used in its pure form. Languages have evolved to accommodate linguistic codes from other languages for better communication and understanding. Such languages are code-mixed and translation of the same becomes tedious, and presently, more essential than ever. Code-mixing of Hindi and English on a day-to-day basis (colloquially called Hinglish) is very common in India. In this paper, we present a mechanism for the translation of Hinglish written in Roman text to English text.

Keywords: Machine translation · Hinglish · Code-mixed

1 Introduction

In this present fast moving, well-connected and global economy, communication has become more essential than ever. Two things that have risen from this is that, one, no natural language is untouched anymore. All languages have adopted words from other languages to supplement their own vocabulary and to make communication easier and accessible. And two, it has made the speed and efficiency of translation more crucial than ever. Code-Switching and Code-Mixing are stable and well-studied linguistic phenomena of multilingual speech communities. Code-Switching is "juxtaposition within the same speech exchange of passages of speech belonging to two different grammatical systems or subsystems" [8], and Code-Mixing refers to the embedding of linguistic units such as phrases, words and morphemes of one language into an utterance of another language [5]. Thus, Code-Switching is usually intersentential while Code-Mixing (CM) is an intrasentential phenomenon. Linguists believe that there exists a continuum in the manner in which a lexical item transfers from one to another of two languages in contact [5].

In the present communication-based Indian society, no natural language seems to have been left untouched by the trends of Hindi-English code-mixing.

A. Bhattacharjee et al. (Eds.): MIND 2020, CCIS 1241, pp. 347–356, 2020.
https://doi.org/10.1007/978-981-15-6318-8_29

This gives rise to a mixed language which is neither totally Hindi nor English language. The Hinglish language poses a new challenge to the problem of machine translation.

Here are a few examples to illustrate the problem at hand along with the required machine translation:

Hinglish text: doctor ne use cough syrup prescribe kiya hai.
Translated text: 'The doctor prescribed him a cough syrup'

Hinglish Text: maine party ke liye uski black dress borrow ki.
Translated Text: 'I borrowed her black dress for the party'

Besides using Hinglish for mere general communication, tag lines of different commercial brands are motivated by the popularity of Hinglish in the Indian society. Domino's Pizza: "Hungry kya?"

Hence, a code-mixed (Hinglish) translation helps the Indian content creators, who tend to make videos, or write blogs using both Hindi and English, in taking their ideas and opinions to a larger audience. As many social media users have adapted to colloquially using Hinglish, translation to English would provide more exhaustive information extraction exploiting social media and user-generated content. Also, it could provide speakers with less knowledge of English to write English text.

As translation is a labour intensive process, automating translation is seen to gain popularity. Difficulties in using the existing machine translation systems is because of the inaccuracy in the translation of code-mixed languages. English has permeated all sections of the society in India and it is used to supplement the vocabulary of native Indian languages. One such hybrid language is Hinglish (a portmanteau for the combination of Hindi and English). Though the MT systems available translate Hindi to English efficiently, Hinglish translation is not as satisfactory.

In this paper, we have adopted a neural machine translation approach. Neural Machine translation (NMT) jointly aligns and translates without the requirement of the predetermined set of features. NMT is a fully trainable model and only the parallel corpora is used to train and tune the model to get maximum translation performance.

2   Related Research

In paper [4], the common social media phenomenon of code-mixing is talked about. It is understood that content generated by social media users who are multilingual, though code mixing and borrowing from different languages can be easily identified, there exist variations in the way the words are spelt, grammar is used and transliterations are made that are unusual to say the least resulting in high complexity to model these computationally. Word level language identification is essential for analysis. This paper, [5] experimented with seven languages to identify language at word level using a novel unsupervised technique and results showed 74% relative error reduction in word level labelling. In paper [9], the authors have collected and annotated code-mixed Hinglish Social media messages taken from Twitter and Facebook and worked on automatic part of speech tagging. In paper [6], the authors have investigated about the various constraints and rules of code-switching in Hinglish language data and also discussed about their procedure for collecting mixed language corpus. In paper [14], the authors have discussed about the grammatical constraints occur in the bilingual switching and hence, investigated about the psycholinguist and neurolinguist studies. In paper [12], a mechanism for machine translation of Hinglish to pure (standard) Hindi and pure English forms is done based on the language of the verb of the sentence. The sentences are classified into Simple Code Mixed Hindi (SCMH), Simple Code Mixed English (SCME) and Complex Code Mixed (CCM). The sentences are fed to Hindi and English Morphological Analyzers and unknown, unmarked words are analyzed for plural forms. The Isolated SCMH and SCME are translated completely to Hindi and the Hindi translation is further translated to English. Though this classification of code-mixed sentences based on grammar is a popular idea for translation, we realise that it fails for some grammar like polysemous verbs, Hindi gerunds and Hindi verb infinitive forms. The approach [7] is similar in a way that there is an embedded language and a matrix language and a sentence in a code-mixed language follows the grammar of the matrix language. Recent papers on machine translation use Neural Machine Translation. In paper [15], different components of Statistical Machine Translation approaches (SMT), the role of deep learning models in improving different components of SMT, have been discussed. This paper helped us to understand end-to-end neural machine translation (NMT) and the basic encoder-decoder based NMT, attention based model. Moreover, our approach is similar to [10] where RNN based deep learning is used for translation of Japanese to English. Further, this paper [3] introduced a code-mixing index to evaluate the level of blending in the corpora and describe the performance of a system developed to separate multiple languages. The word level language detection is experimented with a system based on well-studied techniques, namely N-gram Language Profiling and Pruning, Dictionary-Based Detection and SVM-based Word-Language Detection.

3   Problem Definition

Ideally, content created by Internet users, no matter in which language, should be used to understand the general population that exists on the internet. India has around 560 million internet users and the most common language, Hinglish used is not even a language. Somewhere between two languages, Hindi and English and somewhere between the spoken languages and the written languages, Hinglish content stands as a treasure trove of untapped information. The reality is that most existing systems tuned to extracting data from English text are unable to use this content. Our aim in this research is to create a model that translates Hindi-English (Hinglish) code-mixed text to English (Roman) text. This would enable existing information extractions to be used for this content.

4   Methodology

The following sections describe the methodology followed, the databases used for experimentation and the modelling techniques employed.

4.1   Data Flow Diagram

The data flow diagram is represented in Fig. 1.

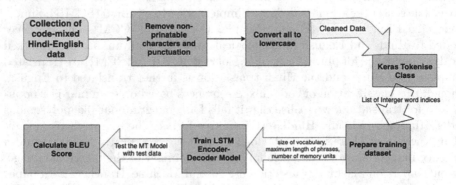

Fig. 1. Data flow diagram

4.2   Databases Used

Though code-mixed data is widely seen on the internet, there does not exist a parallel corpus with code-mixed Hindi-English and its translation. So data collection for this work has involved a combination of identifying data that could be used for this purpose and generating efficient data from it. The datasets used for experimentation in this paper are the Universal Word - Hindi Dictionary [2], Datasets for FIRE 2013 Track on Transliterated Sear [1], Xlit-Crowd: Hindi-English Transliteration Corpus. The sentences selected has about 100–300 characters and are manually translated with help of dictionaries to generate the complete dataset.

4.3   Data Pre-processing

To create a reliable dataset, the following pre-processing steps were followed:

1. All non-printable characters and punctuation characters are removed.
2. Normalisation of the case to lowercase is carried.
3. The non-alphabetic tokens were removed.
4. A final file with both the source and translation separated by a tab space is created.

After cleaning there are about 7000 pairs, from which the training and testing datasets are split.

4.4 Modelling Techniques Used

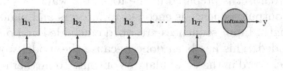

Fig. 2. Recurrent neural network

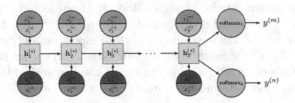

Fig. 3. Architecture of LSTM

1. In order to model the persistence ability of human brain, the Neural Network technology of Deep Learning has been used in this work. But, it is well observed that traditional Neural Networks face shortcomings in classifying the current situation based on previous memory. Hence, Recurrent neural networks have been used to overcome this issue (Fig. 2).
2. Next Recurrent neural networks (RNN) are used. RNNs are the networks which allow information to persist. These networks have loops in them, which facilitate passing of information from one point of the network to another. Basically, RNNs are chains of NNs, each passing the message to its successor.
3. Finally Long Short Term Memory networks has been employed. LSTMs are special RNNs, explicitly designed to avoid the long-term dependency problem namely, remembering information for long periods of time. The Encoder-Decoder LSTM is explicitly designed to address sequence-to-sequence problems, sometimes called seq2seq. LSTM Encoder-Decoder, consists of two RNNs that act as an encoder and a decoder pair. A variable-length source sequence is taken, which is mapped to a fixed-length vector by this encoder, and the vector representation is mapped back to a variable-length target sequence by the decoder (Fig. 3).
   In paper [13], the author describes the fundamental basics of LSTM and RNN.
4. From [11], the architecture of the LSTM model used is shown.

4.5 Proposed Method

The dataset is loaded to start training the neural machine translation model. The English phrases along with the corresponding Hinglish phrases are used to create a combined dataset. The words are thereafter mapped to integers, as needed for modeling. Separate tokenizers are used for the English sequences and the Hinglish sequences.

The training dataset is prepared in the following way:
Each input and output sequence is encoded to integers and padded to the maximum phrase length. Input sequences are word embedded and output sequences are one-hot encoded. This has been done because the model would predict the probability of each word in the vocabulary as output. To further refine the model, an encoder-decoder LSTM model has been used in this work. In this model, a front-end encoder model encodes the input sequence model and then a back-end decoder model decodes each word.

A number of parameters for configuration are taken as input parameters to the model, such as, the model is configured by the size of the input vocabularies, output vocabularies and the maximum length of input and output phrases.

The efficient Adam approach to Stochastic Gradient Descent is used to train the model, which is observed to have minimized the categorical loss function as the prediction problem is framed as a multi-class classification.

4.6   Evaluation with Neural Translation Model

A translation for the input taken has been generated firstly. Thereafter, it is repeated for all the other different inputs. The performance and efficiency of the model across all of the inputs have been evaluated.

It is observed that the model can perform the mapping for each integer in the translation, the result of which is returned as a string of words. This is repeated for every source string in the dataset and then the result is computed by comparing the predicted translation with the target phrase expected.

4.7   Bilingual Evaluation Understudy (BLEU) Score

The BLEU Score is a measure of performance of a translation model and a metric for evaluating a generated sentence with a target sentence. It is calculated to get a quantitative idea of how well a given model has performed. The score achieved is 1.0 in case of a perfect match and 0.0 in case of a perfect mismatch. The BLEU score is calculated using the following formula:

$$BLEU = min\left(i, exp\left(1 - \frac{referencelength}{outputlength}\right)\right)\left(\prod_{i=1}^{4} precision_i\right)^{\frac{1}{4}}$$

with

$$precision_i = \frac{\sum_{snd \, \epsilon \, Cand-corpus} \sum_{i \, \epsilon \, snt} min\left(m_{cand}^i, m_{ref}^i\right)}{w_t^i = \sum_{snd' \, \epsilon \, Cand-corpus} \sum_{j \, \epsilon \, snt'} m_{cand}^j} \; where,$$

m_{cand}^i is the count of i-gram in candidate matching the reference translation

m_{ref}^i is the count of i-gram in the reference translation

w_t^i is the total number of i-grams in candidate translation

snt' Sentences which do not belong to the candidate corpus.

5 Experimental Results and Discussion

5.1 Cleaned Dataset

The dataset is cleaned and each of the English/Hindi word is mapped to the corresponding Hindi/English equivalent word. A sample of the mapping is given below:

[half] ↔ [aadha]
[the manner] ↔ [aacharan]
[habit] ↔ [aadat]
[base] ↔ [aadhaar]
[base] ↔ [aadhar]

5.2 Vocabulary Sizes

- The various parameters as needed for modeling by mapping words to integers have been found. The English sequences and the Hindi-English code-mixed sequences have separate tokenizers.
- The tokenizer is trained on a list of phrases. The maximum length in the list of phrases is obtained by calculating the length of the longest sequence.
- Each input and output sequence is encoded to integers. They are then padded to the maximum phrase length. Every input sequence has a word embedding. The output sequence is encoded using one hot encoding.

The size of the final vocabulary on which the experimentation has been done is the follows:

English Vocabulary size: 46985
Hindi Vocabulary: 73880

5.3 Training

With a total of 42729 sentences in our dataset, we take 37729 sentences for training the model and 5000 sentences for testing. The model is trained for 30 epochs and a batch size of 64 samples.

To ensure that each time the performance of the model is improved, the model is checkpointed and the obtained checkpoints are saved.

5.4 Predictions Obtained

- src = [andrews], target = [andrews], predicted = [andrew]
- src = [bad], target = [bad], predicted = [bad]
- src = [velvet], target = [velvet], predicted = [velvet]
- src = [arnald], target = [arnold], predicted = [arnold]
- src = [august], target = [august], predicted = [august]
- src = [kounse dryer], target = [which dryer], predicted = [which dryer]

- src = [bohot painful], target = [very painful], predicted = [very the painful]
- src = [tribunal times hai], target = [it's tribunal times], predicted = [turn tribunal is]
- src = [main gujarat me ahmedabad se hu], target = [I am from ahmedabad in gujarat], predicted = [I am the gujarat me ahmedabad]
- src = [main class 1 se 12th tak wahi raha], target = [I stayed there from class 1 to 12th], predicted = [I the from class tak 1 to 12 raha]

5.5   BLEU Scores Obtained

Table 1 gives the BLEU scores obtained for unigram (BLEU-1), bigram (BLEU-2), trigram (BLEU-3) and 4-gram (BLEU-4).

Table 1. BLEU score result

Type of BLEU	Value obtained
BLEU-1	30.7779
BLEU-2	1.7283
BLEU-3	8.6567
BLEU-4	12.9506

The low score achieved for 2-grams is because the 2-gram order is larger than the overlap that exists between the reference and hypothesis and thus, corpus BLEU perform poorly in this case. This is because a huge chunk of the dataset is unigrams on account of unavailability of appropriate code-mixed sentences (Table 2).

Table 2. Interpretation of obtained of BLEU scores

BLEU score	Interpretation
Lesser than 10	Almost Useless
10–19	Hard to get the gist
20–29	The gist is clear but has significant grammatical errors
30–40	Understandable to good translations
40–50	High quality translations
50–60	Very high quality, adequate and fluent translations
Greater than 60	Quality often better than humans

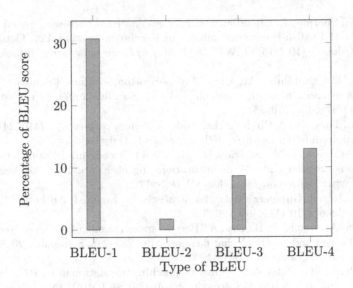

6   Conclusion and Future Work

Substantial amount of work has been done by various researchers using bi-lingual databases. In this work the experimentation has been carried out on a Hindi-English database and an attempt has been made to convert the code-mixed text to English (Roman) text using RNN. The results thus obtained are promising, though not excellent. The uni-gram model is seen to give the best score. This is because it is considering one word at a time. It is reported that the Google translator has a BLEU-1 score of 32 while the BLEU-1 score for this work is 30.779. This is probably because of the much bigger training dataset as compared to the one that is used in this work. While considering sentences, the best score is obtained by using BLEU-4 which is 12.9506. There is no reported literature with a BLEU-4 score as high as this. The reason behind not being able to come up with very high BLEU scores is because of the fact the BLEU scores are the standards for representing the results of conversion from one language to another. Hence they are not expected to work very efficiently with code-mixed languages.

In future an attempt will be made to improve the BLEU score by accumulating more data. As a larger vocabulary is expected to improve the BLEU scores.

References

1. http://cse.iitkgp.ac.in/resgrp/cnerg/qa/fire13translit/
2. http://www.cfilt.iitb.ac.in/~hdict/
3. Amitava Das, B.G.: Identifying languages at the word level in code-mixed Indian social media text. NLP Association of India (2014)

4. Bali, K., Sharma, J., Choudhury, M., Vyas, Y.: "I am borrowing ya mixing?" An analysis of English-Hindi code mixing in Facebook, pp. 116–126, October 2014. https://doi.org/10.3115/v1/W14-3914. https://www.aclweb.org/anthology/W14-3914

5. Davies, E., Bentahila, A.: Carol Myers-Scotton, contact linguistics: bilingual encounters and grammatical outcomes. Lang. Soc. **36** (2007). https://doi.org/10.1017/S0047404507070285

6. Dey, A., Fung, P.: A Hindi-English code-switching corpus, pp. 2410–2413 (2014). http://dblp.uni-trier.de/db/conf/lrec/lrec2014.html#DeyF14

7. Dhar, M., Kumar, V., Shrivastava, M.: Enabling code-mixed translation: parallel corpus creation and MT augmentation approach, pp. 131–140, August 2018. https://www.aclweb.org/anthology/W18-3817

8. Gal, S.: John J. Gumperz's discourse strategies. J. Linguist. Anthropol. **23** (2013). https://doi.org/10.1111/jola.12023

9. Jamatia, A., Gambäck, B., Das, A.: Part-of-speech tagging for code-mixed English-Hindi Twitter and Facebook chat messages, pp. 239–248, September 2015. https://www.aclweb.org/anthology/R15-1033

10. Chaudhary, J.R., Patel, A.C.: Bilingual machine translation using RNN based deep learning. Int. J. Sci. Res. Sci. Eng. Technol. IJSRSET **4**(4), 1480–1484 (2018)

11. Liu, P., Qiu, X., Huang, X.: Recurrent neural network for text classification with multi-task learning. CoRR abs/1605.05101 (2016). http://arxiv.org/abs/1605.05101

12. Sinha, R.M.K., Thakur, T.: Machine translation of bi-lingual Hindi-English (Hinglish) text. IIT Kanpur (2005)

13. Sherstinsky, A.: Fundamentals of recurrent neural network (RNN) and long short-term memory (LSTM) network. CoRR abs/1808.03314 (2018). http://arxiv.org/abs/1808.03314

14. Singh, R.: Grammatical constraints on code-mixing: evidence from Hindi-English. Can. J. Linguist. **30**, 33–45 (1985). https://doi.org/10.1017/S0008413100010677

15. Srivastava, S., Shukla, A., Tiwari, R.: Machine translation: from statistical to modern deep-learning practices, December 2018

Comparative Analysis of Neural Models for Abstractive Text Summarization

Heena Kumari[1]([✉]), Sunita Sarkar[1], Vikrant Rajput[2], and Arindam Roy[1]

[1] Assam University, Silchar, India
heenasingh1995@gmail.com, sunitasarkar@rediffmail.com,
arindam_roy74@rediffmail.com
[2] National Institute of Technology, Silchar, India
vikrantrajput040@gmail.com

Abstract. Abstractive text summarization is the task of generating the summary of text documents like humans do. It's completely laborious and time taking process to summarize the lengthy documents manually. Abstractive text summarization takes a document as input and produces a summary by combining a piece of information from different source sentences and paraphrase them while maintaining the overall meaning of the document. Here, the abstractive text summarization task is done using various sequence-to-sequence (seq2seq) models and their performance has been analyzed on the MSMO dataset. Seq2seq with attention, pointer generator network (PGN) and pointer generator with coverage models are used to generate the summary. To improve accuracy, hyper-parameters were tuned and successfully obtained good results. ROUGE and BLEU scores are used to evaluate the performance of these models. Seq2seq with attention, PGN, and PGN with coverage models achieved ROUGE-1 scores 35.49, 38.19, 37.68 respectively. These neural abstractive text summarization models have also performed effectively in terms of the BLEU score and achieved BLEU-1 scores 40.60, 44.50, 45.20 respectively.

Keywords: Extractive text summarization · Abstractive text summarization · Sequence-to-sequence · Pointer generator network

1 Introduction

The job to summarize a text document is to generate a short summary that consists of a few sentences and captures the main idea of text document. Text summarization is very important in natural language understanding. It gives a precise summary so that humans can understand the gist of long documents in less time.

The text summarization can be broadly classified into two sub-classes. The first one is extractive text summarization (ETS) which is just extracting the important keywords, phrases, sentences and combining them to produce a summary. The second one is abstractive text summarization (ABS) which generates

© Springer Nature Singapore Pte Ltd. 2020
A. Bhattacharjee et al. (Eds.): MIND 2020, CCIS 1241, pp. 357–368, 2020.
https://doi.org/10.1007/978-981-15-6318-8_30

a more powerful summary by generating new keywords, phrases, sentences and combine them to make a summary like humans do.

Lately, by the advancement of computation devices and more research in deep learning, seq2seq models have been introduced for the ATS task which depicts the input document into the output summary. In this paper, various types of encoder-decoder models have used and analyzed based on ROUGE [3] score and BLEU [6] score to quantify the quality of the generated summary.

The remaining part of the paper is divided into sections as follows: Some related work has been concisely discussed in Sect. 2. Different types of ATS models are discussed in Sect. 3. In Sect. 4, the used dataset has been discussed. Section 5 describes the experiments. Section 6, gives detailed results and comparative analysis of results acquired from various systems. Lastly, Sect. 7 ends the paper with conclusions.

2　Related Work

Lots of previously existing summarization approaches are either extractive or abstractive. In extractive summarization, the model extracts only important keywords, phrases and sentences from articles and combines them to produce summary. These kinds of models cannot produce new keywords, phrases, sentences that can be added into the summary so that the summary looks more likely as humans do. Abstractive text summarization produces the summary by paraphrasing the source document and generating new phrases that are not in the source document. In recent five years, lots of research is done in the area of Deep Learning, and it can handle many NLP tasks. Most of the state of the art abstractive text summarization models have used seq2seq models with attention [1]. Many researchers have used the attention model [1] as a base model for their work. Sutskever [9] introduced the seq2seq model for neural machine translation but it had disadvantage that as the length of the document increases the accuracy was decreasing. To get over this disadvantage, Bahdanau [1] introduced an attention mechanism that finds the parts in the source document that are closely related to generate the next word. Later, these seq2seq models were being used for text summarization also. Nallapati [5] used an attentional encoder-decoder model for text summarization and achieved the best result. There were many problems like generation of words which are absent in vocabulary and repetition of words. See [7] introduced the pointer generator network to generates the words which are absent in vocabulary and also used coverage mechanism to get rid of the word repetition problem. Liu [4] used a generative adversarial network for abstractive text summarization. Song [8] used an LSTM-CNN based ATS model to generate the summary.

3　Proposed Models

In this section we narrate our proposed ATS models: (1) Sequence-to-sequence with attention (2) Pointer Generator Network (3) Coverage Mechanism.

3.1   Seq2seq with Attention Model

In prior work, Seq2seq model has been used by Sutskever [9] for machine translation, but there is a problem with this model. If long sentences are encoded into a fixed-length vector, it starts losing the information. So seq2seq with attention mechanism is used to get over this disadvantage. Seq2seq with attention model was introduced by Bahdanau [1] for machine translation and is depicted in Fig. 1. Later it has been used by many researchers as a baseline system for their research work. In this encoder-decoder model, encoder compress input sequence $W = (w_1, w_2, ..., w_{T_x})$ to a fixed-length vector. The decoder produces output at each timestamp. The encoder will produce hidden state z_t by taking word w_t and previous hidden state z_{t-1} in every time step. The output of the last timestamp of the encoder is given to the decoder as initial input. At each timestamp t, the decoder will predict a target word by soft search for the relevant part of the source sentence.

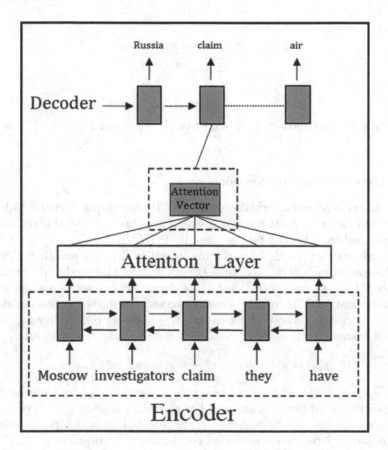

Fig. 1. Seq2seq with attention model Architecture

The decoder will produce the target word o_t by taking the context vector c and all the previously predicted target words $o_1, o_2, \ldots\ldots, o_{t-1}$ as input. The decoder defines the probability of generating word o_i as follows:

$$p(o_i|o_1, ..., o_{i-1}, W) = q(o_{i-1}, m_i, c_i) \tag{1}$$

where, q is a non-linear function that outputs the probability o_i and m_i is the outcome vector of decoder at time i, can be estimated as

$$m_i = f(m_{i-1}, o_{i-1}, c_i) \tag{2}$$

Context vector c_i is determined by the set of hidden states $(z_1, z_2..., z_{T_x})$. z_i contains the details of part of surrounding i^{th} input word.

$$c_i = \sum_{j=1}^{T_x} \alpha_{ij} z_j \tag{3}$$

α_{ij} is computed as:

$$\alpha_{ij} = \frac{exp(e_{ij})}{\sum_{k=1}^{T_x} exp(e_{ik})} \tag{4}$$

where,

$$e_{ij} = a(m_{i-1}, z_j) \tag{5}$$

e_{ij} gives a score that shows the alignment of jth input word and $(i-1)^{th}$ decoder output.

3.2 Pointer Generator Network

The previous model has several disadvantages. It reproduces factual details inaccurately and cannot output the words which are absent in vocabulary and also repeat themselves. This can be overcome by PGN [7].

PGN can extract words from the input article through pointing, that produces the correct factual details, while novel words will be produced through the generator. This network can be called a combination of extractive and abstractive text summarization. The context vector is the same as in the previous model and attention distribution also. For timestamp t, generating probability $p_{out} \in [0, 1]$ is derived from context vector c_t^*, decoder's hidden state z_t and input x_t:

$$p_{out} = sigmoid(w_{c*}^T c_t^* + w_z^T z_t + w_x^T x_t + b_{ptr}) \tag{6}$$

vectors w_{c*}, w_z, w_x and b_{ptr} are trainable weights. p_{gen} gives probability of making output word from vocabulary. For each document extended vocabulary is used, created by the combination of the vocabulary and input document's words. Equation 7 represents extended vocabulary's distribution:

$$P(w) = p_{out} P_{voc}(w) + (1 - p_{out}) \sum_{j:w_j=w} a_j^t \tag{7}$$

If word w is absent in the vocabulary, then P_{voc} of word w is 0 and if w is not in the input article, then $\sum_{i:w_i=w} \alpha_i^t$ is 0. One of the main benefit of pointer generator models is its ability to produce words that are not present in the library.

3.3 Coverage Mechanism

There is a problem of the repetition of words in our previous seq2seq models. So, there is a need for something to keep track of what has been summarized so that the repetition of words can be controlled in the generated summary. So coverage mechanism [7] is used to track what is already summarized. It prevents the repetition of words. In coverage mechanism, coverage vector c^t is calculated as:

$$c^t = \sum_{t'=0}^{t-1} a^{t'} \tag{8}$$

4   Dataset

The dataset that has been used for the experiment is called MSMO Dataset [10]. The dataset has been downloaded from the nlpr website[1]. MSMO Dataset contains text articles, the title of the article, corresponding summaries, images related to the article and captions of the image. In the experiment, only text article files have been taken. The text data file's inside view has been shown in Fig. 2.

Each text file contains article's title, article's body and article's multiple summaries. Article title has been used as an article summary. Article's title and body have been extracted from the text file. A parallel article summary corpus has been created. Dataset statistics have been given in Table 1. Source documents's word distribution is shown in Fig. 3 and the target summary's word distribution is shown in Fig. 4.

Table 1. Dataset statistics.

Data	Data samples
Training data	293760
Validation data	10344
Test data	10251

---

[1] http://www.nlpr.ia.ac.cn/cip/dataset.htm.

```
@title
Was the CIA tailing Woodward and Bernstein ? Newly released documents show the

@body
Newly published documents reveal the CIA was keeping a close eye on the two jou
The information was contained in a massive dump of more than 12 million pages (
Including in the trove of documents were hundreds of pages about Bob Woodward a
There were memos suggesting the agency was investigating the pair , with one sa
It was dated January 31 , 1980 - almost eight years after the Watergate break i


@summary
The CIA published about 13 million declassified documents online on Tuesday

@summary
Including in the file dump are hundreds of pages on the Watergate journalists

@summary
Bob Woodward and Carl Bernstein exposed saga that took down Richard Nixon

@summary
CIA memos from after Watergate said they wanted to know more about the duo
```

Fig. 2. Text data inside view of .txt files

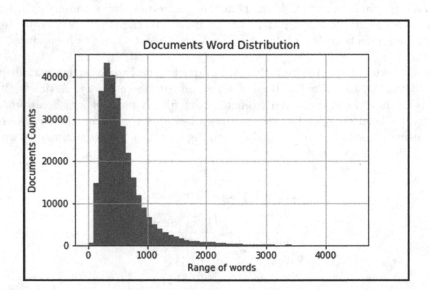

Fig. 3. Source documents word distribution

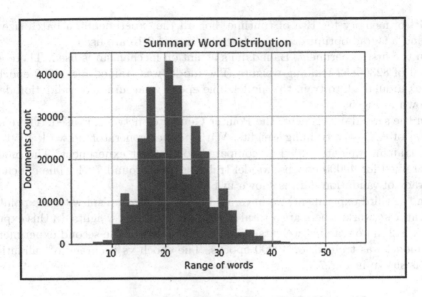

Fig. 4. Target summary word distribution

5   Experiment

5.1   Text Pre-processing

Following steps have been done to pre-process the text data:

1. Converted the text into lower case.
2. Contractions have been expanded.
3. Removed special characters and symbols.
4. Removed those articles in which summary contains less than 6 words.
5. Truncated the source article after 100 words and target summary after 25 words.

5.2   Training

OpenNMT [2] toolkit is used to develop the models. OpenNMT is an open-source toolkit that is used for neural machine translation and neural sequence learning. OpenNMT was started in December 2016 by the Harvard NLP group and SYSTRAN.

In all the experiments, a bi-directional LSTM is used as Encoder which outputs 512-dimensional hidden state with dropout rate 0.3 and an LSTM Decoder which outputs hidden state of 512-dimensions with dropout rate 0.3. Also for all the experiments, source vocabulary is of 210002 words and target vocabulary is of 80004 words. Also, each word is embedded in 128 dimensions. Each model's validation accuracy was checked for every 1000 epochs. All the models have been trained in Google Colaboratory which provides Nvidia's Tesla P100 GPU with

25 GB of memory for 12 h of runtime. For all the experiments, a batch size of 128 and adagrad optimizer with a learning rate of 0.15 are used.

In the first experiment, Bahadanu's attention mechanism is used. There are a total of 82366852 training weights. The model was trained for 50000 epochs. It took around 4 h to train the model. The epoch vs accuracy of validation data is shown in Fig. 5.

In the second experiment, the Pointer Generator network is used. There are a total of 83417477 training weights. With pointer generator network 1050625 more training weights added as compared to the first experiment. The model was trained for 40000 epochs. Model training took around 7.5 h. The epoch vs accuracy of validation data is shown in Fig. 6.

In the third experiment, we have used coverage mechanism with the pointer generator network. There are a total of 83417989 training weights. In this experiment, 512 more training weights added as compared to the second experiment. The model was trained for 40000 epochs. The epoch vs accuracy of validation data is shown in Fig. 7.

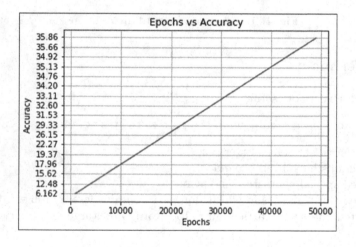

Fig. 5. Seq2seq with attention model validation accuracy graph

6   Results and Analysis

The performance of the proposed model has been evaluated in terms of BLEU [6] Score and ROUGE [3] score. These metrics are the standard performance measures for the summary evaluation task. Moses' multi-bleu.perl script is used to calculate the BLEU score. The script has been downloaded from the github knowledge sharing social group[2]. In further subsection, obtained results have been analyzed and a brief comparative analysis is done with Zhu's MSMO [10] result.

---

[2] https://github.com/moses-smt/mosesdecoder/blob/master/scripts/generic/multi-bleu.perl.

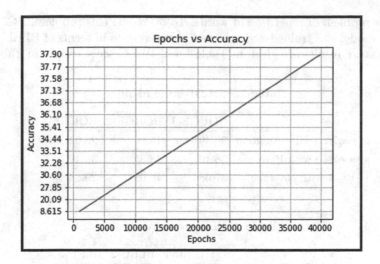

Fig. 6. PGN model validation accuracy graph

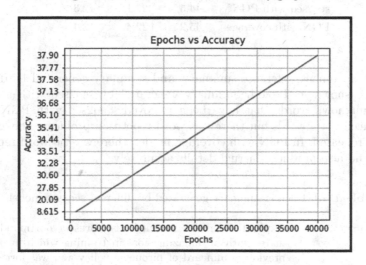

Fig. 7. PGN with coverage model validation accuracy graph

6.1 Results

ROUGE score and BLEU score results of the models are presented in Table 2 and Table 3 respectively. The obtained results reveal that the seq2seq with PGN performed best in terms of ROUGE score and seq2seq with PGN and coverage performed best in terms of BLEU Score.

First, seq2seq with attention model was trained and it achieved good ROUGE score. Afterward, producing the words which are absent in vocabulary, seq2seq with pointer generator model was trained which lead to fine improvements in the result. Then the generated summary was analyzed and it was found that there is a problem of repetition of words. To overcome this problem, PGN with coverage model was trained and achieved better results in terms of BLEU score. ROUGE score results are given in Table 2 and BLEU score results in Table 3.

Table 2. ROUGE score results

Model	ROUGE-1	ROUGE-2	ROUGE-L
seq2seq with attention	35.49	15.96	28.07
seq2seq with PGN	38.19	18.35	30.40
PGN with coverage	37.68	18.08	29.84

Table 3. BLEU score results

Model	BLEU-1	BLEU-2	BLEU-3
seq2seq with attention	40.6	18.7	10.0
seq2seq with PGN	44.5	22.1	12.3
PGN with coverage	45.2	22.4	12.4

A text document, reference summary, and summary generated by different models are shown in Table 4. Summary generated by seq2seq with attention contains unknown words that have been removed. Seq2seq with PGN model has produced novel words but there was word repetition problem. The 'camera' word was repeated. In PGN with coverage model, there was no word repetition problem and also produced factual details accurately.

Table 4. Abstractive summary generated by different seq2seq models

Text document	Raphael Guerreiro stunned his borussia dortmund team mates with an amazing goal in training which involved a previously unheard of pirouette volley and was fortunately caught on a cctv camera
Reference summary	Borussia dortmund defender Raphael Guerreiro scores amazing pirouette volley in training and he is only just returned from a four month injury
seq2seq with attention	Real madrid star raphael guerreiro shows off his skills as he is caught on camera camera
seq2seq with PGN	Borussia dortmund borussia dortmund raphael guerreiro scores amazing goal in training
PGN with coverage	Borussia dortmund goalkeeper raphael guerreiro shows off his amazing goal in training

6.2   Comparative Analysis

When comparing these three seq2seq models with ZHU [10] experiments, seq2seq with attention model has produced better results as compared to ZHU's MSMO base model. Table 5 describes the result comparison with ZHU [10] in terms of ROUGE score.

Table 5. ROUGE score comparison with ZHU [10] experiment

Model	ROUGE-1	ROUGE-2	ROUGE-L
seq2seq with attention (Proposed model)	35.49	15.96	28.07
PGN with coverage (Proposed model)	37.68	18.08	29.84
S2S+attn (ZHU's base model)	32.32	12.44	29.65
PGC (ZHU's base model)	41.11	18.31	37.74

7   Conclusions

Different types of encoder-decoder models are presented in this paper and their performance is analyzed. MSMO text dataset is used to train the models and estimated the ROUGE score which significantly outperformed and gave better results. The traditional neural network methods for ATS is encoder-decoder model approach. The encoder compresses the whole sequence into a constant size vector from which decoder decodes the information. But the problem with this approach is that by encoding long sentences into a fixed-length vector, it starts losing the information. To address this issue seq2seq with attention is used which searches for the relevant part in the input sequence to generate the next output word. Seq2seq with attention model achieved 35.49 ROUGE-1 score and the ROUGE-1 score of existing seq2seq with attention is 32.32 on MSMO data. The ROUGE-1 score of seq2seq with attention is improved by 3.17. Further, It was analyzed that there was a problem in generating the words which are absent in vocabulary and some words were repeating. To address the problem of generating the words which are absent in vocabulary. PGN was used and to address word repetition issue PGN with coverage was used which improved the results significantly. The performance of these models is also evaluated on the BLEU score. Seq2seq with attention model achieved 40.6 BLEU-1 score, PGN achieved 44.5 BLEU-1 score and PGN with coverage achieved 45.2 BLEU-1 score. These models have abilities to generate abstractive summary but a higher level of abstraction can be achieved in future work.

References

1. Bahdanau, D., Cho, K., Bengio, Y.: Neural machine translation by jointly learning to align and translate. In: Bengio, Y., LeCun, Y. (eds.) 3rd International Conference on Learning Representations, ICLR 2015, Conference Track Proceedings, San Diego, CA, USA, 7–9 May 2015 (2015). http://arxiv.org/abs/1409.0473

2. Klein, G., Kim, Y., Deng, Y., Nguyen, V., Senellart, J., Rush, A.: OpenNMT: neural machine translation toolkit. In: Proceedings of the 13th Conference of the Association for Machine Translation in the Americas (Volume 1: Research Papers), Boston, MA, pp. 177–184. Association for Machine Translation in the Americas, March 2018. https://www.aclweb.org/anthology/W18-1817

3. Lin, C.Y.: ROUGE: a package for automatic evaluation of summaries. In: Text Summarization Branches Out, Barcelona, Spain, pp. 74–81. Association for Computational Linguistics, July 2004. https://www.aclweb.org/anthology/W04-1013

4. Liu, L., Lu, Y., Yang, M., Qu, Q., Zhu, J., Li, H.: Generative adversarial network for abstractive text summarization (2018). https://www.aaai.org/ocs/index.php/AAAI/AAAI18/paper/view/16238

5. Nallapati, R., Zhou, B., dos Santos, C., Guİ‡lçehre, Ç., Xiang, B.: Abstractive text summarization using sequence-to-sequence RNNs and beyond. In: Proceedings of the 20th SIGNLL Conference on Computational Natural Language Learning, Berlin, Germany, pp. 280–290. Association for Computational Linguistics, August 2016. https://doi.org/10.18653/v1/K16-1028. https://www.aclweb.org/anthology/K16-1028

6. Papineni, K., Roukos, S., Ward, T., Zhu, W.J.: BLEU: a method for automatic evaluation of machine translation. In: Proceedings of the 40th Annual Meeting of the Association for Computational Linguistics, Philadelphia, Pennsylvania, USA, pp. 311–318. Association for Computational Linguistics, July 2002. https://doi.org/10.3115/1073083.1073135. https://www.aclweb.org/anthology/P02-1040

7. See, A., Liu, P.J., Manning, C.D.: Get to the point: summarization with pointer-generator networks. In: Proceedings of the 55th Annual Meeting of the Association for Computational Linguistics (Volume 1: Long Papers), Vancouver, Canada, pp. 1073–1083. Association for Computational Linguistics, July 2017. https://doi.org/10.18653/v1/P17-1099. https://www.aclweb.org/anthology/P17-1099

8. Song, S., Huang, H., Ruan, T.: Abstractive text summarization using LSTM-CNN based deep learning. Multimed. Tools Appl. **78**(1), 857–875 (2018). https://doi.org/10.1007/s11042-018-5749-3

9. Sutskever, I., Vinyals, O., Le, Q.V.: Sequence to sequence learning with neural networks. In: Ghahramani, Z., Welling, M., Cortes, C., Lawrence, N.D., Weinberger, K.Q. (eds.) Advances in Neural Information Processing Systems, vol. 27, pp. 3104–3112. Curran Associates, Inc. (2014). http://papers.nips.cc/paper/5346-sequence-to-sequence-learning-with-neural-networks.pdf

10. Zhu, J., Li, H., Liu, T., Zhou, Y., Zhang, J., Zong, C.: MSMO: multimodal summarization with multimodal output. In: Proceedings of the 2018 Conference on Empirical Methods in Natural Language Processing, Brussels, Belgium, pp. 4154–4164. Association for Computational Linguistics, October–November 2018. https://doi.org/10.18653/v1/D18-1448. https://www.aclweb.org/anthology/D18-1448

Fraud Detection in Credit Card Data Using Machine Learning Techniques

Arun Kumar Rai[✉] and Rajendra Kumar Dwivedi

Department of IT and CA, MMMUT, Gorakhpur, India
toakrit@rediffmail.com, rajendra.gkp@gmail.com

Abstract. Credit cards have become the part of human life these days. It facilitates users in various sectors. Intruders try to steal credit card information in many ways. Hence, security of sensitive information of credit cards is a major concern. We can apply different machine learning techniques to detect such frauds or anomalies. On basis of our survey, we found two outperforming classifiers of machine learning viz., Logistic Regression (LR) and Naïve Bayes (NB). This paper provides a method of fraud detection in credit card system using Random Forest (RF) classifier. The work is compared with the existing classifiers: LR and NB. Their performance is evaluated on various metrics viz., Accuracy, Precision, Recall, F1 Score and Specificity on some datasets of credit card system. It is observed that Random Forest is outperforming others. Random Forest gives 99.95% accuracy while accuracy of LR and NB is 91.16% and 89.35% respectively.

Keywords: Fraud detection · Anomaly · Random Forest · Naïve Bayes · Logistic Regression

1 Introduction

Advancement in communication and network technology is increasing these days in all sectors. Now everything is being connected with Internet to facilitate the users in many ways [20]. This technology is called Internet of Things (IoT). Although technology is rising fast, the frauds are also increasing day by day. Therefore, security becomes a major concern of research. Frauds can be handled using prevention and detection methods. Prevention can be defined as the method where a protection layer is defined which prevents from outside attacks. It tries to stop frauds beforehand. When the prevention method fails, detection method comes into play. There should be always an ongoing background detection method running due to the fact that one could never know where the breach might occur.

This paper focuses on fraud detection in one of the critical problem viz., credit card applications. Here, financial companies need to enhance the detection methods to avoid the frauds in future. The older transactions of any credit card can be used as data for training the detection system with the goal that faster detection method will get better results. The term 'imbalanced data' defines the class of data of one type has high number of occurrences as compared to another. For example: in credit card frauds, the normal cases have higher count as compared to frauds. To solve this problem, machine

© Springer Nature Singapore Pte Ltd. 2020
A. Bhattacharjee et al. (Eds.): MIND 2020, CCIS 1241, pp. 369–382, 2020.
https://doi.org/10.1007/978-981-15-6318-8_31

learning techniques can be applied for getting balanced classification [6, 7]. Two main methods for getting balanced classification are: Data level and Algorithm level. In data level method, the negative effect of imbalanced class is reduced by applying re-sampling. In algorithm level method, either existing algorithms are modified or new algorithms are developed to select learning towards minority class. This paper presents a machine learning based approach to detect the frauds in credit card system. Then it compares the performance of the three classifiers used for fraud detection in credit card systems viz., RF, LR and NB.

The rest of this paper is organized as follows. Section 2 presents the literature review of the related work. Section 3 presents the proposed work and Sect. 4 provides the performance analysis of various machine learning techniques used for fraud detection in credit card information. Finally, Sect. 5 concludes the work with some future directions.

2 Related Work

Different Fraud Detection Methods (FDM) have been devised in the last few years. Every method had shown its better work on some particular datasets, but there is no method which is appropriate to all type of datasets. There are several techniques for identifying frauds in a credit card. This section presents a brief survey on such techniques.

Maja Puh et al. [1] provided the performance analysis of some machine learning techniques (MLT) such as random forest, logistics regression and support vector machine for fraud detection in real-life transactions. Dejan Varmedja et al. [2] used different types of models of machine learning to categorizing either genuine or fraud one in their transactions. In research, the CCFD dataset used because datasets were highly imbalanced, for oversampling SMOTE methods were used. Navin Kasa et al. [3] addressed to detect their fraud in credit card transactions used by semi-supervised, XGBoost and Random forest algorithm. Sangeeta Mittal et al. [4] explained un-supervised and supervised machine learning models used for the CCFD dataset which are imbalanced. To found that unsupervised learning approaches that can handle the skewness and give the best classification results. Anuruddha Thennakoon et al. [5] focuses on the use of four fundamental fraud events in real world. A sequence of ML techniques are used for addressing each category of fraud and at last the best method is selected using the techniques. The selection provides the result in form of optimal algorithm. Real time fraud detection in credit card is also focused in this approach. Rajeshwari U et al. [8] used the concept of streaming analytics for the detection and prevention of credit card. In the concept of streaming analytics a real-time data is used to make real time actions which depends upon some human decision. The approach uses historical data instead of specific data so that the fraud patterns can be detected. Real time transactions are also analyzed by this approach. Dilip Singh Sisodia et al. [9] used a resampling technique to deal with imbalance problem which occurs in fraud. A sequence of oversampling methods are used on the sampled data. The performance evaluation is done by cost sensitive and ensemble classifier under some metrices like sensitivity, area under ROC, etc. SMOTE ENN is the best method in oversampling techniques for fraud detection and TL technique is best in undersampling for fraud detection.

John O. Awoyemi et al. [10] investigated the performance of logistic regression, k-nearest neighbor (KNN) and naïve Bayes in the credit card fraud dataset. These three types of the method were used at the fact and preprocessed data. In this, the KNN is shown the outcome was well than the LS and NB methods. Andrea Dal Pozzolo et al. [11] proposed three major contributions. In the first approach fraud detection system is formalized which tells the working environment of FDSs for illustration of transaction. In the second approach imbalance problem, drift concept and verification latency strategy is designed and accessed. In the third approach demonstration for the impact of imbalance problem and drift concept is done using real world data. Kuldeep Randhawa et al. [12] devised machine learning schemes that are used for fraud detection in the credit card transaction. Firstly use of standard approaches. Before the use of hybrid schemes that are used of majority voting and AdaBoost, models were applied. To compute the efficiency of the method, that assesses the robustness of the algorithm. The investigational outcomes majority voting algorithm indicates that the accuracy rate is better to detect fraud. Deepti Dighe et al. [13] described Decision Trees, Multi-Layer Perceptron, Naïve Bayes, Chebyshev Functional Link Artificial Neural Network (CFLANN), KNN, Logistic Regression and estimated the results on basis of several metrics.

Apapan Pumsirirat et al. [14] focused on the fraud case which cannot be detected on the basis of supervised learning and to develop a model for the reconstruction of normal transactions. AE uses backpropagation technique. RBM is available in two layers namely visible and hidden. Tensorflow library is used for deep learning approach. Abhimanyu Roy et al. [15] devised the evaluation of subsection topologies of the common artificial neural network by memory components and unlike factors by detail to their efficiency in detection of fraud on a dataset. Akhil Sethia et al. [16] focused on the use of multiple adversarial networks for generating code to elaborate performance. Various parameters are analysed like classifier accuracy, convergence of each model, etc. ANN is used for testing the generated data. Shiyang Xuan et al. [18] analyzed the performance for fraud detection in a transaction to use more than one random forest that differs in their base classifiers to trains the behavior features of abnormal and normal transactions. The data is coming from an online electronic-commerce china based company. Lutao Zheng et al. [19] proposed the logical graph of BP. They computed an "entropy-based diversity coefficient" to identify users' behavior. In contrast, they express a "state transition probability matrix". Thus, BP algorithm is slightly better than the three other approaches to verify that every user is fraud or not in the transaction.

Table 1 presents a comparative study of the related work. On basis of the survey, it can be observed that classification technique of supervised learning is very good in identifying outliers. So, we are focusing our work on classification algorithms. We found LR and NB classifiers are used in fraud detection and given good performance. But this performance can be further improved. It is noticed that RF is an algorithm which may perform better in terms of precision and accuracy over the other existing schemes. Therefore, we have used RF classifier to detect the frauds in credit card system. We compared our work with the existing schemes viz., LR and NB.

Table 1. Comparative study of the related work

Authors	Issues	Techniques used	Environment & mode	Remarks
Maja Puh et al. [1] (2019)	Changing of fraud patterns	RF, SVM, LR	Online, static	Poor performance of SVM on incremental and static learning
Dejan Varmedja et al. [2] (2019)	Fraud detection	MLP, RF, NB	Online, distributed	MLP is better than NB and random forest still better from these
Navin Kasa et al. [3] (2019)	Dynamic and effective fraud detection	RF, XGBoost	Online, distributed	XGBoost works outperform across clusters
Sangeeta Mittal et al. [4] (2019)	Fraud detection on E-commerce	LOF, K–means, SOM	Online, centralized	Kmeans clustering is better performance
Anuruddha Thennakoon et al. [5] (2019)	System fraud detection	SVM, NB, LR	Online, distributed	API model applied for detection of anomalous or not
Rajeshwari U et al. [8] (2016)	Fraud detection on E-commerce	Hidden Markov Model	Online, centralized	Pattern based fraud detection
Dilip Singh Sisodia et al. [9] (2017)	Fraud detection	CSVM, C4.5, Adaboost, bagging	Online, distributed	The method, SMOTE-ENN, is outperform
John O. Awoyemi et al. [10] (2018)	System fraud detection	NB, K-NN, LR	Online, distributed	KNN is performed better results
Andrea Dal Pozzolo et al. [11] (2018)	Fraud detection in bank credit card	Alert feedback FDS	Online, distributed	Tried to improve the accuracy devised alert feedback (FDS) in learning process
Kuldeep Randhawa et al. [12] (2018)	Fraud detection in credit card	AdaBoost and majority voting	Online, distributed	The Majority voting worked better than AdaBoost
Deepti Dighe et al. [13] (2018)	Fraud detection	NB, KNN, decision trees and LR and neural network, (CFLANN)	Online, centralized	MLP perform slightly better than CFLANN
Apapan Pumsirirat et al. [14] (2018)	Detection of fraud in credit card	Auto-encoder; restricted Boltzmann machine	Online, distributed	Auto-encoder, RBM, methods

(*continued*)

Table 1. (*continued*)

Authors	Issues	Techniques used	Environment & mode	Remarks
Abhimanyu Roy et al. [15] (2018)	Fraud detection	LSTM, GRU	Online, distributed	GRU and LSTM performed better result when N/W size increase
Akhil Sethia et al. [16] (2018)	Fraud detection	Minibatch discrimination, GNA	Online, distributed	GAN Minibatch Discrimination is improved
Shiyang Xuan et al. [18] (2018)	Fraud detection in E-commerce	RF, DT	Online, centralized	Tried to improve the accuracy
Lutao Zheng et al. [19] (2018)	Fraud detection	Logical graph of behavior profile (LGBP)	Online, distributed	Behavior profiles outperforming

3 Proposed Approach

Algorithm 1: Fraud Detection Scheme

Input: Dataset of credit card system

Output: Identified anomalies (Detected Frauds)

Begin

   1. Input credit card data

   2. Preprocessing of data:

      (a) Cleaning of data

      (b) Removing redundant data

   3. Feature Selection (Identity, Location, Mode of Payement, Network)

   4. Split data into Training set and Test set

   5. Training and Tesing using RF classifier

      (a) Train the model using RF classifier

         (i)   Create two classes (Anomolous and Non anomolous)

         (ii) **If (**amount and time are changing extremely**)**

            Set the value as anomalous

          Else

            Set the value as non-anomolous

      (b) Apply testing

   6. Report the identified anomaly or the fraud

End

Algorithm 2: Performing Attack (Attack performed by the intruder)

Input: Data from customer's profile
Output: Attack success or failure
Begin
  1. Data collection from transaction history of customers
  2. Initiate to perform a fraud transaction
       If (Fraud detected by the detection system)
            Transaction failed
       Else
            Transaction successful
  3. Report the status to the performer
End

Algorithm 3 Detecting Attack (Detection performed by our detection system)

Input: Dataset of credit card system
Output: Identified anomalies (Detected Frauds)
Begin
  1. Read the input transaction to be performed
       If (fraud detected technique detects it as a fraud transaction)
            Report as fraud transaction and reject the transaction
       Else
            Complete the transaction successfully
  2. Report the status of the input transaction to the system
End

We have used classification technique to detect the frauds. Algorithm 1 shows the steps of fraud detection model which describes that preprocessing is applied on the input dataset to extract the selected features after cleaning the data. Then dataset is split into Training and Test set. After that, training and testing is done using RF classifier. Performance of RF classifier is compared with two other classifiers LR and NB. Algorithm 2 presents the procedure of performing attack by the intruder. It is required to simulate our detection system for getting the input fraud transactions. On basis of customers transaction history, the attackers perform the fraud transactions which must be detected by the detection system. Algorithm 3 shows the procedure of detecting the attack performed by the intruder.

4 Performance Evaluation

4.1 Dataset

We have used the dataset of a credit card system [17] which holds transactions data of European customers during two days in 2013. It contains 31 numeric types of columns with 492 frauds out of 284,807 transactions.

4.2 Techniques Used for Fraud Detection

We have used three machine learning techniques for fraud detection in credit card data. They are explained in short as below:

A. *Random Forest*: It is a technique used in regression and classification problems that consists concepts of decision trees. This technique gives better outcomes when there are higher numbers of tree in the forest. It also prevents model from over-fitting. Every decision tree in forests specifies some outcomes. These outcomes are merged together in order to become more stable and accurate prediction.
B. *Logistic Regression:* It is the most general classification method in the machine learning model. This method defines the correlation between predictor which can be categorical, continuous and binary. The dependent variables can also be binary.
C. *Naive Bayes*: This technique uses Bayesian model that selects decision on basis of conditional probability.

4.3 Setup

Various machine learning models are expecting balance input. Taking into account the values of amount and time extremely changing, the scaling is done in order to bring all features to a similar level of amounts. The experiment is carried out in Python on Ubuntu 18.04 platform. Python libraries used for scientific use are computations are Sklearn, Pandas, Matplotlib, Numpy, and Seaborn.

4.4 Performance Measurement

We have used five performance metrics viz., Accuracy, Precision, Recall, F1 Score and Specificity. The metrics used for performance evaluation are discussed as follows:

A. *Accuracy:* This metric denotes the correctly classified data points. It is shown in Eq. 1.

$$Accuracy = (TP + TN) / (TP + TN + FN + FP) \qquad (1)$$

Here, TP is True Positive, TN is True Negative, FP is False Positive and FN means False Negative.
B. *Precision:* It denotes precision of the classifier and measures the accuracy of positive predictions. It is represented in Eq. 2.

$$Precision = \frac{True\ Positives}{True\ Positives + False\ Positives} \qquad (2)$$

C. *Recall*: It is the ratio of positive instances that are correctly detected by the classifier with the sum of True Positives and False Negatives. Equation 3 describes this metric.

$$Recall = \frac{True\ Positives}{True\ Positives + False\ Negatives} \qquad (3)$$

D. *F1 Score*: F1 Score is calculated using Recall and Precision as shown in Eq. 4. This metric specifies a balance between these two entities. Recall and precision are used to represent the harmonic mean. The mean specifies the equal weight for all values which are regular.

$$F1\ Score = \frac{2}{\frac{1}{Precision} + \frac{1}{recall}} = 2 \times \frac{precision \times recall}{precision + recall} \qquad (4)$$

E. *Specificity:* It is the ratio of True Negative with the sum of True Negative and False Positive which is mentioned in Eq. 5.

$$Specificity = \frac{True\ Negative}{True\ Negative + False\ Positive} \qquad (5)$$

4.5   Confusion Matrix

Confusion matrix is a matrix which represents the performance of any classifier. It visualizes the performance of the classification model very well. Classification matrix of the RF, LR and NB classifiers used in fraud detection is shown in Table 2. RF gives the highest True Negative, the lowest True Positive, the lowest False Positive and the highest False Negative values. It shows that performance of RF is best among RF, LR and NB.

Table 2. Confusion matrix corresponding to various classifiers

Classifier	TN	TP	FP	FN
RF	93816	125	22	24
LR	85582	142	8256	7
NB	83840	139	9998	10

4.6   Results

Fraud Detection algorithm is implemented with three classifiers RF, LR and NB. Their performance comparison is shown in Table 3. It can be seen from the Table 3 that in case of RF, accuracy, precision, f1 score and specificity are the highest while recall is the lowest. It shows that performance of RF is the best among RF, LR and NB.

Table 3. Performance comparison of various classifier

Metrics	Classifiers		
	RF	LR	NB
Accuracy	99.95	91.16	89.35
Precision	0.8503	0.0169	0.0137
Recall	0.8389	0.9530	0.9329
F1 Score	0.8446	0.0332	0.0270
Specificity	0.9998	0.9120	0.8935

Figure 1 presents comparison of precision of various classifiers viz., RF, LR and NB. It can be seen that RF has the highest precsion. Figure 2 shows the comparison of recall of these classifiers and it is observed that recall of RF is the lowest. Figure 3 describes f1 score of these schemes and it can be noticed that RF has the highest f1 score. Figure 4 provides the comparison of specificity of these classification methods and it is found that specificity of RF is the highest. Figure 5 depicts the accuracy of RF, LR and NB and Fig. 6 displays the ROC curve of RF, LR and NB. we can see that RF gives the highest accuracy. Thus, we can say that RF is the best scheme for fraud detection in credit card system.

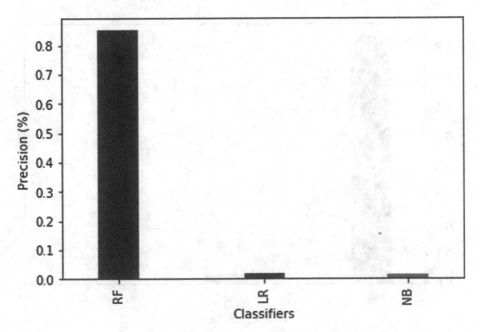

Fig. 1. Comparison of precision

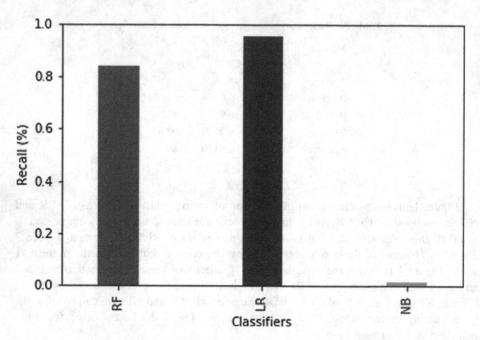

Fig. 2. Comparison of recall

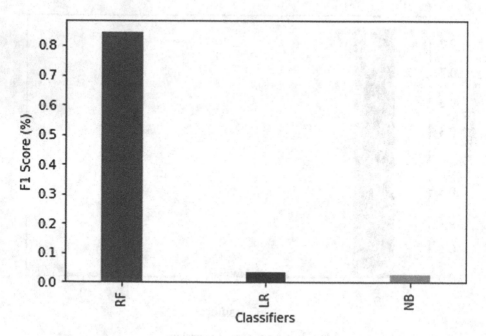

Fig. 3. Comparison of F1 score

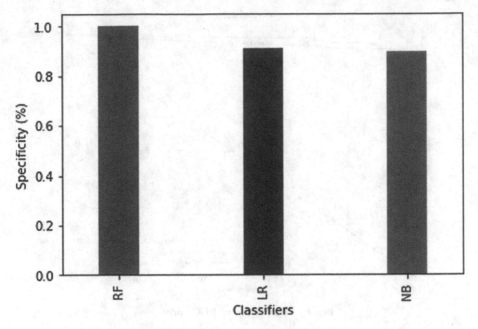

Fig. 4. Comparison of specificity

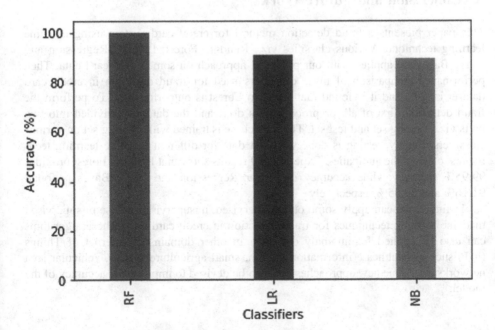

Fig. 5. Comparison of accuracy

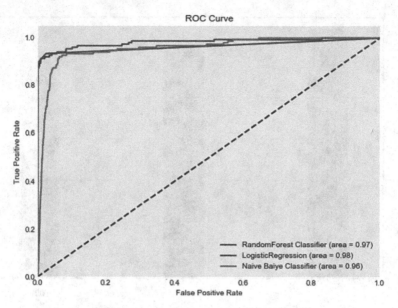

Fig. 6. Comparison of ROC curve

5 Conclusion and Future Work

This paper presents a fraud detection method for credit card system using machine learning technique. Various classifies viz., Random Forest, Logistic Regression and Naive Bayes are applied with our proposed approach on some credit card data. Then performance comparison of these classifiers used for fraud detection in credit card dataset is done and it is found that Random Forest is outperforming. To perform the fraud detection, first of all, preprocessing is done and the dataset is divided into two parts viz., training set and test set. Then, machine is trained with training set on various classifiers. Finally, testing is done with test data for different machine learning techniques to detect the anomalies. Experimental results show that Random Forest provides 99.95% accuracy while accuracy of Linear Regression and Naive Bayes is found 91.16% and 89.35% respectively.

In future, we can apply some other supervised, unsupervised and semi supervised machine learning techniques for fraud detection in credit card data. These algorithms can also be applied for anomaly detection in other domains of Internet of Things (IoT) such as healthcare information system, smart agriculture system, vehicular area networks etc. Some new approaches can also be devised to improve the accuracy of the model.

References

1. Puh, M., Brkic, L.: Detecting credit card fraud using selected machine learning algorithms. In: MIPRO, Opatija Croatia, pp. 250–255. IEEE (2019)
2. Varmedja, D., Karanovic, M., Sladojevic, S., Arsenovic, M., Anderla, A.: Credit card fraud detection - machine learning methods. In: 18th International Symposium INFOTECH-JAHORINA, 20–22 March, pp. 1–5. IEEE (2019)
3. Kasa, N., Dahbura, A., Ravoori, C., Adams, S.: Improving credit card fraud detection by profiling and clustering accounts, pp. 1–6. IEEE (2019)
4. Mittal, S., Tyagi, S.: Performance evaluation of machine learning algorithms for credit card fraud detection. In: 9th International Conference on Cloud Computing, Data Science & Engineering (Confluence), pp. 320–324. IEEE (2019)
5. Thennakoon, A., Bhagyani, C., Premadasa, S., Mihiranga, S., Kuruwitaarachchi, N.: Real-time credit card fraud detection using machine learning. In: 9th International Conference on Cloud Computing, Data Science & Engineering (Confluence), pp. 488–493. IEEE (2019)
6. Dwivedi, R.K., Rai, A.K., Kumar, R.: A study on machine learning based anomaly detection approaches in wireless sensor network. In: 10th International Conference on Cloud Computing, Data Science & Engineering (Confluence), pp. 200–205. IEEE (2020)
7. Dwivedi, R.K., Rai, A.K., Kumar, R.: Outlier detection in wireless sensor networks using machine learning techniques: a survey. In: 2020 International Conference on Electrical and Electronics Engineering (ICE3), pp. 1–6. IEEE (2020)
8. Rajeshwari, U., Babu, B.S.: Real-time credit card fraud detection using streaming analytics. In: 2nd International Conference on Applied and Theoretical Computing and Communication Technology (iCATccT), pp. 439–444. IEEE (2016)
9. Sisodia, D.S., Reddy, N.K., Bhandari, S.: Performance evaluation of class balancing techniques for credit card fraud detection. In: International Conference on Power, Control, Signals and Instrumentation Engineering (ICPCSI), pp. 2747–2752. IEEE (2017)
10. Awoyemi, J.O., Adetunmbi, A.O., Oluwadare, S.A.: Credit card fraud detection using machine learning techniques: a comparative analysis, pp. 1–9. IEEE (2017)
11. Pozzolo, A.D., Boracchi, G., Caelen, O., Alippi, C., Bontempi, G.: Credit card fraud detection: a realistic modeling and a novel learning strategy. IEEE Trans. Neural Netw. Learn. Syst. 29(8), 3784–3794 (2018)
12. Randhawa, K., Loo, C.K., Seera, M., Lim, C.P., Nandi, A.K.: Credit card fraud detection using AdaBoost and majority voting. IEEE Access 6, 14277–14282 (2018)
13. Dighe, D., Patil, S., Kokate, S.: Detection of credit card fraud transactions using machine learning algorithms and neural networks: a comparative study. In: Fourth International Conference on Computing Communication Control and Automation (ICCUBEA), pp. 1–6. IEEE (2018)
14. Pumsirirat, A., Yan, L.: Credit card fraud detection using deep learning based on auto-encoder and restricted Boltzmann machine. Int. J. Adv. Comput. Sci. Appl. (IJACSA) 9(1), 18–25 (2018)
15. Roy, A., Sun, J., Mahoney, R., Alonzi, L., Adams, S., Beling, P.: Deep learning detecting fraud in credit card transactions, pp. 129–134. IEEE (2018)
16. Sethia, A., Patel, R., Raut, P.: Data augmentation using generative models for credit card fraud detection. In: 4th International Conference on Computing Communication and Automation (ICCCA), pp. 1–6. IEEE (2018)
17. Dataset for credit card fraud (2020). https://www.kaggle.com/mlg-ulb/creditcardfraud
18. Xuan, S., Liu, G., Li, Z., Zheng, L., Wang, S., Jiang, C.: Random forest for credit card fraud detection, pp. 1–6. IEEE (2018)

19. Zheng, L., Liu, G., Yan, C., Jiang, C.: Transaction fraud detection based on total order relation and behavior diversity. IEEE Trans. Comput. Soc. Syst. **5**(3), 796–806 (2018)
20. Dwivedi, R.K., Kumari, N., Kumar, R.: Integration of wireless sensor networks with cloud towards efficient management in IoT: a review. In: Kolhe, M.L., Tiwari, S., Trivedi, M.C., Mishra, K.K. (eds.) Advances in Data and Information Sciences. LNNS, vol. 94, pp. 97–107. Springer, Singapore (2020). https://doi.org/10.1007/978-981-15-0694-9_10

Res-VGG: A Novel Model for Plant Disease Detection by Fusing VGG16 and ResNet Models

Ashish Kumar[(⊠)], Raied Razi, Anshul Singh, and Himansu Das

School of Computer Engineering, KIIT Deemed to be University,
Bhubaneswar, Odisha, India
ashish229.ddp@gmail.com, raied.286@gmail.com,
ppriyam.muz@gmail.com, das.himansu2007@gmail.com

Abstract. Agriculture is one of the major growing sectors in India, and plant disease is the key factor that affects the economy of the country to a large extend. Plant disease management has become a challenging task to ensure the food safety and sustainability of agriculture. Deep learning (DL) has recently made some good walk-through in the field of image identification and classification. In this article, we have proposed a new model called Res-VGG that hybridized two different DL models such as VGG16 and ResNet. This model has been used to detect and categorize the symptoms of plant diseases. In our proposed model, we have used a total of 12 layers consisting of 9 convolutional layers, two fully connected layers, and one softmax layer. The effectiveness of this proposed model has been tested and validated using Plant Village dataset. The experimental analysis reveals that the proposed model is superior over the existing models in terms of disease identification so that effective preventive measures can be taken for eliminating these diseases, thus removing the problem of food security.

Keywords: Res-VGG · Plant disease detection · CNN · Deep learning · VGG16 · ResNet · ILSVRC · ReLU

1 Introduction

A plant disease refers to change in the original condition of a plant that influences or alter vital functions of the plant. Plant diseases are caused by some fungal attack, bacteria or micro-animals, which has a great impact on agricultural production. Plant disease identification is of greater importance and plays a key role in the prevention and control of plant diseases so that preventive measures can be taken for good production of plant species. Approximately 20% to 40% of crop yield globally are reduced each year because of damage caused by plant pests and diseases. There are approximately 550 million agricultural farms in the entire world and 83% of them are little scaled under 5 acres, farmers practicing subsistence farming have less knowledge of crop growth and better productivity. Detection of diseases in the plant before time is a great challenge for protecting diseases in crops and increasing crop yields. Initial disease detection is usually done by on-sight assessment [1] and the value of the diagnosis be

© Springer Nature Singapore Pte Ltd. 2020
A. Bhattacharjee et al. (Eds.): MIND 2020, CCIS 1241, pp. 383–400, 2020.
https://doi.org/10.1007/978-981-15-6318-8_32

heavily conditional on the knowledge of humans. On the other hand disease identification based on laboratory analysis is time taking and does get unsuccessful in achieving timely results.

To the above-mentioned context, it is too captivating to develop an automated system that is capable of identifying plant diseases in a fast and efficient manner. Automatic detection of plant diseases by image scanning shows a favorable solution to get over this problem and cut down the lack of good skills in this field. DL [2] currently is a great area of research in artificial intelligence and machine learning (ML) [3–5] that has been successfully been applied in several fields. DL is a subset of ML which has many layers of non-linear data for supervised and unsupervised learning. Moreover, it has been applied to various fields like natural language processing, speech recognition, and computer vision.

There has been great progress for classification task using deep convolution neural network (CNN) [6]. Recently, some modifications of CNN Architecture have been made with a gradual increment in the number of layers. Some of the architectures such as AlexNet [7], GoogleNetInception V4 [8], VGG net [9], Microsoft ResNet [10], DenseNets [11] emerged, more and more researchers used these models to do specific image recognition. These DL architectures may be efficient but have its difficulty and challenges such as a breakdown in accuracy when the network depth is increased, another challenge faced is by changing the data distribution in the input data to the internal layers. However many optimization techniques have been proposed such as transfer learning, Initialization strategies, optimization strategies, batch normalization and layer-wise training.

The training of CNN models requires millions of parameters, so a large number of the training dataset is required for better accuracy. Only when network depth is more, and data samples are enough, then CNN can show good predictions. So, if the sample size is small, it becomes easy for the models to over-fit. Since most of the pre-trained models which are there have the weight of the Imagenet challenge, but the main problem in Imagenet is that it doesn't have the crop and plant image in the dataset which includes 1000 classes.

The objective of this proposed work is to develop a hybrid model called Res-VGG by fusion of VGG16 and ResNet architectural models. This proposed model uses both max and average pooling functions with different kernel sizes that decreases the model size and simultaneously increases the accuracy of the model. This model uses two convolutional layers and on top of it, a batch normalization technique is implemented along with the implementation of a pooling layer. The remaining sections of the paper are as follows: Sect. 2 describes the related works in the field of plant disease identification, Sect. 3 represents the System model. Section 4 includes the result analysis section, and Sect. 5 concludes the paper with the future scope of this research work.

2   Related Work

ILSVRC is an annual computer vision competition that was first started in 2010 and ended in 2017. The VGG16 model won the challenge in the year 2014 with top-5 error rates. The ILSVRC'10, ILSVRC'11, AlexNet, ZFNet are 4 models that were released

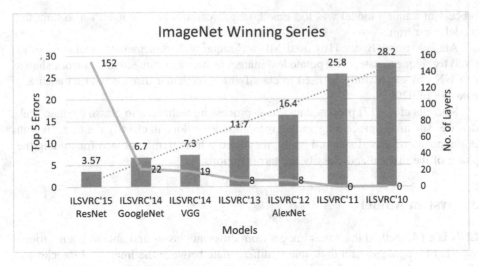

Fig. 1. The graph of winning series of ILSVRC

before VGG16, out of which the first two are not based on the DL technique, whereas VGG16 was the 5th model of ILSVR challenge and 3rd DL model. The accuracy of the models is increasing gradually with the increase in the number of layers of the several DL models is shown in Fig. 1.

Several works have been done in the area of plant disease detection using different algorithmic techniques likewise, DL and several approaches of ML procedures have also been applied for some better results and have been also extensively used in the field of agriculture.

Mohanty et al. [12] in their paperwork used a DL method to detect plant disease on the smartphone-assisted system. They have used a large image dataset of around 54,000 images which included a healthy and infected plant leaf image. Their model was trained to identify 14 crops and 26, they used AlexNet and GoogleNet Architecture, which achieved an accuracy of approx 99.4%, despite a good accuracy their model failed to achieve good results under different conditions.

Similarly, Sladojevic et al. [13] used a DL approach to detect plant disease with the help of leaf images. The model was also able to spot 14 different diseases from leaves and achieved an accuracy of 96.3% on experimental testing.

Likewise, Dyrmann et al. [14] also used DL architectures to recognize weeds and plants using different colored image dataset, the image dataset consisted of 10,413 images which had 22 weeds and crop species. This CNN model has also able to achieved an accuracy of 86.2% only because of a low number of training inputs.

Sa et al. [15] proposed a model called Deepfruits which used image datasets for fruit detection. Its main aim was to build a reliable and accurate fruit detection system so that it played a big role in yield estimation. They used the approach of R-CNN to train their model which was able to achieve an improved result of 0.838 precision and recall in spotting sweet pepper as compared to their previous work. But the entire process of training model was too time taking because it took around 4 h to train the model for a fruit.

Athanikar and Badar [16] used ML technique and implemented neural network (NN) technique to categorize potato leaf images as healthy or infected, this work shown that NN can successfully be used in classifying a particular disease with an accuracy measure of 92%.

Samanta et al. [17] proposed an image processing technique to classify potato scab disease. The image processing and segmentation were done to classify the target region in the potato (diseased spots). Finally, they used a histogram approach for finding the phase of the disease and classify the target regions.

3   System Model

CNN is a DL method that takes images from different classes and able to learn various aspects of the images and thus able to differentiate between the images of the classes. The use of the weight of the ImageNet challenge in the VGG16 model that shows accuracy and loss graph is represented in Fig. 8, which is not achieving better accuracy on the Plant village dataset. One of the reasons may be that from the 1000 classes of the ImageNet dataset, there are no classes of plants or crops. So, the model is not trained on the plant or crop classes. To address this issue, this work is based on the modification of the pre-trained VGG16 model. Since most of the pre-trained model which are available in tools such as tensor flow and PyTorch have the weight of the ImageNet challenge. The main objective of using the pre-trained model (weight) is that it performs with better accuracy on a small dataset. Since the plants or crop classes are not belonging in the ImageNet dataset and the accuracy of the pre-trained model which we have used is not up to the mark. So in this work, a new model is designed to address the real-life problem that cannot be solved by past experiences. However, for new problems, we have to come with a new solution. So, we have created a model with inspiration from both the VGG16 and the ResNet. Generally, any CNN models may have the following components such as convolutional operation, pooling operation, and activation functions.

3.1   Dataset

Plant village dataset [18] is a huge dataset consisting of 14 different plants. It contains healthy as well as contaminated leaves. It has 38 crop disease sets with 26 crop disease categories. The whole dataset is separated into two parts such as training and validation sets, where 80% of data are for training purpose and the leftover 20% of the data are for validation purpose (more specifically 67,848 images are for training purpose, while 16,973 images are for validation purpose). The use of this large dataset makes our prediction more precise and specific with good results. Table 2 shows all the 38 classes with the name of the plant, disease name and number of training and validation datasets.

Table 1. Description of plant village dataset (% is for percentage of images)

Classes	Disease name	Plant name	Train	%	Validation	%
1	Scab	Apple	2016	2.97	504	2.97
2	Healthy	Apple	2008	2.96	502	2.96
3	Cedar apple rust	Apple	1760	2.59	440	2.59
4	Black rot	Apple	1987	2.93	497	2.93
5	Healthy	Blueberry	1816	2.68	454	2.67
6	Healthy	Cherry (including sour)	1826	2.69	456	2.69
7	Powdery mildew	Cherry (including sour)	1683	2.48	421	2.48
8	Cercospora leaf spot gray leaf spot	Corn (maize)	1429	2.11	355	2.09
9	Healthy	Corn (maize)	28	0.04	14	0.08
10	Northern leaf blight	Corn (maize)	1673	2.47	423	2.49
11	Common rust	Corn (maize)	1907	2.81	477	2.81
12	Healthy	Grape	1692	2.49	423	2.49
13	Leaf blight (Isariopsis leaf spot)	Grape	1722	2.54	430	2.53
14	Esca (Black measles)	Grape	1920	2.83	480	2.83
15	Black rot	Grape	1888	2.78	472	2.78
16	Haunglongbing (Citrus greening)	Orange	2010	2.96	503	2.96
17	Bacterial spot	Peach	1838	2.71	459	2.7
18	Healthy	Peach	1728	2.55	432	2.55
19	Bacterial spot	Pepper bell	1913	2.82	478	2.82
20	Healthy	Pepper bell	1987	2.93	497	2.93
21	Healthy	Potato	1824	2.69	456	2.69
22	Early blight	Potato	1939	2.86	485	2.86
23	Late blight	Potato	1939	2.86	485	2.86
24	Healthy	Raspberry	1781	2.62	445	2.62
25	Healthy	Soybean	2022	2.98	505	2.98
26	Powdery mildew	Squash	1717	2.53	426	2.51
27	Leaf scorch	Strawberry	1773	2.61	443	2.61
28	Healthy	Strawberry	1824	2.69	456	2.69
29	Early blight	Tomato	1920	2.83	480	2.83
30	Healthy	Tomato	1925	2.84	481	2.83
31	Tomato mosaic virus	Tomato	1790	2.64	448	2.64
32	Leaf mold	Tomato	1882	2.77	470	2.77
33	Septoria leaf spot	Tomato	1745	2.57	436	2.57
34	Tomato yellow leaf curl virus	Tomato	1961	2.89	490	2.89
35	Target spot	Tomato	1827	2.69	457	2.69
36	Bacterial spot	Tomato	1702	2.51	425	2.5
37	Late blight	Tomato	1705	2.51	433	2.55
38	Spider mites two-spotted spider mite	Tomato	1741	2.57	435	2.56

3.2   Convolution Operation

It is the process of taking an input and estimating a weighted average as shown in
Fig. 2. The kernels are present in different sizes out of which (3 × 3) is the smallest
one. VGG16 has 16 layers out of which 13 layers are convolution layers and rest 3

layers are fully connected layers. The VGG16 model uses a kernel of size (3×3), regularization as ReLU and pooling as max pooling. Kernels are matrices that move throughout the image along with the height and width. Since it is moving on a 3D image but we are using the kernel as 2D. It is of the same depth as the image and thus including the depth it also becomes a 3D matrix.

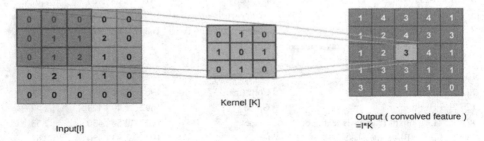

Fig. 2. Convolutional layer

3.3   Pooling

Pooling operation is a process of reducing the resolution of an input image and the resulting image is created without losing the important properties of the input image. It is one of the reasons that we can train the neural network with a lesser number of parameters. It lowers the size of the feature maps. Pooling can be added after the convolutional layer, like in the VGG16 model. In [19] the authors show the importance of pooling and how pooling layers improve the model's efficiency by reducing the number of parameters. Many types of pooling techniques are present such as average pooling, max pooling, and random pooling [20]. Max pooling operation considers only the greatest pixel value present in the pool region as shown in Fig. 3. Average pooling takes an average of the pixel values of a region as shown in Fig. 4.

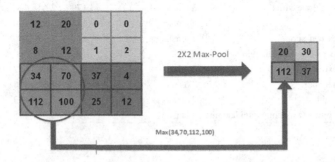

Fig. 3. Max pooling operation

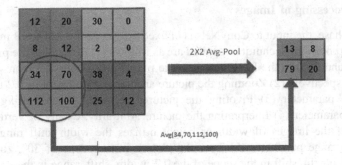

Fig. 4. Avg pooling operation

3.4 Activation

It tells whether a neuron is to be active or not. There are various activation functions present such as logistic, tanh, rectified linear unit (ReLU) and leaky RLU. Figure 5 shows the ReLU activation function. The mathematical representation of the ReLU activation function is shown in Eq. 1.

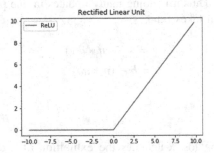

Fig. 5. ReLU graph

$$f(t) = \max(0, t)$$

$$f'(t) = \frac{\partial f(t)}{\partial t} = \begin{cases} 0, & \text{if } t \le 0 \\ 1, & \text{if } t > 0 \end{cases} \tag{1}$$

Here, if the value of t is less than or equal to 0, then the neuron will not be active, it does not saturate in the positive region otherwise it saturates in the negative region. It is easy in terms of computation as it does not have to calculate exponential components. The range of the ReLU activation function is from 0 to infinity. ReLU is half rectified (from bottom), $f(t)$ is zero when t is less than or equal to zero and $f(t)$ is equal to 1 when t is greater than zero.

3.5   Preprocessing of Images

In training phase, the input to ConvNets is of fixed size as 224 × 224 RGB images. The various pre-processing techniques applied are as follows (1) Re-scaling the pixel values (between 0 and 255) to the [0, 1] interim. The pixel value 0 and 255 represents black and white respectively (2) Zooming the picture arbitrarily by a factor of 0.2 utilizes the zoom_range parameter (3) Pivoting the picture arbitrarily by 30° using the rotation_range parameter (4) Interpreting the picture arbitrarily, evenly or vertically by a 0.2 factor of the images of width or height utilizes the width_shift_range and the height_shift_range parameter (5) Turn the picture in the scope of 30°, zoom in the scope of 0.2, height_shift in the scope of the 0.2, width_shift_range in the scope of 0.2.

3.6   Optimization Algorithms

Optimization algorithms are used to change the attributes (weights and learning rate) of the neural networks to reduce the losses. We have used stochastic gradient descent (SGD) optimizer, in which for every x and y, it will update the weights by using Eq. 2. It corrects the error which occurs at that time and not waits for the training of the whole image or the batch size. But in the batch gradient descent, it only updates the weight after training the whole images of the given batch size. So with the help of the SGD, faster updates are made. Thus it is doing many updates in one pass of data. But doing updates in every iteration takes time.

$$w = w - (\eta * dw)$$
$$b = b - (\eta * db)$$

(2)

3.7   Loss Function

Cross-entropy loss or log loss calculates the exhibition of a characterization model whose yield is probability esteem somewhere in the range of 0 and 1. Since we need to anticipate from which class the image has a place with and since we have 38 classes at the yield end of the fully connected layer, thus our model will predict what is the likelihood that the given image has a place with a given class. Cross-entropy loss increments as the anticipated probability diverge from the real label and can be calculated by using Eq. 3.

$$C_m(n) = -\sum_{k=1}^{K} n(y_k).\log(m(y_k))$$

(3)

3.8   Proposed Architecture

The proposed architecture has a total of 12 layers, comprising of nine convolutional layers, two fully connected layers and one SoftMax classifier, as shown in Fig. 6 and compared in Table 1. The precise structure of the proposed model shown in Fig. 6 is as follows:

i. The first convolutional layer is comprised of 64 filters and the size of the kernel used is 3 × 3, excluding padding. As input image (RGB image) passed into the first convolutional layer, dimension changes to 110 × 110 × 64. Then the resulting output is passed to the next convolutional layer with a stride of two.

ii. The second convolutional layer is comprised of 128 filters and the size of the kernel used is 5 × 5, excluding padding with stride one. This layer is trailed by the average pooling layer with stride two and the subsequent yield will be diminished to 53 × 53 × 128.

iii. The third convolutional layer is comprised of 128 filters and the kernel used is 3 × 3, padding of one is used with stride one. The resulting output of dimensions 53 × 53 × 128 is passed to the next convolutional layer.

iv. The fourth convolutional layer is comprised of 256 filters and the kernel used is 3 × 3, padding of one. The layer is trailed by the max-pooling layer and the subsequent yield will be diminished to 26 × 26 × 256 dimensions.

v. The fifth convolutional layer is comprised of 256 filters and the kernel used is 3 × 3, without padding and with stride one. The resulting output of dimensions 24 × 24 × 256 is passed to the next convolutional layer.

vi. The sixth layer is comprised of 384 filters and kernel of size 3 × 3, with padding of one. The layer is followed by an average pooling layer and the resulting output is reduced to 12 × 12 × 384 dimensions.

vii. The seventh layer is comprised of 512 filters and the kernel used is 3 × 3, without padding and with a stride of one. The resulting output of dimensions 10 × 10 × 512 passed to the next convolutional layer.

viii. The eighth layer is comprised of 512 filters and the kernel used is 3 × 3, without padding. The layer is followed by the average polling layer and the resulting output is reduced to 4 × 4 × 512 dimensions.

ix. The ninth layer is comprised of 512 filters and the kernel used is 3 × 3, without padding and with a stride of one. The layer is followed by a max-pooling layer and the resulting output is reduced to 1 × 1 × 512.

x. The 10th and 11th layer are fully connected hidden layers of 4096 units followed by a softmax output layer (12th layer) of 38 units.

Fig. 6. The proposed architecture of Res-VGG model

Table 2. Comparison layers of different methods

Models	Layers	Convolutional layer	Fully connected layer
VGG16	16	13	3
Modified VGG16	15	13	2
New model	12	9	3

3.8.1   Fully Connected Layers

Finally in CNN, the last pooling layer's output (9th layer) can be treated as input of the fully connected layer (4096). There may have one or more number of such layers as shown in Fig. 7.

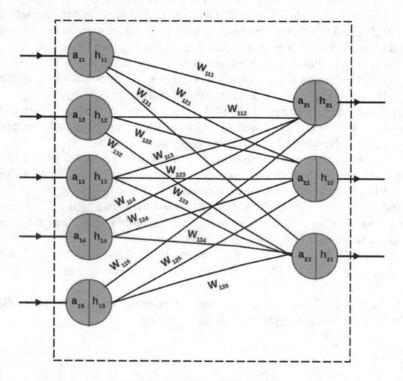

Fig. 7. Fully connected network

This work has described a model by taking the help of both the VGG and ResNet models. VGG uses the only kernel of size 3 × 3, ReLU activation function and max-pooling throughout the layers. It combines two or three convolutional layers and gives an output that is good with respect to the time. ResNet uses the kernel of size 7 × 7 for the 1st convolutional layer and it also used both the pooling functions, max, and average pooling and it also included residual network, due to which the performance gets boosted and it shows top 5 error rate of 3.57.

All hidden layers are equipped with the rectification (ReLU) non-linearity. In our model, we have used pooling after every two layers and at the last i.e. in the 9th convolutional layer, we have used max pooling. We have taken the kernel size of the first layer as five. Since at the input end, the size of the image is large and the features which we have to collect for the next layer can easily be collected using a larger kernel. As in the first pooling we have taken average pooling because the image size is large so by taking the average of the pooling we can extract more important information.

The model has two fully connected layers since the convolution layer is not so deep. So we have to extract information from the fully connected layers. At last, we have one softmax layer to predict 38 classes. Since the fully connected layer are dense (4096, 4096), this may lead to overfitting and thus we have used the dropout as 0.5 between the first two fully connected layers, 0.3 between second fully connected layer and a softmax layer.

Dropout is very useful, they turn the activation of nodes on and off randomly. It helps in stoping the model from overfitting over the given data. And larger dropout values are also not good for the model prediction process. For example, let us set the dropout as 0.7 it means that out of 100 neurons, only 30 is active in giving the prediction and rest are not active, but since more neurons are not active in giving the prediction, so the accuracy may decrease. Hence, during setting the dropout we must consider the model complexity of the model. The importance of the dropout layer is explained in detail in [21].

We have taken the batch size of 128. The batch size characterizes the number of tests that will spread through the system. For example, if we have a dataset of 1280 images and we have set the batch size of 128, then the model takes the first 128 images from the training dataset and trains the network. And again it takes the same number of images and repeats the process again and again till the training of the whole dataset is not completed. Since we train the network using fewer sample images (as we are using the concept to batch) than the datasets so, the overall training procedure requires less memory.

4   Result Analysis

The system configuration that we have used for this experiment is provided by Kaggle (Implemented using Python language on GPU). Kaggle provides free access to NVidia K80 GPUs in kernels. Kaggle provides Intel(R) Xenon(R) CPU @ 2.30 GHz with core 16 processors, with 118 GB RAM. Training on the GPU will speed up the process by approx 12 times that to CPU. The Res-VGG model is used to train from scratch, the learning rate of the model is chosen as 0.005, the number of epochs used is 14, with momentum 0.9, and using loss function as categorical_crossentropy, the batch size used is 128. To reduce overfitting, a regularization technique is used to the network, dropout is also used. We have used a decay value 5×10^{-5}, during optimization, it needs to move fast using a higher learning rate but when it reaches to the points which are near to the relatively optimal point, we have to reduce the learning rate in order not to miss the optimal point. So in each epoch, we are decreasing the learning rate by decaying factors as mentioned above.

Figure 8(a, b) shows the relationship between the accuracy and loss of VGG16 and the modified VGG16 (mVGG) model. As can be seen from Fig. 8(a), the final training accuracy of VGG16 and mVGG model is 84% and 87% as shown in Table 3, respectively. In the Fig. 8(b), the final training loss of VGG16 and mVGG model is 0.50 and 0.48 respectively. Thus, from both the graphs we conclude that if we use a pre-trained neural network then we are not getting better loss and accuracy.

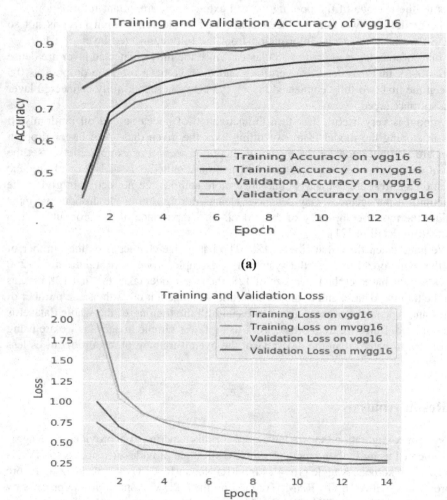

Fig. 8. (a) Training and validation accuracy of VGG16 and mVGG, (b) Training and validation loss of VGG16 and mVGG

Figure 9(a) shows the accuracy of the Res-VGG model varying with the number of epochs. As we can see that the training accuracy starts from 0.38 at epoch one and it goes to 98.56 at epoch 14 as shown in Table 3. For the validation accuracy, it starts at

0.09 and goes to 98.27 at the end as shown in Table 3. Since we see that the validation accuracy curve deviates much because we are using SGD as an optimizer and it changes its values for every single x y and Fig. 9(b) shows the loss of the Res-VGG model that decreases with the number of epochs. As we can see that the training loss at epoch one is 2.4 and it goes to 0.05 at epoch 14. Validation loss at epoch one is 7.3 and it goes to 0.02 at epoch 14.

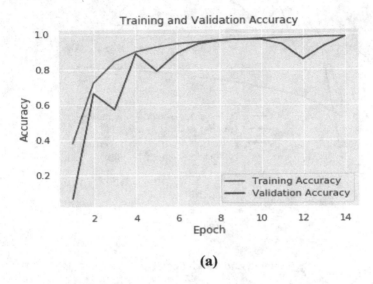

(a)

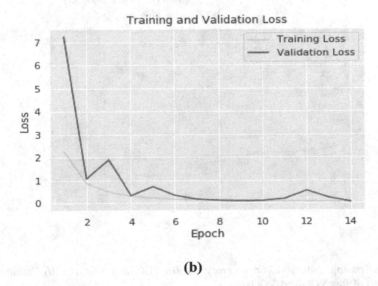

(b)

Fig. 9. (a) Training and validation accuracy of Res-VGG model, (b) Training and validation loss of Res-VGG model

Figure 10(a), 10(b) shows the comparison between the accuracy and loss of the Res-VGG model and the VGG16 model. Here we can see that the Res-VGG model is getting higher accuracy and lower loss as compared to the VGG16 model.

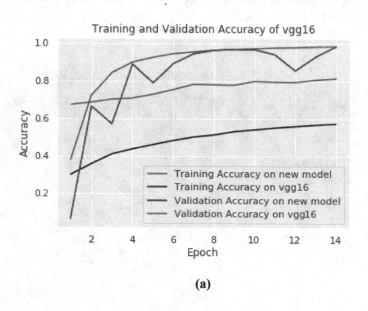

(a)

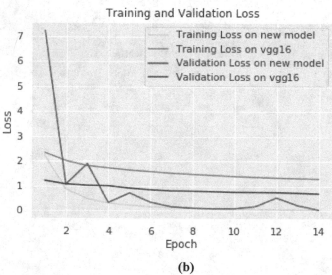

(b)

Fig. 10. (a) Training and validation accuracy of Res-VGG and VGG16, (b) Training and validation loss of Res-VGG and VGG16

Loss is the mistake made by the model while making expectations. It either takes the best one or else top-5 error rates. Top-5 error rates are part of images that are absent in the expectation of top-5. For instance, if the article is a pen and the framework distinguishes the main five classes as container, pen, keys, mobile and book and the best 5 suppositions that are right and afterward it isn't chosen. If the prediction does not

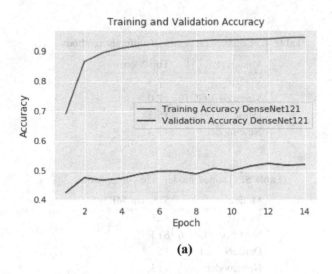

(a)

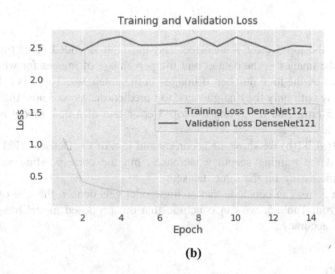

(b)

Fig. 11. (a) Training and validation accuracy of DenseNet121, (b) Training and validation loss of DenseNet121

Table 3. Comparison results of different methods

Models	Training accuracy (in %)	Validation accuracy (in %)
VGG16	84	90
Modified VGG16	87	90.23
DenseNet121	97.3	53.2
New model	98.56	98.27

Table 4. Comparison errors of different methods

Models	Top-5 errors
VGG16	7.3
Modified VGG16	7.0
DenseNet121	15.5
New model	3.3

Table 5. Trained model size comparison

Models	Size (in MB)
VGG16	865
Modified VGG16	813
DenseNet121	156
New model	113

contain pen then the top-5 error is incorrect and the fault is added. This process is repeated for all the images in the dataset and the percentage of images for which it is not true is divided by the total number of images in the databases. Top-1 is calculated in an identical way with only the first guess or top prediction. As we know that for the VGG16 the top-5 error rate is 7.3 and the top-5 error rate of a new model is 3.3 as shown in Table 4.

From Fig. 11(a), 11(b) we show the accuracy and loss of the DenseNet121 model. Here we see that the training accuracy increases, but the corresponding validation accuracy is not increasing on the same dataset.

As per Table 5, we can conclude that as the model gets denser, the size of model increases. And from Table 5, we can conclude that our proposed model has smaller size, with higher accuracy.

5   Conclusion

This paper has examined the pre-trained model (VGG16), modified VGG16 (mVGG) and the proposed model (Res-VGG) and compare the results. To achieve an effective and efficient model, we have tuned the kernel size, pooling layer, convolutional layer, and optimization techniques. This proposed model (Res-VGG) eliminates the problems of the pre-trained model (VGG16) and modified model (mVGG16) that is experimentally shown with the Plant-Village dataset. The fact that the proposed model outperforms than the existing models because of using the kernel of different sizes and both the pooling algorithm i.e. max and average pooling. In this proposed model, we have used 5×5 kernels at the input end and also both the max and average pooling functions. The use of large kernel size or dropout may lead to a decade of the performance of the model. In the future, any large dataset may be trained using this proposed model or it can be modified accordingly for better performance. This can be suitable for farmers to detect the diseases and take preventive measures accordingly.

As we have datasets of only 38 crop diseases. So, in the future, if more classes of crop diseases are available, the model which is proposed in this paper can be used or if required it can be modified and trained on the available datasets. This can help farmers in many ways as we can detect diseases with our model and help them in protecting their crops from diseases. Since, as we know that food is a very important part and for the production of crops so, we can help them with our technology, and provide the chance to see a new future.

References

1. Barbedo, J.G.A.: A review of the main challenges in automatic plant disease identification based on visible range images. Biosys. Eng. **144**, 52–60 (2016)
2. LeCun, Y., Bengio, Y., Hinton, G.: Deep learning. Nature **521**(7553), 436–444 (2015)
3. Panigrahi, K.P., Das, H., Sahoo, A.K., Moharana, S.C.: Maize leaf disease detection and classification using machine learning algorithms. In: Das, H., Pattnaik, P.K., Rautaray, S.S., Li, K.-C. (eds.) Progress in Computing, Analytics and Networking. AISC, vol. 1119, pp. 659–669. Springer, Singapore (2020). https://doi.org/10.1007/978-981-15-2414-1_66
4. Das, H., Naik, B., Behera, H.S.: An experimental analysis of machine learning classification algorithms on biomedical data. In: Kundu, S., Acharya, U.S., De, C.Kr., Mukherjee, S. (eds.) Proceedings of the 2nd International Conference on Communication, Devices and Computing. LNEE, vol. 602, pp. 525–539. Springer, Singapore (2020). https://doi.org/10.1007/978-981-15-0829-5_51
5. Das, H., Naik, B., Behera, H.S.: Classification of diabetes mellitus disease (DMD): a data mining (DM) approach. In: Pattnaik, P.K., Rautaray, S.S., Das, H., Nayak, J. (eds.) Progress in Computing, Analytics and Networking. AISC, vol. 710, pp. 539–549. Springer, Singapore (2018). https://doi.org/10.1007/978-981-10-7871-2_52
6. Sahoo, A.K., Pradhan, C., Das, H.: Performance evaluation of different machine learning methods and deep-learning based convolutional neural network for health decision making. In: Rout, M., Rout, J.K., Das, H. (eds.) Nature Inspired Computing for Data Science. SCI, vol. 871, pp. 201–212. Springer, Cham (2020). https://doi.org/10.1007/978-3-030-33820-6_8
7. Krizhevsky, A., Sutskever, I., Hinton, G.E.: ImageNet classification with deep convolutional neural networks. In: Advances in Neural Information Processing Systems, pp. 1097–1105 (2012)
8. Szegedy, C., Ioffe, S., Vanhoucke, V., Alemi, A.A.: Inception-v4, inception-ResNet and the impact of residual connections on learning. In: Thirty-First AAAI Conference on Artificial Intelligence, February 2017

9. Simonyan, K., Zisserman, A.: Very deep convolutional networks for large-scale image recognition. arXiv preprint arXiv:1409.1556 (2014)
10. He, K., Zhang, X., Ren, S., Sun, J.: Deep residual learning for image recognition. In: Proceedings of the IEEE Conference on Computer Vision and Pattern Recognition, pp. 770–778 (2016)
11. Huang, G., Liu, Z., Van Der Maaten, L., Weinberger, K.Q.: Densely connected convolutional networks. In: Proceedings of the IEEE Conference on Computer Vision and Pattern Recognition, pp. 4700–4708 (2017)
12. Mohanty, S.P., Hughes, D.P., Salathé, M.: Using deep learning for image-based plant disease detection. Front. Plant Sci. **7**, 1419 (2016)
13. Sladojevic, S., Arsenovic, M., Anderla, A., Culibrk, D., Stefanovic, D.: Deep neural networks based recognition of plant diseases by leaf image classification. Comput. Intell. Neurosci. **2016**, 1–11 (2016)
14. Dyrmann, M., Karstoft, H., Midtiby, H.S.: Plant species classification using deep convolutional neural network. Biosys. Eng. **151**, 72–80 (2016)
15. Sa, I., Ge, Z., Dayoub, F., Upcroft, B., Perez, T., McCool, C.: Deepfruits: a fruit detection system using deep neural networks. Sensors **16**(8), 1222 (2016)
16. Athanikar, G., Badar, P.: Potato leaf disease detection and classification system. Int. J. Comput. Sci. Mob. Comput. **5**(2), 76–88 (2016)
17. Samanta, D., Chaudhury, P.P., Ghosh, A.: Scab disease detection of potato using image processing. Int. J. Comput. Trends Technol. **3**(1), 109–113 (2012)
18. Hughes, D., Salathe, M., et al.: An open access repository of images on plant health to enable the development of mobile disease diagnostics. arXiv preprint arXiv:1511.08060 (2015)
19. Scherer, D., Müller, A., Behnke, S.: Evaluation of pooling operations in convolutional architectures for object recognition. In: Diamantaras, K., Duch, W., Iliadis, L.S. (eds.) ICANN 2010. LNCS, vol. 6354, pp. 92–101. Springer, Heidelberg (2010). https://doi.org/10.1007/978-3-642-15825-4_10
20. Sheng, J., Chen, C., Fu, C., Xue, C.J.: EasyConvPooling: random pooling with easy convolution for accelerating training and testing. arXiv preprint arXiv:1806.01729 (2018)
21. Srivastava, N., Hinton, G., Krizhevsky, A., Sutskever, I., Salakhutdinov, R.: Dropout: a simple way to prevent neural networks from overfitting. J. Mach. Learn. Res. **15**(1), 1929–1958 (2014)

A Novel Algorithm for Salient Region Detection

Rajesh Kumar Tripathi[✉]

Computer Engineering and Applications, IET, GLA University, Mathura,
Uttar Pradesh, India
`rajesh.tripathi@gla.ac.in`

Abstract. Salient region is the most prominent object in the scene
which attracts to the human vision system. This paper presents a novel
algorithm that is based on the separated Red, Green and Blue colour
channels. Most prominent regions of all the three channels of RGB colour
model are extracted using mean value of the respective channels. Pixels of extracted salient region of RGB channels are counted and then
some specified rules are applied over these channels to generate final
saliency map. To evaluate the performance of the proposed novel algorithm, a standard dataset MSRA-B has been used. The proposed algorithm presents better result and outperformed to the existing approaches.

Keywords: Salient object · RGB channel · Algorithm · Prominent
region

1 Introduction

Salient region detection is a challenging research field of the image processing and
computer vision. Human vision system is highly capable to separate the distinct
object in the scene and mostly have a deep focus on the most prominent part
of the scene. The object or portion of the image, which attracts to the human
vision system in first sight is called as salient region or salient object in the
scene. Colours play important role to highlight the salient object in the image.
RGB image has three basic colours red, green, and blue which has contribution
in some specific ratio to complete an image. Image has background as well as
foreground objects. These foreground objects may be the salient object.

Most important issue is to detect these most attractive salient regions in the
image through an intelligent machine. Salient region or salient object detection
reduces computational complexity in the various applications-object detection
and recognition, video and image compression, segmentation, and image classification.

Proposed algorithm is robust to salient region detection in the image with
the following features:

1. The proposed algorithm is able to detect the saliency region in cluttered
   background.

© Springer Nature Singapore Pte Ltd. 2020
A. Bhattacharjee et al. (Eds.): MIND 2020, CCIS 1241, pp. 401–410, 2020.
https://doi.org/10.1007/978-981-15-6318-8_33

2. The proposed algorithm is better to extract the correct saliency region with almost complete portion of the salient object under illumination effects.
3. The proposed algorithm outperformed to almost all the exiting approaches on the basis quantitative measures - precision and recall.

The rest parts of the paper is arranged as follows: Sect. 2 discusses some existing approaches for finding salient region, Sect. 3 discusses the proposed algorithm, Sect. 4 presents the result analysis, and Sect. 5 presents the conclusion.

2   Related Work

This section discusses the progress of the existing approaches of the recent decade in the field of salient region detection. In the recent years, many salient region extraction approaches have been developed. Itti et al. [12] introduced saliency model for rapid scene analysis using orientation, luminance and color opposition. The works of saliency region findind can be categorized into three ways: i) local-contrast ii) global-contrast and iii) statistical-learning based models.

Local contrast based approaches detects the salient region by extracting features of small regions and higher weightage is assigned to high contrast. Harel et al. [8] applied Markovian approach check the dissimilarity feature of histogram of surrounding the center. Goferman et al. [7] utilized both local and global saliency map to generate final salient region of the image. Klein and Frintrop [15] applied KL Divergence to compute prominent part and extraction of correct salient region. Jiang et al. [13] presented saliency based on a super pixel which is multi-scale and boundary pair that is closed. Yan et al. [23] introduced a hierarchical-model by applying features based on contrast at different scales of a scene and then fusion is applied by graphical model. Hou et al. [10] used informative divergence to represent non-uniform visual information's distribution of an image. Zhu et al. [26] proposed an optimization framework for modeling the background measure.

Global contrast based approaches utilize color contrast over the whole image globally for saliency detection. These approaches are less complex on the basis of computational complexity. Achanta et al. [2] extracted the saliency with the help of frequency domain by using luminance and colour of the scene. Cheng et al. [4] introduced spatial weighted coherence and global contrast differences to extract salient region. Shen and Wu [22] presented decomposition of low-rank matrix to extract foreground and background separately. He and Lau [9] exploited brightness of prominent region to generate final saliency map using pairs of flash and no flash image. Statistical learning based approaches employ models based on Machine learning. In these methods, accuracy of the saliency map is increased and complexity of computation is also increased. Wang et al. [21] presented an auto context model which combined salient region finding and segmentation using trained classifier. Borji and Itti [3] computed saliency map based on rarity of different color spaces using local-global patch dictionary learning. Yang et al. [24] used graph based manifold to assign the rank to regions of image based on similarity. Li et al. [16] computed saliency region using sparse and dense representation errors of the image region. Jiwhan et al. [14] applied local and global contrast approach, spatial distribution, center prior and backgroundness as a set of features for salient region finding. Sikha et al. [20] proposed a hybrid approach for saliency driven transition using DMD to generate saliency map. The proposed algorithm used colour channels mean and rules on the basis of pixel count to extract salient region of the image.

Algorithm 1 The proposed algorithm-extraction of R, G, B channels foreground

---

Require: Image I
Ensure: Salient Region I_S
1: Read an Image I
2: Split the image I into R, G, B channel i.e. I_R, I_G, I_B respectively
3: Applied the Gaussian Filter of the I_R, I_G, I_B to remove the noise from each regions of the channel
4: Compute the mean of each channel R, G, B region i.e. $M_{I_R}, M_{I_G}, M_{I_B}$
5: Compute overall average: $M_{R,G,B} = \frac{M_{I_R} + M_{I_G} + M_{I_B}}{3}$
6: Compute r and c as rows and columns of an image respectively.
7: **for** $i = 1$ **to** r **do**
8:     **for** $j = 1$ **to** c **do**
9:         **if** $M_{R,G,B} < M_{I_R(i,j)}$ **then**
10:             $M_{I_{R_1}}(i,j) \leftarrow 1$
11:         **end if**
12:         **if** $M_{R,G,B} < M_{I_G(i,j)}$ **then**
13:             $M_{I_{G_1}}(i,j) \leftarrow 1$
14:         **end if**
15:         **if** $M_{R,G,B} < M_{I_B(i,j)}$ **then**
16:             $M_{I_{B_1}}(i,j) \leftarrow 1$
17:         **end if**
18:     **end for**
19: **end for**
20: Apply the dilation followed by erosion over $M_{I_{R_1}}, M_{I_{G_1}}, M_{I_{B_1}}$
21: $c1 \leftarrow 0$
22: $c2 \leftarrow 0$
23: $c3 \leftarrow 0$
24: **for** $i = 1$ **to** r **do**
25:     **for** $j = 1$ **to** c **do**
26:         **if** $M_{I_{R_1}}(i,j) == 1$ **then**
27:             $c1 \leftarrow c1 + 1$
28:         **end if**
29:         **if** $M_{I_{G_1}}(i,j) == 1$ **then**
30:             $c2 \leftarrow c2 + 1$
31:         **end if**
32:         **if** $M_{I_{B_1}}(i,j) == 1$ **then**
33:             $c3 \leftarrow c3 + 1$
34:         **end if**
35:     **end for**
36: **end for**

---

3   Proposed Work

This section presents the functionality of the proposed algorithm that is able to extract most prominent region of the image. The proposed algorithms is robust to most prominent region of the image through red, green and blue channels. A region-based rules are applied over the region of RGB channels to find the salient region, that is highly focused by human vision system. The proposed approach consists of two algorithms: Algorithm 1 is responsible to extract the most of the prominent region of RGB channels which plays important role in the removal of background details. Output generated by Algorithm 1 is passed to Algorithm 2, where Algorithm 2 apply rules on count of pixels present in the RGB channels to decide salient object.

Algorithm 1 presents its well defined steps for background removal which are non-salient region. Steps 1–5 takes an colored input image, RGB channels are extracted as I_R, I_G, I_B and gaussian filter is utilized to remove the noise. Mean of each channel is computed as $M_{I_R}, M_{I_G}, M_{I_B}$ and average of mean of RGB channels is computed. Dimension r and c is computed to process the image of any dimension in step 6. Steps 7–19 preserves those pixels of each channels which are more than the average mean of RGB channels. Morphological operations are applied over these obtained RGB images. Pixels of RGB regions are counted and represented as $c1$, $c2$ and $c3$ respectively.

Algorithm 2 uses the region count of RGB channel to decide the prominent region of the image. Algorithm 2 extracts the saliency region of an image after applying its rule over the segmented R, G, and B images. Therefore, proposed approach is robust to find salient region of the image correctly with complete portion of the object in complex background.

4   Performance Analysis

To measure and analyze the performance of the proposed novel algorithm, 1000 complex and challenging images of standard dataset MSRA-B [4] have been used. The implementation of the proposed algorithm has been done on a computer having configuration- Intel Core i7 8th Gen CPU, 8GB DDR 3 RAM, windows 10 operating system using Matlab 2016a.

Performance analysis of the proposed algorithm has been done by quantitative as well as qualitative. Quantitative analysis has been performed using two frequently used measures-precision and recall. Qualitative analysis have presented as salient region of the image with respect to ground truth. The quantitative and qualitative results have been compared with the following existing approaches: DMD [20], SUN [25], FES [18], SIM [17], SR [11], SER [19], SWD [6], HDCT [14], HC [4], GC [5], FT [2], MC [13], GB [8], AC [1].

Algorithm 2 The proposed algorithm-salient region detection based on some rules

Require: Segmented Image of R, G, B channel-$M_{I_{R_1}}$, $M_{I_{G_1}}$, $M_{I_{B_1}}$, and Count $c1$, $c2$, $c3$ respectively.
Ensure: Salient Region R
1: Compute size of image as r and c
2: **if** $c1 > c2$and$c1 > c3$and$c2 > c3$ **then**
3:    $R \leftarrow (M_{I_{R_1}} \mathbf{xor} M_{I_{G_1}})$
4:    $R \leftarrow (M_{I_{R_1}} - M_{I_{B_1}}) * M_{I_{B_1}} + M_{I_{G_1}}$
5:    $R \leftarrow (M_{I_{G_1}} * M_{I_{B_1}})$
6: **else if** $c1 > c2$and$c1 > c3$and$c3 > c2$ **then**
7:    $R \leftarrow (M_{I_{R_1}} - M_{I_{B_1}}) * M_{I_{B_1}} + M_{I_{G_1}}$
8: **end if**
9: **if** $c2 > c1$and$c2 > c3$and$c1 > c3$ **then**
10:   $R \leftarrow (M_{I_{G_1}} - M_{I_{R_1}}) * M_{I_{R_1}} + M_{I_{B_1}}$
11: **else if** $c2 > c1$and$c2 > c3$and$c3 > c1$ **then**
12:   $R \leftarrow M_{I_{G_1}} \mathbf{xor} M_{I_{B_1}}$
13:   $R \leftarrow M_{I_R} * M_{I_{R_1}}$
14: **end if**
15: **if** $c3 > c1$and$c3 > c2$and$c1 > c2$ **then**
16:   $R \leftarrow (M_{I_{B_1}} - M_{I_{R_1}}) * M_{I_{R_1}} + M_{I_{G_1}}$
17: **else if** $c3 > c1$and$c3 > c2$and$c2 > c1$ **then**
18:   $R \leftarrow (M_{I_{G_1}} - M_{I_{R_1}}) * M_{I_{B_1}}$
19:   **if** $r * c - c3 > Threshold1$ **then**
20:     $M_{I_{B_1}} \leftarrow (1 - M_{I_{B_1}})$
21:     $R \leftarrow M_{I_{B_1}}$
22:   **end if**
23:   **if** $r * c - c3 < Threshold2$ **then**
24:     $R \leftarrow (M_{I_{G_1}} - M_{I_{R_1}}) * M_{I_{B_1}} + M_{I_{G_1}}$
25:   **end if**
26: **end if**

The precision and recall quantitative measures have been utilized to analyze the performance according to the presented formulas: Precision refers to accurate salient region detection, and it is defined as the ratio of the total number of pixels of ground truth's salient region to the total count of the pixels of extracted salient region. It is represented as equation given below:

$$Precision = \frac{|F \cap G|}{F} \tag{1}$$

Recall refers to the portion of the extracted salient region, and it can be defined as the ratio of pixels of the extracted salient region to the total count of the pixels of ground truth salient region. It is represented as equation given below:

$$Recall = \frac{|F \cap G|}{G} \tag{2}$$

where F is the binary foreground and G is the ground truth binary image. In other ways, precision refers to correct salient region detection while recall refers to the how much portion of the correct salient region is detected in comparison to the ground truth.

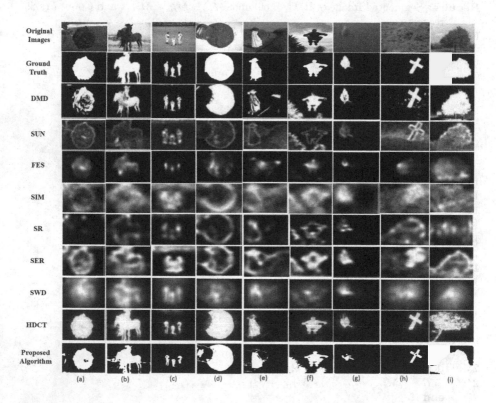

Fig. 1. Comparative study of visual saliency results of the proposed algorithm and different existing approaches on complex images.

Table 1 shows the performance of the proposed algorithm and above mentioned existing approaches in terms of precision and recall. The proposed algorithm outperformed to some existing approaches and comparable to a few approaches.

It has been observed that the methods SUN [25], FES [18], SR [11] and AC [1] failed to detect few of the saliency map due to the use of limited set of local features. A few algorithms-SIM [17], SER [19], SWD [6] and GB [8] are failed to detect salient region with better resolution. Although some methods GB [8], SER [19], FT [2], SIM [17], GC [5], MC [13], HC [4], SWD [6], and SEG detected most of the saliency map and some non saliency map were also detected. The proposed algorithm outperformed to the following existing approaches-SUN [25], FES [18], SIM [17], SR [11], SER [19], SWD [6], HC [4], GC [5], FT [2], GB [8], AC [1] in terms of precision and recall measures excepting DMD [20], HDCT [14], and MC [13].

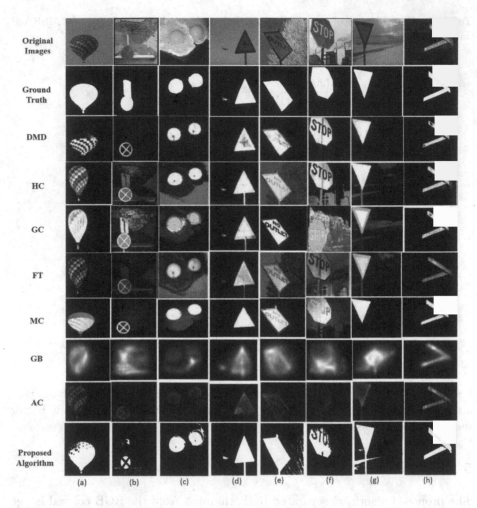

Fig. 2. Comparative study of visual salient region obtained by the proposed algorithm and different existing approaches.

Figure 1 shows the qualitative results for analysis of correctly salient region detection as well as how much portion of the salient region detected. The proposed algorithm can be compared with the following approaches-DMD [20], HDCT [14], and MC [13] as qualitative and quantitative as well. The proposed algorithm is lacking in terms of precision from DMD [20], HDCT [14] by small margin i.e. .001 and .004 respectively while outperformed both by small margin in terms of recall. The proposed algorithm is lacking by small margin in terms of recall by MC [13] but outperformed in terms of precision.

Figure 2 shows results of some challenging images of the proposed algorithm and the existing approaches. Result of proposed algorithm for image a, b, d, h is better than existing approaches. Result of c is very close to DMD [20] and

Table 1. Performance of proposed algorithm and existing approaches on MSRA-B dataset.

Approaches	Precision	Recall
GB (2006) [8]	.775	.829
SR (2007) [11]	.655	.997
SUN (2008) [25]	.449	.995
AC (2008) [1]	.704	.964
SER (2009) [19]	.654	.999
FT (2009) [2]	.698	.988
FES (2011) [18]	.767	.921
SIM (2011) [17]	.464	.647
SWD (2011) [6]	.890	.599
GC (2013) [5]	.875	.997
MC (2013) [13]	.892	.933
HC (2015) [4]	.582	.938
HDCT (2015) [14]	.901	.829
DMD (2018) [20]	.898	.848
Proposed algorithm	**.897**	**.851**

better than other approaches. Result of images e, f and g are better than other approaches excepting DMD [20]. In comparison to DMD [20], result is better including small noise.

5   Conclusion

The proposed algorithm separated RGB channels from the RGB colored image and extracted the most prominent region using the mean value of the three channel images. Some rules have been applied based on pixel count of the salient region of three channels to find final salient region.

The proposed approach performed well and outperformed to the existing approaches, excepting a few approaches with which lacking by a small margin. In future, improvement in the algorithm is required which can improve both the precision and recall measures simultaneously.

References

1. Achanta, R., Estrada, F., Wils, P., Süsstrunk, S.: Salient region detection and segmentation. In: Gasteratos, A., Vincze, M., Tsotsos, J.K. (eds.) ICVS 2008. LNCS, vol. 5008, pp. 66–75. Springer, Heidelberg (2008). https://doi.org/10.1007/978-3-540-79547-6_7

2. Achanta, R., Hemami, S., Estrada, F., Süsstrunk, S.: Frequency-tuned salient region detection. In: IEEE International Conference on Computer Vision and Pattern Recognition (CVPR 2009), pp. 1597–1604 (2009). For code and supplementary material http://infoscience.epfl.ch/record/135217

3. Borji, A.: Exploiting local and global patch rarities for saliency detection. In: Proceedings of the 2012 IEEE Conference on Computer Vision and Pattern Recognition (CVPR), CVPR 2012, pp. 478–485. IEEE Computer Society, Washington (2012). http://dl.acm.org/citation.cfm?id=2354409.2354899

4. Cheng, M.M., Mitra, N.J., Huang, X., Torr, P.H.S., Hu, S.M.: Global contrast based salient region detection. IEEE TPAMI **37**(3), 569–582 (2015)

5. Cheng, M.M., Warrell, J., Lin, W.Y., Zheng, S., Vineet, V., Crook, N.: Efficient salient region detection with soft image abstraction (2013)

6. Duan, L., Wu, C., Miao, J., Qing, L., Fu, Y.: Visual saliency detection by spatially weighted dissimilarity, pp. 473–480 (2011)

7. Goferman, S., Zelnik-Manor, L., Tal, A.: Context-aware saliency detection. IEEE Trans. Pattern Anal. Mach. Intell. **34**(10), 1915–1926 (2012). https://doi.org/10.1109/TPAMI.2011.272

8. Harel, J., Koch, C., Perona, P.: Graph-based visual saliency. In: Proceedings of the 19th International Conference on Neural Information Processing Systems, NIPS 2006, pp. 545–552. MIT Press, Cambridge (2006). http://dl.acm.org/citation.cfm?id=2976456.2976525

9. He, S., Lau, R.W.: Saliency detection with flash and no-flash image pairs. In: Proceedings of European Conference on Computer Vision, pp. 110–124 (2014)

10. Hou, W., Gao, X., Tao, D., Li, X.: Visual saliency detection using information divergence. Pattern Recogn. **46**(10), 2658–2669 (2013). https://doi.org/10.1016/j.patcog.2013.03.008

11. Hou, X., Zhang, L.: Saliency detection: a spectral residual approach (2007)

12. Itti, L., Koch, C., Niebur, E.: A model of saliency-based visual attention for rapid scene analysis. IEEE Trans. Pattern Anal. Mach. Intell. **20**(11), 1254–1259 (1998). https://doi.org/10.1109/34.730558

13. Jiang, B., Zhang, L., Lu, H., Yang, C., Yang, M.H.: Saliency detection via absorbing Markov chain. In: 2013 IEEE International Conference on Computer Vision, pp. 1665–1672 (2013)

14. Kim, J., Han, D., Tai, Y., Kim, J.: Salient region detection via high-dimensional color transform and local spatial support. IEEE Trans. Image Process. **25**(1), 9–23 (2016)

15. Klein, D.A., Frintrop, S.: Center-surround divergence of feature statistics for salient object detection. In: 2011 International Conference on Computer Vision, pp. 2214–2219 (2011)

16. Li, Z., Tang, K., Cheng, Y., Hu, Y.: Transition region-based single-object image segmentation. AEU Int. J. Electron. Commun. **68**(12), 1214–1223 (2014)

17. Murray, N., Vanrell, M., Otazu, X., Párraga, C.A.: Saliency estimation using a non-parametric low-level vision model, pp. 433–440 (2011)

18. Rezazadegan Tavakoli, H., Rahtu, E., Heikkilä, J.: Fast and efficient saliency detection using sparse sampling and kernel density estimation. In: Heyden, A., Kahl, F. (eds.) SCIA 2011. LNCS, vol. 6688, pp. 666–675. Springer, Heidelberg (2011). https://doi.org/10.1007/978-3-642-21227-7_62

19. Seo, H., Milanfar, P.: Static and space-time visual saliency detection by self-resemblance. J. Vis. **9**(15), 1–27 (2009)

20. Sikha, O., Kumar, S.S., Soman, K.: Salient region detection and object segmentation in color images using dynamic mode decomposition. J. Comput. Sci. **25**, 351–366 (2018)

21. Wang, L., Xue, J., Zheng, N., Hua, G.: Automatic salient object extraction with contextual cue. In: Proceedings of the 2011 International Conference on Computer Vision, ICCV 2011, pp. 105–112. IEEE Computer Society, Washington (2011). https://doi.org/10.1109/ICCV.2011.6126231

22. Wu, Y.: A unified approach to salient object detection via low rank matrix recovery. In: Proceedings of the 2012 IEEE Conference on Computer Vision and Pattern Recognition (CVPR), CVPR 2012, pp. 853–860. IEEE Computer Society, Washington (2012). http://dl.acm.org/citation.cfm?id=2354409.2354676

23. Yan, Q., Xu, L., Shi, J., Jia, J.: Hierarchical saliency detection. In: Proceedings of the 2013 IEEE Conference on Computer Vision and Pattern Recognition, CVPR 2013, pp. 1155–1162. IEEE Computer Society, Washington (2013). https://doi.org/10.1109/CVPR.2013.153

24. Yang, C., Zhang, L., Lu, H., Ruan, X., Yang, M.: Saliency detection via graph-based manifold ranking. In: 2013 IEEE Conference on Computer Vision and Pattern Recognition, pp. 3166–3173, June 2013

25. Zhang, L., Tong, M.H., Marks, T.K., Shan, H., Cottrell, G.W.: SUN: a Bayesian framework for saliency using natural statistics. J. Vis. **8**, 32 (2008)

26. Zhu, W., Liang, S., Wei, Y., Sun, J.: Saliency optimization from robust background detection. In: Proceedings of the 2014 IEEE Conference on Computer Vision and Pattern Recognition, CVPR 2014, pp. 2814–2821. IEEE Computer Society, Washington (2014). https://doi.org/10.1109/CVPR.2014.360

Exploiting Topic Modelling to Classify Sentiment from Lyrics

Maibam Debina Devi[(✉)] and Navanath Saharia

IIIT Manipur, Imphal, India
{debina,nsaharia}@iiitmanipur.ac.in

Abstract. With the increase in an enormous amount of data, text analysis has become a challenging task. Techniques like classification, categorization, summarization and topic modeling have become part of every natural language processing activity. In this experiment, we aim to perform sentiment class extraction from lyrics using topic modeling techniques. We have use generative statistical model Latent Dirichlet Allocation (LDA) which is also the most widely explored model in topic modeling and another nonparametric bayesian based approach model Heuristic Dirichlet Process (HDP) to extract the topics from 150 lyrics samples of Manipuri songs written using Roman script. We observe this unsupervised techniques, able to obtain the underlying different sentiment class of lyrics in the form of topics.

Keywords: Lyrics · Sentiment classification · Topic modelling ·
Latent Dirichlet allocation · Hierarchical Dirichlet process

1 Introduction

The text being written format of data, the field of text analysis is becoming one of the most focus areas under natural language processing. Understanding the concept of the underlying idea, meaning, the structure of the text is called text analysis. Topic modeling is a statistical approach of text analysis and it aims to discover the discrete or abstract form of topic in collection of documents and deals with the finding of the semantic structure of the text. It comes under natural language processing and information retrieval. It is largely used in several applications like classification, topic discovery, finding entities relationship, etc. It is the process of uncovering the hidden structure of data and follow the generative process. In this, the model documents representation is in mixture of topics, with probability distribution of topics. It can also be consider as dimension reduction of data other way summarizing the larger context, way of automatically organizing data. Comparison is done through clustering techniques, where some clusters, number of topics act as hyperparameters. For every, it requires collection of documents containing texts, and vocabulary which consist set of unique words in the collection.

© Springer Nature Singapore Pte Ltd. 2020
A. Bhattacharjee et al. (Eds.): MIND 2020, CCIS 1241, pp. 411–423, 2020.
https://doi.org/10.1007/978-981-15-6318-8_34

At the very beginning, topic modeling is considered to be an information retrieval tool, used to browse large collections of documents. Day by day text data is available in enormous amounts and beyond processing capacity. Topic modeling became the technique which helps to organize a large collection of unstructured data. The topic represents a relevant concept or hidden theme about the documents out of an enormous collection of data. It can learn the hidden set of word distributions for collection of documents, where each document is assigned to the topic and each topic is formed by a cluster of semantic similar words. Following the probabilistic approach, discover the text's latent semantic structure. It differs from model to model of deciding number of topics for modeling. Model like latent Dirichlet allocation works with user defined value where as HDP model can pull many topics required for the data-set. The most suitable "k" value, k define total number of topics to be generate. [24] present a heuristic approach for determining the k value.

Over the past reported work mainly latent Dirichlet allocation (LDA) and latent semantic analysis has been the most used applications in topic modeling. Evaluation strategies over topic modeling require an opinion of experts and comparison concerning various parameters is explain under [7]. Besides performance ground truth comparison require human judgment. Modeling of the collective document remains to be a challenging task and an active area. Applying the concept of LDA model performance in sentiment classification is reported in [16] work.

Many work implemented is under large data, mostly documents or articles. Our contribution includes to perform sentiment classification over lyrics using topic modeling technique. Using latent Dirichlet allocation which is the famous algorithm in topic modeling and also heuristic Dirichlet process, which outperforms in our experiment with the retrieval of a different dimension of the sentiment of happy and sad. We have explored in Manipuri lyrics, Manipuri language is a low-resource language, agglutinative and highly inflectional, challenges occurs and no work has been reported till now. The next section explains so far reported work in topic modeling. The workflow of this experiment and implementation is described in Sect. 3. Results achieve and observations obtain from this experiment are explained in the following two sections. The last section describes the conclusion made from the experiment of this paper.

2   Related Work

The methodology of topic modeling and require enhancement is clearly explained in paper [7]. It gives a figure of 33 papers based on topic modeling in information system. Topic modeling is broadly reached out in many applications, few works have been reported under lyrics. Work of [5] used the latent Dirichlet allocation modeling technique to recognize the emotion of song, where sequence of words is considered as features with occurrence probability and secure 72% accuracy with manual evaluation. Another solution for mining over topics proposed by [21] gives collective idea over different type of text, taking Wikipedia and twitter data separate experiment is performed. It explore LDA technique taking 1000 documents with k value as 50, *alpha* is set as 1 and *beta* value as 0.1. In topic modeling, *alpha* value gives the document-topic density, with its higher value means the document is contributed to many topics. When it comes to density of words contributing a topic *beta* value represents. The model is train with jensen-shannon divergence [12] as similarity measurement. On the other side work reported by [4] explain approach with the word topic model, finds the co-occurrence relationship among the words. Besides referring documents from collection of documents for topic mixture model, each word is regarded as a word topic model, for finding the existence of particular word. The concept of qualitative and quantitative analysis on topic modeling is described clearly [15]. The automatic categorization of software using LDA [20] is performed to analyze documents and index accordingly as probabilistic topics. Every mention work on topic modeling is mostly explored with rich data that describe the subject in a clear context. Report work by [10] is based on Indonesians song lyrics. It aims for topic interpretation of songs using the LDA model.

3   Baseline Algorithm

This section describes the basic and most widely used algorithm in topic modeling, most reported work either compared or take the reference to this algorithm.

3.1   Latent Dirichlet Allocation

Latent Dirichlet allocation is a generative statistical model proposed by [4] which is a widely used algorithm in topic modelling [3]. It considers a set of fixed topics. The set of words contributes to the representation of each topic. LDA aims to map documents to topics with references to words in documents and topics. It uses bag-of-words as a feature for the topic discovery through posterior inference. Vocabulary refers to the feature set, with the word as a feature. Every document contains a number of topics, each topic has a distribution of words associated with it. It has counted one of the popular topic modeling probabilistic base techniques. Documents have a probability distribution over topics.

LDA Parameter. From the training set, it derived parameters alpha α and beta β which act as hyper-parameter. α behave Dirichlet prior on the per-document distribution of topic. A high value of α indicates the document consists of a mixture of topics and low indicate less mixture of topics. So it is upon to the data-set likely to set α value. α define topic density of the documents which range from 0.1 to 1. β is also Dirichlet prior to per-topic word distributions. Theta θ define random matrix where distributed across where $\theta(i, j)$ means the probability of the ith document word contain belong to j^{th} topic. Eta η is a parameter vector for each topic, which governs the distribution of words in each topic.

$$P(\Theta_{1:M}, z_{1:m}, \beta_{1:k} \mid D; \alpha_{1:M}, \eta_{1:k}) \tag{1}$$

where 1:M defines the set of documents range from 1 till M, with each document have N words and word is generated by one topic from the total number of topic k. With join posterior probability of θ, β and z with N topics for each document and D define the text corpus.

In the LDA modeling, user need to specify k that is number of topics, which in some case it might not truly highlight the real distribution which in result, may pull down the performance of the model. Dirichlet topic distribution does not have the capability to capture correlation. As bag-of-word does not maintain the sentence structure, in some scenarios violate the sense in modeling topic.

4 Experiment

Lyrics is a written form of songs, it carries high sentimental expression. The structure and word sequences and distribution of lyrics are normally differ from normal text. This experiment aims to implement the concept of topic model namely latent Dirichlet allocation, latent semantic analysis and hierarchical Dirichlet process in the field of Manipuri lyrics. The experiment starts with collection of lyrics written in roman script from kangleilyrics.com and manipurisonglyrics.com. This source is the known option for the collection of songs and lyrics for Manipuri song lyrics. We collect 150 lyrics sample from the sources considering two sentiment polarity lyrics that are sad and happy. For the experiment, we labeled each lyric with its corresponding sentiment manually, for classification and topic sentiment analysis. To justify the sentiment we have validated the labeled from native person and to refer for ground truth analysis of topics generated by the model. The given Fig. 1 give the distribution of the two sentiment category that is happy and sad over 150 lyrics.

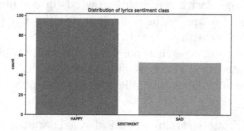

Fig. 1. Lyrics sentiment distribution

Preprocessing plays an important role in natural language processing. The performance of the model also dependent upon how clean and type of the input data is passed to a model. There is no certain fix rule or steps of preprocessing, it needs to perform according to the requirement. In this experiment as part of preprocessing we find the length of each lyric as a basic step to observe the word count distribution for all data-set as given in Fig. 2. Most lyrics happen to have many unwanted char and words which do not contribute to deciding the topic and which does not contribute to defining a sentiment. As the first step, we create a list that includes all the unwanted char observe in data-set and removal is done. Next removal of punctuation and string which length is less than three. And finally tokenization and convert into lowercase.

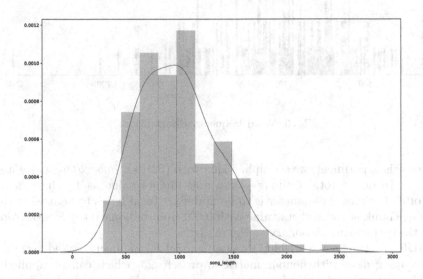

Fig. 2. Lyrics length distribution graph

The topic modeling model requires two certain input dictionary and corpus. A dictionary is created with 5323 words for 150 lyrics, where for each unique word in the lyrics is retrieve and unique id is assigned to it. Concerning the dictionary, a corpus is created with two attribute word id and frequency of the word is assigned. Both the dictionary and corpus are pass to the model for topic modeling. Figure 3 give the overview structure of word frequency count distribution with a number of lyrics. With it, the mean value, median and standard deviation are also obtained.

Finding optimal number of topics plays an important factor in deciding the quality of the model. For the LDA model, a total number of topics k value is user define. Choosing the right value of k marks interpretable and meaningful topics. There does not exist a benchmark value of k, it depends upon corpus and text structure. The higher value of k might result in granular sub-topics or on the otherwise, it can also even retrieve the same keywords among topics. Lesser value might result in the shrinking of important topics. For training the model in latent Dirichlet allocation, along with the input we set the number of topics k as 5, increase in topic can also divert the semantic term relationship in topic, it may also create a scenario where all topics happen to be similar. LDA model hyperparameters affect topic sparsity.

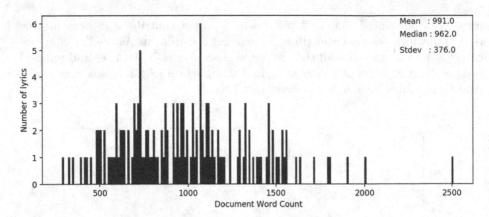

Fig. 3. Word frequency distribution

For this experiment, we set alpha value with $(0.01 * number of topics)$. Passes value as 10 define total training passes and update value as 1, which defines how often the model parameter is to be updated. Total lyrics to be used in each training chunk is 100 and eta value with 0.001 and dictionary key length. Along with the corpus and dictionary to the model.

HDP (Hierarchical Dirichlet Process) model is an unsupervised technique for grouping data with nonparametric approach [23] which can be applied to mixed-membership data. Being a generative model, the document is considered as a group with observed words over terms, it aims to discover low-dimensional latent structure, unlike LDA. It can be represented with a tree-like structure, each node associates a Dirichlet Process [19] and child node being conditionally independent to their parent node. The concept of HDP with the Chinese restaurant process is clearly explained in [2]. HDP learns from data to define a maximum number of topics rather than pre-specification. It captures uncertainty in a number of topics, selects a common base distribution and represents a variant set of possible topics, from it. For this experiment with id to word, we set an alpha value as $(0.01 * number of topics)$ as we observe our lyrics data does not possess much mixture topic and eta value as $(0.001 * dictionary key length)$, random state as none and gamma to 1.

Topic modeling comes under an unsupervised approach for the extraction of topics. The interpretability of topics is not guaranteed it requires a measure. Topic coherence is a method to evaluate topic models. Coherence is a measuring technique in order to make distinguish between bad and good topics. The coherence value is an aggregated form of a segmented set of word subsets S and P word probabilities based on reference corpus. These consist of 2 ways of coherence calculation, intrinsic and extrinsic measurement. Intrinsic measure based with conditional log-probability and coherence representation is done using **UMass-coherence** proposed in [14]. Compare word only with neighbour words and giving pairwise score function, given formula (2) is use to calculate coherence, for given list of words $\mathbf{L} = w_1...w_m$ and ratio of total lyrics which contain words and total number of lyrics **D** with word probabilities define as $\mathbf{p}(w_m, w_l)$. The extrinsic measure uses **Point wise mutual information** (PMI). Here pairing is done in word to word manner, and the topic is decided by its pairing score. For this experiment we are using extrinsic measurement [18] with **c_v measure** based on word PMI and sliding window method by obtaining co-occurrence counts for given words. Using this count it is used to calculate NPMI (normalized PMI) of every top word to top word and result in a vectors set. The similarity is measure among the sum of all top word vectors and every top word vector.

$$(C_{UMass}(L) = \sum_{m=2}^{M} \sum_{l=1}^{m-1} log(\frac{p(w_m, w_t) + \frac{1}{D}}{p(w_l)}) \tag{2}$$

5 Result

Topic modeling refers to discovering the latent or hidden topics of the corpus whereas, lyrics are about underlying mood expressing in different forms. Implementing topic modeling in lyrics remains a challenging task as unlike document lyrics exhibit the nature of the expression of the subject in hidden or indirect form.

This experiment aims to exploit the concept of topic modeling to classify the sentiment of lyrics. Two topic modeling technique is used to classify the sentiment of lyrics. Before fitting to model, words in lyrics that don't contribute to defining sentiment is stored in a list called the stopword list. This list has been filter out at the preprocessing phase, example of few stop words are *nang: you, ei: me, nanggi: yours*.

In lyrics without being refer or mention, the actual sentiment can be emotionally loaded. For example emotion like "happy" or "sad" need not mention in lyrics to define context or emotional load of lyric [22]. Lyric happens to possess distinct characteristics compared to normal text document [13] with its structure, statistical information and other specific information like the presence of slang language.

In this experiment, we consider 150 lyrics with an average length of the lyrics is about 127 words, with the total words in the corpus, which is about 19077 words. With it, there consist of 5323 unique words. Each lyric tells about an underlying sentiment class. With low statistical information and underlying conceal emotion and with metaphoric expressions form find topic modeling as a challenging task. To support model performance and to measure the topic quality, coherence value is considered.

According to the topic generated and word distribution by the models, all topics happen to describe the secondary feature of two labeled sentiment in different dimensions. The core concept of the model is retrieved despite challenges with the language. After overall observed, words obtain for the topic reflects semantic weightage. This experiment perform one level sub-sentiment classification of lyrics. Consider lyrics consist two sentiment polarity *happy* and *sad*.

For the performance evaluation of the model, we have considered the coherence score and Table 1 to describe the obtain score for each model in this experiment. Word to exclude in topic generation is decided by filter size. Filter size defines the word present in the number of lyrics. Condition for word to filter is to remove word in modeling if the occurrence of the word is less than filter size (number of lyrics). Different 3 filter size is implemented1 and it is observed, for this corpus with minimum filter size equal to 2 obtained coherence score for the models is high, with HDP model giving the highest score.

Table 1. Model coherence score

Model	No filter	Filter size = 2	Filter size = 5
LDA	0.38	**0.57**	0.48
HDP	0.75	**0.76**	0.62

Given below figures are the obtained coherence graph shown for the models. For the LDA model, Fig. 4 shows that the coherence score decrease with an increase in a number of topics, set peak value with 5 and with its inference topic is assigned. The coherence graph of the HDP model refer Fig. 5, gives peak value at different numbers of topics. As cases observe keywords repetition occurs for a large value of k, it always requires a human role for deciding better value of k. Along with its consideration of dictionary size, quality topics can be obtain with less value of k. Therefore for this experiment HDP model retrieves 20 topics as described above.

LDA model the topics inferences with best coherence score are describe below Table 2, keywords shown are the words that contribute high sentiment intensity to the topic and possess relation among them to define the inferences topic. It is describe with its base language and literal meaning corresponding to it. The text in the bold are the inferences topics for the model. Taking account with retrieve keyword. Five generated topics are **Inequitable love**, second topic define **Expressive love** with keywords address mostly when a person falls in love or to describe beauty. Thirdly **Deeply in love**, **Separation** and last topic as **Sacrifice**.

For HDP, concerning the coherence graph and score model itself generate twenty topics with the best fit contributed keywords. Topics are **Desperate, Confident, Love, Ignorance, Restless, Happy, Regret, Interest, Attention, Acceptance, Dejected, Rejection, Embarrassment, Hopeless, Hopeful, Blessful, Enjoyment, Painful, Expectation, Rejoice**.

Each topic defines the sub-level of both the sentiment of two polarities happy and sad. For both the model it shows a clear result that all the generated topic refers to a sentimental class of happy and sad. Hence applied technique able to extract the different forms of happy and sad expression used in lyrics to describe the sentiment.

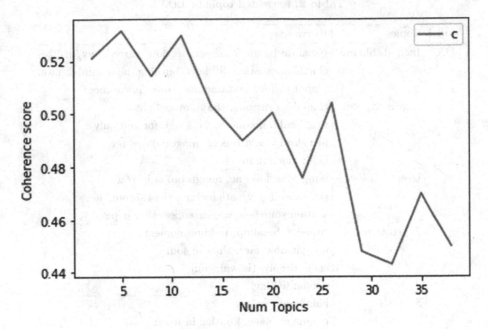

Fig. 4. Coherence graph for LDA

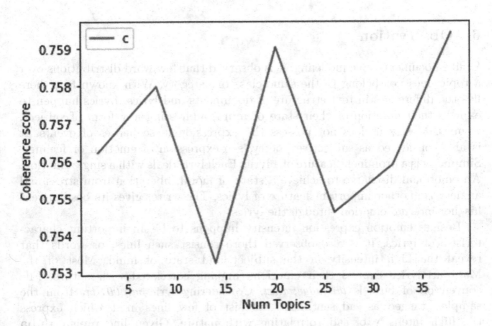

Fig. 5. Coherence graph for HDP

Table 2. Extracted topic by LDA

Model	Topics	Keywords
LDA	Inequitable love	nanakta: beside you, pamde: dont agree/deny/dislike, chakliba: emotionally hurt/burning, nongdamba: fate, mapokse: life, saktamduna: your appearance
	Expressive love	chanabi: dear one, thaja: moonlight ngaohanlli: madness, nangtagi: for you only liri: slowly/cold breeze, ningol: daughter helli: much more
	Deeply in love	nungshibi: loveone, nangtabu: only you, penna:willingly/satisfactory, thawai:soul/life, saktam:your face/appearance, asha: hopeful
	Seperation	kainaba: breakup, mikup: moment nongdamba: fate, thawai: soul asuk: deeply, thawai: soul penna: willingly
	Sacrifice	haipham: restless mapham: place, khutka: in hand pubiro: take me, nungcba: love punshise: life

6   Observation

Unlike document topic modeling, it is observed that few word distributions over a topic does not belong to the same class or category. With known fact there lies the differences in text structure of documents and lyrics. Lyrics happen to express their emotion or their state of mind, addressing any form of subject, rhymes. Mostly it does not possess the expression in sequences of events. It is also considered as subjective poetry, self-expression of emotion or feelings. Simplicity is a prominent feature of a lyric. Each lyric deals with a single emotion. An emotional discharge to achieve a state of moral, liberation from stress and anxiety is another important feature of lyrics. The writer gives its best to vent his/her internal emotion through the lyrics.

Besides emotion expression intensity happens to be an important characteristic of lyrics. It is also observed there consist such lines, or words that reveal the high intensity of the subject and state of mind. Most of the Manipuri lyrics express their emotions making correlated with nature. File convention of lyric is *language:id:txt*. Considering lyric *mn.001.txt* from the samples, tagged as sad sentiment. Consist of few lines in it which express the high intensity of sad correlating with nature. Given line **meisa puba nongni madi** literal meaning, meisa: *"burning"* puba: *"carries"* nongni: *"rain"* madi: *"him"*. Which is a hyperbolic metaphor phrase, which tends to exaggerate the emotion meaning *he is a heartbreaker*. Another line **nungshiba khanglamdragabu kainabada pirang tarudara** with literal words as Nungshiba: *"love"* khanglamdragabu: *"without knowing"* Kainabada: *"breakup"* pirang: *"tears"* tarudara: *"shed"*. Reference meaning *"without falling in love, how will we know the cost of tears for breakup"*. Normally express in broken love. Certainly, Manipuri lyrics have its indigenous flavor of relating the emotion or comparing the emotion with nature. Can be term as multi-dimensional emotion expression. Which is applicable in both negative and positive polarities. The expressed phrase of *mn.001.txt* is an example of negative polarity defining "sad" sentiment. When it comes to this experiment topic modeling, for deciding word contributing a topic frequency plays an important factor. With consideration of both lyric and topic modeling features, there is a possibility that few words may contribute to a topic, even if it may not contribute to the domain or inferences subject. All the inferences topics are decided based on the intensity of retrieve keyword's sentiment and semantic contributed keywords relation.

7 Conclusion

This experiment starts with 150 samples of sentiment labeled Manipuri lyrics. And implement the topic model algorithm LDA and HDP for sentiment classification. Being an unsupervised approach it is observed that, the topic models results happen to retrieve that topics which is one subclass of labeled sentiment *happy or sad*. Which relates and carries the ground-truth label of sentiment. Lyrics being written form of songs, it possess their characteristics to express in poetic, rhymes and carry the theme. With the ground labeled two-class, this model obtains different sub-categories of two sentiment polarity i.e happy and sad. LDA model happens to hold the ground truth with the topic generated. HDP model extracts its number of topics for this experiment it generates 20 topics, which describe different dimensions of happy and sad class. It can be concluded that the using topic model this experiment is able to retrieve the subdivision of two define sentiment class in an unsupervised manner. The topics can be considered as the different dimensions of positive and negative sentiment expressed in lyrics. The generated topics describe the different-variation of two sentiment classes, which holds the ground truth of this experiment. Unsupervised topic modeling technique applied in the classification of lyrics, able to obtain underlying sentiment which is express in lyrics in the form of topics.

References

1. Bashri, M.F., Kusumaningrum, R.: Sentiment analysis using latent Dirichlet allocation and topic polarity wordcloud visualization. In: 2017 5th International Conference on Information and Communication Technology (ICoIC7), pp. 1–5. IEEE (2017)
2. Blei, D.: Cos 597c: Bayesian nonparametrics. Lecture Notes in Priceton University (2007). http://www.cs.princeton.edu/courses/archive/fall07/cos597C/scribe/20070921.pdf

3. Blei, D.M., Ng, A.Y., Jordan, M.I.: Latent Dirichlet allocation. J. Mach. Learn. Res. **3**(Jan), 993–1022 (2003)
4. Chen, B.: Latent topic modelling of word co-occurence information for spoken document retrieval. In: 2009 IEEE International Conference on Acoustics, Speech and Signal Processing, pp. 3961–3964. IEEE (2009)
5. Dakshina, K., Sridhar, R.: LDA based emotion recognition from lyrics. In: Kumar Kundu, M., Mohapatra, D.P., Konar, A., Chakraborty, A. (eds.) Advanced Computing, Networking and Informatics - Volume 1. SIST, vol. 27, pp. 187–194. Springer, Cham (2014). https://doi.org/10.1007/978-3-319-07353-8_22
6. Ding, W., Song, X., Guo, L., Xiong, Z., Hu, X.: A novel hybrid HDP-LDA model for sentiment analysis. In: 2013 IEEE/WIC/ACM International Joint Conferences on Web Intelligence (WI) and Intelligent Agent Technologies (IAT), vol. 1, pp. 329–336. IEEE (2013)
7. Eickhoff, M., Neuss, N.: Topic modelling methodology: its use in information systems and other managerial disciplines (2017)
8. Landauer, T.K., Foltz, P.W., Laham, D.: An introduction to latent semantic analysis. Discourse Process. **25**(2–3), 259–284 (1998)
9. Landauer, T.K., McNamara, D.S., Dennis, S., Kintsch, W.: Handbook of Latent Semantic Analysis. Psychology Press, London (2013)
10. Laoh, E., Surjandari, I., Febirautami, L.R.: Indonesians' song lyrics topic modelling using latent Dirichlet allocation. In: 2018 5th International Conference on Information Science and Control Engineering (ICISCE), pp. 270–274 (2018)
11. Lee, D.D., Seung, H.S.: Learning the parts of objects by non-negative matrix factorization. Nature **401**(6755), 788 (1999)
12. Lin, J.: Divergence measures based on the shannon entropy. IEEE Trans. Inf. Theory **37**(1), 145–151 (1991)
13. Mayer, R., Neumayer, R., Rauber, A.: Rhyme and style features for musical genre classification by song lyrics. In: ISMIR, pp. 337–342 (2008)
14. Mimno, D., Wallach, H.M., Talley, E., Leenders, M., McCallum, A.: Optimizing semantic coherence in topic models. In: Proceedings of the Conference on Empirical Methods in Natural Language Processing, pp. 262–272. Association for Computational Linguistics (2011)
15. Nikolenko, S.I., Koltcov, S., Koltsova, O.: Topic modelling for qualitative studies. J. Inf. Sci. **43**(1), 88–102 (2017)
16. Onan, A., Korukoglu, S., Bulut, H.: LDA-based topic modelling in text sentiment classification: an empirical analysis. Int. J. Comput. Linguist. Appl. **7**(1), 101–119 (2016)
17. Poria, S., Chaturvedi, I., Cambria, E., Bisio, F.: Sentic LDA: improving on LDA with semantic similarity for aspect-based sentiment analysis. In: 2016 International Joint Conference on Neural Networks (IJCNN), pp. 4465–4473. IEEE (2016)
18. Röder, M., Both, A., Hinneburg, A.: Exploring the space of topic coherence measures. In: Proceedings of the Eighth ACM International Conference on Web Search and Data Mining, pp. 399–408 (2015)
19. Teh, Y.W., Jordan, M.I., Beal, M.J., Blei, D.M.: Sharing clusters among related groups: hierarchical Dirichlet processes. In: Advances in Neural Information Processing Systems, pp. 1385–1392 (2005)
20. Tian, K., Revelle, M., Poshyvanyk, D.: Using latent Dirichlet allocation for automatic categorization of software. In: 2009 6th IEEE International Working Conference on Mining Software Repositories, pp. 163–166. IEEE (2009)

21. Tong, Z., Zhang, H.: A text mining research based on LDA topic modelling. In: International Conference on Computer Science, Engineering and Information Technology, pp. 201–210 (2016)
22. Van Zaanen, M., Kanters, P.: Automatic mood classification using TF* IDF based on lyrics. In: ISMIR, pp. 75–80 (2010)
23. Wang, C., Paisley, J., Blei, D.: Online variational inference for the hierarchical Dirichlet process. In: Proceedings of the Fourteenth International Conference on Artificial Intelligence and Statistics, pp. 752–760 (2011)
24. Zhao, W., et al.: A heuristic approach to determine an appropriate number of topics in topic modeling. In: BMC Bioinformatics, vol. 16, p. S8. BioMed Central (2015)

Crucial Gene Identification
for Esophageal Squamous Cell Carcinoma
Using Differential Expression Analysis

Pallabi Patowary[✉] and Dhruba K. Bhattacharyya[✉]

Department of Computer Science and Engineering, Tezpur University,
Tezpur, Assam, India
{ppallabi,dkb}@tezu.ernet.in

Abstract. This paper attempts to identify a set of crucial genes for
Esophageal Squamous Cell Carcinoma (ESCC) using Differential Expression analysis supported by gene enrichment analysis. Initially, we identify a subset of up-regulated and down-regulated genes based on *adjusted
P-value* and *log fold change* value. Then, we construct co-expression network and PPI network on selected genes to investigate the interactions
and associations among these genes. Finally, enrichment analysis is performed to filter out the most crucial subset of genes which are also evi-
denced to be associated with the ESCC. Three genes, namely TNC,
COL1A1, and FN1 are found most closely relevant to ESCC.

Keywords: RNA-seq · ESCC · Differential expression analysis ·
Topological network · Gene enrichment analysis

1 Introduction

During Esophageal Cancer (EC), healthy cells start growing uncontrollably along
the surface of the esophagus. Esophageal Squamous Cell Carcinoma (ESCC)
and Adenoarcinoma (EAC) are the two main types of esophageal cancer. ESCC
develops from regular squamous cells, running along the surface of the esophagus. ESCC is considered as the ninth most frequently diagnosed melanoma
worldwide [3]. It is reported that the survival rate of ESCC patient is declining
from 20% to 4% in the advanced cases [7]. For all stages combined, survival
is the lowest for cancers of the esophagus (19%) [8]. Unfortunately, it has one
of the lowest survival rates, since esophageal cancer is rarely diagnosed early.
For this cause, doctors and researchers are constantly seeking better methods of
detection and diagnosis, as well as more effective treatments. Late diagnosis and
few therapeutic options increase the mortality rate. Therefore, the identification of crucial genes which might be biomarkers for ESCC is very important. It
also helps in the early detection of ESCC and development of new drugs target.
The information carried out by a gene in terms of gene expression is used in
the synthesis of a functional gene product. Differential Gene Expression Analysis (DEA) helps quantify the statistically significant change of gene expressions

A. Bhattacharjee et al. (Eds.): MIND 2020, CCIS 1241, pp. 424–436, 2020.
https://doi.org/10.1007/978-981-15-6318-8_35

between two experimental conditions and Differentially Expressed Genes (DEGs) have biological significances. The RNA-Seq technology is found very useful for differential expression analysis. In this paper, we perform a systematic analysis based on publicly available ESCC RNA-seq data to identify interesting genes in ESCC. Significant differential behaviour of genes between ESCC and normal samples are analyzed with DESeq2 [4] tool and DEGs are identified. Topological behaviour is studied across the conditions followed by biological validation and existing literature evidences. Our study reveals that TNC, COL1A1, and FN1 are crucial genes for ESCC and these three genes have a significant role while the disease is in progression.

2   Materials and Method

RNA-seq data (SRA: SRP008496, GEO: GSE32424) used in this paper is downloaded from Recount2[1]. It contains 12 clinical samples from ESCC from homosapiens and 58,037 genes. Among 12 clinical samples, seven samples are tumors (SRR349741, SRR349742, SRR349743, SRR349744, SRR349745, SRR349746, and SRR349747) and other five samples are non-tumors (SRR349748, SRR349749, SRR349750, SRR349751, and SRR349752). DEGs helps to find out which genes are crucial in the progression of ESCC. We have used R [11] software platform for the downstream analysis of the dataset. DESeq2 [4] is a popular and widely used differential expression analysis tool available in R [11] which is used to identify the DEGs.

The conceptual framework for the identification of crucial genes of ESCC in progression RNA-seq data is shown in Fig. 1. The raw count data (GSE32424) is pre-processed and analyzed by R language software. We extract the differentially expressed genes using DESeq2 [4] from the processed data to obtain the up and down regulated genes. Up-regulated genes have the log fold change value greater than 0 and down-regulated genes have the log fold change value lower than 0. The top 10 Up-regulated and top 10 down-regulated DEGs are identified based on their *log fold change* value, say this is the *list1*, presented in Table 1 and 2. Fold change is a parameter for measuring change in the expression level of a gene during analysis of gene expression data. The DEGs with highest *log fold change* might not have the lowest adjusted P-value. The adjusted P-value can be defined as the smallest familywise significance at which a specific comparison is considered statistically significant as part of multiple comparative tests. A set of significant DEGs are identified with reference to an adjusted P-value cut-off lower than 0.05. We consider top 100 DEGs from this set of genes, say *list2* shown in Table 3 and examined how many genes are mapped from *list1* with higher significance level. Our aim is to consider the most significant genes based on adjusted P-value (*list2*) as well as *log fold change* value. Hence, the common genes from *list1* and *list2* are found out. Among the 20 genes from *list1*, 8 genes are considered because they are more significant from our research point of view i.e. these 8 genes are found common to both the lists. The rest of the genes are

---

[1] https://trace.ncbi.nlm.nih.gov/Traces/sra/?study=SRP008496.

neglected because remaining genes from *list1* are randomly scattered in *list2* and there is a difference of significance level of selected 8 DEGs from the remaining genes. These eight genes are considered as the initial set of crucial genes and used for the downstream analysis. Co-expression, gene regulatory, and PPI networks are constructed with these initial set of genes and finally, gene enrichment and pathway analysis are performed to validate the set of suspected genes. The final set of genes are further studied in the existing literature to establish the roles of these genes in the progression of ESCC.

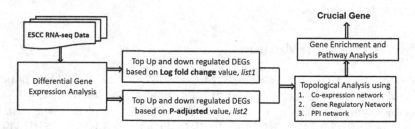

Fig. 1. Conceptual framework for identification of crucial genes for ESCC RNA-seq data

2.1   Differential Expression Analysis

Differential expression analysis with DESeq2 [4] package involves several steps. DESeq2 [4] models the raw count using normalization factors (size factors) to account for library depth variations. Further, it estimates the gene-wise dispersions which help to shrink these estimates resulting in more accurate estimates of dispersion to model the counts. Finally, the testing of hypothesis using the Wald test or Likelihood ratio test is performed by DESeq2 with the help of the negative binomial model.

2.2   Co-expression Network Analysis

Co-expression networks are constructed by using the correlation matrix where genes represent nodes and edges represent computed pairwise correlation between pairs of co-expressed genes. It is a systems biology method for describing the correlation patterns among genes across microarray or RNAseq samples. Most of the tools use pearson correlation to detect co-expression between samples. It identifies group of tightly correlated genes associated with biological processes.

2.3   Gene Regulatory Network Analysis

Gene regulatory networks define how the genes are connected to interpret the biological insights among them [12]. For this network, we need transcription factors and target genes. Transcription factors act as regulators and target genes are the remaining genes from the lists. The transcription factor has the different characteristics and it is identified based on the ability to bind to DNA and to recruit RNA polymerase/alter transcription of a gene [12].

2.4   PPI Network Analysis

A network of protein-protein interactions (PPIs) is a platform from which we have this ability to systematically recognise disease-related genes from the associations between proteins with similar functions.

2.5   Gene Enrichment Analysis

In analysis of gene enrichment, biological importance of a set of genes are examined and assigned functions and roles in biological processes from the previously studied records.

3   Results

Pre-filtering of GSE32424: The low counts are removed by considering the genes with at most 1 zeroes. Version numbers from raw GTEx (GENCODE) Gene IDs (Ensembl) are removed using "cleanid" function available in R. Ensembl IDs are again mapped with Symbol IDs. Occurrences of "NA" in our dataset are deleted and finally, we filter out a total of 12,903 transcripts. Dataset is not normalized since DESeq2 takes input in terms of raw value (data type integer). DEseq2 [4] performs normalization during the execution process.

3.1   Identification of DEGs

DESeq2 [4] is applied in the processed dataset with 12,903 transcripts and 12 samples to identify the differentially expressed genes between normal and ESCC samples. In this analysis, 3,474 (27%) up-regulated (log2FoldChange > 0) and 3,906 (30%) down-regulated genes (log2FoldChange < 0) are identified. Most recent studies consider cut off criteria for identifying DEGs at padj $< .05$ [6]. Also, we extracted the 3,087 number of up-regulated and 3,439 down-regulated DEGs with reference to this threshold.

Here, top 10 DEGs (up-regulated and down-regulated) are extracted based on higher *logfoldchange* value (positive and negative) shown in Table 1 and 2. Again, top 100 genes shown in Table 3 are also selected from DEGs list with a cutoff *padj* value lower than 0.05. The top 10 up and down-regulated genes (Table 1 and 2) are matched with the DEGs of top 100 (Table 3) and common genes are marked in bold. Total eight common genes are identified such as FMO2, PRSS27, FN1, COL1A1, TNC, COL12A1, POSTN, and VCAN.

Table 1. Top 10 Up-regulated DEGs, ranked by *log2FoldChange* value

Gene name
MAL
KRT4
KRT78
CLCA4
FAM25A
CAPN14
FMO2
PRSS27
CNFN
SPRR3

Table 2. Top 10 Down-regulated DEGs, ranked by *log2FoldChange* value

Gene name
FN1
COL1A1
SPP1
TNC
COL12A1
POSTN
VCAN
LOC101927136
TRIM74
SPATA13

Table 3. Top 100 Up and Down-regulated DEGs, ranked by *padj* value, Bold gene: common gene

Gene	baseMean	log2FoldChange	lfcSE	stat	pvalue	padj
THY1	4829.780025	−6.346169979	0.345707208	−18.35706585	2.90E−75	1.98E−71
COL1A1	79691.08739	−8.413805944	0.458422037	−18.35384267	3.08E−75	1.98E−71
LAMC2	37275.82834	−5.542758525	0.308612186	−17.96027112	3.99E−72	1.71E−68
ADAMTS2	4920.146397	−6.061987268	0.341390392	−17.75676005	1.53E−70	4.92E−67
FN1	181649.5053	−8.222104419	0.474595349	−17.32445215	3.08E−67	7.93E−64
PIM1	42755.71584	3.854282258	0.22276014	17.30238745	4.51E−67	9.69E−64
COL12A1	47856.70431	−6.672382153	0.400244028	−16.67078506	2.14E−62	3.94E−59
COL5A2	18280.45918	−6.429870927	0.390642863	−16.4597169	7.14E−61	1.15E−57
ST3GAL4	8995.995796	3.954588218	0.241013217	16.40817989	1.67E−60	2.39E−57

(*continued*)

Table 3. (*continued*)

Gene	baseMean	log2FoldChange	lfcSE	stat	pvalue	padj
CXCR2	4920.643462	6.072532962	0.376603248	16.12448376	1.72E−58	2.21E−55
RMND5B	13440.99001	3.456259672	0.219586365	15.7398647	8.06E−56	9.45E−53
POSTN	40952.11114	−7.747065835	0.497745713	−15.56430449	1.27E−54	1.37E−51
ADAM12	4826.287217	−6.15294879	0.397145909	−15.49291746	3.87E−54	3.84E−51
TRIP10	16056.88274	3.986371988	0.261954274	15.21781616	2.69E−52	2.48E−49
LUM	45988.43525	−4.951477482	0.329347359	−15.0342104	4.38E−51	3.77E−48
LAMA3	15311.98511	−3.625304579	0.242251039	−14.96507338	1.24E−50	1.00E−47
FMO2	29124.0302	7.062021632	0.47636551	14.82479627	1.01E−49	7.68E−47
LEXM	3256.659762	6.18141436	0.419963727	14.71892443	4.87E−49	3.49E−46
TMEM40	31612.7687	5.152150988	0.353738479	14.56485875	4.70E−48	3.19E−45
C6orf132	22551.56257	3.890906817	0.267420679	14.54976045	5.86E−48	3.78E−45
SPARC	118600.3026	−4.841257552	0.336428876	−14.3901368	5.97E−47	3.66E−44
RNF222	3565.500282	5.633596299	0.393950789	14.3002539	2.18E−46	1.28E−43
SERPINB1	123343.2718	4.770905492	0.334812385	14.24948926	4.52E−46	2.53E−43
COL4A1	14627.27515	−4.557388882	0.320552572	−14.21729003	7.16E−46	3.84E−43
RHCG	709479.5522	6.434233656	0.455121165	14.13740813	2.23E−45	1.11E−42
CSTB	1372242.639	5.511962738	0.389883505	14.13746073	2.23E−45	1.11E−42
TNC	64376.6442	−6.463542179	0.458039345	−14.11132525	3.23E−45	1.54E−42
TCP11L2	25709.84086	4.013446948	0.284902751	14.08707684	4.56E−45	2.10E−42
PRSS27	37234.17027	6.718938671	0.478985004	14.02745099	1.06E−44	4.55E−42
UBL3	36513.15223	4.229885666	0.301528583	14.02814164	1.05E−44	4.55E−42
COL4A2	20274.78159	−4.316236534	0.309005665	−13.96814694	2.44E−44	1.01E−41
CD276	3158.72067	−3.565675805	0.256654281	−13.89291384	6.99E−44	2.82E−41
COL5A1	11586.49807	−5.912263015	0.428061337	−13.81171927	2.17E−43	8.46E−41
ALDH9A1	19624.9843	2.965937691	0.215162691	13.78462816	3.15E−43	1.20E−40
VCAN	34011.33394	−6.485585193	0.473516046	−13.69665347	1.06E−42	3.92E−40
AIF1L	21917.32824	5.36849827	0.39481115	13.59763589	4.14E−42	1.48E−39
GRHL1	32056.55097	3.198778742	0.235710599	13.57078871	5.97E−42	2.08E−39
TMEM2	7160.360127	−2.507931141	0.184932304	−13.56134696	6.79E−42	2.30E−39
MXD1	69316.50753	3.966933834	0.295599565	13.41995828	4.62E−41	1.53E−38
KRT13	3444280.396	6.265108333	0.467551522	13.39982447	6.06E−41	1.95E−38
KAT2B	17491.4411	4.055043137	0.303202256	13.3740533	8.57E−41	2.70E−38
DPYSL3	17228.92587	−4.344984457	0.328673845	−13.21974511	6.75E−40	2.07E−37
GMDS	10089.58508	4.122008091	0.312083659	13.20802284	7.89E−40	2.36E−37
LAMC1	10221.65459	−3.775912692	0.286258235	−13.19058189	9.94E−40	2.91E−37
BICDL2	7343.039247	4.441014816	0.336907252	13.18171332	1.12E−39	3.20E−37
PTK6	30586.50244	4.762290492	0.361906168	13.15890945	1.51E−39	4.24E−37
PITX1	91905.99949	4.271973924	0.32961395	12.96053739	2.05E−38	5.62E−36
EHD3	22683.50204	3.836940993	0.297148233	12.91254859	3.82E−38	1.03E−35
CALU	11381.19778	−3.135307865	0.243172743	−12.89333592	4.91E−38	1.29E−35
CALD1	25305.63373	−3.577924467	0.277775088	−12.88065281	5.78E−38	1.49E−35
RANBP9	19274.4568	2.990187779	0.232873675	12.84038556	9.74E−38	2.46E−35
TMPRSS11E	118884.2098	5.929667306	0.461934614	12.83659445	1.02E−37	2.54E−35
CDH11	6210.810544	−5.927628626	0.461864286	−12.83413506	1.06E−37	2.57E−35
ACTA2.AS1	6173.680836	−4.850089176	0.381201425	−12.72316644	4.40E−37	1.05E−34
SPINT1	29984.9069	3.555776328	0.279529745	12.72056511	4.55E−37	1.07E−34

(continued)

Table 3. (*continued*)

Gene	baseMean	log2FoldChange	lfcSE	stat	pvalue	padj
GALE	8795.210953	3.443019304	0.270770858	12.7156199	4.84E−37	1.11E−34
AGFG2	14294.89654	4.333237683	0.342744779	12.6427533	1.23E−36	2.77E−34
FAM129B	95382.00311	3.37513708	0.267166487	12.63308552	1.39E−36	3.08E−34
BGN	7441.279285	−4.533584372	0.359019456	−12.62768436	1.49E−36	3.25E−34
AQP3	232059.326	6.040920179	0.480490879	12.57239304	3.00E−36	6.43E−34
MFSD5	9545.879161	2.265874497	0.18045964	12.55612888	3.68E−36	7.77E−34
ESPL1	5890.654444	3.345698311	0.267073883	12.52723883	5.30E−36	1.10E−33
HOPX	176753.4791	5.933176055	0.473852517	12.52114496	5.72E−36	1.17E−33
SPAG17	4679.285588	4.428817534	0.353773302	12.5188009	5.89E−36	1.19E−33
IL1RN	283189.9994	5.623433999	0.449487646	12.51076432	6.52E−36	1.29E−33
THBS1	33937.76103	−4.687751038	0.375422515	−12.4866007	8.83E−36	1.72E−33
ACPP	13258.13474	3.563615188	0.285412904	12.48582363	8.92E−36	1.72E−33
TGFBI	34296.5564	−4.134967061	0.332247269	−12.44545086	1.48E−35	2.81E−33
KRT7	166890.2056	8.313731856	0.671314957	12.3842494	3.18E−35	5.94E−33
GRPEL2.AS1	1660.483921	4.748874436	0.384009207	12.36656399	3.96E−35	7.30E−33
WDR26	28894.85354	2.48702274	0.202212381	12.29906266	9.16E−35	1.66E−32
CARHSP1	16441.46779	3.020013399	0.246829055	12.23524274	2.02E−34	3.61E−32
PDLIM3	2436.469936	−4.887648845	0.402268773	−12.15020695	5.72E−34	1.01E−31
LOC440434	3491.220659	2.52137897	0.207738486	12.13727421	6.70E−34	1.17E−31
N4BP3	3251.494204	4.048901462	0.334171113	12.11625216	8.66E−34	1.49E−31
ACADM	12716.78695	2.848985866	0.235192358	12.11342873	8.97E−34	1.52E−31
NCCRP1	68372.79468	6.268609098	0.51855541	12.08860033	1.21E−33	2.03E−31
COL6A3	37965.73171	−5.059818655	0.418759069	−12.08288735	1.30E−33	2.15E−31
EPHA2	22450.99902	3.342511137	0.276909142	12.07078651	1.51E−33	2.46E−31
ABLIM3	11188.47785	4.942711439	0.410193382	12.04971035	1.95E−33	3.14E−31
TAGLN	16206.02829	−4.786646146	0.397711983	−12.03545869	2.31E−33	3.68E−31
TMPRSS2	10933.52417	5.820889372	0.485062485	12.0002877	3.54E−33	5.57E−31
STN1	7850.852744	3.591563246	0.299431636	11.99460182	3.79E−33	5.89E−31
SEMA3C	3735.783579	−5.541321276	0.462375765	−11.98445442	4.29E−33	6.58E−31
SESN2	8749.522319	3.918387959	0.327071806	11.98020704	4.51E−33	6.84E−31
MMP2	14805.05584	−5.089611929	0.425399971	−11.96429777	5.47E−33	8.19E−31
SDCBP2	4725.015159	3.70781534	0.310018836	11.95996794	5.76E−33	8.53E−31
LYPD3	63034.79089	3.599396791	0.301606025	11.93410109	7.86E−33	1.15E−30
PMM1	9737.844398	3.5076909	0.295355445	11.87616803	1.57E−32	2.28E−30
FBN1	14840.78056	−4.957674005	0.41792637	−11.86255369	1.85E−32	2.65E−30
WDR66	2551.195043	−4.142504875	0.350739228	−11.8107829	3.43E−32	4.86E−30
SLC35C1	5801.432072	3.263112906	0.277059328	11.77766844	5.09E−32	7.13E−30
PDGFRB	7465.757153	−3.637579521	0.310365774	−11.72029852	1.00E−31	1.39E−29
GPR157	8360.437935	3.02043467	0.258529819	11.68311912	1.55E−31	2.13E−29
FKBP10	5449.581025	−5.418447488	0.46403527	−11.67680096	1.67E−31	2.27E−29
IL18	27793.41571	4.875775621	0.417985018	11.66495307	1.93E−31	2.58E−29
DDR2	4394.368264	−4.0064582	0.34450708	−11.62953808	2.92E−31	3.88E−29
DUSP5	39611.84658	5.126600523	0.441421291	11.61384969	3.50E−31	4.61E−29
ANKRD22	5112.400757	3.00641139	0.259231553	11.5973976	4.25E−31	5.53E−29
GIPC1	41835.05319	2.911257142	0.25107735	11.59506081	4.37E−31	5.63E−29

3.2   Construction of Co-expression Network

In this study, two different co-expression networks are formed for normal and disease conditions as shown in Fig. 2 and 3. For these networks, we consider only the eight suspected DEGs. In these networks, the genes are connected if the Pearson's correlation coefficient is greater than 0.01. Here, considered Pearson's correlation coefficient is greater than 0.01 because the size of our adjacency matrix is very small i.e. 8×8 and all the values with Pearson's correlation coefficient lower than and equal to 0.01 are 0. By comparing these two networks, it is observed that the connectivity of genes with their immediate neighbours in normal condition are lesser (edge connectivity is 5) than the connectivity of genes with their immediate neighbours in disease condition (edge connectivity is 13). When genes transmit from normal to disease conditions, their edge connectivity with neighbours increases and topological behaviour (network connectivities) are significantly different from each other across conditions.

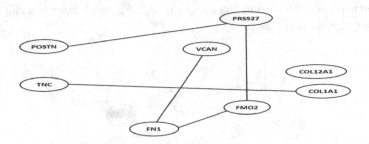

Fig. 2. Co-expression network of the suspected eight genes across the states (i.e. Normal and disease). The total number of edge connectivity is 5.

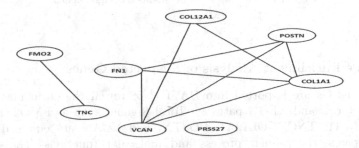

Fig. 3. Co-expression network of the suspected eight genes across the disease condition. The total number of edge connectivity is 13.

3.3   Construction of Gene Regulatory Network (GRN)

Transcription factors among 52 genes are identified with TFcheckpoint[2] tool. Among the 52 genes (Genes from Table 1, 2 and 3), we found only three genes

---

[2] http://www.tfcheckpoint.org/index.php/search.

such as PITX1, GRHL1, and MXD1 as transcription factors. To analyze the different behaviour of GRN in normal and disease conditions, only edge connectivity among regulators (transcriptions factors) and target gene are shown in Table 4 and 5. GENIE3 [2] package available in R platform is used to construct GRN.

3.4 Construction of PPI Network

The STRING website presents an interaction network of the DEGs FMO2, PRSS27, FN1, COL1A1, TNC, COL12A1, POSTN, and VCAN. This network is formed based on the evidences of known interactions among genes from curated databases, text mining, experiments, co-expression, neighbourhood, gene fusion, and co-occurrence with a confidence score of 0.5. Figure 4 describes the interaction among the eight DEGs.

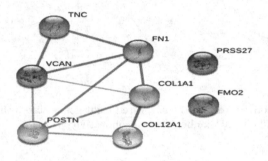

Fig. 4. PPI network of the suspected eight genes

3.5 Gene Enrichment Analysis of Suspected Genes

The eight DEGs are imported into DAVID[3] to reveal the enrichment analysis of GO terms and KEGG pathway. Total 8 genes such as FMO2, PRSS27, FN1, COL1A1, TNC, COL12A1, POSTN, and VCAN are enriched in biological process, the cellular process and molecular functions. The enriched GO terms of these 8 DEGs are GO:0043062 extracellular structure organization (TNC, COL12A1, POSTN, and COL1A1), GO:0030198 extracellular matrix organization (COL12A1, POSTN, and COL1A1), GO:0007155 cell adhesion (TNC, COL12A1, POSTN, and FN1), GO:0022610 biological adhesion (TNC, COL12A1, POSTN, and FN1), GO:0001501 skeletal system development (COL12A1, POSTN, and COL1A1), and GO:0030199 collagen fibril organization (COL12A1 and COL1A1).

---

[3] https://david-d.ncifcrf.gov/.

Table 4. Topological statistics of GRN among 3 regulatory gene and 8 suspected genes in normal state

RegulatoryGene	TargetGene	Weight
PITX1	TNC	0.718599097
GRHL1	COL12A1	0.530555566
GRHL1	POSTN	0.485545356
MXD1	FMO2	0.484461331
MXD1	FN1	0.469279134
MXD1	PRSS27	0.426127752
PITX1	POSTN	0.41000477
GRHL1	FMO2	0.409450798
MXD1	COL12A1	0.396999557
GRHL1	PRSS27	0.396835715
GRHL1	VCAN	0.395777311
GRHL1	COL1A1	0.380200849
MXD1	VCAN	0.353484894
GRHL1	FN1	0.339335059
MXD1	COL1A1	0.332040763
PITX1	COL1A1	0.287758388
PITX1	VCAN	0.250737794
PITX1	FN1	0.191385808
PITX1	PRSS27	0.177036534
GRHL1	TNC	0.145307643
MXD1	TNC	0.13609326
PITX1	FMO2	0.106087871
MXD1	POSTN	0.104449874
PITX1	COL12A1	0.072444878

After the KEGG pathway analysis of the 8 DEGs, two pathways are found enriched such as hsa04512: ECM-receptor interaction (Shared by TNC, COL1A1, and FN1) and hsa04510: Focal adhesion (Shared by TNC, COL1A1, and FN1). The cutoff for adjusted p-value was set as less than 0.01 for the significantly enriched biological processes and the KEGG pathway analysis, adjusted p-value cut off is set as less than 0.05.

Table 5. Topological statistics of GRN among 3 regulatory gene and 8 suspected genes in disease state

RegulatoryGene	TargetGene	Weight
PITX1	FN1	0.514260159
MXD1	TNC	0.511935998
PITX1	COL1A1	0.458977461
PITX1	FMO2	0.396016814
GRHL1	COL12A1	0.381068216
GRHL1	PRSS27	0.378760255
PITX1	COL12A1	0.37851948
GRHL1	POSTN	0.378347311
PITX1	VCAN	0.371907687
MXD1	POSTN	0.343706288
MXD1	PRSS27	0.320786888
GRHL1	VCAN	0.316487829
MXD1	FMO2	0.314507509
MXD1	VCAN	0.311604484
PITX1	PRSS27	0.300452857
MXD1	COL1A1	0.29652297
GRHL1	FMO2	0.289475676
GRHL1	TNC	0.285323713
PITX1	POSTN	0.277946401
GRHL1	FN1	0.250241668
GRHL1	COL1A1	0.244499569
MXD1	COL12A1	0.240412304
MXD1	FN1	0.235498173
PITX1	TNC	0.202740288

4   Discussion

We identify FN1, COL1A1, and TNC among 8 DEGs as suspected genes for ESCC, because these genes are significantly differentially expressed based on *adjusted P-value,* and *log fold change* values between normal and disease conditions. Further, these genes are found highly enriched in terms of GO terms and KEGG pathway analysis. From the observation (Fig. 2 and 3), it is seen that COL1A1 is only associated with TNC in normal condition but in disease condition, the degree of COL1A1 is 4. The degree of FN1 and TNC in normal condition are 2 and 1 and in disease condition, their degrees are 3 and 1 respectively. Again, from Table 4 and 5, it is observed that PITX1 regulates TNC with the highest weight rank in normal condition but in tumor they are connected with the lowest weight rank. In tumor, the top 3 genes which are regulated by the transcription factors with the highest weight rank are FN1, TNC, and COL1A1. The PPI network also depicts the experimentally known interaction from several evidences among these genes, TNC, FN1, and COL1A1 or directly and indirectly connected with each other. FN1, the metastasis marker of ESCC, was observed in the marginal cells of ESCC and was strongly expressed in the cytoplasm of the tumor cells [10]. FN1 was found overexpressed in ESCC and it activates ERK pathway which was experimented by Western blot test and RT-PCR analysis [10]. By up-regulation of FN1 and PDGFRB, SATB1 performs an oncogenic role in ESCC [9]. COL1A1 is reported as a crucial gene for ESCC [1]. TNC, an extracellular matrix protein, is associated with a poor prognosis of ESCC [5].

5 Conclusion

In this study, we analyze RNA-seq data (GSE32424) for Esophageal Squamous Cell Carcinoma. Differential expression analysis is performed to identify differentially expressed genes. Then, the topological behaviour of networks at normal and disease conditions are studied. Finally, gene enrichment analysis is done for validation of the identified genes. From differential expression analysis, topological analysis, and functional enrichment analysis, we find TNC, COL1A1, and FN1 genes which are found to be associated with ESCC and these genes are considered as crucial genes for ESCC. These genes need further investigation to uncover their other activities while the disease is in progression.

Acknowledgements. The authors are thankful to the Ministry of HRD, Government of India for supporting this work financially under the FAST scheme.

References

1. Fu, J.H., Wang, L.Q., Li, T., Ma, G.J., et al.: RNA-sequencing based identification of crucial genes for esophageal squamous cell carcinoma. J. Cancer Res. Ther. **11**(2), 420 (2015)
2. Irrthum, A., Wehenkel, L., Geurts, P., et al.: Inferring regulatory networks from expression data using tree-based methods. PloS One **5**(9), e12776 (2010)
3. Lagergren, J., Smyth, E., Cunningham, D., Lagergren, P.: Oesophageal cancer. The Lancet **390**(10110), 2383–2396 (2017)
4. Love, M.I., Huber, W., Anders, S.: Moderated estimation of fold change and dispersion for RNA-seq data with DESeq2. Genome Biol. **15**(12), 550 (2014)
5. Ohtsuka, M., et al.: Concurrent expression of C4. 4A and Tenascin-C in tumor cells relates to poor prognosis of esophageal squamous cell carcinoma. Int. J. Oncol. **43**(2), 439–446 (2013)
6. Peng, H., Wang, S., Pang, L., Yang, L., Chen, Y., Cui, X.B.: Comprehensive bioinformation analysis of methylated and differentially expressed genes in esophageal squamous cell carcinoma. Mol. Omics **15**(1), 88–100 (2019)
7. Siegel, R.L., Miller, K.D., Jemal, A.: Cancer statistics, 2016. CA: Cancer J. Clin. **66**(1), 7–30 (2016)

8. Siegel, R.L., Miller, K.D., Jemal, A.: Cancer statistics, 2019. CA: Cancer J. Clin. **69**(1), 7–34 (2019)
9. Song, G., et al.: SATB1 plays an oncogenic role in esophageal cancer by up-regulation of FN1 and PDGFRB. Oncotarget **8**(11), 17771 (2017)
10. Sudo, T., et al.: Expression of mesenchymal markers vimentin and fibronectin: the clinical significance in esophageal squamous cell carcinoma. Ann. Surg. Oncol. **20**(3), 324–335 (2013)
11. Team, R.C., et al.: R: a language and environment for statistical computing (2013)
12. Yu, D., Lim, J., Wang, X., Liang, F., Xiao, G.: Enhanced construction of gene regulatory networks using hub gene information. BMC Bioinform. **18**(1), 186 (2017)

HRV Signal Feature Estimation and Classification for Healthcare System Based on Machine Learning

Ranjeet Kumar[1]([⊠]) [iD], Agya Ram Verma[2], Manoj Kumar Panda[2], and Papendra Kumar[2]

[1] Madanapalle Institute of Technology and Science, Madanapalle 517325, Andhra Pradesh, India
ranjeet281@gmail.com
[2] G.B. Pant Engineering College, Pauri Garhwal 246194, Uttarakhand, India
agyaram06ei03@gmail.com, pandgbpec@gmail.com,
papendra1@yahoo.co.in

Abstract. A system for heartbeat classification is provided a solution against the mortality due to cardiac arrest. Here, an automated real-time system proposed to identify and classify the abnormalities in the electrocardiogram (ECG) signal or its variability. In healthcare services, multiple monitoring systems are available to monitor cardiac health conditions. Although, efficient monitoring and the alert system needed for prevention from any health loss or mortality. In this work, a public database is utilized named MIT-BIH Arrhythmia (MITA) ECG Database and Normal Sinus Rhythm Database (NSRDB). In the classification process features play a key role to identify the class of the signal that may indicate the particular health condition. Here, a statistical technique is used for the analysis of HRV data of ECG signad and decision tree for classification of parameters extracted from HRV signals. In this paper, a method developed for arrhythmia detection using time and time-frequency domain statistical features. Therefore, five statistical parameters of HRV signals were computed and considered as features of normal and arrhythmia HRV signals, used in training and test data in the decision tree classifers. The use of multiple sizes of training dataset gives accuracy variation as well as the classification rate. As per the comparison of both feature sets and training dataset, Time-frequency feature is efficiently employable for identification of signal class that represents the cardiac health condition, its accuracy in classification reached up to 99.2% with 20:80 data distribution as a training and testing dataset.

Keywords: Arrhythmia · Sinus rhythm · ECG signal · Feature extraction · Classification

1 Introduction

In field of ECG signal processing, classification of ECG signals and its accuracy is most important and challenging task due to complex signal nature and associated health risk. Here, HRV signal itself a characteristic/feature; its exploited for the classification

© Springer Nature Singapore Pte Ltd. 2020
A. Bhattacharjee et al. (Eds.): MIND 2020, CCIS 1241, pp. 437–448, 2020.
https://doi.org/10.1007/978-981-15-6318-8_36

of ECG characteristics [1]. It is very important in study of cardiac heath condition. In the classification process features plays key role to identify the class of the signal that may indicate the particular health condition. These features basically consider as signature or characteristics of large data size samples.

In this study, the HRV signal that is a time-series data of *R-R intervals* in ECG signal is analyzed with its time domain and wavelet-based time-frequency domain statistical parameters to classify the signal classes; these classes directly explain the cardiac health condition. In the continuation of the introductory section, a short review of machine learning techniques in ECG signal processing. In Sect. 2, the time domain and wavelet-based time-frequency domain statistical parameters/features of the HRV signal are discussed, and its classification analysis is briefly explained in Sect. 3. Further, results, discussion, and a conclusion are elaborated in Sects. 4 and 5 respectively.

1.1   Machine Learning in ECG Signal Processing

Nowadays, automated, artificial intelligence or machine with intelligence system helps a lot in many services similar to healthcare; its intelligent machines work as assistive tool or system that help to medical experts in decision or healthcare planning. In the past two decades, several techniques are reported in the literature as systems developed for health monitoring and decease detection based on the vital features form signals and images [2–8]. Here, Machine learning (ML) techniques make the rules based on the labelled data in a system training; it can work as substitute of expert or physician involvement in case of accurate label data [9–13]. In the ECG signal processing, classification problems such as diagnosis of myocardial infarction (MI), arrhythmia detection, super ventriculus condition, etc. causes cardiac arrest are identified and classified and 85% to 99% accuracy achieved with different machine learning methods using several ECG signal features and transform techniques [14]. However, ECG signal or variability feature are not standardized due to several conditions like age, stress, activity, lifestyle. Therefore, an ECG signal having a similar waveform pattern like *P*, *QRS*, *T*, and *U* in humans with normal health conditions; although it's different in individuals with abnormalities [1, 2]. Such that very difficult task for cardiologist or data scientist to recommend a common subjective feature for different health conditions to train the ML classifier.

The primary observation with ECG is heart rate and its variability that reflect the several cardiac conditions similar to waveforms. Although, heart rate variability (HRV) is itself a feature for the health interpretation by the physician. Here, HRV signal further explored for the classification of cardiac health condition using ML techniques.

2   HRV Signal and Feature Estimation

An automated real-time system helps to identify and classify the abnormalities in electrocardiogram (ECG) signal or its variability such as heart rate (HR).

The HRV signal are represent the variation of heart rate, it can be measured in term of R-R intervals. The variance of R-R intervals clearly represents the variability in cardiac rhythm; it may be normal/abnormal or specific cardiac decease. Here, different feature is calculated for two different domains such as time and wavelet-based time-frequency features. In Fig. 1, *R-R intervals* shown for the 1-min duration of arrhythmia and normal sinus rhythm ECG signal [15].

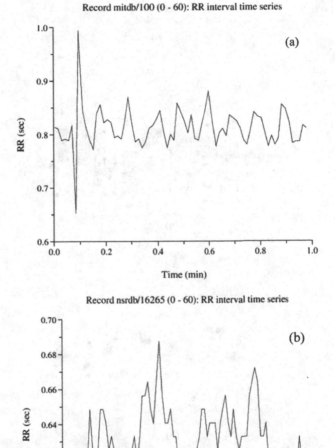

Fig. 1. *R-R interval* variability for the two different ECG signals: (a) MIT-BIH arrhythmia Rec. 100, and (b) NSR Rec. 16265 [15].

As per the pattern of *R-R interval* and HR for any ECG signal doctors or physician can identify the abnormality or normal condition with very short duration of time-series data. It is very difficult to identify or classify the cardiac health condition or pathological class with long duration time-series data or during real-time/ambulatory monitoring. The main feature for the any time-series data are mean, standard deviation, skewness and kurtosis that represent the center tendency, group deviation from mean value, symmetric behavior around the mean, and the tails of a distribution differ from the tails of normal distributed data respectively [15].

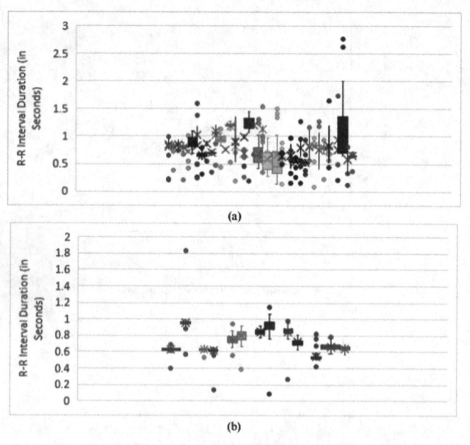

Fig. 2. R-R Interval distribution of different signals for 1-minute duration data from (a) MIT-BIH Arrhythmia (MITA), (b) Normal Sinus Rhythm Database (NSRDB). It represents the values from lower to upper quartile and the central line is representative of the centre data tendency.

In the Fig. 1 and 2, its clearly shown the variability of *R-R interval* for different signals from the both datasets. Although, range of variability is clearly visible for both groups of signals such as arrhythmia signal HRV spread between 0.5–1.2 s and NSR HRV spread between the 0.6–0.9 s. However, these range of variability are overlapped with some signals of both the records, in such cases difficult to separate both case from each other.

Further, statistical measure evaluated for the different analysis like time-domain and time-frequency based on the wavelet coefficients. These statistical measures considered as features for the classifier as shown in Fig. 3 and summarized as follow:

Step-1: HRV Signal Extracted for ECG Signal/database
Step-2: Feature estimation in time/time-frequency domain
Step-3: feature index and data label for the classification
Step-4: Classification.

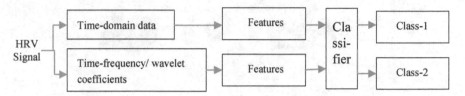

Fig. 3. Feature estimation for HRV signals in time-domain and time-frequency domain, and classification.

As discussed above, five features such as heart rate (HR), and mean, standard deviation (S_d), skewness (S_k) and kurtosis (K_t) estimated for the time domain data and wavelet domain time-frequency data [16]. Here, HRV data is decomposed at two-level with the coiflet (coif-5) wavelet function that produces one-approximation and three-detailed coefficients bands as reported in many literatures of wavelet and filter bank theory [17–22]. Therefore, features computed in both the domain such as time and time-frequency.

2.1 Time Domain Feature Analysis of HRV Signal

The detailed illustration is presented with Fig. 4 that represent the feature variability for both datasets. A comparison of both the dataset is illustrated in Fig. 4 with Box-plots and whisker diagram that represent the data/value distribution with its mean/median value of heart rate (HR), Mean, S_d, S_k, K_t features. The median HR is 78 and 81, Mean is 0.9 and 0.7, S_d is 0.09 and 0.05, S_k is −1.8 and −0.8, K_t is 10 and 5 for MITA and NSRDB database respectively. Here, some features are clearly separable like S_d, S_k, and K_t and some are not clearly separable in both the dataset of R-R interval time series data. It may affect the performance of classification.

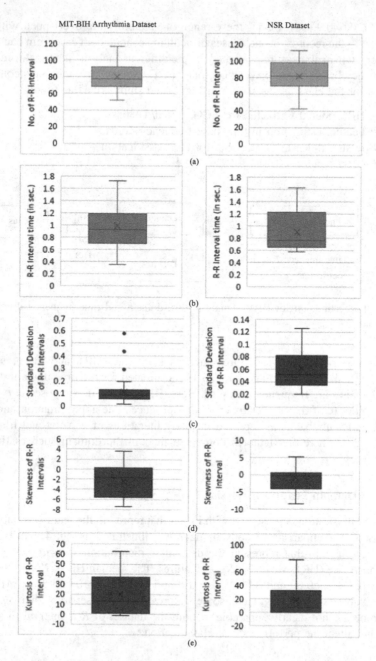

Fig. 4. Distribution of different time features from center tendency of different signals for MIT-BIH Arrhythmia (MITA), Normal Sinus Rhythm Database (NSRDB). The box represents the values from lower to upper quartile and the central line is representative of the median. The whiskers are expanded from lower to upper values. (a) HR, (b) mean, (c) standard deviation, (d) skewness, and (e) kurtosis

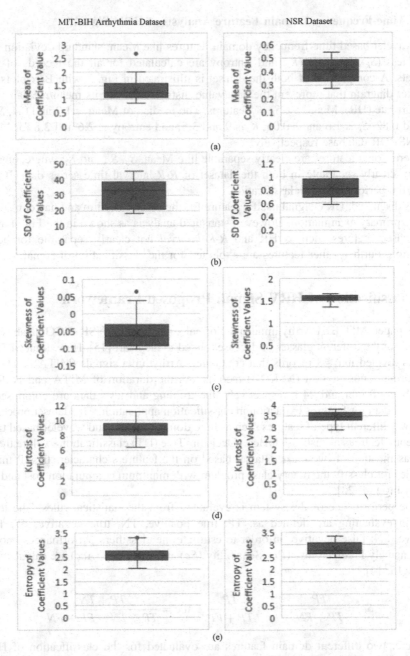

Fig. 5. Distribution of different wavelet-based time-frequency features of different signals for MIT-BIH Arrhythmia (MITA), Normal Sinus Rhythm Database (NSRDB). The box represents the values from lower to upper quartile and the central line is representative of the median. The whiskers are expanded from lower to upper values of wavelet coefficients. (a) mean, (b) standard deviation, (c) skewness, (d) kurtosis, and (e) entropy.

2.2   Time-Frequency Domain Feature Analysis of HRV Signal

The wavelet-based time-frequency domain features like Mean, standard deviation (S_d), Skewness (S_k), Kurtosis (K_t) and Entropy are calculated for all the records of both datasets. A comparison of both the dataset is illustrated in Fig. 5 with Box-plots and whisker diagram that represent the data/value distribution with its mean/median value of heart rate (HR), Mean, S_d, S_k, K_t features. The median of Mean is 1.2 and 0.4, S_d, is 35 and 0.82, S_k is 1.6 and −0.06, K_t is 9 and 3.5, and entropy is 2.6 and 2.8 for MITA and NSRDB database respectively.

Here, some features are clearly separable like Mean, S_d, S_k, and K_t; where, entropy are not clearly separable in both the dataset of R-R interval time series data. It may affect the performance of classification.

As discussed, HRV signal itself a feature for the cardiac rhythm and nay considered for the primary examination. However, statistical analysis as shown in the Fig. 4 and 5 time based features such as HR and R-R *interval* not clearly separable for health condition. Further, other features are exploited for the classification of signal.

3   Classification of HRV Signal: Proposed Framework

In this paper, MIT-BIH Arrhythmia and Normal sinus rhythm (NSR) ECG databased is studied for the different classes of decease related to the heart [15]. Here, total 61 HRV signals divided into 48 records that containing Arrhythmia signals (MITA) beats and 13 Normal sinus rhythm (NSRDB) records. As the duration of MITA and NSRDB records is 30 min and 24 h respectively, the training and tests data are composed as 1 min of data for features extraction in classification application. The dataset processed with two different type of features such as time domain feature and wavelet-based time-frequency features as discussed. Here, Decision-Tree (DT) classification explore the for the classification of two-class data set based on the feature's characteristics; it makes the rules for classify the binary class problem with minimum computation cost and fast processing [14, 23].

The performance of the system is evaluated from the statistical rules. The terms used in evaluating are defined as: TP: true positive, TN: true negative, FP: false positive, FN: false negative. In order to estimate the classifiers performances another index namely Predictability (*Pr*), Sensibility (*Se*) and Accuracy (*Acc*) are calculated as follow [5, 14]:

$$Se = \frac{TP}{TP + FN}, \; Pr = \frac{TP}{TP + FP}, \; Acc = \frac{TP + TN}{TP + TN + FP + FN}$$

Here, two different domain features are evaluated for the classification of HRV signal such as Arrhythmia and Normal Sinus classes. As per the Fig. 4 and 5, it is clearly shown the time domain features are not clearly separated for the different class and wavelet-based time-frequency features are clearly distinguishing to each other. It is clearly illustrated through statistical data in Table 1 and 2. Here, both the feature dataset is divided as training and test dataset as ratio of 10:90, 20:80, and 40:60 respectively, further dataset exploited for classification based on the decision-tree method.

4 Results and Discussion

In Table 1, signals are classified 80%, 79.6%, and 78.4% as a TP for 10%, 20% and 40% dataset as training set from time-domain features of total 61 signals respectively. Similarly, signals are classified 78.2%, 99%, and 99% as a TP for 10%, 20% and 40% dataset as training set from wavelet-based time-frequency domain features of total 61 signals respectively as listed in Table 2.

Table 1. Statistical data result for time domain features

Parameters	Size of training dataset (in %)		
	10	20	40
TP	0.8	0.796	0.784
TN	0	0	0
FP	0.2	0.204	0.216
FN	0	0	0

Table 2. Statistical data result for wavelet-based time-frequency domain features

Parameters	Size of training dataset (in %)		
	10	20	40
TP	0.782	0.99	0.99
TN	0	0	0
FP	0.218	0	0
FN	0	0	0

As discussed, previous section, training and test feature datasets are classified using the decision tree algorithm. From Tables 3 and 4, it clearly shown that wavelet-based feature is more suitable for the classification task. The analysis of features as illustrated in Figs. 4 and 5 is also support the achieved results of classifier, because of time based feature are not distinguish in between two classes.

Table 3. Performance of classifier for time domain features

Performance	Size of training dataset (in %)		
	10	20	40
Sensitivity (%)	100	100	100
Predictivity (%)	80	79.6	78.4
Accuracy (%)	80	79.6	78.4

Table 4. Performance of classifier wavelet-based time-frequency domain features

Performance	Size of training dataset (in %)		
	10	20	40
Sensitivity (%)	100	100	100
Predictivity (%)	78.2	99.2	99.2
Accuracy (%)	78.2	99.2	99.2

The performance of classifier based on two features dataset is summarized in Table 3 and 4 as sensitivity, predictivity and accuracy parameters. The accuracy of wavelet-based time-frequency features is 99.2% for 20% and 40% of training dataset. Where, maximum accuracy 80% for 10% of training dataset time domain feature.

These results achieved based on the separable and non-separable features of time-series and time-frequency data for the binary class problem using the decision tree technique.

5 Conclusion

A system for heart rate variability (HRV) classification is provided assistance to the cardiologist in the planning of healthcare against the mortality due to cardiac arrest. Here, a statistical technique is used for analysis of HRV data and decision tree for classification of parameters extracted from HRV signals. Different separable and non-separable statistical features/parameters of HRV signals were computed and considered as features of normal and arrhythmia HRV signals, used in training and test data in the Decision Tree classifiers. Further, division in feature dataset in multiple size as training dataset give variation in accuracy as well as classification rate. As per comparison of both feature sets and training dataset, Time-frequency feature are efficiently employable for identification of signal class that represent the cardiac health condition. It gives the 99.2% accuracy and classification rate with 20% and 40% size of training dataset due to clear separation of both domain features.

Acknowledgement. This work is supported by research grant under Competitive Research of Technical Education Quality Improvement Programme (TEQIP-III) of Uttarakhand Technical University, Dehradun.

References

1. Acharya, U.R., Joseph, K.P., Kannathal, N., Lim, C., Suri, J.: Heart rate variability: a review. Med. Biol. Eng. Comput. **44**, 1031–1051 (2006)
2. Navin, O., Kumar, G., Kumar, N., Baderia, K., Kumar, R., Kumar, A.: R-peaks detection using shannon energy for HRV analysis. In: Rawat, B.S., Trivedi, A., Manhas, S., Karwal, V. (eds.) Advances in Signal Processing and Communication. LNEE, vol. 526, pp. 401–409. Springer, Singapore (2019). https://doi.org/10.1007/978-981-13-2553-3_39

3. Budoff, M.J., Shinbane, J.S.: Cardiac CT Imaging: Diagnosis of Cardiovascular Disease. Springer, Berlin (2016). https://doi.org/10.1007/978-1-84882-650-2

4. Ceylan, R., Özbay, Y.: Comparison of FCM, PCA and WT techniques for classification ECG arrhythmias using artificial neural network. Expert Syst. Appl. **33**, 286–295 (2007)

5. Fujita, H., et al.: Sudden cardiac death (SCD) prediction based on nonlinear heart rate variability features and SCD index. Appl. Soft Comput. **43**, 510–519 (2016). https://doi.org/10.1016/J.ASOC.2016.02.049

6. Bahadure, N.B., Ray, A.K., Thethi, H.P.: Comparative approach of MRI-based brain tumor segmentation and classification using genetic algorithm. J. Digit. Imaging **31**(4), 477–489 (2018). https://doi.org/10.1007/s10278-018-0050-6

7. Avola, D., Cinque, L., Placidi, G.: Customized first and second order statistics based operators to support advanced texture analysis of MRI images. Comput. Math. Methods Med. **2013**, 213901 (2013). https://doi.org/10.1155/2013/213901

8. Banday, S.A., Mir, A.H.: Statistical textural feature and deformable model based brain tumor segmentation and volume estimation. Multimed. Tools Appl. **76**(3), 3809–3828 (2016). https://doi.org/10.1007/s11042-016-3979-9

9. Salem, A.M., Revett, K., El-Dahshan, E.A.: Machine learning in electrocardiogram diagnosis. In: 2009 International Multiconference on Computer Science and Information Technology, pp. 429–433 (2009)

10. Jambukia, S.H., Dabhi, V.K., Prajapati, H.B.: Classification of ECG signals using machine learning techniques: a survey. In: 2015 International Conference on Advances in Computer Engineering and Applications, pp. 714–721 (2015)

11. Zubair, M., Kim, J., Yoon, C.: An automated ECG beat classification system using convolutional neural networks. In: 2016 6th International Conference on IT Convergence and Security (ICITCS). pp. 1–5 (2016)

12. Hegde, V.N., Deekshit, R., Satyanarayana, P.S.: Comparison of characterizing and data analysis methods for detecting abnormalities in ECG. In: 2011 Second Asian Himalayas International Conference on Internet (AH-ICI), pp. 1–5 (2011)

13. Yu, S.-N., Chen, Y.-H.: Electrocardiogram beat classification based on wavelet transformation and probabilistic neural network. Pattern Recognit. Lett. **28**, 1142–1150 (2007). https://doi.org/10.1016/J.PATREC.2007.01.017

14. Alarsan, F.I., Younes, M.: Analysis and classification of heart diseases using heartbeat features and machine learning algorithms. J. Big Data **6**(1), 1–15 (2019). https://doi.org/10.1186/s40537-019-0244-x

15. Mark, R., Moody, G.: The impact of the MIT-BIH arrhythmia database history, lessons learned, and its influence on current and future databases (2001)

16. Alekseev, M.A.A.: Statistical methods of ECG signal processing in diagnostics of coronary artery disease. Int. J. Cardiovasc. Res. **7** (2018). https://doi.org/10.4172/2324-8602.1000339

17. Kumar, A., Singh, G.K., Kumar, R.: Electrocardiogram signal compression using singular coefficient truncation and wavelet coefficient coding. IET Sci. Meas. Technol. **10**, 266–274 (2016). https://doi.org/10.1049/iet-smt.2015.0150

18. Kumar, R., Kumar, A., Singh, G.K.: Electrocardiogram signal compression based on singular value decomposition (SVD) and adaptive scanning wavelet difference reduction (ASWDR) technique. AEU - Int. J. Electron. Commun. **69**, 1810–1822 (2015). https://doi.org/10.1016/j.aeue.2015.09.011

19. Kumar, R., Kumar, A., Singh, G.K.: Electrocardiogram signal compression using singular coefficient truncation and wavelet coefficient coding. IET Sci. Meas. Technol. **10** (2016). https://doi.org/10.1049/iet-smt.2015.0150

20. Ranjeet, K., Kumar, A., Pandey, R.K.: ECG signal compression using different techniques. In: Unnikrishnan, S., Surve, S., Bhoir, D. (eds.) ICAC3 2011. CCIS, vol. 125, pp. 231–241. Springer, Heidelberg (2011). https://doi.org/10.1007/978-3-642-18440-6_29
21. Ranjeet, K., Farida, J.: Retained signal energy based optimal wavelet selection for denoising of ECG signal using modified thresholding. In: 2011 International Conference on Multimedia, Signal Processing and Communication Technologies, IMPACT 2011 (2011)
22. Kumar, A., Ranjeet: Wavelet based electrocardiogram compression at different quantization levels. In: Das, V.V., Thomas, G., Lumban, G.F. (eds.) Information Technology and Mobile Communication. AIM 2011. Communications in Computer and Information Science, vol. 147. Springer, Heidelberg (2011). https://doi.org/10.1007/978-3-642-20573-6_69
23. Sannino, G., De Pietro, G.: A deep learning approach for ECG-based heartbeat classification for arrhythmia detection. Futur. Gener. Comput. Syst. **86**, 446–455 (2018). https://doi.org/10.1016/J.FUTURE.2018.03.057

Securing Face Recognition System
Using Blockchain Technology

Saumya Shankar, Jitendra Madarkar[✉], and Poonam Sharma

Computer Science and Engineering, VNIT, Nagpur, Maharashtra, India
jitendramadarka475@gmail.com, dr.poonamasharma@gmail.com

Abstract. Facial recognition is a wide area of a computer vision which is mostly used for security purpose. The main motive of the face recognition system is to authentic a person from a given training database. The face-based biometric system and surveillance cameras are deployed everywhere, for that need a strong face recognition system. The recognition system needs a large number of training samples that need to store in any storage center but when the face data is collected and stored, that time hackers can access and manipulate that data. So, a platform is presented that is secure and tamper-proof from these data breaches as well as hacks and is not compromising with data availability, by using blockchain to store face images. The absolute infeasibility of editing a historical record in a blockchain makes it tamper-proof (immutable) ensuring security. The storage of data on multiple computers provides accessibility. For face recognition, VGGFace deep neural network is used for automatic extraction of features and logistic regression for classification. ...

Keywords: Face recognition · Blockchain · VGGFace · Logistic regression

1 Introduction

In today's era, the face-recognition (FR) system is mostly used in biometrics for authentication purposes. It maps a person's facial features mathematically and stores those pixel values so that whenever a live capture comes, it can be compared with stored ones and an individual's identity can be verified. But there may be chance of security threats to the face recognition system, like the FR system can be fooled from outside and illegitimate access can be gained to manipulate the critical data, or the face database can even be hacked to manipulate the legitimate user's list. So a platform is needed that is secure and tamper-proof (immutable) from these data breaches and hacks and is not compromising with data availability. Blockchain can help in building that platform. Blockchain most certainly has the potential to enhance security and ensure accessibility. The absolute infeasibility of editing a historical record in a blockchain makes it tamper-proof ensuring security which is achieved by hashes. Data is stored on multiple computers, so making the ledger public gives accessibility.

A. Bhattacharjee et al. (Eds.): MIND 2020, CCIS 1241, pp. 449–460, 2020.
https://doi.org/10.1007/978-981-15-6318-8_37

Access and manipulation of data can result in damage of whole databases which makes face recognition very challenging, inhibiting the smooth execution of the job. Not only this, misuse of the data, can severely affect law enforcement. So it is very necessary to invest resources in data security also. In the past, various approaches have been discovered to provide security to the face database. For example, to gain confidentiality, database encryption can be used. Improper disclosure of data can be controlled by the various access control mechanism. Loss of data can be made up by replication of the database. Data integrity can be ensured by again backups and immutability. But these mechanisms have to be applied together to combat every angle of data insecurity. Blockchain technology can provide security to face database with a desired characteristics such as tamper-proof, immutable, and decentralized.

The raimaining paper is organized as follows. Section 3, discusses the blockchain technology. The proposed model is provided in Sect. 4. Section 5 discusses result and its analysis. The paper concludes in Sect. 6.

2 Related Work

A lot of work has been done to enhance data security. To detect spoofing, a major threat to gain illegitimate access and manipulation the data, an algorithm [1] base line face recognition including ISV and ICP was put forward, but with the advancement in 3D technology, 3D masks were getting cheaper and thus could not hinder spoofing attacks. Another method was employed for detecting the face spoofing [2] which used a colour texture analysis rather than relying only on luminance information which achieved stable performance on all the database, proving that colour texture seems to be of greater help in unknown conditions compared to its gray-scale counterparts. Thus helped in countering spoofing attacks.

So fooling a face recognition system (and getting the access) can be reduced to a great extent but what if the database is hacked and contents are changed. For this encryption [3] can be used, so that even when it is hacked, the hackers can't make out something from it, thus protecting critical data. But encryption scheme is not 100% secure, when the encryption algorithm is compromised then all the databases is open for tampering.

Fragmenting the data [4] can further improve database security. Based on the level of security that is provided by the encryption algorithm, the databases were distributed across the clouds. It enhanced security with acceptable overhead. But data availability is an issue not handled by this cloud storage. Also it underestimated the communication and processing delays.

The data availability can be conquered by using system like the blockDS [6] that used blockchain to store encrypted data. It allows private keyword search rather than downloading the whole data and then searching, after verifying the client's access by a legitimate access certificate issued by the data owner, without knowing about him (who is he and how many times he came).

Another very different approach to database security is secret image sharing technique [7]. This technique distributes a secret image to n shadow images which is there with n participants. At least k images are needed out of n shadow images to construct the secret image. Less than k images will not produce the secret image.

Lossless recovery [8] can be ensured to an extent if mechanisms like GF(2r) (Power-of-Two Galois Fields) based on the (t, n) threshold scheme is used. But it is susceptible to leakage of colour values [9]. So, using an Information Dispersal Algorithm [10] instead of a secret sharing algorithm in the above technique can further improve share generation and secret reconstruction. Steganography can also be used to further enhance image security and privacy [5].

The blockchain has proved its usefulness in many areas [11] such as E-Voting [12], healthcare industry [13], smart cities [14], IOT [15], corporate Governance [16] etc. In E-Voting recording system [12], each vote can be entered as a transaction in blockchain when the ledger is brought to every node. So that when the number of e-votes and sound votes are compared, the hint of tampering can be deduced, thus providing security.

It can also benefit healthcare industry [13]. In public health management, user-oriented medical research based on personal patient data as well as drug counterfeiting are done smoothly, since direct transactions became possible by blockchains.

This technology can also help in securing smart devices, in smart cities [14]. Data is transmitted ubiquitously even from remote locations, making it prone to security attacks. So, blockchain can help in improved reliability, better fault tolerance capability, faster and efficient operation, and scalability, providing a secure communication platform. Blockchains can also be integrated with IOT [15] to facilitate the sharing of resources. Transparency and better record keeping of blockchains can also help corporate governance [16].

As far as face recognition is concerned, convolutional neural networks (CNN) is a very popular deep learning model in the field of computer vision. CNN has shown better performance than MLP [17] for image classification. It can also be combined with logistic regression classifier (LRC) to improve the classification [18]. Stochastic gradient descent algorithm [19] can also be used along with CNN. This method has achieved a recognition rate of 98.95% and 98.30% respectively, on ORL and AR face database. The network with above technique has shown excellent convergence and strong robustness. But the attenuation coefficient lambda (0.0005 recommended here) which significantly improves the classification accuracy is difficult to find. Also accuracy increases very slowly and smoothly by increasing the number of training iteration.

Along with the above strategy, dimensionality reduction can also be used [20] using LDA and WPCA. It has showed more accuracy compared to PCSNet and DCTNet. Also is was more straightforward. But in many scenarios the dimensionality reduction is always not suitable because it may lead to data loss.

To make training faster non-saturating neurons and GPU [21] can be used. A pre-trained CNN can also be used for extracting features and a classifier can be used for classification. This pre-training model reduces training time. While training CNN and the classifier adjustment of certain parameters is needed.

For example, the final batch size, decay co-efficient and the parameter y are not easy to choose if one use SVM as a classifier [22]. Batch Normalization [23] can also be used for the outputs of the first and final convolutional layers with softmax classifier, which has showed an increased accuracy rate upto 98.8% in 35 epochs.

3   Blockchain Technology

Structure: Blockchains are cryptographically linked chains of blocks of data. Each "block" represents a number of transactional records, and the "chain" component links them all together with a hash function. As records are created, they are confirmed by a distributed network of computers and paired up with the previous entry in the chain, thereby creating a chain of blocks or a blockchain.

Working: One of the nodes requests a transaction. That transaction is broadcasted to all the nodes of the network. Those nodes when receiving the request, validate it using an algorithm, and that transaction is inserted into block and paired with the chain.

Availability: The blockchain is replicated on every computer that is a part of the network, so even though one or two computers fails, data is available with us.

Accessibility: If a node becomes a member of blockchain, then it would be given a complete snapshot of blockchain. Since every computer has a complete copy of the data, accessibility is ensured.

Immutability: The data is bundled into blocks before being added to the blockchain database. Along with data, previous block's hash is also stored in the block. As each block includes the previous block's hash as part of its data, a chain of blocks is formed. So when anyone tries to modify a block, the hash is computed again and that hash no longer matches with the hash stored in next block's previous hash field. So, immutability is guaranteed (immutable ledger).

This built-in layer of protection was not possible with a standard centralized database of information.

3.1   Blockchain and Face Recognition

Face recognition is a way to identify people. It has found its way everywhere. Law enforcement is greatly benefitted from this technology. Various approaches are provided to improve face recognition accuracy. But little incentives are taken to provide security to the face database. The database is prone to unauthorized access and manipulation of data, resulting in severe consequences. The solution lies in one of the disruptive technology blockchains. The face database when stored in blocks becomes very secure because of the immutability property of blockchains. And it also ensures accessibility of data to all members (all those nodes who are interested in uploading face images for the identification or are interested in identifying) of the blockchains as the ledger is public.

4   Proposed Model

The face pixel values (the identifying data) are extracted and placed in blockchain (on every verifying node), that acts like an immutable distributed ledger. If the ID (pixel values of a face) is on the chain, then that ID can't be manipulated. This way access and manipulation of the data can be prevented by hackers.

Now when every node has the complete snapshot of blockchain, The features are extracted using VGGFace which used chain of CNN layers and also used a pre-trained weights of the VGGFace for face recognition. The features are extracted from the user-specified layer (pool5 and pool4 in this case) of the model as shown in Fig. 2. The logistic regression is used for classification.

When a test image is brought, its features are also extracted and are fed to the model for classification to find a match.

4.1   Methdology

Algorithm 1.

1: The pixel value of a train image are stored in a block and are distributed to all the nodes to create blockchain at every node.

2: For recognition, pixel values are retrieved from the blockchain and images are reconstructed.

3: Features are extracted using a deep neural network and the model is trained using logistic regression.

4: Similarly features are extracted from the testing images and prediction is generated for it using the trained logistic regression classifier model.

5: The accuracy is estimated by equation 8.

Creation of Blockchain. Each block of the blockchain has four attributes:

$$Block(index, previousHash, data, hash) \tag{1}$$

Grayscale Conversion and Reshaping of Data: First, the images are converted into grayscale images and reshaped into 1-D vectors. All these vectors are inserted into a matrix, column-wise. So each column of the matrix corresponds to pixel values of one image. Now each of the columns serves as the data part for each block.

Calculation of Hash and Creation of Blocks: The hash of the previous block and the current block is calculated using SHA-256 provided by System.Security.Cryptography namespace. These hashes are inserted into the block along with the data (pixel values).

$$block = Block(index, previousHash, data, hash) \tag{2}$$

Formation of Blockchain: These blocks are paired up and thus a blockchain is formed as shown in Fig. 1.

$$blockchain(end + 1) = block \tag{3}$$

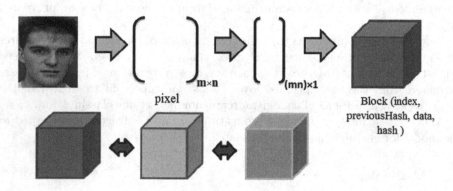

pixel

Block (index, previousHash, data, hash)

Fig. 1. Creation of blockchain

Broadcasting the Data into the Network: The matrix is sent to other nodes as well where they extract the columns and insert them into blocks, in the same manner, to form a blockchain there also. Now the data is available to all the participating nodes, the nodes can go for the training of their model to classify unseen images.

Training. Reconstruction of Images and Extraction of Features: The pixel values are retrieved from the blockchain and images are reconstructed. A pre-trained VGG-Face CNN descriptor as shown in Fig. 2 is used as a feature extractor. It comprises 11 blocks. The first eight such blocks are convolutional. The last three blocks are fully connected. The images are fed into this pre-trained network and features are extracted.

Training the Model: The features and labels extracted from our dataset which were stored in the HDF5 file are loaded. And then logistic regression [25] is used for training [18].

Linear Regression Equation:

$$y = \beta_0 + x_1\beta_1 + x_2\beta_2 + x_3\beta_3 + ... + x_n\beta_n \tag{4}$$

where, y is dependent variable and x1, x2 ... and Xn are explanatory variables.

Sigmoid Function:

$$p = 1/1 + e^{-y} \tag{5}$$

Logistic regression is formed by applying sigmoid function on linear regression:

$$p = 1/1 + e^{-(\beta_0 + x_1\beta_1 + x_2\beta_2 + x_3\beta_3 + ... + x_n\beta_n)} \tag{6}$$

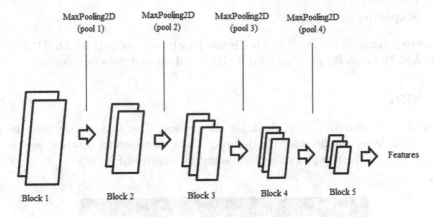

Fig. 2. VGG-Face CNN descriptors

This simple logistic regression classifier has showed highest classification accuracy and lowest classification time as compared to other classifier like NaiveBayes, NaiveBayesSimple, NaiveBayesUpdateable, MultiLayerPerceptron, RBFNetwork, SimpleLogistic, Support Vector Machine, IB1, IBk, LWL i.e. Local Weighted Learning, Classification via regression methods, BFTree, FT, LMT and SimpleCart [18].

Now this logistic regression classifier model can be used for recognition.

Recognition. Generating the Prediction: Features are extracted in the similar manner from the test images and prediction is generated for it using the trained logistic regression classifier model.

$$testData = [X1\,X2\,X3\ldots Xn] \tag{7}$$

The logistic regression classifier as shown in Eq. 6:

Calculation of Accuracy: The accuracy of FR is estimated by comparing the correct output of the classifier and the testing labels as shown in Eq. 8.

$$Accuracy = (Count_correct_classified/size(testLabels)) \tag{8}$$

5   Results and Analysis

Three datasets ORL, LFW, and FEI datasets are used. The dataset is divided into ratios of 90:10, 70:30 and 50:50 for training and testing respectively. The model was first tested without pre-training and then with pre-training. Also, output layers were changed to see the results. Results were better with pre-training and required less time.

5.1 Experiment Setup

In the experimentation, python 3.6.7 is used with processor-AMD A6-6310 APU with AMD radeon R4 graphics and 4 GB RAM on 64-bit os (windows).

5.2 ORL

Total 40 individuals, 1 individual has 10 images, The images are capture in different lighting conditions with different facial expressions. Each image is of size 92×112. The samples of an individual as shown in Fig. 3.

Fig. 3. Samples of ORL database images

Table 1. Results of ORL database with pool5 as the output layer

Train dataset	Test dataset	Accuracy pretrained weights	Accuracy random weights
90%	10%	100	100
70%	30%	100	98.33
50%	50%	100	95

Table 2. Results of ORL database with pool4 as the output layer

Train dataset	Test dataset	Accuracy pretrained weights	Accuracy random weights
90%	10%	100	100
70%	30%	99.16	97.5
50%	50%	97.5	97.5

Analysis. Table 1 shows the results of the ORL database with pool5 as the output layer and logistic regression as the classifier. Since the images are taken in a very constrained environment in which background is homogeneous and the images are in an upright frontal position, the accuracy of the system with pretrained is very good (almost 100%). But when the output layer was changed to pool4, the accuracy is less as shown in Table 2.

5.3   FEI

Total of 2800 images, 14 images for each of individuals. Each image is of size 640 × 480. For experimentation, 650 images are taken of 50 people. The samples of an individual as shown in Fig. 4

Fig. 4. Samples of FEI database images

Table 3. Results of FEI database with pool5 as the output layer

Train dataset	Test dataset	Accuracy pretrained weights	Accuracy random weights
90%	10%	98.46	87.69
70%	30%	96.41	89.23
50%	50%	95.00	87.07

Analysis. The experimental results of the FEI Database is much better with pre-training (more than 95%) weights. The experimental results are shown as in Table 4 and 3 and the results of FEI database is slightly lower than the ORL database because of pose variation. The changes in the output layer (from pool5 to pool4) of CNN architecture also fluctuated the results.

Table 4. Results of FEI database with pool4 as the output layer

Train dataset	Test dataset	Accuracy pretrained weights	Accuracy random weights
90%	10%	100	93.84
70%	30%	97.43	93.3
50%	50%	95.38	91.38

5.4   LFW

The images are collected from the web and there are more than 13,000 images. The images are labeled. For experimentation, 9 images each of 35 people are taken after cropping the face. Each image is of size 115 × 115. The samples of an individual as shown in Fig. 5

Fig. 5. Samples of LFW database images

Table 5. Results of LFW database with pool5 as the output layer

Train dataset	Test dataset	Accuracy pretrained weights	Accuracy random weights
90%	10%	96.96	51.51
70%	30%	98.97	37.75
50%	50%	99.38	30.86

Table 6. Results of LFW database with pool4 as the output layer

Train dataset	Test dataset	Accuracy pretrained weights	Accuracy random weights
90%	10%	93.75	56.25
70%	30%	91.57	55
50%	50%	79.11	37.97

Analysis. The experimental results of the LFW database as shown in Table 5 with pool5 and Table 6 with pool4 as an output layer. The results are far better with Pre-trained weights as compared to without pre-trained weights. With the output layer as pool4, the accuracy is less than pool5 as shown in Table 6.

6   Conclusion

The face-database is very much susceptible to breaches to gain illegitimate access to manipulate the critical data. To provide better security and immutability to our face-database, blockchain is used. The pixel values are inserted into the blocks to keep it tamper-proof and that block is broadcasted to all other nodes to achieve accessibility. This concludes that the manipulation of data can be greatly eradicated by this disruptive technology. For face recognition, VGGFace deep neural network was used for feature extraction and logistic regression as a classifier which resulted in increased accuracy in less time.

Declaration
Acknowledgements. The work was supported by Visvesvaraya PhD scheme, Govt of India.

Funding. This study was funded by the Ministry of Electronics and Information Technology (India) (Grant No.: MLA/MUM/GA/10(37)B).

References

1. Khan, J.K., Upadhyay, D.: Security issues in face recognition. In: 5th International Conference - Confluence The Next Generation Information Technology Summit (Confluence) (2014)
2. Boulkenafet, Z., Komulainen, J., Hadid, A.: Face spoofing detection using colour texture analysis. IEEE Trans. Inf. Forensics Secur. **11**, 1818–1830 (2016)
3. Singh, P., Kaur, K.: Database security using encryption. In: International Conference on Futuristic Trends on Computational Analysis and Knowledge Management (ABLAZE) (2015)
4. Alsirhani, A., Bodorik, P., Sampalli, S.: Improving database security in cloud computing by fragmentation of data. In: International Conference on Computer and Applications (ICCA) (2017)
5. Wu, W.-C., Yang, S.-C.: Enhancing image security and privacy in cloud system using steganography. In: IEEE International Conference on Consumer Electronics - Taiwan (ICCE-TW) (2017)
6. Do, H.G., Ng, W.K.: Blockchain-based system for secure data storage with private keyword search. In: IEEE World Congress on Services (SERVICES) (2017)
7. Tso, H.-K., Lou, D.-C., Wang, K.-P., Liu, C.-L.: A lossless secret image sharing method. In: Eighth International Conference on Intelligent Systems Design and Applications (2008)
8. Chien, M.-C., Hwang, J.-I.G.: Secret image sharing using (t, n) threshold scheme with lossless recovery. In: 5th International Congress on Image and Signal Processing (2012)
9. Mohanty, M., Gehrmann, C., Atrey, P.K.: Avoiding weak parameters in secret image sharing. In: IEEE Visual Communications and Image Processing Conference (2014)
10. Ahmadian, A.M., Amirmazlaghani, M.: Computationally secure secret image sharing. In: Iranian Conference on Electrical Engineering (ICEE) (2017)
11. Zyskind, G., Nathan, O., Pentland, A.S.: Decentralizing privacy: using blockchain to protect personal data. In: IEEE Security and Privacy Workshops (2015)
12. Hanifatunnisa, R., Rahardjo, B.: Blockchain based e-voting recording system design. In: 11th International Conference on Telecommunication Systems Services and Applications (TSSA) (2017)
13. Mettler, M.: Blockchain technology in healthcare: the revolution starts here. In: IEEE 18th International Conference on e-Health Networking, Applications and Services (Healthcom) (2016)
14. Biswas, K., Muthukkumarasamy, V.: Securing smart cities using blockchain technology. In: IEEE 18th International Conference on High Performance Computing and Communications; IEEE 14th International Conference on Smart City; IEEE 2nd International Conference on Data Science and Systems (HPCC/SmartCity/DSS) (2016)
15. Christidis, K., Devetsikiotis, M.: Blockchains and smart contracts for the Internet of Things. IEEE (2016)
16. Yermack, D.: Corporate governance and blockchains. Rev. Financ. **21**, 7–31 (2017). NYU Stern School of Business and National Bureau of Economic Research

17. Lawrence, S., Giles, C.L., Tsoi, A.C., Back, A.D.: Face recognition: a convolutional neural-network approach. IEEE Trans. Neural Networks **8**, 98–113 (1997)
18. Khalajzadeh, H., Mansouri, M., Teshnehlab, M.: Face recognition using convolutional neural network and simple logistic classifier. In: Snášel, V., Krömer, P., Köppen, M., Schaefer, G. (eds.) Soft Computing in Industrial Applications. AISC, vol. 223, pp. 197–207. Springer, Cham (2014). https://doi.org/10.1007/978-3-319-00930-8_18
19. Yan, K., Huang, S., Song, Y., Liu, W., Fan, N.: Face recognition based on convolution neural network. In: 36th Chinese Control Conference (CCC) (2017)
20. Wan, L., Liu, N., Huo, H., Fang, T.: Face recognition with convolutional neural networks and subspace learning. In: 2nd International Conference on Image, Vision and Computing (ICIVC) (2017)
21. Krizhevsky, A., Sutskever, I., Hinton, G.E.: ImageNet classification with deep convolutional neural networks. Commun. ACM **60**, 84–90 (2017)
22. Guo, S., Chen, S., Li, Y.: Face recognition based on convolutional neural network and support vector machine. In: IEEE International Conference on Information and Automation (ICIA) (2016)
23. Coşkun, M., Uçar, A., Yildirim, Ö., Demir, Y.: Face recognition based on convolutional neural network. In: International Conference on Modern Electrical and Energy Systems (MEES) (2017)

A Hybrid Symmetric Key Cryptography Method to Provide Secure Data Transmission

Pankaj Kumar Keserwani(✉) and Mahesh Chandra Govil

Department of Computer Science and Engineering, National Institute of Technology
Sikkim, Burfang Block, South Sikkim, Ravangla 737139, India
pankaj.keserwani@gmail.com, govilmc@gmail.com

Abstract. Confidentiality of data is required when it travels over the insecure network such as e-mail transfer using Pretty Good Privacy (PGP), image transfer, etc. The proposed symmetric cryptographic algorithm is suitable for such data transfer. A number of other algorithms can be formulated by combining the existing algorithms to incorporate the algorithms in the relevant applications. The modified algorithm for session key generation is a combination of Affine cipher and hill cipher. A systematic study of the symmetric-key algorithm consisting of multiple keys with regular dependency has been carried out in order to show the efficacy. Security analysis of the proposed algorithm reveals the weakness of the algorithm.

Keywords: Pretty Good Privacy (PGP) · Encryption · Decryption · Symmetric · Algorithm · Sender · Receiver

1 Introduction

The enhancement in the technology such as Internet and in the technological devices such as computers, laptops, smartphones, etc. have converted the life in such a way that the user can get easy and friendly environment to receive the digital data in the form of texts, images, audio, videos files, emails using PGP, etc. Diagram(s) in the digital image file provides more clear and precious information than text and audio files. Sometimes, it is required to send or exchange private and confidential information through the nonsecure channel. In the nonsecure channel anyone can get the data or message form the path. The secure channel demands high costs. The primary requirement of privacy is that only authorized people should be allowed to access private information. To fulfill this basic requirement many approaches are there, such as cryptography, stenography, virtual private networks (VPNs), etc. The orientation of our work is towards the cryptography. Cryptography is a combination of encryption and decryption processes. In the encryption data or message is changed into the non-understandable form i.e. a form in which the original sense of message is being

© Springer Nature Singapore Pte Ltd. 2020
A. Bhattacharjee et al. (Eds.): MIND 2020, CCIS 1241, pp. 461–474, 2020.
https://doi.org/10.1007/978-981-15-6318-8_38

lost, known as ciphertext. The ciphertext is obtained with the help of the key. The ciphertext is then sent over the nonsecure channel to the receiver. When the receiver receives the ciphertext the decryption process comes into the place to extract the original message. In decryption, the ciphertext is changed into it original form with the help of the relevant key known as plaintext or original message at the receiver end. Cryptography generally is of two types namely asymmetric key cryptography and symmetric key cryptography. In asymmetric key cryptography sender and receiver both have different key pairs known as the public key and private key. In the encryption process, the sender encrypts the message on the public key of the receiver and in the decryption process the receiver uses his private key to decrypt the message which has been encrypted to his public key. In symmetric-key cryptography, the same session key is used for encryption and decryption process both. The encryption and decryption algorithms used in symmetric key cryptography are inverses of each other. The symmetric key cryptography method is highly preferable for encrypting large messages due to its quick and speeding processing nature (Fig. 1).

Symmetric Encryption

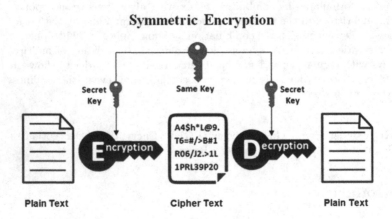

Fig. 1. Symmetric key cryptography [8]

Application layer data transfer such as mail transfer using PGP, image transfer demands the simple security approach. To fulfill the requirement Jha et al. [10] have proposed the symmetric key cryptography algorithm using matrix property with the help of a hill cipher technique only for data security. Here, the proposed symmetric key cryptography system uses the property of Affine Cipher and Hill Cipher both for better security on the data. Affine cipher is a combination of additive and multiplicative ciphers, which require two keys one for additive cipher and other for multiplicative cipher in encryption and decryption of the message. Hill cipher uses the property of matrices such as multiplication of matrices, the inverse of a matrix, etc. which require one key in encryption and decryption process. Hence, the use of three keys makes the algorithm strong enough to provide security from an intruder for the hacking of the message.

As the contributions through the proposed scheme are discussed to overcome the limitations of Jha et al. [10] work, which are the following:

1. **Key domain:** In a previous algorithm [10] only one key is used and the key domain is very small. Jha et al.'s algorithm is only dependent on the property of the inverse of metrics but according to Kirchhoff's principle, it can be assumed that the attacker has access to the encryption/decryption algorithm. The robustness of the ciphertext from any kind of attack depends on the secrecy of the used key for encryption and decryption, so a large key domain is considered that will reduce the possibility of guess by the intruder. Instead of one key, three keys have been used in our proposed protocol for encryption and decryption. Out of three keys, first is a digit representing a symbol and this key needs to be a member in Z_{27}^*, so the key domain range is 18 only because there is no multiplicative inverse for all with respect to modulo 27. The second key is also a single digit belongs to Z_{27} and it has the key domain of 27. The third key is a metrics key of size $m * m$ and the key domain for the third key is $(m * m)^{27}$. So, the total key domain for our proposed protocol is $18 * 26 * (m * m)^{27}$, making it one of the strongest cipher for session key generation.

2. **Number of steps:** In the previous algorithm [10] there are only two steps for encryption, one is for adding the message with a key and other is for simply finding the inverse of the result from the first step. In the proposed protocol, there is a total of three steps and every step is working with the corresponding key. Because every step is using a corresponding key, the proposed protocol has become a very complicated protocol that is very difficult for the intruder to find our plaintext as it has been using three sets of keys (two for Affine cipher and one as $m * m$ matrix for Hill cipher) consequently.

3. In the proposed system, matrix multiplication is used. Matrices multiplication provides high diffusion [17].

4. The proposed scheme is traced with the help of a suitable example.

5. Confusion and diffusion have also been calculated. Confusion is the change in the number of characters or bits in the ciphertext on changing one character or bit in the key. Diffusion is the change in the number of characters or bits in the ciphertext on changing one character or bit in the plaintext.

The rest of the paper is arranged as follows. The related survey has been discussed in Sect. 2. Section 3 discusses the proposed encryption and decryption algorithm with the implementation. Section 4 provides a detail discussion with the help of one suitable example for the encryption and decryption process of the proposed scheme. Section 5 presents the diffusion and confusion property of the proposed scheme. Security analysis of the proposed scheme has been discussed in Sect. 6 and the paper ends with a conclusion in Sect. 7.

2   Literature Survey

The theme to bring variation in symmetric key encryption is not new. Symmetric key encryption performs very important role for secure communication in an open network [1,2,14,16]. Computation between symmetric key Cryptography and other approaches have taken the center stage in the paper published by Chen et al. [5]. The asymmetric key block cipher algorithm based on Principal Component Analysis (PCA) of order (n * m) has been presented by S. Roy [13]. Comparison of algorithms related to symmetric and asymmetric key cryptography has been presented by Chandra et al. in [4]. A comprehensive comparative analysis of many symmetric key cryptography algorithms with different attributes such as architecture, scalability, flexibility, reliability, security, and limitation required for secure communication has been presented in [6]. A comprehensive study between the symmetric key and asymmetric key encryption algorithms has been made which may enhance the data security in the cloud computing system in [18]. Kumar et al. [11] has presented the diffusion model through cryptography to enhance data security. Sundaram et al. [15], implemented security for IoT through the combination of encryption as well as hashing technique. Due to small size i.e. 64-bits per block, the implemented solution fails for large amounts of data transmission. Hence, suffer from slow performance.

Chandra et al. [3], proposed a double encryption algorithm based on content through symmetric key cryptography. In the encryption process, the algorithm uses middle operations such as binary addition, folding and shifting. Purnama et al. [12], and Goval et al. [7], worked on the modification for the Caesar cipher in different ways to get the ciphertext. Imran et al. [9], combines three different methods to develop an encryption algorithm but the encrypted data was readable. The survey shows that different symmetric key algorithms were presented for the data security purpose over the network. In the present work, the proposed scheme is the combination of affine cipher and hill cipher methods to simply encrypt the message to provide difficulty to understand the ciphertext. Due to the non-understanding nature of the ciphertext, it is not easy to get the original message from the ciphertext without applying the authorize and the right process.

3   Proposed Symmetric Key Cryptography System

The proposed symmetric key cryptography system is consists of two parts: encryption and its corresponding decryption.

3.1   Encryption

The encryption process is shown by the flowchart (Fig. 2):

The steps of the encryption process are mentioned below as:

1. Select a key K_1 from Z_{27}^*. Key should have the multiplicative inverse modulo 27. The total number of symbols used is 27 where 0 indicates padding symbol, 1 indicates A, Z is presented by numeric value 26 and so on.
2. Select another key K_2 from Z_{27}.

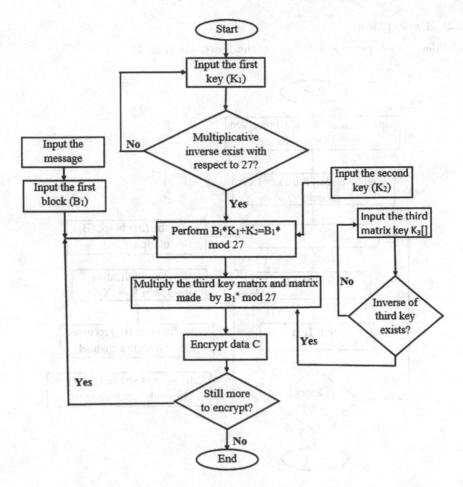

Fig. 2. Flowchart of the encryption process of the proposed algorithm

3. Select third key K_3 of $m * m$ matrix type. Determine the determinant of the matrix $|A|$. If $|A| \neq 0$ then $n * m$ matrix is selected. Otherwise, a new $n * m$ matrix is considered for testing. Only the matrics with non zero determinants will be considered. Again, as determinant exists only for a square matrix, only $m * m$ matrix will be considered.
4. Convert the plaintext into digits as $A = 1$, $B = 2$ and so on up to $Z = 26$.
5. Compute $C^* = (P * K_1) + K_2$. Where C^* is the intermediate encrypted message and P is the plaintext.
6. Divide the C^* into n blocks matrix. Put padding if necessary. Padding is usually indicated by zero (0) in the symbol set.
7. Multiply K_3 with every block. The result is the final encrypted message as $C = (C^* * K_3)$
8. Repeat till the last block.

3.2   Decryption

The decryption process is shown by the flowchart (Fig. 3):

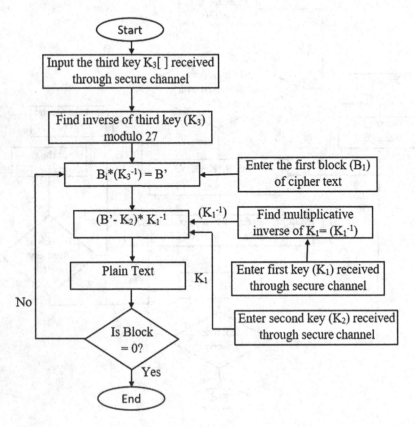

Fig. 3. Flowchart of the decryption process of the proposed algorithm

The steps of the decryption process is mentioned as follows:

1. Find the inverse of the key matrix K_3 modulo 27 received through a secure channel K_3^{*-1} is the calculated inverse to be multiplied to the ciphertext as some of the steps towards decryption.
2. Find the multiplicative inverse of K_1 modulo 27 received through a secure channel K_1^{*-1} is the inverse with which intermediate ciphertext to be multiplied.
3. Separate the ciphertext blocks and multiply every block with K_3^{*-1}. This is the intermediate plaintext P^*.
4. Compute $P^* = (C * K_3^{*-1})$
5. Repeat till the last block of ciphertext.
6. Subtract the P^* corresponding to K_2 character and then multiply it by the K_1^{*-1}.
7. $P = (P^* - K_2) * K_1^{*-1}$.

4   Traced Example Based on the Proposed Algorithm

Consider the three secret keys for encryption: $K_1 = 7K_2 = 2$ and $K_3 = \begin{bmatrix} 3 & 7 \\ 5 & 12 \end{bmatrix}$

The message to be encrypted is "ENCRYPT". Firstly, the characteristics are convert it into digits $E = 5, N = 14, C = 3, R = 18, Y = 25, P = 16$ and $T = 20$. There is a total of 7 digits that cannot be put into matrix form hence we have to take an extra digit 0 which is known as the padding character.

Encryption: In first step we have multiply every digit by first K_1 and then add with second key K_2.

```
E = (05 * 7) + 2 = 37 mod 27 = 10
N = (14 * 7) + 2 = 100 mod 27 = 19
C = (03 * 7) + 2 = 23 mod 27 = 23
R = (18 * 7) + 2 = 128 mod 27 = 20
Y = (25 * 7) + 2 = 177 mod 27 = 15
P = (16 * 7) + 2 = 114 mod 27 = 6
T = (20 * 7) + 2 = 142 mod 27 = 7
```

In second step we have to put these results into a matrix which can be multiply easily by the third key K_3.

$$\begin{bmatrix} 10 & 19 \\ 23 & 20 \\ 15 & 6 \\ 7 & 0 \end{bmatrix} * \begin{bmatrix} 3 & 7 \\ 5 & 12 \end{bmatrix} = \begin{bmatrix} 125 & 298 \\ 169 & 401 \\ 75 & 177 \\ 21 & 49 \end{bmatrix} mod\,27 = \begin{bmatrix} 17 & 1 \\ 7 & 23 \\ 21 & 15 \\ 21 & 22 \end{bmatrix}$$

The matrix can be presented as ciphertext as being converted to alphabetic character set.

```
17 = Q
01 = A
07 = G
23 = W
21 = U
15 = O
21 = U
22 = V
```

"QAGWUOUV" is the corresponding ciphertext of the plain text "ENCRYPT" with one padding digit.

Decryption: We have evaluated the inverse of the K_3 as

$$K_3^{-1} = \begin{bmatrix} 12 & -7 \\ -5 & 3 \end{bmatrix}$$

In the decryption, first multiply the encrypted message and then multiplicative inverse of third key K_3^{-1}:

$$\begin{bmatrix} 17 & 1 \\ 7 & 23 \\ 21 & 15 \\ 21 & 22 \end{bmatrix} * \begin{bmatrix} 12 & -7 \\ -5 & 3 \end{bmatrix} = \begin{bmatrix} 199 & -116 \\ -31 & 20 \\ 177 & -102 \\ 142 & -81 \end{bmatrix} = \begin{bmatrix} 10 & 19 \\ 23 & 20 \\ 15 & 6 \\ 7 & 0 \end{bmatrix}$$

Now in the second stage, we have to first subtract all these results one by one except 00 by the third key K_3^{-1} and the multiply it with the inverse of second key K_2.

```
(10-2) * 4 = 32 mod 27 = 05 = E
(19-2) * 4 = 68 mod 27 = 14 = N
(23-2) * 4 = 84 mod 27 = 03 = C
(20-2) * 4 = 72 mod 27 = 18 = R
(15-2) * 4 = 52 mod 27 = 25 = Y
(6-2)  * 4 = 16 mod 27 = 16 = P
(7-2)  * 4 = 20 mod 27 = 20 = T
```

"ENCRYPT" is the plain text obtained after decryption.

Kirchhoff's Principle has been followed in the proposed algorithm. Ciphers are no more hidden algorithms and ciphers are regularly published in journals and magazines. It is understood that a hacker is familiar with all the techniques of encryption and decryption whether it is substitution cipher or transposition. Based on Kirchhoff's principle it is assumed that the adversary Eve keeps herself updated with all the encryption and decryption algorithms. Hence, the total resistance of the cipher to attack the cipher must be based on the secrecy of the key. Therefore, the key should have the property of a very large domain on key space so that a brute force attacks could not occur. The other property of the key is that the key should be of a proper length so that repetition in the ciphertext is minimum. Also, confusion should be more than average in order to devoid cryptanalysis. The properties are maintained in the proposed algorithm and a simplified version of the proposed algorithm has been enacted to verify the result regarding confusion and diffusion.

The secrecy depends on the key size. Anyone of the keys in the proposed algorithm is more than 128 bits and the key is being exchanged using a secure protocol such as Diffie-Hellman-Key-Exchange etc. then the security is considered full-proof. It is also possible to choose the matrix in such a way so that matrix is itself is more than 128 bits. All the key properties are ensured in the proposed algorithm.

The implementation of the algorithm in the machine using python code with the above example has been shown in video link: https://youtu.be/D7tZ-dYg7WM (Fig. 4 and Fig. 5).

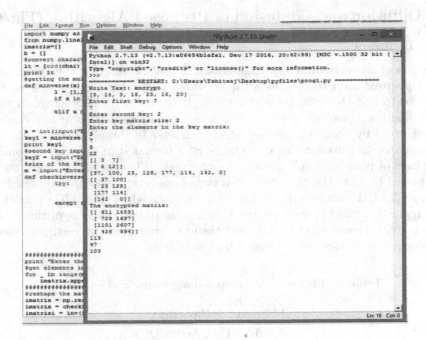

Fig. 4. Screen-shot to show the output of encryption process

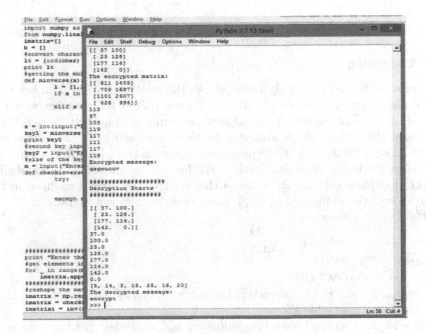

Fig. 5. Screen-shot to show the output of decryption process

5   Diffusion and Confusion of Proposed Algorithm (Fig. 6)

5.1   Diffusion

Diffusion of an encryption algorithm shows the relationship between plain text and ciphertext such that if the attacker wants to get the plain text from the ciphertext(s), it the diffusion which hides the relationship between plain text and ciphertext. In other words, diffusion is the number of bits or one characters changed by changing the one bit or character in the plain text (Table 1). For example, as shown in the above table, SI-1 is related to the original considered case of plain text and generated ciphertext. When in SI-2 a character R is replaced by M in the plain text then two characters GW of the ciphertext is changed by UH. Similarly in SI-3 when C is replaced by T in plain text then WU replaced by MS in the ciphertext. Hence, in the proposed algorithm when a character is changed in the plain text then two characters are getting changed in the ciphertext which shows that diffusion is 2.

Table 1. Diffusion of the proposed algorithm from examples

S.I	Plaintext	Ciphertext
1	ENCRYPT	QAGWUOUV
2	ENCMYPT	QAUHUOUV
3	ENTRYPT	QAMSUOUV

5.2   Confusion

Confusion of an encryption algorithm shows the relationship between key used in the algorithm and generated ciphertext such that if the attacker wants to get the key used in the encryption algorithm from the ciphertext(s) then it the confusion which hides the relationship between key used in the algorithm and generated ciphertext. Here in the proposed algorithm three keys K_1, K_2 and K_3 have been used. K_1 for multiplication, K_2 for addition and K_3 as matrix for matrix multiplication mod 26. When a character of the digit is changed in the different keys the changes in the ciphertext have been shown in Table 2:

The Original Values are:

$$K_1 = 7 \quad K_2 = 2 \ and \quad K_3 = \begin{bmatrix} 3 & 7 \\ 5 & 12 \end{bmatrix}$$

Plaintext = ENCRYPT
Ciphertext = QAGWUOUV

_ represents the Bogus character. Bogus = 0. Average Confusion = 6.78 as calculated from the table above.

Here in the proposed algorithm diffusion and confusion has been made by using multiplication, addition and modulus operators with a combination of K_1, K_2 and K_3. Confusion of the proposed algorithm is better than diffusion.

Table 2. Confusion of the proposed algorithm from examples.

S.I	Changed key value	Changed ciphertext	Confusion
1	$K_1 = 3$	AZPTRQUV	6
2	$K_1 = 5$	LYHHJIL	8
3	$K_1 = 11$	FCYZTYRO	8
4	$K_1 = 17$	CFYQEM_R	8
5	$K_2 = 3$	YTOOBGXB	8
6	$K_2 = 5$	NDDZRRCP	8
7	$K_2 = 9$	SZIUWMOQ	8
8	$K_2 = 11$	HJYELXUD	8
9	$(K3)_{11} = 11$	PABWFOWV	6
10	$(K_3)_{11} = 13$	IAUWIOJV	7
11	$(K_3)_{01} = 11$	QIGCUIUV	5
12	$(K_3)_{01} = 13$	QTGPUUUV	5
13	$(K_3)_{00} = 5$	QHGDULUI	6
14	$(K_3)_{10} = 11$	WASWCOUV	4

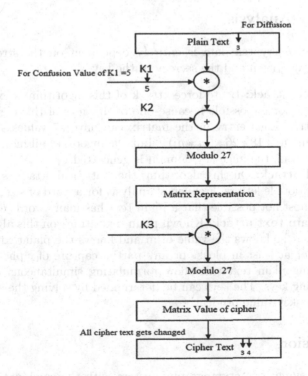

Fig. 6. Diffusion and Confusion for the ciphertext

5.3   Disadvantages of the Proposed Algorithm

– There are three keys to the proposed protocol. The first key is used for multiplication in the encryption side and in the decryption side multiplicative inverse is required but it is not necessary that every key has the multiplicative inverse with respect to modulo 27. The key domain gets reduced in such conditions.
– The third key is a matrix. The decryption side inverse of the key matrix is required to decrypt the message. It is not necessary that every key has a multiplicative inverse. In fact, if by imprudent selection, $|A| = 0$, then inverse becomes nonexistent.
– Known plain text attack on this algorithm may be possible. If he knows the value of m and knows the plain text and ciphertext pairs for at least m blocks or any partial capture of ciphertext and its corresponding plain text will allow formulating simultaneous linear equations in corresponding keys. The keys can be determined by solving the equation and selecting the key values prudently. It gives rise to a set of m linear equations in a number of unknown m. The set of the simultaneous linear equation is solvable if the number of unknowns $\leq$ the number of simultaneous equations. The proposed algorithm comes under the scanner of solvability.

6   Security Analysis

The security of encrypted data is entirely dependent on the strength of the cryptographic algorithm and the secrecy of the key.

– **Brute force attack:** Brute force attack of this algorithm is extremely difficult though not impossible because one of the keys of this algorithm is an m * m matrix. Each entry in the matrix can have 27 values so the size of this key domain is $18 * 26 * (m * m)^{27}$ but the inverse of all matrix key is not possible but still, the huge key domain is generated.
– **Statistical attack:** On this algorithm, the statistical attack is not possible on single or double letters. Frequency analysis for a word of size m may work but it is almost not possible that a plain text has many words of size m.
– **Known plain text attack:** Known plain text attack on this algorithm may be possible. If he knows the value of m and knows the plaintext and ciphertext pairs for at least m blocks or any partial capture of ciphertext and its corresponding plain text will allow formulating simultaneous equations in corresponding keys. The keys can be determined by solving the equation and selecting the key-value prudently.

7   Conclusion

The proposed symmetric cryptography system with the combination of Affine cipher and Hill cipher technique is able to provide better security. The matrix property of the hill cipher technique provides the required robustness for the system. It is simple to understand and it is of average complexity. It can be easily implemented in various platforms which leads to faster conversion of text. The generation of the shared symmetric key will serve the purpose of the session key in an e-mail application having PGP in place. It can be used for encryption and decryption purposes in different fields such as chat systems, file transfer systems, etc. that uses sessions. The key will serve the purpose of a shared symmetric session key.

Acknowledgment. The authors express deep sense of gratitude to Computing Centre of National Institute of Technology, Sikkim India, where the work has been carried out.

References

1. Agrawal, M., Mishra, P.: A comparative survey on symmetric key encryption techniques. Int. J. Comput. Sci. Eng. **4**(5), 877 (2012)
2. Beaulieu, R., Treatman-Clark, S., Shors, D., Weeks, B., Smith, J., Wingers, L.: The Simon and Speck lightweight block ciphers. In: 2015 52nd ACM/EDAC/IEEE Design Automation Conference (DAC), pp. 1–6. IEEE (2015)
3. Chandra, S., Mandal, B., Alam, S.S., Bhattacharyya, S.: Content based double encryption algorithm using symmetric key cryptography. Procedia Comput. Sci. **57**, 1228–1234 (2015)
4. Chandra, S., Paira, S., Alam, S.S., Sanyal, G.: A comparative survey of symmetric and asymmetric key cryptography. In: 2014 International Conference on Electronics, Communication and Computational Engineering (ICECCE), pp. 83–93. IEEE (2014)
5. Chen, L., Zhou, S.: The comparisons between public key and symmetric key cryptography in protecting storage systems. In: 2010 International Conference on Computer Application and System Modeling (ICCASM), vol. 4, pp. V4–494. IEEE (2010)
6. Ebrahim, M., Khan, S., Khalid, U.B.: Symmetric algorithm survey: a comparative analysis. arXiv preprint arXiv:1405.0398 (2014)
7. Goyal, K., Kinger, S.: Modified caesar cipher for better security enhancement. Int. J. Comput. Appl. **73**(3), 0975–8887 (2013)
8. Guide, I.: Name the difference between symmetric and asymmetric cryptography (2016). https://itinterviewguide.com/difference-between-symmetric-and-asymmetric/. Accessed 29 Aug 2018
9. Imran, E.I., Abdulameerabdulkareem, F.: Enhancement Caesar cipher for better security. IOSR J. Comput. Eng. (IOSR-JCE) **16**(3), 01–05 (2014)
10. Jha, D.P., Kohli, R., Gupta, A.: Proposed encryption algorithm for data security using matrix properties. In: 2016 International Conference on Innovation and Challenges in Cyber Security (ICICCS-INBUSH), pp. 86–90. IEEE (2016)
11. Kumar, S., et al.: Cryptographic construction using coupled map lattice as a diffusion model to enhanced security. J. Inf. Secur. Appl. **46**, 70–83 (2019)
12. Purnama, B., Rohayani, A.H.: A new modified caesar cipher cryptography method with legibleciphertext from a message to be encrypted. Procedia Comput. Sci. **59**, 195–204 (2015)

13. Roy, S., Nandi, S., Dansana, J., Pattnaik, P.K.: Application of cellular automata in symmetric key cryptography. In: 2014 International Conference on Communications and Signal Processing (ICCSP), pp. 572–576. IEEE (2014)
14. Saranya, K., Mohanapriya, R., Udhayan, J.: A review on symmetric key encryption techniques in cryptography. Int. J. Sci. Eng. Technol. Res. (IJSETR) **3**(3), 539–544 (2014)
15. Sundaram, B.V., Ramnath, M., Prasanth, M., Sundaram, V.: Encryption and hash based security in internet of things. In: 2015 3rd International Conference on Signal Processing, Communication and Networking (ICSCN), pp. 1–6. IEEE (2015)
16. Wang, C., Wang, Q., Ren, K., Cao, N., Lou, W.: Toward secure and dependable storage services in cloud computing. IEEE Trans. Serv. Comput. **5**(2), 220–232 (2012)
17. Williams, S.: Cryptography and Network Security: Principles and Practices, p. 17. Pearson Education, Upper Saddle River (2006)
18. Yassein, M.B., Aljawarneh, S., Qawasmeh, E., Mardini, W., Khamayseh, Y.: Comprehensive study of symmetric key and asymmetric key encryption algorithms. In: 2017 International Conference on Engineering and Technology (ICET), pp. 1–7. IEEE (2017)

Trust-Based Detection of Malicious Nodes for Wireless Mesh Networks

Amit Kumar Roy[1]($\boxtimes$) (iD), Ajoy Kumar Khan[2](iD), and Hridoy Jyoti Mahanta[3](iD)

[1] NIT Mizoram, Aizawl, Mizoram, India
amitkroy12@gmail.com
[2] Mizoram University, Aizawl, Mizoram, India
ajoyiitg@gmail.com
[3] Assam Don Bosco University, Guwahati, Assam, India
hridoy69@gmail.com

Abstract. Wireless Mesh Networks (WMNs) becomes the most widely growing network topology in today's era due to its distributed nature and multi-hopping communication environment. WMNs do not rely on any centralized administration. Therefore, security is the major issue in WMNs. Due to its distributed nature and multi-hop environment; it suffers from certain types of internal attacks which increases the vulnerability of routing protocols. These internal attacks degrade the overall performance of WMNs by dropping the packets by introducing the malicious node towards the destination. Therefore, to ensure secure routing, it is essential to compute the trustworthiness of each node and to detect the malicious nodes within the WMNs. Therefore, we have proposed a trust-based detection algorithm that ensures the detection of malicious nodes at the backbone of WMNs where we have considered the nodes as mesh routers (MRs). Through simulation results, the performance of our proposed protocol achieves a higher detection rate of a malicious node in WMNs.

Keywords: Wireless Mesh Networks · Malicious nodes · Detection mechanism

1 Introduction

Wireless Mesh Networks has emerged as a key technology for next-generation wireless networks due to its self-organizing, self-configuring and minimal upfront investment in deployment. WMNs have divided into three tiers, the top-tier consists of gateway routers, the middle-tier is also known as the backbone of WMNs consists of mesh routers (MRs), and the bottom-tier consists of mesh clients (MCs). Gateway routers are connected to the Internet through wired networks, the mesh routers (MRs) also act as access points (APs) in the backbone are connected to the gateway routers using multi-hop communication [1]. Therefore, when a mesh client wants to get access the Internet, it sends its request to MRs and then the MRs forwards the request towards the gateway router in a

© Springer Nature Singapore Pte Ltd. 2020
A. Bhattacharjee et al. (Eds.): MIND 2020, CCIS 1241, pp. 475–485, 2020.
https://doi.org/10.1007/978-981-15-6318-8_39

multi-hop fashion. Therefore, cooperation and coordination among mesh routers (MRs) is an important factor for WMNs to influence its performance. The major functionality of mesh routers in a backbone is to offer secure network services to its clients [2,3]. Therefore, a secure routing protocol for forwarding data packets towards the gateway is required for WMNs. At the backbone of WMNs, some of the mesh routers (MRs) deny to forward the data packets for other mesh routers (MRs) and behaves as a malicious node by violating the rules of routing protocols. This misbehavior act allows the malicious node to preserve their bandwidth and power by not utilizing them without forwarding the data packets for other nodes. Therefore, the selfish behavior of MRs degrades the overall performance of WMNs by dropping packets in a massive amount. Therefore, security is one of the major issues in WMNs. As the traffic of the end-user is forwarded in multi-hop fashion among MRs at the backbone, therefore, confidentiality and preservation of the user traffic is a major requirement. The nature of traffic transmission in a broadcast fashion through multi-hop communications among MRs leads to various security issues in WMNs. One of the important parts of WMNs is their routing services among MRs that are vulnerable to a number of threats from adversaries both internal and external to the network. A detailed survey of such routing attacks had made in [4]. Therefore, to enforce secure cooperation and coordination among nodes, various collaboration schemes had proposed in the literature [5] to detect the selfish nodes in the networks.

Several mechanisms had proposed that are based on frameworks to trust and believe the nodes in the networks and attempt to identify misbehaving nodes by suitable decision-making systems and then isolate or punish them [6]. In this paper, we had presented a detection algorithm that detects the malicious nodes in WMNs. Our proposed algorithm is mainly designed for the detection of malicious nodes that violets the rule of AODV routing protocols at the backbone of WMNs.

2   Literature Survey

To forward the packets securely between source to destination through intermediate nodes, certain secure routing protocols had designed in the past. As routing is one of the major functionalities of a network, an attacker could easily target the routing protocol to compromise the security of a network. Even though a lot of works had done in the past for resolving security issues for routing protocol, still the existing work suffers from vulnerabilities and other issues as discussed in this section.

In 2008, Sen proposed an efficient algorithm for the detection of selfish packet dropping nodes in Wireless Mesh Networks [7]. The algorithm is an extension work to [8] based on local observation of each node in the network. The algorithm involves the clustering technique which observed the nodes behavior locally within fixed a range or domain. The algorithm involves two nodes, monitor node and monitored node where the monitor node observes the behavior of the monitored node locally by using a finite state machine. However, the algorithm suffers from computational overhead due to the clustering of WMNs. Moreover, the detection is based on local observation which is not efficient for large networks as WMNs. In 2002, Papadimitratos and Haas proposed a secure routing protocol for mobile ad hoc networks that secure the route discovery process against non-colluding Byzantine adversaries [9]. The protocol assures secure routing between the source node and the destination node. Without relying on any intermediate nodes the protocol provides end-to-end security association through the addition of extra fields in the routing protocol header that contains the query sequence number QSEC, query identifier number QID, and a 96 bit MAC field. The destination node responds to RREQ with an appropriate QSEC and QID to the source node. The source node validates the destination node by comparing the QSEC and QID in RREP send by the destination node. If the QSEC and QID of currently pending query matches with the QSEC and QID in RREP, then the source node accepts an RREQ. Vulnerabilities of SRP are identified in [10,11] employing a formal verification approach. In 2017, Regan, and Man-ickam proposed an adaptive learning technique for Wireless Mesh Networks to ensure security against wormhole attacks [12]. The protocol is based on one-level and two-level security mechanisms. The first level is concerned with the security of mesh nodes and the second level is concerned with the security of cluster head. However, the cluster head in the proposed protocol suffers from traffic overhead with the increase in a malicious node which results in an authentication delay. In 2015, Subhash et al. proposed a secure neighbour discovery in Wireless Mesh Networks. Their protocol used connectivity information technique that authenticated mesh peering exchange and allows MRs to search their peer's neighbours securely [13]. Gao et al. in 2016 proposed a proxy group signature scheme based on identity which allows mutual authentication between mesh entities. Proxy group signature is combined with the identity-based group signature to further allow the mutual authentication among mesh entities [14]. Later, in 2017, Niizuma and Goto proposed an automatic authentication path generation protocol to decreases the system deployment costs [15]. In their proposed work the authentication took place between the users and APs by locally verifying the digital certificates as the authentication credentials. In 2015, Gaur and Pant proposed a trust computation metric based on nodes impulsive behavior to detect malicious nodes in ad hoc networks. The proposed protocol offers trustworthy communication in real life applications such as healthcare through secure and trusted clustering to ensure security [16]. Later, in 2016, Singh et al. proposed a hybrid technique to ensure security against the wormhole attack (WRHT) [17]. The protocol is based on two schemes-watchdog and Delphi for dual detection of wormhole attacks. The WHRT makes the decision on two parameters- time delay probability and packet loss probability to establish a secure path between source and destination. Guo et al. in 2013, proposed a secure access control mechanism to ensure guarding against internal attacks in distributed networks [18]. The protocol is based on a secure and efficient trust model using Bayesian theory and Diffie-Hellman key agreement protocol. The trust model detects the malicious nodes in the network by calculating the trust values of each individual node in the network to establish a secure route between the source node and the destination node. The protocol involves the clustering technique where each domain consists of a cluster head which calculates the trust values of nodes within each domain. Although the effectiveness of the low-energy adaptive clustering hierarchy(LEACH) routing protocol had demonstrated, security is one of its problems. Moreover, if the cluster head gets malicious the protocol fails to provide secure routing in distributed networks. Zhang et al. in 2013 proposed a virtual currency to simulate cooperation in self-organized mobile ad hoc networks based on a reward-based scheme [19]. To simulate the cooperative packets among each individual node in the wireless ad hoc network the reward-based scheme uses virtual currency. This virtual currency is assumed as a credit provided to each node in the network based on their forwarding behavior. All nodes need to forward for others to earn credits for their own expenses. Also, reward-based scheme employee tamper-proof hardware technique, that prevents illegal credit manipulation from adversaries. However, the proposed scheme suffers from inconsistency where, the nodes not having any packets to forward may not get a chance to earn any credits in the network, especially nodes at the edge of the WMN topology. Abdel-Azim et al. in 2018 proposed an intrusion detection system to ensure security against anomalies within the network [20]. The protocol is based on the Fuzzy Inference System (FIS) which is further optimized via an Adaptive Neuro-Fuzzy Inference System (ANFIS) using the Genetic Algorithm (GA) to detect the anomalies.

Although a variety of work had done in the past, related to secure routing in different types of networks, but still, they suffer from vulnerabilities and other issues as mentioned above. Moreover, some of the existing works are not suitable for WMNs due to their distributed environment. Therefore, in our proposed protocol we had designed a detection algorithm to detect the malicious nodes in WMNs, which drops the packets which it requires to forward for other nodes. Through experimental result, our proposed protocol ensures an efficient detection of the malicious node with a higher detection capability.

3   Detection of Malicious Nodes

The proposed protocol is based on the detection of malicious nodes that drop packets of other nodes during multi-hop forwarding between source and destination. The proposed protocol allows the routing protocol to choose an alternate secure path towards the destination once the malicious nodes are detected between source and destination. Based on the trust values of each node, our proposed protocol detects the malicious nodes in WMNs. The trust value of each node depends on its current behavior which the monitor node experiences from its neighboring nodes. We set a threshold value μ to 10% for the packet drop ratio. When a monitor node experiences its neighboring node dropping more than 10% of the packets, the trust value for this neighbor node is upgraded.

3.1 Proposed Detection Mechanism

Starting phase: This phase assigns a default trust value to every node in a network which signifies that the monitoring node neither trusts nor distrusts its neighboring nodes.

Upgrading phase: This phase is used for upgrading the trust value based on the current behavior of the neighboring nodes. We use the following criteria to upgrade the trust value for the neighboring nodes. The upgraded trust value T_u is given as

$$T_u = PacketDropRatio(DR) \tag{1}$$

Database phase: This phase stores the trust information of each node and allows to extract information about stored trust values.

Monitor phase: This phase is used to adjust the trust values of neighboring nodes by fixing the threshold value between 0 to 1. We set the threshold value μ to 10% which equals to 0.5 between 0 to 1. If the drop rate of a neighboring node is higher than 10%, then the trust value of the neighbor node is decreased. If the drop rate of a neighboring node is lower than 10%, then the trust value of the neighbor node is increased.

Path Selector phase: This phase selects the path between two nodes with higher trust values. If the trust value between two nodes is less than the threshold value μ than that path is ignored and an alternate path is selected with trust value greater than the threshold value (Fig. 1).

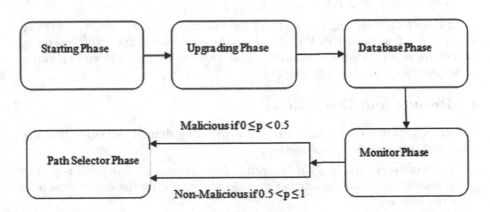

Fig. 1. Trust model.

3.2 Detection Algorithm

1. Initially the trust value is set to 0.5 for each node. At this point, the neighbor nodes could neither be trusted nor distrusts by the monitor node.
2. If the neighbor node had more than 10% of packet drops, then its trust value reduces starting from 0.5 towards 0 and then concludes as a malicious node.

$$0 \le p < 0.5 \tag{2}$$

where, p is a probability. Decrease of trust value from 0.5 towards 0, increases the chances of more packet drop beyond 10%.

3. If the neighbor node had less than 10% of packet drops, then its trust value increases starting from 0.5 towards 1 and then concludes as a non-malicious node.

$$0.5 < p \leq 1 \tag{3}$$

where, p is a probability. The increase of trust value from 0.5 towards 1, increases the chances of less packet drop below 10%.

3.3 Trust-Based Relationship(R) Among Nodes in Wireless Mesh Networks

1. Neighbor node j is an Acquaintance (A) to monitor node i at the initial stage.

$$R(node i \rightarrow node j) = A \tag{4}$$

if trust value= 0.5.
2. Neighbor node j is Friend (F) to monitor node i.

$$R(node i \rightarrow node j) = F \tag{5}$$

if trust value= $(0.5 < p \leq 1)$.
3. Neighbor node j is malicious (M) to monitor node i.

$$R(node i \rightarrow node j) = M \tag{6}$$

if trust value= $(0 \leq p < 0.5)$.

Note: If both the two neighbor nodes of the monitor node are between the range of $0.5 < p \leq 1$ as shown in Eq. (5), than their relation status will depend on their trust values. A node with higher trust value will treat as Friend and other as Acquaintance as shown in Fig. 2.

4 Results and Discussion

The proposed algorithm is simulated with NS3. The simulation results had analyzed with three performance metrics.

1. Packet delivery ratio (PDR): The ratio of the number of data packets sent by the source node and the number of packets received by the destination node in the next hop.

$$PDR = \left(\frac{R_x}{T_x}\right) \times 100 \tag{7}$$

where, R_x is the total packets received and T_x is the total packet send.
2. Packet Drop Ratio (DR): If a sending node i sends "x" number of packets to a receiving node j and the receiving node j only forwards "y" number of packets.

$$DR = \left(\frac{x - y}{x}\right) \times 100 \tag{8}$$

3. Detection Rate: The detection of a malicious node in WMNs increases with the increase in packets drop ratio above 10% by the malicious node.

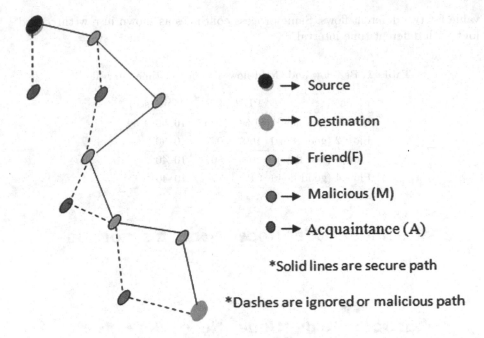

Fig. 2. Trust-based relationship

4.1   Performance Analysis

To evaluate the effectiveness of our proposed protocol, we consider 49 nodes (mesh routers MRs) in the presence of malicious node and analysis the fluctuations in the packets drop of the flows. These fluctuations reflect the detection rate of a malicious node in Wireless Mesh Networks (WMNs). We start a flow between MR 0 denoted as Sender1 and MR 48 denoted as Receiver in the presence of malicious nodes during the time period 10–100 s shown in Fig. 3. MR 7 as a neighbor node to MR 0, it convinces the MR 0 that it has a shorter path towards the destination node MR 48; therefore MR 0 forwards the packets to MR 7. On receiving the packets, MR 7 drops all the packets which it requires to forward on behave of MR 0 at the time interval of 10–50 s (bad flow) shown in Fig. 4. At the same time period 10–50 s (good flow) shown in Fig. 4, the flow from MR 7 enjoys good packet delivery towards its destination node MR 48. Therefore, this misbehavior act of MR 7 in regards of packets send and packets drop, allows the MR 0 to conclude MR 7 as a malicious node. After detection of a malicious node, MR 0 purges their routing entry through MR 7 and re-route their traffic. This process continues for each flow between sender and receiver shown in Fig. 5 for the detection of malicious nodes at different time intervals.

Table 1 shows two different flows performed by malicious node MR 1. Row one shows that MR 1 drops all the packets received from MR 0 at the time interval of 10–50 s. Row two shows that MR 1 forwards all of its packets to the destination node MR 24 at the same time intervals of 10–50 s. In columns two and three, PDR and DR are the Packet Delivery Ratio and Packet Drop Ratio

value for two different flows. Same process continues as shown in row three and
four with different time interval.

Table 1. Bad flow and Good flow at different time intervals

Flows	PDR	DR	Time (sec)
Flow 1 (bad flow)	0%	100%	10–50
Flow 2 (good flow)	100%	0%	10–50
Flow 3 (bad flow)	20%	80%	10–40
Flow 4 (good flow)	91%	9%	10–40

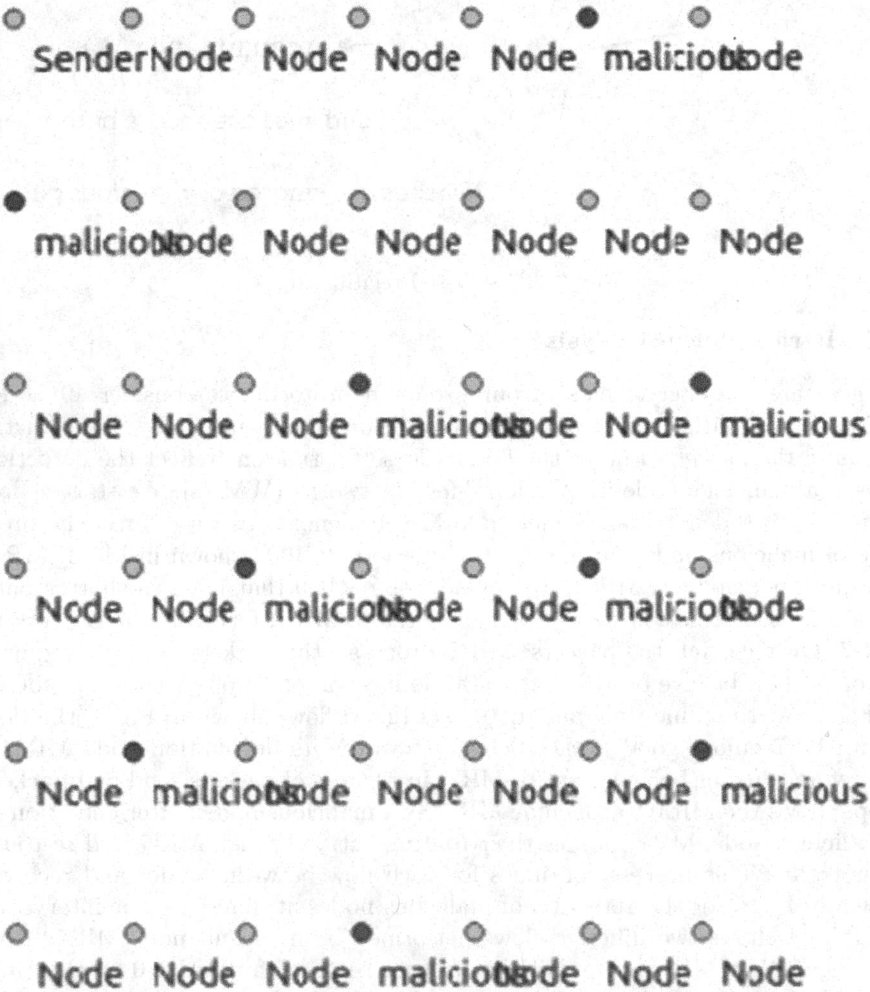

Fig. 3. Mesh routers setup

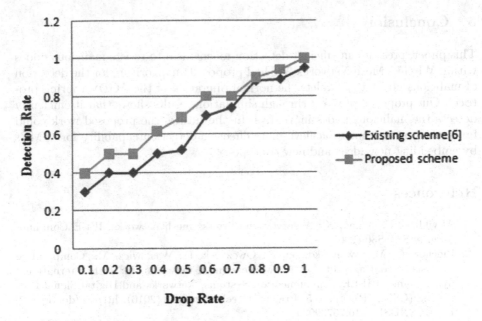

Fig. 4. Flow 1 (bad flow) vs. Flow 2 (good flow)

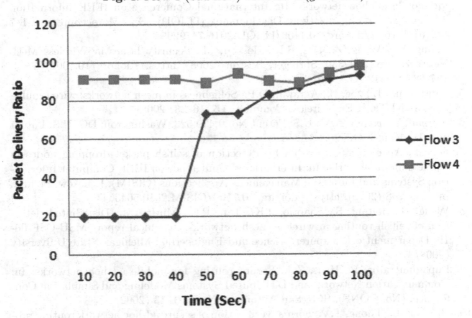

Fig. 5. Flow 3 (bad flow) vs. Flow 4 (good flow)

5   Conclusion

This paper, presents an efficient detection mechanism to resists malicious nodes within Wireless Mesh Networks. We had proposed an algorithm for the detection of malicious nodes that violets the normal operation of the AODV routing protocol. Our proposed protocol through simulation results shows that it efficiently detects the malicious nodes in WMNs. In the future, the proposed work could be further carried out to achieve more effective detection capability for WMNs by embedding new ideas and new concepts.

References

1. Akyildiz, I.F., Wang, X.: A survey on wireless mesh networks. IEEE Commun. Mag. **9**, S23–S30 (2005)
2. Piechowiak, M., Zwierzykowski, P., Owczarek, P., Wasłowicz, M.: Comparative analysis of routing protocols for wireless mesh networks. In: 10th International Symposium on IEEE Communication Systems, Networks and Digital Signal Processing (CSNDSP), pp. 1–5, Prague, Czech Republic (2016). https://doi.org/10.1109/CSNDSP.2016.7573902
3. Moudni, H., Er-rouidi, M., Mouncif, H., El Hadadi, B.: Secure routing protocols for mobile ad hoc networks. In: International Conference on IEEE Information Technology for Organizations Development (IT4OD), Fez, Moroccopp, pp. 1–7 (2016). https://doi.org/10.1109/IT4OD.2016.7479295
4. Zhang, W., Wang, Z., Das, S.K., Hassan, M.: Security Issues in Wireless Mesh Networks, pp. 309–330. Springer, Boston (2008). https://doi.org/10.1007/978-0-387-68839-8_12
5. Santhanam, L., Xie, B., Agrawal, D.P.: Selfishness in mesh networks: wired multihop MANETs. IEEE Wireless Commun. **15**, 16–23 (2008)
6. Altman, Y., Keren, A.Y.: U.S. Patent No. 9,479,523. Washington, DC. U.S. Patent and Trademark Office
7. Sen, J.: An efficient algorithm for detection of selfish packet dropping nodes in wireless mesh networks. In: International Conference on IEEE Computer Information Systems and Industrial Management Applications (CISIM), Krackow, Poland, pp. 283–288 (2010). https://doi.org/10.1109/CISIM.2010.5643647
8. Wang, B., Soltani, S., Shaprio, J.K., Tan, P.N., Mutka, M.: Distributed detection of selfish routing in wireless mesh networks. Technical report MSU-CSE-06-19, Department of Computer Science and Engineering, Michigan State University (2008)
9. Papadimitratos, P., Haas, Z.J.: Secure routing for mobile ad hoc networks. In: Communication Networks and Distributed Systems Modeling and Simulation Conference, (No. CONF), SCS, San Antonio, TX, pp. 1–13 (2002)
10. Buttyan, L., Thong, T.V.: Formal verification of secure ad-hoc network routing protocols using deductive model-checking. In: Proceedings of the Wireless and Mobile Networking Conference (WMNC), pp. 1–6. IEEE, Budapest (2010). https://doi.org/10.1109/WMNC.2010.5678752
11. Pervaiz, M.O., Cardei, M., Wu, J.: Routing Security in Ad Hoc Wireless Networks, pp. 117–142. Springer, Boston (2005). https://doi.org/10.1007/978-0-387-73821-5-6

12. Regan, R., Manickam, J.M.L.: Detecting and denying malicious behavior using adaptive learning based routing protocols in wireless mesh network. Appl. Math. Inf. Sci. **11**, 1155–1162 (2017)
13. Subhash, P., Ramachandram, S.: Secure neighbour discovery in wireless mesh networks using connectivity information. In: International Conference on IEEE Advances in Computing, Communications and Informatics (ICACCI), Kochi, India, pp. 2061–2066 (2015). https://doi.org/10.1109/ICACCI.2015.7275920
14. Gao, T., Peng, F., Guo, N.: Anonymous authentication scheme based on identity-based proxy group signature for wireless mesh network. EURASIP J. Wireless Commun. Network. **2016**(1), 1–10 (2016). https://doi.org/10.1186/s13638-016-0685-2
15. Niizuma, T., Goto, H.: Easy-to-deploy wireless mesh network system with user authentication and WLAN roaming features. IEICE Trans. Inf. Syst. **100**, 511–519 (2017)
16. Gaur, M.S., Pant, B.: Trusted and secure clustering in mobile pervasive environment. Hum. Centric Comput. Inf. Sci. **5**(1), 1–17 (2015). https://doi.org/10.1186/s13673-015-0050-1
17. Singh, R., Singh, J., Singh, R.: WRHT: a hybrid technique for detection of wormhole attack in wireless sensor networks. Mob. Inf. Syst. (2016). https://doi.org/10.1155/2016/8354930
18. Guo, J., Zhou, X., Yuan, J., Xu, H.: Secure access control guarding against Internal attacks in distributed networks. Wireless Pers. Commun. **68**, 1595–1609 (2013)
19. Zhang, Z., Long, K., Wang, J.: Self-organization paradigms and optimization approaches for cognitive radio technologies: a survey. IEEE Wirel. Commun. **20**, 36–42 (2013)
20. Abdel-Azim, M., Salah, H.E.D., Eissa, M.E.: IDS against black-hole attack for MANET. IJ Network Secur. **20**, 585–592 (2018)

Evidence Building for Ad Click or Web Access on Cloud

Pankaj Kumar Keserwani[1](✉), Mahesh Chandra Govil[1],
and Pilli Emmanuel Shubhakar[2]

[1] Department of Computer Science and Engineering, National Institute of
Technology Sikkim, Burfang Block Ravangla, South Sikkim 737139, India
pankaj.keserwani@gmail.com, govilmc@gmail.com
[2] Department of Computer Science and Engineering, Malaviya National Institute
of Technology Jaipur, JLN Marg, Jaipur, Rajasthan, India
espilli.cse@mnit.ac.in

Abstract. Web related illegal activities are increasing beyond expectation in recent years. Association of National Advertisers has reported that businesses lost more than $6.5 billion in 2017 due to fraudulent activities of ad frauds. Website of Github was down on 28 February, 2018 due to Distributed Denial of Services (DDoS) attack. The attack of DDoS was conducted through memcached servers. Analysis on relevant log data (web access log or ad click log) is required to identify such illegal incidents in digital forensics investigation. An evidence building methodology is proposed and implemented to generate required log data. The proof of concept is provided by coding three scripts, two in python and one in JavaScript. Virtual Machine (VM) on Amazon Web Service (AWS) has been utilized to execute one python script for log separation. Second python script is executed on client database server to store fingerprint of each click or web access. Fingerprint is a generated hash value unique for each device accessing a website or clicking an advertisement (ad). The third JavaScript code is to be embedded in client web page(s) or ad. The verification of log data has also been discussed with the help of fingerprints. The verification process allows regenerating the fingerprints of log data stored in AWS data store. The regenerated fingerprints are being matched with fingerprints stored in client's database server. The proposed methodology can identify malicious intention of the cloud service provider (CSP) or the investigator or attacker. The proposed methodology can be extended to cloud forensics.

Keywords: Cloud computing web access · Ad click · Evidence ·
Forensic · Virtual Machine (VM) · Amazon Web Service (AWS)

© Springer Nature Singapore Pte Ltd. 2020
A. Bhattacharjee et al. (Eds.): MIND 2020, CCIS 1241, pp. 486–500, 2020.
https://doi.org/10.1007/978-981-15-6318-8_40

1   Introduction

There are legal rules which provide a direction in transportation, management, communication, and presentation of evidence so that the evidence can be accepted in Court of Law. When a user is utilizing the cloud for business(es), it is very difficult to obtain a log of business-related activities. The cloud user has limited control over different layers of the cloud. There is no way to collect logs from a terminated VM due to its volatile nature. Generally, the collection of VM log data is dependent on CSP. Investigator has no way to verify that the CSP is providing valid logs or malicious logs which is generated by exploiting the logging system [5,6,35]. Such evidence guide the investigator to have full faith on CSP but the adversary can perform unethical activities such as hosting a botnet server, launching a bot program, setting-up a spam email server, phishing website, etc. The investigator may also turn to be malicious and tamper with logs. Evidence logs are affected before presenting to the legal institutions. The following hypothetical scenarios can illustrate the situations addressed in the proposed methodology of evidence building:

Scenario 1: *Suppose Alice is a very successful lady in her business and she runs her business through a popular website. Eve, a competitor of Alice, hired some virtual machines (VMs) in a cloud environment and launches a Distributed Denial of Service (DDoS) attack on Alice's website. As a result, Alice's website was down for two hours. Alice experienced a very negative impact on her business in terms of profit and goodwill both. Consequently, Alice asked a forensic investigator to handle the case. After analyzing the logs of Alice's web server, the investigator found that the website was flooded by some IP addresses owned by a cloud service provider (CSP). Eventually, the investigator issued a subpoena to the CSP to provide him network logs for identified IP addresses.*

Scenario 2: *Suppose Alice is a businesswoman and she wants to advertise her business in such a way that she may get the attention of more users to get more customers. Hence, her intention is to gain popularity and profit. She has made a digital ad for her product(s) and service(s). The ad is provided to Eve (a publisher) to publish on pay per click policy. The publisher, Eve hired some VMs in a cloud environment and launched a bot attack to generate a number of clicks on the ad. Alice realizes forgery from Eve after receiving the false reports. Consequently, Alice asked a forensic investigator to handle the case. After analyzing the entries in the log, the investigator found that many clicks were made by bots generated from some IP addresses, owned by a cloud service provider (CSP). Eventually, the investigator issued a subpoena to the CSP to provide him the network logs for those particular IP addresses.*

Similarly, the third scenario may be considered the same as scenario 2, when the publisher wants to resell the ads to other publishers to profit as a broker. In this case, the publisher acts as an advertiser and the sub-publishers act as publisher.

– The possible outcomes for the above scenarios are:

- **Case 1:** Eve may compromise with the CSP for altering the logs. The investigator has no way to verify the CSP for the correctness of the provided logs. A crime committed in this case, impossible to detect.
- **Case 2:** Eve may terminate the hired VMs leaving no traces of the attack. The CSP may fail to produce relevant logs to the investigator.
- **Case 3:** Eve may claim that the investigator and the CSP are colluded with each other to frame him by altering the logs.

Many authors proposed various methods towards mitigation of challenges in cloud forensics, but the tampering log could not be stopped as a whole. The log acquisition process was suggested through read-only APIs [8,10] but the confidentiality and integrity of log lost if the CSP is dishonest. Privacy and integrity of logs were suggested through initial secret but it depends on the intention of CSP. Since the malicious CSP may collude with the investigator or the external attacker to share the initial secret [2,6,12,17].

The proposed methodology addresses all issues mentioned in the above three cases. Section 5 describes the methods in detail.

1.1 Motivation

Fingerprints log of remote hosts has generated in localhost OS automatically if a remote OS accesses the localhost. The fingerprint of OS contains generally serial number, time, source IP, destination IP, source port, destination port, protocol, length, and information.

Accessibility of OS fingerprint is not an easy task. The log includes actions of all the Cloud Service Users (CSUs) who share the same OS platform which produces evidence segregation issues. The log information of the host OS works as proprietary information of CSP. Generally, most of the CSPs implement their propriety technology (e.g. Amazon Web Services (AWS) CloudWatch, AWS data store, etc.) which makes the investigation task complex. Collection of required log data demands co-operation of CSPs, but it is difficult [28]. Taking over the full control by the customers for enabling and configuring the logging services is not effective from a forensic point of view. The criminals will oppose enabling and configuring the logging services and will make an effort to erase all the traces of evidence. Due to multi-tenancy on the cloud environment, one CSU log may be shaking hands for co-mingling with another CSU logs, which is another issue to ensure privacy.

Therefore, the above issues motivate to design a fingerprint-based log under the control of external users which has been implemented in the proposed methodology. The proposed methodology satisfying the forensic and incident handling needs of internal as well as external entities.

The rest of the paper is organized as Sect. 2 provides the background study and related work. Section 3 is a discussion of the proposed methodology. Section 4 is the detail discussion of the use of the proposed methodology for cloud forensics investigation. Section 5 narrates the limitation of the proposed methodology. Section 6 describes the implementation of the proposed methodology. Section 7 presents the comparison of work from other work and Sect. 8 concludes the paper.

2 Background Study and Related Work

2.1 Background Study

The background study contains the definition and description of the terminology that appears in the proposed methodology:

- **Evidence:** Evidence should have legal significance, logical conceptions to prove the relevancy and it should have the strength and exclusionary rules to fulfill the evidential completeness [1].
- **Cloud Forensics:** Application of digital forensics in a cloud computing environment is known as cloud forensics. As per the NIST, "The application of scientific principles, technological practices, and derived as well as proven methods to reconstruct past cloud computing events through identification, collection, preservation, examination, interpretation, and reporting of digital evidence" [20]. There are many cloud forensics challenges in comparison to traditional digital forensics [26,29,30]. The cloud forensics has the ability of reconstruction and analysis of stored log of cloud computing events to investigate cloud-based cybercrimes or incidents. The cloud forensics situation can be visualized (Fig. 1) as:

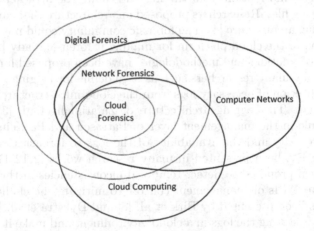

Fig. 1. Cloud forensics

2.2 Related Work

In cloud computing scenario identification and collection, the evidence is difficult due to distributed locations of physical systems, which support the cloud environment [26,29]. Digitally admissible evidence is necessary to trusted third parties (TTP) which are maintained in an audit trail for cloud forensics [20]. Capturing a trustworthy log from a valid set of logs provides guidance to perform cloud forensics at different layers with the help of CSP. The trust was built up by the process of convincing the observers that a system/model/design is correct and secured [23]. A Digital Certificate based distribution and methodology can be used to increase the trust level where the certificates are produced on the basis of technical, legal, financial and structural inputs [19]. A method to identify and to extract the forensically relevant log entries from the Linux operating system and security logs has been suggested by Zafarullah et al. [3]. The experiment has been conducted for producing fingerprints in the cloud to reconstruct an event. Some popular forensic data acquisition tools used by Dykstra et al. [9] to extract volatile and non-volatile data from the cloud environment and explored at different trust levels of cloud. One Forensic Open Stack Tool (FROST) was also developed by them. The objective was the collection of logs from different virtual disks, firewall logs, and application logs. Zawoad et al. [36] proposed a Secure-Logging-as-a-service (SecLaaS) scheme to store logs of VMs and the storage can be accessed for performing forensic in a secured way. The proposed work was able to ensure the integrity of the log in case of the malicious intention of cloud actors such as the CSU, the CSP, and the investigator [35]. A layered based cloud logging design with monitoring capability was proposed by Patrascu et al. [25]. One scheme to keep the audit log on an untrusted machine has been suggested by Marty [18]. The researchers proved that if an attacker gains control over the untrusted machine, the scheme can lock the attacker with a minute or zero information from the log and limits the attacker's ability for corrupting the log files. Researchers proposed an architecture that can be applied for cloud logging architecture [4]. The forensic community could not manage the implementation of the cloud platform for making it forensic ready [29].

A number of solutions and methodologies have been proposed for digital evidence creation by many researchers such as a guideline for logging standards by Marty [18], collection of necessary logs from the cloud infrastructure by Zafarullah et al. [3] etc. The logging architecture of Zafarullah et al. [3] and cloud forensics module in the management layer of Patrascu and Patriciu [25] in not ensuring the security and the availability of the logs to forensics investigators. Secure logging has been presented in many research works [2,12,17,34]. A log auditor has been proposed to detect temporal inconsistencies in the timeline of VM [33]. Public APIs or management console to mitigate the challenges of log acquisition has been presented by Birk et al. [8] and Dykstra et al. [10].

No scheme is storing the logs in a cloud environment and make it available to the user or investigators by ensuring integrity and secrecy. Keeping terminated VM logs is costly due to the ephemeral nature of VM. Forensic capable data must be collected from the VM log data set as evidence. The evidence must be stored in particular storage to create the logs under the control of cloud service users and other stakeholders. The proposed methodology presents the storage of web accesses or ad clicks logs in the cloud. The fingerprint for each event (web access or ad click) has been generated and stored on the client database server. The fingerprint helps to ensure integrity and secrecy. In a combination of the previous solutions, the proposed methodology is more user-friendly for cloud forensics.

3 Proposed Methodology

Evidence building procedure of online activities such as ad clicks, web page access has been presented (Fig. 2):

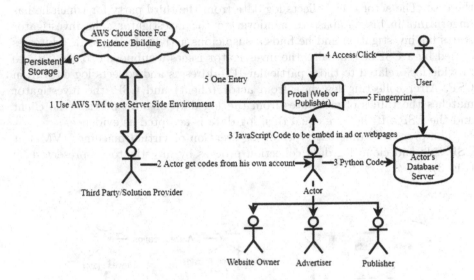

Fig. 2. Process methodology

Explanation of the proposed methodology:

1. The third party or solution provider set up the server side environment to accept and store values of attributes related to web access or ad click on AWS data store.
2. The third party provides the two scripts (One in JavaScript and other in python) to the actor (website owner, advertisement or publisher) on request for the solution. The actor requests for solution from his own account.
3. The actor embeds the JavaScript code to his ads or web pages and executes python script to his database server to accept and store the fingerprint value for each ad click or web access.
4. The cloud user accesses the web page or clicks ad.
5. One row for values of attributes is added to third party AWS data store and one row for fingerprint of values of attributes is added to actor's database corresponding to ad click or web page access.
6. Generated log at AWS data store is transferred to a persistent storage periodically.

4   Detail Description of Proposed Methodology for Cloud Forensics Investigation

When the actor (website owner/advertiser/publisher) suspects the illegal activity to his website or advertisement, subsequently he hires the investigator to handle the case. The actor then collects log data from the third party for which he has fingerprints in his database to handover to the investigator. The investigator starts his investigation and he finds a suspicious activity for some IP addresses owned by a CSP. Eventually, the investigator issues a subpoena to the CSP to provide logs related to those particular IP addresses and collects log data from CSP. After collecting log data from actor (client) and CSP, the investigator matches the values of attributes from the log data of both parties (the client and the CSP). If they are equal then log data is accepted as evidence.

The process of different types of log creation of virtual machines (VMs) at CSP side and cloud log data collection process by investigator is presented by (Fig. 3):

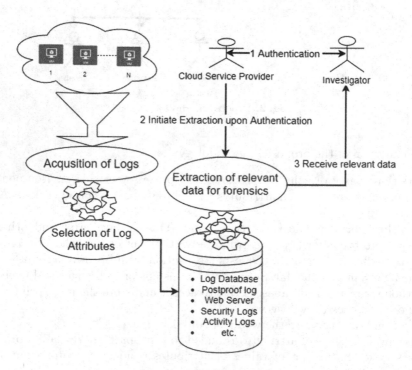

Fig. 3. The process of different types of log creation of virtual machines (VMs) at CSP side and cloud log data collection process by investigator

Explanation of Fig. 3:

– Log creation of VMs by CSP:

1. The CSP acquires data of all VMs periodically in acquisition process.
2. The CSP selects values of different attributes for different types of logs in selection of log attributes process.
3. Values of attributes of different logs such as web server, security logs, activity logs etc. are saved into a persistent data store.

- Cloud log data collection process by investigator:
  1. The CSP and the investigator authenticate each other.
  2. The CSP initiate the log extraction process from persistent data store for certain duration as per demand.
  3. The investigator receives log data.

The discussion verifies the CSP partially for small portion of logs. This may be the base to increase the confidence on CSP correctness.

4.1 Use of Fingerprint to Address the Illegal Intentions of CSP or Investigator or Attacker

- **Case 1:** If Eve (the attacker) compromises with the CSP for altering the logs then the generated fingerprints on collected log data will differ from the stored fingerprints at the actor's database server and creates inconsistency. Due to this inconsistency, the CSP will be in a suspect for altering the log data.
- **Case 2:** If Eve (the attacker) terminates the hired VMs then logs of those hired VMs before termination is with the third party from which malicious intention of Eve can be identified.
- **Case 3:** If Eve (the attacker) claims that the investigator and the CSP both collude to frame him by altering the logs, then consistency of CSP log data and actor's data can be verified with each other. Eve claims will be nullified in case of consistency.

5 Limitation of Proposed Methodology

1. The proposed methodology is limited to identification of illegal activities related to web accesses or ad clicks.
2. It is mandatory to know the common attributes at CSP side as well as third party side. The fingerprint for common attributes can be stored to database server of actor for verification of log data.
3. The publisher can use the third party solution of proposed methodology until the advertiser is not aware or not using the solution of proposed methodology.

6 Implementation of Proposed Methodology

In the implementation of proposed methodology of evidence building, three scripts have been used as follows:

– One scripts in python is executed by the third party or solution provider to accept and store the log of each event on AWS data store.

Pseudo code of the script to accept and store the log to AWS data store:

```
1) Import required dependencies from flask as Flask,
request, redirect, url_for, Response, MySQL;
2) Open database connection;
3) accept all values of attributes
at server interface;
4) Insert value of all attributes to the AWS data store;
```

Figure 4 show the values of some attributes generated through the python script on AWS data store.

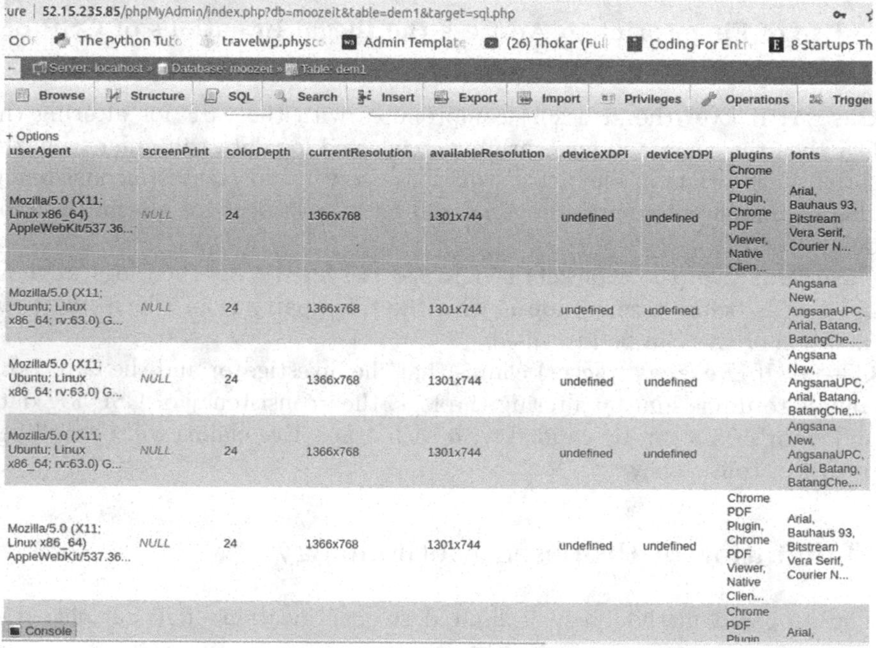

userAgent	screenPrint	colorDepth	currentResolution	availableResolution	deviceXDPI	deviceYDPI	plugins	fonts
Mozilla/5.0 (X11; Linux x86_64) AppleWebKit/537.36...	NULL	24	1366x768	1301x744	undefined	undefined	Chrome PDF Plugin, Chrome PDF Viewer, Native Clien...	Arial, Bauhaus 93, Bitstream Vera Serif, Courier N...
Mozilla/5.0 (X11; Ubuntu; Linux x86_64; rv:63.0) G...	NULL	24	1366x768	1301x744	undefined	undefined		Angsana New, AngsanaUPC, Arial, Batang, BatangChe,...
Mozilla/5.0 (X11; Ubuntu; Linux x86_64; rv:63.0) G...	NULL	24	1366x768	1301x744	undefined	undefined		Angsana New, AngsanaUPC, Arial, Batang, BatangChe,...
Mozilla/5.0 (X11; Ubuntu; Linux x86_64; rv:63.0) G...	NULL	24	1366x768	1301x744	undefined	undefined		Angsana New, AngsanaUPC, Arial, Batang, BatangChe,...
Mozilla/5.0 (X11; Linux x86_64) AppleWebKit/537.36...	NULL	24	1366x768	1301x744	undefined	undefined	Chrome PDF Plugin, Chrome PDF Viewer, Native Clien...	Arial, Bauhaus 93, Bitstream Vera Serif, Courier N...
							Chrome PDF Plugin	Arial,

Fig. 4. Part of attributes on AWS data store

– Two scripts are provided to the actor on demand for solution from his own account. First code in JavaScript is to be embedded in advertisement or web pages as per situation for following:

• to capture ad click or web access log.
• to send to values of attributes to AWS data store.
• to generate fingerprint from values of attributes.
• to send the generated fingerprint to the database server of actor.

Algorithm for JavaScript code

```
1) Capture values of attributes of ad click or
web page access in the objects;
2) Store all values of attributes into an array;
3) Send that array to AWS data store using post method;
4) Pass the array to murmurhash3_32_gc function
to generate fingerprint as output;
5) Send the fingerprint in post method to actor's database server;
```

The fingerprint is the hash value of sixteen attributes, namely, screenprint, color depth, current resolution, available resolution, device XDPI, device YDPI, plugin list, local storage, session storage, time zone, font list, language, system language, cookies, canvas print, and user agent. The description of fingerprint's attributes explained below as:

- **User agent:** A computer program that represents human behavior such as a browser for a web-based network environment. A user agent could also be a bot scraping web page, a download manager, or another app accessing the web page.
- **Screen Print:** It generates and saves an image of what is currently being displayed.
- **Color Depth:** The number of bits used to hold a screen pixel. Also called "pixel depth" and "bit depth," the color depth is the maximum number of colors that can be displayed.
- **Current Resolution:** The current resolution or display resolution or display modes of a device is the number of distinct pixels in each dimension that displayed with the current request.
- **Available Resolution:** Available resolution is the maximum display resolution of a device. The resolution has been described by the number of pixels arranged horizontally and vertically on a monitor, for example, $720 \times 360 = 259200$ pixels
- **Device XDPI & Device YDPI:** It is dots per inch (DPI) of a device on HTTP request which is equal to xdpi/ydpi.
- **Canvas Print:** It is gallery-wrapped which is being displayed after converted into a frame.
- **Plugin list:** It shows the list of plugins currently installed on the browser.
- **Time Zone:** It tells the time zone of the user device.
- **Font List:** It tells about the list of fonts installed on the user device. A Font is a particular size, weight, and style of a typeface.
- **Language:** It is the language of the browser/webpage.
- **System language:** It is the language currently used by the system.
- **Local Storage:** It is storage available after completion of a session.
- **Session Storage:** The session storage is the storage where the data is stored until the browser (or tab) is closed for a particular session.
- **Cookie:** A small text file value created by the JavaScript code on the device of the user.

The fingerprint has been created through Murmur hash function which is faster and has very good collision resistance. Murmur family contains general-purpose hash functions. It is used for the non-cryptographic purposes. It has the following benefits:

- It is very simple and provides better distribution since it passes chi-squared tests for all keysets and bucket sizes.
- It contains good avalanche behavior with a max bias of 0.5%. Hence, it passes the avalanche test.
- Its collision resistance is better.
- It uses three basic operations as a whole multiply, rotates and XOR.

The second script in python to store fingerprint value in the database server of actor. Algorithm to insert data in the database server of actor (Fig. 5).

```
1) Import required dependencies from flask as Flask,
request, redirect, url_for, Response, MySQL;
2) Open database connection;
3) accept fingerprint value at database at server interface;
4) Insert fingerprint value to the database;
```

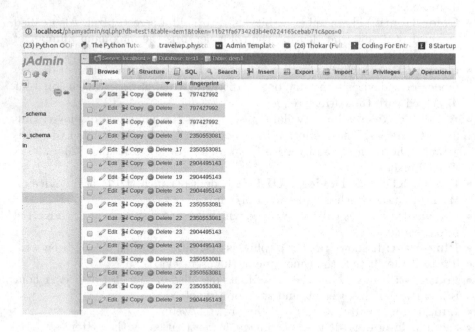

Fig. 5. Storage of fingerprint value in actor's database

7   Comparison of Proposed Work from Other's Work

Table 1 presents the comparisons of the proposed work from other's work.

- **Secure logging (1 for Yes, 0 for No):** It prevents the leak of data.
- **Dependence on third party (0 for Yes, 1 for No):** If the scheme is not self-dependent, and depends on third party, some leaks may occur.
- **Backup for logs (1 for Yes, 0 for No):** To check frauds.
- **Software Assurance (1 for Yes, 0 for No):** A necessity of CC.
- **Data Analysis (1 for Yes, 0 for No):** Analysis of data can be used to check for unauthorized users or frauds.
- **Elasticity of service (1 for Yes, 0 for No):** The flexibility of service allows the scheme to work in various scenarios.
- **Chance of frauds (0 for Yes, 1 for No):** The risk of frauds is harmful to the user.
- **Cloud monitoring (1 for Yes, 0 for No):** Monitoring of data over cloud can help find anomalies.
- **Client blocking (1 for Yes, 0 for No):** Client blocking is useful when too many calls are made from the same client. It prevents DoS attacks.

Table 1. Comparison of proposed work from other works

Paper Ref	Proposed	[35]	[22]	[24]	[21]	[32]	[13]	[11]	[7]	[27]	[31]	[14]	[15]	[16]
Secure logging	Yes	Yes	Yes	No	Yes	No	Yes	No	Yes	Yes	Yes	Yes	No	No
Dependence on third party	No	Yes	No	Yes	Yes	Yes	Yes	No	Yes	Yes	Yes	Yes	Yes	Yes
Backup for logs	Yes	No	Yes	No	No	No	No	No	No	No	No	No	No	No
Software assurance	Yes	No	No	No	No	Yes	Yes	No	Yes	Yes	Yes	Yes	No	No
Data analysis	Yes	Yes	No	Yes	Yes	Yes	No	Yes	No	Yes	No	No	Yes	No
Elasticity of service	Yes	Yes	Yes	No	No	Yes	Yes	Yes	Yes	Yes	No	Yes	Yes	No
Chance of frauds	No	No	No	Yes	No	Yes	No	Yes	Yes	No	No	No	No	Yes
Cloud monitoring	Yes	Yes	Yes	Yes	Yes	Yes	No	No	No	No	No	No	Yes	No
Blocking for client	No	No	No	No	No	No	No	No	No	No	No	No	No	Yes
Score	8	5	6	2	4	4	3	3	4	5	3	3	4	1

8   Conclusion

The paper proposed a methodology of an evidence building of web accesses or ad clicks on the AWS environment using scripts coded in python and JavaScript. It uses the fingerprint concept to verify the integrity of data. It also verifies the consistency of CSP log with third party log for common attributes with the help of fingerprint. Fingerprint in this paper is the hash value of 16 attributes where two-bit to each value has been reserved. The generated log is helpful for different actors such as website owners, advertisers, and publishers. MySql database server is used for the AWS data store as well as the actor's database server.

References

1. The legal concept of evidence (stanford encyclopedia of philosophy). https://plato.stanford.edu/entries/evidence-legal/. Accessed 12 Sept 2018
2. Accorsi, R.: On the relationship of privacy and secure remote logging in dynamic systems. In: Fischer-Hübner, S., Rannenberg, K., Yngström, L., Lindskog, S. (eds.) SEC 2006. IIFIP, vol. 201, pp. 329–339. Springer, Boston, MA (2006). https://doi.org/10.1007/0-387-33406-8_28
3. Anwar, F., Anwar, Z., et al.: Digital forensics for eucalyptus. In: 2011 Frontiers of Information Technology, pp. 110–116. IEEE (2011)
4. Battistoni, R., Di Pietro, R., Lombardi, F.: Cure-towards enforcing a reliable time-line for cloud forensics: model, architecture, and experiments. Comput. Commun. 91, 29–43 (2016)
5. Bellare, M., Yee, B.: Forward integrity for secure audit logs. Technical report, Computer Science and Engineering Department, University of California (1997)
6. Bellare, M., Yee, B.: Forward-security in private-key cryptography. In: Joye, M. (ed.) CT-RSA 2003. LNCS, vol. 2612, pp. 1–18. Springer, Heidelberg (2003). https://doi.org/10.1007/3-540-36563-X_1
7. Bhattacharya, S.S., et al.: Systems and methods for log generation and log obfuscation using SDKs, uS Patent 9,411,708, 9 August 2016
8. Birk, D., Wegener, C.: Technical issues of forensic investigations in cloud computing environments. In: 2011 IEEE Sixth International Workshop on Systematic Approaches to Digital Forensic Engineering (SADFE), pp. 1–10. IEEE (2011)
9. Dykstra, J., Sherman, A.T.: Acquiring forensic evidence from infrastructure-as-a-service cloud computing: exploring and evaluating tools, trust, and techniques. Digit. Invest. 9, S90–S98 (2012)
10. Dykstra, J., Sherman, A.T.: Design and implementation of frost: digital forensic tools for the openstack cloud computing platform. Digit. Invest. 10, S87–S95 (2013)
11. Hamooni, H., Debnath, B., Xu, J., Zhang, H., Jiang, G., Mueen, A.: LogMine: fast pattern recognition for log analytics. In: Proceedings of the 25th ACM International on Conference on Information and Knowledge Management, pp. 1573–1582. ACM (2016)
12. Holt, J.E.: Logcrypt: forward security and public verification for secure audit logs. In: Proceedings of the 2006 Australasian workshops on Grid computing and e-research-Volume 54, pp. 203–211. Australian Computer Society, Inc. (2006)
13. Karande, V., Bauman, E., Lin, Z., Khan, L.: SGX-Log: securing system logs with SGX. In: Proceedings of the 2017 ACM on Asia Conference on Computer and Communications Security, pp. 19–30. ACM (2017)

14. Kraenzel, C.J., Immerman, J.D., Mills, W.A., Lu, J.J.: System and method for developing and administering web applications and services from a workflow, enterprise, and mail-enabled web application server and platform, uS Patent 9,805,337, 31 October 2017

15. Kurakami, H.: Log analyzing device, information processing method, and program, uS Patent 9,860,278, 2 January 2018

16. Lee, J.H.: Client session blocking method and apparatus of web application server, uS Patent App. 15/798,639, 3 May 2018

17. Ma, D., Tsudik, G.: A new approach to secure logging. ACM Trans. Storage (TOS) **5**(1), 2 (2009)

18. Marty, R.: Cloud application logging for forensics. In: Proceedings of the 2011 ACM Symposium on Applied Computing, pp. 178–184. ACM (2011)

19. Mell, P., Grance, T.: National institute of standards and technology. The NIST definition of cloud computing, 2011

20. Mell, P., Grance, T.: Nist cloud computing forensic science challenges. Draft Nistir **8006** (2014)

21. Moh, M., Pininti, S., Doddapaneni, S., Moh, T.S.: Detecting web attacks using multi-stage log analysis. In: 2016 IEEE 6th International Conference on Advanced Computing (IACC), pp. 733–738. IEEE (2016)

22. Muthurajkumar, S., Ganapathy, S., Vijayalakshmi, M., Kannan, A.: Secured temporal log management techniques for cloud. Procedia Comput. Sci. **46**, 589–595 (2015)

23. Nagarajan, A., Varadharajan, V.: Dynamic trust enhanced security model for trusted platform based services. Future Gener. Comput. Syst. **27**(5), 564–573 (2011)

24. Neelima, G., Rodda, S.: Predicting user behavior through sessions using the web log mining. In: 2016 International Conference on Advances in Human Machine Interaction (HMI), pp. 1–5. IEEE (2016)

25. Patrascu, A., Patriciu, V.V.: Logging system for cloud computing forensic environments. J. Control Eng. Appl. Inform. **16**(1), 80–88 (2014)

26. Pichan, A., Lazarescu, M., Soh, S.T.: Cloud forensics: technical challenges, solutions and comparative analysis. Digit. Invest. **13**, 38–57 (2015)

27. Plante, J.: Vehicle event recorders with integrated web server, uS Patent 8,996,240, 31 March 2015

28. Raju, B., Moharil, B., Geethakumari, G.: FaaSeC: enabling forensics-as-a-service for cloud computing systems. In: Proceedings of the 9th International Conference on Utility and Cloud Computing, pp. 220–227. ACM (2016)

29. Reilly, D., Wren, C., Berry, T.: Cloud computing: pros and cons for computer forensic investigations. Int. J. Multimedia Image Proces. (IJMIP) **1**(1), 26–34 (2011)

30. Ruan, K., Carthy, J., Kechadi, T., Crosbie, M.: Cloud forensics. In: Peterson, G., Shenoi, S. (eds.) DigitalForensics 2011. IAICT, vol. 361, pp. 35–46. Springer, Heidelberg (2011). https://doi.org/10.1007/978-3-642-24212-0_3

31. Semba, S.: Communication terminal and secure log-in method acquiring password from server using user id and sensor data, uS Patent 9,479,496, 25 October 2016

32. Swapna, A., Guptha, K.G., Geetha, K.: Efficient approach for web search personalization in user behavior supported web server log files using web usage mining (2017)

33. Thorpe, S., Ray, I.: Detecting temporal inconsistency in virtual machine activity timelines. J. Inf. Assur. Secur. **7**(1) (2012)

34. Yavuz, A.A., Ning, P.: BAF: an efficient publicly verifiable secure audit logging scheme for distributed systems. In: 2009 Annual Computer Security Applications Conference, pp. 219–228. IEEE (2009)
35. Zawoad, S., Dutta, A., Hasan, R.: Towards building forensics enabled cloud through secure logging-as-a-service. IEEE Trans. Dependable Secure Comput. 1, 1–1 (2016)
36. Zawoad, S., Dutta, A.K., Hasan, R.: SecLaaS: secure logging-as-a-service for cloud forensics. In: Proceedings of the 8th ACM SIGSAC Symposium on Information, Computer and Communications Security, pp. 219–230. ACM (2013)

Security Analysis of MITM Attack on SCADA Network

Debasish Deb[1(✉)], Sagorika Raj Chakraborty[2], Mahendra Lagineni[1],
and Kirani Singh[1]

[1] Centre for Development of Advanced Computing, Silchar, India
debasishd@cdac.in
[2] Cachar College, Silchar, India
http://www.cdac.in

Abstract. Cybersecurity is one of the major concerns in the Supervisory Control and Data Acquisition Technique (SCADA) systems. The main goal of this paper is to check how secure the power SCADA System is? In SCADA systems, attackers either disable the system or attempt to damage the SCADA network by pushing out improper data or commands for disrupting communications. SCADA systems are most vulnerable to malicious attackers due to their interconnectivity in smart grids and usage of standard plain text protocols. In SCADA systems due to legacy communication infrastructure and protocols, they have cybersecurity vulnerabilities because systems were initially designed with less cyber threat consideration. This paper analyses the possibility of conducting Man-in-the-middle (MITM) attacks on SCADA communication, which uses an International Electrotechnical Commission (IEC 60870-5-104) SCADA communication protocol standard. The Packet Inspection method on SCADA systems is used for detection of MITM attacks conducted based on ARP Poisoning method. SCADA communication networks are used to control various infrastructures and play vital roles for utility companies and the process industries including the power sector, gas, oil, water, etc. This paper is used to analyze security threats in Remote Terminal Unit (RTU)-control center communication using packet sniffing on IEC-60870-5-104 standard compliance SCADA communications and by conducting MITM attacks on it.

Keywords: SCADA · Man-In-The-Middle attack · ARP poisoning · IEC 60870-5-104

1 Introduction

1.1 SCADA System

Supervisory Control and Data Acquisition are popularly known as SCADA can be considered as a computer-based system, used to collect field data, analyze and control in real-time. The computer processes the data and displays it on

© Springer Nature Singapore Pte Ltd. 2020
A. Bhattacharjee et al. (Eds.): MIND 2020, CCIS 1241, pp. 501–512, 2020.
https://doi.org/10.1007/978-981-15-6318-8_41

a screen in real-time. SCADA technology saves and makes historian data in a database. SCADA is mostly used in industries and an industrial control network is an interconnected equipment that are used to control and monitor field devices in industrial environments [2]. Industrial control systems (ICS) generally use SCADA techniques mostly deployed in industries to control and used to keep tracking devices in the fields [7]. SCADA technology plays a very important role in power system network communications and operation. SCADA systems are composed of a large communication network therefore the network is complex itself. SCADA systems have Remote Terminal Unit (RTU) [10] and Master Terminal Unit (MTU), Human Machine Interface, historian, analytics server, reporting server, etc. Communications happen between RTU and MTU can be sniffed. The smart grids in electrical fields are mostly the prospect of cyber-attacks from malicious sources. SCADA communication networks having networks infrastructure and having protocols not generally considered cybersecurity issues as a threat in the past. SCADA systems can be considered as a target (legitimate) by malicious attackers to gain unauthorized access to a SCADA system at vulnerable points [9,12]. Thus, we need to provide a SCADA communication network that level of security from being unauthorized access. Protecting the SCADA system from cyber attackers is a need of the hour.

Some of the research activities based on the exploitation of SCADA protocols are as follows

1. Sniff the communication between RTU and MTU.
2. Tamper the data between RTU and MTU.
3. Hold the data in a temporary buffer and replay the data between RTU and MTU.
4. Data modification/Man in the middle attack: After sniffing the communication between RTU and MTU, measured data/indication data can tamper.
5. After sniffing the communication, data can be provided to MTU for every request. In this case, the attacker behaves like RTU.
6. As an attacker, conduct DoS attacks on RTU or MTU. DoS attack can be conducted at various layers, i.e. data link layer, transport layer and application layer.

1.2 SCADA Network and Architecture

The SCADA network consists of an MTU to interact with the RTU for data collection and control. The system also hosts an HMI to display the data acquired from the RTU. This MTU server is in LAN connection with other systems like historians, reporting systems, etc. The MTU, with the help of a router, connects to the substation RTUs which is in a different network. Figure 1 shows the basic SCADA architecture.

The rest of the paper is organized as follows. Section 2 discusses COPS SCADA Research laboratory, which is used for conducting MITM attacks. Section 3 discusses IEC 60870-5-104 standard SCADA communication protocol and its vulnerabilities. Section 4 discusses MITM Attacks. Section 5 presents

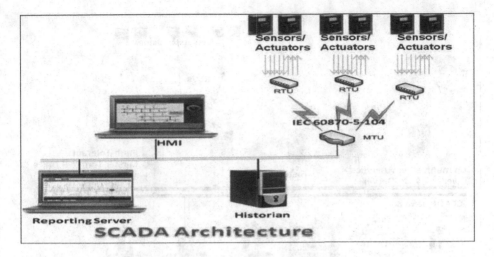

Fig. 1. Simple SCADA system architecture.

the MITM experiment attacks conducted on SCADA networks and Sect. 6 ends
with the conclusion.

2   COPS SCADA Research Laboratory

CDAC's open process solutions (COPS) is a generic SCADA system. COPS
solutions are being deployed in many different sectors including power for energy
management. In COPS SCADA system communications are based on IEC 60870-
5-101/104 standard protocol compliance. The main usages of these domains
include SCADA Research Laboratory [11] in Educational Institutions for conducting research, training, capacity building in the area of SCADA system and
used in the process Industry. SCADA uses IEC 60870-5-101/104 compliant master called MTU and a remote terminal unit called RTU. SCADA System data is
also integrated with a device called the human-machine interface (HMI). HMI
is responsible for displaying the activities in the control center. COPS is integrated with IEC 101 to IEC 104 converter for enabling interoperability features
between IEC 101 devices with IEC 104 networks and vice versa. This resolves
the interoperability issues in the SCADA communication networks with legacy
devices.

Figure 2 shows COPS SCADA Research Laboratory, and the lab has the
following features:

- RTU and field signal simulation kit
- RTU software simulator and field data simulation
- Master Terminal Unit
- SCADA Human Machine interface
- Historian, Reporting Server

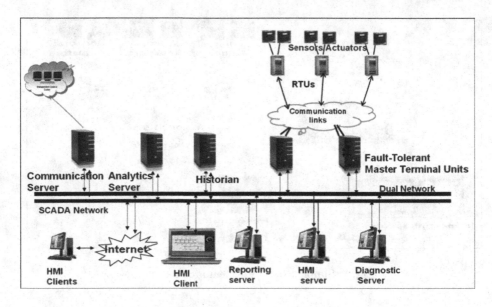

Fig. 2. COPS SCADA research laboratory.

- Data Analytics Server
- Diagnostic server
- Tag Database configuration
- Alarm/Event Management tools

RTU is configured to process 24 measurand values (analog input card) for inputs and 16 indication signals for both inputs (digital input) and outputs (digital output) and 8 analog outputs. The analog input cards were configured for measurement ranges of 0–10 V/0–20 mA/4–20 mA. The RTU Analog Input card, when connected to the RTDS/sensors/transducers, senses the analog electrical signals at the connection points and converts them to digital information (using 15-bit ADC) before passing it to the MTU. Similarly, RTU Digital Input card, when connected to the RTDS/sensors/transducers, senses the analog electrical signals at the connection points and converts them to digital information (either 0- OFF or 1-ON) before passing it to the MTU. RTU receives the digital output/analog output control commands from the control center and sends equivalent electrical signals to field actuators for needful control.

3   IEC 60870-5-104 Standard Protocol and Its Vulnerabilities

3.1   Introduction to the SCADA Protocol in the Power System

IEC 60870-5-104 (IEC 104) is a standard protocol that is ethernet based and mostly used in tele-control in the SCADA system in the power system automation applications. IEC 104 is a protocol that is used for network communication

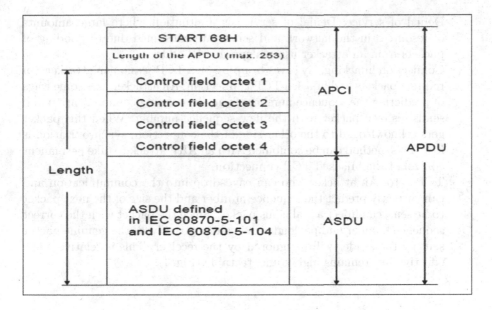

Fig. 3. IEC104 protocol packet format.

in the control region of SCADA that is communication between MTU/Control center and RTU devices. This protocol uses a similar frame format used by IEC 60870-5-101, a serial line protocol and uses an open TCP/IP interface for communication and standard RTU listening port number is 2404. As shown in Fig. 3, IEC 60870-5-104 frame format is divided into two parts namely Application Protocol Control Information (APCI) and Application Service Data Unit (ASDU). The ASDU part deals with the actual information being transferred and also its metadata. The APCI part has 6 octets in length and contains a start character, the specification of the length of the ASDU and 4 octets of the control field [13]. IEC 60870-5-104 protocol basically supports many types of data to be exchanged in SCADA communication like measured (voltage, current, power, oil temperature, winding temperature, frequency, etc.) and indication (circuit breaker status, isolator status, etc.) data acquisition from RTU to MTU, control commands from MTU to RTU, transfer of files, time synchronization data, etc. Data acquisition and control commands are the basic core of SCADA communications.

3.2 SCADA Communication Vulnerabilities

Vulnerabilities [9] of IEC 60870-5-104 can broadly be listed as follows:

1. Vulnerabilities are due to the TCP/IP stack.
2. Vulnerabilities in the protocol due to the lack of inbuilt security mechanisms.

1. A plain TCP connection may be attacked in a variety of ways resulting in unwanted/compromised situations like the following:

- Denial of service: Denial of service is a situation where large amounts of resources in the network and server are consumed due to flooding of packets from an attacker using a spoofed IP address.
- Connection hijacking: By eavesdropping on a TCP session an attacker can redirect packets and hijack a TCP connection. An attacker uses some ways of predicting the sequence numbers from the ongoing communication and sends his own packet with the new sequence number. When this packet gets acknowledged to the other side of the connection, synchronization is lost. This method can be combined with an ARP attack to take permanent control of the hijacked TCP connection.
- TCP veto: An attacker who can eavesdrop into the communication and can correctly predict the sequence number and the size of the next packet to be sent, can inject a malicious packet. Since the packet with the correct sequence number and payload size is already received, the genuine packet sent by the sender will be ignored by the receiver. This is relatively less effective but remains highly undetectable (Fig. 4).

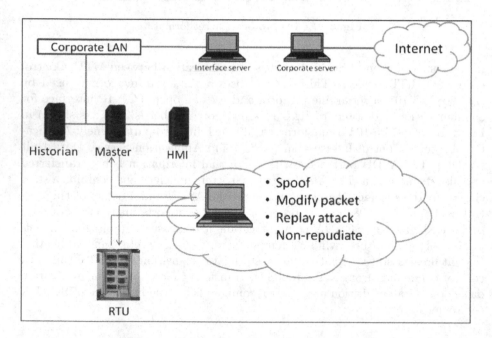

Fig. 4. SCADA communication vulnerabilities.

2. Due to no special care taken to provide security in the protocol, IEC 60870-5-104 communication is always vulnerable for an attack as below:

- Confidentiality: Since this is a plain text communication, it is easy for an eavesdropper to have access to the actual data being transferred. The protocol, being an open standard, makes it easier for an attacker to interpret the packets appropriately.
- Integrity: For an attacker who is successful in launching a man-in-the-middle attack, with enough knowledge about the protocol, it can modify the packet in its transit to MTU to indicate wrong measurement values and incorrect status of the devices. This can in turn force the operator to take inappropriate action.
- Authenticity: The protocol has no provision to authenticate the communicating device. This makes it possible for an intruder to inject a packet to send it to RTU. The injected packet can have a command to perform a task that results in a catastrophic situation in substation [5].

There are other threats like MITM attack [3] and non-repudiation. While replay attacks can be countered, only to an extent and not completely, by effective use of the sequence numbers that inherently feature in the protocol, non-repudiation doesn't fall in the same threat level that is being discussed in this paper.

4   MITM Attack

Man-in-the-middle is a cyberattack where a malicious party enters into a conversation between two devices, impersonates both the devices and accesses the information of the two parties while exchanging the data and control messages [8]. The main objective of MITM attack is to steal credential information of one's or during transmission of field data and control commands information. In this paper Ettercap [6] installed system would act as a MITM, that attacks the SCADA Network and disrupts the confidentiality of both RTU and MTU. MITM attack uses a technique called ARP poisoning. It can be done by exploiting the two-device security. The first thing is the response of an Address Resolution Protocol is trusted. Any malicious device connected will be trusted by the network to deviate and intercept SCADA network traffic. Additionally, MITM attack allows the third party to intercept and capture the data for further results, and modify the data in real-time before its being forwarded to the victim [4]. The ARP attack once completed, the users can be intercepted while the field data is sent and control commands received. This activity can be monitored using Wireshark [7] which is an open and free packet analyzer. Wireshark is a platform and can run on Windows, Linux, etc. Network securing with an intrusion detection system. Network administrators shall be good network hygiene to mitigate a MITM poisoning. Analyzing traffic patterns to identify unusual behavior. Network shall have strong firewalls and internet protocols to prevent unauthorized access. Use third-party penetration software, tools and Hypertext Transfer Protocol Secure (HTTPS) encryption to help detecting and blocking of eavesdropping attempts. To secure Install high active virus and malware protected software that includes a scanner and that runs on the system to reboot. Man-in-the-middle attacks (MITMs) attacks often rely on malware. Running updated anti-virus software is secure. The best defense to protect against communication interception is Encrypted form. The effective procedure to stop Internet Protocol (IPs) hijacking is to enable two-factor authentication. In addition to authenticating your system, use a password.

4.1 ARP Poisoning

ARP is an abbreviation for Address Resolution Protocol where the attackers send modifies ARP messages over a LAN to link MAC Address of attackers to make the server legitimate [1]. In this paper, we used ARP Poisoning to poise or change the identity of SCADA units. Finally, when the third system MAC address is connected to an authenticated IP address it will begin receiving any data that is intended for IP address. ARP poisoning can intercept any malicious system and can modify or stop data transition. ARP poisoning attacks can only occur on LAN that as a SCADA network is wired connection.

4.2 Ettercap -G

Ethernet capture in short Ettercap -G, which is a graphical user interface suited for a man-in-the-middle attack. In this paper, we have done a MITM attack on the SCADA network using this tool. Firstly, we have checked for an ethernet port in which both RTU and MTU communication was going on. In this experiment, we have chosen the third system and installed Ettercap -G and performed the MITM poisoning. The basic representation of the attack is explained in the illustrated Fig. 5. Secondly, we have connected the Ettercap system in the SCADA through the switch, then we scanned available hosts in the network. After scanning we have found RTU's and MTU's IP addresses and MAC addresses in the network These two IPs we have chosen for cyber-attack using the Ettercap tool as shown in the figure below.

5 Experiment: MITM Attacks on SCADA Networks

With all the vulnerabilities mentioned in the last section, it is to be concluded that the SCADA network is not immune to a cyber-attack. Now, the consequence of any such cyber attacker also has to be established. For this purpose, an experiment has been conducted at C-DAC SCADA research laboratory by using the COPS SCADA Lab kit and other tools associated with this experiment are Ettercap for attacking the specific IP either RTU or MTU and Wireshark for monitoring packet data. The purpose of the experiment is to carry out the research work that can implement or affect a cyber-attack on the SCADA network. In this paper, we have attacked both the RTU and MTU side of the SCADA network. The third-party known as MITM Attacker enters into the SCADA network and disrupt the RTU and MTU communication by changing the address of the respective system. In earlier cases communication between RTU and MTU are continuous and both systems are having the same machine address. We used the Ettercap tool, that sniffed the packets and changed the machine address of the RTU and MTU in the network. We used an Ettercap tool to change the identity of the system of RTU and MTU. That means in earlier case RTU is getting a response from MTU and MTU is getting a response from RTU, but when due to interruption of the third party in the SCADA network, third-party changes the system address and replaces the address of the system with its address.

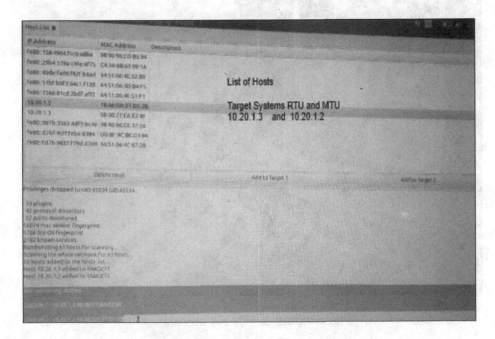

Fig. 5. Scanned for RTU and MTU IP and machine details.

5.1 Launching MITM Attack on SCADA Network

The experiment that has been performed in SCADA Laboratory with the help of the Ettercap tool. The MAC addresses of the RTU and MTU have been modified by the attacker's MAC as shown in the Fig. 7.

1. MTU/10.20.1.2 18:66:da:97:d5:2b
2. RTU/10.20.1.3 08:00:27:ea:e2:8f
3. Attacker/10.20.1.4 8c:16:45:c4:98:71

The following diagram explains the network architecture. Attack has been made using Ettercap installed system which entered the SCADA networks and did the attack on both RTU and MTU and losses both RTU's and MTU's identity.

The experiment that has been performed in SCADA Laboratory using Etter-cap. Tabular data as shown in Table 1 and Table 2 shows that the change in MAC addresses of the RTU and MTU systems.

The MAC addresses of the RTU and MTU have been modified by the attacker's MAC address. As shown in the figure below (Fig. 6):

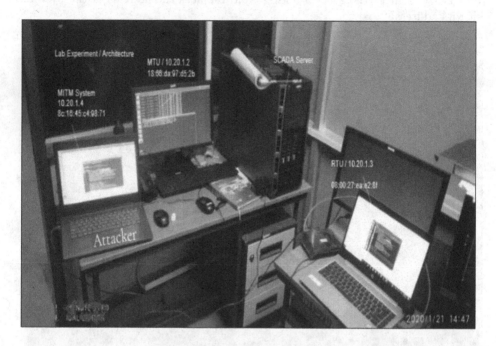

Fig. 6. Attack on SCADA network

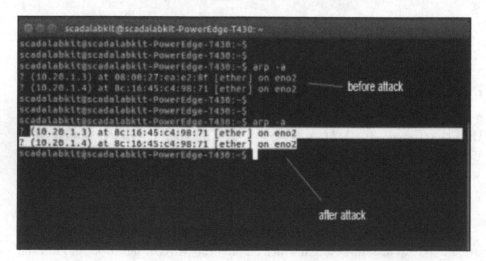

Fig. 7. Attack on SCADA network

Table 1. Tabular data showing the change on MAC of RTU after MITM attack

Sl No	Source	MAC1	Destination	MAC2	Remarks
1	MTU	18:66:da:97:d5:2b	RTU	08:00:27:ea:e2:8f	No disruption
2	RTU	08:00:27:ea:e2:8f	MTU	18:66:da:97:d5:2b	No disruption
3	Attacker	8c:16:45:c4:98:71	RTU	8c:16:45:c4:98:71	Disruption happens

Table 2. Tabular data showing the change on MAC of MTU after MITM attack

Sl No	Source	MAC1	Destination	MAC2	Remarks
1	MTU	08:00:27:ea:e2:8f	MTU	18:66:da:97:d5:2b	No disruption
2	RTU	18:66:da:97:d5:2b	RTU	08:00:27:ea:e2:8f	No disruption
3	Attacker	8c:16:45:c4:98:71	MTU	8c:16:45:c4:98:71	Disruption happens

6 Conclusion

SCADA networks, like any communication network are vulnerable to cyber-attacks. Adoption of open standard IEC 60870-5-104 protocols overcame the interoperability problems in SCADA systems but came with vulnerabilities as these protocols are not designed with security in view. With the added vulnerabilities that TCP/IP networks bring, SCADA communication is more vulnerable. IEC 60870-5-104 is a plain text protocol with no authentication mechanism. MITM attacks are conducted on the SCADA network more easily as data communication in plain text format and proved that it is more vulnerable for various attacks. Unfortunately, the risk from cyber threat is much greater, while conducting control commands on the field environment. SCADA communication requires authentication, authorization, encryption, end-point security, communication security, etc. for reliable operation of the power system. So, one needs to be proactive to study the vulnerabilities and analyze the risk involved and implement appropriate security steps to prevent access to unauthorized users from a third-party system or communication network.

References

1. Amaraneni, A., Lagineni, M., Kalluri, R., Senthilkumar, R.K., Ganga Prasad, G.L.: Transient analysis of cyber-attacks on power SCADA using RTDS. Power Res. **11**(1), 79–92 (2015)
2. Galloway, B., Hancke, G.P.: Article introduction to industrial control networks. IEEE Commun. Surv. Tutorials **15**(2), 860–880 (2013). https://doi.org/10.1109/SURV.2012.071812.00124
3. Prabadevi, B., Jeyanthi, N., Abraham, A.: An analysis of security solutions for ARP poisoning attacks and its effects on medical computing. Int. J. Syst. Assur. Eng. Manag., 1–14 (2019)
4. Nenovski, B., Mitrevski, P.: Real-world ARP attacks and packet sniffing, detection and prevention on windows and android devices. In: The 12th International Conference for Informatics and Information Technology (CIIT 2015) (2015)

5. Pidikiti, D.S., Kalluri, R., Senthil Kumar, R.K., Bindhumadhava, B.S.: SCADA communication protocols: vulnerabilities, attacks and possible mitigations. CSI Trans. ICT **1**(2), 135–141 (2013)
6. https://www.ettercap-project.org/
7. https://www.wireshark.org/
8. https://www.vskills.in/certification/tutorial/tag/web-application-attacks/
9. Kalluri, R., Mahendra, L., Senthil Kumar, R.K., Ganga Prasad, G.L., Bindhumadhava, B.S.: Analysis of communication channel attacks on control systems— SCADA in power sector. In: Pillai, R.K., et al. (eds.) ISGW 2017: Compendium of Technical Papers. LNEE, vol. 487, pp. 115–131. Springer, Singapore (2018). https://doi.org/10.1007/978-981-10-8249-8_11
10. Mahendra, L., Kalluri, R., Senthil Kumar, R.K., Bindhumadhava, B.S., Ganga Prasad, G.L.: SCADA research lab kit for educational institutes. IETE J. Educ. (2019) https://doi.org/10.1080/09747338.2019.1628666
11. Wikipedia contributors: Remote terminal unit. Wikipedia, The Free Encyclopedia. Wikipedia, The Free Encyclopedia, 8 February 2020. Web 17 February 2020
12. Shaw, W.T.: SCADA system vulnerabilities to cyber attack. https://electricenergyonline.com/energy/magazine/181/article/SCADA-System-Vulnerabilities-to-Cyber-Attack.htm
13. Yang, Y.: Man-in-the-middle attack test-bed investigating cyber-security vulnerabilities in Smart Grid SCADA systems. In: IET. IEEE Xplore, 04 April 2013

A Large-Scale Investigation to Identify the Pattern of App Component in Obfuscated Android Malwares

Md. Omar Faruque Khan Russel,
Sheikh Shah Mohammad Motiur Rahman$^{(\boxtimes)}$ [iD], and Takia Islam$^{(\boxtimes)}$

Department of Software Engineering, Daffodil International University,
Dhaka, Bangladesh
{russel35-1170,motiur.swe,takia35-1014}@diu.edu.bd

Abstract. Number of smartphone users of android based devices is growing rapidly. Because of the popularity of the android market malware attackers are focusing in this area for their bad intentions. Therefore, android malware detection has become a demanding and rising area to research in information security. Researchers now can effortlessly detect the android malware whose patterns have formerly been recognized. At present, malware attackers commenced to use obfuscation techniques to make the malwares incomprehensible to malware detectors. For this motive, it is urgent to identify the pattern that is used by attackers to obfuscate the malwares. A large-scale investigation has been performed in this paper by developing python scripts to extract the pattern of app components from an obfuscated android malware dataset. Ultimately, the patterns in a matrix form has been established and stored in a Comma Separated Values (CSV) file which will conduct to the primary basis of detecting the obfuscated malwares.

Keywords: Android malware · Obfuscated malware · App component pattern · Pattern identification

1 Introduction

For the expanding number and complicated nature of capacities, android smartphones have become more trendy than other platforms. Other than PCs, smartphones offer a lot more administrations and applications. Unluckily, malware attackers main goal is now obtaining users sensitive information illegally. Financial benefit is the reason to target mobile devices [1]. Android devices can be affected by injecting malicious applications, by spreading malicious spam emails [2] etc. Therefore, it is a popular way to infect malware on Android devices. The easiest way to get access in android, by installing Android Application Packages (APKs) from unknown and unverified application market or sources. To spread malware, in most cases third party sources make a simpler

© Springer Nature Singapore Pte Ltd. 2020
A. Bhattacharjee et al. (Eds.): MIND 2020, CCIS 1241, pp. 513–526, 2020.
https://doi.org/10.1007/978-981-15-6318-8_42

way [3]. Those services that are threat to sensitive information and user's privacy, malicious activity can be performed using background services. These dangerous services normally run by malicious software without user's attention. Some common operations have been performed by malware. For example: stealing text messages, user's contacts, login details, without user's attention, do subscription with premium services [4]. Recent statistics show that in the first quarter of 2018, android based smartphones have been sold worldwide 80% of the smartphone market [5]. As a result, mobile users' personal information is at risk. Malware attackers are exploiting mobile devices restricted areas and taking advantages of absence of standard security, by spreading portable explicit malware that get touchy information, access the client's phone credit or remove access of some device functionalities. 121 thousands new variations of portable malware have been found in China by March 2019. Now-a-days, Code obfuscating alters the program code to create posterity duplicates which have a similar usefulness with various byte grouping. The new code isn't perceived by antivirus scanner [6]. Thus android malware detection has been a tremendous area to research [7]. Various researchers found many solutions and its increasing day by day. Malicious codes behaviour [8], security policies [9,10], intrusion detection system (IDS) [11], privacy specific [12], privilege escalation [13,14] typed specific attacks are focused on those studies to enforce the data security. Some observable downsides exist to those proposed solutions. Quick inconstancy of new keen attacks [15], the utilization of AI methods has been expanded in the digital cyber security area [16]. Two major categories of android malware detection mechanisms [17] are static analysis [18] and dynamic analysis [19]. Distinguishing the suspicious pattern is called Static analysis by reviewing the source code. Static Analysis has been acted in most extreme antivirus organizations. Also, behavior based inspection is known as dynamic analysis [20]. The core contribution of this paper is given below:

- Static analysis has been performed on obfuscated Android malware application.
- Proposed an approach to extract the app component from obfuscated malwares in android.
- The seven obfuscated techniques such as Trivial Encryption, String Encryption, Reflection Encryption, Class Encryption, Combination of Trivial and String Encryption, Combination of Trivial, String and Reflection Encryption, Combination of Trivial, String, Reflection and Class Encryption has been considered.
- The pattern of app components has been represented in matrix.
- Identify the usage trends of app components by Obfuscated Android Malware.

The structure of this paper is organized as follows. The Literature Review is described in Sect. 2. Research methodology is illustrated and described in Sect. 3. Section 4 presents the result analysis and discussion. Section 5 concludes the paper.

2   Literature Review

Application components are the fundamental structure squares of an Android application. Every component is a section point through which the framework or a client can enter your application [21]. These parts are inexactly coupled by the application show record AndroidManifest.xml that depicts every segment of the application and how they connect [22]. Some of them depend on others. Also, Some malware families may have an equivalent name of parts. For instance, a few variations of the DroidKungFumalware utilize a similar name for specific administrations [23] (e.g., com.google.search). There are the following four types of component used in Android application:

- **Activities.** An action is the section point for communicating with the client. It speaks to a solitary screen with a UI. For instance, an email application may have one movement that demonstrates a rundown of new messages, another action to create an email, and another action for perusing messages. In spite of the fact that the exercises cooperate to shape a durable client involvement in the email application, everyone is free of the others. All things considered; an alternate application can begin any of these exercises if the email application permits it. For instance, a camera application can begin the movement in the email application that makes new mail to enable the client to share an image.
- **Services.** An administration is a broadly useful section point for keeping an application running out of sight for a wide range of reasons. An administration is a part that keeps running out of sight to perform long-running activities. An administration does not give a UI. For instance, an administration may play music out of sight while the client is in an alternate application, or it may get information over the system without blocking client connection with a movement.
- **Broadcast Receivers.** A broadcast receiver is a part that empowers the framework to convey occasions to the application outside of standard client stream, permitting the application to react to framework wide communication declarations. Since communication collectors are another all-around characterized section into the application, the framework can convey communicates even to applications that aren't as of now running. Thus, for instance, an application can plan an alert to present a warning on enlightening the client regarding an up and coming occasion... Also, by conveying that caution to a BroadcastReceiver of the application, there is no requirement for the application to stay running until the alert goes off. In spite of the fact that communication recipients don't show a UI, they may make a status bar warning to alarm the client when a communication occasion happens [17].
- **Content Providers.** A content provider part supplies information from one application to others on solicitation. The information might be put away in the record framework, the database or elsewhere altogether. Through the content provider, different applications can inquiry or change the information if the content provider permits it. For instance, the Android framework gives a content provider that deals with the client's contact data. Content providers

are additionally helpful for perusing and composing information that is private to your application and not shared.

In this way, the hugeness of app component pattern has been seen from state-of-art arranged in Table 1 From Table 1, it's been expressed that app component pattern analysis has remarkable impact to develop anti-malware tools or to recognize the malwares in android gadgets.

Table 1. Recent works on android app component to detect malware.

Ref	Feature set	Samples	Accuracy	Year
[22]	8 features including App Component	8,385	99.7%	2017
[24]	4 features including App Component	1,738	97.87%	2012
[25]	7 features including App Component	35,331	98.0%	2018
[26]	3 features including App Component	308	86.36%	2014
[27]	7 features including App Component	19,000	≈99%	2018
[28]	8 features including App Component	5,560	97.0%	2019

2.1 Obfuscated Techniques

By means of the term obfuscation, they [29] suggests that any adjustment of the Android executable bytecode (i.e., .dex file) and/or .xml files (for example AndroidManifest.xml or String.xml), that doesn't influence the key functionalities of the application. They divided techniques into two sets that they obtained. One set is Trivial Obfuscation Techniques and the other set is Non-Trivial Obfuscation Techniques. There are four key principal procedures alongside the blend of those procedures in all out seven [29] methods as indicated by dataset are considered in this analysis.

Trivial Obfuscation Technique. These strategies just adjust strings in the classes.dex record without changing the bytecode directions. This strategy can adjust names everything being equal, techniques, classes, fields and source codes of an Android application with unpredictable letters. Dismantling, reassembling and repacking the classes.dex files are involved for these exercises.

Non-Trivial Obfuscation Strategies. Both strings and byte-codes of the executable are affected by these techniques. Reflection and Class Encryption are pretty much effective against anti-malware systems that explore the bytecode indication to detect malware. Similarly, various kinds of strings (e.g., constants) are changed, and this may handle machines which resort to explore them so as to perform recognition.

- **Reflection.** Reflection is basically the property of a class of evaluating itself, thus, getting information on its strategies, fields, etc. They [25] utilize the reflection property for summons. Three summons are used to return the first: i) forName, finds a class with a specific name ii) getMethod, gives the point object method and iii) conjure, aftereffect of the second summon and plays out the correct conjuring on the technique object. It is utilized distinctly in code advancement under specific circumstances since misuse of bytecode instructions.
- **String Encryption.** This technique obfuscates each string that is described inside a class by infers of a computation subject to XOR tasks. At runtime, the correct string is made by passing the encoded string. In spite of the way that this framework doesn't fall back on DES or AES algorithms, it is significant that it is more puzzling than various techniques for string encryption that have been proposed in the composition, which grasped a Caesar move [30].
- **Class Encryption.** They [29] got this system as generally potential and initiating method from others procedures they received. This obfuscation strategy totally scrambles and shrink (with GZIP calculation) each class and stores its subtleties in an information exhibit. During the execution of the jumbled application, the obfuscated class ought to be first decoded, decompressed, and a while later stacked in memory. This strategy can incredibly manufacture the overhead of the application as a lot of bearings are incorporated. In any case, it makes it greatly difficult for a human specialist to perform static investigation.

3   Methodology

The action plan and procedure used in this study work has demonstrated in Fig. 1 and described in this section.

Dataset. The dataset used in this study that is analyzed is PRAGuard [29, 31], an obfuscated android malware dataset. It contains 10479 samples. MalGenome [32] and the Contagio Minidump datasets [33] samples were obfuscated in this dataset. Seven obfuscation techniques were applied and each technique has 1497 samples.

Environment Used. For examination, HP i5 2.30 GHz 8 GB computerised working environment has been utilized. Working system is Windows 10, Programming language is Python 3.7 and python modules Matplotlib, Pandas, Androguard [34].

Data Preprocessing. As a preprocessing part, APKs are check whether APKs are in great configuration or not. In the wake of preprocessing, 62 APKs were unconsidered. Furthermore, the concluding dataset contains 10,417 obfuscated malware applications where Trivial, String, Reflection, Class, Trivial + String, Trivial + String + Reflection and Trivial + String + Reflection + Class encryption (enc.) with the quantity of tests 1485, 1486, 1486, 1486, 1492, 1492, and 1492 correspondingly.

App Component Extraction. A python script with Androguard has been created to dismantle the APKs. This content can dismantle APKs and concentrate the app component from the APKs. APKs extraction time of each obfuscation technique has taken normal 40 min time on the exploratory condition.

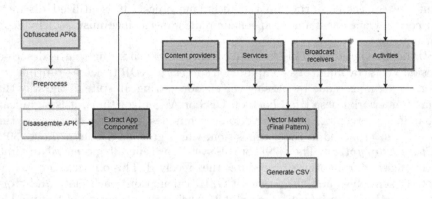

Fig. 1. Overview of proposed approach

Vector Metrics (Final Pattern). In this part a 2D vector metrics pattern are created from the obtaining process of app component. This metric pattern is made up of rows and columns. Columns act for the names of the app component and rows are marked as a 0 or 1. If the app component found in APKs associated with the column, it will be 1 else 0. A comma-separated values file (CSV) produced to represent the pattern. For every APK, one vector matrix has originate. A vector is a list of 0 or 1 which are in a row format.

4   Results and Discussion

This section represents the results obtained from experiments. This section has 7 subsections based on the seven obfuscation techniques. The name of the app component, for example Receiver, MainA, BaseABroadcastReceiver, MainActivity, BootReceiver,..............,NotificationActivity has been denoted as AC_1, AC_2, AC_3, AC_4, AC_5.............., AC_N. The maximum usage of app components are found from four basic techniques: Receiver, c, d, a, g, e, i, MainA etc.

Trivial Encryption (enc.). The APKs which have used only trivial obfuscation techniques are analyzed and got in total 1774 app components are used. Top 50 app components from 1774 are depicted in Fig. 2. The trends of top 27 app components used in trivial encryption technique are found from Fig. 2. Which includes: Receiver, c, d, a, g, i, e, MainA, f, h, b, p, BaseABroadcastReceiver, R, Q, O, M, N, BootReceiver, MainActivity, j, Y, k, NotificationActivity, BaseBroadcastReceiver, OperaUpdaterActivity and AutorunBroadcastReceiver in total 468, 450, 393, 287, 280, 276, 267, 252, 248, 228, 207, 191, 186, 185, 183,

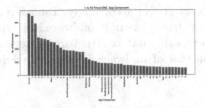

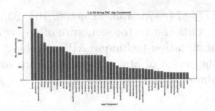

Fig. 2. Top 50 app components used in Trivial encryption technique

Fig. 3. Top 50 app components used in String encryption technique

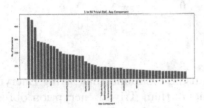

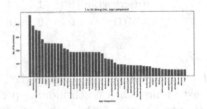

Fig. 4. Top 50 app components used in Reflection encryption technique

Fig. 5. Top 50 app components used in Class encryption technique

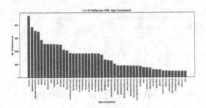

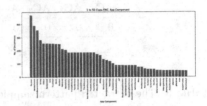

Fig. 6. Top 50 app components used in Trivial + String enc. technique

Fig. 7. Top 50 app components used in Trivial + String + Reflection enc. technique

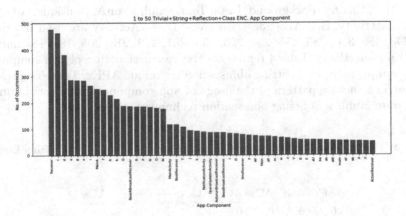

Fig. 8. Top 50 app components used in Trivial + String + Reflection + Class enc. technique

177, 174, 173, 133, 118, 108, 104, 93, 89, 89, 87 APKs accordingly. Table 2 represents the vector structure of app component from a sample malware in trivial obfuscation technique APKs. Table 3 represents the matrix structure pattern of the usage of app component from some samples of malware families in trivial obfuscation techniques APKs.

Table 2. The extracted pattern sample in vector matrix of one APKs (Trivial Encryption).

AC_1	AC_2	AC_3	AC_4	AC_5	————	AC_N
0	0	0	0	1	————	0

Table 3. The extracted pattern sample of family wise APKs (Trivial Encryption).

Family	AC_1	AC_2	AC_3	AC_4	AC_5	————	AC_N
jSMSHider	0	0	0	0	0	————	0
AnserverBot	0	1	1	0	0	————	0
ADRD	0	0	0	1	0	————	0

String Encryption (enc.). From the investigation, it's found that String Encryption technique has much more app components than Trivial encryption obfuscation technique, 2381 number of app components found. The top 50 app component of the string encryption technique has depicted in Fig. 3. The trends of top 15 app components used in string encryption technique are found from Fig. 3. Which includes: Receiver, UpdateService, AdwoAdBrowserActivity, Dialog, Setting, History, Background, Lists, TextDetail, MainA, Boutique, AdActivity, MainActivity, BaseABroadcastReceiver, BaseAActivity are used in around 469, 390, 356, 350, 285, 255, 254, 253, 253, 251, 249, 213, 205, 185, 184 number of APKs respectively. Table 4 represents the vector structure of app component from a sample malware in String obfuscation technique APKs. Table 5 represents the matrix structure pattern of the usage of app component from some samples of malware families in String obfuscation techniques APKs.

Table 4. The extracted pattern sample in vector matrix of one APKs (String Encryption).

AC_1	AC_2	AC_3	AC_4	AC_5	————	AC_N
0	0	0	0	0	————	1

Table 5. The extracted pattern sample of family wise APKs (String Encryption).

Family	AC_1	AC_2	AC_3	AC_4	AC_5	————————	AC_N
DroidKungFu1	1	0	0	0	0	————————	0
Bgserv	0	0	0	0	1	————————	0
KMin	0	0	0	1	1	————————	0

Reflection Encryption (enc.). Second highest number of app components have been used by Reflection enc. 2429 app components applied in this technique. The top 50 app component of the reflection encryption technique has depicted in Fig. 4. The trends of top 15 app components used in string encryption technique are found from Fig. 4. Which are: Receiver, UpdateService, AdwoAdBrowserActivity, Dialog, Setting, History, Background, Lists, TextDetail, MainA, Boutique, AdActivity, MainActivity, BaseABroadcastReceiver, BaseAActivity are used in around 469, 384, 356, 349, 286, 256, 255, 254, 254, 252, 250, 211, 205, 186, 183 number of APKs respectively. Table 6 represents the vector structure of app component from a sample malware in Reflection obfuscation technique APKs. Table 7 represents the matrix structure pattern of the usage of app component from some samples of malware families in Reflection obfuscation techniques APKs.

Table 6. The extracted pattern sample in vector matrix of one APKs (Reflection Encryption).

AC_1	AC_2	AC_3	AC_4	AC_5	————————	AC_N
0	0	0	0	0	————————	1

Table 7. The extracted pattern sample of family wise APKs (Reflection Encryption).

Family	AC_1	AC_2	AC_3	AC_4	AC_5	————————	AC_N
BaseBridge	0	1	0	0	0	————————	0
AnserverBot	0	1	1	0	0	————————	0
DroidKungFu3	1	0	0	1	0	————————	0

Class Encryption (enc.). Highest number of app components have been seen in Class encryption technique. 2733 app components found in this obfuscation technique. The top 50 app component of the class encryption technique has depicted in Fig. 5. The trends of top 15 app components used in class encryption technique are found from Fig. 5. Which are: Receiver, UpdateService, AdwoAdBrowserActivity, Setting, History, Background, Lists, TextDetail, MainA, Boutique, AdActivity, MainActivity, FirstAActivity, SecondAActivity, ThirdAActivity are used in around 468, 389, 355, 281, 255, 254, 253, 253, 251, 249, 211, 204, 186, 186,

186 number of APKs respectively. Table 8 represents the vector structure of app component from a sample malware in Class obfuscation technique APKs. Table 9 represents the matrix structure pattern of the usage of app component from some samples of malware families in Class obfuscation techniques APKs.

Table 8. The extracted pattern sample in vector matrix of one APKs (Class Encryption)

AC_1	AC_2	AC_3	AC_4	AC_5	—————	AC_N
0	0	0	1	0		0

Table 9. The extracted pattern sample of family wise APKs (Class Encryption).

Family	AC_1	AC_2	AC_3	AC_4	AC_5	—————	AC_N
DroidDream	0	0	0	0	0		0
RogueSPPush	0	0	0	1	0		0
YZHC	0	0	0	0	1		0

Combination of Trivial and String Encryption (enc.). 1579 app components have been found from this combination technique. Number of app components usage are less in all combination techniques than all above single obfuscation techniques. Figure 6. depicts the top 50 app components of the Trivial + String encryption technique. The trends of top 27 app components used in class encryption technique are found from Fig. 5. Which are: C, Receiver, d, a, g, e, i, MainA, f, h, b, P, R, Q, BaseABroadcastReceiver, O, N, M, BootReceiver, MainActivity, NotificationActivity, OperaUpdaterActivity, AutorunBroadcastReceiver, Y, k, j, BaseBroadcastReceiver are used around 475, 473, 418, 286, 283, 277, 271, 254, 249, 228, 214, 191, 189, 186, 182, 179, 177, 121, 114, 111, 109, 109, 108, 92, 88, 87 number of APKs respectively. Table 10 represents the vector structure of app component from a sample malware in Trivial + String obfuscation technique APKs. Table 11 represents the matrix structure pattern of the usage of app components from some samples of malware families in Trivial + String obfuscation techniques APKs.

Table 10. The extracted pattern sample in vector matrix of one APKs (Trivial + String Encryption)

AC_1	AC_2	AC_3	AC_4	AC_5	—————	AC_N
0	0	0	0	1		0

Table 11. The extracted pattern sample of family wise APKs (Trivial + String Encryption).

Family	AC_1	AC_2	AC_3	AC_4	AC_5	————	AC_N
FakePlayer	0	0	0	0	0	————	0
zHash	0	0	0	1	0	————	0
AnserverBot	0	1	1	0	0	————	0

Combination of Trivial, String and Reflection Encryption (enc.). Number of app components found from this obfuscation technique is 1439. This is the second lowest amount extracted among all other techniques. Figure 7. depicts the top 50 app components of the Trivial + String + Reflection encryption technique. The trends of top 27 app components used in class encryption technique are found from Fig. 5. Which are: Receiver, c, d, a, g, e, i, MainA, f, h, b, P, R, Q, BaseABroadcastReceiver, N, O, M, MainActivity, BootReceiver, Y, k, NotificationActivity, j, OperaUpdaterActivity, AutorunBroadcastReceiver, BaseBroadcastReceiver are used around 478, 460, 386, 289, 289, 282, 265, 255, 252, 229, 219, 191, 187, 187, 187, 182, 181, 177, 118, 117, 104, 93, 89, 89, 87, 87, 87 number of APKs respectively. Table 12 represents the vector structure of app component from a sample malware in Trivial + String + Reflection obfuscation technique APKs. Table 13 represents the matrix structure pattern of the usage of app component from some samples of malware families in Trivial + String + Reflection obfuscation techniques APKs.

Table 12. The extracted pattern sample in vector matrix of one APKs (Trivial + String + Reflection Encryption)

AC_1	AC_2	AC_3	AC_4	AC_5	————	AC_N
0	0	0	0	1	————	0

Table 13. The extracted pattern sample of family wise APKs (Trivial + String + Reflection Encryption).

Family	AC_1	AC_2	AC_3	AC_4	AC_5	————	AC_N
FakePlayer	0	0	0	0	0	————	0
zHash	0	0	0	1	0	————	0
AnserverBot	0	1	1	0	0	————	0

Table 14. The extracted pattern sample in vector matrix of one APKs (Trivial + String + Reflection + Class Encryption)

AC_1	AC_2	AC_3	AC_4	AC_5	————	AC_N
0	0	0	0	0	————	1

Table 15. The extracted pattern sample of family wise APKs (Trivial + String + Reflection + Class Encryption).

Family	AC_1	AC_2	AC_3	AC_4	AC_5	————	AC_N
GoldDream	0	0	0	0	0	————	0
DroidKungFu2	1	0	0	1	0	————	0
NickySpy	0	0	0	0	1	————	0

Combination of Trivial, String, Reflection and Class Encryption (enc.). Compared to other obfuscation techniques, the lowest number of app components found in this technique, is 1365. Figure 8. depicts the top 50 app components of the Trivial + String + Reflection + Class encryption technique. The trends of top 27 app components used in class encryption technique are found from Fig. 5. Which are: Receiver, c, d, a, g, e, i, MainA, f, h, b, Q, BaseABroadcastReceiver, R, P, N, O, M, MainActivity, BootReceiver, Y, j, k, NotificationActivity, OperaUpdaterActivity, AutorunBroadcastReceiver, BaseBroadcastReceiver are used around 478, 464, 382, 288, 286, 285, 266, 253, 250, 229, 216, 188, 187, 186, 186, 184, 180, 177, 117, 117, 108, 94, 92, 89, 87, 87, 86 number of APKs respectively. Table 14 represents the vector structure of app component from a sample malware in Trivial + String + Reflection + Class obfuscation technique APKs. Table 15 represents the matrix structure pattern of the usage of app component from some samples of malware families in Trivial + String + Reflection + Class obfuscation techniques APKs.

5   Conclusion

From the above study, it's been recapitulated that obfuscated android malwares has trends to use a tremendous number of app components. It's also been observed that the total number of app component usage decreases accordingly with the combination of those techniques. The final pattern obtained from these obfuscation techniques will lead a strong basement to detect the obfuscated android malwares in future.

References

1. Sen, S., Aysan, A.I., Clark, J.A.: SAFEDroid: using structural features for detecting android malwares. In: Lin, X., Ghorbani, A., Ren, K., Zhu, S., Zhang, A. (eds.) SecureComm 2017. LNICSSITE, vol. 239, pp. 255–270. Springer, Cham (2018). https://doi.org/10.1007/978-3-319-78816-6_18
2. Mamoun, A., Roderic, B.: Spam and criminal activity. Trends and Issues in Crime and Criminal Justice (Australian Institute of Criminology) **52** (2016)
3. Arp, D., Spreitzenbarth, M., Hubner, M., Gascon, H., Rieck, K., Siemens, C.E.R.T.: DREBIN: effective and explainable detection of android malware in your pocket. In: NDSS, vol. 14, pp. 23–26 (2014)
4. Saracino, A., Sgandurra, D., Dini, G., Martinelli, F.: Madam: effective and efficient behavior-based android malware detection and prevention. IEEE Trans. Depend. Secure Comput. **15**, 83–97 (2016)
5. Number of smartphones sold to end users worldwide from 2007 to 2020 (in million units). https://www.statista.com/statistics/263437/global-smartphone-sales-to-end-users-since-2007/. Accessed 25 Nov 2019
6. Huda, S., Abawajy, J., Alazab, M., Abdollalihian, M., Islam, R., Yearwood, J.: Hybrids of support vector machine wrapper and filter based framework for malware detection. Fut. Gener. Comput. Syst. **55**, 376–390 (2016)
7. Reina, A., Fattori, A., Cavallaro, L.: A system call-centric analysis and stimulation technique to automatically reconstruct android malware behaviors. EuroSec, April (2013)
8. Alazab, M.: Profiling and classifying the behavior of malicious codes. J. Syst. Softw. **100**, 91–102 (2015)
9. Backes, M., Gerling, S., Hammer, C., Maffei, M., von Styp-Rekowsky, P.: AppGuard – enforcing user requirements on android apps. In: Piterman, N., Smolka, S.A. (eds.) TACAS 2013. LNCS, vol. 7795, pp. 543–548. Springer, Heidelberg (2013). https://doi.org/10.1007/978-3-642-36742-7_39
10. Bugiel, S., Davi, L., Dmitrienko, A., Fischer, T., Sadeghi, A.R., Shastry, B.: Towards taming privilege-escalation attacks on Android". In: NDSS, vol. 17, p. 19 (2012)
11. Vinayakumar, R., Alazab, M., Soman, K.P., Poornachandran, P., Al-Nemrat, A., Venkatraman, S.: Deep learning approach for intelligent intrusion detection system. IEEE Access **7**, 41525–41550 (2019)
12. Gibler, C., Crussell, J., Erickson, J., Chen, H.: AndroidLeaks: automatically detecting potential privacy leaks in android applications on a large scale. In: Katzenbeisser, S., Weippl, E., Camp, L.J., Volkamer, M., Reiter, M., Zhang, X. (eds.) Trust 2012. LNCS, vol. 7344, pp. 291–307. Springer, Heidelberg (2012). https://doi.org/10.1007/978-3-642-30921-2_17
13. Viswanath, H., Mehtre, B.M.: U.S. Patent No. 9,959,406. Washington, DC: U.S. Patent and Trademark Office. (2018)
14. Zhong, X., Zeng, F., Cheng, Z., Xie, N., Qin, X., Guo, S.: Privilege escalation detecting in android applications. In: 2017 3rd International Conference on Big Data Computing and Communications (BIGCOM), pp. 39–44. IEEE (2017)
15. Aafer, Y., Du, W., Yin, H.: DroidAPIMiner: mining API-level features for robust malware detection in android. In: Zia, T., Zomaya, A., Varadharajan, V., Mao, M. (eds.) SecureComm 2013. LNICST, vol. 127, pp. 86–103. Springer, Cham (2013). https://doi.org/10.1007/978-3-319-04283-1_6

16. Demontis, A., et al.: Yes, machine learning can be more secure! a case study on Android malware detection. IEEE Trans. Depend. Secure Comput. (2017)
17. Egele, M., Scholte, T., Kirda, E., Kruegel, C.: A survey on automated dynamic malware-analysis techniques and tools. ACM Comput. Surv. (CSUR) **44**(2), 6 (2012)
18. Papadopoulos, H., Georgiou, N., Eliades, C., Konstantinidis, A.: Android malware detection with unbiased confidence guarantees. Neurocomputing (2017)
19. Shabtai, A., Moskovitch, R., Elovici, Y., Glezer, C.: Detection of malicious code by applying machine learning classifiers on static features: a state-of-the-art survey. Inf. Secur. Techn. Rep., **14**(1), 16–29 (2009)
20. Burguera, I., Zurutuza, U., Nadjm-Tehrani, S.: Crowdroid: behavior-based malware detection system for android. In: Proceedings of the 1st ACM Workshop on Security and Privacy in Smartphones and Mobile Devices, pp. 15–26. ACM (2011)
21. App components. https://developer.android.com/guide/components/fundamentals. Accessed 25 Nov 2019
22. Wang, X., Zhang, D., Xin, S., Li, W.: Mlifdect: android malware detection based on parallel machine learning and information fusion. Security and Communication Networks **2017** (2017)
23. Android - Application Components. https://www.tutorialspoint.com/android/android_application_components.htm. Accessed 25 Nov 2019
24. Wu, D.-J., Mao, C.-H., Wei, T.-E., Lee, H.M., Wu, K.P.: Droidmat: android malware detection through manifest and API calls tracing. In: 2012 Seventh Asia Joint Conference on Information Security, pp. 62–69. IEEE (2012)
25. Kim, T.G., Kang, B., Rho, M., Sezer, S., Im, E.G.: A multimodal deep learning method for android malware detection using various features. IEEE Trans. Inf. Foren. Secur. **14**(3), 773–788 (2018)
26. Shen, T., Yibing, Z., Zhi, X., Bing, M., Huang, H.: Detect android malware variants using component based topology graph. In: 2014 IEEE 13th International Conference on Trust, Security and Privacy in Computing and Communications, pp. 406–413. IEEE (2014)
27. Li, C., Mills, K., Niu, D., Zhu, R., Zhang, H., Kinawi, H.: Android malware detection based on factorization machine. IEEE Access **7**, 184008–184019 (2019)
28. Motiur Rahman, S.S.M., Saha, S.K.: StackDroid: evaluation of a multi-level approach for detecting the malware on android using stacked generalization. In: Santosh, K.C., Hegadi, R.S. (eds.) RTIP2R 2018. CCIS, vol. 1035, pp. 611–623. Springer, Singapore (2019). https://doi.org/10.1007/978-981-13-9181-1_53
29. Maiorca, D., Ariu, D., Corona, I., Aresu, M., Giacinto, G.: Stealth attacks: an extended insight into the obfuscation effects on android malware. Comput. Secur. **51**, 16–31 (2015)
30. Rastogi, V., Chen, Y., Jiang, X.: Droidchameleon: evaluating android anti-malware against transformation attacks. In: Proceedings of the 8th ACM SIGSAC Symposium on Information, Computer and Communications Security, pp. 329–334. ACM (2013)
31. Android PRAGuard Dataset. http://pralab.diee.unica.it/en/AndroidPRAGuard Dataset. Accessed 25 Nov 2019
32. MalGenome. http://www.malgenomeproject.org/. Accessed 25 Nov 2019
33. Contagio. http://contagiominidump.blogspot.com/. Accessed 25 Nov 2019
34. Androguard. https://github.com/androguard/androguard. Accessed 25 Nov 2019

An AHP-TOPSIS Based Framework for the Selection of Node Ranking Techniques in Complex Networks

Kushal Kanwar$^{(\boxtimes)}$, Sakshi Kaushal, and Harish Kumar

UIET, Panjab University, Chandigarh 160014, India
kushalneo@gmail.com, {sakshi,harishk}@pu.ac.in

Abstract. Disparate natural and artificial systems are modelled as complex networks to understand their structural properties and dynamics of phenomena occurring on them. Identification of key components (nodes) of a complex network and ranking them has both theoretical and practical applications. The node ranking techniques are compared on three categories of criteria, namely, Differentiation, Accuracy and Computational Efficiency. Having multiple criteria for technique selection and a number of alternative ranking techniques available renders ranking technique selection in the domain of complex networks as Multi-Criteria Decision Making (MCDM) problem. A number of MCDM methods are accessible in the literature, but no treatment is available for the selection of node ranking techniques based on systematic decision making. In this paper, Analytic Hierarchy Process (AHP), followed by Technique for Order Preference by Similarity to Ideal Solution (TOPSIS), are used in tandem to propose a framework that objectively compares and select node ranking techniques for complex networks. The working of the proposed framework is demonstrated with a dataset of complex networks.

Keywords: MCDM · AHP · TOPSIS · Node ranking · Technique selection · Complex networks

1 Introduction

Complex networks around us are in diverse forms such as social networks, infrastructure networks, technological networks, brain networks, ecological networks, metabolite networks and so on [1]. A complex network can be modelled as undirected graph $G = (V, E)$ where $V = \{v_1, v_2, v_3, ..., v_{|V|}\}$ is the set of nodes and it represents entities of complex network and $E = \{e_1, e_2, e_3, ..., e_{|E|}\}$ is the set of edges and it encodes interaction among entities. Studying the structure of complex networks and dynamical phenomena occurring over them is a challenging task due to the existence of multiple interacting entities. Complex networks have a multitude of nodes, and it is infeasible to study them all together. Hence, it is advantageous to select a few important nodes to study as it saves time and effort. Node ranking techniques have applications in viral marketing,

© Springer Nature Singapore Pte Ltd. 2020
A. Bhattacharjee et al. (Eds.): MIND 2020, CCIS 1241, pp. 527–542, 2020.
https://doi.org/10.1007/978-981-15-6318-8_43

information dissemination, finding important points in infrastructure networks, inducting health awareness and so on. A number of ranking techniques are available in literature and new ones are being reported regularly [2,4,5,8,9,13,16–19,22,23,25,27,29]. Based on the nature of the information used, node ranking techniques for unweighted undirected networks are classified into four categories, i.e., local, semi-local, global and hybrid. Further, node ranking techniques are compared on a set of evaluation parameters (criteria) like Differentiation, Accuracy and Computational Efficiency. Results of evaluation parameters are usually presented in tabular or graphical form. In literature, no method is available that accommodates domain knowledge and user requirement for selection of a node ranking technique given a set of node ranking technique(s) and complex network(s). In this scenario, the following decision making issue needs to be addressed:

"which node ranking technique(s) is most suitable for a given complex network(s) under user requirements and application constraints."

Further, this issue has following specific depictions:

- Which node ranking technique is best for a given complex network?
- Which node raking technique is best for specific types of complex networks?
- Which node ranking technique is best for a mixed dataset of complex networks?
- Which category of node ranking techniques performs better overall on evaluation parameters?

An amalgamation of domain knowledge and systematic judgement is required to address these issues. These issues can be modelled as Multi-Criteria Decision Making (MCDM) problem (described in Sect. 2) and can be solved by using AHP and TOPSIS in tandem, called as AHP-TOPSIS method [10,11,21]. Analytic Hierarchy Process (AHP) method allows merging domain knowledge and subjective judgment to derive relative weights for each criterion under consideration for decision making that assimilates application constraints and user requirements [21]. Whereas, Technique for Order Preference by Similarity to Ideal Solution (TOPSIS) is a well established and well suited technique for solving MCDM problems. It is used to systematically order the alternative solutions (node ranking techniques in our case) as per the chosen criteria [10,11]. In this paper, an AHP-TOPSIS based framework is proposed to give solutions to the above stated issues.

The rest of the paper is organized in the following sections. The parameters on which ranking techniques can be compared and how to model node ranking technique selection as an MCDM problem are given in Sect. 2. The description of AHP and TOPSIS is given in Sect. 3. Section 4 demonstrates the working of AHP-TOPSIS based framework to address above stated issues. Conclusion and future scope is given in Sect. 5.

2   Background

This section presents the detail of different node ranking techniques and how their selection can be viewed as a Multi-Criteria Decision Making (MCDM) problem. In first subsection, five node ranking techniques are presented which have been further used to demonstrate the working of proposed framework. The second subsection includes details of evaluation criteria for ranks produced by node ranking techniques.

2.1   Node Ranking Techniques

A brief description of node ranking techniques that are used to demonstrate the working of proposed framework is as follows:

– Degree Centrality (D) is the oldest centrality measure used to quantify influence of a node in the graphs [9]. The influence of a node is computed as number of its immediate neighbours, i.e., degree.
– k-shell (KS) decomposition assigns an index, namely, k_s to every node to assign it a coreness score [13]. This method works in passes, and a pass can go through multiple iterations. In the first pass, 1-degree nodes are removed, unless remaining nodes have a degree greater ≥ 2. All removed nodes are assigned the value as, $k_s = 1$. In the second pass, 2-degree nodes are removed unless the remaining nodes have a degree ≥ 3. The nodes removed in this step are assigned the value as, $k_s = 2$. This process is repeated until all nodes are assigned a k_s value and hence removed from the graph.
– Extended Neighborhood Coreness (Cnc+): As per this method, a node is considered more influential if it has neighbors with high k_s value, i.e., neighbors being close to the core of the graph [2]. The information of k_s index of the first and second-order neighborhood is used to improve the ranking accuracy. The Neighbourhood Coreness Centrality ($C_{nc}(v)$) for a node v is defined as Eq. (1):

$$C_{nc}(v) = \sum_{u \in N_v} k_s(u) \tag{1}$$

where N_v is set of neighbours of v, and $k_s(u)$ is k_s index of node u, such that $u \in N_v$. The extended neighborhood coreness centrality ($C_{nc} + (v)$) for a node v is given in Eq. (2):

$$C_{nc+}(v) = \sum_{u \in N_v} C_{nc}(u) \tag{2}$$

– k-shell Iteration Factor (KSIF) is also derived from the k-shell decomposition method. In this method, the same process of the k-shell decomposition is followed but nodes with the same k_s index are assigned differently centralities by taking account of iteration in each step of the k-shell [25]. The δ value for each node v is computed using Eq. (3):

$$\delta(v) = k_s(1 + n/m) \tag{3}$$

where n is the total number of iterations in s^{th} pass of k-shell decomposition and m is the iterations within the sth pass in which v is removed. For example, suppose total 7 iteration are required to remove all 1-degree nodes (1st pass) and a node v_c (a 1-degree node) gets removed in 4th iteration, then for this node v_c, $k_s = 1$, $m = 7$ and $n = 4$. Finally, Influence Capability (IC) of node v in KSIF method is defined as per Eq. (4):

$$IC(v) = \delta(v)d_v + \sum_{u \in N_v} \delta(u) * d_u \qquad (4)$$

where d_u and N_v are degree and set of neighbours of the nodes u and v, *respectively.*

– Zareie and Sheikhahmadi, improvised the k-shell method and named it Hirearicahl k-shell (HKS) method [27]. HKS value for a node v is computed using Spreading influence ($S(v)$) as Eq. (5):

$$HKS(v) = \sum_{u \in N_v} S(u) \qquad (5)$$

where $S(v)$ is defined as follows:

$$S(v) = \sum_{u \in N_v} d_u(b_u + f_u) \qquad (6)$$

In Eq. (6), b_u and f_u stands for b value and f value of node u, respectively. The procedure to compute b and f values is given in [27]. This method is highly formidable because it has the capability to assign different ranks to nodes with high accuracy.

These techniques act as alternative solutions when node ranking technique selection is viewed as MCDM problem.

2.2   Evaluation Criteria for Node Ranking Techniques

In this subsection, it is explained how to evaluate ranks produced by a node ranking technique. The ranks produced by a node ranking technique for the nodes of a graph are evaluated on a set of three criteria, namely, Differentiation, Accuracy and Computational Efficiency.

– *Differentiation* is the ability of a ranking technique to assign different ranks to the nodes. Monotonicity (M) [2], number of nodes (NN) [18,27] in different ranks and complimentary commutative distribution function (CCDF) [27] are the methods to assess differentiation ability of a ranking technique. NN and CCDF are methods of visual comparison while Monotonicity (M) is a value in the range [0, 1]. Further, the results of M, NN and CCDF are highly correlated, therefore, only M is used in the proposed work.

- *Correctness* of a ranking technique is its ability to generate correct ranks. It is assessed by comparing ranks generated by ranking technique and influence scores given by Susceptible-Infected-Recovered (SIR) simulation to the nodes of the graph [12,20]. Kendall's Tau (τ) and Rank-Biased Overlap (RBO) are the two measures to assess correctness [12,26]. The value of Kendall's Tau (τ) varies in the range $[0, 1]$, where 0 represents no correlation between ranks given by ranking technique and influence scores of SIR simulation, 1 represents identical ranking/scoring by both. RBO value varies in the range $[-1, 1]$, where -1, 0, and 1 represent negative correlation, no correlation, and a total correlation, respectively, between ranks of ranking technique and influence scores given by SIR simulation.
- *Computation Efficiency* of a ranking algorithm is the time efficiency of a ranking algorithm. Conventionally, time efficiency of an algorithm is evaluated with $\mathcal{O}(n^c)$ notation [24] and empirical running time, here c is a real constant and n is the input size of the problem [6]. In proposed framework, all ranking algorithms have same input size (n, i.e., number of nodes in the graph) and expression for their computation complexity is $\mathcal{O}(n^c)$. Theoretically, comparing real number c (exponent of n) among algorithms is the best idea to evaluate computational efficiency of a ranking algorithm. Although, $\mathcal{O}(n^c)$ notation is very useful to compare computational performance of ranking algorithms but with same expression algorithms can have significant difference in their Empirical Running Time (ERT) due to hidden constants [6]. In this paper, ERT is also used as a sub-criterion under computational efficiency. A pass is the one iteration performed over all the nodes of a graph in the process of generating ranks and in this way a ranking technique can be a single pass or multi-pass method. The number of passes taken by a ranking algorithm is named as Iteration Count (IC). IC is useful in comparing ranking algorithms' ability to compute ranks with less number of operations, and less the value of IC is, better it is.

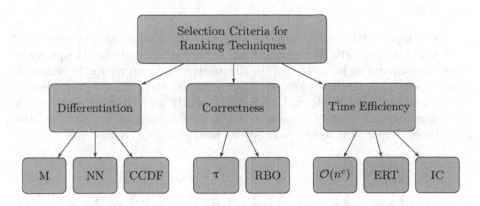

Fig. 1. Criteria and Sub-criteria for ranking technique selection.

Whenever a new node ranking technique is proposed, results of the same are analyzed and compared with existing state of the art methods and are usually presented in tabular or graphical form. Since, it is not possible for a ranking technique to be the best on all criteria, hence to objectively select the most suitable node ranking technique for a given dataset(s), a concrete procedure is required.

Multi-criteria Decision Making (MCDM) methods are used for systematic selection of alternative solutions given a selection criteria. This work presents that MCDM methods can be deployed for the systematic selection of ranking techniques. As shown in Fig. 1, ranking techniques act as alternative solutions and Monotonicity (M), Kendall's Tau (τ), Rank-Biased Overlap (RBO), constant c of $\mathcal{O}(n^c)$, Empirical Running Time (ERT) and Iteration Count (IC) functions as selection criteria. A number of methods are available for solving MCDM problems [7,28]. Among these methods, Analytic Hierarchy Process (AHP) and Technique for Order Preference by Similarity to Ideal Solution (TOPSIS) methods are used in tandem (AHP-TOPSIS) to establish a framework for systematic selection of ranking technique [3,7,10,11,21,28]. It is chosen because it is easy to comprehend and is successfully applied to other similar decision making problems. Also, the results produced by TOPSIS have high correlation to other frequently used MCDM methods.

3   AHP and TOPSIS Based Framework for Node Ranking Technique Selection

In this section, proposed framework is presented that systematically resolve the issues related to node ranking techniques selection. Figure 2 schematically presents the proposed framework. The following section presents the details of AHP and TOPSIS methods.

3.1   AHP

Saaty developed AHP method to model subjective decision making process based on multiple criteria [21]. The central idea of AHP is to synthesize the priorities based on comparative judgement of the alternatives and the criteria. In this work, Monotonicity (M), Kendall's Tau (τ), RBO, ERT, IC and c of $\mathcal{O}(n^c)$ are selection criteria and ranking techniques D, KS, Cnc+, KSIF and HKS are alternatives. For comparison of a set of criteria in a pairwise fashion as per their relative importance weight, a pair-wise comparison matrix is used as shown in (7):

$$
A = \begin{bmatrix} a_{11} & \cdots & a_{1j} & \cdots & a_{1m} \\ \vdots & & \vdots & & \vdots \\ a_{i1} & \cdots & a_{ij} & \cdots & a_{im} \\ \vdots & & \vdots & & \vdots \\ a_{m1} & \cdots & a_{mj} & \cdots & a_{mm} \end{bmatrix}, a_{ii} = 1, a_{ij} = 1/a_{ji}, (\forall a_{ij} \in A, a \neq 0) \quad (7)
$$

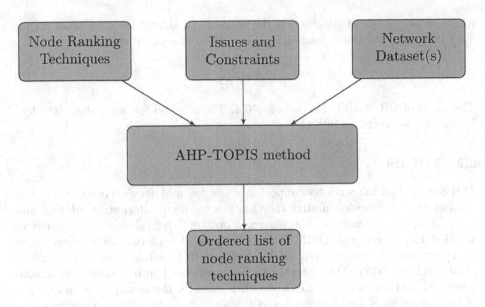

Fig. 2. AHP-TOPSIS based framework for node ranking technique selection.

where a_1, a_2, ..., a_m are criteria. Table 1 give linguistic terms for comparing two criteria and corresponding weights, intermediate weights 2, 4, 6 and 8 can be used to accommodate intermediate judgments for comparison of criteria. The comparative weights are obtained by computing the eigenvector W with respect to highest eigenvalue (λ_{max}) of the matrix A and it satisfies the relation (8):

$$A \cdot W = \lambda_{max} \cdot W \tag{8}$$

Table 1. The weights

Weight	Interpretation
1	Equally important
3	Slightly more important
5	Strongly more important
7	Demonstrably more important
9	Absolutely more important

Consistency index (CI) and consistency ratio (CR) are computed to ascertain the consistency of the subjective perception and the accuracy of the comparative weights. The CI is computed as (9):

$$CI = \frac{\lambda_{max} - m}{m - 1} \tag{9}$$

where m is number of criteria and the value of CI should be lower than 0.1 for a confident result. The consistency ratio (CR) is computed as (10):

$$CR = \frac{CI}{RI} \tag{10}$$

The value of CR should also be below 0.1. The method for computing Random Index (RI) is described in [21].

3.2 TOPSIS

TOPSIS method takes relative importance weights and decision matrix as inputs to operate. The decision matrix (DM) is $n \times m$, for n alternative solution and m criteria; $(i, j)^{th}$ entry of the matrix represents the value of ith alternative solution for j^{th} criteria. TOPSIS method ranks the alternative solution based on their closeness to positive ideal solution (PIS) and farness from negative ideal solution (NIS). The criteria can be categorized into beneficial and non-beneficial attributes depending upon their nature, for example, running time of an algorithm is non-beneficial and it should be minimized and accuracy is beneficial and should be maximized.

TOPSIS method consists of following steps:

1. Obtain the normalize decision (ND) matrix by normalizing the columns using following expression (11):

$$nd_{ij} = \frac{x_{ij}}{\sqrt{\sum_{i=1}^{n} x_{ij}^2}}, \; j = 1, 2, \ldots, m; \quad i = 1, 2, \ldots, n. \tag{11}$$

   where x_{ij} is the $(i, j)^{th}$ entry of Decision Matrix (DM).
2. Multiply the jth column of normalized decision matrix by corresponding relative weight W_j obtained in Eq. (8) using AHP method, described in Subsect. 3.1. This results in a weighted and normalized decision matrix (V) computed using Eq. (12):

$$V_{ij} = nd_{ij} W_j, \; j = 1, 2, \ldots, m; \quad i = 1, 2, \ldots, n. \tag{12}$$

3. PIS is a vector which contains maximum value from normalized decision matrix (V) for beneficial attribute (criteria) and minimum value for non-beneficial attribute, Eqs. (13) and (14):

$$PIS = \{V_1^+, V_2^+, \ldots, V_m^+\}, \; j = 1, 2, \ldots, m. \tag{13}$$

$$V_i^+ = \begin{cases} max(V(:, i)), & \text{If } i^{th} \text{ attribute is beneficial.} \\ min(V(:, i)), & \text{If } i^{th} \text{ attribute is non-beneficial.} \end{cases} \tag{14}$$

4. NIS is a vector which contains minimum value from normalized decision matrix (V) for beneficial attribute (criteria) and maximum value for non-beneficial attribute, Eqs. (15) and (16):

$$NIS = \{V_1^-, V_2^-, \ldots, V_m^-\}, \ j = 1, 2, \ldots, m. \tag{15}$$

$$V_i^- = \begin{cases} min(V(:, i)), & \text{If } i^{th} \text{ attribute is beneficial.} \\ max(V(:, i)), & \text{If } i^{th} \text{ attribute is non-beneficial.} \end{cases} \tag{16}$$

5. To evaluate goodness of an alternative solution, its distance is computed from both PIS and NIS using Euclidean distance as given in Eqs. (17) and (18):

$$S_i^+ = \sqrt{\sum_{j=1}^{m}(V_{ij} - PIS_j)^2}, \ j = 1, 2, \ldots, m; \ i = 1, 2, \ldots, n. \tag{17}$$

$$S_i^- = \sqrt{\sum_{j=1}^{m}(V_{ij} - NIS_j)^2}, \ j = 1, 2, \ldots, m; \ i = 1, 2, \ldots, n. \tag{18}$$

6. The relative closeness to the PIS is computed as shown in Eq. (19):

$$C_i = \frac{S_i^-}{S_i^+ + S_i^-}, \ i = 1, 2, \ldots, n.; \ 0 \leq C_i \leq 1. \tag{19}$$

The higher value of C_i implies that rank is better.

4 Application of AHP-TOPSIS Based Method for Ranking Technique Selection

In this section, application of TOPSIS method in conjunction with AHP is demonstrated for node ranking technique selection.

4.1 Dataset for Demonstration

To demonstrate the ranking by TOPSIS method, a dataset of seven networks is chosen [14,15] as shown in Table 2, where d_{max}, d_{avg}, r, and C stand for maximum degree, average degree, assortativity, and Cluster Coefficient, respectively [1]. Further, five simple ranking techniques, *namely*, Degree (D) [9], k-shell decomposition (KS) [13], Neighborhood Coreness (Cnc+) [2], k-shell iteration factor (KSIF) [25] and hierarchical k-shell (HKS) [27] are chosen as alternatives for demonstration. In Table 3, Monotonicity (M) and its average is given for chosen ranking methods for dataset mentioned in Table 2. In Table 4, the values for Kendall's Tau (τ) are mentioned along with epidemic threshold (β_{th}) and rate of infection (β) for each network. The rate of infection (β) is the value slightly above β_{th} with which SIR simulation has been performed [20]. SIR simulation is repeated for 1000 times and the average number of recovered nodes are recorded as influence score of a node.

Table 2. A small dataset of complex networks with statistical properties.

Name	$|V|$	$|E|$	d_{max}	d_{avg}	r	C
Zebra	27	111	14	8.2222	0.71770	0.8759
Karate	34	78	17	4.5882	−0.47561	0.5706
Contiguous	49	107	8	4.3673	0.23340	0.4967
Copperfield	112	425	49	7.5892	−0.12935	0.1728
Netscience	379	914	34	4.8232	−0.0817	0.7412
Euroroad	1174	1417	10	2.1440	0.12668	0.0167
Chicago	1467	1298	12	1.7696	−0.50402	0.0000

Table 3. The monotonicity (M) values for selected ranking techniques.

Name	M(D)	M(KS)	M(Cnc+)	M(KSIF)	M(HKS)
Zebra	0.5786	0.3478	0.8786	0.8786	0.8786
Karate	0.7079	0.4958	0.9472	0.9542	0.9542
Contiguous	0.6973	0.1666	0.9848	0.9949	1.0
Copperfield	0.8661	0.5990	0.9968	0.9997	0.9997
Netscience	0.7642	0.6421	0.9893	0.9947	0.9947
Euroroad	0.4442	0.2129	0.9175	0.9632	0.9963
Chicago	0.0530	0.0000	0.4115	0.6049	0.7660
Average value	0.5873	0.3520	0.8751	0.9129	0.9414

Table 4. The Kendall's Tau (τ) values for selected ranking techniques.

Name	β_{th}	β	$\tau(D)$	$\tau(KS)$	$\tau(Cnc+)$	$\tau(KSIF)$	$\tau(HKS)$
Zebra	0.091	0.10	0.7415	0.7308	0.8504	0.8504	0.8504
Karate	0.129	0.15	0.7462	0.6819	0.8745	0.8224	0.8332
Contiguous	0.203	0.25	0.7519	0.6282	0.8852	0.8914	0.9201
Copperfield	0.073	0.10	0.8586	0.8231	0.8733	0.8516	0.9079
Netscience	0.125	0.15	0.6003	0.5549	0.8246	0.7941	0.8811
Euroroad	0.333	0.35	0.6001	0.6042	0.8198	0.7975	0.8633
Chicago	0.185	0.20	0.3706	0.0000	0.7112	0.6992	0.7139
Average value	–	–	0.6670	0.5747	0.8341	0.8152	0.8528

Table 5. The RBO values for selected ranking techniques at $p = 0.9$.

Name	RBO(D)	RBO(KS)	RBO(Cnc+)	RBO(KSIF)	RBO(HKS)
Zebra	0.4173	0.4696	0.6353	0.6256	0.6353
Karate	0.7918	0.4648	0.7983	0.5934	0.7839
Contiguous	0.6136	0.1891	0.8277	0.8278	0.8777
Copperfield	0.8238	0.2333	0.7843	0.7692	0.8197
Netscience	0.4709	0.6916	0.8058	0.729	0.8550
Euroroad	0.2967	0.051	0.6296	0.596	0.6307
Chicago	0.0140	0.0002	0.5795	0.6779	0.6315
Average value	0.4897	0.2999	0.7229	0.6884	0.7477

Last row in the Table 4 shows the average value of ranking techniques over seven networks. RBO values for all five ranking techniques over seven datasets is shown in Table 5, and in last row, the average of each technique is mentioned in corresponding column. The value for c of $\mathcal{O}(n^c)$ and iteration count (IC) is tabulated in Table 6 and empirical running time (ERT) is mentioned in Table 7.

Table 6. The c value of $\mathcal{O}(n^c)$ and Iteration Count (IC) for all ranking techniques.

Technique	c	IC
Degree	1	1
KS	1	1
Cnc+	1	3
KSIF	1	2
HKS	1	4

Table 7. Running time of ranking techniques for all seven datasets.

Name	D	KS	Cnc+	KSIF	HKS
Zebra	0.0009	0.0017	0.0034	0.0017	0.0067
Karate	0.0006	0.0011	0.0022	0.0018	0.0062
Contiguous	0.0012	0.0024	0.0047	0.0017	0.0064
Copperfield	0.0029	0.0057	0.0114	0.0061	0.0215
Netscience	0.0084	0.0168	0.0335	0.0162	0.0596
Euroroad	0.0263	0.0526	0.1051	0.0330	0.1328
Chicago	0.0123	0.0247	0.0493	0.0361	0.0787
Average value	0.0075	0.0150	0.0299	0.0138	0.0446

4.2   Criteria Weighting Using AHP

To derive criteria weights using AHP comparison matrix is formed by selecting Monotonicity (M), Kendall's Tau (τ), RBO, c of $\mathcal{O}(n^c)$, ERT and IC as criteria (or decision making attributes). In Table 8, relative importance matrix for six selected attributes is shown. The relative weights are derived with the help of following important points:

- A ranking method should have high accuracy as well as it must be theoretically computationally efficient.
- Theoretically computationally efficient is more important then ERT and IC.
- High differentiation of a ranking technique is desirable but accuracy is preferred over differentiation.
- IC is least sought after feature since $\mathcal{O}(n^c)$ and ERT is more important.

In Table 9, weight of the attribute and whether it is beneficial or non-beneficial is mentioned. The beneficial criteria is depicted by $+1$ and a -1 represents a non-beneficial attribute (criteria). The values obtained for CI is 0.0703 and CR is 0.0567. Both are less than 0.1, hence, it implies that weights are reliable.

Table 8. Comparison Matrix

	τ	RBO	c	M	ERT	IC
τ	1	1	1	3	3	5
RBO	1	1	1	3	3	5
c	1	1	1	3	3	5
M	1/3	1/3	1/3	1	3	5
ERT	1/3	1/3	1/3	1/3	1	5
IC	1/5	1/5	1/5	1/5	1/5	1

Table 9. Weights obtained via AHP and Beneficial/Non-beneficial criteria.

	τ	RBO	c	M	ERT	IC
AHP Weights	0.2467	0.2467	0.2467	0.1289	0.0931	0.0380
(Non)Beneficial	$+1$	$+1$	-1	$+1$	-1	-1

4.3   Ranking via TOPSIS Method

TOPSIS is applied in this section to address two issues raised in Sect. 1 of this paper. The solution of first and third issue is demonstrated here and on the same line others can be resolved. The **first issue** is "Which node ranking technique is best for a given complex network". To address this issue using TOPSIS method, "Zebra" network is chosen and Table 10 represents decision matrix for this purpose and values are taken from Tables 3, 4, 5, 6, and 7. The PIS and NIS are computed using Eqs. 13 and 16, *respectively*. The distances from the PIS and NIS and the relative closeness (C_i) to the ideal solution are computed using Eqs. (17, 18, 19) and the results are listed in Table 11. The result shows that KSIF is best technique for ranking nodes of "Zebra" network followed by Degree (D) and Cnc+ methods as per the chosen criteria and relative weights derived by AHP method.

To resolve **third issue**, *i.e.*, "Which node ranking technique is best for a mixed dataset of complex networks?", TOPSIS method is applied on decision matrix given in Table 12. The data for this Decision matrix is average value of criteria corresponding to ranking technique extracted from Tables 3, 4, 5, 6, and 7.

Table 10. Decision matrix for Zebra network.

Name	M	τ	RBO	c	ERT	IC
Degree (D)	0.5786	0.7415	0.4173	1	0.0009	1
k-core (KS)	0.3478	0.7308	0.4696	1	0.0017	1
Cnc+	0.8786	0.8504	0.6353	1	0.0034	3
KSIF	0.8786	0.8504	0.6256	1	0.0017	2
HKS	0.8786	0.8504	0.6353	1	0.0067	4

Table 11. TOPSIS ranks for ranking technique for Zebra network.

Alternative	S_i^+	S_i^-	C_i	Rank
Degree (D)	0.0022	0.0081	0.7868	2
k-shell (KS)	0.0067	0.0049	0.4242	5
Cnc+	0.0029	0.0080	0.7342	3
KSIF	0.0018	0.0101	0.8483	1
HKS	0.0069	0.0065	0.4818	4

Table 12. Decision matrix for dataset of Table 2

Name	M	τ	RBO	c	ERT	IC
Degree (D)	0.5747	0.6670	0.4897	1	0.0075	1
k-core (KS)	0.3520	0.5747	0.2999	1	0.0150	1
Cnc+	0.8751	0.8341	0.7229	1	0.0299	3
KSIF	0.9129	0.8152	0.6884	1	0.0138	2
HKS	0.9414	0.8528	0.7477	1	0.0446	4

Table 13. TOPSIS ranks for ranking technique on dataset given in Table 2

Alternative	S_i^+	S_i^-	C_i	Rank
Degree (D)	0.0047	0.0073	0.6101	2
k-shell (KS)	0.0090	0.0092	0.5047	4
Cnc+	0.0074	0.0077	0.5116	3
KSIF	0.0051	0.0105	0.6742	1
HKS	0.0104	0.0088	0.4584	5

Algorithm 1. Procedure for evaluating performance of different category of node ranking technique.

Input: Weights obtained by AHP method.

Step 1: Select a dataset of complex networks as per the requirement.

Step 2: Choose all categories of ranking techniques that needs to be compared and name their group as $RT_1, RT_2, ..., RT_n$.

Step 3: Compute average values of Monotonicity (M), Kendall's Tau (τ), Rank-Biased Overlap (RBO), constant c of $\mathcal{O}(n^c)$, Empirical Running Time (ERT) and Iteration Count (IC) for each group RT_i, $i \in 1, 2, ..., n$ for selected dataset.

Step 4: Create a decision matrix where rows corresponds to i^{th} group of ranking techniques (RT_i) and columns corresponds to decision criteria Monotonicity (M), Kendall's Tau (τ), Rank-Biased Overlap (RBO), constant c of $\mathcal{O}(n^c)$, Empirical Running Time (ERT) and Iteration Count (IC). The entries of this matrix are filled from average values obtained from previous step.

Step 5: Apply TOPSIS on decision matrix formulated in **Step 4** to obtain ranks for group of techniques.

The PIS and NIS was computed using Eqs. 13 and 16, *respectively*. The distances from the PIS and NIS is the relative closeness (C_i) to the ideal solution and are computed using Eqs. (17, 18, 19) and the results are given in Table 13. The result shows that KSIF is the best technique for dataset given in Table 2 followed by Degree (D) and Cnc+ methods as per the selection criteria and relative weights derived by AHP method. Whenever there is change in relative importance matrix (designed by other domain expert) for the same dataset, the ranks may change. This is suitable for accommodating application requirements and resource constraints.

The **second issue**, *i.e.*, "Which node ranking technique is best for specific types of complex networks?" can be resolved as follows. Select a dataset of complex networks originating from a specific domain and alternative ranking techniques. Compute the values and average of Monotonicity (M), Kendall's Tau (τ), Rank-Biased Overlap (RBO), constant c of $\mathcal{O}(n^c)$, Empirical Running Time (ERT) and Iteration Count (IC). Then create decision matrix and obtain ranks by TOPSIS method as done for **third issue**. The **fourth issue**, *i.e.*, "Which category of node ranking techniques performs better overall?" can be addressed by procedure given in **Algorithm** 1. It includes the steps to determine which category of node ranking techniques is better compared to others for complex networks.

Hence, the proposed framework is able to address the issues related to the selection of node ranking techniques for complex networks in a systematic and user-oriented manner.

5   Conclusion and Future Scope

In this paper, it is proposed that MCDM methods can be deployed for the systematic selection of ranking techniques in a user-oriented manner. An AHP-TOPSIS based framework is presented to objectively select and provide solutions for issues of node ranking technique selection for complex networks. It enables accommodation of domain knowledge and expert's judgment, and it is better than traditional approaches. The utility of the proposed framework is demonstrated using a dataset of complex networks to address issues related to node ranking technique selection. Further, a domain expert can create own relative importance matrix according to the resource constraints and application requirements to select the most suitable node ranking technique.

In future, AHP-TOPSIS based framework presented in this letter can be extended by including more decision criteria and refining criteria weighting process for weighted complex networks.

References

1. Albert, R., Barabási, A.L.: Statistical mechanics of complex networks. Rev. Modern Phys. **74**(1), 47 (2002)
2. Bae, J., Kim, S.: Identifying and ranking influential spreaders in complex networks by neighborhood coreness. Phys. A: Stat. Mech. Appl. **395**, 549–559 (2014)
3. Behzadian, M., Otaghsara, S.K., Yazdani, M., Ignatius, J.: A state-of the-art survey of topsis applications. Expert Syst. Appl. **39**(17), 13051–13069 (2012)
4. Borgatti, S.P.: Identifying sets of key players in a social network. Comput. Math. Organ. Theory **12**(1), 21–34 (2006)
5. Chen, D., Lü, L., Shang, M.S., Zhang, Y.C., Zhou, T.: Identifying influential nodes in complex networks. Phys. A: Stat. Mech. Appl. **391**(4), 1777–1787 (2012)
6. Cormen, T.H., Leiserson, C.E., Rivest, R.L., Stein, C.: Introduction to Algorithms. MIT press, Cambridge (2009)
7. Figueira, J., Greco, S., Ehrgott, M.: Multiple Criteria Decision Analysis: State of the Art Surveys. Springer, New York (2005). https://doi.org/10.1007/b100605
8. Freeman, L.C.: A set of measures of centrality based on betweenness. Sociometry **40**, 35–41 (1977)
9. Freeman, L.C.: Centrality in social networks conceptual clarification. Soc. Netw. **1**(3), 215–239 (1978)
10. Hwang, C.L., Lai, Y.J., Liu, T.Y.: A new approach for multiple objective decision making. Comput. Oper. Res. **20**(8), 889–899 (1993)
11. Hwang, C.L., Yoon, K.: Methods for multiple attribute decision making. In: Multiple attribute decision making, pp. 58–191. Springer, Heidelberg (1981)

12. Kendall, M.G.: The treatment of ties in ranking problems. Biometrika **33**(3), 239–251 (1945)
13. Kitsak, M., et al.: Identification of influential spreaders in complex networks. Nat. Phys. **6**(11), 888–893 (2010)
14. Kunegis, J.: Konect: the koblenz network collection. In: Proceedings of the 22nd International Conference on World Wide Web, pp. 1343–1350. ACM (2013)
15. Leskovec, J., Krevl, A.: SNAP Datasets: Stanford large network dataset collection. http://snap.stanford.edu/data, June 2014
16. Li, C., Wang, L., Sun, S., Xia, C.: Identification of influential spreaders based on classified neighbors in real-world complex networks. Appl. Math. Comput. **320**, 512–523 (2018)
17. Liu, Y., Wei, B., Du, Y., Xiao, F., Deng, Y.: Identifying influential spreaders by weight degree centrality in complex networks. Chaos, Solitons Fractals **86**, 1–7 (2016)
18. Liu, Y., Tang, M., Zhou, T., Do, Y.: Identify influential spreaders in complex networks, the role of neighborhood. Phys. A: Stat. Mech. Appl. **452**, 289–298 (2016)
19. Lü, L., Zhou, T., Zhang, Q.M., Stanley, H.E.: The h-index of a network node and its relation to degree and coreness. Nature Commun. **7**, 10168 (2016)
20. Pastor-Satorras, R., Vespignani, A.: Epidemic dynamics and endemic states in complex networks. Phys. Rev. E **63**(6), 066117 (2001)
21. Saaty, T.L., Decision, H.T.M.A.: The analytic hierarchy process. Euro. J. Oper. Res. **48**, 9–26 (1990)
22. Sabidussi, G.: The centrality index of a graph. Psychometrika **31**(4), 581–603 (1966)
23. Salavati, C., Abdollahpouri, A., Manbari, Z.: Bridgerank: A novel fast centrality measure based on local structure of the network. Statistical Mechanics and its Applications, Physica A (2017)
24. Schmidt, F.K.: Analytische zahlentheorie in körpern der charakteristikp. Mathematische Zeitschrift **33**(1), 1–32 (1931)
25. Wang, Z., Zhao, Y., Xi, J., Du, C.: Fast ranking influential nodes in complex networks using a k-shell iteration factor. Phys. A: Stat. Mech. Appl. **461**, 171–181 (2016)
26. Webber, W., Moffat, A., Zobel, J.: A similarity measure for indefinite rankings. ACM Trans. Inf. Syst. (TOIS) **28**(4), 20 (2010)
27. Zareie, A., Sheikhahmadi, A.: A hierarchical approach for influential node ranking in complex social networks. Expert Syst. Appl. **93**, 200–211 (2018)
28. Zavadskas, E.K., Turskis, Z., Kildiene, S.: State of art surveys of overviews on mcdm/madm methods. Technol. Econ. Dev. Econ. **20**(1), 165–179 (2014)
29. Zeng, A., Zhang, C.J.: Ranking spreaders by decomposing complex networks. Phys. Lett. A **377**(14), 1031–1035 (2013)

Security Enhancement of IoT Based Smart Home Using Hybrid Technique

Saijshree Srivastava[✉] and Shiva Prakash

Information Technology and Computer Application,
M.M.M.U.T, Gorakhpur, India
swatisrivastava817@gmail.com, shiva.plko@gmail.com

Abstract. Internet of Things is an advance technology which is used all across the globe for sensing and collecting the data. Due to such unique nature of the network, various types of security attacks are possible on the network. Various enhanced security techniques had been proposed in previous years to overcome the problems of various attacks but there is no such technique which provides full security because day to day new attacks are arrived. Hybrid Technique in IoT security is enhanced security techniques which provide better security in IoT devices. In this paper, we proposed a Hybrid Security Technique which enhances the security and encryption speed of smart home appliances than the traditional algorithm. The purpose of the hybrid security algorithm is data security, confidentiality and integrity for IoT.

Keywords: Security in Internet of Things · Encryption technique · Decryption technique · Hybrid algorithm · TwoFish · NTRU

1 Introduction

The Internet of Things (IOT) is a set of several related objects, programs, individuals & devices that connect, exchange knowledge and data to accomplish a shared purpose across various fields and applications. IoT has a wide range of fields of operation such as travel, forestry, education, electricity generation, and distribution. IoT devices follow an approach to Identity Management identifying themselves in a collection of like & heterogeneous devices. A region in the IoT can also be classified by an IP address, but every entity has a single IP address in each region. IoT's goal is to change the way that we work together by completing everyday activities and projects with intelligent tools around us. The words IoT important are intelligent homes, intelligent towns, smart transport, and utilities, etc. There are various IoT application domains, from entity to company. IoT users communicate with their environments and human users can proceed to create social connections through applications within the personal and social fields. [1]. Within the IoT network devices, the real-world environment is provided by the RFID and sensors which are already available within numerous technologies as shown in Fig. 1 [4].

This paper comprises proposed Hybrid security technique which enhances the smart home security. As general techniques are not much secure than hybrid security technique. A lot of work has already been done in IoT security, and various hybrid

© Springer Nature Singapore Pte Ltd. 2020
A. Bhattacharjee et al. (Eds.): MIND 2020, CCIS 1241, pp. 543–558, 2020.
https://doi.org/10.1007/978-981-15-6318-8_44

Home appliances

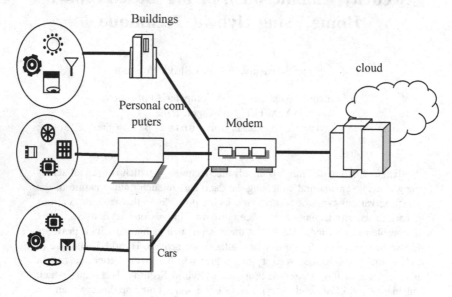

Fig. 1. Architecture of IoT

security techniques had been proposed but in this paper we proposed an enhancement in the security by using hybrid security technique i.e., TwoFish and NTRU algorithm. TwoFish is a symmetric algorithm whom speed is faster than AES, while increasing the RAM, and also for sound encryption it performs better than AES algorithm [9]. NTRU is an asymmetric algorithm used in proposed method for encryption and decryption process as NTRU algorithm provide strong security in various IoT devices thus we used NTRU algorithm so that security may high. In previous work *Amirhossein Safi*, [10] proposed a hybrid security technique in which AES and NTRU algorithm was used, as AES algorithm provide strong security but it does not overcome some security i.e., Brute Force attack. To overcome this attack we used TwoFish algorithm, which may provide better security.

The rest of the paper is structured as: Sect. 2 gives an outline of the taxonomy of an IoT security. Section 3 defines the related work on IoT security techniques. Section 4 define a problem formulation and suggested method. Section 5 gives brief description of proposed approach. Section 6 analyses the result. Finally, the conclusion is presented in Sect. 7.

2 Taxonomy

This section is organized as it gives an overview on IoT Security and further describes issues in IoT. To accomplish objectives in different fields & technologies, IoT gathers integrated objects, resources, individuals, and devices that can communicate, exchange information, and data. IoT may be carried out in many ways, including travel, agriculture, education, electricity production and delivery, and many other sectors, which include Internet-based connectivity to cleverly carry out business operations without human intervention. IoT systems typically adopt an ID strategy to be classified in a community of comparable and specific systems. An IP address may be defined for an IoT area, but in that area, each organization has its special ID.

2.1 Architecture of IoT

The roles and tools included in the network of an IoT framework are described by each node. In terms of the number of IoT levels, specific information is available. However, the IoT essentially uses on three layers of awareness, network, and device unit, according to many investigators. Every IoT layer has inherent security problems. The key design of IoT is the three levels for each structure concerning the systems and technologies as shown in Fig. 2.

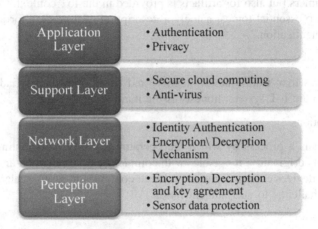

Fig. 2. IoT security layer

1. Perception Layer

The "sensor" layer in IoT is named the vision unit. The explanation for this layer is to collect sensor data from the environment. This layer tracks gathers, manages, and passes data from sensors to the layer of the network. However, this layer can also be used in local and short networks to merge the IoT node.

2. Network Layer

IoT network layer carries out a function of data propagation various connectivity across the Internet between various IoT hubs and computers. Internet gateways, switches, networking tools, etc. are available on this layer.

3. Application Layer

The application layer ensures that the data are authentic, complete as well as confidential. The purpose of IoT to build intelligent ecosystems is fulfilled in this layer [2]. For virtually any iot system that has either been deployed or is currently developing, security is extremely important [3].

2.2   Security Issues of IoT

For all communications utilizing computers and networks, the same fundamental protection principle of secrecy, fairness, and accessibility is required to control the protection of IoT.

1. Confidentiality

It ensures access and modification of the data to authorized entities. Authorization not only for consumers but also for artifacts is provided in the IoT context. Confidentiality will answer two essential topics, namely a description of a process for access control and entity authentication.

2. Integrity

It's nothing less than truthfulness, integrity, and trust. With the myriad devices and users linked to the IoT system, honesty is the main security issue.

3. Authentication

Authentication is a process by which the operator or entity participating in communiqué checks its originality. It operates with completeness, anonymity, and consent. As the amount of devices connecting to the internet continues to grow, scalability presents a significant challenge to user authentication.

4. Authorization

Authorization is issued to the device or identity of the user. Everybody has the same identification to access details from the IoT world. Without permission, nobody may access data or devices in this field.

5. Non-repudiation

It's the guarantee you can't deny. A node does not reject its notification or its knowledge submitted to the other node or user in the IoT setting.

6. Availability

Accessibility to the IOT requires stability and durability. The explosive amount of data is available throughout the world by a highly distributed Io T environment. Once linked to the internet, any computer will produce data and attempt to store data anywhere.

7. Privacy

An individual (person) shall have the freedom to decide the volume of knowledge that they are prepared to share. Data security would become a major concern regardless of something relevant to IoT. Most committed individual details may be rendered without the user's knowledge [4].

3 Related Work

This section describes in details of security techniques and hybrid security techniques used in IoT and its applications.

Aikaterini Roukounaki et al. [2019] in recent years there has been an increasing increase in solutions relevant to Internet protection problems and applications utilizing computer learning and in-depth research techniques. The creation of flexible infrastructures to collect and process IoT systems and devices for security-related datasets is a crucial pre-condition for such strategies. This paper presents a scalable as well as configurable IoT security data collection architecture [5].

Tenzin Kunchok et al. [2018] This paper proposed a lightweight, hybrid encryption system that uses ECDH key exchange mechanisms to generate keys & to establish connections, digital authentication signature as well as subsequently an AES algorithm to encrypt as well as decrypt user data files. The suggested combination is called a "three-way protected data encryption method" that interprets all the 3 authentication safety, information security, and control schemes with lower cost and faster speed characteristics, allowing it more resistant against hackers to crash the security system and therefore to have a defense for transmitting data [6].

Mohamed Elhoseny et al. [2018] this paper explores the protection of medical photos in IoT using an advanced cryptographic paradigm of techniques for optimization. For the majority of instances, medical records are held in the hospital as a cloud service, which ensures privacy is important. This requires another framework for secure transmission as well as efficient storage of medical images interwoven with patient data [7].

Marwan Ali Albahar et al. [2018] in this paper, we suggested the modern triple algo of Bluetooth that is currently by 128-bit AES for encryption in its latest version (Bluetooth 4.0–5.0), focused on RSA (rivest-Shamir-Adleman, AES (Advanced Encryption Standard) & TwoFish. Furthermore, older Bluetooth 1.0 A – 3.0 + HS (High-Speed) systems are using the E0 stream chip for encoding that has been shown by various researchers to below. In our current strategy, the three-fold security of AES, RSA & TWOFISH will increase] safety standard that prevents Bluetooth data transmission [8].

Eman Salim Ibrahim Harba et al. [2017] Powerful encoding/authentication schemes use various techniques to prevent access to unencrypted passwords and to ensure that an intruder will make no use of the authentication data that is sent and processed. Throughout this paper, we also suggested a way to secure data sharing utilizing 3 hybrid encryption approaches: symmetric AES mostly used for crypto bursts, asymmetric RSA for AES password encryption and the HMAC framework to encrypt symmetric keys & data to ensure a protected transmitting of the in-between client and server as well as server clients and clients [11].

Chandu Y et al. [2017] the planet is heading to an interactive, interactive, and continuously increasing age of technology. In this respect, IOT plays a crucial role because everything is cloud-based storage as well as remote access. The next big problem for IOT is the privacy and security of knowledge. Whichever the technique to obtain information created by the edge computer, the transmission to the cloud is not safe. A synthetic, secure algorithm for data transfer and storage in the cloud is suggested in this report. The proposed algorithm enables the edge computer, until transferring to the cloud, to encrypt data produced using AES. Through the usage of the RSA encryption program origin of AES is authenticated. The authenticated RSA key is submitted via electronic mail to the designated individual [12].

Garrett S. Rose [2016] this paper provides examples of rudimentary nanoelectronic protection which explores how these circuits or structures can be used in developing IoT applications. Since the traditional IoT devices are powerful, their onboard computer systems do have to be simple in that they are compact and consume limited electricity. Nevertheless, in the development of IoT systems, the IoT itself raises fresh privacy and protection issues. To ensure robust protection with a minimal area and overhead strength, IoT Safety is focused on nanoelectronic primitives and nano-enabled safety protocols to have robust security [13].

Jonathan Charity Talwana et al. [2016] the growth of Broadband Internet is also raising due to the rising number of internet users. As a result, Wi-Fi and built-in system sensors and the full amount of devices can be linked using a standard network, the communication cost will be minimized. The technology called IOT has evolved to meet all these requirements. IoT may be viewed as a bridge between mobile devices such as cell phones, coffee makers, washing machines, internet wearable devices. IoT creates a network, connects "information" and users by creating ties between computers, people, and objects. With the rise in the number of system contacts, the safety risk decreases. Protection in all companies around the world is the biggest problem for IoT [14].

Rufai Yusuf Zakari et al. [2015] Mobile technology has been flourishing more rapidly than any other technology in history in the developing world over the past dozen years. Digital money is the newest trend brought on by mobile technologies. is popular as well as user-friendly mobile communication technology. In this review a secured short Message service (SMS) which is peer-to-peer hybrid cryptography is analyzed which provide the security services, it uses symmetric (AES Rijndael) and asymmetric (NTRU) algorithm to achieve more robust functionality and the use of hashing algorithm SHA-1 is suggested to be replaced with HMAC-SHA256 because of its vulnerability. The protocol is proposed to be used in the mobile money short message service communication channel [15].

Gaurav R. Patel et al. [17] in the paper, two main RSA algorithms combined and the Diffie Hellman algorithm proposes hybrid approaches. Compared to RSA, this hybrid encryption algorithm provides greater stability. The findings are also obtained from the paper [16].

4 Problem Formulation

This section describes the description about the problem formulation.

To receive IoT advancement, it is essential to make a user's well known about its security and data protection which convey that using this technology, there would not be any possibility of risk of data integrity confidentiality, security and protection in smart home tools.

A lot of solutions are available for security in IoT. As one of the author *Amirhossein Safi*, [10] proposed a hybrid security technique in their previous work in which AES and NTRU algorithm was used, as AES algorithm provide strong security but it unable to resolve some attack i.e., Brute Force attack.

To resolve this attack, the proposed method used TwoFish algorithm which may provide better security and confidentiality than AES algorithm in IoT Smart Home.

The primary goal of the network and data protection is to provide security and confidentiality. This paper proposes a Hybrid security technique for IoT which is based on mixing of two algorithms which enhances the security and speed. The proposed model uses asymmetric algorithm i.e., NTRU based on multinomial usage in IoT, and symmetric algorithm i.e., TwoFish which gives better performance in IoT security. As TwoFish algorithm gives better performance when RAM is increased thus the speed of TwoFish algorithm is also fast during encryption.

5 Proposed Approach

As above, we identify the problem as AES algorithm is unable to resolve some attack i.e., Brute Force attack, for that we provide solution. Our proposed methodology is based on a smart home security system i.e. Home Security Technique (HST) that provides technological support to make smart home more secure, easier and confidential. The proposed system consists of three stages – *Key generation, Encryption, Decryption*. The proposed method uses TwoFish algorithm in place of AES algorithm to provide more security, integrity and confidentiality. As on the basis of methodology used for encryption and decryption, the proposed methodology is used for security of IoT applications like smart home and evaluation is to be done on smart home tools.

Steps of Home Security Technique are as follows:

- The sender or home resident has a public key which is generated from symmetric encryption i.e. TwoFish.
- Now messages or tools which are needed to be encrypted, are encrypted by asymmetric encryption techniques i.e. NTRU algorithm.
- Then the encrypted message will be sent to the receptor (television, door, almirah, refrigerator, etc.) in the internet surroundings.
- Receptors own a private key which is unaware from senders.
- Hackers or attackers cannot guess the password of smart home tools because of the hybrid approach and it can also enhances IoT security in HST.

- Receptors now decrypt the message from the sender or user using the private key and cipher text. In our proposed method we present a new hybrid approach in IoT security and increasing speed of encryption and decryption using the combination of two algorithms of TwoFish and NTRU in Fig. 3.

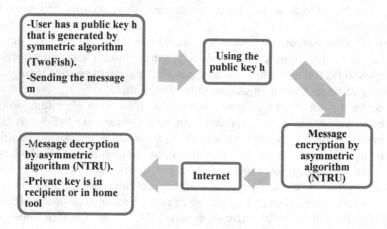

Fig. 3. Proposed model of HST

5.1   Key Creation

For Key production process in TwoFish is used to create a key. It is flexible; it may use in various network applications where keys are changed frequently and used in applications where there is little or no RAM and ROM available. TwoFish also has something called "Whitening" in which prewhitening is done and create a public key k. Each 128 bit key is broken up into four by four byte. These four bytes (the S-boxes have 8-bit input and output) are combined with MDS (Maximum Distance Separable) matrix and give two 64-bit words. These two 64-bit words then combined with PHT (Pseudo-Hadamard Transform), further added two round sub keys, and then right half of the text is XORed by mixing of operation. The main aim of creating a public key is to hide the message from sender to receiver and provide security and safety of message.

Therefore NTRU algorithm is used for encryption process and hacker should not identify public key as hybrid approach is used for providing more security and confidentiality.

5.2   Encryption

Let Plaintext is sent to the receiver from the sender. Here for Encryption we use NTRU algorithm and message is mapped into a polynomial or multinomial form. The key (k) which is generated by TwoFish and random polynomial r is XORed and make a new polynomial.

Now we have encrypted message and sender should not revealed it (Fig. 4).

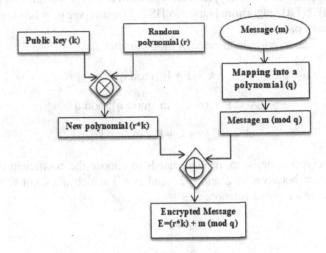

Fig. 4. Flowchart of hybrid encryption HST

$$\text{Encrypted Message } E = r * k + m \ (\text{mod } q) \qquad (1)$$

Following steps are performed in Hybrid Encryption process:

1. Begin
2. Creating a public key k using TwoFish algorithm.
3. Choose random polynomial r and q
4. X OR between public key h and random polynomial r
5. Calculate new polynomial r*k
6. From input message m and mapped into polynomial q
7. Calculate a new polynomial (m (mod q))
8. X OR between new polynomial (r* k) and new polynomial(m (mod q))
9. Calculate Encrypted message using NTRU algorithm

$$E = (r * k) + m \ (\text{mod } q)$$

10. End

5.3   Decryption

When receiver received the encrypted message from sender, receiver tries to decrypt it. For decryption, NTRU algorithm is used in HST. The receiver now has both the private keys i.e., F and Fp.

First step of decryption is to calculating parameter A:

$$A = F * E \ (\text{mod } q) \tag{2}$$

$$A = F * [r * k + m \ (\text{mod } q)] \text{mod } q \tag{3}$$

$$A = [F * r * k + F * m \ (\text{mod } q)] \tag{4}$$

To avoid a decryption problem, receiver needs to choose the coefficient of a lie in an interval of length between –q/2 and q/2. And p = 3 which does not effected on the procedure thus from above relation.

$$r * k = 0 \tag{5}$$

$$A = F * m \ (\text{mod } q) \tag{6}$$

Receiver then center lifts mod q and obtain B:

$$B = A \ (\text{mod } p) \tag{7}$$

Then finally receiver reduces a (mod p) and uses another secret key Fp to get the message.

$$\text{Decryption } m = Fp * B \tag{8}$$

Whenever Decryption = plaintext, we will sure that message will reach its destination with security and confidentiality (Fig. 5).

Following steps are performed in Hybrid Decryption process:

1. Begin
2. Secret key F and Fp using NTRU algorithm
3. X OR between F and Encrypted message e

$$\text{Calculate } A = F * E \ (\text{mod } q)$$

4. Make all coefficients positive and shift a coefficient into [–q/2, q/2]
5. Calculate new polynomial B = A (mod p) and reduces coefficient of (A (mod p))
6. X OR between secret key Fp and new polynomial B
7. Calculate Decrypted message using NTRU algorithm

$$m = Fp * B$$

8. if Decrypted message = message

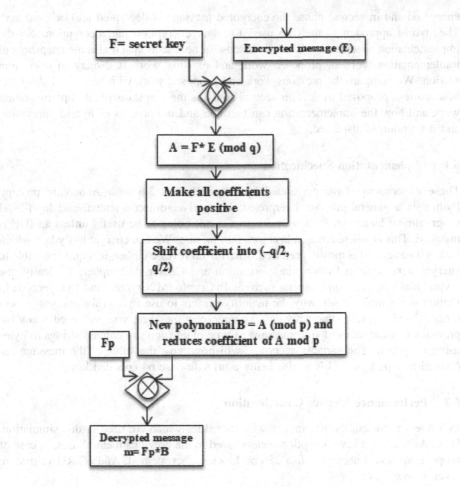

Fig. 5. Flowchart of hybrid decryption HST

9. then successful
10. End
11. else unsuccessful
12. End

6 Result and Analysis

This section describes the brief description of result on the basis of comparison and analysis of our proposed work with existing algorithm, which gives the better result in IoT Smart Home Security. We have employed our idea by means of Anaconda framework and Python language for coding. Our main aim is to enhance the security and execution speed. This can be done in two phases, In first phase the input message is encrypted and in second phase the encrypted message is decrypted into original text. The hybrid approach is then be used for data encryption and decryption. So the implementation specification is briefly discuss in next section and also the snapshots of implementation work of proposed work and existing work is display in upcoming section. We compare the previous work and proposed work with result and show the best result of proposed work. This section contains the snapshots of all implementation work and how the implementation can be done and the process of hybrid encryption and decryption is displayed.

6.1   Implementation Specification

These experiments have performed by using Python 3.6 with Anaconda prompt. Python is a general-purpose interpreted, interactive, object-oriented, and high-level programming language. Python on its own is not going to be useful unless an IDE is installed. This is where Anaconda comes into picture. We can encrypt in Python which makes it easier and is mostly preferred. Apart from reverse cipher, it is quite possible to encrypt a message in Python via substitution and Caesar shift cipher. Typically, the cryptography library and others such as PyCrypto, M2Crypto, and PyOpenSSL in Python is the main reason why the majority prefers to use Python for encryption and other related cryptographic activities. To encrypt a message, you will need a key (as previously discussed) and your message as type bytes (you can convert strings to bytes using encode()). The variable encrypted will now have the value of the message encrypted as type bytes. This is also being a url safe base 64 encoded key.

6.2   Performance Metrics Consideration

In Table 1 represent the parameters with its values which are used in this simulation. Here, AES 256-bit key encryption method used in the previous method. But, in case of propose method it uses Two-fish 256-bit block cipher method. And NTRU values are given below Table 1.

Table 1. Parametric table

Parameters	Values
AES	256-bit key
AES block size	16-bits
N	251
P	3
Q	128
D	2
Two-fish	256-bit block cipher

6.3   Snapshots of Implementation

This section shows the whole procedure of implementation of proposed approach and existing approach and also shows how it is being executed as encryption and decryption. In the home screen we here shows some icons as buttons. Each buttons has perform different function as "Generate Key" is used to creating a key, "Encrypt password" embeds the secret message or password text into byte. Get Private Key" is used in the decryption process and "Decrypt password" is used in decryption of password.

Figure 6 represents the first screen appeared when no encryption has performed. At this time no key exist.

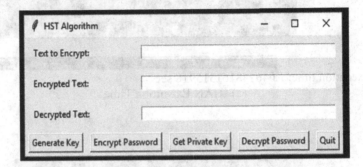

Fig. 6. Home screen

6.3.1   Execution Time

After Decryption, "Quit" button is pressed and get total execution time on prompt as shown in Fig. 7. In Fig. 7 (a) this is done by HAN encryption method (NTRU and AES) and in Fig. 7 (b) this is done by HST encryption method (NTRU and Two-fish) in which execution time of both techniques displayed.

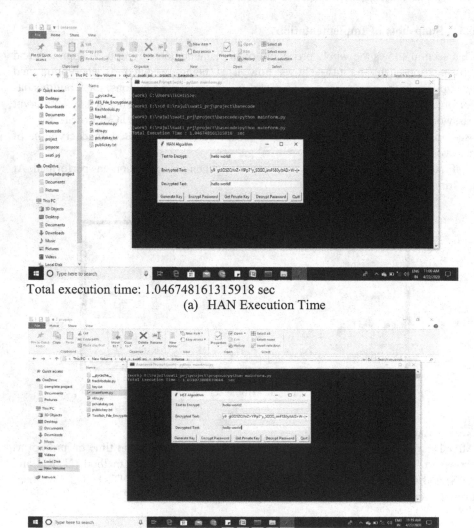

Total execution time: 1.046748161315918 sec
(a) HAN Execution Time

Total Execution Time: 1.031073808670044 sec
(b) HST Execution Time

Fig. 7. Total execution time

6.3.2   Comparison Graph

The Anaconda Prompt is used to perform the experiment and measure the efficiency of the proposed algorithm and also compare it with the existing algorithm. In order to compare the two algorithms i.e. (HAN and HST) we use performance metrics. We can measure the performance metrics on the basis of its execution time of both the hybrid algorithms as shown in Fig. 8.

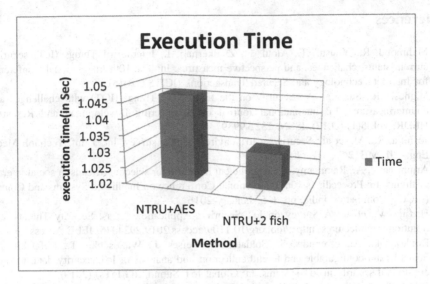

Fig. 8. Time comparison graph

As HAN algorithm shows good execution time but HST algorithm gives better result. It means HST can provide more security, confidentiality and also better execution time.

Methods	HAN Algorithm(NTRU + AES)	HST Algorithm (NTRU + TwoFish)
Execution time	1.046748161315918	1.031073808670044

7 Conclusion

Internet of Things mainly provides the way to analyses collected sensing data, from across the world to taking decision over the situation. Due to such unique nature security is major challenge to protect it from various types of attacks. We provided a hybrid security algorithm that enhanced the security of smart home. The proposed hybrid home security algorithms are combination of TwoFish symmetric encryption algorithm and NTRU asymmetric encryption algorithm. This algorithm has high speed key creation, encryption and decryption, therefore overall enhancement of security in Smart Home of IoT due to TwoFish algorithm and NTRU as a multinomial usage in encryption and decryption to accomplish correct message which is more secure than prior hybrid approaches. We present proof and results verification of proposed methodology, in our research work.

References

1. Mahmoud, R., Yousuf, T., Aloul, F., Zualkernan, I.: Internet of Things (IoT) security: current status, challenges, and perspective measures. In: The 10th International Conference for Internet Technology and Secured Transactions (ICITST-2015)
2. Vignesh, R., Samurai, A.: Security on the Internet of Things (IOT) with challenges and countermeasures. In: International Journal of Engineering Development and Research, IJEDR, vol. 5(1) (2017). ISSN: 2321-9939
3. Joshitta, R.S.M., et al.: Security in IoT environment: a survey. Int. J. Inf. Technol. Mech. Eng.- IJITME, 2(7), 1–8 (2016)
4. Arjunasamy, A., Ramasamy, T.: A proficient heuristic for selecting friends in social internet of things. In: Proceedings 10th International Conference on Intelligent Systems and Control (ISCO), Coimbatore India, pp. 1–5, January 2016
5. Hassija, V., et al.: A Survey on IoT Security: Application Areas, Security Threats, and Solution Architectures. https://doi.org/10.1109/access.2019.2924045. IEEE Access
6. Roukounaki, A., Efremidis, S., Soldatos, J., Neises, J., Walloschke, T., Kefalakis, N.: Scalable and configurable end-to-end collection and analysis of IoT security data: towards end-to-end security in IoT systems. In: Global IoT Summit (G IoTs) (2019)
7. Kunchok, T., Kirubanand, V.B.: A lightweight hybrid encryption technique to secure IoT data transmission. Int. J. Eng. Technol. 7(26), 236–240 (2018)
8. Elhoseny, M., Shankar, K., Lakshmanaprabu, S.K., Maseleno, A., Arunkumar, N.: Hybrid optimization with cryptography encryption for medical image security in Internet of Things. Neural Comput. Appl. 1 (2018)
9. Rizvi, S.A.M.: Performance analysis of AES and TwoFish encryption schemes. In: International Conference on Communication Systems and Network Technologies (2011)
10. Safi, A.: Improving the security of internet of things using encryption algorithms. Int. J. Comput. Inf. Eng. 11(5), 5 (2017)
11. Albahar, M.A., Olawumi, O., Haataja, K., Toivanen, P.: Novel hybrid encryption algorithm based on AES, RSA, and TwoFish for bluetooth encryption. J. Inf. Secur. 9, 168–176 (2018)
12. Harba, E.S.I.: Secure Data Encryption Through a Combination of AES, RSA, and HMAC. Eng. Technol. Appl. Sci. Res. 7(4), 1781–1785 (2017)
13. Chandu, Y., Rakesh Kumar, K.S., Prabhukhanolkar, N.V., Anish, A.N., Rawal, S.: Design and implementation of hybrid encryption for security of IOT data. In: International Conference On Smart Technologies For Smart Nation (Smart TechCon) (2017)
14. Rose, G.S.: Security meets Nanoelectronics for the Internet of things applications. In: International Great Lakes Symposium on VLSI (GLSVLSI) (2016)
15. Talwana, J.C., Hua, H.J.: Smart world of Internet of Things (IoT) and its security concerns. In: IEEE International Conference on Internet of Things (I Things) and IEEE Green Computing and Communications (Green Com) and IEEE Cyber, Physical and Social Computing (CPS Com) and IEEE Smart Data (Smart Data) (2016)
16. Zakari, R.Y., Suleiman, A., Lawa, Z.K., Abdulrazak, N.: A review of SMS security using hybrid cryptography and use in mobile money system. Am. J. Comput. Sci. Eng. 2(6), 53–62 (2015)
17. Patel, G.R., Pancha, K.: Hybrid encryption algorithm. IJEDR 2(2) (2014)

Insider Threat Detection Based on User Behaviour Analysis

Malvika Singh[1,2](✉), B.M. Mehtre[1](✉), and S. Sangeetha[2](✉)

[1] Centre of Excellence in Cyber Security, Institute for Development and Research in Banking Technology, Established by Reserve bank of India, Hyderabad, India
singh23malvika23@gmail.com, bmmehtre@idrbt.ac.in
[2] Department of Computer Applications, National Institute of Technology, Tiruchirappalli, India
sangeetha@nitt.edu

Abstract. Insider threat detection is a major challenge for security in organizations. They are the employees/users of an organization, posing threat to it by performing any malicious activity. Existing methods to detect insider threats are based on psycho-physiological factors, statistical analysis, machine learning and deep learning methods. They are based on predefined rules or stored signatures and fail to detect new or unknown attacks. To overcome some of the limitations of the existing methods, we propose behaviour based insider threat detection method. The behaviour is characterized by user activity (such as logon-logoff, device connect-disconnect, file-access, http-url-requests, email activity). Isometric Feature Mapping (ISOMAP) is used for feature extraction and Emperor Penguin Algorithm is used for optimal feature selection. The features include time based features (time at which a particular activity is performed) and frequency based features (number of times a particular activity is performed). Finally, a Multi-fuzzy-classifier is used with three inference engines F1, F2, F3, to classify users as normal or malicious. The proposed method is tested using CMU-CERT insider threat dataset for its performance. The proposed method outperforms on the following metrics: accuracy, precision, recall, f-measure, and AUC-ROC parameters. The insider threat detection results show a significant improvement over existing methods.

Keywords: Insider threat detection · User behaviour analysis · Isometric Feature Mapping (ISOMAP) · Time based features · Frequency based features · Emperor Penguin Algorithm (EPA) · Multi-fuzzy-classifier

1 Introduction

Insider threats are the major cause of security breach in organizations. Tremendous growth in the number of insider threats and the amount of damage caused by them, highly motivates us to detect potential insider threats present within

© Springer Nature Singapore Pte Ltd. 2020
A. Bhattacharjee et al. (Eds.): MIND 2020, CCIS 1241, pp. 559–574, 2020.
https://doi.org/10.1007/978-981-15-6318-8_45

the organization. Users with legitimate access rights often poses the most danger to an organization's security. Therefore, detecting insider threat helps in preventing an insider attack which may be launched by insiders in future by means of performing any malicious activity. It can be detected by analyzing user's behaviour at different intervals of time.

Insider threats can be detected using various behaviour based techniques which helps in discovering unusual behaviour change in an individual's usual behaviour. The unusual behaviour pattern is then detected and is compared with his past usual behaviour. Based on the amount of deviation in an individual's behaviour an anomaly is detected and that individual is considered as a potential insider threat.

Based on the above idea insider threat detection problem is usually modelled as problem of detecting anomaly. Behaviour analysis to detect an anomaly present in an individual's behaviour can be applied using various methods. They are mainly based on psychological and physiological factors that affects user's behaviour. Based on these factors an insider threat can be detected using various methods which are as follows: Statistical Analysis Methods, Machine Learning Methods, Deep Learning Methods. These methods detect any unusual change in user's normal behaviour pattern and flag it as an anomaly/malicious behaviour. That particular user is then considered as a potential insider threat. Existing methods to detect insider threats consider only stored signatures or predefined rules thus in turn fail to detect any new or unknown threat. Some behaviour based methods consider only week to week user behaviours while missing the anomalous behaviour happening within a day. Other methods require explicit feature engineering which may not extract a rich feature set which in turn results in low threat detection accuracy. Therefore, in this work we aim to overcome some of the limitations of the existing methods and provide an improved method for insider threat detection with reduced number of false positives.

The rest of the paper is organised as follows: Sect. 2 presents the Related Work. Proposed Methodology is presented in Sect. 3. Section 4 presents Results & Discussion. Section 5 presents Conclusion and Future Work.

2 Related Work

In general many methodologies are introduced for mitigating insider threats [1]. Statistical Analysis [15], Machine Learning [16] and Deep Learning [4] are few such methodologies which help in detecting insider threats.

Insider threats are determined using time series features based on pre-defined insider threat scenarios in [7]. Authors in [5] used the mechanism of encrypted honeypots sensors to detect insider threats and reduce false positives.

In [10] user behaviour is modelled to detect anomalies for threat detection using LDA (Latent Dirichlet Allocation). In [6] authors developed an Intent Based Access Control (IBAC) system for insider threats detection based on user's intention. Authors in [11] proposed a new framework named RADISH. It is a statistical based method to discover anomalies from heterogeneous data streams.

In [12] a tree structure profiling approach is proposed in which anomalous behaviour of each user is represented by using a tree structure and Principal Component Analysis (PCA). In [8] three distance measurement metrics are used for detecting any changes in user behaviour. In [9] authors proposed a hybrid model for Across Domain Anomaly Detection (ADAD) and Across Time Anomaly Detection (ATAD) for improved Hidden Markov Models (HMM). They used Principal Component Analysis (PCA). They are machine learning based methods.

Recurrent neural networks are deployed in the field of cyber security for detecting insider threats in [2–4]. In [13] authors implemented a deep neural network using Long Short Term Memory (LSTM) and Convolution Neural Network (CNN), where insider threats are detected by profiling or modelling user's behaviour language from their daily activit ies.

The insider threat detection is deployed using various approaches for detecting insiders by using efficient feature processing. However, in majority of the existing literature present for insider threat detection, explicit feature engineering is required along with the requirement to extract more relevant feature sets. Therefore, it is essential to potentially detect insider threat with improved efficiency, reduced false positives, and less threat detection time. For this purpose, in this work we extracted both time series based features as well as frequency based features to construct an efficient feature set for insider threat detection. For feature processing, we used global feature extraction algorithm Isometric Feature Mapping (ISOMAP) and an optimal bio-inspired Emperor Penguin Algorithm (EPA) for feature selection. Finally the optimally selected features are feed to multi-fuzzy-classifier to classify users as normal or malicious.

3 Proposed Methodology

This section describes the proposed methodology in detail. It consists of the following four modules: data preprocessing, feature extraction, feature selection and classification. The data preprocessing steps process the dataset for efficient feature processing, further feature processing is implemented where both time and frequency based features are extracted and selected optimally from user's behaviour. User's behaviour represents the sequence of actions performed by each individual user over a fixed interval of time. In this work user behaviours are extracted and selected based on five different type of user activities (logon-logoff, device, file, email, http) from CMU-CERT r4.2 dataset using Isometric Feature Mapping and Emperor Penguin Algorithm respectively. User behaviour features are extracted from the preprocessed dataset's real vector values X_i, in a high dimensional space R_D. Subsequently a neighbour graph is constructed and shortest path is estimated to extracted behaviour features. Each vector represents the attribute of each field. Likewise, individual features and their corresponding user's information are extracted. The individual behaviour features present in the dataset are separated and then optimization is involved to select best features using Emperor Penguin Algorithm. Finally, a multi fuzzy classifier with three fuzzy inference engines F1, F2 and F3 is used. Input to fuzzy F1 and F2 are time based and frequency based features respectively. Finally third fuzzy inference engine F3 classify the users as normal or malicious based on fuzzy 3 output values.

3.1 Model Overview

Figure 1 illustrates the overview of the proposed method.

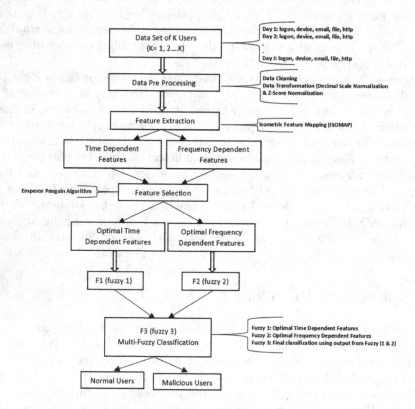

Fig. 1. Overview of the proposed methodology

It consists of the following four modules:

1. Data Pre-processing
2. Feature Extraction
3. Feature Selection
4. Classification

Finally, the proposed method is tested for its performance using the following metrics:

- Accuracy
- Precision
- Recall
- F-Measure
- AUC-ROC Curve

Description of the proposed method and its analysis is detailed below:

3.2   Data Pre-processing

Raw data contains noise in the form of missing values, redundant values, null values, unsupported data format etc. Therefore, incorporating data pre-processing steps helps in improving the detection rate and classifier's accuracy. In the proposed work, we implemented the data pre-processing steps which are as follows:

1. Data Cleaning: In this step, we labeled the missing categorical features as "Missing", and for missing numerical data we flagged and filled the missing values with 0.

2. Data Transformation: It is the combination of two methods:
   - Decimal Scale Normalization: This step is performed for numerical data present in the data set. It is computed by:

$$X_{s(i)} = \frac{x_i}{10^j} \tag{1}$$

   ,In Eq. 1, x_i is the original data value, $X_{s(i)}$ is the normalized data value, and smallest integer is denoted by j such that $max(|(X_{s(i)}|) < 1$.

   - Z-Score: It is computed based on standard deviation and mean of the values in the data. It is computed using the following formula:

$$Z_{s(i)} = \frac{x - \bar{M}}{\sigma_S} \tag{2}$$

   In Eq. 2, $Z_{s(i)}$ is the normalized data value, x denotes the actual data value, σ_S is standard deviation of all values, and $\bar{M}$ is the mean of all values.
   Here data transformation is implemented as:

$$D_T = (X_{s(i)}, Z_{s(i)}) \tag{3}$$

   In Eq. 3, D_T represents data transformation function, $X_{s(i)}$ represents the decimal scale normalization, and $Z_{s(i)}$ represents the z score normalization which is used to ensure the avoidance of redundant data and data dependency.

3.3 Feature Extraction

Once the complete pre-processed dataset is loaded, feature extraction is performed. In existing methods, time series based features are mainly taken in account. However, to enhance the threat detection rate in this work, the time dependent features (logon/log off time, removable events etc.) and frequency dependent features (number of e-mail sent, number of USB connected, number of logins/logoffs etc) are extracted from user behaviour using ISOMAP (Isometric Feature Mapping) [17]. Unlike other existing feature extraction methods which preserve the local features, ISOMAP preserves the global non-linear feature space hence providing with complete feature set for classification. Authors in [18] used ISOMAP as a dimensionality reduction algorithm for fault prediction in electromechanical equipment. In [19,20] authors used a modified ISOMAP algorithm as a feature extraction method for intrusion detection system.

To implement ISOMAP, let us consider a system S of K users containing N real value data vectors V_n in R_D in higher dimensional. Here, ISOMAP is implemented to obtain the high dimensional data R_D in observational space while preserving the distance between the data projecting it onto a lower dimensional space R_d such that $(d < D)$.

ISOMAP algorithm is implemented in three steps as follows:

1. Construction of neighbour graph G: For each set of data point (i, j) in the high dimensional space, construct the neighbour graph G, using the Euclidean distance between each point (i, j), if j is located around k nearest points of i. The distance is thus denoted by $d_x(i, j)$.

2. Calculation of shortest path: For each two points in the above constructed neighbour graph G, calculate using Floyd Warshall algorithm, the shortest path between (i, j) denoted by $d_G(i, j)$. Note down the estimate distance between those points which is known as geodesic distance in topological space M denoted by $d_M(i, j)$

3. Embedding into lower dimensional space: Using Multidimensional Space (MDS) algorithm, construct a d dimensional space Y, preserving the above constructed topological space M on $d_G(i, j)$ which is the distance matrix constructed in previous step. Now, calculate the Euclidean distance matrix for data points in d dimensional space denoted by D_Y, where y_i is the coordinate vector which is obtain through minimizing the error using the following equation:

$$E = \|\tau(D_G) - \tau(D_Y)\|_2 \tag{4}$$

where

$$\tau_D = \frac{HSH}{2} \tag{5}$$

where H represents a centralized matrix

$$Hx_ix_j = \frac{\delta x_ix_j - 1}{1} \tag{6}$$

and S represents a squared distance matrix

$$Sx_ix_j = D^2x_ix_j \tag{7}$$

In above Eq. (4), minimum value is achieved with the help of feature vectors which are corresponding to feature vectors of matrix $\tau(D_G)$. Using ISOMAP algorithm's rules we can determine the dimensionality which needs to be reduced. To measure dimensionality reduction error we calculate the residual error e_d as

$$e_d = 1 - R^2(D_G, D_Y) \tag{8}$$

where R^2, represents the linear correlation coefficient. We implemented the feature extraction using ISOMAP and extracted time dependent features, frequency dependent features. The number of k neighbours considered for the proposed method are 13 with uniform weights.

Table 1 presents the list of extracted time and frequency dependent features using ISOMAP.

Table 1. List of Extracted Features

Extracted feature type	List of extracted features
Time based features	#logon time, #logoff time, #device connect time, #device disconnect time, #file accessed time, #email send time, #email receive time, #http request send time
Frequency based features	#total number of logins, #total number of device connected, #total number of device disconnected, #total number of files accessed, #total number of emails sent, #total number of email receive, #total number of attachments in email, #size of the attachment, #total number of http requests sent(url visited)
Others	#employee name, #user id, #pc id, #email-cc, #email-bcc, #email-to, #email-from, #file name, #urls, #logon-logoff activity, #psychometric features (O,C,E,A,N)

3.4 Feature Selection

For selecting optimal features from a complete feature set we implemented feature selection. Existing methods for feature selection for insider threat detection may not be optimum. Therefore, in the proposed work, we implemented feature selection using Emperor Penguin Algorithm [21] for optimal feature selection. It is a bio inspired algorithm in which emperor penguin's huddling behaviour is being mimic. The main motivation of using this algorithm is the fact that most of the population based algorithms are better than single solution based methods as they are best suited for efficient function evaluations. They explore the complete search space (globally optimum solution), while avoiding local optima until optimal result is obtained. There are four main steps in emperor penguin algorithm. They are as follows:

1. Step 1: Compute the huddle boundary for emperor penguins. It is calculated based on the observation fact that emperor penguins usually huddle in a polygon shape boundary having at least two neighbours chosen randomly. Huddle boundary is then generated based on the wind flow around the huddle. Let the wind velocity is denoted by ω, and its gradient is deoted by ψ as represented in Eq. 9.

$$\omega = \psi \tag{9}$$

$$F = \psi + i\omega \tag{10}$$

In Eq. 10, the analytical function is denoted by F on the polygon plane.

2. Step 2: In this step the temperature T' is computed which is the temperature around the huddle boundary. It is computed by

$$T' = T - \frac{Max_{iteration}}{x - Max_{iteration}} \tag{11}$$

In Eq. 11, it is assumed that, when polygon radius $R > 1$, then $T = 0$ and when polygon radius $R < 1$ then $T = 1$. Time to compute the optimal feature set is denoted by T and $Max_{iteration}$ is the number of maximum iterations, polygon radius is denoted by R and x denotes current iteration.

3. Step 3: Distance between emperor penguins is calculated by:

$$D_{ep} = Abs(SF(A).P(x) - C.P_{ep}(x)) \tag{12}$$

In Eq. 12, the distance between emperor penguins is denoted by D_{ep}, x represents current iteration, to avoid the collision between emperor penguins A and C are used, P represents the best optimum solution, position vector of emperor penguin is represented by P_{ep}, SF is the social factors for emperor penguins which helps to move towards best optimal solution. A and C are computed from:

$$A = (MP \times (T' P_{grid}(Accu)) \times Ran()) - T' \tag{13}$$

$$P_{grid}(Accu) = Abs(P - P_{ep}) \tag{14}$$

$$C = Ran() \tag{15}$$

In Eq. 13, MP represents the movement parameter to avoid collisions by maintaining a gap between emperor penguins which is set to 2 here, polygon grid accuracy is represented by $P_{grid}(Accu)$, $Ran()$ represents a random function within the range [0,1]. $SF()$ is calculated by:

$$SF(A) = (\sqrt{f.e^{\frac{-x}{T}} - e^{-x}})^2 \tag{16}$$

In Eq. 16, to calculate social factors SF, e denotes the expression function, selected control parameters are obtained by f and l to obtain better exploration and exploitation.

4. Step 4: Last step is to relocate the effective mover. Based on the optimal solution achieved, emperor penguin's positions are continuously updated. Emperor penguin's next position is updated by

$$P_{ep}(x + 1) = P(x) - A.D_{ep} \tag{17}$$

In Eq. 17, $P_{ep}(x + 1)$ represents next updated position of emperor penguin's.

Table 2 presents the parameter settings of emperor penguin algorithm. Table 3 presents the list of selected optimal features.

Table 2. Parameter settings of EPA

EPA's parameters	Values
Population size	32
Temperature (T')	[1,1000]
Social factors SF()	[0, 1.5]
Movement parameter (MP)	2
Control parameters (F & L)	F= [2,3] & L = [1.5,2]
Vector A	[−1.5,1.5]
Vector C	[0,1]

Table 3. List of selected features

Extracted feature type	List of extracted features
Time based features	#date-time, #logon activity, #http activity, #File activity, #email activity, #device activity
Frequency based features	#total number of logins, #total number of device connected, #total number of device disconnected, #total number of emails sent, #total number of email receive, #total number of attachments, #size of the attachment, #total number of http requests sent(url visited), #total number of files accessed
Others	employee name, #user id, #pc id, #email-to, #email-from, #psychometric features (O,C,E)

3.5   Classification

Finally, in this section the users are classified as normal or malicious using a multi-fuzzy-classifier [22]. This classifier is composed of multiple interference engines which parallel operates and obtain result. We consider three fuzzy interference engines (F1, F2, F3) in which they are fed with,

1. F1: Optimal Time dependent features
2. F2: Optimal Frequency dependent features
3. F3: Final classification of users into normal or malicious

As per the above mentioned input in each fuzzy the output is extracted and fed into third fuzzy for final classification of users. According to the optimal features the membership functions are dynamically generated for fuzzy 1 and fuzzy 2. Finally, fuzzy 3 classifies the users as normal or malicious.

Figure 2 illustrates the flow chart of the classification module.

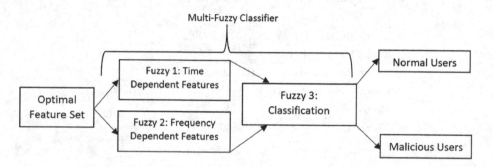

Fig. 2. Multi fuzzy classifier flow chart

The existing methods to classify users as normal or malicious are based on crisp values of each user to be classified as the member of only one of the class either normal or malicious. It means classification is based on the binary values 0 or 1, where it is denoted that a user is either 100% normal or 100%malicious. Where as using fuzzy classification, each user will be associated with its membership value. The more the membership value, the more strongly that particular user is associated with that particular class. In the proposed work, the third fuzzy F3 classify the users as normal or malicious. Subsequently by analyzing the output values of the third fuzzy inference engine F3, for different threshold values, such a value is chosen which gives the minimum number of false positives. For this reason, the users with membership value < 0.4 are classified as normal users, where as the users with membership value > 0.4 are classified as malicious users.

4   Results and Discussion

Experimental results and discussion for the proposed method is described in this section. Each of the subsections elaborately describes the data set used to implement the proposed method, environmental setup, and the performance metrics used for evaluating the proposed and existing methods respectively.

4.1   Data Set Description

CMU-CERT r4.2 Data Set [14] is used to analyze the performance of the proposed method. The results are compared with four existing methods [8,11–13]. The data set contains data of 1000 users, generated over five type of activities (logons, device, file, http, and email) over 18 months of time starting from December 2009 to May 2011. Each activity file contains the following fields: name, time-stamp, user-id, pc-id, action-details. Additional to these there is a psychometric.csv file containing the score of 5 types of personality traits of each user. Also, there is one LDAP folder containing eighteen .csv files containing the list of all the users for each month along with their names, user id, email, role, business unit, functional unit, department, supervisor. The train-test split of the above described data set used for implementation is in the ratio of 80:20, for training and testing respectively.

4.2   Experimental Environment

The proposed method has been implemented using the environmental setup presented in Table 4.

Table 4. Environmental setup

Dataset	CMU CERT r4.2	
Hardware	Operating system	Windows 10 - 64 bit Single OS
	Processor	Intel I Core I i3-7100 CPU@3.90 GHz
	Processor speed	3.90 GHz
	RAM	4 GB
Software	IDLE	Python IDLE 3.6.6 (64bit)

4.3   Performance Metrics and Result Analysis

After implementing the proposed method for the given dataset, we analyzed it using five different performance metrics : Accuracy,Precision, F-Measure, Recall, and AUC-ROC. The results are analyzed using confusion matrix presented in Table 5. It is described using the following four outcomes: True Positives (TP) which represents the number of users which are predicted as normal and are

Table 5. Confusion matrix

Confusion matrix		Predicted class	
		Normal users	Malicious users
Actual class	Normal users	Ture positive (TP)	False negative (FN)
	Malicious users	False positive (FP)	True negative (TN)

actually normal only; True Negatives (TN) which represents the number of users which are predicted as malicious and are actually malicious only; False Positives (FP) which represents the number of users which are predicted as normal but are actually malicious; and False Negatives (FN) which represents the number of users which are predicted as malicious but are actually normal. Using the confusion matrix presented in Table 5, the experimental results are presented below:

1. Accuracy: It is used to evaluate the percentage of correctly classified users compared to all the users. It is represented as:

$$Accuracy = \frac{TP + TN}{TP + TN + FP + FN} \tag{18}$$

It is observed that the proposed method obtains higher accuracy compared to the existing methods due to effective and efficient data pre-processing, feature extraction, feature selection and classification operations. For better accuracy the threshold value for classification is selected in such a manner that it minimizes the false positives and increases the true positives for the proposed method.

Table 6 presents the average accuracy of the proposed method with respect to the existing methods.

2. Precision: This metric is used to evaluate the number of users in the data set which are classified correctly. Raising the threshold value for classification would probably give better precision as it decreases false positives, but raising the classification threshold beyond a limit will decrease the true positive rate, therefore, in the proposed method selecting the appropriate classification threshold results in higher precision. It is represented as:

$$Precision = \frac{TP}{TP + FP} \tag{19}$$

It is observed that the proposed method obtains higher precision compared to the existing methods due to optimal feature selection and classification operations.

Table 6 presents the average precision of the proposed method with respect to the existing methods.

3. Recall: It is used to evaluate the number of correctly classified insider threats with respect to the total number of users. It is also known as True Negative Rate (TNR) or sensitivity. Raising the threshold value for classification will make the recall to decrease or remain constant, therefore after analyzing different threshold values, an appropriate threshold vale is selected in such a manner that number of true positives as well as number of false negatives remains constant as much as possible. It is represented as:

$$Recall/(TNR) = \frac{TP}{TP + FN} \tag{20}$$

It is observed that the proposed method obtains higher recall value as compared to the existing methods due to effective and efficient feature processing operations.

Table 6 presents the average recall of the proposed method with respect to the existing methods.

4. F-Measure: This metric is use to evaluate combined precision and recall's performance. For a better classification model precision value should be increased without compromising any reduction in recall value, likewise recall value should be increased without compromising any reduction in precision value. Therefore, for the proposed method, we looked at both precision and recall together. It represents harmonic mean of precision and recall. It is represented as:

$$F_{Measure} = 2 \times \frac{Precision \times Recall}{Precision + Recall} \tag{21}$$

It is observed that the proposed method obtains higher f-measure compared to the existing methods.

Table 6 presents the average f-measure of the proposed method with respect to the existing methods.

5. AUC-ROC: Area under Curve- Receiver Operating Characteristic Curve is another major metric to evaluate the performance of the proposed method. The curve is generated using FPR (False Positive Rate) and TPR (true Positive Rate) against each other on x-axis and y-axis respectively. Figure 3 shows the plots of AUC-ROC parameter for existing methods compared to the proposed method. It is observed that the proposed method obtains higher AUC-ROC curve values as compared to the existing methods. Higher the obtained AUC-ROC Curve value, higher the probability of distinguishing a normal user from malicious user.

Table 6 presents the average AUC-ROC curve values of the proposed method with respect to the existing methods.

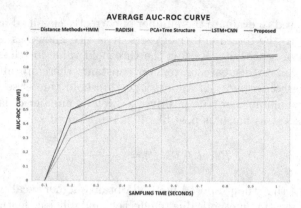

Fig. 3. Average AUC-ROC

Table 6 presents the combined results obtained for the proposed method for the following five performance evaluation metrics: accuracy, precision, recall, f-measure and AUC-ROC. The results are compared with the following four existing methods: Distance Measurement Methods[8], RADISH[11], PCA + Tree Structure[12], and LSTM + CNN [13].

Table 6. Results comparison

Methods	Accuracy	Precision	Recall	F-Measure	AUC-ROC
Distance measurement methods [8]	71.1	64..1	55.9	61.7	0.79
RADISH [11]	54	47.5	44.2	44.9	0.67
PCA + Tree structure [12]	64.8	58.7	56.2	56.5	0.57
LSTM + CNN [13]	75.3	71.8	68.1	68.6	*0.90*
Proposed	**87.3**	**84.9**	**81.7**	**81.9**	**0.89**

5   Conclusion and Future Work

We proposed an insider threat detection method based on user's behaviour to classify users as normal or malicious. ISOMAP is used as a global optimal feature extraction method. Emperor Penguin Algorithm, is used for feature selection. Finally, a multi-fuzzy-classifier is used for classification of users.

The proposed method is tested using CMU-CERT r4.2 dataset. The results are compared with four existing methods: Distance Measurement Methods, RADISH, PCA with Tree Structure, and LSTM-CNN. The following five performance metrics are used for evaluation of the proposed method: Accuracy, Precision, Recall, F-Measure, AUC-ROC. From the results it is evident that the proposed method outperforms the existing methods. The main advantage of the proposed method is that along with classifying a user as normal or malicious, it also gives the membership value of each user associated with either of the class : normal or malicious.

In future, we plan to work on prevention of insider threats.

References

1. Insua, D.R., et al.: An Adversarial Risk Analysis Framework for Cybersecurity. Risk Analysis, Wiley Periodicals (2019). arXiv preprint arXiv:1903.07727
2. Al-mhiqan, M.N., et al.: New insider threat detection method based on recurrent neural networks. **17**(3), 1474–1479 (2020)
3. Lu, J., Wong, R.K.: Insider threat detection with long short-term memory. In: Proceedings of the Australasian Computer Science Week Multiconference, pp. 1–10 (2019)
4. Yuan, F., Cao, Y., Shang, Y., Liu, Y., Tan, J., Fang, B.: Insider threat detection with deep neural network. In: Shi, Y., et al. (eds.) ICCS 2018. LNCS, vol. 10860, pp. 43–54. Springer, Cham (2018). https://doi.org/10.1007/978-3-319-93698-7_4
5. Yamin, M.M., Katt, B., Sattar, K., Ahmad, M.B.: Implementation of insider threat detection system using honeypot based sensors and threat analytics. In: Arai, K., Bhatia, R. (eds.) FICC 2019. LNNS, vol. 70, pp. 801–829. Springer, Cham (2020). https://doi.org/10.1007/978-3-030-12385-7_56
6. Almehmadi, A.: Micromovement behavior as an intention detection measurement for preventing insider threats. IEEE Access **6**, 40626–40637 (2018)
7. Chattopadhyay, P., Wang, L., Tan, Y.-P.: Scenario-based insider threat detection from cyber activities. IEEE Trans. Comput. Soc. Syst. **5**(3), 660–675 (2018)
8. Lo, O., Buchanan, W.J., Griffiths, P., Macfarlane, R.: Distance measurement methods for improved insider threat detection. Security and Communication Networks (2018)
9. Lv, B., Wang, D., Wang, Y., Lv, Q., Lu, D.: A hybrid model based on multi-dimensional features for insider threat detection. In: Chellappan, S., Cheng, W., Li, W. (eds.) WASA 2018. LNCS, vol. 10874, pp. 333–344. Springer, Cham (2018). https://doi.org/10.1007/978-3-319-94268-1_28
10. Kim, J., Park, M., Kim, H., Cho, S., Kang, P.: Insider threat detection based on user behavior modeling and anomaly detection algorithms. Appl. Sci. **9**(19), 4018 (2019)
11. Böse, B., Avasarala, B., Tirthapura, S., Chung, Y.-Y., Steiner, D.: Detecting insider threats using radish: a system for real-time anomaly detection in heterogeneous data streams. IEEE Syst. J. **11**(2), 471–482 (2017)
12. Legg, P.A., Buckley, O., Goldsmith, M., Creese, S.: Automated insider threat detection system using user and role-based profile assessment. IEEE Syst. J. **11**(2), 503–512 (2015)
13. Singh, M., Mehtre, B.M., Sangeetha, S.: User behavior profiling using ensemble approach for insider threat detection. In: 2019 IEEE 5th International Conference on Identity, Security, and Behavior Analysis (ISBA), pp. 1–8 (2019)
14. Insider Threat Dataset, Software Engineering Institute, Carnegie Mellon University. https://ftp.sei.cmu.edu/pub/cert-data/
15. Leslie, N.O., Harang, R.E., Knachel, L.P., Kott, A.: Statistical models for the number of successful cyber intrusions. J. Defen. Model. Simul. **15**(1), 49–63 (2018)

16. Xin, Y., Kong, L., Liu, Z., Chen, Y., Li, Y., Zhu, H., Gao, M., Hou, H., Wang, C.: Machine learning and deep learning methods for cybersecurity. IEEE Access 6, 35365–35381 (2018)
17. Isometric Feature Mapping. https://en.wikipedia.org/wiki/IsomapAlgorithm/
18. Iranmanesh, S.M., Mohammadi, M., Akbari, A., Nassersharif, B.: Improving detection rate in intrusion detection systems using FCM clustering to select meaningful landmarks in incremental landmark isomap algorithm. In: Zhou, Q. (ed.) ICTMF 2011. CCIS, vol. 164, pp. 46–53. Springer, Heidelberg (2011). https://doi.org/10.1007/978-3-642-24999-0_7
19. Xu, X., Tao, C.: ISOMAP algorithm-based feature extraction for electromechanical equipment fault prediction. In: IEEE 2nd International Congress on Image and Signal Processing, pp. 1–4 (2009)
20. Zheng, K., Xu, Q., Yu, Z., Jia, L.: Intrusion detection using ISOMAP and support vector machine. In: IEEE International Conference on Artificial Intelligence and Computational Intelligence, vol. 3, pp. 235–239 (2009)
21. Dhiman, G., Kumar, V.: Emperor penguin optimizer: a bio-inspired algorithm for engineering problems. Knowl.-Based Syst. 159, 20–50 (2018)
22. Multi-Fuzzy-Classification. https://en.wikipedia.org/wiki/Fuzzy-classification/

Layer-2 Performance Analysis of LTE-A and HetNets for 5G Networks

Krishna Reddy[✉], Irani Acharjamayum[✉], and Arup Bhattacharjee[✉]

Department of Computer Science and Engineering,
National Institute of Technology Silchar, Silchar, India
krishna9reddy9@gmail.com, irani.acharj@gmail.com, 1971.arup@gmail.com

Abstract. 5G mobile networks major challenge is in improving system capacity and service demands. In wireless networks, there has been a tremendous growth in traffic demands which can be solved using Het-Net (Heterogeneous Network). In our case, we considered LTE and WiFi for HetNet support. At the same time due to rapid increase of wireless devices and applications, the demand for wireless radio spectrum increases. Carrier Aggregation (CA) has been introduced in LTE-A with the sole purpose of additional bandwidth requirements. Experimentation takes place to estimate achievable performance of LTE and HetNet. Performance patterns of LTE, LTE-A and HetNets has been examined extensively.

Keywords: LTE · LTE-A · HetNet · 5G · CA · Performance

1 Introduction

Wireless devices and applications advancement have resulted into growing demand for wireless radio spectrum. Gaming and video enabled applications in cellular and Personal Area Network (PAN) devices generate large volume of wireless traffic. From user perspective, traffic has completely become unpredictable in terms of speed, additional bandwidth, etc. Although bandwidth may be underutilized for most of the time, still users are ready to pay for additional bandwidth during peak time. Wireless communication require only spectrum, which is naturally available. As the number of wireless devices are increasing, this spectrum allocations are becoming congested day by day. With the inclusion of machines in the communication platform, a completely different paradigm of communication has emerged. Machines which are wireless devices like sensors, actuators exchange information without or with restricted human intervention. As the number of machines increases manifold that surpasses the human centric communication devices, M2M communication is a key solution in future network. M2M communication [18] objective is to achieve ubiquitous connectivity over a wide coverage area. Its applications requires machines to achieve mobility support, reliability, coverage, power consumption, bandwidth, cost etc. The network architecture for M2M communication requires communication technologies

© Springer Nature Singapore Pte Ltd. 2020
A. Bhattacharjee et al. (Eds.): MIND 2020, CCIS 1241, pp. 575–587, 2020.
https://doi.org/10.1007/978-981-15-6318-8_46

which provide low cost, low data rate that covers in long range. It is witnessed about increased demand for intercommunication between heterogeneous devices. Wireless technologies such as WiFi (IEEE 802.11b) and LTE [15] are considered by interconnecting devices in a form of large heterogeneous network. A key point to note is that, low frequency signals can travel over longer distance compared to higher frequency signals. Also, higher frequency signals need to spend more energy compared to low frequency signals. In this paper it is proposed for performance analysis explicitly in LTE and HetNets.

These technologies or protocols have different benefits and drawbacks when it comes to IOT. To overcome the challenges of M2M communication, interconnecting the cellular network to other wireless networks i.e. HetNet is one of the promising solution.

1.1   Long Term Evolution (LTE)

Long Term Evolution (LTE) is data enabled cellular technology, standardized by 3rd Generation Partnership Project (3GPP). First standardization of LTE was released in 2008, for achieving 300 Mb/s for delay of 5 ms. LTE technology is able to operate in multiple modes FDD, TDD, QPSK, TD-SCDMA, OFDM, and IMT. Basically LTE cellular standards are aimed to meet mobility and QoS at defined distance limitations. LTE infrastructure is able to provide service up to 30 km distance limitations at line of sight. However, service providers need to take care of inter-cell interference caused by neighbour cells. Service providers are allocated licensed spectrum for LTE operations according to country policies. As stated earlier, licensed spectrum is a precious physical layer parameter (Fig. 1).

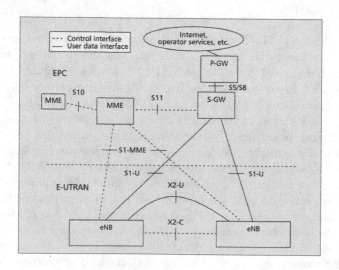

Fig. 1. LTE architecture [12]

In general, LTE services are made operational in infrastructure mode only. A legitimate LTE User Equipment (UE) generated traffic is carried forward from LTE base station (evolved node B or eNB) to gateway type device called Mobility Management Entity (MME) or Packet data network Gateway (PGW). LTE traffic at gateway will be routed in public networks as per operator routing policies. Layers involved in radio protocol stack are Packet Data Convergence Protocol (PDCP), Radio Link Control (RLC), MAC and PHY. As per standards, LTE wireless hop is allowed to operate in channels from 180 KHz to 20 MHz range [1,6,19].

1.2   Long Term Evolution Advanced (LTE-A)

Carrier Aggregation (CA) future has been introduced in LTE-Advanced (LTE-A) which forms the basis of 5G communication. The objective of CA is to increase available bandwidth to facilitate increased bitrate. Each aggregated carrier is termed to as a Component Carrier (CC) which can provide additional bandwidth of 1.4, 3, 5, 10, 15 or 20 MHz. Upto five component carriers can be aggregated, and thus maximum available bandwidth can be 100 MHz. LTE facilitates multi-user access through OFDM, by allocating sub carriers to users within the same transmission interval [2,3,21].

1.3   HetNet

Fifth Generation (5G), the next generation wireless standard is designed to enclose Heterogeneous Networks (HetNets). Ubiquitous connectivity are expected to achieve through 5G HetNets [4]. One major challenge in 5G mobile networks is to improve system capacity and service demands. HetNets is the most promising technology to solve this problem. There has been a tremendous growth in traffic demands in wireless networks with the increase in the usage of smart devices. This tremendous increase in traffic can only be assisted by wireless networks densification and Heterogeneous Network (HetNet) architectures deployment. The continuous development of wireless technologies leads to the coexistence of different wireless technologies like LTE, IEEE 802.11 based WiFi network etc (Fig. 2).

In the 5G era, LTE-Wi-Fi networks [13] is an emerging solution for providing widespread network capacity. With the joint operations of LTE cellular network and WiFi network, higher capacity and data rate with less power consumption requirements are expected to be fulfilled. Their collaborative operations can provide wider coverage area as well as indoor coverage. WiFi works on Industrial, Scientific and Medical (ISM) 2.4 GHz band while LTE works efficiently over the licensed spectrum from 700 MHz to 2.6 GHz. WiFi technology are low power with high capacity which has been adopted as the most successful indoor wireless solution in unlicensed bands. LTE on the other hand provides long range communication and outdoor coverage. To acquire capacity growth, 3GPP are on its effort [5]. The unlicensed 2.4 GHz band as well as the 5 GHz spectrum which is currently being used by WiFi, Zigbee and other communication systems are

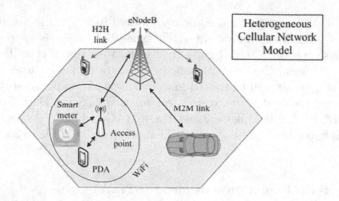

Fig. 2. Heterogeneous Network of LTE and WiFi [5]

to be enabled for the cellular networks in order to achieve capacity as well as reducing co-channel interference.

In the next section, research work related to performance analysis of LTE and HetNet were briefly discussed. In Sect. 3, designing of the system model has been explained. In Sect. 4, some analysis has been performed to understand the traffic pattern of LTE. Finally, conclusion briefly discussed in Sect. 5.

2   Related Work

In this paper [13], a brief summary of two HetNet architecture has been discussed i.e. LTE-WLAN Aggregation (LWA) and LTE-WLAN radio level integration with IP security tunnel (LWIP). Some simulation results shows the performance of potential gains of LWA and LWIP features w.r.t different load conditions. Based on the result, it is shown that LWA outperforms LWIP.

In this paper [11], HetNet with WiFi and LTE interfaces throughput performance has been studied. In order to make users benefit on cell edges, LTE average throughput is investigated. In addition to this, WiFi offloading optimal setting is studied. Under interferences, the proposed analysis provides users fair services.

In this paper [8], extensive local experiments were conducted and studied the LTE network performance. Comparison of performance with other types of mobile networks is studied. LTE has higher downlink and uplink throughput as compared to WiFi has been observed in this paper. With comparison to WiFi, LTE power efficient is less based on the study. Processing power of UE becomes more of a bottleneck based on the study.

In this paper [14], for downlink transmission, LTE PHY layer performance evaluation is conducted using Single-Input and Single-Output (SISO) and Multi-Input and Multi-Output (MIMO) techniques. Moreover, LTE performance analysis comprehensive investigation has been conducted.

In this paper [17], LTE-A random access channel and Access Class Bearing (ACB) performance analysis has been conducted. Certain configuration parameters has been modified in order to improve the LTE-A performance in massive M2M scenarios.

In this paper [7], to compare the performances of dual connectivity (to deal high data rate demand in 5G networks), an analytical framework has been proposed. Mobile terminals (MTs) data rate demands, arrival pattern of traffic and condition of the channel has been considered in their work.

In this paper [10], LTE network performance has been analysed using throughput, average throughput and jitter in various spectral bands. It has been observed that average throughput is lesser as compared to throughput. With the increase in the number of nodes, average throughput decreases. Jitter analysis does not show a normal specific trend.

In the paper [20] a Markov chain-based analytic model has been proposed capable of analyzing licensed-assisted access (LAA) network performance. Accuracy of the proposed analytic model has been checked by demonstrating comparison between analysis and simulation results.

In the paper [9], LTE wireless network MAC layer performance has been analyzed thoroughly. Main key factors which impact LTE networks performance index has been discussed. To achieve the system to have a good performance, reasonable LTE communication scheme has been on focused under different conditions.

3   System Models

Generally in computer networks, achievable performance is based on the number of active users in the network. Theoretically when active users are increasing in the network, performance will drop down. This performance completely depends on the competition among the active users to hold the available channel. At certain threshold time, this competition causes congestion [16] in the network. Congestion happens because of lack of sufficient wireless frequency needed to support other WiFi devices. This is called as Spectrum Crunch. Spectrum Crunch is a major risk in telecommunications and has profound implications in the immediate future. In-view of LTE network, experimental study has been done with respective to achievable performance at later-2 taking consideration of the number of active users. To validate achievable performance of LTE, system model mentioned in Fig. 3 has been considered. Depends on perspective, number of users and parameters of traffic models are considered.

Carrier Aggregation (CA) is expected to increase additional bandwidth at physical layer. Logically in CA, at physical layer additional channel is added to all active users. So at physical layer all active users are equally holding available carriers. It is necessary to understand growth rate of achievable performance at Layer-2 to feasibility of additional bandwidth requirement. With respect to each additional carrier, set of experimental studies has been conducted to understand bandwidth share among active users with similar applications. Along with this,

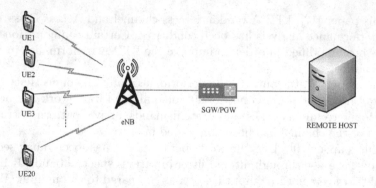

Fig. 3. LTE system model

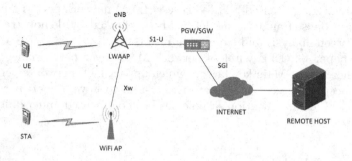

Fig. 4. HetNet system model

experimentation conducted for different applications with respective to various component carriers. However for carrier aggregation scenarios, same Fig. 3 system model is considered.

For supporting inter-working schemes like LTE and WiFi, different NS-3 modules and wireless technologies were used. Based on the system model for HetNet given in Fig. 4, WLAN AP is connected to eNB with the standardized interface Xw. This model is based on the LTE-WLAN Aggregation (LWA) introduced in 3GPP Release 13 [4]. At the Packet Data Convergence Protocol (PDCP) layer of eNB, LTE-WLAN is integrated efficiently. The HetNet model includes eNB, WiFi Access Point (AP), WiFi station (STA), User Equipment (UE). Here in this model, WiFi unlicensed bandwidth is combined with the licensed LTE bandwidth. A new sublayer called LWA Adaptation Protocol (LWAAP) adds the Data Radio Bearer (DRB) ID to the PDCP frames and transmitted to the WiFi interface. This layer makes multiple bearers to be offloaded to the WiFi network (Table 1).

Table 1. Simulation parameters

Parameters	Values	Parameters	Values
Carrier frequency	2 GHz	No. of UEs	1–20
Bandwidth	5 MHz	No. of eNBs	01
Traffic flow	UDP	No. of RHs	01
Interval	1 ms	Simulation time	20 s
Carriers	1–5	No. of AP & STA	01

4   Results and Analysis

To know the traffic pattern in LTE, experimentation done with standard LTE architecture. Achievable MAC layer performance has reported with simple UDP application. Initially performance measured with one number of active UE, and iterated same experimentation with increased number of UEs up to 20. It is observed that performance is dropping down non-linearly. It is noted that performance degradation is because of competition to hold channel among active users, corresponding performance is shown in Fig. 5. For LTE users from 1 to 20, simple UDP-CBR traffic model has been considered with interval 1 ms and packet size 1472.

$$Number\ Of\ LTE\ Users \propto \frac{1}{Performance} \tag{1}$$

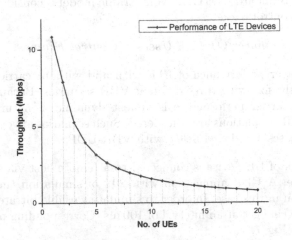

Fig. 5. Performance with respective to no. of UEs

To overcome additional bandwidth requirements, additional carriers are being added with primary carriers. It is observed that the initialization of communication happens after certain control frames exchanges. In LTE protocol stack, RRC is responsible to initialize control packets and communication with the support from RLC and MAC. An experimentation takes place to estimate additional control frames requirement for each appended carrier up to 20 LTE

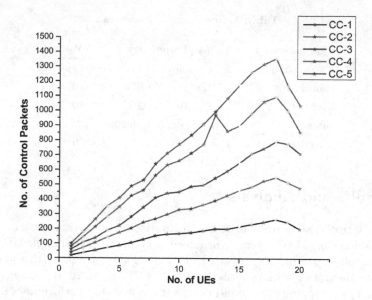

Fig. 6. LTE control packet requirement with respective to UEs

users. Requirement of control messages for each additional carrier with respective to users is found to be non-linear. Growth of control packets is found to be non-stationarily distributed with increase in active users. Such non-stationarity is not healthy for any system. Additional frame requirements statistics mentioned in Fig. 6. Standard LTE GBR-Voice traffic model is considered to analyse requirement of control packets.

$$Number \ Of \ LTE \ Users \propto Control \ Frames \qquad (2)$$

The MAC layer performance of LTE with and without carrier aggregation is evaluated in the following three different VBR scenarios. Because in realtime scenarios, LTE carrier performance is almost dynamic in nature. So in that perspective, VBR simulations are considered. Such scenarios are categorized into three different cases mentioned below with VBR-UDP.

– **Case 1:** 1 no. of UE device is connected to a remote host via standard LTE infrastructure. A UDP application with 20 s of simulation time is used for the simulation in this case. In order to simulate variable bitrate, the application datarate changes at an interval of 100 ms. Corresponding performance is mentioned in Fig. 7.
– **Case 2:** 20 no. of UE devices are connected to a remote host via standard LTE infrastructure. All applications are generating UDP traffic. UE no. 1 is active during 20 s of simulation time to generate variable bitrate for every 100 ms. UE no. 2 to UE no. 20 starts and stops randomly within the simulation time. Corresponding performance is mentioned in Fig. 8.
– **Case 3:** This is same as Case-2 except that, 5 component carriers are aggregated. Corresponding performance is mentioned in Fig. 9.

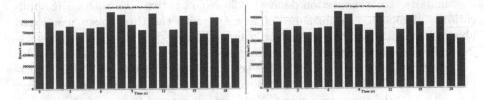

Fig. 7. Performance of LTE network while only 1 UE is active

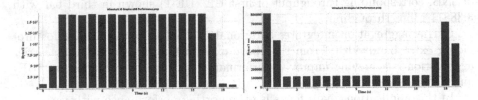

Fig. 8. Performance of LTE network with 20 UEs

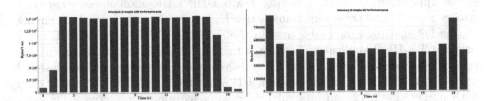

Fig. 9. Performance of LTE network with 20 UEs & CA-5

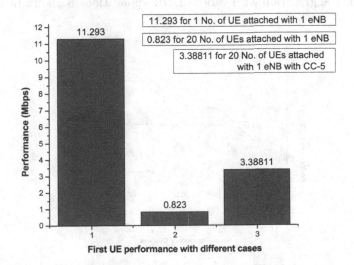

Fig. 10. Performance of LTE network with CBR application

Similarly, experimentation done with 20 No. of active UEs with CBR application and reported performance of first UE with the three cases mentioned above. With the assumption that only first UE is legitimate user and expecting additional bandwidth. Corresponding first UE performance shown in Fig. 10. For mentioned simulation, CBR-UDP scenarios were considered. With attachment of 1 no. of UE with 1 no. of eNB, corresponding throughput shown in first bar with 11.293 Mbps throughput. With attachment of 20 no. of UEs with 1 no. of eNB, corresponding throughput of only first UE (UE-1) shown in second bar with 0.823 Mbps throughput. With attachment of 20 no. of UEs with 1 no. of eNB, corresponding throughput of first UE (UE-1) shown in third bar with 3.38811 Mbps throughput.

Carrier aggregation integrates additional channel at physical layer for providing extra bandwidth. From the above experiments, it is noted that carrier aggregation is achieving improved performance on both User Equipment (UE) and Evolved Node B (eNB).

In this application, main focus is on reporting performance with variety of application scenarios. So three different application scenarios are considered with component carriers from CC-1 to CC-5 for each set of applications. In the first set of application, UE no. 1 having 1 Mb UDP CBR-onoff application with packet size 1472 whereas remaining active LTE users from UE no. 2–20 having the packet size 1024 interval 25 ms. In the second set of application, UE no. 1 having CBR-UDP application with packet size 1472 and interval 1 msec whereas remaining active LTE users from UE no. 2–20 having the packet size 1024 interval 25 ms. In the third set of application, UE no. 1 having CBR-UDP application with packet size 1472 and interval 1 msec whereas remaining active LTE users from UE no. 2–20 having packet size, interval and active time are different from each other. Overall LTE MAC layer performance from UE no. 1's perspective versus carrier aggregation with various UDP applications is shown in Fig. 11.

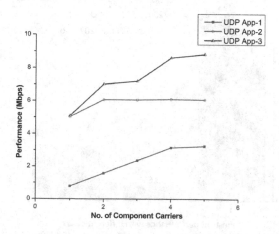

Fig. 11. Performance of LTE network from CC-1 to CC-5 with different applications

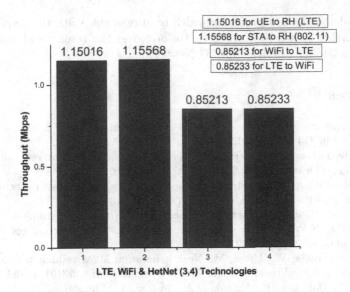

Fig. 12. Performance of intercommunication among HetNet devices

However even after appending additional channel to UEs, it is observed that aggregated carrier is shared among all active users. This results that a legitimate users may not be fulfilling additional datarate requirements as user is expecting.

For validating working principles of heterogeneous network, experimentation take place among heterogeneous technologies explicitly in LTE and WiFi. Initialization of communication of LTE with heterogeneous technology is done at PDCP. With the heterogeneous architecture [4], exhibited performance is reported in Fig. 12 with LTE only, WiFi only, HetNet technologies. In above simulation, UE-RH, STA-RH, WiFi-UE, UE-WiFi exhibiting performance 1.15016, 1.15568, 0.85213, 0.85233 respectively. These simulations has been iterated with interval 10 ms, packet size 1472, number of packets 100.

5   Conclusion and Future Work

In this article, performance of different technologies, explicitly in LTE and Het-Nets has been reported. These technologies act as key enablers of 5G Networks to serve large volumes of data around the globe. In-view of such key enabler technologies, achievable layer-2 performance has been reported with various test cases. It is observed that when number of LTE users are increasing, achievable performance of each user is decreasing exponentially. For additional bandwidth, whenever carrier aggregation is used, control packets requirement is becoming non-stationary. In congested LTE simulations, appending of five component carriers are also not exhibiting expected performance. It has been found that LTE infrastructure proves to provide hassle free services to heterogeneous devices also. It is noted that in congested channels further improvements are necessary to fulfil on-demand additional bandwidth requirements. With this experimental analysis, further it has been directed to look over the resource allocation and resource availability problems for 5G Networks.

References

1. Lte; evolved universal terrestrial radio access (e-utra); layer 2 - measurements. ETSI TS 136 314 V15.1.0 (07 2018)
2. Lte; evolved universal terrestrial radio access (e-utra); medium access control (mac) protocol specification. ETSI TS 136 321 V15.3.0 (10 2018)
3. Lte; evolved universal terrestrial radio access (e-utra); radio resource control (rrc); protocol specification. ETSI TS 136 331 V15.1.0 (10 2018)
4. Afaqui, M.S., Cano, C., Kotzsch, V., Felber, C., Nitzold, W.: Implementation of the 3GPP LTE-WLAN inter-working protocols in ns-3. In: Proceedings of the 2019 Workshop on ns-3, pp. 25–32 (2019)
5. Ali, A., Hamouda, W., Uysal, M.: Next generation M2M cellular networks: challenges and practical considerations. IEEE Commun. Mag. **53**(9), 18–24 (2015)
6. Astély, D., Dahlman, E., Furuskär, A., Jading, Y., Lindström, M., Parkvall, S.: LTE: the evolution of mobile broadband. IEEE Commun. Mag. **47**(4), 44–51 (2009)
7. Ghosh, S.K., Ghosh, S.C.: Performance analysis of dual connectivity in control/user-plane split heterogeneous networks. Comput. Commun. **149**, 370–381 (2020)
8. Huang, J., Qian, F., Gerber, A., Mao, Z.M., Sen, S., Spatscheck, O.: A close examination of performance and power characteristics of 4G LTE networks. In: Proceedings of the 10th International Conference on Mobile Systems, Applications, and Services, pp. 225–238 (2012)
9. Huang, M., Zhang, X., Hu, D., Liu, N.: Performance analysis of MAC layer for LTE networks. In: 2017 11th IEEE International Conference on Anti-counterfeiting, Security, and Identification (ASID), pp. 109–113. IEEE (2017)
10. Imran, M., Jamal, T., Qadeer, M.A.: Performance analysis of LTE networks in varying spectral bands. In: 2016 IEEE International Conference on Engineering and Technology (ICETECH), pp. 50–55. IEEE (2016)
11. Kao, Y.H., Chiu, H.L., Wu, S.H., Chao, H.L., Gan, C.H.: Throughput analysis of LTE and WiFi heterogeneous dense small cell networks. In: 2019 IEEE Wireless Communications and Networking Conference (WCNC), pp. 1–6. IEEE (2019)
12. Larmo, A., Lindström, M., Meyer, M., Pelletier, G., Torsner, J., Wiemann, H.: The LTE link-layer design. IEEE Commun. Mag. **47**(4), 52–59 (2009)
13. Laselva, D., Lopez-Perez, D., Rinne, M., Henttonen, T.: 3G PP LTE-WLAN aggregation technologies: functionalities and performance comparison. IEEE Commun. Mag. **56**(3), 195–203 (2018)
14. Layer, L.P.: LTE physical layer: performance analysis and evaluation (2017)
15. Nossenson, R.: Long-term evolution network architecture. In: 2009 IEEE International Conference on Microwaves, Communications, Antennas and Electronics Systems, pp. 1–4. IEEE (2009)
16. Reddy, K., Dey, B.: Near field communication over cognitive radio networks: an overview. Int. J. Comput. Intell. IoT **1**(2) (2018)
17. Tello-Oquendo, L., et al.: Performance analysis and optimal access class barring parameter configuration in LTE-a networks with massive M2M traffic. IEEE Trans. Veh. Technol. **67**(4), 3505–3520 (2018)

18. Verma, P.K., et al.: Machine-to-machine (M2M) communications: a survey. J. Netw. Comput. Appl. **66**, 83–105 (2016)
19. Ye, Y., Wu, D., Shu, Z., Qian, Y.: Overview of LTE spectrum sharing technologies. IEEE Access **4**, 8105–8115 (2016)
20. Yi, J., Sun, W., Park, S., Choi, S.: Performance analysis of LTE-LAA network. IEEE Commun. Lett. **22**(6), 1236–1239 (2017)
21. Yuan, G., Zhang, X., Wang, W., Yang, Y.: Carrier aggregation for LTE-advanced mobile communication systems. IEEE Commun. Mag. **48**(2), 88–93 (2010)

Placement Issues in Network Function Virtualization

Khem Prosad Sharma$^{(\boxtimes)}$ and Arup Bhattacharjee

National Institute of Technology Silchar, Silchar, India
khemnitm@gmail.com

Abstract. Network function virtualization(NFV) is being widely recognized as a network paradigm potentially suitable for current and future dynamic network service environment. NFV introduces flexible network function ordering in network service provisioning by proposing separation of network functions from the underlying hardware. Virtualized implementation of network functions as software modules can make network service provisioning simpler by reducing capital expenditure(CAPEX) and operational expenditure(OPEX) among various other advantages. NFV is being discussed with cloud computing framework to provide network functionalities as a cloud service. The placement of virtualized software modules on physical space is a very crucial step in NFV service provisioning. Overall service delivery is greatly affected by the way Virtualized network functions are placed in physical space. In this paper a formal introduction of the placement problem, importance of efficient placement, challenges faced in placement and study of various solution approaches is presented.

Keywords: Virtualization · Algorithm · MILP · NFV · Placement · Heuristic · VNF

1 Introduction

In the past few years, with the incremental growth of network data traffic, network services have become more diverse and dynamic [1]. NFV is an emerging networking paradigm that has the potential to become a key enabling technology for providing such services. Specifically, NFV framework through the Service Chaining (SC) model [2] can provide the necessary flexibility to offer a wide range of network services customized for the specific requirements of service users.

NFV [4–6] is currently one of the trending research area in academic and industry circle because of its immense possibilities. It proposes virtual softwarized implementation of network functions using general purpose servers [7]. Flexible service provisioning in NFV may help in addressing various developmental issues in the current networking infrastructure [3]. The softwarized implementation of network function is referred to as Virtual Network Function(VNF). VNFs are basic unit of service delivery in NFV environment. VNFs allow one to

A. Bhattacharjee et al. (Eds.): MIND 2020, CCIS 1241, pp. 588–599, 2020.
https://doi.org/10.1007/978-981-15-6318-8_47

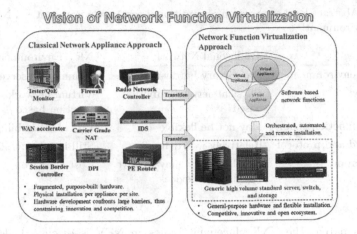

Fig. 1. Vision of NFV [3]

instantiate network services on cloud data centres or local servers as a software instance. This would allow dynamic and on demand provisioning of network services at a reasonable cost. One of the major challenges in service provisioning is the allocation of resources for VNFs in the servers. Usually VNFs needs to be placed in servers. The servers are usually substrate network nodes. Algorithms related to placement of VNFs on substrate network, i.e on servers or cloud, are very crucial for efficient service delivery. VNF placement is a crucial phase in network service provisioning in NFV environment. Devising a strategy to place the VNFs optimally onto servers plays crucial role in the efficiency of overall service delivery (Fig. 1).

Software implementation of the network functions makes it possible to instantiate multiple copies of same network function as per requirement. The proper implementation of NFV technology will significantly lower the CAPEX and OPEX of network service providers. As a result of NFV, there can be a clear separation between the service provider and the Infrastructure providers. The infrastructure providers will be responsible for providing the underlying hardware and service providers will use the hardware to implement the services over the hardware. Because of the virtualization technology, the implementation of the services will be less time and cost intensive. Since services are no longer dependent of the hardware, migration from one server to another server will be simple (Table 1).

NFV has received a lot of attention from industry recently. NFV is seen as a strategy to optimize cost efficiency, reduce time-to-market, and enhance the innovativeness in network service provisioning. However, efficiently running virtualized services is a multi stage process. The process of service provisioning involves mapping of virtual network functions onto physical networks, and thereafter scheduling virtual functions execution in order to optimize service availability. The problem of mapping VNFs onto substrate network is usually referred to as *placement problem*. It is explored in various research articles.

Table 1. Abstract level comparison of traditional service environment Vs. NFV based service environment

	Traditional Network	NFV Environment
Service environment	Proprietary hardware	Commodity server
Strategy	Physical network function based	Virtual network function based
Service function chain	May not be flexible	Provides flexibility
Standard and protocol	Relatively well defined	Still in nascent stage
Modification	Usually costly, may involve buying new devices	Cost effective

In this paper, the VNF placement issues in NFV is discussed along with importance and challenges. In Sect. 2, a formal introduction to VNF placement is presented in terms of service function chaining. The importance of an efficient placement strategy is also highlighted in Sect. 2. In subsect. 2.1, the effect of flexibility in service function chaining introduced by NFV is highlighted with an example. In subsect. 2.2, some of the placement approaches proposed by the researchers are discussed and a comparative table for some of the proposed approaches is presented. In subsect. 2.3, some of the major challenges in placement of VNFs for service function chaining is discussed. Section 3, concludes the paper.

2   VNF Placment in NFV

NFV is a concept having potential to revolutionize the network function development and deployment. NFV proposes to drastically change the network service provisioning environment by allowing network functions to be deployed in general purpose servers instead of proprietary hardware.

Fig. 2. Traffic through multiple VNFs of a network service

VNF placement is a crucial issue in NFV effecting the overall service delivery in NFV. A number of VNFs together make up a network service as in Fig: 2. The network traffic is routed through the constituent VNFs for applying the intended service. Placement of VNFs efficiently can affect the service response time. NFV aims to replace or complement the services provided using traditional proprietary hardware. Even if, proprietary hardware are expensive and difficult to maintain, the service response time is considerably good. Network service in

NFV environment has to match the service response time of proprietary hardware based services in order to be able to replace or co-exist with the traditional hardware based service delivery. In NFV, a service delivery involves, initialization of multiple VNFs in the server. Efficient utilization of the resources i.e. memory, bandwidth etc. will play a crucial role in service response time. Response time of the services will depend considerably on the efficient placement of the VNFs in the servers/commodity hardware. Importance of Efficient VNF placement may be emphasized by some of the following points,

☐ **On-demand Initialization**
NFV proposes on-demand initialization of network functions to support the flexibility introduced in service function ordering. Placement of VNFs modules in network nodes should be in such a way which can support on demand initialization, by being able to satisfy necessary resource requirements.

☐ **Routing of Traffic**
Routing traffic via the VNFs can be unpredictable, non optimal placement may lead to traffic congestion. Placement approach should insure that the placement layout of the VNFs on physical nodes, should try to avoid or minimize traffic congestion which may lead to service disruption.

☐ **Response Time for Service**
Transition to NFV is hugely dependent on service response time in NFV environment. Even if proprietary hardware based network services have various developmental disadvantages, but hardware based services usually tend to have relatively less response time as compared to services based out of a cloud environment. Similarly, NFV based services may also have the issues. Placement of VNFs will greatly effect the overall service response time.

☐ **Static vs. Dynamic resource allocation**
A user may not be continuously using a service for long. If a service is not being used and the constituent VNFs of the service are not being shared with some other service, the VNFs will remain idle. Utilization level of VNFs at all times may not constant. Static allocation of resources may lead to over provisioning of limited available resources.

☐ **Dynamic Nature of Service Request**
Frequent changes in user service requests may change the order of the placed VNFs leading to change in placement. The placement approach should be able to cope with such scenarios.

☐ **Fault Tolerance**
Mitigation against sudden failure of some VNFs in the sequence of VNFs deployed for a specific network service.

☐ **Scalability**
The service function chain placement approach should be scalable. VNF as a service(VNFaaS) a concept in discussion and early stages of implementation. In VNFaaS distributed VNF placement is explored for scalability.

2.1 The Problem

The placement problem in NFV is to allocate resources, such as storage, processing etc., to the VNFs in the physical hardware. Physical resources has limitations in terms of capacity and availability. Whenever a VNF is instantiated as per requirement, it has to be allocated some resources based on its requirements on some physical node in the network. The host node of the VNF should be able to support the computation requirement whenever the VNF will be in use and the links between the host nodes of different VNFs need to support the bandwidth requirement whenever traffic starts to traversed through the VNFs. The Utilization level of physical resources also plays an important role in overall cost so, efficient utilization of resources while going for VNF placement is highly desirable.

As NFV introduces flexibility in service chain formation for the constituent VNFs, deciding an optimum order for the VNFs is an decision problem in NFV. If there are n constituent VNFs for a service there may be $n!$ possibilities. Taking each possible formation and evaluating after placement is a computation intensive task and may not be feasible in practical environment supporting on demand requests. Randomly selecting a formation and going for placement may also not be good option considering the fact that random order may not be the optimum order or ever worse, it may be the worst order in terms of resource utilization (Table 2).

As for example, we take a service request with two VNFs where the service request has two VNFs in it which can be placed in an arbitrary order. These VNFs need to be traversed between given service endpoints. Input data rates and ratio of outgoing to incoming data rate for VNFs are chosen randomly. Resource requirements of each VNF increases linearly with data rate that enters the VNF and the resource requirement for a unit of data rate is also chosen randomly (Table 3).

Service request:

$$p1 \rightarrow (vnf_1, vnf_2) \rightarrow p2 \tag{1}$$

where $p1$ and $p2$ are the end point of the service request and vnf_1, vnf_2 can be arranged randomly among themselves.

Along with the set of VNFs some other information is assumed to be provided with the service request.

(i) Initial data_rate, which is considered as 1000 data_rate unit.
(ii) Value of outgoing to incoming data rate ratio, represented by "r". Value of outgoing data rate will be given by the product of incoming data rate and "r".
(iii) Resource requirement of the VNFs, for per unit of data rate, represented as "R". Total resource requirement for a VNF, vnf_i, will be given by the product of R_i with the total incoming data rate to vnf_i.

For the above service request two possible chaining options are possible.

$$p1 \rightarrow vnf_1 \rightarrow vnf_2 \rightarrow p2 \tag{2}$$

$$p1 \rightarrow vnf_2 \rightarrow vnf_1 \rightarrow p2 \tag{3}$$

Table 2. Resource requirement calculation

VNF	r	R	data_rate(in)	data_rate(outgoing)	Computational resources (data_rate(in)*R)
p1	1	0	1000	1000	0
vnf_1	0.8	0.55	1000	800	550
vnf_2	2.0	0.7	800	1600	560
p2	1	0	1600	1600	0

Table 3. Resource requirement calculation

VNF	r	R	data_rate(in)	data_rate(out)	Computational resources (data_rate(in)*R)
p1	1	0	1000	1000	0
vnf_2	2.0	0.7	1000	2000	700
vnf_1	0.8	0.55	2000	1600	1100
p2	1	0	1600	1600	0

☐ For service chain in Eq. 2,

Total computational resources requirement: 1110 resource units
total data_rate requirement: 3400 data_rate units

☐ Similarly for service chain in Eq. 3,

Total computational resources requirement: 1800 resource units
total data_rate requirement: 4600 data_rate units

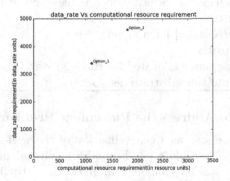

Fig. 3. Trade-off between computational resources and data rate requirement

From the above evaluation it evident that service chain option in Eq. 2 is better suited for placement as compared to option in Eq. 3. The overall resource consummation after the actual placement may change because of various issues. Still choosing the first service chain for placement may serve as the better option for overall resource utilization (Fig. 3).

VNF placement problem is very similar to the Virtual Network Embedding(VNE) problem. VNE problem is NP-complete and similarly VNF placement problem is also NP- complete. Solving a problem using exact algorithm in less time is very difficult. So most of the solution approaches usually try to apply heuristic methods to achieve some meaningful and realistic solutions which may be applicable to the actual NFV scenario. Exact algorithms give a good solution with near optimal or optimal result but the rate of convergence is very low, i.e. time taken for generating the solutions is very high. Time is going to be very crucial in NFV is it has to achieve its promising objectives.

Summary of VNF Placement

☐ **Problem statement**: Mapping of VNFs along with their links into the substrate network
☐ **Challenges**:
  • Limited resources, such as storage and computing, availability in Substrate network(links and nodes).
  • Inherent processing and traversing delay in the substrate network.
  • There may be various other network specific challenges.
☐ **Objectives**:
  • Optimize service response
  • Minimize the delay
  • Optimization of resources utilization by VNFs.
  • There may be other objects based on situation.
☐ **Input**:
  • VNFs and links among them
☐ **Output**:
  • Resource allocated for the VNFs and the links into the substrate network

---

2.2   Approaches to Address the Placement Problem

NFV placement can be seen as a generalization of the well-known Virtual Network Embedding(VNE) problem [8]. Embedding virtual networks in a SN is the main resource allocation challenge in network virtualization and is usually referred to as the VNE problem. VNE deals with the allocation of virtual resources both in nodes (mapped to substrate nodes) and links (mapped to substrate paths). Computing optimal VNEs is a NP-hard optimization problem [9] (Table 4).

Table 4. Abstract level comparison of VNE and VNF placement problem

	Input	Flexibility
VNE problem	Fixed virtual network	No
VNF Placement problem	List of VNFs and links among them	Usually yes

The term, Placement or Embedding, in case of NFV, generally means mapping the Virtualized Network Function onto physical resources. The VNFs are mapped to physical nodes whereas the links among the VNFs may be mapped into a physical link or inside a physical node. More than one VNF nodes can be mapped into the same node in the substrate network. Thus the mapping of VNFs into physical nodes is a n:1 relationship [5]. If two VNFs are mapped to same physical node then the link between the VNFs is also mapped to that particular physical node. Usually VNF instances of the same VNF are allocated to single node subject to the resource availability.

Resource requirements of the VNFs may be different based on the functionality provided by the VNF. Some VNFs maybe computation intensive or some VNFs may be networking specific. The node to which the VNFs are going to be mapped should be able to satisfy these requirements. Accordingly VNFs are mapped to storage or networking or computing nodes in the physical network. There are multiple number solutions proposed to address the VNF placement problem considering the respective constraints and optimization goals. Various exact and heuristic algorithm based proposals are tried to effectively address the placement/embedding. Integer programming has been used by various techniques to efficiently model the VNF placement problem.

In [10], the authors have proposed to divide the VNF placement problem into two separate sub problems . First, form a sequence of VNFs i.e. a chain of VNFs using a heuristic algorithm and then apply Mixed Integer Quadratic Constrained Program(MIQCP) model formulation for placing the VNFs on substrate network. MIQCP gives an exact solution but is very computation intensive. Based on the situation and requirement, objective for optimization of VNF placement may vary. In [10], the authors have given more importance to optimisation of energy efficiency, path latency and remaining data rate of the physical network links. The technique proposed in [11] uses a heuristic approach for VNF placement. Using heuristic makes the solution less computation intensive. It begins with a possible sequence of the VNFs which are to be placed and starts placing one VNF at a time in the substrate network. Initially the first VNF in the service chain is embedded into a substrate node having sufficient resources. Then the next VNF is taken up for embedding on the next suitable node. Search for the next placement node in substrate network is limited to one hop distance. Heuristically the nodes in one hop distance are checked one by one for embedding. Backtracking is used in this techniques. Next VNF in the sequence is tried to be placed into a node which is in one hop distance from the node where last embedding was done, if embedding is unsuccessful, backtracking is performed and again check for other nodes in one hop distance. In [12], the placement problem is formulated as an ILP formulation. But since VNF placement is an NP complete problem, it proposes heuristic technique to solve the placement problem. It starts with a initial feasible and tries to improve the solution step by step (Table 5).

2.3 Challenges

Placing of VNFs on substrate network has various challenges. Placement strategy has to consider the capabilities of the substrate network along with the

Table 5. Some of the Techniques Proposed to address the VNF placement and related issues in NFV environment

Reference	Primary Objectives	Optimization Techniques Used	Remarks
[10]	Formalizing requests VNF chain formation Placement of VNF sequence	CFG for parsing request Heuristic for chain composition MIQCP solving placement problem	Heuristic may not give optimum result MIQCP may limit Dynamic provisioning
[13]	Distributed Service Function Chaining(DSFC)	MILP Heuristic	MILP is time and computation intensive
[14]	VNF placement	ILP	Resiliency against single-node or link failure
[15]	Distributive deployment of multiple VNF instances	MIP	Combines heuristice of MIP
[16]	Composition of VNF chains	Heuristic	Heuristic method(CoordVNF) to coordinate the composition of VNF sequences and their embedding
[17]	Virtual Network Function Placement	ILP	Computation intensive
[18]	VNF placement and chaining	Heuristic	Minimize required resource allocation Dynamic composition not considered
[19]	Network function placement and chaining	ILP heuristic	Formulates the placement problem as an ILP Heuristic for large networks

requirements of VNFs in service provisioning. Some of the major challenges can be listed as,

☐ **Chaining**
NFV service provisioning request is usually supposed to have the list of VNFs along with the requirements. It is usually the responsibility of the service provider to define the order of the VNFs. The possible service chains for the requested list of VNFs is usually very large, there may be $n!$ for a VNF service request involving n number of VNFs. Finding out the optimal chain or order among the possible options is a challenge.

☐ **Large search space**
The search space for finding the optimal service function chain is very large. If every service chain needs to be evaluated for finding out the chain to be placed, the representation of the all the possible combinations may also an issue.

☐ **NP-Hard Problem**
VNF placement is an NP-hard problem as the VNE problem [8]. Solving an NP-hard problem with conventional methodology may not be enough. Innovative solution strategies have to applied to achieve an reasonable and practically applicable solution.

☐ **Resource Constraints**
The physical resource utilization needs to be optimized while deciding placement strategy. Allocation strategy may go for static or dynamic allocation. The comparison of Static allocation against Dynamic allocation based on resource requirement needs to evaluated. While Static allocation might be less computation intensive but may lead to over provisioning of limited resources. Whereas dynamic allocation might lead to near optimum resource utilization but may need complex calculation and continuous tracking of resource utilization level.

☐ **Sustainable Business**
NFV clearly introduces the flexibility of separation of services form underlying hardware. There can be independent service providers and independent infrastructure providers. Service provides can solely focus on providing services using the infrastructure provided by infrastructure providers. This model is dependent on sustainable business model. Service providers business depends on the customer satisfaction, which is dependent on service quality. If services can be made available on demand and within a reasonable time frame as compared to traditional hardware based services, NFV provides a sustainable business model.

3   Conclusion

Placement of VNFs in NFV environment is a core issue having the potential to affect the success of NFV in real world. The migration from current networking infrastructure to NFV based infrastructure depends on the ability to provide the services within a reasonable response time. Dynamic traffic may need different network functionality at different time, compelling initialization of multiple different VNFs at the same time, the placement algorithms should be able to do it with considerably less response time while maintaining minimum level of resource wastage. Placement is still a open research area where the scope of improvement and contribution is very large.

References

1. Otokura, M., Leibnitz, K., Koizumi, Y., Kominami, D., Shimokawa, T., Murata, M.: Application of evolutionary mechanism to dynamic virtual network function placement. In 2016 IEEE 24th International Conference on Network Protocols (ICNP), pp. 1–6. IEEE (2016)
2. John, W., et al.: Research directions in network service chaining. arXiv preprint arXiv:1312.5080 (2013)
3. D'Oro, S., Palazzo, S., Schembra, G.: Orchestrating softwarized networks with a marketplace approach. Procedia Comput. Sci. **110**, 352–360 (2017)
4. Li, Y., Chen, M.: Software-defined network function virtualization: a survey. IEEE Access **3**, 2542–2553 (2015)
5. Mijumbi, R., Serrat, J., Gorricho, J.-L., Bouten, N., De Turck, F., Boutaba, R.: Network function virtualization: state-of-the-art and research challenges. IEEE Commun. Surv. Tutorials **18**(1), 236–262 (2016)
6. Yi, B., Wang, X., Li, K., Huang, M., et al.: A comprehensive survey of network function virtualization. Comput. Netw. **133**, 212–262 (2018)
7. Bronstein, Z., Roch, E., Xia, J., Molkho, A.: Uniform handling and abstraction of NFV hardware accelerators. IEEE Netw. **29**(3), 22–29 (2015)
8. Fischer, A., Botero, J.F., Beck, M.T., De Meer, H., Hesselbach, X.: Virtual network embedding: a survey. IEEE Commun. Surv. Tutorials **15**(4), 1888–1906 (2013)
9. Han, B., Gopalakrishnan, V., Ji, L., Lee, S.: Network function virtualization: challenges and opportunities for innovations. IEEE Commun. Mag. **53**(2), 90–97 (2015)
10. Mehraghdam, S., Keller, M., Karl, H.: Specifying and placing chains of virtual network functions. In: 2014 IEEE 3rd International Conference on Cloud Networking (CloudNet), pp. 7–13. IEEE (2014)
11. Beck, M.T., Botero, J.F.: Coordinated allocation of service function chains. In: 2015 IEEE Global Communications Conference (GLOBECOM), pp. 1–6. IEEE (2015)
12. Luizelli, M.C., da Costa Cordeiro, W.L., Buriol, L.S., Gaspary, L.P.: A fix-and-optimize approach for efficient and large scale virtual network function placement and chaining. Comput. Commun. **102**, 67–77 (2017)
13. Ghaznavi, M., Shahriar, N., Kamali, S., Ahmed, R., Boutaba, R.: Distributed service function chaining. IEEE J. Sel. Areas Commun. **35**(11), 2479–2489 (2017)
14. Hmaity, A., Savi, M., Musumeci, F., Tornatore, M., Pattavina, A.: Virtual network function placement for resilient service chain provisioning. In: 2016 8th International Workshop on Resilient Networks Design and Modeling (RNDM), pp. 245–252. IEEE (2016)
15. Ghaznavi, M., Shahriar, N., Ahmed, R., Boutaba, R.: Service function chaining simplified. arXiv preprint arXiv:1601.00751 (2016)
16. Hwang, J., Ramakrishnan, K.K., Wood, T.: NetVM: high performance and flexible networking using virtualization on commodity platforms. IEEE Trans. Netw. Serv. Manag. **12**(1), 34–47 (2015)

17. Moens, H., De Turck, F.: VNF-P: a model for efficient placement of virtualized network functions. In: 10th International Conference on Network and Service Management (CNSM) and Workshop, pp. 418–423. IEEE (2014)
18. Nejad, M.A.T., Parsaeefard, S., Maddah-Ali, M.A., Mahmoodi, T., Khalaj, B.H.: vSPACE: VNF simultaneous placement, admission control and embedding. IEEE J. Sel. Areas Commun. **36**(3), 542–557 (2018)
19. Luizelli, M.C., Bays, L.R., Buriol, L.S., Barcellos, M.P., Gaspary, L.P.: Piecing together the NFV provisioning puzzle: efficient placement and chaining of virtual network functions. In: 2015 IFIP/IEEE International Symposium on Integrated Network Management (IM), pp. 98–106. IEEE (2015)

A Novel Graph Based Approach to Predict Man of the Match for Cricket

Kaushik Ravichandran$^{(\boxtimes)}$, Lalit Gattani, Advithi Nair, and Bhaskarjyoti Das

PES University, Bengaluru, India
kaushikrchandran@gmail.com, lalit16.gattani@gmail.com,
advithi.nair@gmail.com, bhaskarjyoti01@gmail.com

Abstract. The advent of computational intelligence has only accelerated the motive to automate manual processes. In sports, the award of
the best player is questionable in many cases and requires the opinion
of multiple distinguished experts in the sport. This often results in an
unfair judgement of the situation, given the time constraint for making
this decision, and the dependence on pure human skill and reasoning.
This calls for a reliable and fair system to fairly award the man of the
match, taking into account the numerous variables. Though there are
machine learning based approaches trying to model the game for predicting win/loss outcome, it is hard to model the "man of the match" in
a cricket game using the same approach. We propose a novel graph based
approach to award the "man of the match" to a player for a cricket game.
We model the game as a directed graph with each player as a node and
an interaction between two players as an edge. We use ball by ball delivery details to construct this graph with a heuristics to calculate the edge
weights and compute node centrality of every player using the Personalized Pagerank algorithm to find the most central player in the game.
A high centrality indicates a good overall performance of the player.
Comparison with existing game data showed encouraging results.

Keywords: Personalized Pagerank (PPR) · Social Network Analysis
(SNA) · Graphs · Cricket · Man of the Match (MOM)

1 Introduction

Cricket is entering its golden age of statistical analysis in India, with a lot of
teams and managers relying on technology to make important player purchases
and employ game winning strategies. This dependence on technology is also
extended to post game analysis to keep the cricket community live and active
between games in a season. Outcome of a match prediction has been a prime area
of interest to statisticians due to its simplicity yet complexity, being a binary
classification problem and at the same time relying on countless non quantifiable
parameters.

An important question asked after a match is that of awarding the best
overall performer of the game. This decision is usually taken by distinguished

© Springer Nature Singapore Pte Ltd. 2020
A. Bhattacharjee et al. (Eds.): MIND 2020, CCIS 1241, pp. 600–611, 2020.
https://doi.org/10.1007/978-981-15-6318-8_48

experts of the game, notwithstanding which is often a matter of ambiguity due to the number of parameters that affect this situation. Extensive research using learning based techniques have been studied for predicting the outcome of the game, but none on predicting the best player. In this paper, we propose a novel graph based approach to predict the man of the match of a cricket game. We aim to obtain a fair result, which accounts for any outcome for every ball played in a match. This guarantees that every ball of the game is equally important and could influence the outcome of the game, as is in the real world case.

2 Related Work

Games have lot of followings and people spend considerable amount of time as well as energy trying to guess the outcome of popular games. So, for obvious reasons, predicting outcome of games has attracted lot of research. With the advent of artificial intelligence and specifically that of data mining, machine learning and social network analysis, significant amount of research work has been done trying to predict the game outcomes. However, majority of the existing research uses various machine learning techniques leveraging game data. Also, the games which have attracted researchers' outcome are mainly basketball and football. Famous basketball tournaments such as NBA and football tournaments such as NFL have been subjected to lot of research whereas cricket has been attracting researchers' attention only recently.

Leung et al. [16] predicted outcome of college football based on historical results. Machine learning model based approaches to predict outcome of basketball and football games have been attempted by several researchers [9,12,17]. O'Donoghue et al. [20] did a probabilistic neural network learning the intricate relationship between different match factors. Instead of match factors, social media [32] has also been used to predict match outcomes. An alternative approach leveraging tweets has also been attempted for game outcome prediction [8,27]. Victoria J Hodge et al. [10] recently investigated the problem of win prediction in a multi-player battle oriented e_sports and has concluded that up to 85% accuracy is possible in short duration game play. These methods are novel, but do not tackle the task of predicting match results using actual match data, but rather rely on twitter data.

Most of the research conducted around cricket in recent years, has been to predict the outcome of games. MA Uddin et al. [31] proposed a framework using simple algorithms and neural networks that supports a variety of cricket predictions, including predicting the man of the match. However, results they obtained for the predictions were not mentioned. The authors used parameters such as age, player rating, score predicted for the match and runs/ wickets taken in the past to train their network. Somaskandhan et al. [29] identified the optimal feature set for high impact end result of Indian Premier League. Sankaranarayana et al. [24] used a subset of match parameters from historical as well current match data to predict outcome of one day international cricket leveraging classical machine learning and clustering techniques. Singh et al. [26]

combined linear regression along with Naive Bayes algorithms to predict both win as well as score. Kaluarachchi et al. [14] adopted a comprehensive approach considering not only game parameters but also environmental parameters to predict the probability of a win. Duckworth-Lewis method brings in uncertainty in match outcome in cricket and Ananda Bandulasiri [3] built a machine learning model to predict outcome in such cases. F Ali et al. [2] attempts to address the same shortcoming of Duckworth-Lewis method by considering player's quality and ranking in their proposed model. These approaches perform very well on predicting match outcomes such as win/loss and score, but the primary focus was not on predicting the man of the match, which is more of a deterministic problem with ambiguous answers.

Some researchers have focused on team selection and comparatively fewer researchers have focused on player performance, player style etc. in cricket. Deep convolution network has been used to identify the batting shot of cricketer [15]. A critical combination of players are often instrumental in win. Saraswat et al. [25] used weighted associated rule mining to analyze performance of Indian cricket teams in various tournaments. Solanki et al. [28] used association rule mining for selection of team. Chaudhary et al. [6] used Data Envelopment Analysis (DEA) model for team selection. Saikia et al. [23] built an artificial neural network based model to predict the performance of bowlers in Indian Premiere League (IPL). Iyer et al. [13] adopted a similar approach to predict selection of players in IPL. Hossain et al. [11] used genetic algorithm for team selection. H Ahmad et al. [1] used generative as well as discriminative models to classify players into different categories i.e. stable star, falling performance, rising star etc. Bruce G Charlton [5] proposed a performance model of a bowler in cricket using extra run saved per match instead of just number of wickets.

However, social network based approaches have rarely been used in the field of sports, to analyze games. Vaz de Melo et al. [18] investigated utility of network statistics such as clustering coefficient and degree for predicting game outcome and subsequently built team network models trying to predict outcome in NBA tournament [19]. Yoonjae Cho et al. [7] recently used a combined approach by using social network analysis metrics as independent variables in machine learning approaches. S Roy et al. [22] obtained the dataset from ESPN Cricinfo for all international matches for a period of ten years and formed a social network with the players where an edge represented a co-player relationship. Detailed social network analysis such as centrality analysis and validation of small world network characteristics were done using a composite framework of Hadoop, MapReduce and Giraph. They delivered this composite framework for future applications. Tripathy et al. [30] also used data from Cricinfo and attempted to model cricket as a complex network. Separate social networks were formed for different categories of games for each country i.e. one day, test match and IPL. Social network analysis such as centrality, clustering coefficient etc. were done on each of these social graphs but these social graphs were not used for any specific application such as team selection, result prediction or man of match. Also the work just focused on batsmen (and gave an incomplete perspective of the game) where the edge weight between two nodes was formed by the fraction of runs scored in partnership as compared to total runs scored. The bowlers were left out. The approach used by these authors captures relation between the players of a game, which can be exploited to predict man of the match, which directly relies on the interactions of a single player with the remaining players of the game.

As far as the game of cricket is concerned, the existing work mostly tries to predict the win/loss outcome of the match and in doing that, a set of factors have been used to put together a model. These factors play a huge role in deciding the winning team of a match but less so on the man of the match. Factors affecting man of the match is an entirely different set and can be the form, morale, performance of a player in previous games etc. It is hard to quantify such attributes to model into a machine learning algorithm when using this approach for 22 players makes the computation combinatorially expensive.

3   Model

3.1   Overall Approach

A directed graph is constructed by iterating through the dataset where each player playing represents a node and each interaction between two players represents an edge. The edge is weighted and the weights indicate the severity or importance of the interaction between the two players. Every ball played is accounted for. Based on the outcome of a ball, one or more edge(s) are either added or their weight(s) are updated using a heuristic defined by the edge weighting function, parameterized by the actors involved and the nature of their interaction. When the match ends, the Pagerank algorithm is used to evaluate the node centrality score of each node iteratively. The player or node with the highest centrality score is awarded man of the match. The remainder of this section is structured as follows:

We give a brief discussion of the dataset used in Sect. 3.2 followed by a discussion of the algorithm used in Sect. 3.3 and the edge weighting functions used in Sect. 3.4.

3.2   Dataset

The data used for testing our model consisted of match details of about 750 cricket matches, played in the Indian Player League season 2008–2016. It was collected manually as the cricket matches were played and obtained from Kaggle who in turns obtained it from Retrosheet. The information used here was obtained free of charge from and is copyrighted by Retrosheet. Interested parties may contact Retrosheet at "www.retrosheet.org".

The metadata of the dataset used is given in Table 1.

Table 1. Dataset metrics: (A) Dataset size (B) Match data attributes

No. of Matches	756
No. of Deliveries	179078
No. of Match Attributes	17
No. of Delivery Attributes	20

(A)

Innings	Bat team	Bowl team	Over
Ball	Batsman	Non-striker	Bowler
Issuperover	Wide runs	Bye runs	Legbye runs
No-ball runs	Penalty runs	Batsman runs	Extra runs
Total runs	Player out	Out type	Fielder

(B)

3.3 Pagerank Algorithm

Pagerank [21] measures the stationary distribution of a random walk that starts from a random vertex and in each iteration jumps to a random vertex with a predefined probability p and with probability 1-p, follows a random outgoing edge of the current vertex. Pagerank is usually conducted on a graph with homogeneous edges. The personalized Pagerank algorithm is built on this algorithm, such that the nodes or edges are weighted so as to affect teleport and transition probabilities in this random surfer model [4].

The personalized Pagerank weight update rule is given by Eq. 1. $M(p_i)$ is the set of all incoming vertices to the node p_i. $E(p_i)$ is the edge weight of node p_i. The dampening factor controls how much of the weight is transferred across an edge during one iteration of the pagerank algorithm. Since this is an iterative algorithm, we run it for some number of iterations until we notice a significant difference between the most central node and the second most central node.

$$PR(p_i) = \frac{1-d}{N} + d * \sum_{p_j \epsilon M(p_i)} \frac{PR(p_j) * E(p_j)}{\sum_{p_j \epsilon M(p_i)} E(p_j)} \tag{1}$$

where:

$PR(p_i)$ = Pagerank of node p_i
d = dampening factor
N = number of nodes
$M(p_i)$ = all incoming vertices of a p_i
$E(p_j)$ = gives the edge weight of node p_j

Algorithm 1: Graph Construction

Result: Graph G
adj_matrix;
for *every ball played* **do**
    if *wicket* **then**
        | adj_matrix[Batsman][bowler]+=weight_update();
        | adj_matrix[Batsman][fielder]+=weight_update() ;
    else if *run* **then**
        | adj_matrix[bowler][Batsman]+=weight_update() ;
        | adj_matrix[bowler][non_striker]+=weight_update() ;
    else if *boundary* **then**
        | adj_matrix[bowler][Batsman]+=weight_update();
    else if *extra* **then**
        | adj_matrix[bowler][Batsman]+=weight_update();
    else
        | adj_matrix[Batsman][bowler]+=weight_update();
    end
end
G=construct_graph(adj_matrix)

3.4 Edge Weighting Functions

An edge weighting function is triggered whenever an interaction takes place. All possible general interactions are given below. We have avoided mentioning particular cases such as when the fielder who took the catch is the bowler himself as that would also be handled by the more general case.

– Batsman hits the ball and scores some runs
– Batsman hits the ball for a boundary
– Bowler bowls a dot ball
– Bowler takes a wicket
– Bowler takes a wicket and a fielder is involved in a catch
– Bowler takes a wicket and a fielder is involved in a run out
– Extras including overthrows and penalties
– A match is won or lost

The chosen edge weights are purely based on the nature of the interaction between the players, for every ball. The algorithm used to construct the adjacency matrix of the graph is given in Algorithm 1. A detailed explanation of the same is given below.

For every ball that was played in the match, there can be a maximum of four possible actors: batter, non striker, bowler, fielder. Based on the outcome of the ball, a minimum of one and a maximum of $^4C_2$ weights are updated. For example, when the batter scores any number of runs off a bowler, the weight of the directed edge from the bowler to the batter is increased, as well the weight of the edge from the bowler to the non striker(in the case it was not a boundary). Similarly for a wicket, the weight of the edge from the batter to the bowler/fielder is increased. The direction of the edge signifies the flow of "points" from one player to another, and the magnitude of the weight update signifies the importance of the interaction(A wicket or a boundary should be given more weight than a dot ball). Similarly, a win would results in a weight update of the edges from all players of the losing team to all players of the winning team(121 total weight updates). This is relevant as the man of the match is usually from the winning team, with certain rare exceptions(which is captured by choosing the right weight updates of other interactions, in our model). The values for these weight updates were chose based on knowledge of cricket and multiple trials of observing the predictions. Further tuning of these weights can be done for a better accuracy of the model.

3.5 Implementation

The code was written in Python 3.7.2. Networkx 2.2 was used for the Pagerank algorithm. An alpha value of 0.85 was used and the Pagerank was computed for 100 iterations. All nodes started with an equal Pagerank of $1/N$, with no bias. The values chosen for alpha, maximum iterations and weights were chosen from repeated experimentation and are discussed further in Sect. 5.

4   Evaluation and Results

The model was tested on real match data collected from the IPL match dataset, which was constructed based on real ball by ball details of matches played in the IPL between 2008–2016. Although we do not aim to rate our model based on the accuracy of prediction, we have presented the results obtained in Table 2.

Table 2. Results

Type	Correct predictions	Total matches	Accuracy
Exact prediction	494	756	65.34
Top two predictions	537	756	71.03

An accuracy $> 60\%$ could be used to substantiate that there is not much disparity in awarding man of the match between our model and the actual outcome. The main focus of this paper is to develop a model that is just and fair to all the players and minimize human error. Example scenarios that could depict the performance of our model is discussed in Sect. 5. Figure 1 shows the Pagerank of all the players as computed by our algorithm. Each subfigure is our algorithm applied on different matches. The key value pairs are the player name and his pagerank respectively. The highest Pagerank corresponding to the most central player of that match, who is awarded man of the match by our algorithm. The actual man of the match awardee is also meentioned for a comparison.

Predicted List:
('BA Stokes', 0.073948486479488)
('GJ Maxwell', 0.0614730961656016)
('Imran Tahir', 0.0560972239657121)
('AR Patel', 0.05389347117704542)
('DT Christian', 0.05293108919532141)
('MP Stoinis', 0.050236827673055894)
('SPD Smith', 0.04822923087413726)
('DA Miller', 0.047812817312472826)
('RD Chahar', 0.04775571291019469)
('AB Dinda', 0.04705933185992377)
('HM Amla', 0.04704893455657219)
('WP Saha', 0.04615227906803456)
('MK Tiwary', 0.04398280370185393)
('MM Sharma', 0.042597421590899968)
('M Vohra', 0.04247890247953342)
('R Bhatia', 0.03885514655052097)
('Sandeep Sharma', 0.0382306980223293)
('T Natarajan', 0.03814065510542923)
('AM Rahane', 0.03639413213008835)
('Swapnil Singh', 0.0319349968490259)
('MS Dhoni', 0.0280001322534382894)
('MA Agarwal', 0.026745519798376707)
Actual Value: GJ Maxwell

(a)

Predicted List:
('AJ Tye', 0.07854619043806824)
('Imran Tahir', 0.068011030822389)
('DR Smith', 0.06479243489224143)
('P Kumar', 0.06367573479446717)
('BB McCullum', 0.0625470710248421)
('SPD Smith', 0.060069395462376134)
('RA Jadeja', 0.05814552373499297)
('Ankit Sharma', 0.05478638484204403)
('MK Tiwary', 0.053028887103697034)
('BA Stokes', 0.04824027885753221)
('RA Tripathi', 0.04783550762747681)
('LH Ferguson', 0.04489652285012342)
('AJ Finch', 0.0427400588111831)
('SK Raina', 0.04200477577936497)
('MS Dhoni', 0.035468785863551316)
('SN Thakur', 0.03278191754279856)
('RD Chahar', 0.03216843589811547)
('SB Jakati', 0.0270621952304416888)
('Basil Thampi', 0.025765347667350235)
('KD Karthik', 0.023551674579543325)
('AM Rahane', 0.022088293968510798)
('Ishan Kishan', 0.011168993047529642)
Actual Value: AJ Tye

(b)

Fig. 1. Screenshot of computed pagerank of the players of a match

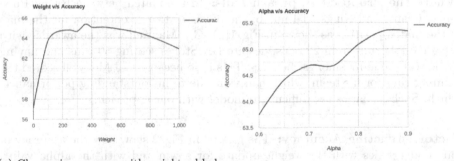

(a) Change in accuracy with weight added for a win

(b) Change in accuracy with alpha

Fig. 2. Change in accuracy

5 Analysis

The proposed approach aims at finding the most fair results efficiently. Alternative to treating the infractions as scalar values, we treat them as vectors where they can change over time. By making the interactions weighted we establish that any two interactions of the same kind will (and should) have a different impact on the game.

Example: Our proposed approach was accurate in a general case as shown in Fig. 1(b). In a game between Rising Pune Supergiants and Guharat Lions, A J Tye was awarded the man of the match for taking 5 wickets, with an economy of 4.25.

Tie Game: A game between Gujarat Lions and Mumbai Indians was tied and won in the one over eliminator by Mumbai Indians. K H Pandya was awarded man of the match, for taking 3 wickets with an economy of 3.5. Our model was accurate again. Our model also predicted Parthiv Patel(Who had scored 70 of the 153 runs) and James Faulkner(Who had taken 2 important wickets) to be next in contention for man of the match, which seems to be coherent with their performance.

Where Humans Fail: When there is a contention for the award between two bowlers with a similar economy, a bowler who has taken more wickets is preferred to be given the award. In a case where a bowler takes 3 wickets, he is awarded the man of the match, over someone who has taken 2 wickets. What we fail to capture is the importance of the wickets taken. If the latter bowler has taken the wicket of a Batsman who had a very high strike rate, he must be given credit for this as well. This is seldom taken into consideration while awarding the man of the match, but is captured in our model.

Where the Proposed Approach Fails: In the match between Rising Pune Super Giants and Kings XI Punjab, there was a strong contention for the man of the match position as shown in Fig. 1(a). G J Maxwell was the awardee with a score off 44 runs from 20 balls, despite BA Stokes scoring 50 runs and having the lowest economy amongst bowlers. This is so because G J Maxwell scored the winning runs for his team, which had won due to his outstanding performance, which. Such scenarios are difficult to model with our approach.

Factors Affecting Accuracy: The graphs in Fig. 2 show how the accuracy of our model varies with the weight update for a win and with the alpha value. The accuracy increases with increase in the weight update, and then gradually starts decreasing.

6 Conclusion

Cricket is filled with technologies. From the complicated ball tracker to simple in-match analysis, technology has had a major impact in the game. A large amount of research has been done on analysis of games. Since there are many aspects to a game of cricket, with each game being a complex combination of multiple dynamically changing parameters, there are a lot of applications using new technologies that have not yet been explored. There have been attempts to model a game in the form of neural networks, and other machine learning based models. We explore the possibility of modelling a cricket game in the form of a graph. Since social network analysis using graphs is an emerging field in research, this gives a large scope for improvement and analysis that can be done.

In this paper, we propose a novel approach to award the man of the match as opposed to generally used manual methods. We construct a weighted bi directional graph based on in-game interactions to model the weights. Each player corresponds to a node, and each interaction accounts for the weights between the nodes in the graph. We use a personalised pagerank centrality algorithm on this graph to compute the node centrality of every node. This ensures that the edge weights are accounted for while calculating the importance of every player. With extensive research and analysis, we find the most appropriate weights associated with interactions that give the best accuracy. With appropriate tuning of parameters, to model the game, as well as for the algorithm used we achieve an accuracy of about 65% for exact predictions and 71% for top two predictions. We also analyse the results obtained by our approach, and highlight how it performs in extreme cases, and sometimes even proves to be more fair than human judgement.

7   Future Work

This paper is a first look into automating one of many components of cricket. Awarding the man of the match has many times been an ambiguous question, with an accepted answer, given by the umpires. With this approach, we try to provide a concrete solution to this problem. Ensembling the results from this algorithm with the results of other well known learning based techniques would result in a more accurate outcome prediction. A continuous function with multiple parameters, as opposed to a set of discrete values could be used to model the weights for every interaction. Furthermore, psychological instances such as pressure of winning, form of the player and other anthropogenic factors that play a huge effect in the performance of a player could also be modeled to capture a more realistic view of the scenario. A detailed analysis of the factors affecting our model could be done to get a deeper understanding of the influential factors that could improve the performance and make the system more just.

References

1. Ahmad, H., Daud, A., Wang, L., Hong, H., Dawood, H., Yang, Y.: Prediction of rising stars in the game of cricket. IEEE Access **5**, 4104–4124 (2017)
2. Ali, F., Khusro, S.: Player ranking: a solution to the duckworth/lewis method problems. In: 2018 14th International Conference on Emerging Technologies (ICET), pp. 1–4. IEEE (2018)
3. Bandulasiri, A.: Predicting the winner in one day international cricket. J. Math. Sci. Math. Educ. **3**(1), 6–17 (2008)

4. Blum, A., Chan, T.H., Rwebangira, M.R.: A random-surfer web-graph model. In: 2006 Proceedings of the Third Workshop on Analytic Algorithmics and Combinatorics (ANALCO), pp. 238–246. SIAM (2006)
5. Charlton, B.G.: The bowling equivalent of the batting average: quantitative evaluation of the contribution of bowlers in cricket using a novel statistic of 'extra runs saved per match'(ERS/M). OR Insight **20**(4), 3–9 (2007)
6. Chaudhary, R., Bhardwaj, S., Lakra, S.: A dea model for selection of indian cricket team players. In: 2019 Amity International Conference on Artificial Intelligence (AICAI), pp. 224–227. IEEE (2019)
7. Cho, Y., Yoon, J., Lee, S.: Using social network analysis and gradient boosting to develop a soccer win-lose prediction model. Eng. Appl. Artif. Intell. **72**, 228–240 (2018)
8. Godin, F., Zuallaert, J., Vandersmissen, B., De Neve, W., Van de Walle, R.: Beating the bookmakers: leveraging statistics and twitter microposts for predicting soccer results. In: KDD Workshop on Large-Scale Sports Analytics (2014)
9. Heit, E., Price, P.C., Bower, G.H.: A model for predicting the outcomes of basketball games. Appl. Cogn. Psychol. **8**(7), 621–639 (1994)
10. Hodge, V.J., Devlin, S.M., Sephton, N.J., Block, F.O., Cowling, P.I., Drachen, A.: Win prediction in multi-player Esports: live professional match prediction. IEEE Trans. Games (2019)
11. Hossain, M.J., Kashem, M.A., Islam, M.S., Marium, E., et al.: Bangladesh cricket squad prediction using statistical data and genetic algorithm. In: 2018 4th International Conference on Electrical Engineering and Information & Communication Technology (iCEEiCT), pp. 178–181. IEEE (2018)
12. Huang, K.Y., Chang, W.L.: A neural network method for prediction of 2006 world cup football game. In: The 2010 International Joint Conference on Neural Networks (IJCNN), pp. 1–8. IEEE (2010)
13. Iyer, S.R., Sharda, R.: Prediction of athletes performance using neural networks: an application in cricket team selection. Expert Syst. Appl. **36**(3), 5510–5522 (2009)
14. Kaluarachchi, A., Aparna, S.V.: Cricai: A classification based tool to predict the outcome in ODI cricket. In: 2010 Fifth International Conference on Information and Automation for Sustainability, pp. 250–255. IEEE (2010)
15. Khan, M.Z., Hassan, M.A., Farooq, A., Khan, M.U.G.: Deep CNN based data-driven recognition of cricket batting shots. In: 2018 International Conference on Applied and Engineering Mathematics (ICAEM), pp. 67–71. IEEE (2018)
16. Leung, C.K., Joseph, K.W.: Sports data mining: predicting results for the college football games. Procedia Comput. Sci. **35**, 710–719 (2014)
17. Loeffelholz, B., Bednar, E., Bauer, K.W.: Predicting NBA games using neural networks. J. Quant. Anal. Sports **5**(1), 1–17 (2009)
18. Vaz de Melo, P.O., Almeida, V.A., Loureiro, A.A.: Can complex network metrics predict the behavior of NBA teams? In: Proceedings of the 14th ACM SIGKDD international conference on Knowledge discovery and data mining, pp. 695–703. ACM (2008)
19. Vaz de Melo, P.O., Almeida, V.A., Loureiro, A.A., Faloutsos, C.: Forecasting in the NBA and other team sports: network effects in action. ACM Trans. Knowl. Discovery Data (TKDD) **6**(3), 13 (2012)
20. O'Donoghue, P., Dubitzky, W., Lopes, P., Berrar, D., Lagan, K., Hassan, D., Bairner, A., Darby, P.: An evaluation of quantitative and qualitative methods of predicting the 2002 FIFA world cup. J. Sports Sci. **22**(6), 513–514 (2004)
21. Page, L., Brin, S., Motwani, R., Winograd, T.: The pagerank citation ranking: Bringing order to the web. Technical report, Stanford InfoLab (1999)

22. Roy, S., Dey, P., Kundu, D.: Social network analysis of cricket community using a composite distributed framework: From implementation viewpoint. IEEE Trans. Comput. Soc. Syst. **5**(1), 64–81 (2017)
23. Saikia, H., Bhattacharjee, D., Lemmer, H.H.: Predicting the performance of bowlers in IPL: an application of artificial neural network. Int. J. Perform. Anal. Sport **12**(1), 75–89 (2012)
24. Sankaranarayanan, V.V., Sattar, J., Lakshmanan, L.V.: Auto-play: a data mining approach to odi cricket simulation and prediction. In: Proceedings of the 2014 SIAM International Conference on Data Mining, pp. 1064–1072. SIAM (2014)
25. Saraswat, D., Dev, V., Singh, P.: Analyzing the performance of the indian cricket team using weighted association rule mining. In: 2018 International Conference on Computing, Power and Communication Technologies (GUCON), pp. 161–164. IEEE (2018)
26. Singh, T., Singla, V., Bhatia, P.: Score and winning prediction in cricket through data mining. In: 2015 International Conference on Soft Computing Techniques and Implementations (ICSCTI), pp. 60–66. IEEE (2015)
27. Sinha, S., Dyer, C., Gimpel, K., Smith, N.A.: Predicting the NFL using twitter. arXiv preprint arXiv:1310.6998 (2013)
28. Solanki, U.J., Vala, J.: Selection for balanced cricket team fourth coming ICC championship 2017. In: 2017 2nd International Conference on Communication and Electronics Systems (ICCES), pp. 794–797. IEEE (2017)
29. Somaskandhan, P., Wijesinghe, G., Wijegunawardana, L.B., Bandaranayake, A., Deegalla, S.: Identifying the optimal set of attributes that impose high impact on the end results of a cricket match using machine learning. In: 2017 IEEE International Conference on Industrial and Information Systems (ICIIS), pp. 1–6. IEEE (2017)
30. Tripathy, R.M., Bagchi, A., Jain, M.: Complex network characteristics and team performance in the game of cricket. In: Bhatnagar, V., Srinivasa, S. (eds.) BDA 2013. LNCS, vol. 8302, pp. 133–150. Springer, Cham (2013). https://doi.org/10.1007/978-3-319-03689-2_9
31. Uddin, M.A., Hasan, M., Halder, S., Ahamed, S., Acharjee, U.K.: CRICRATE: a cricket match conduction and player evaluation framework. In: Abraham, A., Dutta, P., Mandal, J.K., Bhattacharya, A., Dutta, S. (eds.) Emerging Technologies in Data Mining and Information Security. AISC, vol. 755, pp. 491–500. Springer, Singapore (2019). https://doi.org/10.1007/978-981-13-1951-8_44
32. Yu, S., Kak, S.: A survey of prediction using social media. arXiv preprint arXiv:1203.1647 (2012)

Construction of Identity Based Signcryption Using Learning with Rounding

Dharminder Dharminder and Dheerendra Mishra[✉]

Department of Mathematics, The LNM Institute of Information Technology,
Jaipur, India
{dharminder.y16,dheerendra.mishra}@lnmiit.ac.in

Abstract. Current technology, quantum computing is a big threat to the security based on essentially number-theoretic cryptographic constructions. Shor's algorithm forces one to understanding and working on quantum resistant problems. Therefore, we need a reliable communication especially which can provide both confidentiality and authenticity in a single step. This paper presents an identity based signcryption using learning with rounding (IBSCLR) scheme in a random lattice. The security is based on the worst-case hardness of learning with rounding (LWR) problem. This scheme uses short signature and ensures security in widely acceptable standard model. Furthermore, the scheme illustrates security in the quantum era and can be applied to practical application vehicular, crowdsourcing, internet of things based structure in the modern computation world.

Keywords: Signcryption · Security · Authentication · Discrete Gaussian · Learning with rounding

1 Introduction

An advanced cryptographic tool signcryption was proposed by Zheng et al. [25] in the year 1997. Most of the signcryption techniques [14,25] have been proved secure in the random oracle model. Therefore, many of the schemes [6,7,12,13, 19,22,23] are presented in the standard model. However, the presented schemes are based on the discrete logarithm problem or elliptic curve discrete logarithm problem. But Shor [20] presented a polynomial-time algorithm to kreak down the assumptions factorization and discrete logarithm problems, which is a serious threat to the security of existing number-theory based cryptosystems.

The quantum attacks [8,18] are best resisted by lattice, thus making it one of the most powerful cryptographic tool. Lattice-based cryptography plays an important role as its security assumption assumes the worst-case hardness in some lattice, where the cryptographic parameters depend only on modular operations (addition and multiplication). The above mentioned two flexible features

© Springer Nature Singapore Pte Ltd. 2020
A. Bhattacharjee et al. (Eds.): MIND 2020, CCIS 1241, pp. 612–626, 2020.
https://doi.org/10.1007/978-981-15-6318-8_49

of lattice-based cryptography has introduced a series of developments i.e. encryption [9,11,16,17], signature [8,9,16,17], homomorphic encryption [4,5], and functional encryption [2]. Thus, designing an IBSC in some of the lattices based on worst to average case assumptions is of both theoretical aspect and practical aspect (Fig. 1).

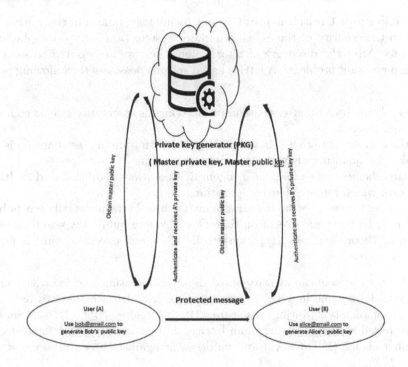

Fig. 1. A formal communication model of identity-based signcryption

This paper presents an IBSCLR scheme based on learning with rounding (LWR) assumption. This construction is inspired by the techniques as: Agrawal-Boneh-Boyen's [1] ID-based scheme, an efficient identity-based encryption due to Water et al.'s scheme [21] and Boyen's [3] lattice-based signature. Moreover, this IBSCLR scheme is being selective-ID secure without any requirement of random oracle model. Furthermore, it is also extendable to adaptive chosen identity attacks using the techniques [1,21]. The proposed IBSCLR has the following three features: (1) This framework for IBSCLR scheme is flexible such that the concerned encryption is deterministic or probabilistic. Moreover, the IBSCLR scheme can be proven indistinguishable against adaptive chosen ciphertext (INDCCA2). (2) The signature used in the scheme is much compact. Moreover, we have combined the form of identity [1,21] and the technique [3] to get an ID-based shorter signature. In addition, the IBSCLR scheme involves an efficient pre-image sampling, SampleRight, and ID-based encryptions. The

SampleRight is constructed to sample a preimage e to hold $Ae = b$ using the trapdoor of $\Delta^{\perp}(B)$, where $A = [A_1||A_1R + HB||C]$. The ordinary process executes both SampleBasisright and Samplepre consecutively. Moreover, the cost of Sampleright in answering for a single IBSCLR query is about eighth part of the ordinary technique if the extraction's query for the identically same ID has been submitted, otherwise approximately $\frac{1}{O(nlogn)}$ times of the ordinary method.

Motivation and Contribution: Current technology, quantum computing is a threat to the security of the existing number system based cryptographic constructions. After the discovery of Shor's algorithm, we are excited to work on quantum resistant problems. A lattice based scheme possesses the following properties.

1. This scheme uses worst-case assumption, which is essentially safe as compare to average-case.
2. In the current, the scheme based on learning with rounding assumption is not broken by quantum algorithms in polynomial time.
3. These schemes use simple linear algebraic operations (addition and multiplication), which requires low computation.
4. Assuming the security parameter κ, a lattice based scheme usually has public-key in size $O(\kappa^2)$ and execution time $O(\kappa^2)$, where public key size reduces in number theoretic classic cryptosystem i.e. $O(\kappa)$ and execution time is $O(\kappa^3)$ respectively.

This paper presents an identity based signcryption using learning with rounding (IBSCLR) scheme in a well studied lattice. IBSCLR scheme uses only non zero bits of plaintext during signature [21]. Therefore, IBSCLR uses shorter identity based signature in a random lattice. This scheme is secure against chosen cipher attack (IND-CCA2) and unforgeable against chosen message attack (EUF-CMA).

2 Preliminaries

In this manuscript, one can easily observe that $\mathbb{Z}$ stands for the set of integers, $\mathbb{R}$ denotes the set of real numbers, and $\mathbb{Z}_q$ residue class modulo prime "q". In the similar way, $\mathbb{Z}^n$ has tuples containing n integer elements, $\mathbb{Z}_q^n$ has tuples containing integers modulo "q", $\mathbb{Z}^{n \times m}$ denotes the set of matrices with m column vectors, each having $n > 0$ integer is necessarily the dimension of concerned lattice.

2.1   Lattice

A lattice (a two dimensional lattice shown in Fig. 2) is a discrete subgroup of R^m as follows in definition.

Definition 1. Let $a_1, a_2, \dots, a_m \in R^n$ be linearly independent tuples, then a lattice (Δ) generated by independent tuples $A = \{a_1, a_2, \dots, a_m\}$ is denoted

$\Delta = L(a_1, a_2, \dots, a_m) = \{Ax = \Sigma_i x_i \, a_i \ : \ x \in \mathbb{Z}^m\}$. The integers m and n denotes rank of concerned matrix, dimension of given lattice respectively.

$$\Delta = \mathbf{A} \cdot \mathbf{x} = \begin{bmatrix} | & | & & | \\ a_1 & a_2 & \dots & a_m \\ | & | & & | \end{bmatrix} \cdot \begin{bmatrix} x_1 \\ x_2 \\ \vdots \\ x_m \end{bmatrix}$$

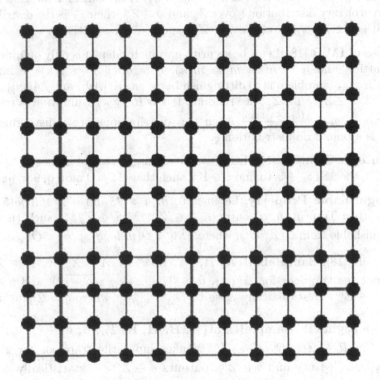

Fig. 2. Two dimensional lattice

The **q-ary lattice** satisfies $Z_q^m \subseteq \Delta \subseteq Z^n$, where $q > 0$ is an odd prime, and it is called q-ary lattice as q times vector belongs to the lattice. We are given a matrix modulo $q = poly(n)$ (depends only dimension of lattice) denoted $A \in Z_q^{n \times m}$ there are two types of n-dimensional $q - ary$ lattices $\Delta_q^{\perp} = \{x \in Z^n : A\,x = 0 \bmod q\}$ and $\Delta_q^u = \{x \in Z^n : u = A\,x \bmod q \mid x \in Z^m\}$, where m, n and q are integers and $m > n$.

$$\mathbf{A} \cdot \mathbf{x} = \begin{bmatrix} | & | & & | \\ a_1 & a_2 & \dots & a_m \\ | & | & & | \end{bmatrix} \cdot \begin{bmatrix} x_1 \\ x_2 \\ \vdots \\ x_m \end{bmatrix} = \begin{bmatrix} 0 \\ 0 \\ \vdots \\ 0 \end{bmatrix}$$

$$\mathbf{A} \cdot \mathbf{x} = \begin{bmatrix} | & | & & | \\ a_1 & a_2 & \cdots & a_m \\ | & | & & | \end{bmatrix} \cdot \begin{bmatrix} x_1 \\ x_2 \\ \vdots \\ x_m \end{bmatrix} = \begin{bmatrix} u_1 \\ u_2 \\ \vdots \\ u_m \end{bmatrix}$$

The lattices $\Delta_q^u(A)$ is essentially a coset of $\Delta_q^\perp(A)$ i. e. $\Delta_q^u(A) = \Delta_q^\perp(A) + z$ for arbitrary z satisfying $A\,z = u\,mod\,q$. If $b \in Z_q^n$, then a coset of q-ary lattice is given as $\Delta_b^\perp(A) = \{a \in Z^n : A\,a = b\,mod\,q\}$. Now, consider integers $n > 0$, $q > 2$, an arbitrary distribution ξ over Z_q and $\vartheta \in Z_q^n$, then $_{\vartheta,\xi}$ is the distribution of $(a, a^t\vartheta + e) \in Z_q^n \times Z_q$, where $a \leftarrow Z_q^n$, and $e \leftarrow \xi$ respectively.

Hardness of LWR [18]. Let κ be security parameter depends only on dimension of the lattice, and $n = n(\kappa)$, $m = m(\kappa)$, $q = q(\kappa)$, $p = p(\kappa)$ be integers, then $LWR_{n,m,p,q}$ problem is to distinguish between $(A, [A\vartheta])$ and $(A, [u])$, where $A \in Z_q^{m \times n}$, $\vartheta \in Z_q^m$, $u \in Z_q^m$ are random. If $LWR_{l,q,n,\xi}$ assumption is true and $q > 2\alpha\gamma mnp$, $n > \frac{(l+\lambda+1)log\,q}{log\,2\gamma+2\lambda}$, then two distributions are indistinguishable, where α is a bound on distribution ξ.

Small Integer Solution [15]. Let $q > 0$ be an integer, a real number $\zeta > 0$, and $A \in Z_q^{n \times m}$, then $SIS_{q,\zeta}$ is to find $z \in Z^m$ such that $Az = 0\,mod\,q$, $0 < ||z|| < \zeta$.

Indistinguishable Property. Let $\eta > 0$, $m, q > 2$, and $n > mlogq(5 + 3\eta)$ be given, then Trap(m, n, q) outputs $A \in Z_q^{m \times n}$, $S \in Z_q^{n \times n}$, such that A is indistinguishable from $U(Z_q^{m \times n})$, where $||S|| < O(m\,logq)$, $||\tilde{S}|| < O(\sqrt{m\,logq})$.

SampleLeft [18]: **SampleLeft(A, B, T_A, b, ϑ)** $\leftarrow A \in Z_q^{n \times m}$, $B \in Z_q^{n \times m'}$ takes input the trapdoor for $\Delta^\perp(A)$, $\vartheta > ||\tilde{T}_A||.\omega(log\,\sqrt{n+n'})$, and $b \in Z^m$, outputs $e \in Z^{m+m'}$ statistically close to $D_{\Delta_b^\perp(A||B),s}$, where $q > 2$ and $m > n$ are integers.

SampleRight [18] **SampleRight(A, B, H, R, T_B, b, ϑ)** $\leftarrow A \in Z_q^{n \times m'}$, $B \in Z_q^{n \times m}$, $R \in Z_q^{m' \times m}$, $H \in Z^{n \times n}$ takes input the trapdoor for $\Delta^\perp(B)$, $\vartheta > ||\tilde{T}_B||.\vartheta.\omega(log\,m)$, and $b \in Z^m$, outputs $e \in Z^{m+m'}$ statistically close to $D_{\Delta_b^\perp(A||AR+HB),s}$, where $q > 2$ and $m > n$ are integers, H is a non singular matrix.

2.2 Security-Notions

IBSCLR necessarily follows two well known notions of security, (1) indistinguishable under chosen cipher attack (IND-CCA2) and existential unforgeable against chosen message attack (EUF-CMA) [7,21,23]. One can observe that IND-CCA2 security is essential to ensure confidentiality of the signcryption.

Phase-1: IND-CCA2 phase is necessarily executed between a challenger $(\mathcal{C})$ and polynomial times adversary $(\mathcal{A})$. In the beginning, $\mathcal{C}$ executes the set up and sends output to $\mathcal{A}$, then $\mathcal{A}$ submits polynomial times queries as:

Extraction-queries: $\mathcal{A}$ submits an identity $\mathbb{ID}$ to $\mathcal{C}$, then $\mathcal{C}$ executes $Extraction(\mathbb{ID}) = K_{\mathbb{ID}}$ and returns the corresponding private key.

Signcryption: $\mathcal{A}$ submits two identities $\mathbb{ID}_s$, $\mathbb{ID}_r$ and a message (μ) to $\mathcal{C}$, then $\mathcal{C}$ computes $K_{\mathbb{ID}_s} = Extraction(\mathbb{ID}_s)$ corresponding to $\mathbb{ID}_s$ and executes Signcryption (μ, $K_{\mathbb{ID}_s}$, $\mathbb{ID}_r$) returns output to $\mathcal{A}$.

Unsigncryption: $\mathcal{A}$ submits two identities $\mathbb{ID}_s$, $\mathbb{ID}_r$ and a cipher (c), then $\mathcal{C}$ computes $K_{\mathbb{ID}_r} = Extraction(\mathbb{ID}_r)$, and Unsigncryption(c, $K_{\mathbb{ID}_r}$, $\mathbb{ID}_s$) and sends output to $\mathcal{A}$.

Challenge: If $\mathcal{A}$ completes phase 1, then he selects essentially two messages μ_0, μ_1 and $\mathbb{ID}_s^*$ and $\mathbb{ID}_r^*$ for the challenge. If $\mathcal{A}$ has never executed queries on $\mathbb{ID}_r^*$ in phase 1, then $\mathcal{C}$ tosses a coin and chooses a bit $b \in \{0,1\}$ and generates $c^* = Signcryption(\mu_b, K_{\mathbb{ID}_s}^*, \mathbb{ID}_r^*)$, and sends back to $\mathcal{A}$.

Phase-2: $\mathcal{A}$ arbitrarily asks polynomial times queries as in phase (1), except submitting the special extraction on $\mathbb{ID}_r^*$ and unigncryption on c^* to get the corresponding message. At last, $\mathcal{A}$ chooses a bit $b' \in \{0,1\}$, where $Adv(\vartheta) = |Pr[b' = b] - \frac{1}{2}|$ is the advantage in the game.

Definition 3. IBSCLR is IND-CCA2 if no $\mathcal{A}$ could gain the advantage more than arbitrary small ϵ however, $\mathcal{A}$ executes polynomial bounded extractions, signcryptions and unsigncryptions in the IND-CCA2 game.

EUF-CMA-Game: A similar game as phase (1) is executed between two parties $\mathcal{C}$ and $\mathcal{A}$. Now, $\mathcal{C}$ executes setup algorithm under security parameter (κ) and outputs public parameters and sends to $\mathcal{A}$, then $\mathcal{A}$ submits queries as in phase (1), and $\mathcal{A}$ guesses a tuple (c', $\mathbb{ID}_s'$, $\mathbb{ID}_r'$) as a forgery, where $K_{\mathbb{ID}_s}'$ is never queried before. $\mathcal{A}$ wins, he recovers the message from Unsigncryption (c', $K_{\mathbb{ID}_r}'$, $\mathbb{ID}_s'$).

Definition 4. IBSCLR is EUF-CMA if no $\mathcal{A}$ could gain information more than arbitrary small ϵ under polynomially bounded extractions, signcryptions and unsigncryptions queries respectively.

3 Proposed Post-quantum IBSCLR Scheme

We here describe how the mathematics of linear algebra has been used to define the cryptographic scheme called signcryption. The security mainly depends on worst case hardness in some lattices which are important mathematical objects. Some parameters used in the scheme is described below.

1. **Setup phase:** The $\mathcal{PKG}$ inputs security parameter κ and outputs public parameters along with private master key as following:
   (a) $\mathcal{PKG}$ chooses h: $Z_q^n \to Z_q^{n \times n}$, where h is a hashing under full rank differences [1].
   (b) $\mathcal{PKG}$ chooses five integers τ_1, τ_2, τ_3, τ_4, τ_5 and various collision resistant hashing $h_1 : \{0, 1\}^* \times \{0, 1\}^{\tau_1} \times Z_q^n \to \{0, 1\}^{\tau_2}$, $h_2 : \{0, 1\}^{\tau_3} \times Z_p^n \times Z_p^n \to \{0, 1\}^{\tau_4}$, and $H_\Lambda : \{0, 1\}^{\tau_5} \times \{r \in Z^{m'} : ||r|| < \tilde{\sigma}\sqrt{m'}\} \to Z_q^n$, where $\tilde{\sigma} = O(\sqrt{n \log q})\omega(\sqrt{\log n})$ and H_Λ is a matrix as in [1] and described as $\Lambda = [\Lambda_0 || \Lambda_1]$, where $\Lambda_0 \in Z_q^{n \times \tau_5}$ and $\Lambda_1 \in Z_q^{n \times m'}$.

(c) This algorithm generates random $A_0 \in Z_q^{n \times m}$ along with trapdoor $T_{A_0} \in Z_q^{m \times m}$ for $\Delta^\perp(A_0)$. Now, it selects random A_1, A_2, B_1, $B_2 \in Z_q^{n \times m}$, $G \in Z_q^{n \times \tau_5}$, $Q = \{Q_i \in Z_q^{n \times m}\}_1^n$, a nonzero vector $b \leftarrow Z_q^n$, then outputs public parameters $\{A_0, A_1, A_2, B_1, B_2, G, b, Q, h, h_1, h_2, H_\Lambda\}$, and master private key T_{A_0} along with a Gaussian parameter σ.

2. **Extraction phase:** Let $ID \in Z_q^n$ be an identity and SK_{ID} be the corresponding secret key. Now, the $\mathcal{PKG}$ executes $T_{ID} \leftarrow SampleLeft(A_0, [A_1 + H(ID)B_1], T_{A_0}, \sigma) \in Z^{m \times m}$, where T_{ID} is a trapdoor for $\Delta^\perp(A_{ID})$ with $A_{ID} = [A_0 || A_1 + H(ID)B_1]$, where $A_{ID} E_{ID} = G \in Z_q$ and vectors of E_{ID} as column vector e_{id} follows the distribution $D_{\Delta_q^{e_{id}}(A_{ID}), \sigma}$. Finally, it sends private key $SK_{ID} = T_{ID}$ to the owner of corresponding identity.

3. **Signcryption phase:** The sender with identity ID_s chooses a message $\mu \in \{0, 1\}^*$, his own secret key T'_{ID_s}, and identity ID_r of the receiver.

(a) Sender chooses a random number $r_1 \in \{0, 1\}^{\tau_1}$, and computes $\varrho = h_1(\mu, r_1, ID_r)$. Furthermore, the sender computes $ID_{sr} = \sum_{i \in U}(-1)^i Q_i$, where U is the subset of $\{1, 2, \ldots, n\}$ be the set of positions where $\varrho[i] \neq 0$. Now, he computes $\omega = (\omega_1, \omega_2)$ as $z = ID_{sr} \omega_2$, where $\omega_2 \leftarrow D_{Z^n, \sigma_1, 0}$ with Gaussian σ_1, and samples $\omega_1 \leftarrow SamplePre(T'_{ID_s}, b - z, \sigma_1)$ respectively.

(b) Now, the sender transforms ω in to (ρ_1, ρ_2) two strings of finite lengths. Then, the sender encrypts ρ_1 under the identity ID_r with a random $r_2 \in D_{Z^{n'}, \tilde{\sigma}}$ and computes $t = H_\Lambda(\rho_1, r_2)$, if $t = 0$, then he repeats the process.

(c) Now, he generates the matrix $A_{ID_r} = [A'_{ID_r} || A_2 + h(t)B_2]$, where $A'_{ID_r} = [A_0 || A_1 + h(ID_r)B_1]$ as in extraction phase. Furthermore, the sender chooses a nonzero vector $\vartheta \leftarrow Z_q^m$, R, $Q \in \{1, -1\}^{n \times n}$, and computes $c_0 = [G^t \vartheta] + \rho_1[\frac{p}{2}]$ modulo p, $c_1 = [A_{ID_r}^t \vartheta] - [0, [R^t \epsilon_0], [Q^t \epsilon_0]]^t$ modulo p, where $\epsilon_0 = (\frac{p}{q})A_0^t \vartheta - [A_0^t \vartheta]_p$, where 't' denotes the transpose of a matrix.

(d) The sender computes $c_2 = h_2(\rho_1, c_0, c_1) \oplus (\rho_2, r_1, r_2, \mu)$, and outputs a cipher $c = (t, c_0, c_1, c_2)$.

4. **Unsigncryption phase:** The receiver decrypts $c = (t', c'_0, c'_1, c'_2)$ with his own secret key T_{ID_r}, proceeds for the authentication as:

(a) First he checks t' is nonzero, then sample $e_i \leftarrow D_{Z^n, \vartheta}$, and computes $e'_i = [A_2 + h(t)B_2]e_i$ for $0 < i < \tau_5$. Furthers the receiver computes $E_{ID_r} = [\delta_1, \delta_2, \ldots, \delta_{\tau_5}, e_1, e_2, \ldots, e_{\tau_5}]$, where $\delta_i \leftarrow SamplePre(T_{ID_r}, A_{ID_r}, g_i - e_i, \vartheta)$, $A_{ID_r} = [A_0 || A_1 h(ID)B_1]$, and g_i is i^{th} column of G.

(b) Now, the receiver computes $b = c_0 - E_{ID_r}^t c_1$, and verifies, if $||b[j] - [\frac{p}{2}]|| < [\frac{p}{4}]$, then $\rho_1[j] = 1$, otherwise $\rho_1[j] = 0$.

(c) The receiver recovers $(\rho_2, r_1, r_2, \mu) = h_2(\rho_1, c_0, c_1) \oplus c_2$. Now, he transform $\rho = (\rho_1, \rho_2)$ in to ω. Furthers if $||\omega|| > \vartheta_1 \sqrt{3n}$, then he rejects, otherwise he computes $\varrho = h_1(\mu, r'_1, ID_r)$, $ID_{sr} = \sum_{i \in U}(-1)^i Q_i$, where U is the subset of $\{1, 2, \ldots, n\}$ be the set of positions where $\varrho[i] \neq 0$. Now, the receiver verifies $[A_0 || A_1 + h(ID_s)B_1 || \tilde{ID}_{sr}]\omega \neq b$ then rejects, otherwise outputs μ.

Correctness with Parameters. The length of every parameter of error vector is less than $O(n^2)$ during the decryption process. As we know, during the decryption step we computes as:

$$\omega = c_0 - E_{ID_r}^t c_1$$
$$= ([G^t \vartheta]_p + \rho_1[\frac{p}{2}]) - E_{ID_r}^t c_1$$
$$= ([G^t \vartheta]_p + \rho_1[\frac{p}{2}]) - E_{ID_r}^t((\frac{p}{q})(A_{ID_r}^t \ \vartheta) - \epsilon_1 - [0, \ [R^t \ \epsilon_0], \ [Q^t \ \epsilon_0]]^t)$$
$$= ([G^t \vartheta]_p + \rho_1[\frac{p}{2}]) - ((\frac{p}{q})E_{ID_r}^t(A_{ID_r}^t \ \vartheta) - E_{ID_r}^t \epsilon_1 - E_{ID_r}^t[0, \ [R^t \ \epsilon_0], \ [Q^t \ \epsilon_0]]^t)$$
$$= \rho_1[\frac{p}{2}] + (E_{ID_r}^t \epsilon_1 + E_{ID_r}^t[0, [R^t \epsilon_0], [Q^t \epsilon_0]]^t - \epsilon_2)$$

Where $\epsilon_0 = (\frac{p}{q})A_0^t \vartheta - [A_0^t \vartheta]_p \in [0,1)^n$, $\epsilon_1 = (\frac{p}{q})A_{ID_r}^t \vartheta - [A_{ID_r}^t \vartheta]_p \in [0,1)^{3n}$, $\epsilon_2 = (\frac{p}{q})E_{ID_r}^t A_{ID_r}^t \vartheta - [E_{ID_r}^t A_{ID_r}^t \vartheta]_p \in [0,1)^{3n}$.

It can be observed each entry of error vector $E_{ID_r}^t \epsilon_1 + E_{ID_r}^t[0, \ [R^t \epsilon_0], \ [Q^t \epsilon_0]]^t - \epsilon_2$ is $\epsilon = e_{ID_r}^t \epsilon_1 + e_{ID_r}^t[0, \ [R^t \epsilon_0], \ [Q^t \epsilon_0]]^t - \epsilon_2'$, where $||\epsilon|| < C'n^2$, where C' is a constant.

If one claims the correctness, then the following must hold:

1. The LWR assumption is hard under $q \geq 2(\alpha \ \gamma \ n \ m \ p)$ and $\sigma \ q > 2\sqrt{n}$.
2. Trapdoor algorithm ensures correctness for $m \geq 6 \ n \ (log \ q)$ and error should be small enough $(C'm^2 \leq [\frac{p}{4}])$.
3. Both **SampleLeft** and **SampleRight** algorithms ensure correctness when $\sigma_1 > O(m)\sqrt{log \ m}$ holds.

4 Security Analysis

In the IBSCLR scheme, SampleRight is used to sample the pre-image. Only the trapdoor T_B of $\Delta^{\perp}(B)$ is known for the matrix $A = [A_1||A_1R + HB||C] \in Z_q^{m \times (2n+\kappa)}$ and a vector $b \in Z_q^m$, where H is invertible matrix. Furthermore, it can be observed that SamplePre is run only once by SampleRight, where $[-Ra, \ a, \ e]^t$ is the pre-image of b.

Theorem 1. In the standard model, the proposed IBSCLR scheme is indistinguishable under chosen ciphers attack (IND-CCA2) for the given instance $LWR_{m, \ n, \ g, \ p}$ of the problem.

Proof. The security of IBSCLR is described under a number of games executed between a challenger ($\mathcal{C}$) and an adversary ($\mathcal{A}$) as:

Game G_0: In the IND-SID-CCA2, $\mathcal{C}$ knows the trapdoor T_{A_0} for $\Delta^{\perp}(A_0)$, hence he can reply all of the submitted legal queries.

Game G_1: Initially, $\mathcal{C}$ chooses a random $R^* \leftarrow \{-1, 1\}^{m \times m}$, then he computes $A_1 = A_0 R^* - h(ID_r^*)B_1$, where ID_r^* is an identity for the challenge. Now, $\mathcal{C}$ chooses $Q^* \leftarrow \{-1, 1\}^{m \times m}$, $t^* \in Z_q^n$ and computes $A_2 = A_0 \ Q^* - H(t^*)B_2$

and $\mathcal{C}$ replies all the legal queries. However, one can observe that a challenge cipher $[R^{*t}\epsilon_0]$, $[Q^{*t}\epsilon_0]$ reveals some information about R^* as well as Q^*, where $\epsilon_0 \leftarrow [0, 1)^n$. But, the information guessed about R^* and Q^* due to $[R^{*t}\epsilon_0]$, $[Q^{*t}\epsilon_0]$ is no more than $R^{*t}[q\epsilon_0]$, and $Q^{*t}[q\epsilon_0]$. According to leftover hash lemma, A_0, $A_0 R^*$, $R^{*t}[q\epsilon_0]$ has negligible statistical distance from A_0, A'_r, $R^{*t}[q\epsilon_0]$, $A'_r \in Z_q^{m \times n}$ random matrices. Therefore, $\mathcal{A}$'s advantage is negligible in the games G_0 and G_1.

Now, we will analyze the fact that $[R^{*t}\epsilon_0]$ does not reveal any information about R^* more than $R^{*t}[q\epsilon_0]$ modulo "q", where $\epsilon_0 \leftarrow [0, 1)^m$ is random. If one assumes $b \approx R^{*t}[q\epsilon_0]$ modulo "q" for some matrix $R^* \leftarrow \{-1, 1\}^{m \times m}$, then $Pr[R^{*t}[q\epsilon_0] \bmod q = b] = q^{-m}$ i. e. for a fixed "b" the number of matrices R^* are approximately $q^{-m}2^{m^2}$. Therefore, it has entropy $\vartheta' = -log_2((2m)^{-m}2^{m^2}) = m^2 - m \ log_2 \ m$ which means $[R^{*t}\epsilon_0]$ does not leaks information no more than $R^{*t}[q\epsilon_0]$ respectively.

Game G_2: $\mathcal{C}$ uses chameleon hash function H_C in place of the hash function H_Λ, but retains the trapdoor corresponding to H_C to itself. Following the same lines as game G_1, $\mathcal{C}$ can reply all the valid queries. Therefore, one can observe that the view of adversary $\mathcal{A}$ is indistinguishable in both G_1 and G_2 games.

Game G_3: The way of generating A_0, B_1 and B_2 is slightly being changed by $\mathcal{C}$. The challenger $\mathcal{C}$ chooses random $A_0 \leftarrow Z_q^{n \times m}$ and generates B_1, $B_2 \leftarrow Trap(m, n, q)$, where both A_1 and A_2 are same as in G_2, and answers all the queries except corresponding to ID_r^* and the tag t^* simultaneously.

However, it can be easily observed that G_2 and G_3 are independent in the view of the adversary, where $\mathcal{C}$ can reply all the legal queries except $ID_r = ID_r^*$, $t = t^*$ simultaneously. In both G_2 and G_3 public key is $A_{ID_r} = [A_0||A_1 + h(ID_r)B_1||A_2 + h(t)B_2] = [A_0||A_0 R^* + (h(ID_r) - h(ID_r^*))B_1||A_0 Q^* + (h(ID_r) - h(ID_r^*))B_2]$, where in G_2, $A_0 \leftarrow Trap(m, n, q)$, in G_3, $A_0 \leftarrow Z_q^{m \times n}$ is a random matrix. Hence, these two matrices follows indistinguishable property discussed in preliminaries section in this chapter. Therefore, both the games G_2 and G_3 has indistinguishable public key in the form of matrices.

Game G_4: $\mathcal{C}$ generates a challenge ciphertext c^* in a slightly different way. Following the same lines as in G_3, $\mathcal{C}$ chooses a random vector $r_2 \leftarrow D_{Z^{n'}, \sigma_1}$, where $||r_2|| \leq \sigma_1 \sqrt{m'}$. Now, $\mathcal{C}$ essentially chooses r_2 such that $H_C(\varrho_1, r_2) = t^*$ and $||r_2|| \leq \vartheta_1 \sqrt{m'}$ using the trapdoor of chameleon hashing H_C, where ϱ_1 is a substring of signed message (μ). Therefore, $\mathcal{C}$ easily replies all the legal queries in the game. Now, one claims the main difference between G_3 and G_4 are indistinguishable. In G_3, $H_\Lambda(\rho_1, r_2)$ follows the uniform random distribution according to chameleon hashing. In G_4, $H_\Lambda(\rho_1, r_2) = t^*$, $t^* \leftarrow Z_q^m$ is random and hidden before generating the challenge cipher. Therefore, $\mathcal{A}$ has negligible advantage to distinguish $t = H_\Lambda(\rho_1, r_2)$ and t^* which completes the argument.

Game G_5: $\mathcal{C}$ again generates a challenge cipher c^* by choosing $(c_0^*, c_1^*) \leftarrow Z_p^m \times Z_p^m$, where $\mathcal{C}$ could reply any number of polynomial times queries. One claims $\mathcal{A}$ cannot distinguish between games G_4 and G_5, otherwise we can model a $\mathcal{C}$, who can solve the hard assumption "LWR" problem. Here, one can observe that $c_2 = h_2(\rho_1, c_0, c_1) \oplus (\rho_2, r_1, r_2, \mu)$, where h_2 is collision resistant hashing. Therefore, c_2 is completely random, whenever the inputs c_0, c_1 are random. Hence, in the view of $\mathcal{A}$, cipher c_2 is not distinguishable from a random string. The indistinguishable property in the game G_4 and G_5 implies the complete randomness between c_0^*, c_1^* under the LWR encryption. Moreover, a LWR instance is constructed either in $\mathcal{O}_1$ pseudo random oracle or in $\mathcal{O}_2$ completely random oracle. The challenger $\mathcal{C}$ can use $\mathcal{A}$ as a subroutine in these two pseudo-random and random cases as:

Initialization $\mathcal{C}$ sends a request to the oracle $\mathcal{O}$ and receives an instance $(\phi_i, \psi_i) \in Z_q^n \times Z_p$ for $0 < i < [n + \tau_5]$ and publish the relevant parameters.

Key-generation $\mathcal{A}$ selects an identity ID_r^* as a target identity, then $\mathcal{C}$ generates master key as:

1. $\mathcal{C}$ chooses a matrix A_0, fixing i^{th} column as $(A_0)_i = \phi_i$ for $0 < i < n$, the $\mathcal{C}$ composes "G", where $(G)_i = \phi_{i+n}$ for $0 < i < \tau_5$.
2. $\mathcal{C}$ selects B_1, B_2 as a output of $Trapgen(m, n, q)$.
3. $\mathcal{C}$ selects and publishes public parameters $\{A_0, A_1, A_2, B_1, B_2, G, b, \mathbb{Q}, h, h_1, h_2, H_A\}$.

Phase 1: $\mathcal{C}$ follows the instruction as in G_4 and G_5 and replies all the polynomial times queries.

Challenge. If $\mathcal{A}$ submits a message μ, identities ID_s and ID_r such that $ID_r^* \neq ID_r \neq ID_s$, then $\mathcal{C}$ generates a challenge cipher as:

1. Consider an "LWR" instance (ϕ_i, ψ_i) as discussed above, and $\mathcal{O} = \mathcal{O}_1$, $\psi = [< \phi_i, \sigma >]$, where $\mathcal{O}_1$ is pseudo-random oracle.
2. Set $\chi_2^* = [\psi_{n+1}, ..., \Psi_{n+\tau_5}]^t$, $c_0^* = \chi_2^* + \rho_1^*[\frac{q}{2}]$.
3. Set $\chi_1^* = [\psi_1, ..., \psi_n]^t$, $\chi_1^{*'} = R^{*t}\chi^*\chi_1^{*''} = Q^{*t}\chi^*$, where $c_1^* = [\chi^*, \chi_1^{*'}, \chi_2^{*''}]$
4. Finally, $\mathcal{C}$ sends a challenge cipher $c = (c_0^*, c_1^*)$ to an adversary $\mathcal{A}$.

It can be observed that preceding (c_0^*, c_1^*) is a part of challenge $(t^*, c_0^*, c_1^*, c_2^*)$ generated in game G_4 under assumption $\mathcal{O} = \mathcal{O}_1$. Now, one observes that encryption matrix corresponding to receiver is $A'_{ID_r} = [A_0 || A_0 R^* + (h(ID_r) - h(ID_r^*))B_1] = [A_0 || A_0 R^*]$. Now, $\mathcal{C}$ chooses a random r_2 such that $H_C(\varrho_1, r_2) = t^*$ holds using the trapdoor for H_C, and ϱ_1 is a part of the signature. Therefore, the encryption matrix is $A_{ID_r}^* = [A_0 || A_0 R^* + (h(ID_r) - h(ID_r^*))B_1 || A_0 Q^* + (h(t^*) - h(t^*))B_2] = [A_0 || A_0 R^* || A_0 Q^*]$. Now, we check the challenge cipher in case (1) and case (2) respectively.

Case 1: If $\mathcal{O} = \mathcal{O}_1$, then ψ_i satisfies $\psi_i = [< \phi_i, \vartheta >]$ for $n < i < n + \tau_5$, as $G = [\phi_{1+m}, \phi_{2+m}, ..., \phi_{\tau_5+m}]$, and $[G^t \vartheta] + \rho_1[\frac{p}{2}] = [\psi_{m+1}, ..., \psi_{m+\tau_5}]^t + \rho_1[\frac{p}{2}] = \chi_2^* + \rho_1[\frac{p}{2}] = c_0^*$. Furthermore, this c_0^* is consistent with the c_0^* in the game G_4 and ψ_i is $\psi_i = [< \phi_i, \vartheta >]_p$ for $1 \leq i \leq m$. If $A_0 = [\phi_1, \phi_2, ..., \phi_m]$, and $\chi_1^* = [\psi_1, \psi_2, ..., \psi_m]^t = [A_0^t \vartheta]_p$, then c_1^* is computed as below.

$$c_1^* = \begin{bmatrix} \chi_1^* \\ \chi_1^{*'} \\ \chi_1^{*''} \end{bmatrix} = \begin{bmatrix} [A_0^t \vartheta]_p \\ R^{*t}[A_0^t \vartheta]_p \\ Q^{*t}[A_0^t \vartheta]_p \end{bmatrix} = \begin{bmatrix} [A_0^t \vartheta]_p \\ R^{*t}((\frac{p}{q})A_0^t \vartheta - \epsilon_0) \\ Q^{*t}((\frac{p}{q})A_0^t \vartheta - \epsilon_0) \end{bmatrix}$$

One observes that it is essentially same as c_1^* in the game G_4.

Case 2: If $\mathcal{O} = \mathcal{O}_2$, then χ_2^* is completely random in Z_p^n which means c_0^* is also completely random element.

Phase 2: $\mathcal{A}$ makes queries to $\mathcal{C}$ similar to phase 1, but he could not perform unsigncryption queries corresponding to ID_r^*.

Guess. After polynomial times queries to $\mathcal{C}$, $\mathcal{A}$ answers as a guess to "LWR" oracle. Furthermore, if $\mathcal{O} = \mathcal{O}_1$, then $\mathcal{A}$ has an advantage as in game G_4. Moreover, if $\mathcal{O} = \mathcal{O}_2$, then $\mathcal{A}$'s view as in the game G_5. Therefore, a simulator's $\mathcal{O}$ advantage to solve an instance of "LWR" problem is same as $\mathcal{A}$'s advantage.

Theorem 2. The proposed IBSCLR scheme is unforgeable under selective identity and chosen message (EUF-SID-CMA) assuming $SIS_{q, \varsigma}$ is hard for large $\varsigma = \vartheta n (2C' + \sqrt{2\kappa}\vartheta_1)$.

Proof. Let us assume that $\mathcal{A}$ can forge a valid signature, then one can model $\mathcal{C}$ to solve $SIS_{q, n, \varsigma}$ with non negligible advantage.

Initialization: If $\mathcal{A}$ chooses an identity ID_s^* and decleres it target identity, then $\mathcal{C}$ generates B_1, B_2 gets $\in Z_q^{n \times m}$ with corresponding trapdoors T_{B_1}, $T_{B_2} \in Z_q^{m \times m}$ under kernel lattices $\Delta^\perp(B_1)$, $\Delta^\perp(B_2)$ with the help of $TrapGen(m, n, q)$ respectively. Furthermore, $\mathcal{C}$ chooses random matrices $A_0 \leftarrow Z_q^{m \times n}$, $A_2 \leftarrow Z_q^{m \times n}$, $G \leftarrow Z_q^{m \times \tau_5}$, then samples $Q_i' \leftarrow D_{Z^n, \vartheta}^{m \times m}$, and constructs $Q_i = A_0 Q_i'$ for $0 < i < \tau_2$, $\mathcal{C}$ samples R^*, $Q^* \leftarrow \{0, 1\}^{m \times m}$, fixes $A_1 = A_0 R^* - h(ID_s^*)B_1$, and samples $x \leftarrow D_{Z^n, \vartheta, 0}$ and computes $b = A_0 x$, until we get "b" is a nonzero value. Finally, $\mathcal{C}$ publishes the parameters $\{A_0, A_1, A_2, B_1, B_2, G, b, \mathbb{Q}, h, h_1, h_2, H_A\}$, where $\{h, h_1, h_2, H_A\}$ are same as in the set up phase in the proposed scheme.

Queries-Phase: If $\mathcal{A}$ submits any of the queries extraction, signcryption, unsigncryption, then $\mathcal{C}$ proceeds as:

1. **Extraction-queries:** $\mathcal{A}$ submits $ID_i \neq ID_{s^*}$, then $\mathcal{C}$ executes $T_{ID_i} \leftarrow SampleBasisright(A_0, B_1, h(ID_i) - h^*(ID_{s^*}), R^*, T_{B_1}, \vartheta)$, and returns T_{ID_i} to $\mathcal{A}$.

2. **Signcryption-queries:** If $ID_s \neq ID_s^*$, then $\mathcal{C}$ calls SampleBasisright( ) to gets cipher c, and sends it to $\mathcal{A}$. Furthermore, if $ID_s = ID_s^*$, then $\mathcal{C}$ selects a random $r \in \{0, 1\}^{\tau_5}$, computes $\rho = h_1(\mu, r, ID) \in \{0, 1\}_2^\tau$ and $ID_{sr}' = \sum_{i \in U}(-1)^i Q_i$, where U is the subset of $\{1, 2, \ldots, n\}$ be the set of positions where $\varrho[i] \neq 0$. Now, $\mathcal{C}$ samples $\omega_2 \in D_{Z^{2n}, \vartheta, 0}$ and computes $b_1 = [R^*||ID_{sr}']\omega_2$, $\omega_1 = x - b_1$, where $(r, [\omega_1, \omega_2]^t)$ is a correct signature on message μ corresponds to ID_s^* and proves the claim in the following two aspects.

   First, one observes $\rho = h_1(\mu, r, ID)$, $ID_{sr} = \sum_{i \in U}(-1)^i Q_i$, and $[A_0||A_1 + h_1(ID_s^*)B_1||ID_{sr}'][\omega_1, \omega_2]^t = b$ respectively. $[A_0||A_1 + h_1(ID_s^*)B_1||ID_{sr}']$ $[\omega_1, \omega_2]^t$

$$= [A_0||A_0 R^* + (h_1(ID_s^*) - h_1(ID_s^*))B_1||A_0 ID'_{sr}][\omega_1, \ \omega_2]^t$$
$$= [A_0||A_0 R^* + A_0 ID'_{sr}][\omega_1, \ \omega_2]^t$$
$$= [A_0||A_0(R^*||ID'_{sr})][\omega_1, \ \omega_2]^t$$
$$= A_0\omega_1 + A_0(R^* ID'_{sr}) \ \omega_2$$
$$= A_0(x - b_1) + A_0 b_1 = A_0 x = b$$

Second, one can see $||[\omega_1 \ \omega_2]^t|| = ||[x - b_1 \ \omega_2]^t|| \leq ||x - b_1|| + ||\omega_2|| \leq ||x|| + ||\omega_2|| + ||\omega_2|| \leq \vartheta \ m(2C + \sqrt{2}\tau_3\vartheta_1) = \zeta$. Finally, $\mathcal{C}$ encrypts the information and sends it to $\mathcal{A}$.

3. **Unsigncryption-queries:** If $ID_r \neq ID_s^*$, then $\mathcal{C}$ decrypts cipher c and gets corresponding signature $(r, \ \omega)$ under message μ using trapdoor for ID_r. If $(r, \ \omega)$ is a legal signature on the message μ under corresponding identity ID_s, then $\mathcal{C}$ sends back μ to $\mathcal{A}$. On the other hand, if $ID_r = ID_s^*$, then encryption matrix is $A_{ID_r} = [A_0||A_0 R^*||A_0 Q^* + (h(t) - h(t^*))B_2]$, but $\mathcal{C}$ does not have any information about T_{ID}, he can use trapdoor of $\Delta^{\perp}(B_2)$ for the decryption process.

   $\mathcal{A}$ could not guess a cipher with $t = t^*$ as the tuple "t^*" is hidden and "t" is secure due to collision resistant hashing. Therefore, $\mathcal{C}$ can change unsigncryption process as $\vartheta_i = Sample-Right(A_0, \ B_2, \ h(t)-h(t^*), \ Q^*, \ 0, \ T_{B_2}, \ g_i, \ \sigma)$, where $0 \leq i \leq \tau_2$ and g_i is i^{th} column of matrix "G" and $E_{ID_r} = [s_1, \ ..., \ s_{\tau_2}] \leftarrow Z^{2m \times \tau_2}$. Now, one has $A_{ID_r} E_{ID_r} = G$ and the tuples ϑ_i are same as in unigncryption step of the proposed scheme. Therefore, $\mathcal{C}$ can get correct "b" and executes unsigncryption to answer the queries.

4. **Forgery:** At last, $\mathcal{A}$ outputs a signcryption "c" corresponding to ID_s^* and ID_r. Now, $\mathcal{C}$ decrypts "c" and obtains a legal signature $(r', \ [\pi_0', \ \pi_1', \ \pi_2']^t)$ corresponding to message μ, and identity ID_s^* respectively. Furthermore, if signcryption of μ assuming $ID_s^* = ID_s$ is never queried in any of the phases, then $(r', \ [\pi_0', \ \pi_1', \ \pi_2']^t)$ is an existential forgery, where $\pi_0' \leftarrow Z_q^n$, $\pi_1' \leftarrow Z_q^n$, and $\pi_2' \leftarrow Z_q^n$. Furthermore, one can observe $A_0 x = b$, if one assumes $x_1 = \pi_0' + R^*\pi_1' + ID'_{sr}\pi_2' - x$, then $A_0 x_1 = 0$ and $Pr[x_0 = 0] = 0$ is arbitrary small. The norm x_1 satisfies the inequality $||x_1|| = ||\pi_0' + R^*\pi_1' + ID'_{sr}\pi_2' - x|| \leq \zeta$. Therefore, if $\mathcal{A}$ find existential forgery, then $\mathcal{C}$ solves $SIS_{q, \ m, \ \zeta}$ problem.

   Moreover, if signcryption of μ assuming $ID_s^* = ID_s$ is queried in any of the phases, then $(r', \ [\pi_0', \ \pi_1', \ \pi_2']^t)$ is a strong existential forgery, where $\pi_0' \leftarrow Z_q^n$, $\pi_1' \leftarrow Z_q^n$, and $\pi_2' \leftarrow Z_q^n$. Therefore, it can be observed that $[A_0||A_0 R^*||A_0 ID''_{sr}][\pi_0', \ \pi_1', \ \pi_2']^t = b$ and $\varrho' = h_1(\mu, \ r', \ ID_r)$. Furthermore, the sender computes $ID''_{sr} = \sum_{i \in U}(-1)^i \ Q_i$, where U is the subset of $\{1, \ 2, \ ..., \ m\}$ be the set of positions where $\varrho'[i] \neq 0$. If $(r, \ [\omega_1, \ \omega_2]^t)$ is a legal signature, then $[\omega_1, \ \omega_2]^t$ is written as $[\pi_0', \ \pi_1', \ \pi_2']^t$ and implies $[A_0||A_0 R^*||A_0 ID'_{sr}][\pi_0, \ \pi_1, \ \pi_2]^t = b$ and $\varrho = h_1(\mu, \ r, \ ID_r)$. Furthermore, the sender computes $ID'_{sr} = \sum_{i \in U}(-1)^i \ Q_i$, where U is the subset of $\{1, \ 2, \ ..., \ m\}$ be the set of positions where $\varrho[i] \neq 0$.

   If $x_1 = (\pi_0' - \pi_0) + R^*(\pi_1' - \pi_1) + ID'_{sr}(\pi_2' - \pi_2)$, then $A_0 x_1 = 0$ and $Pr[x_0 = 0] \leq \frac{1}{3}$ and norm of x_1 satisfies the inequality $||x_1|| = ||(\pi_0' - \pi_0) + R^*(\pi_1' - \pi_1) + ID'_{sr}(\pi_2' - \pi_2)|| \leq \zeta$. Therefore, if $\mathcal{A}$ find existential forgery, then $\mathcal{C}$ solves $SIS_{q, \ m, \ \zeta}$ problem with non negligible probability.

5   Performance Analysis

This section provides computation cost **IBSCLR** and compares it with the other relevant protocols. Zhang et al. scheme [24] describes various choices of parameters in a lattice generated by an ideal. We have set system parameters $n = 1024$ bits, τ an odd prime, and Gaussian distribution $log\ \rho = 17.01$ for **IBSCLR** scheme, where ρ is standard deviation [10,18]. If one considers **IBSLR** under a security parameter κ, then the size of public key is $O(\kappa^2)$ and time taken $O(\kappa^2)$, where it becomes $O(\kappa)$ and time of computation $O(\kappa^3)$ in view of number-theoretic cryptosystems respectively [10]. Furthermore, a lattice based cryptosystem using learning with rounding [18] can reduced size of public key $\tilde{O}(\kappa)$.

We here analyzed performance of presented IBSCLR scheme. In LWR we have assumed $q = O(\kappa), x = O(\kappa log q), n = O(\kappa log q)$ for security parameter κ respectively. If one considers $q = \kappa^2$, $x = \kappa log\ q$, $n = 2\kappa log\ q$, then a lattice-based cryptosystem costs for $x + r^T E, Ar$ is $n|q|$ or $m|q|$ and for matrix A is $16\kappa^2 log^3 k$ in bits. Whereas for the discrete logarithm space used and communication cost is $log(q)$ with $q \approx 2^\kappa$ in bits. The public key possesses complexity $O(\kappa^3 log^5 \kappa)$ and costs of $x'^t + rE$ as well as verification costs $O(\kappa^2 log^4 \kappa)$. Our **IBSCLR** scheme has secret key size nm as in Table 1 and verification key size $4n^2 log\ q$ respectively. The public key size is $O(\kappa^2 log \kappa)$ and secret key size $n^2 log\ q$.

Table 1. Performance comparison with classical scheme

Protocols	Primitive	Bit-size
DLP Storage	$g \in Z_p^*$	$k' = log p$
DLP communication	$g^r, r^{-1}(P - X_A h) \in Z_p^*$	$k' = log p$
LWR Storage	$A \in Z_q^{m \times n}$	$((5 + \kappa)n + \tau_5 + 1)m log q$
LWR signcryption	$\omega_1 \leftarrow SamplePre(T'_{ID_s}, b - z, \vartheta_1), Z_q^*$	$m^2 n + 4nm + m\tau_5$
LWR unsigncryption	$\omega_1 \leftarrow SamplePre(T'_{ID_r}, b - z, \vartheta'_1), Z_q^*$	$m^2 n + 4nm + 3\tau_5 n$

In IBSCLR signcryption phase, a Gaussian sample is taken with dimension n, and a preimage sample is taken in dimension 2m. The cost of multiplication over Z_q is approximately $m^2 n + 4nm + m\tau_5$, whereas the cost of unsigncryption is $m^2 n + 4nm + 3\tau_5 n$, number of multiplication cost is $3\tau_5 n$ over Z_q. The ciphertext in IBSCLR scheme is $c = (t, c_0, c_1, c_2)$, where size of c_2 is given as $|c_2| = |r_1| + |r_2| + |\mu|$. Therefore, the length of signcryption output is given as $|t| + |c_0| + |c_1| + |r_1| + |r_2| + |\mu|$ as in Table 1. Moreover, the signcryption phase of the proposed IBSCLR scheme requires n discrete Gaussian sampling and 2n preimage sampling. In addition to this, on the receiver side needs 3mn multiplication over Z_q. Furthermore, a solution to $Ae = b$, needs the Gaussian elimination process to be executed, and resultant matrix could also be stored for efficient computation. The total number of multiplicative operations over Z_q in back substitution process is $[n-(m-1)] + [n-(m-2) + \ldots + n + (m-m)] = mn - \frac{1}{2}m(m-1)$.

6   Conclusion

Here we have presented a new identity-based signcryption under the assumption of Learning With Rounding (LWR) lattice problem. This scheme got motivated by the fundamental Water et al.'s identity-based signature and Agrawal et al.'s identity-based encryption schemes. The presented protocol is easy to implement because of simplicity and parallel linear algebraic operations (additions and multiplications) in a random lattice. The security analysis of this given protocol shows that the presented scheme is resistant against the quantum computing technology and has better efficiency in terms of computation and communication cost than the fundamental scheme based on ordinary number system based technique.

References

1. Agrawal, S., Boneh, D., Boyen, X.: Efficient lattice (H)IBE in the standard model. In: Gilbert, H. (ed.) EUROCRYPT 2010. LNCS, vol. 6110, pp. 553–572. Springer, Heidelberg (2010). https://doi.org/10.1007/978-3-642-13190-5_28
2. Agrawal, S., Freeman, D.M., Vaikuntanathan, V.: Functional encryption for inner product predicates from learning with errors. In: Lee, D.H., Wang, X. (eds.) ASIACRYPT 2011. LNCS, vol. 7073, pp. 21–40. Springer, Heidelberg (2011). https://doi.org/10.1007/978-3-642-25385-0_2
3. Boyen, X.: Lattice mixing and vanishing trapdoors: a framework for fully secure short signatures and more. In: Nguyen, P.Q., Pointcheval, D. (eds.) PKC 2010. LNCS, vol. 6056, pp. 499–517. Springer, Heidelberg (2010). https://doi.org/10.1007/978-3-642-13013-7_29
4. Brakerski, Z., Gentry, C., Vaikuntanathan, V.: (Leveled) fully homomorphic encryption without bootstrapping. ACM Trans. Comput. Theor. (TOCT) 6(3), 13 (2014)
5. Brakerski, Z., Vaikuntanathan, V.: Efficient fully homomorphic encryption from (standard) LWE. SIAM J. Comput. 43(2), 831–871 (2014)
6. Dharminder, D., Mishra, D.: Understanding signcryption security in standard model. Secur. Priv., e105 (2020)
7. Dharminder, D., Obaidat, M.S., Mishra, D., Das, A.K.: SFEEC: provably secure signcryption-based big data security framework for energy-efficient computing environment. IEEE Syst. J., 1–9 (2020)
8. Ducas, L., Durmus, A., Lepoint, T., Lyubashevsky, V.: Lattice signatures and bimodal gaussians. In: Canetti, R., Garay, J.A. (eds.) CRYPTO 2013. LNCS, vol. 8042, pp. 40–56. Springer, Heidelberg (2013). https://doi.org/10.1007/978-3-642-40041-4_3
9. Gentry, C., Peikert, C., Vaikuntanathan, V.: Trapdoors for hard lattices and new cryptographic constructions. In: Proceedings of the Fortieth Annual ACM Symposium on Theory of Computing, pp. 197–206. ACM (2008)
10. Goldreich, O., Goldwasser, S., Halevi, S.: Public-key cryptosystems from lattice reduction problems. In: Kaliski, B.S. (ed.) CRYPTO 1997. LNCS, vol. 1294, pp. 112–131. Springer, Heidelberg (1997). https://doi.org/10.1007/BFb0052231
11. Gupta, D.S., Biswas, G.: Design of lattice-based ELGamal encryption and signature schemes using SIS problem. Trans. Emerging Telecommun. Technol. 29(6), e3255 (2018)

12. Jin, Z., Wen, Q., Du, H.: An improved semantically-secure identity-based signcryption scheme in the standard model. Comput. Electr. Eng. **36**(3), 545–552 (2010)
13. Li, F., Takagi, T.: Secure identity-based signcryption in the standard model. Math. Comput. Modell. **57**(11–12), 2685–2694 (2013)
14. Malone-Lee, J.: Identity-based signcryption. IACR Cryptology ePrint Archive **2002**, 98 (2002)
15. Micciancio, D., Regev, O.: Worst-case to average-case reductions based on Gaussian measures. SIAM J. Comput. **37**(1), 267–302 (2007)
16. Peikert, C.: Public-key cryptosystems from the worst-case shortest vector problem. In: Proceedings of the Forty-First Annual ACM Symposium on Theory of Computing, pp. 333–342. ACM (2009)
17. Peikert, C.: Lattice cryptography for the internet. In: Mosca, M. (ed.) PQCrypto 2014. LNCS, vol. 8772, pp. 197–219. Springer, Cham (2014). https://doi.org/10.1007/978-3-319-11659-4_12
18. Regev, O.: On lattices, learning with errors, random linear codes, and cryptography. J. ACM (JACM) **56**(6), 34 (2009)
19. Selvi, S.S.D., Vivek, S.S., Vinayagamurthy, D., Rangan, C.P.: ID based signcryption scheme in standard model. In: Takagi, T., Wang, G., Qin, Z., Jiang, S., Yu, Y. (eds.) ProvSec 2012. LNCS, vol. 7496, pp. 35–52. Springer, Heidelberg (2012). https://doi.org/10.1007/978-3-642-33272-2_4
20. Shor, P.W.: Polynomial-time algorithms for prime factorization and discrete logarithms on a quantum computer. SIAM Rev. **41**(2), 303–332 (1999)
21. Waters, B.: Efficient identity-based encryption without random oracles. In: Cramer, R. (ed.) EUROCRYPT 2005. LNCS, vol. 3494, pp. 114–127. Springer, Heidelberg (2005). https://doi.org/10.1007/11426639_7
22. Wei, G., Shao, J., Xiang, Y., Zhu, P., Lu, R.: Obtain confidentiality or/and authenticity in big data by id-based generalized signcryption. Inf. Sci. **318**, 111–122 (2015)
23. Yu, Y., Yang, B., Sun, Y., Zhu, S.L.: Identity based signcryption scheme without random oracles. Comput. Standards Interfaces **31**(1), 56–62 (2009)
24. Zhang, J., Zhang, Z., Ding, J., Snook, M., Dagdelen, Ö.: Authenticated key exchange from ideal lattices. In: Oswald, E., Fischlin, M. (eds.) Annual International Conference on the Theory and Applications of Cryptographic Techniques, pp. 719–751. Springer, Heidelberg (2015). https://doi.org/10.1007/978-3-662-46803-6_24
25. Zheng, Y.: Digital signcryption or how to achieve cost(signature & encryption) << cost(signature) + cost(encryption). In: Kaliski, B.S. (ed.) CRYPTO 1997. LNCS, vol. 1294, pp. 165–179. Springer, Heidelberg (1997). https://doi.org/10.1007/BFb0052234

Deep Detection of Anomalies in Static Attributed Graph

Prakhyat G. Kulkarni[✉], S. Y. Praneet, R. B. Raghav[✉],
and Bhaskarjyoti Das

PES University, Bengaluru, India
prakhyat2612@gmail.com, praneetsy@gmail.com, rbongole@gmail.com,
bhaskarjyoti01@gmail.com

Abstract. While online social media is one of the greatest innovations of modern man, it often gets used to perform a barrage of malicious activities which can be anomalous in nature. The area of anomaly detection deals with this challenging task. In this paper, we methodically investigate anomaly detection for the modern content driven attributed graphs. Since labeled graph data is not available for scientific research, we work with a synthetically generated dataset with an unsupervised learning approach to prove that both attribute as well as structure should be considered. We also investigate whether deep learning in this context brings an additional advantage in anomaly detection. We extend the recent work in this area, with an innovative combination of attributed graph embedding with graph convolution technique.

Keywords: Anomaly detection · Attributed graph · Static graph · Social graph · Network embedding · Node2vec embedding · Graph convolutional network · Accelerated Attributed Network Embedding · Isolation Forest · Autoencoder

1 Introduction

Anomaly detection is the process of identifying unexpected items or events in a data set. For a graph, this is about identifying structural entities that differ significantly from the majority of the nodes in the graph. Though anomaly detection is an established area of research for unstructured non-graph data, it is different when applied to graph data. This is mainly due to the fact that graph data has structural components that affect the attributes of the graph nodes. In that sense, nodes of a graph along with their attributes cannot be assumed as IID (independent and identically distributed). Apart from scale and associated complexity in a modern graph data set (For example: Facebook has more than a billion nodes), there is also large search space that is associated with such a graph. Hence, traditional data mining techniques of anomaly detection cannot be applied on such graph datasets. Below are few examples of several domains that can be represented graphically and will benefit from anomaly detection:

© Springer Nature Singapore Pte Ltd. 2020
A. Bhattacharjee et al. (Eds.): MIND 2020, CCIS 1241, pp. 627–640, 2020.
https://doi.org/10.1007/978-981-15-6318-8_50

1. Anomaly detection can be an important task in accounting networks where suspicious transactions are done on particular accounts that are typically related. Similar risk labels can be assigned to such accounts using graph based methods.
2. Another important application is in the context of auction networks where fraudsters gain legitimacy by trading with accomplices but subsequently commit frauds. Based on these interaction characteristics, fraudsters can be identified.
3. In financial trading networks, the fraudsters typically operate in a group and they can be identified using graphical methods.
4. Opinion networks with fake reviews are common in the social network domain. The nodes contributing fake reviews and opinions are part of the social network. Considering various graph based approaches, an honesty score can be arrived at to detect such users/nodes.
5. On networks such as Facebook and Twitter, the content and structure can be used to detect fake opinions and malicious users spreading spams.

A graph based analysis involving both attribute as well as edges can be carried out for most of the examples cited above and can be considered as useful applications of the work described in this paper.

2   Related Work

David Savage et al. [1] and R Yu et al. [2] provide an excellent overview of how anomaly detection as an area evolved from unstructured to structured data. On a graph dataset, anomaly detection techniques emerging from data mining domain as well as graph based approaches have been used.

2.1   Types of Anomalies in a Graph

Anomaly itself can be classified differently for a graph dataset i.e.

1. **On the basis of nature of the anomaly:** Point anomaly or global anomaly is when a sample point deviates appreciably from the rest of the points. However, how much of the deviation is sufficient to brand a point as anomalous is hard to decide. Collective anomaly is a situation when a collection of sample points deviates appreciably from the rest of the points. Contextual anomaly can be defined as a point anomaly or a collective anomaly based on the context. For example, the income of a node in a social graph of college friends can point to a contextual anomaly if the income is abnormal compared to similarly qualified individuals in the current scenario.
2. **On the basis of nature of graphs:** In case of dynamic graphs, a sequence of graphs are examined and an anomalous graph snapshot is identified along with the structural elements that contribute to the anomaly. These are examples of dynamic anomalies. On the contrary, static anomalies are captured when no time dimension is involved.

3. **On the basis of whether node and edge attributes are used:** Labeled anomalies are for attributed graphs and unlabeled anomalies are for unattributed graphs.
4. **On the basis of behavior:** This sort of classification is useful for an anomaly that deviates significantly from others (white crow) vs. anomaly that deviates marginally from the rest of the graph and cannot be easily concluded as anomalous (in-disguise).
5. **On the basis of interaction pattern:** The interaction anomalies are best captured by the graph/subgraph structures built using interaction data. Sudden occurrence of a very sparsely connected node or a set of densely connected nodes in the form of a clique can both indicate possible anomaly.

2.2   Data Mining Approaches for Anomaly Detection

Anomaly detection started as a research area in the field of data mining. This is still relevant for graph data even though the data itself is in graph form. From the perspective of how data is mined, anomaly detection typically uses either of the three approaches i.e.

1. **Supervised:** In the presence of labeled datasets, researchers have used methods such as Bayesian (both Naive Bayes and probabilistic graphical model) [3,4], Support Vector Machine (both one and multi-class SVM) [5–8] and Artificial Neural Networks [9,10]. However, since the anomaly constitutes a very small fraction of a dataset, the dataset is typically imbalanced and the classifier so designed should be chosen based on classifier recall rather than accuracy. For single class classification, the data that cannot be classified is an anomaly whereas for multi-class classification, ambiguity in predicted class itself can be an anomaly.
2. **Unsupervised:** This is used when labeled datasets are not available. It mainly uses various clustering methods [11,12] assuming that normal data points tend to fit into clusters and the data points that do not belong to a cluster or belong to a very small cluster are anomalous. Clustering approach has been used [13] to identify nodes showing anomalous behavior in online social networks.
3. **Semi-supervised:** This method is used when only a limited amount of labeled data is available. The available labeled data is used to make a classifier which is then utilised to label the unlabeled data and anomaly is detected using various distance metrics.

2.3   Unsupervised Anomaly Detection by Isolation Forest and Deep Autoencoder

As discussed in the previous section, availability of labeled dataset is a real challenge for social graphs. Supervised approaches are not really practical in such cases and an unsupervised learning approach is more viable. Isolation Forest [14] has been considered the preferred unsupervised mechanism in investigating structure and attribute oriented approaches in anomaly detection by numerous researchers [15–18] in the past. Instead of profiling normal points (which many of the common approaches perform), Isolation Forest works by isolating anomalies. The core principle behind the algorithm of the Isolation Forest is that, there is a tendency that anomalous instances separate (are isolated) more easily than normal data points. The algorithm proceeds by randomly selecting an attribute and randomly selecting a split value for the attribute (using allowed values of the attribute). Eventually, after generating such partitions recursively, a tree is built. The main idea behind this approach is that leaf nodes in the tree which are closer to the root are probably anomalous as they are easier to isolate.

However, a method such as Isolation Forest is a shallow machine learning method. Another interesting unsupervised approach is deep autoencoder. Jinwon An et al. [19] used a deep auto encoder that used the reconstruction error as an indicator of anomaly.

2.4   Anomaly Detection for a Social Graph

Online social networks have attracted the attention of researchers in the past few years due to explosive growth of such networks and their ever increasing prominence in our lives. Researchers group techniques of anomaly detection in social graphs into three types:

1. **Behaviour based:** This approach uses the structure and content associated with normal users. It does this by dealing with behaviour of the users or their posts that are typically captured as attributes of nodes and edges in a social graph. This includes the number of posts, the number of messages sent to friends, the content of these posts and messages, number of likes and shares etc. However, nowadays spammers are smart enough to at least remain structurally similar to normal users. One possible approach [20] is to make a supervised classifier based on features derived from the structure and content of legitimate users. Zheng et al. [21] have handpicked a variety of user and content based features followed by SVM classifier to detect spammers on a large dataset of a chinese social media site. Vimal Biswanath et al. [22] adopted a content based approach and employed Principal Component Analysis (PCA) technique to separate out users with anomalous behaviour from the regular users from the data comprised of two years of recorded user behavior from nearly 14,000 to 100,000 users of Facebook, Yelp and Twitter.
2. **Structure based:** This approach mainly evaluates structural properties of nodes, substructures and ego networks [23] in social graphs. Examples include centrality based properties, local clustering coefficient of nodes, dyad level features such as reciprocity, ego net features and graph level features such as number of connected components, global clustering coefficient etc. Ravneet Kaur et al. [24] correlates negative ties (behavior) with anomalies and then uses a centrality based analysis. Leman Akolglu et al. [25] proposed Oddball algorithm that extracts egonet features and validates the patterns that pairs of such features follow in large social graphs. J Huang et al. [26] proposed

an approach based on evolutionary networks where anomalies are identified by overlapping communities. Doostari et al. [27] used a novel hybrid approach that uses fuzzy logic and combines both parametric and non-parametric approaches to spot anomalies. They detect abnormal users in complete subgraphs (cliques) of users in an online social network. Cliques are employed as the basic blocks since it is laborious to evaluate the entire social network. Detection of communities in dynamic networks [28] has also been employed for anomaly detection. The proposed approach was used on evolutionary networks where anomalies were identified by overlapping communities.

3. **Spectral property based:** This uses the spectral properties of the social graph dataset. In a graph, spectral analysis can be done on the graph Laplacian and based on this technique, spectral clustering is possible. The rest of the method follows the general principle of cluster based anomaly detection approach. Ying et al. [29] detected spam attackers using their spectral coordinate characteristics.

2.5   Network Embedding Methods

Network embedding is a recently emerged technique that fits a graph data to the machine learning paradigm. Hamilton et al. [30] discusses graph embedding from an encoder-decoder perspective. The encoder attempts to build a low dimensional vector for each node such that similar nodes have similar vectors and will be adjacent in the embedding space. The decoder uses these embedding to decode some structural information about the graph. In other words, the decoder when applied to a pair of such embedding provided by the encoder should closely mimic the proximity feature of the graph as calculated for the considered nodes. An appropriate loss function is then defined and minimized for the best representation embedding of the nodes. Cai et al. [31] classify embedding techniques from the perspective of algorithm or technique used and the problem setting perspectives. From the problem setting perspectives, when we consider the input to the embedding process, it can be embedding for homogeneous (for example, user-user graph in a recommendation system scenario) or heterogeneous (user-item graph in a recommendation system scenario) graphs. When we consider the output of the embedding process, it can be embedding for nodes, edges, sub-graphs or even combination of graph components such as node and community. So, clearly representation learning or embedding depends on the chosen task. From the algorithm perspective, there are methods that use matrix factorization and there are other methods that use random walk with deep learning.

Random Walk Based Method Such as Node2Vec. Embedding methods such as DeepWalk [32] and Node2Vec [33] discover the node representations using random walk. Here the input is a homogeneous graph and the output is node embedding. They employ a relatively shallow learning method where depth of the random walk is truncated by a parameter. Additionally, Node2Vec uses a biased random walk. Also, their optimisation approaches for the loss function are different. Internally, they adopt the SkipGram model from natural language processing where the nodes visited in a random walk started from a node are equivalent to the words that appear in a sample window in SkipGram model. However, this approach focuses on structural aspect of the graph alone. There are other variants of random walk based approaches other than DeepWalk and Node2Vec. The other main deep learning approach uses autoencoder [34,35] that transforms high dimensional neighbourhood vector to a low dimensional embedding. However, this approach has a limitation in terms of generalization capability across evolving graph as the size of the auto-encoder fixed and it also depends only on the local neighbourhood. Similarly, the random walk approach works well for only the nodes that are visited in random walk and cannot generalize across unseen nodes.

Network Neighbourhood Aggregation Method Such as Graph Convolutional Network. The encoder in the Graph Convolution networks (GCN) [36] aggregates the attributes of the nodes connected to each node in the graph in an iterative fashion. In the first iteration, attributes of a node decide the embedding of a node. In each successive iteration, the attributes of the neighbour nodes are aggregated using an aggregation function and the embedding is updated. The updated embedding is passed through a deep neural network for certain number of iterations. In this way, this method provides an embedding which is based on deep neighbourhood of the graph nodes and combines both node neighbourhood as well as neighbourhood attribute information. The GraphSAGE algorithm [37] essentially follows the same approach with a different aggregation scheme. Recently, GCNs have been used by Zheng et al. [38] to find anomalous edges in a network using semi-supervised learning. Kaize Ding et al. [39] has detected anomalies by making use of GCN with auto-encoder based reconstruction so that the reconstruction error points out anomalous nodes.

Efficient Modelling of Joint Space of Structure and Attribute by Accelerated Attributed Network Embedding. From a social graph perspective, if we recall the principle of homophily(birds of a feather flock together), it is clear that modeling embedding should be done in a joint space of neighbourhood information of network structure as well as node attributes. For a very large social graph, this has a computational challenge as most optimisation algorithms use gradient descent or eigen decomposition. The recent work on Accelerated Attributed Network Embedding (AANE) by Huang et al. [40] provides an embedding that combines structures with the attribute information in a rather efficient manner. They achieve the efficiency by implementing a distributed optimization algorithm.

2.6   Graph Anomaly Detection Dataset

One particular challenge with anomaly detection based on datasets of social graph is lack of labeled data. Most datasets that are available with existing research are method specific and rather small in size. For example, Enron dataset [41] has been extensively used for anomaly detection but is rather small or too well-understood to remain a good anomaly detection dataset in the social media setup. Manual labeling of huge social media dataset is not practical. So, synthetic generation of such dataset has to be done for any such research. Vengertsev et al. [42] have proposed a way to construct synthetic graphs where the anomalies have been injected considering the substructure patterns that are global, neighbor-based and community-based. These graphs are then examined with various graph based anomaly detection methods. Christine Largeron et al. [43] provided a new synthetic generator for an attributed network that has communities following patterns of real world networks. This generator offers an extensive set of parameters such as number of vertices, maximum within and between community edges for each vertex, minimum number of edges in the graph, number of communities, number of members in the generated community etc.

2.7   Observations

From the discussion above, several observations can be made:

1. There are different anomaly detection approaches with no appreciable overlap and the researchers have had some success in detecting anomaly using all of these methods in various domains and datasets. So, the existing research of anomaly detection is somewhat domain and dataset specific. It is hard to say that any particular approach is vastly superior compared to all other approaches in all domains.
2. In modern social networks, in addition to the structure, attributes of the nodes and edges play a very important role due to the content they represent. Neither attribute alone nor structure alone represent such a dataset completely as structure influences the attributes of nodes and edges. Most of the existing research around graph anomalies did not give much attention to such attributed networks.
3. The existing researches on graph anomaly detection are predominantly shallow learning mechanisms that focus on a fraction of the graph i.e. node, community, ego nets etc.
4. Due to lack of availability of labeled dataset of social graphs, supervised learning techniques should be less preferred than unsupervised methods.
5. Network embedding that takes care of both node attribute as well as node neighbourhood information should be more effective.

3   Methodology

The focus of our work is anomaly detection on static graph using behavioral and structural information. From the anomaly terminology discussed, this work focuses on static anomaly, point anomaly, labeled anomaly and anomalies that can be called "white crow" type. From the perspective of anomaly detection methods for social graph, this work does not use spectral methods. From the perspective of data mining techniques, due to lack of labeled data, unsupervised learning is used. We hypothesize that:

1. Considering both structure and attribute is better than considering either individually. Deep neighbourhood information is more effective than shallow neighbourhood information.
2. Deep learning approach will be more effective to detect anomalous node as compared to shallow machine learning approaches.

There are multiple approaches which can be employed for solving anomaly detection problem for a graph data set. We systematically categorize these approaches into the following categories:

1. Considering only nodal attributes
2. Considering only network structure
3. Considering both nodal attributes and network structure

The step by step methodology is summarized below:

1. **Considering only nodal attributes**: We ignore the relationship between nodes and treat the attribute vectors of each node as independent of the other nodes in the network. For representing the nodal attributes, we have an attribute matrix $\mathbf{X} \in \mathbf{R}^{n \times d}$ where n is the number of nodes in the network and d is the number of attributes per node. We apply Isolation Forest [14] for detection of anomaly.
2. **Considering only network structure**: We apply Node2Vec [33] embedding technique on the Adjacency matrix to get a more structured form of the topological structure of the graph. On the embedding matrix obtained, a standard method like Isolation Forest is applied to obtain different anomalies present based on structure.
3. **Considering both nodal attributes and network structure using AANE embedding with Isolation Forest**: We use an embedding technique which is called Accelerated Attributed Network Embedding [40]. This technique attempts to generate a continuous vector representation for each node in the network which preserves node proximity both in the network space and the attribute space. This technique enforces the preservation of node proximity in the network space by penalizing the difference between the vector representation of two connected nodes when the edge weight between them is low. This ensures that the vector representations of strongly connected nodes are similar. The technique enforces the preservation of node proximity in the attribute space by factorizing the attribute affinity matrix symmetrically and imposing that the dot product of the vector representations of two connected nodes be same as the similarity measure of their attribute vectors. AANE offers an efficient method for jointly learning both of the above simultaneously. We feed in the $\mathbf{A}$ as well as $\mathbf{X}$ to the AANE algorithm and obtain an embedding matrix which integrates both nodal attributes and network structure wherein each row can now be treated as an independent vector in

this embedding space. We then apply Isolation Forest on the obtained embedding matrix to detect anomalous nodes.

4. **Considering both nodal attributes and network structure using AANE embedding with deep auto encoder**: We then move on to deep learning for the anomaly detection task at hand. We adopt the method described in Kaize Ding et al. [39] that obtains a node embedding representation which models both network structure and nodal attributes by means of GCN with the idea of deep autoencoders. The decoder for the deep autoencoder reconstructs the network structure and the nodal attributes from the node embeddings. The reconstruction errors of the adjacency matrix and the attribute matrix are combined (weighted sum) to form the loss function for the deep architecture. The reconstruction errors post-training are used for ranking the nodes based on its abnormality (or anomaly). The idea here is that, the more anomalous the node, the harder it is for the decoder to reconstruct (deviation from pattern). Hence, the anomalous nodes have higher reconstruction errors. We present a tweak to the aforementioned GCN based solution that takes as input the attribute matrix $\mathbf{X}$ in the first layer and uses the adjacency matrix $\mathbf{A}$ in each layer as a part of the forward propagation rule. We experiment by feeding in the AANE embedding matrix instead of the attribute matrix. The intuition for this being that each layer of GCN recursively captures the information of the next hop neighbors, and since the number of layers which can be trained is limited, GCN may not be able to learn the full scope of the network. Hence, by feeding in the AANE embedding matrix, we provide the GCN model more information about the network which was not available previously, without adding extra layers. With this change in the aforementioned technique, we carry out the task of anomaly detection.

4   Dataset

Since there is a dearth of datasets with ground truth labels for anomalies, we choose two datasets and inject anomalies in them. Table 1 lists the dataset used in this work.

1. Firstly, we synthesize a small dataset by using an existing software developed by Christine Largeron et al. [43].
2. Secondly, we utilize the Amazon product co-purchase network dataset [44]. In this dataset, each node represents a product and there is an edge between two nodes if the two corresponding products are frequently co-purchased.

At this point, anomalies are injected in the datasets for our work.

1. **Injecting Structural Anomalies**: We create n small cliques of size m based on the intuition that, in many real-world scenarios, there is presence of small cliques where the nodes are linked closer to each other than the average. The algorithm we follow is given below:

(a) Select m nodes randomly and connect them together fully to form a clique and label these nodes as anomalous

(b) Repeat this process n times.

(c) We obtain $m \times n$ anomalies which are structural in nature.

2. **Injecting Attribute Anomalies**: We also create $m \times n$ attribute based anomalies. The algorithm we employed is as follows:

(a) Select k nodes from graph randomly

(b) Obtain node j by finding the node which has maximum deviation of attribute vector based on euclidean distance from node i

(c) Attributes of node j is set to node i

Table 1. Data set

Data set	# of Nodes	# of Edges	# of Attributes
Synthetic	10000	17848	2
Amazon product	1418	3695	21

Table 2. Results

ROC-AUC scores			
Methodology	Aspect considered	Amazon	Synthetic
Attribute matrix + Isolation Forest	Attributes	0.27	0.40
Node2vec embedding + Isolation Forest	Structure	0.36	0.44
AANE embedding + Isolation Forest	Attributes + Structure	0.46	0.51
AANE embedding + Deep auto encoder	Attributes + Structure	0.51	0.52

5   Experimental Results

Table 2 shows the methodology used, aspects of the network considered and the AUC scores of the ROC curve for each method on both Amazon and the synthetic dataset. Considering only the node attributes with an unsupervised anomaly detection method such as Isolation Forest predictably gives the lowest performance. Similarly considering only the structure information provided by Node2Vec along with Isolation Forest provides a slightly better performance. However, whether the node attributes or the network structure is more important depends on the nature of the network itself. The key observation is that considering both the structure information and attributes gives a better result than considering each individually. In the last option, the Isolation Forest based anomaly detection technique is replaced with a deep auto-encoder based anomaly detection where the quantum of reconstruction error for the embedding helps in detection of anomaly. As expected, replacing isolation forest with a deep anomaly detection technique further improves efficiency.

6   Conclusion

In this paper, we present a systematic and organized study on the problem at hand by looking at four different methodologies. Due to the lack of unlabeled graph data, we used existing research to synthetically generate graph data with injected anomaly. We start with a naive approach of ignoring either the topology or the structural aspects of the graph, then gradually increase the knowledge of the considered graph and finally take into account both the topology and the nodal attributes of the graph. The detection efficiency improves further with a deep learning approach in anomaly detection. This step by step approach clearly shows an increase in performance at each step which validates our prior hypothesis. The contribution of this investigation is two fold i.e. investigating the utility of unsupervised method such as Isolation Forest with embedding provided by Node2Vec [33] and AANE [40] to prove the first hypothesis and combining embedding provided by AANE [40] with GCN [36] to prove the second hypothesis.

As future work, this sequence of experiments may be redone on a much larger graph data with more than a million nodes. Also, to remove the constraint of static graph, robust anomaly detector may be developed that quickly readjusts itself in case of changing adversarial strikes. The work in this paper deals with static graphs and as future work, it can be extended for dealing with time-evolving graphs.

References

1. Savage, D., Zhang, X., Xinghuo, Y., Chou, P., Wang, Q.: Anomaly detection in online social networks. Soc. Netw. **39**, 62–70 (2014)
2. Rose, Y., Qiu, H., Wen, Z., Lin, C.Y., Liu, Y.: A survey on social media anomaly detection. ACM SIGKDD Explor. Newsl. **18**(1), 1–14 (2016)
3. Abraham, B., Box, G.E.P.: Bayesian analysis of some outlier problems in time series. Biometrika **66**(2), 229–236 (1979)
4. Kruegel, C., Mutz, D., Robertson, W., Valeur, F.: Bayesian event classification for intrusion detection. In: Proceedings 19th Annual Computer Security Applications Conference, pp. 14–23. IEEE (2003)
5. Ma, J., Perkins, S.: Time-series novelty detection using one-class support vector machines. In: Proceedings of the International Joint Conference on Neural Networks, vol. 3, pp. 1741–1745. IEEE (2003)
6. Ma, J., Perkins, S.: Online novelty detection on temporal sequences. In: Proceedings of the Ninth ACM SIGKDD International Conference on Knowledge Discovery and Data Mining, pp. 613–618 (2003)

7. Li, K.L., Huang, H.K., Tian, S.F., Xu, W.: Improving one-class SVM for anomaly detection. In: Proceedings of the 2003 International Conference on Machine Learning and Cybernetics (IEEE Cat. No. 03EX693), vol. 5, pp. 3077–3081. IEEE (2003)

8. Perdisci, R., Ariu, D., Fogla, P., Giacinto, G., Lee, W.: McPAD: a multiple classifier system for accurate payload-based anomaly detection. Comput. Netw. **53**(6), 864–881 (2009)

9. Moradi, M., Zulkernine, M.: A neural network based system for intrusion detection and classification of attacks. In: Proceedings of the IEEE International Conference on Advances in Intelligent Systems-Theory and Applications, pp. 15–18 (2004)

10. Augusteijn, M.F., Folkert, B.A.: Neural network classification and novelty detection. Int. J. Remote Sens. **23**(14), 2891–2902 (2002)

11. Pires, A., Santos-Pereira, C.: Using clustering and robust estimators to detect outliers in multivariate data (2005)

12. Eskin, F., Portnoy, L., Stolfo, S.: Intrusion detection with unlabeled data using clustering. In: Proceedings of ACM CSS Workshop on Data Mining Applied to Security (2001)

13. Beutel, A., Xu, W., Guruswami, V., Palow, C., Faloutsos, C.: Copycatch: stopping group attacks by spotting lockstep behavior in social networks. In: Proceedings of the 22nd International Conference on World Wide Web, pp. 119–130 (2013)

14. Liu, F.T., Ting, K.M., Zhou, Z.H.: Isolation forest. In: 2008 Eighth IEEE International Conference on Data Mining, pp. 413–422. IEEE (2008)

15. Puggini, L., McLoone, S.: An enhanced variable selection and isolation forest based methodology for anomaly detection with oes data. Eng. Appl. Artif. Intell. **67**, 126–135 (2018)

16. Sun, L., Versteeg, S., Boztas, S., Rao, A.: Detecting anomalous user behavior using an extended isolation forest algorithm: an enterprise case study. arXiv preprint arXiv:1609.06676 (2016)

17. Susto, G.A., Beghi, A., McLoone, S.: Anomaly detection through on-line isolation forest: an application to plasma etching. In: 2017 28th Annual SEMI Advanced Semiconductor Manufacturing Conference (ASMC), pp. 89–94. IEEE (2017)

18. Xu, D., Wang, Y., Meng, Y., Zhang, Z.: An improved data anomaly detection method based on isolation forest. In: 2017 10th International Symposium on Computational Intelligence and Design (ISCID), vol. 2, pp. 287–291. IEEE (2017)

19. An, J., Cho, S.: Variational autoencoder based anomaly detection using reconstruction probability. Spec. Lect. IE **2**(1), 1–18 (2015)

20. Xiao, C., Freeman, D.M., Hwa, T.: Detecting clusters of fake accounts in online social networks. In: Proceedings of the 8th ACM Workshop on Artificial Intelligence and Security, pp. 91–101 (2015)

21. Zheng, X., Zeng, Z., Chen, Z., Yuanlong, Y., Rong, C.: Detecting spammers on social networks. Neurocomputing **159**, 27–34 (2015)

22. Viswanath, B., et al.: Towards detecting anomalous user behavior in online social networks. In: 23rd {USENIX} Security Symposium ({USENIX} Security 14), pp. 223–238 (2014)

23. Hassanzadeh, R., Nayak, R., Stebila, D.: Analyzing the effectiveness of graph metrics for anomaly detection in online social networks. In: Wang, X.S., Cruz, I., Delis, A., Huang, G. (eds.) WISE 2012. LNCS, vol. 7651, pp. 624–630. Springer, Heidelberg (2012). https://doi.org/10.1007/978-3-642-35063-4_45

24. Kaur, R., Kaur, M., Singh, S.: A novel graph centrality based approach to analyze anomalous nodes with negative behavior. Procedia Comput. Sci. **78**, 556–562 (2016)

25. Akoglu, L., McGlohon, M., Faloutsos, C.: Oddball: spotting anomalies in weighted graphs. In: Zaki, M.J., Yu, J.X., Ravindran, B., Pudi, V. (eds.) PAKDD 2010. LNCS (LNAI), vol. 6119, pp. 410–421. Springer, Heidelberg (2010). https://doi.org/10.1007/978-3-642-13672-6_40

26. Huang, J., Sun, H., Han, J., Deng, H., Sun, Y., Liu, Y.: Shrink: a structural clustering algorithm for detecting hierarchical communities in networks. In: Proceedings of the 19th ACM International Conference on Information and Knowledge Management, pp. 219–228 (2010)

27. Doostari, M.A., Zeinali, R., Lashkari, H., Ajamzamani, M.: Fuzzy node-fuzzy graph (2013)

28. Chen, Z., Hendrix, W., Samatova, N.F.: Community-based anomaly detection in evolutionary networks. J. Intell. Inf. Syst. **39**(1), 59–85 (2012). https://doi.org/10.1007/s10844-011-0183-2

29. Ying, X., Wu, X., Barbará, D.: Spectrum based fraud detection in social networks. In: 2011 IEEE 27th International Conference on Data Engineering, pp. 912–923. IEEE (2011)

30. Hamilton, W.L., Ying, R., Leskovec, J.: Representation learning on graphs: methods and applications. arXiv preprint arXiv:1709.05584 (2017)

31. Cai, H., Zheng, V.W., Chang, K.C.C.: A comprehensive survey of graph embedding: problems, techniques, and applications. IEEE Trans. Knowl. Data Eng. **30**(9), 1616–1637 (2018)

32. Perozzi, B., Al-Rfou, R., Skiena, S.: Deepwalk: online learning of social representations. In: Proceedings of the 20th ACM SIGKDD International Conference on Knowledge Discovery and Data Mining, pp. 701–710 (2014)

33. Grover, A., Leskovec, J.: node2vec: scalable feature learning for networks. In: Proceedings of the 22nd ACM SIGKDD International Conference on Knowledge Discovery and Data Mining, pp. 855–864 (2016)

34. Wang, D., Cui, P., Zhu, W.: Structural deep network embedding. In: Proceedings of the 22nd ACM SIGKDD International Conference on Knowledge Discovery and Data Mining, pp. 1225–1234 (2016)

35. Cao, S., Lu, W., Xu, Q.: Deep neural networks for learning graph representations. In: Thirtieth AAAI Conference on Artificial Intelligence (2016)

36. Kipf, T.N., Welling, M.: Semi-supervised classification with graph convolutional networks. arXiv preprint arXiv:1609.02907 (2016)

37. Hamilton, W., Ying, Z., Leskovec, J.: Inductive representation learning on large graphs. In: Advances in Neural Information Processing Systems, pp. 1024–1034 (2017)

38. Zheng, L., Li, Z., Li, J., Li, Z., Gao, J.: Addgraph: anomaly detection in dynamic graph using attention-based temporal GCN. In: Proceedings of the 28th International Joint Conference on Artificial Intelligence, pp. 4419–4425. AAAI Press (2019)

39. Ding, K., Li, J., Bhanushali, R., Liu, H.: Deep anomaly detection on attributed networks. In: Proceedings of the 2019 SIAM International Conference on Data Mining, pp. 594–602. SIAM (2019)

40. Huang, X., Li, J., Hu, X.: Accelerated attributed network embedding. In: Proceedings of the 2017 SIAM International Conference on Data Mining, pp. 633–641. SIAM (2017)

41. Klimt, B., Yang, Y.: The enron corpus: a new dataset for email classification research. In: Boulicaut, J.-F., Esposito, F., Giannotti, F., Pedreschi, D. (eds.) ECML 2004. LNCS (LNAI), vol. 3201, pp. 217–226. Springer, Heidelberg (2004). https://doi.org/10.1007/978-3-540-30115-8_22

42. Vengertsev, D., Thakkar, H.: Anomaly detection in graph: unsupervised learning, graph-based features and deep architecture (2015)
43. Largeron, C., Mougel, P.N., Rabbany, R., Zaïane, O.R.: Generating attributed networks with communities. PloS one, 10(4), 54–62 (2015)
44. Leskovec, J., Adamic, L.A., Huberman, B.A.: The dynamics of viral marketing. ACM Trans. Web (TWEB) 1(1), 5 (2007)

Author Index

Printed in the United States
By Bookmasters